Border Management Modernization

Editors

Gerard McLinden

Enrique Fanta

David Widdowson

Tom Doyle

 THE WORLD BANK

Washington, D.C.

© 2011 The International Bank for Reconstruction and Development/The World Bank
1818 H Street NW
Washington DC 20433
Telephone: 202-473-1000
Internet: www.worldbank.org

1 2 3 4 13 12 11 10

This volume is a product of the staff of the International Bank for Reconstruction and Development/The World Bank. The findings, interpretations, and conclusions expressed in this volume do not necessarily reflect the views of the Executive Directors of The World Bank or the governments they represent.

The World Bank does not guarantee the accuracy of the data included in this work. The boundaries, colors, denominations, and other information shown on any map in this work do not imply any judgement on the part of The World Bank concerning the legal status of any territory or the endorsement or acceptance of such boundaries.

Rights and Permissions

ISBN: 978-0-8213-8596-8
eISBN: 978-0-8213-8597-5
DOI: 10.1596/978-0-8213-8596-8

Library of Congress Cataloging-in-Publication data has been requested.

Cover design by Drew Fasick. Text editing, design, and layout by Nick Moschovakis and Elaine Wilson of Communications Development Incorporated, Washington, DC.

Foreword

Trade is an important driver of economic growth and development: integration into world markets allows producers to specialize and reap the benefits of economies of scale. Trade also gives firms and households the opportunity to buy goods, services, and knowledge produced anywhere in the world.

Developing countries face many challenges in fully utilizing the opportunities offered by participation in the global economy. Some of these are associated with traditional trade barriers: tariffs and nontariff measures that impede market access. While such barriers continue to be important for products in which many developing countries have a comparative advantage—such as agricultural goods—the average level of tariffs has fallen significantly in recent decades. Moreover, many of the poorest countries have duty free access to high income markets. It is increasingly recognized that a key factor determining the competitiveness of developing country exporters is the national investment climate and business environment, as this is a major determinant of the costs—and thus the profitability— of production.

An important part of the agenda to lower operating costs is to reduce administrative red tape and remove unnecessary regulation. While there is nothing countries can do to improve their geography or resource endowments, they can take action to facilitate trade and to eliminate unnecessary administrative burdens for traders when moving goods across borders. Many developing countries have taken steps to simplify trade procedures and to use information technology to implement risk management systems to facilitate trade. However, progress has often been halting and has yet to make a real difference in many countries. On average it still takes three times as many days, nearly twice as many documents, and six times as many signatures to import in poor countries as it does in rich ones.

The development community, including the World Bank, has invested heavily in the reform and modernization of customs administrations around the world, and the results achieved in terms of reduced clearance times have at times been very impressive. But recent data compiled in the World Bank's Logistics Performance Indicators suggest that customs authorities are only responsible for approximately one third of the delays traders encounter at the border. An array of other government institutions are responsible for the majority of the problems traders face at the border. It matters little if customs are fully automated if traders still need to carry bundles of paperwork to a multitude of other government agencies that continue to process them manually. Likewise, it matters little if customs employ sophisticated risk management techniques to limit the number of time consuming physical inspections they perform if other agencies continue to require containers to be opened for routine inspection.

Focusing exclusively on customs reform is therefore unlikely to realize the sorts of breakthroughs necessary to significantly improve the competitiveness of traders in developing countries. A wider and much more comprehensive 'whole of government' approach is necessary. While there is no shortage of blueprints and reform tools available to guide the customs reform agenda, this is not the case for the many other agencies involved in clearing goods. In contrast to customs agencies that are linked into the World Customs Organization, most of these agencies are not connected through an intergovernmental body that acts as a focal point for the development of international instruments and the sharing of good practice approaches.

The objective of this book is to summarize and provide guidance on what constitutes good practices in border management—looking beyond customs clearance. The contributions to the volume make clear that there are no simple or universally applicable solutions. Instead, the aim is to provide a range of general guidelines that can be used to better understand the complex border management environment and the interdependencies and interrelationships that collectively need to be addressed to secure meaningful change and improvement.

While the editors have tried to be as comprehensive as possible in the choice of the topics addressed in the book, they have also been selective. Thus, the book does not focus on subjects that have been dealt with in some depth in other publications or on which there is already significant resource material. For example, customs reform is the subject of a 2005 World Bank publication on customs modernization and is therefore not addressed in great depth in this book. Instead the focus is on those emerging issues that present the most perplexing challenges for efficient border management.

I hope that the advice, guidelines, and general principles outlined in the book will help government officials, the trade community, and development practitioners to better understand both the importance of effective border management and the challenges of and options for making the border less of a barrier for traders. Designing and implementing practical initiatives and programs that make a positive difference to national competitiveness is conditional on governments giving priority to border management reform and modernization. There are costs associated with launching the kind of comprehensive border management modernization agenda outlined in this book. Reform in this area can be a long, complex, and at times frustrating process. But the costs and risks associated with ignoring this very important dimension of trade competitiveness are significant.

Bernard Hoekman
Director, International Trade
Department, The World Bank

Foreword

Acknowledgments

The chapters included in this handbook are a product of a collaborative effort, involving many World Bank colleagues and border management experts from around the world, that was supported by a grant from the government of the Netherlands through the Bank-Netherlands Partnership Program (BNPP).

Preparation of the book was led by Gerard McLinden of the World Bank's International Trade Department with support from a dedicated team of co-editors: Enrique Fanta, David Widdowson, and Tom Doyle. The editors are particularly grateful for the assistance provided by Patricia Wihongi, who took on the painstaking task of coordinating the final editing and publication process in a thoroughly professional manner.

The project would not have been possible without the support and advice of many World Bank colleagues, including Monica Alina Mustra, Jean-François Arvis, Charles Kunaka, Olivier Cadot, Sebastián Sáez, Yue Li, John Wilson, Ramesh Sivapathasundram, Munawer Sultan Khwaja, Hamid Alavi, Jean-Christophe Maur, Philip Schuler, Jose Eduardo Gutierrez Ossio, Amer Zafar Durrani, and Maryla Maliszewska, as well as former Bank staff Kees van der Meer, Luc De Wulf, and Robin Carruthers. Another former Bank official, Michel Zarnowiecki, not only authored two chapters but provided valuable feedback on the overall scope and content of the publication. Special acknowledgment also must go to Bernard Hoekman (Director, International Trade Department), who provided invaluable advice at several stages of the project, and to Mona Haddad (Sector Manager), who provided strong leadership and enthusiastic encouragement for the team and ensured the timely completion of the book.

The editors would also like to acknowledge the contribution of the chapter authors not mentioned above who showed great patience with the many demands and revisions suggested by the editors and reviewers: Stephen Holloway, Andrew Grainger, Robert Ireland, Darryn Jenkins, Erich Kieck, Frank Janssens, Laura Ignacio, and Michaela Prokop. Without their valuable expertise and insights on the complex issue of border management, the preparation of this handbook would not have been possible. In addition, Alan Hall, Johan du Plooy, and David Knight prepared chapters that due to size constraints we were unable to include in the final volume, but that will be published at a later time.

Special appreciation goes to our experienced team of peer reviewers, which shared its international expertise and made significant contributions to the scope and content of the publication: Kunio Mikuriya (Secretary General of the World Customs Organization), Graeme Ludlow (Deputy Division Chief, Fiscal Affairs Division, International Monetary Fund), and Roger Smith (Counsellor Customs, New Zealand Embassy, Washington, DC). All gave generously of their time and made a genuine difference to the quality and relevance of the project.

We are also grateful to the many officials in various international organizations who provided ideas and advice on the scope and content of the book, particularly the staff of the World Customs Organization's Capacity Building and Facilitation Directorates. Special recognition should also go to Tadatsugu (Toni) Matsudaira, who, while joining the Bank midway through the project, contributed as both an author and a peer reviewer.

Finally, the project benefited from the patient, professional, and extremely competent support provided by the administrative team in the International Trade Department, including Amelia Yuson, Anita Nyajur, Rebecca Martin, and Cynthia Abidin-Saurman. Special thanks also to Charumathi Rama Rao, who provided support on the financial aspects of the project, and to Stacey Chow, who so effectively coordinates the International Trade Department's publication program.

Acknowledgments

Contents

Boxes

Contents

Figures

Tables

Contents

1 Introduction and summary

Gerard McLinden

This book provides border management policymakers and reformers with a broad survey of key developments in and principles for improving trade facilitation through better border management, including practical advice on particular issues. In contrast to the traditional border management reform agenda, with its focus on improving customs operations, this book addresses both customs reform and areas well beyond customs—a significant broadening of scope. The book thus presents a new, more comprehensive approach to trade facilitation through border management reform: an approach that embraces a much wider, "whole of government" perspective.

Facilitating legitimate trade through better border management: the problem

In recent years countries have realized, perhaps more than ever, the importance of trade to achieving sustainable economic growth. Accordingly, they have lowered tariffs, established regimes to encourage foreign investment, and pursued opportunities for greater regional integration. Yet progress in trade facilitation is still slow in many countries—and progress is hampered by high costs and administrative difficulties at the border.

Outdated and overly bureaucratic border clearance processes imposed by customs and other agencies are now seen as posing greater barriers to trade than tariffs do. Cumbersome systems and procedures and poor infrastructure both increase transaction costs and lengthen delays to the clearance of imports, exports, and transit goods.

Such costs and delays make a country less competitive—whether by imposing deadweight inefficiencies that effectively tax imports, or by adding costs that raise the price of exports. Moreover, inefficient border management deters foreign investment and creates opportunities for administrative corruption.

While border clearance processes are among the most troublesome links in the global supply chain, they are especially so in poor countries, where it frequently takes three times as many days to import goods as it does in rich ones. Imports to poor countries require nearly twice as many documents and six times as many signatures (World Bank and IFC 2006). In Africa the difficulties are particularly severe: excessive physical inspections are a major source of delays, and the time between accepted customs declaration and customs clearance is four days, while in Organisation for Economic Cooperation and Development countries it is one (Arvis and others 2007).

Governments and donors are responding to the problem of inefficient border management by investing in border management reform, with measures designed to make countries more competitive by removing unnecessary barriers to legitimate trade. Virtually all countries now agree that trade facilitation reform will bring benefits to all. Recent bilateral and regional trading agreements include many border management provisions to ease trade. And many countries desire enhanced multilateral rules for trade facilitation within the World Trade Organization—part of an overhaul of the trade facilitation provisions in the General Agreement on Tariffs and Trade, which are now over 50 years old. Trade facilitation reform is a key element of the global Aid for Trade initiative.

Even so, customs and other border management agencies in many countries pay no more than lip service to trade facilitation. Traditionally the roles of these agencies have focused on the control of goods for revenue collection, industry assistance, and community protection. Over the last two decades these traditional roles have widened to include—in principle—the facilitation of legitimate trade. In practice, however, this new objective is honored only so far as it does not infringe on the agencies' existing border control practices.

Border management agencies in many countries regard trade facilitation as a secondary function. A Director General of Customs, from a developing country in Africa, explains the problem:

> My job relies entirely on my capacity to reach revenue collection targets. When the minister calls he has never once asked about clearance times. He is interested only in revenue collection. That's why I have a big board in my office detailing monthly, weekly, and daily collection results. I don't even have reliable information on clearance times. My job doesn't depend on knowing those numbers.

In developed countries, by contrast, border control regimes may focus more on national security than on revenue collection. Still, border management officials in all countries face similar tensions—and apparent contradictions—among the various objectives they are expected to meet.

How then can governments balance the need to facilitate legitimate commercial activities by compliant traders with the need for effective regulatory control—the main aim of traditional border management? This book explores the prospects for improvement, in part by shedding new light on the problems. With its 20 chapters and associated online tools, it can help development professionals and policymakers learn what works, what doesn't, and why.

To help officials meet their traditional control responsibilities while facilitating legitimate trade, the contributors to this book discuss three broad themes: the need for more investment in border management reform, the development of a new approach to border management, and the implications of institutional and political-economic factors for border management reform. In particular, the chapters in the book propose answers to the following questions:

- How can agencies develop and implement cost effective, trade friendly clearance processes and mechanisms while maintaining regulatory control?
- How can risk management and selective intervention techniques, increasingly employed by customs authorities, be extended to all agencies operating at the border?
- How can compliance improvement regimes that appropriately mix incentives with disincentives, and that progressively encourage higher levels of voluntary compliance, be established across border agencies?
- What hard infrastructure and information and communications technology (ICT) can be designed and deployed to appropriately achieve the most cost effective border clearance processes?
- Most important, how can policymakers build and maintain the political will and institutional commitment needed to undertake meaningful reform; to overcome strong vested interests; and to manage change?

Each chapter can be read in isolation or, preferably, as part of the whole.

The book has several intended audiences. First, it should help development professionals not specializing in border management—especially World Bank staff members engaged in customs and trade facilitation projects and diagnostic work—to have better informed discussions about policy choices with client governments, private sector counterparts, and public sector officials, notably by providing diagnostic tools and performance metrics. Second, it should help border management officials carry out reform and modernization initiatives by presenting sound guidance on designing, running, and monitoring programs, including good practice examples and reference tools. Third, it should nurture the political will and commitment to initiate and sustain meaningful border management reform, both among the high level government officials who are often called upon to assess and sponsor reform efforts and among participants engaged in the World Trade Organization negotiations on trade facilitation. Finally, it should help policymakers put into practice such regional integration activities as customs unions and regional trade agreements—agreements that invariably include provisions related to trade facilitation or other measures requiring changes at the border. The book aims especially to illuminate areas of the border management reform agenda that are not well addressed in other publications, or for which no practical resources already exist. It thus complements, without replacing, earlier reference guides such as the World Bank's *Customs Modernization Handbook* (De Wulf and Sokol 2005). Other useful materials and tools are mentioned in the text (and are more fully summarized in chapter 11).

What the book does not do is present off the shelf solutions. Managing borders is a complex task. Border management officials are presented with multiple, sometimes contradictory, objectives. Experience has shown that solutions must be tailored to national circumstances. But while there are no universal prescriptions for reform, many successful and promising initiatives are under way around the world. Many examples of good practice can be studied, adapted, and replicated elsewhere.

For the international customs community there is the World Customs Organization, which helps to shape that community's reform agenda. In other areas of border management reform, however, there have been few attempts to identify and document changing needs and concerns—leaving policymakers and development professionals generally in the dark. They work to address similar problems, but they do so independently, without the benefit of guidelines or good practice examples. As a result, reformers' efforts are duplicated, resources are wasted, and outcomes are less than ideal. The problem is acute in Sub-Saharan Africa, which lags badly behind other regions in trade facilitation. For example, in one African region several donors are financing separate one stop border programs for regional countries. Likewise, several countries are developing single window systems, with minimal sharing of models and information and little attention to making the systems regionally uniform and integrated.

An opportunity has been created by a broad range of initiatives to spur regional trade integration—but that opportunity is being missed. With the help of this book, World Bank staff and others will be better equipped to recapture it.

Border management reform: more than customs modernization

The new agenda for better border management is about more than customs clearance. Driving the new agenda are seven key developments, none of them exclusively related to customs:

- A rise in global competition for foreign investment.
- A growing awareness of the costs created for traders by outdated, inefficient border formalities.
- An expectation of prompter, more predictable processing for imports and exports (the result of increased private sector investment in advanced logistics and just-in-time manufacturing regimes).
- A multiplication of policy and procedural requirements directly related to international commitments (for example, World Trade Organization accession).
- A proliferation of regional trading agreements, making customs work more complex.
- An increased expectation of and respect for integrity and good governance.
- A heightened awareness of the need for customs and other border management agencies to play a more central national security role.

Customs agencies have typically led border management reform efforts, and improving the performance of customs remains a high priority for many countries. But customs is only one of the agencies involved in border processing, and evidence suggests it is often responsible for no more than a third of regulatory delays. Data from the World Bank's Logistics Performance Indicators (Arvis and others 2010) suggest that traders are much more satisfied with the performance of customs than with that of other border management agencies. The data highlight the need to reform and modernize border management in areas other than customs, such as health, agriculture, quarantine, police, immigration, and standards. Moreover, in many developing countries, time release studies—using the methodology adopted by the World Customs Organization (WCO 2002)—suggest that improvements meant to speed goods through customs are undermined by the comparative failure of other border management agencies to reform and modernize using similar modern approaches and risk based selective inspection techniques.

Border management agencies other than customs have not received much attention from the development community—so progress has been patchy at best. There is little knowledge of diagnostic tools, reform and modernization guidelines, or international best practices. Where such tools are available they generally are confined to customs; other border agencies lack the internationally agreed instruments and blueprints that have guided much of the customs reform agenda (in part because they have nothing equivalent to the World Customs Organization). Few practical mechanisms have been developed to help these agencies cooperate and share information. And little work has been done to analyze the political-economy factors and dynamics that affect their ability to cooperate meaningfully.

Because clearance times are largely determined by the weakest link in a border processing chain, meaningful trade facilitation presupposes comprehensive reform initiatives across the whole of border management. There must be cooperation and information sharing among all agencies involved. The keen interest of many developing countries in harmonizing, streamlining, and simplifying border management systems and procedures has led to such initiatives as:

- *Coordinated border management.* This can include information sharing, co-located facilities, close interagency cooperation, delegation of administrative authority, and crossdesignation of officials.
- *One stop border posts.* Neighboring countries coordinate import, export, and transit processes, so that traders need not duplicate regulatory formalities on both sides of a border.
- *Single window systems.* Traders can submit all import, export, and transit information required by regulatory agencies at one time—through a single electronic gateway—rather than submit essentially the same information repeatedly to various government entities.

These initiatives, which have some common themes, promise significant improvement in border management and clearance. Yet they face political, technical, institutional, and procedural problems that so far have proved extremely difficult to overcome. As a result, the conceptual and technological leaps made elsewhere in the business world have not yet transformed border management. Even where progress has been made, most strategies and results have not been distilled, documented, or shared with the wider trade facilitation and development community. And the information that has been shared typically focuses on narrow technical issues. It does not address a much greater challenge: that of securing the political and institutional will and commitment needed to design and carry out cost effective border management reform.

The need for leadership, a clear vision, and strong political commitment

Comprehensive border management reform requires both a very clear vision and strong political will and commitment. If either the clear vision or the political commitment is lacking, reformers will be unlikely to prevail against the strong influence of domestic constituencies that benefit from existing business process inefficiencies, interdependencies, and relationships. In addition, reformers often need knowhow and financial resources that can be hard to access—especially in developing countries, where governments face many pressing challenges and competing development priorities.

Chapter summaries

The preceding discussion has framed this book's approach to modern border management reform by surveying the complex activities, operations, and interdependencies that occur at borders and that can be improved through careful reform. The remaining 19 chapters of the book, addressing specific reform topics in detail, are summarized below.

Chapter 2 articulates a new strategic vision for modern border management and offers a rationale for the new paradigm. Modern initiatives—such as coordinated border management, one stop border posts, and single window regimes—are explored, and their common themes and advantages are expressed in a unified vision of collaborative border management. Tom Doyle presents this new model as a fundamental shift from the physical control of goods to the control of information, through a combination of customer analysis and segmentation and intelligence driven risk management. In this emerging model, imports, exports, and transit shipments can be processed well before their physical arrival at the border, with much of the time consuming processing conducted during transportation. An appropriate mix of incentives and disincentives can encourage high trader compliance.

Collaborative border management challenges traditional thinking, suggesting that officials need not see a tradeoff between securing regulatory compliance and facilitating legitimate trade. A new, more transparent and industry friendly regulatory framework promotes competitiveness and growth, even as it ensures regulatory compliance and protects the community. But the model presented here does not require radical change in existing institutional structures. Government agencies have their own aims and objectives, and typically they devote much time and attention to ensuring their own survival. Under the model outlined in chapter 2, collaboration to meet shared objectives does not presuppose organizational amalgamation, rationalization, or elimination. Finally, chapter 2 describes how to develop and implement a phased transition or transformation plan calibrated to the needs, capabilities, and political realities reformers face.

Chapter 3 puts border management modernization in the context of the larger trade supply chain. Monica Alina Mustra highlights the need to identify bottlenecks by carefully analyzing the entire trade and transport logistics network. Drawing on recently available data sources such as the World

Bank's Logistics Performance Indicators (Arvis and others 2007 and 2010) and on new insights into global supply chains and their operations around the world, the author identifies factors affecting countries' ability to connect to regional and global markets and identifies the possible locations of binding constraints facing countries and regions. The chapter will help reformers and policymakers identify key reform opportunities and set clear priorities for change based on national circumstances.

Also surveyed in chapter 3 are the data sources that can help reformers compare their countries' border management performance with that of neighbors and key competitors. Officials in many developing countries often cite inadequate infrastructure—ports, roads, border stations, and the like—as a major cause of trade bottlenecks and delays in the clearance of goods. Although some such complaints are accurate, recent data suggest that in many cases governments would have done much better to invest in less costly forms of border management reform and modernization. For example, a new port or container handling terminal might not be needed if containers can be kept in port for just 1 or 2 days, rather than for 13 or 14.

In **chapter 4** Michel Zarnowiecki shows how the modern concept of the border has evolved and describes present approaches to border control throughout the world, focusing on the design, management, and operation of border facilities and related infrastructure. Partly because of new security imperatives, and partly because of new approaches to managing border compliance, the concept of a border has changed in recent years. The resulting new challenges and opportunities have major implications for border management professionals.

Unfortunately, in many countries—despite the advent of global supply chains, advanced logistics systems, and affordable new technological solutions—the border crossing experience remains largely as it has been for centuries. Nevertheless, there are good practice models that can guide meaningful reform. Chapter 4 explores their advantages and disadvantages, identifying key issues for reformers. Zarnowiecki highlights how well designed border posts, related infrastructure, and effective operating modalities can support reform across the whole of the border and, at the same time, promote facilitation and security objectives. Modern tools—X-ray equipment, cargo tracking systems, information technology—can ease trade while boosting regulatory compliance.

Chapter 5 begins with a summary of the extensive research that has been done to put reform investments into an economic development context. Authors Yue Li, Gerard McLinden, and John S. Wilson first highlight the trade and economic gains that can be achieved through sensible, well targeted investments. They then describe how to present key decisionmakers with a robust business case. How can a cost-benefit analysis demonstrate that border management reform is a sound business investment—not merely a cost?

Competition for resources is intense. To obtain the political support and commitment needed to initiate and sustain meaningful reform, reformers need a strong business case. Chapter 5 will help them do the needed analysis and present it convincingly.

Chapter 6 analyzes core border management disciplines and competencies that should underpin all modernization efforts. In particular, it emphasizes the need to apply risk management principles to improve inspection-detection ratios and to enable border management agencies to more effectively target suspect or high risk shipments while speeding the release of low risk ones. David Widdowson and Stephen Holloway provide practical guidance on establishing a sound compliance management and improvement regime, with an appropriate mix of incentives and disincentives to boost voluntary compliance by traders. Among customs officials such disciplines are in many cases well understood, even if they are not always consistently practiced. But experience suggests that among many noncustoms border management officials such disciplines are both poorly understood and poorly practiced. Part of chapter 6 accordingly focuses on describing the application of these disciplines in a wider context that extends across all aspects of border management.

Chapter 7 reviews the critical supporting role of ICT. Tom Doyle offers an overview of recent developments, not as a technology manual, but as a nontechnical introduction to the issues that border management officials and policymakers must consider and the major decisions they must make. ICT can play an important part in meeting business objectives and achieving world class performance. New tools make it much easier to do things that, only a decade ago, were impossible or out of the reach of developing countries.

In outlining some of these developments chapter 7 describes close interdependencies among policies, processes, implementation strategies, governance models, organizational structures, development frameworks, and supporting infrastructures. At present these technological developments and interdependencies are not sufficiently understood by most policymakers. As a result, ICT is not selected or deployed as effectively as it should be.

In **chapter 8** (closely related to chapter 7), Ramesh Siva outlines critical issues facing single window systems for trade. Over the past few decades some countries have undertaken serious, systematic efforts to make trade more efficient by implementing national systems of this kind. Where the systems have succeeded they have greatly improved countries' processing of import, export, and transit consignments and have drastically lowered trade transaction and compliance costs. Other countries, especially in the developing world, have noted this correlation and sought to create their own single windows for better border management. And regional initiatives—such as the Association of Southeast Asian Nations Single Window—have encouraged the development of national single windows as a prerequisite to joining the regional systems.

Experience is beginning to identify interlinked areas that ultimately determine success or failure. National single windows can help realize the collaborative border management model outlined in chapter 2.

Chapter 9 explores the often difficult process of ICT procurement. Tom Doyle stresses how such technology has been proven to make business processes more effective and, at the same time, increase control and transparency in border management. Yet its procurement can be complex, time consuming, and fraught with dangers.

Three types of factors—external, technological, and institutional—affect ICT procurement in ways that can be critical to the success or failure of border management reform. To make the procurement process more efficient and effective, some of its features, including its present limitations, must be taken into account. Doyle outlines some emerging best practices in ICT procurement, and he proposes a new procurement approach for wider use in border management modernization.

In **chapter 10** Andrew Grainger focuses on the important, but often overlooked, role of the private sector—as a key stakeholder—in supporting sustainable border management reform. After outlining some consultation mechanisms available for identifying appropriate reform initiatives, Grainger considers the private sector as a partner in ensuring that regulatory control objectives are met, discussing management tools and instruments for encouraging compliant behavior by people involved in legitimate trade. What private sector services can be contracted to underpin the government's activities, augmenting its resources and capabilities? Areas addressed include regulation, outsourcing (preshipment inspection, destination inspection, and management contracts), and the assessment of intermediaries and logistics providers (such as customs brokers and transporters and freight forwarders) for competency and compliance.

Chapter 10 also considers models for securing genuine business government cooperation, including so-called procommittees along with private-public partnerships. Various private sector communities have different interests, and those interests may not be aligned. Yet dedicated local, national, regional, and international trade facilitation committees can convene private sector representatives to explore a shared vision for reform. Such committees can also be effective vehicles for soliciting political patronage and for assigning priorities to reform requirements.

Chapter 11 discusses the role of international instruments in the field of trade facilitation as guides for multiple stakeholders working together to achieve common goals. Robert Ireland and Tadatsugu Matsudaira survey best practice approaches and internationally agreed instruments and implementation tools for trade facilitation and coordinated border management, including those developed by the World Customs Organization. A phased approach is provided suggesting how best to work toward the adoption of international instruments. The authors argue that stakeholder engagement and ownership of the instruments through participation in their design and development is of significant importance.

Chapter 11 also presents a typology of the international instruments and discusses how countries can work toward adopting them. An annex briefly describes many of the key international instruments, tools, and best practice approaches currently available to reformers.

Chapter 12 explores key issues for border management reformers, including how to build and sustain political will and commitment; the importance of managing stakeholder relationships and expectations; the role of institutions (with the advantages and disadvantages of various institutional models and organizational structures); and the critical need for human resource management policies that create incentives for sustained reform. Discussing the core components of effective human resource management, Darryn Jenkins and Gerard McLinden identify key strategic principles for managing change in border management. They highlight the importance of developing a robust communication strategy for internal and external stakeholders, to provide a balanced and comprehensive consultation and education program. And they examine border management arrangements recently put in place around the world, with some of the strategies and philosophies that have guided organizations through transformation. What were the key challenges? How were they overcome? The authors focus on several approaches that have succeeded in practice—and on the reasons for their success.

Chapter 13 focuses on the proliferation of nontariff measures affecting trade. Such measures can significantly increase trader transaction costs and make countries less competitive. Often they are seen as more burdensome and less transparent than traditional trade barriers applied at the border, such as tariffs, quotas, licensing, and prohibitions. As a result, international trade negotiations have developed new and complex rules for the adoption of nontariff measures by national governments. Authors Olivier Cadot, Maryla Maliszewska, and Sebastián Sáez define the problem of nontariff measures, explain the international regulations governing them, and propose policies for managing them more effectively to ensure that they restrict trade as little as possible.

Chapter 14 maps the main border management provisions typically included in regional integration agreements and customs unions. Analytically comparing the key features of customs unions—whose member states share a goal of promoting economic integration—Erich Kieck and Jean Christophe Maur show how such unions present an ideal springboard for coordinated border management. On the one hand, the authors recognize that trade facilitation reform efforts within customs unions so far have adopted a narrow customs perspective. On the other hand, common reform has occurred in some areas, while challenges remain.

Discussing how reform provisions can be made effective and how regional groupings can be used to mobilize support for effective border management reform, chapter 14 explores unionwide approaches to risk management, mutual recognition, joint and one stop controls, trusted traveler and trader schemes, and the real time exchange of information within and between countries. All create opportunities for a more effective approach to regional integration and coordinated border management.

Chapter 15 addresses the role of ICT in supporting regional integration. Tom Doyle and Frank Janssens offer a case study of how the European Union has applied such technology in customs, providing other customs unions with guidance for economic integration. How has the union achieved its present technical and functional integration? What issues must be considered by reformers seeking ICT solutions to facilitate other regional integration initiatives?

Chapter 16 focuses on the effective management of sanitary and phytosanitary (SPS) controls at the border, with special attention to the World Trade Organization's SPS agreement. All food and agricultural and products face SPS controls as part of the border release process. Such products are often comparatively important for developing countries, while the shipments are fairly small. For both reasons, a considerable part of trade for developing countries faces SPS handling.

How SPS controls are managed can significantly affect trade facilitation. As authors Kees van der Meer and Laura Ignacio explain, the segmentation of food and agricultural markets poses special challenges for safety management and trade promotion. SPS clearance differs in two major respects from customs clearance. First, export promotion (market access) is a major aim of SPS services, and it can receive more resources than import control receives. Second, efforts made away from the border can be much larger than efforts at the border. Noting the lack of cooperation between SPS services and customs at present, the authors conclude that SPS agencies should be actively engaged in initiatives designed to rationalize and improve the coordination of border management modernization efforts.

Chapter 17 examines transit cargo management. While often problematic, transit cargo management is especially problematic for landlocked countries. Such countries generally suffer a large disadvantage compared with countries possessing coastlines and deep sea ports (countries that tend to be linked by the world's most active trade corridors, whether in Europe, North America, or developing regions). Furthermore, landlocked developing countries—many of them in Sub-Saharan Africa—depend on comparatively inefficient trade corridors.

In chapter 17 author Jean-François Arvis focuses on transit regimes: sets of provisions enabling goods not yet cleared by customs for consumption to reach their international or inland destinations, or, more narrowly, customs regulations and procedures for goods in transit. Transit regimes are essential to international trade corridors, since goods are cleared at the country of destination where duties and value added tax are collected. Transit regimes are also increasingly important for domestic trade corridors—which may have features very similar to those of international corridors—since the regimes allow traders more flexible clearance options.

Chapter 18 addresses the ramifications of radical changes in the national security environment since the September 11, 2001 attacks on the United States, discussing how the newer security requirements affect border operations. Authors David Widdowson and Stephen Holloway consider how added security can be seamlessly incorporated into border operations without sacrificing trade facilitation. Focusing on recent regulatory supply chain security initiatives, the authors examine the possible impact of such initiatives on regulatory activities at the border, and they assess the consistency of various regulatory responses with the objectives of risk management and commercial practicality. The authors then identify key elements of a modern compliance management strategy, describing how each can be applied to mitigate risk. Based on an analysis of several specific risks to the security of the international supply chain—and of the compliance management strategies intended to address them—Widdowson and Holloway recommend policy responses and operational strategies to guide policymakers and administrators in formulating regulatory responses to identified risks.

Chapter 19 examines issues facing fragile states and postconflict countries—places where traditional approaches may be inappropriate for addressing border management problems. Outlining a typology of fragile states, and describing lessons learned over the past decade of donor support, Luc De Wulf discusses experiences carrying out various types of border management improvement, and he suggests broad strategies and approaches as most appropriate for each type. The chapter focuses on the responsibilities of customs, particularly in raising revenue: a priority for both governments and donors, for which several well documented initiatives have already been put into practice. Nontraditional approaches to customs support include management contracts, foreign technical experts, preshipment inspection and destination inspection services, and reforms driven by ICT.

Chapter 20 focuses on the critical issue of corruption at the border. While poor governance significantly impairs the revenue generation and trade facilitation effectiveness of many countries, it is also recognized as a major barrier to the implementation of many border management reform initiatives. In this chapter Amer Durrani, Michaela Prokop, and Michel Zarnowiecki present a new and innovative approach to assessing and addressing organizational governance vulnerabilities. The authors examine a recently developed integrity risk modeling tool that draws on several different, yet complementary models to yield a comprehensive understanding of governance dimensions from both bottom up and top down perspectives. Although the methodology was designed initially for application in customs administration, chapter 20 outlines how it could be adapted successfully for whole-of-border modernization efforts.

References

Arvis, J.-F., M.A. Mustra, J. Panzer, L. Ojala, and T. Naula. 2007. *Connecting to Compete 2007: Trade Logistics in the Global Economy—the Logistics Performance Index and Its Indicators.* Washington, DC: The World Bank.

———. 2010. *Connecting to Compete 2010: Trade Logistics in the Global Economy—the Logistics Performance Index and Its Indicators.* Washington, DC: The World Bank.

De Wulf, L., and J. Sokol, eds. 2005. *Customs Modernization Handbook.* Washington, DC: The World Bank.

WCO (World Customs Organization). 2002. *Guide to Measure the Time Required for the Release of Goods.* Brussels: WCO.

World Bank and IFC (International Finance Corporation). 2006. *Doing Business 2007: How to Reform.* Washington, DC: The World Bank.

1

Introduction and summary

CHAPTER 2

The future of border management

Tom Doyle

This chapter explores the central themes of contemporary border management and articulates a new strategic vision for border processing and clearance. The chapter brings several key concepts together into a holistic new approach known as collaborative border management.

The foundations of collaborative border management are relationship management with the trading community and regulatory authorities and collaborative engagement with transport and supply chain partners. Through *customer segmentation* and *intelligence driven risk management,* the clearance (admissibility processing) of goods and passengers can be carried out electronically in advance of physical arrival at the border.

Customer segmentation enables border agencies to tailor information and services to the needs of customer groups. This can be done through:

- Grouping website information by customer group—or even by individual.
- Offering dedicated information and trade portals.
- Using account managers for large business customers.
- Providing specialist enquiry services.
- Hosting seminars and training events, direct mail marketing, and outreach campaigns.
- Making direct calls to targeted companies.

Intelligence driven risk management enables border agencies to accurately carry out prearrival and predeparture identity assurance for trusted traders and passengers (with eligibility entitlements), while targeting the rest for intervention. A common source of regulatory admissibility and preclearance information is made available once and only once to all relevant border management agencies, partners, and customers through a single window (see chapter 8).[1] Collaborative border management benefits governments by:

- Lowering the overall cost of border management.
- Enhancing security.
- Improving intelligence and enforcement.
- Boosting trader compliance.
- Deploying resources more effectively and efficiently.
- Increasing integrity and transparency.

Collaborative border management also benefits the private sector by:

- Cutting costs through reducing delays and informal payments.
- Enabling faster clearance and release.
- Explaining rules, making their application more predictable.
- Allowing the more effective and efficient deployment of resources.
- Increasing transparency.

Collaborative border management adds efficiencies in processing goods and passengers—even while increasing regulatory compliance—by obtaining information directly—connecting with upstream supply chain processes and systems at the earliest possible time, either through a single window portal or directly with the customer's or designated agent's information systems. Within collaborative border management, trusted clients—such as authorized economic operators—would be entitled to facilitated, streamlined border clearance facilities, and could even be allowed to discharge their regulatory obligations in a differentiated way (for example, through prearrival clearance processing, postclearance periodic self assessment, and direct connection with trader information systems), as recommended by the World Customs Organization.[2]

Policymakers frequently believe they must choose between regulatory control and trade facilitation. Collaborative border management challenges this commonly held view (Grainger 2008). Its regulatory framework—more transparent, friendlier to industry—promotes growth and competitiveness while ensuring regulatory compliance.

The evolution and challenges of present border management arrangements

Traditionally the role of customs and other border management agencies has been to keep undesirable goods and people out while collecting revenue and taxes on goods that are allowed in. Now, however, there is increased emphasis on facilitating trade.[3] A new vision for border management was introduced in a document presented at the 50th session of the World Customs Organization Policy Commission (Gordhan 2007). Some of its key principles were:

- The need to increase the contribution of international trade to economic growth and development as much as possible through effective, efficient customs controls.
- The need to foster certainty and predictability by establishing clear, precise standards.
- The development of capacity to promote compliance in a way that facilitates legitimate international trade.

The current Doha Round of World Trade Organization negotiations has also stressed the contribution that improved border management can make to economic development and poverty reduction by reducing red tape for goods moving across borders.[4]

Some countries recently have attempted to further secure their borders by assimilating customs agencies into new, more widely focused integrated border management agencies. One approach to accomplishing this is by creating a single border management authority. Another is through a virtual model whereby agencies cooperate without sharing the same corporate identity (sharing the same vision and goals and using the same electronic infrastructure).

Integrating border management agencies requires significant organizational change—yet it has not always fully exploited the available efficiencies, in knowledge sharing and in the improved achievement of government objectives, that might be obtained through collaborative border management. And it has created its own problems, as various entities struggle to retain their identities and protect their mandates and resources.

The limits and constraints of present border management arrangements

The forces now generally driving the border management agenda include:

- A heightened awareness of costs.
- Rising expectations in the private sector.
- Increased policy and procedural requirements.
- Competition for foreign investment.
- The demand for integrity and good governance.
- Political pressure for the agencies to increase competiveness.

Customs and other border management agencies are required to respond to these forces and deliver more varied services more efficiently, often with diminished funding. There is a widely acknowledged need to eliminate delays and duplication in international supply chains—problems caused by multiple reporting requirements and inspection regimes—and to encourage compliance with standards by clearly defining the benefits of trade facilitation. Customs reforms alone will not address the challenges (see chapter 1).

Customs and other border management agencies cannot continue to use an exclusively transaction based approach to controlling the movement of physical goods across borders—one where each shipment received is assessed individually, with little regard for the customer's compliance history or for commercially available information that could ground admissibility checks and preclearance decisions. Information is still typically collected and stored individually by each border agency involved in the clearance process. This information is rarely shared across agencies. So the burden is on the customer to supply similar sets of information to multiple agencies, which then individually process data before regulatory requirements for admissibility and clearance can be met. To complicate the process further, some government agencies are automated and some not—often requiring traders not only to supply the same or very similar data to different entities, but to do so using a variety of paper and electronic forms.

The call for higher rates of export-led economic growth will continue to put customs and other border agencies in the spotlight, creating opportunities for these agencies to demonstrate their willingness and capability to contribute. The European Union's target is to cut red tape by 25 percent by 2012.[5] Similarly ambitious targets have been set by the Association of Southeast Asian Nations and the Asia-Pacific Economic Cooperation. To meet the challenges a holistic approach to border management reform—rather than a narrow technical focus—is needed. Inevitably, the pace of reform in some major trading countries and the onerous demands they make of their trading partners will stretch the administrative capacity of developing countries. Capacity constraints in developing countries, especially in the least developed countries, often hinder effective cooperation among customs and other border management agencies.

Table 2.1	Key aspects of collaborative border management	
Practice type	**Common practice**	**Collaborative border management practice**
Policy	• Balance between facilitation and control • Mistrust of supply chain actors • Limited customer segmentation • Limited incentives for compliance • Focus on physical border controls • Adversarial relationship with trade • Limited cooperation and data exchange	• Optimization of both facilitation and control • Trusted collaboration of supply and transport chain partners • Customer treatment based on differentiation and service culture • Strong incentives for compliance • Focus on virtual border controls • Constructive partnership with trade • Extensive collaboration and information sharing
Processes	• Output based functional model • Focus on goods and revenue • Single treatment for all clients • Agency specific risk management • High levels of physical inspection • Transaction based procedures	• Outcome based process model • Focus on information • Flexible solutions for different clients • Cross-agency, intelligence-driven risk management • Intervention by exception • Exception based procedures and audit based control
People	• Physical control at the border • Limited transparency • Organizational performance measurement • Standard training, mainly administrative	• Customer compliance focus through intelligence driven risk management • Full transparency • Clear measures of individual and collective performance • Capability modeling, commercial and administrative
Information and communications technology (ICT)	• Black box systems—systems viewed solely through input, output, and transfer characteristics, without knowledge of their internal workings—using proprietary software • Isolated data capture and information processing • National silo based solutions • ICT security limited to intrusion protection • Emphasis on back office transaction processing • Reliance on outmoded commercial off the shelf or nationalistic solutions	• Extensive use of open source software systems (free software whose inner components or logic are available for inspection) • Service oriented architecture • Regionally integrated common solutions • Business continuity assured through security and contingency arrangements • Move toward self service, front office solutions and direct access to trade systems • Shared services build of common component solutions
Infrastructure and facilities	• Agencies operating on a standalone basis • Individual trader integration with multiple agencies • Predominance of in-house build and delivery • Output based procurement	• Single window interagency collaboration • One stop shop • Value added outsourcing • Outcome based procurement

Source: Author's compilation.

The concept of collaborative border management

Whereas the international community has discussed integrated border management and coordinated border management, this book—to denote more than mere coordination, while avoiding the more threatening connotations of organizational integration—uses the term *collaborative border management*. Collaborative border management is based on the need for agencies and the international community to work together to achieve common aims. The model suggests that border management agencies can increase control while providing a more efficient service, and that they can do so while retaining their own organizational mandates and integrity.

In collaborative border management a virtual border encompasses the entire transport and supply chain, assessing goods and passengers for admissibility and clearance in advance of arriving at the physical border (see chapter 4). Border management agencies work together, sharing information. As they gather, collate, and share more data, a complete view of risks and opportunities emerges, encouraging a knowledge sharing culture and a border management strategy built on proactive decisionmaking.

Typically collaborative border management is not achieved through forced organizational change—which invariably creates conflict—but by creating an overarching governance body charged with establishing a border management vision and ensuring that all stakeholders work together to achieve it. This requires strong political will and commitment and appropriate incentives and disincentives. While collaborative border management can be achieved under a single border management agency, the creation of such an agency is not a precondition for success. Well managed, collaborative border management results in reduced documentation, a more appropriate treatment of traders through more thorough and accurate data collection and analysis, and a combination of lower costs and greater control for border management agencies. It can also preserve the independence and specific mandates of customs and other agencies involved in border management. Collaborative border management also benefits the customer, reducing administrative and compliance costs while saving time and making service more predictable.

Collaborative border management makes possible a set of defined business outcomes, including:

- Distinctive border management agency operations in areas that make a real difference to trade and industry.
- Objective measures of performance in all key result areas.
- Cost savings through the avoidance of unnecessary duplication of effort.
- A trading environment that is more business friendly and responsive.

Key aspects of collaborative border management

Key aspects of collaborative border management—grouped under policy, processes, people, information and communications technology, and infrastructure and facilities—are summarized in table 2.1. Although many collaborative border management practices are already being achieved through discrete reform initiatives, collaborative border management brings these innovations together in a holistic approach.

Policy

Collaborative border management enables a shift in the primary focus of border management agencies from a weighted, balanced approach to control and facilitation toward a highly facilitated and optimized compliance management approach. Collaborative border management is grounded in the efficacy of compliance management but recognizes that the vast majority of travel and trade is legitimate. Trusted partnership arrangements improve both regulatory control and customer service. More comprehensive compliance management makes agency staff operate more efficiently, targeting only high risk passengers and consignments for intervention. And tangible benefits accrue to compliant customers, even as equally visible enforcement sanctions discourage the less compliant.

Collaborative border management demands improved intergovernmental and interagency networking arrangements, allowing agencies to cooperate in accordance with common and agreed standards. Information is centrally located and a single view of each customer is provided, while customer segmentation allows agencies to deliver enhanced, value added services. The consistency of information across border management agencies provides more accurate intelligence, allowing agencies to focus their resources on risk-driven intervention. By working with neighboring and participating countries, all partners benefit from the piecing together of previously disparate information, and the customer experience is more efficient and consistent across border management agencies and jurisdictions.

Collaborative border management takes advantage of the availability of information at the earliest point in the transport and supply chain at which border management agencies can become involved. This could be at a factory while goods are being packaged for shipment, at a port on the point of departure, or indeed at any time before the physical destination border is reached. Ensuring compliance at the virtual border reduces clearance time at the physical border, so border management agencies can focus on the audit and examination of higher risk shipments and passengers.

Processes

Collaborative border management requires border management agencies to define outcome based processes, such as increased customer compliance and greater export competitiveness, rather than output based processes, such as the volume of transactions processed. Looking at desired outcomes from both agencies' and customers' points of view allows processes to be defined that satisfy both sets of needs. In addition, looking at border management operations as a whole allows certain common outcomes—such as reduced counterfeiting—to be identified, creating opportunities to boost efficiency and make service delivery more cost effective.

Collaborative border management enables border management agencies to concentrate on the intelligent treatment of customers. Having a single view of the customer enables border management agencies to cooperatively analyze and assess information and to make more informed, rigorous decisions. Customers benefit from streamlined, simplified interactions with multiple border management agencies. And services can be designed to improve the customer experience across all interactions.

Intelligent data analysis at the customer level also enables agencies to concentrate on auditing higher risk customers and shipments. Trusted customer relationships are developed, and information shared across agencies allows greater efficiencies.

People

Collaborative border management demands that border management agency officials be well equipped with the skills, knowledge, behavior, and experience to manage new processes. The role of skilled, experienced, committed officials is the driving force. A comprehensive capability assessment of the administrative capacity of each border management agency should ensure a focus on delivering quality collaborative border management while minimizing compliance and administrative costs. The assessment should yield a set of recommended transformation actions, including, for example, organizational change through outsourcing certain functions.[6] In addition, the assessment could result in a change management program enabling border management agency staff whose previous responsibilities may have become less essential to discharge their new responsibilities more effectively. Staff should be trained and designated to perform cross agency tasks where appropriate, eliminating redundancy, reducing duplication, and creating customer service efficiencies.

Information and communications technology

Collaborative border management promotes the technical development and interaction that is needed for more effectively sharing information and identifying risks. It implies significantly closer national, regional, and international collaboration for government agencies and for the international travel and transport industries. This can be achieved through technology systems that share and link information. In addition, bilateral, regional, and multilateral agreements may be required that facilitate policies and strategies for collaborating, information sharing, and developing interoperable systems.

The aims of timely, effective clearance and border operation interoperability are difficult to meet using traditional databases and database queries. A vast amount of data must be analyzed and auctioned in minutes—while data may be erroneous, incomplete, nonspecific, and created without international standards (where what is required in one country is not required in another). Fuzzy logic can improve identity assurance and compliance management by helping border agencies make differentiations using data that may be absent, imprecise, or wrong. Matching with fuzzy logic is particularly useful for finding information that best fits diverse, complex conditions, such as when it is necessary to access large amounts of data stored in multiple formats (structured and unstructured, image and biometric coding).

Fuzzy logic search and match, as opposed to relational database searching, is based on four principles:

- Some search criteria are more important than others, so search criteria may be weighted. For example, a description of goods may have less weight than a country of origin or intelligence on container handling arrangements.
- Some data may be missing from a cargo or passenger manifest.
- Some data may be imprecise. For example, different datasets are collected at different times by different parties, as governments have not agreed on dataset standards.
- Some data may be inaccurate. For example, textual data, such as locations, dates, and container and identity numbers, are all prone to typing errors.

Fuzzy logic searching and matching against interagency risk profiles would greatly increase the chance of successful identity management and preclearance admissibility decisions prior to arrival at the physical border. It would also improve other compliance management functions, such as surveillance and investigation.

Systems and business processes—across countries, organizations, and the like—should be interoperable. Linking both structured and unstructured information across border management agencies prevents redundant processing and averts the inefficiencies inherent in standalone, or stovepiped, information silos.

Infrastructure and facilities

Infrastructures at ports of entry often have designs that predate today's security, trade, and travel demands and priorities. Facilities at ports of entry often are inadequate. Upgrading these facilities, in collaboration with both other border management agencies and neighboring countries, is an important step in cost effective trade facilitation and regulatory control improvements.

Collaborative border management enables the creation of a shared services environment where a collaborative operating model and facilities could be created using industry leading-edge practices. Significant economies of scale could be realized through such arrangements. In a regional setting, a shared service environment could save agency specific country development costs, interagency country development costs, and the country and regional costs of maintaining support technologies. The key features of a shared service approach are:

- A common vision and orientation toward delivery and service levels.
- A culture of continuous improvement.
- Strong performance metrics.

The shared services approach would require some consensus on the construction of an efficient, effective operating model and an agreement on the common core processes to be managed. It would allow participating agencies to rapidly reach the capability level of the most efficient agency and to reduce their operating costs, while the leading agency would set the pace of modernization. Governments and their border agencies typically are at different stages in their reform and modernization programs. While modern technologies and facilities have matured to the point where shared service could greatly improve operations for border agencies and their customers, political will—for this and other new infrastructure and facilities management approaches—is needed.

Outsourcing also provides specialized services more cost effectively. Software application development, maintenance, and operations can be outsourced. Technology infrastructure can also be outsourced—with hardware and associated services contracted out, border management agencies are free to concentrate on the delivery of core business strategies. The current trend is toward value added outsourcing, with the following objectives kept in mind:

- Provision of new technology and expertise.
- Standardization or centralization of operations.
- Improvement in the speed and quality of service.
- Transformation of the agency or department.
- Improvement in the focus of officials.
- Improvement in ability to handle demand fluctuations.
- Compensation for the inability to hire suitably qualified staff.

- Improvement in management discipline and transparency.
- Substitution of expense spending for capital spending.
- Reduction of costs.
- Motivation of organizational change.
- Increase in revenues.

The challenges of outsourcing include:

- Shaping the relationship to the situation.
- Negotiating and contracting effectively.
- Managing workforce issues.
- Managing the ongoing relationship.
- Ensuring strong performance.
- Institutionalizing flexibility and innovation.

The risks of outsourcing include:

- Economic espionage.
- Access to valuable or sensitive code.
- Data privacy.
- Business continuity.

As with shared services, the principal barriers to outsourcing are a lack of understanding at border agencies about savings from the approach and their agencies' unwillingness to change their procurement policies.

A public-private partnership, or contractual agreement between a public agency and a private sector entity, can allow greater private sector participation in many types of projects (figure 2.1).

A single window can benefit from a public private partnership (see chapter 8). Core functions are converged and streamlined to benefit all border management agencies using the available services. For example, a shared document management function could reduce the rate of growth of documentation stored at each agency.

Transformation considerations for collaborative border management

Transformation to collaborative border management requires a detailed understanding and articulation of the work to be carried out, with six steps to successful transformation:

Step 1. Creating a vision.
Step 2. Establishing leadership and governance.
Step 3. Making the business case.
Step 4. Conducting a diagnostic assessment.
Step 5. Defining processes and determining capabilities.

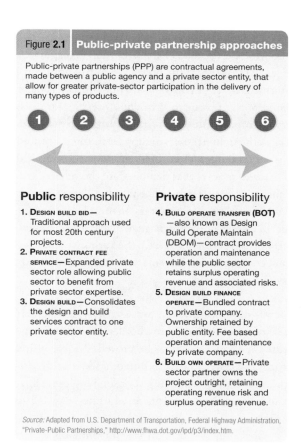

Figure 2.1 | Public-private partnership approaches

Public-private partnerships (PPP) are contractual agreements, made between a public agency and a private sector entity, that allow for greater private-sector participation in the delivery of many types of products.

Public responsibility

1. DESIGN BUILD BID— Traditional approach used for most 20th century projects.
2. PRIVATE CONTRACT FEE SERVICE—Expanded private sector role allowing public sector to benefit from private sector expertise.
3. DESIGN BUILD—Consolidates the design and build services contract to one private sector entity.

Private responsibility

4. BUILD OPERATE TRANSFER (BOT) —also known as Design Build Operate Maintain (DBOM)—contract provides operation and maintenance while the public sector retains surplus operating revenue and associated risks.
5. DESIGN BUILD FINANCE OPERATE—Bundled contract to private company. Ownership retained by public entity. Fee based operation and maintenance by private company.
6. BUILD OWN OPERATE—Private sector partner owns the project outright, retaining operating revenue risk and surplus operating revenue.

Source: Adapted from U.S. Department of Transportation, Federal Highway Administration, "Private-Public Partnerships," http://www.fhwa.dot.gov/ipd/p3/index.htm.

Step 6. Planning for transformation.

Creating a vision. Creating a clear vision, with associated outcomes, is vital. The vision needs to be developed jointly with all stakeholders and must be owned by all. It needs to be simple and easily understood, but it must contain sufficient detail to provide clear direction. It needs to be seen as a win for all participants, or it is unlikely to be democratically accepted or implemented.

Establishing leadership and governance. The leadership at each border management agency must agree to the vision and commit to delivering the agreed business outcomes. Critically, to make this commitment the leadership needs a mandate from government. Even so—since a wide stakeholder group from the public and private sectors needs to be engaged and actively involved—policymakers must understand that the change likely will take longer than the tenure of any government, and bipartisan support for the effort is required.

A governance structure is needed to direct and monitor performance. Each border management agency must secure the political and financial commitment to tailor collaborative border management concept to its own requirements, assess its administrative capacity, develop its transformation program, select the right partners to support the program, and evolve and align its business models and technical strategies in ways that demonstrate the value of collaborative border management to both governments and citizens. A common mission must be created for participating border management agencies. The governance structure must have the authority to define and coordinate implementation, operations, and resource management.

Making the business case. Since various stakeholders must buy into collaborative border management, the case for change needs to be proved. A clear vision with associated business outcomes can start this process. But for achieving sponsorship, leadership, and stakeholder commitment, a business case is also critical.

Governments, and all the stakeholders in the supply chain that interact in any way with border management agencies, need to understand the benefits that collaborative border management can bring them. Among the central benefits are more predictable goods clearance and reduced compliance costs. In analyzing resourcing decisions it is critical to understand and map the relationship between effective investments and their impact on overall business outcomes. It should be carefully ensured that positive actions for one area or agency (such as adding cost efficiencies to its information and communications technology management) do not harm efforts in another area or agency. Increased information and communications technology investments, though often cited as a principal means to business outcomes, can be of limited value if considered without attention to other variables such as overall productivity and staff deployment levels.

Conducting a diagnostic assessment. For border management agencies setting out on a transformation journey, business operations need to continue uninterrupted. To begin the journey, an agency's current position must be assessed against its target position,

with a diagnostic framework established to understand the current or baseline position. Lessons from within and outside the country should be incorporated. There should be a method for each agency to follow in determining its required collaborative border management capabilities, the solutions it requires, the impact of any resulting changes, and its roadmap to transformation.

Defining processes and determining capabilities. Establishing a process catalog—mapping all the key processes associated with collaborative border management—promotes seamless integration, with all border management agencies mandated to support trade facilitation and regulatory control. Useful for re-engineering individual processes, process groups, and end-to-end processes, the process catalog can quickly reveal duplication and redundancy in business operations, identify best practices, and distinguish between core and noncore processes.

A capability assessment provides a basis for determining where each agency needs improved administrative capacity. A well designed capability assessment should focus on operations efficiency and having a knowledgeable, skilled, and motivated workforce in the right place at the right time. It should lead to greater flexibility and speed of execution, increasing partner effectiveness and satisfaction.

Planning for transformation. The previous steps focus on design issues for reform and modernization. In transformation itself, the rigorous planning of development, testing, and operational readiness is extremely important. Critical requirements for a plan—best articulated as a transformation roadmap—include socializing and documenting the transformation approach (development and implementation considerations) and examining the nature, scale, and impact of collaborative border management transformation management. The transformation roadmap should include:

- The roadmap itself, preferably a graphic showing key milestones representing new services or capabilities.
- A business process direction plan defining major business processes, organizational roles, required legislation, and required policy changes.

- An information and communications technology plan describing the future reference architecture.
- A communication plan for both internal and external audiences.
- A testing and conversion plan for adapting reference data to the new operating environment.
- A training performance and support plan.

The final element in transformation planning is the selection of contracting partners and delivery suppliers. There are numerous examples of public agencies pursuing public-private partnership engagement arrangements—in some cases requiring the private sector to fund the entire program—that, at the time of contracting, revert to traditional and adversarial contract negotiations. At the time of negotiation it is critical that the client and vendor teams understand the type of relationship that is being contracted and that they have experience in it. Without such understanding and experience the long term relationship will be jeopardized and the form of the contract will not be ideal for either party.

Criteria that the tender should seek to evidence should include:

- The vendor's relevant experience in a transformation program of this type and scale. This may include a minimum number of completed programs or a minimum number of years of experience in such programs.
- The strength of the vendor's relevant reference sites. This would consider the relevance of the experience gained at reference sites and the outcomes achieved.
- The strength of the vendor's proposed program management and delivery team.
- The scale and track record of the vendor in the local market. This is required to ensure that an international candidate will operate effectively.
- The vendor's financial ability to support a program of this scale.

An example of the goods clearance process under collaborative border management

The following example outlines a core border process—goods clearance—within collaborative border management. A single window is best used in conjunction with a back office processing system (chapter 8). This provides border management agency staff, customers, and other supply chain partners with a single view of the customer and a single way to input and read customer and transaction information, examination results, and the like. The processing work, such as risk analysis or document validation, is done by the border management agencies either collaboratively or individually, as appropriate, with the results available to view through the single window. For example, common single window services could allow customers to register new authorizations or customs clearance documents.

A high level process model for goods clearance is outlined in figure 2.2. In a full process model the subtasks in each process step would need to be defined.

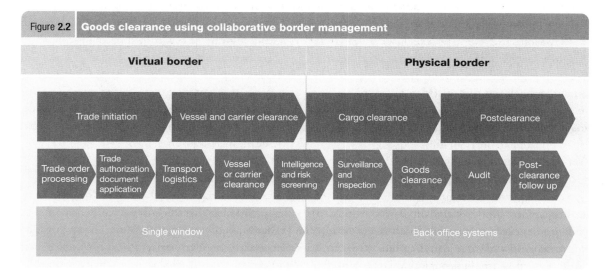

Figure **2.2** | **Goods clearance using collaborative border management**

Trade initiation

The trade initiation component includes the establishment of new trader licenses and authorizations and the initial declaration of planned goods transport. It can be further broken down as follows:

- *Trade order processing.* Traders negotiate contracts and prepare for the application of a trade authorization document, such as a permit or license.
- *Trade authorization document application.* Trade authorization documents, such as licenses, permits, authorizations, and certifications, are applied for and issued.
- *Transport logistics.* Traders organize the logistics of goods transport, from the point of supply to the point of demand, notifying regulatory authorities of the location of relevant trade documents (licenses, authorization, customs clearance) to facilitate the loading or unloading of goods.

Vessel and carrier clearance

This component involves the submission of port formality documents, applications for the clearance of vessels, flights, and crews, and port health formalities. It occurs before the arrival or departure of the shipment. Carriers submit their manifests electronically through the single window as soon as the information is commercially available or, in any event, prior to the arrival and discharge of the vessel.

For each cargo a unique consignment reference is created. The unique consignment reference can then be used as a single tracking reference for all consignments through to clearance and postclearance audit. Port operators also have access to manifest submissions, and part of the supporting documentation should include an application for the loading and unloading of the goods. Upon approval of loading and unloading, the port operators can compare unloaded goods against the lodged manifest and use this to produce outturn reports of landed goods.

Cargo clearance

Occurring when the goods actually arrive or depart, this component involves:

- *Intelligence and risk screening.* Consignments are identified for surveillance and inspection. A cargo search and match of selected cargo intelligence data is completed. Details of the consignments and related importers and exporters are matched against the watch list and the target list stored in the risk analysis system. Preliminary identity approval codes are assigned to trusted customers, to allow express movement of their consignments to their premises immediately on vessel discharge without regard to followup regulatory control. Special constraint codes are issued for consignments that require additional manual checking by border management agencies, so that there is a single and consistent approach to cargo clearance.
- *Surveillance and inspection.* This follows the screening of manifests. Officers are directed to perform cargo surveillance and inspection at designated locations. This could be at the trusted customers' premises for designated consignments or at the terminal operator inspection bays for other customers. The record of customer authorizations and surveillance and inspection actions is reconciled with the goods declaration as required.
- *Goods clearance.* Customers submit their declarations through the single window. This can then be used to track and update the declaration—from registration to assessment, payment, inspection, and release.
- *Trusted customers receiving their goods automatically on vessel discharge.* The inspection officers perform the physical inspection where required, at their premises, within a designated time. The trusted trader can also be authorized to make a periodic (for example, monthly) declaration of all goods received—subsequent to their discharge—and to settle outstanding fiscal liabilities at that time.
- *Standard customers being required to have their goods and documentation checked before clearance to the customers' premises.* Goods will be released after examination and after payment or guarantee of fiscal liabilities.

Postclearance activities

Following examination and inspection, each border management agency will have sufficient data to evaluate trends in contraventions, and, depending on the audit team's resources and capacity, to decide which audits will be conducted and when. New rules

Table **3.1**

Average transaction times for cross border trade, by region (Logistics Performance Index data, 2010)					
Region or income classification	**Customs clearance time (days)**		**Physical inspection (percentage of shipments)**	**Time to export (days)**	**Time to import (days)**
	Without physical inspection	**With physical inspection**			
Region					
East Asia and Pacific	1.55	3.36	25	3.58	4.93
Europe and Central Asia	1.48	1.89	26	2.77	3.00
Latin America and Caribbean	1.62	3.41	23	3.84	5.50
Middle East and North Africa	1.78	2.91	45	2.75	7.22
South Asia	2.17	3.20	35	1.88	3.30
Sub-Saharan Africa	2.83	4.94	36	7.79	7.05
Income classification					
High income	0.83	1.83	2.49	2.53	3.86

Note: Time to export (days) is the median export lead time for the port and airport supply chains. Time to import (days) is the median import lead time for the port and airport supply chains. The Logistics Performance Index methodology uses the World Bank classification of countries (for detailed information, visit http://worldbank.org/data).
Source: Logistics Performance Index 2010 (http://www.worldbank.org/lpi).

ratings, especially when neighboring and competitor countries scored higher on key indices.

The evidence highlights the wide gap in performance between low and high income countries, but it also indicates significant differences between countries at similar development levels. A useful outcome measure of logistics performance is the time taken to complete trade transactions (table 3.1). Clearance times for imported goods, as measured by the LPI, differ greatly by region: in the East Asia and Pacific region they are approximately 1.5 days, but in Sub-Saharan Africa they can be twice as long. Clearance times as a percentage of total lead times also differ considerably across regions. For example, in the Middle East and North Africa region clearance without physical inspection represents 25 percent of the total lead time, compared with 50–60 percent in the Europe and Central Asia and South Asia regions. These data suggest that logistics performance is not simply an issue of national income or development but depends heavily on national governments' policy and investment choices.

The growing awareness of the need for trade facilitation also appears in the many provisions of bilateral and regional trade agreements that concern it. The Doha Round of multilateral trade negotiations includes efforts to overhaul and modernize the World Trade Organization trade facilitation rules, now more than 50 years old (Eglin 2008). The negotiations have expanded beyond their initial mandate to include issues outside the fairly narrow domain of customs procedures.

Logistics and trade competitiveness

Effective connections with international markets depend on supply chain reliability. A key message of the LPI is that, while costs and timeliness are important, traders are primarily concerned with overall reliability and predictability, which can heavily affect their cost competitiveness and are thus the most important aspects of logistics performance.

Supply chain unreliability takes many forms. Long delays and unpredictable goods clearance times result from poor infrastructure, inadequate services, and excessively bureaucratic border processing systems and procedures. Excessive physical inspection and overreliance on inspector discretion cause large variations in clearance times, with multiple inspections frequent. Also, increasingly strict safety and security measures impair service in all but the top ranked countries.

High degrees of unpredictability prompt operators to adopt costly hedging strategies, such as maintaining large inventories or switching to more reliable—and expensive—transportation modes (Guasch and Kogan 2003). Recent research suggests that these induced costs on the supply chain can be even higher than direct freight costs (Arvis, Raballand, and Marteau 2007). So unreliability makes firms less competitive. At the same time, it makes it difficult for developing countries to diversify into more time sensitive commodities.

Exporters in Malawi and Mozambique, for example, face tradeoffs between direct transportation costs

3

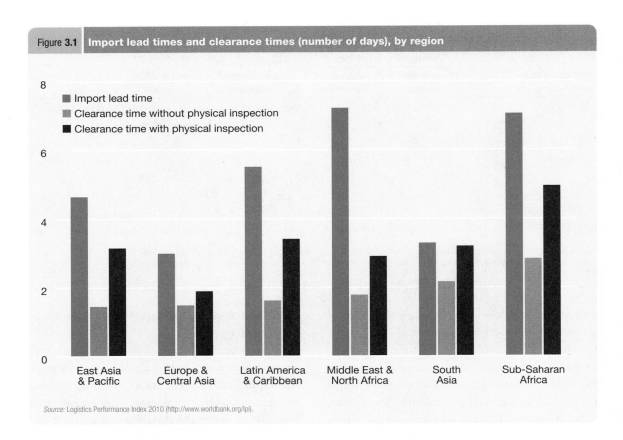

Figure **3.1** | Import lead times and clearance times (number of days), by region

8

■ Import lead time
■ Clearance time without physical inspection
■ Clearance time with physical inspection

6

4

2

0

East Asia & Pacific   Europe & Central Asia   Latin America & Caribbean   Middle East & North Africa   South Asia   Sub-Saharan Africa

Source: Logistics Performance Index 2010 (http://www.worldbank.org/lpi).

and induced costs. Exporters of sugar—a commodity that is inexpensive and not time sensitive—save money by sending their product by an unreliable railway to a small and fairly unproductive port (Nacala in northern Mozambique) for intermediate storage. In contrast, garment manufacturers participating in the preferential African Growth and Opportunity Act program with the United States pay to truck goods to the more distant, but efficient, South African ports of Durban and the Cape (World Bank forthcoming).

Delays tend to rise steeply with lower logistics performance, as illustrated by a stark difference in reliability between countries at the bottom and top of the LPI (Arvis, Mustra, and others 2007; Arvis and others 2010). In the highest performing countries import and export shipments nearly always arrive on schedule. In low performing countries they do not, according to about half of survey respondents. In the fourth through second quintiles there is also a considerable gap in performance between exports and imports: the export supply chain appears substantially more reliable. Curbing unreliability in inland transit, clearance processes, and other services is therefore crucial to logistics upgrading in low performance countries.

Delivery delays may be more important to logistics performance than import and export lead times are. Surprisingly, lead times are relatively lower—at least in developing countries—than was previously thought (Arvis and others 2010). Usually they are much lower than typical ocean shipping times to distant markets.

The first generation of reform projects: infrastructure and customs

Trade facilitation requires a commitment to investment and reform in three main areas: trade related infrastructure, border processing and clearance systems and procedures, and logistics services. Unlike multilateral trade liberalization, which requires international coordination, trade facilitation often consists primarily of initiatives carried out for just one country or region. It can require bilateral or regional cooperation in some cases—for example, in trade facilitation for land border trade and for landlocked country transit trade.

During the last two decades trade facilitation projects in developing countries have focused mainly on trade related infrastructure (port, road,

3

Border management modernization and the trade supply chain

and rail) and on systems and procedures for customs processing and clearance. Such efforts to make the flow of trade cheaper, faster, and more reliable have achieved much progress—though more work is needed. The 2007 and 2010 LPIs (Arvis, Mustra, and others 2007; Arvis and others 2010) show encouraging trends, reflecting successful trade facilitation projects. For example, in port management, the separation of commercial activities from statutory and regulatory missions of the port authority is now the norm in developing countries, with many examples of successful private sector participation in container terminal operations. Automated customs procedures are now commonplace—few countries lack them. A study by the World Bank, the International Monetary Fund, and the World Customs Organization found that each developing country customs agency included in the study had an automated declaration processing system, some sort of formalized risk management, a formalized process for private sector consultation, an active dialogue with the customs administrations in neighboring countries, and a general understanding of the need to balance control and revenue collection with trade facilitation (World Bank 2006). None of these were found in any of the other border management agencies engaged in processing and clearing import, export, and transit consignments.

Offering grounds for hope, the latest LPI (Arvis and others 2010) reveals modest but positive trends in key areas such as customs, investment in private services, and the use of information and communications technology for trade. Customs are still ahead of other border agencies across all performance levels, though the gap remains wider for countries with low index rankings. Customs procedures in all regions—including high income Organisation for Economic Co-operation and Development (OECD) countries—are converging and, with wide use of pre-arrival clearance, online submission, and postclearance audit, have improved much more than have procedures at other border agencies. Logistics overperformers (countries higher on the LPI than their incomes would predict) have consistently invested in reforms and improvements. Highlighted in the LPI are new areas that need more attention, such as the coordination of agencies involved in border

clearance and the quality of domestic trucking and customs brokerage services.

Customs accounts for about a third of total clearance time (Arvis, Mustra, and others 2007)—a fact that underlines the continued importance of facilitation efforts to further integrate border agencies. In some regions additional coordination efforts are needed to reduce multiple inspections of shipments. For instance, while in South Asia only 3 percent of shipments are inspected on more than one occasion, the rate is up to four times as high in other regions (East Asia and Pacific, Europe and Central Asia, Sub-Saharan Africa). Accordingly, discussions on improving border agency cooperation and the developing single window regimes remain crucial.

Clearance times vary greatly by region (figure 3.1). While the clearance of imported goods takes about 1.5 days in the East Asia and Pacific region, it takes as long as 3 days in Sub-Saharan Africa. Moreover, clearance time as a percentage of total lead time also differs substantially by region. For example, clearance without physical inspection represents 25 percent of total lead time in the Middle East and North Africa, but 50–60 percent in Europe and Central Asia and in South Asia.

Nearly every country uses some information and communications technology for customs. But most countries need to upgrade information technology for other border management agencies—to rationalize and simplify agency procedures, and to better exchange information with other trade related agencies and with trading community members (for example, freight forwarders).

In the most recent LPI (Arvis and others 2010), a large percentage of survey respondents describe certain areas of the logistics environment in each LPI quintile "improved" or "much improved" since 2005. Progress for some areas is more noticeable in the higher LPI quintiles (table 3.2). Yet even in the fifth (bottom) quintile, marked improvement was seen for information and communications technology (ICT) infrastructure, private logistics services, and logistics regulations. Progress for border agencies other than customs—and for transport infrastructure and corruption—seems less widespread in the fifth quintile.

Ports and corridors in Central and Eastern Africa face the most severe trade facilitation challenges.

Table **3.2**	**Percentages of international freight forwarders reporting an "improved" or "much improved" logistics environment since 2005, by logistics area and by country quintile on the Logistics Performance Index (2010)**

Logistics area	Country's quintile on the Logistics Performance Index (2010)				
	First (top) quintile	Second quintile	Third quintile	Fourth quintile	Fifth (bottom) quintile
Customs	66	56	53	54	48
Border agencies other than customs	57	37	33	40	38
ICT infrastructure	77	78	63	56	66
Private logistics services	70	78	66	62	63

Source: Logistics Performance Index 2010 (http://www.worldbank.org/lpi).

Evidence suggests that, thanks to various trade facilitation initiatives, the time taken for containers to clear the port has been reduced in some of the poorer countries. Thus Douala, Cameroon has improved import processing with a single window—and Mombasa, Kenya has done so with a similar port community initiative. Container dwell times in both ports have been halved over the last decade, though the average still exceeds 10 days (Arvis and others 2010).

Trade corridor infrastructure is critical, especially for landlocked developing countries. The rehabilitation of that infrastructure and the provision of sustainable resources for its maintenance are given high priority by development agencies. Governments, therefore, have been upgrading and expanding road networks with help from the development community. Most road corridors in Africa are now fairly good, or at least passable, and consequently poor roads have become less likely to cause major costs and delays (Arvis, Raballand, and Marteau 2007; World Bank 2008b). Even in landlocked developing countries, major commercial centers are now generally connected by allweather routes.

Shifting priorities and needs: improving transit, improving services, and reforming border management generally

The emphasis of border management reform is now shifting from customs reform, and from first generation investments in port and road infrastructure, to new areas. Trade constraints in these new areas are crosscutting and more institutionally complex. The new reform agenda will need to address issues such as:

- Improving transport policies and regulations to strengthen market structure.

- Increasing competition in trade related services, such as trucking, forwarding, and railways.
- Improving collaboration among agencies involved in border processing and the private sector.

In addition, more attention will be demanded by problems that are best addressed regionally.

The expanding scope of trade facilitation and logistics reform is demonstrated in various development projects being carried out around the world, as well as in the trade facilitation negotiations taking place in the World Trade Organization (where the focus has been on extending the coverage of General Agreement on Tariffs and Trade articles V, VIII and X to areas not previously covered comprehensively in the first generation of reforms described above). Work to facilitate trade through transit corridors for the benefit of landlocked developing countries is the special focus of another international initiative: the Almaty Programme of Action, launched in 2003 under United Nations auspices.[2]

Reducing clearance times through collaboration. Key to the new border management agenda is a more holistic approach to goods clearance. Such an approach requires better collaboration among all border management agencies—such as standards, sanitary, phytosanitary, transport, and veterinary agencies—and it requires a modern regulatory compliance strategy. Little is achieved when a customs agency adds automation, or when it adopts risk management principles allowing the selective examination of imports, so long as other agencies are not automated and continue to routinely inspect goods regardless of the level of risk involved.

Clearance times have been reduced by a trade facilitation project for border management in the

Border management modernization and the trade supply chain

3

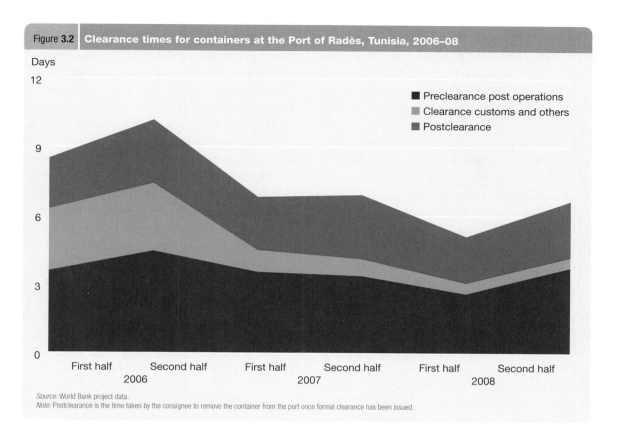

Figure 3.2 Clearance times for containers at the Port of Radès, Tunisia, 2006–08

Days

Legend:
- Preclearance post operations
- Clearance customs and others
- Postclearance

First half / Second half 2006   First half / Second half 2007   First half / Second half 2008

Source: World Bank project data.
Note: Postclearance is the time taken by the consignee to remove the container from the port once formal clearance has been issued.

Port of Radès, Tunisia (figure 3.2). The project, supported by the World Bank, has focused on integrating the clearance procedures of various agencies. As a result, procedures that previously accounted for a third of dwell time have been significantly reduced. Further gains are expected once electronic manifest transmission—and an e-payment system—are in place.

Making transit regimes more efficient. The new agenda will also need to make control more efficient for goods that must cross more than one border to reach their final destination. A cost effective transit regime that reliably guards against leakage into transit country markets requires bilateral and regional cooperation. Such a transit regime is most critical to the economies of landlocked developing countries, whose access to foreign markets is often constrained. Yet transit regimes along important corridors in the developing world are often ineffective. True, there are some exceptions: efficient regional transit systems, such as the Transports Internationaux Routiers (TIR) and common transit systems, developed in Europe after World War

II, allow seamless door-to-door operation across several borders. But overregulation and a focus on costly, inefficient controls prevail in many regions, resulting in transit times that can amount to several weeks (World Bank 2008). In most of Africa regional treaties provide for regional systems similar to the European mode—but a lack of sound implementation mechanisms and poor cooperation among countries have made the systems less effective than they should be.

The international trade community now accepts that improving transit is a top priority, especially for landlocked developing countries. Infrastructure investments are unlikely to facilitate trade unless accompanied by transit regime improvements.

Improving logistics and related services. Finally, another essential part of the new agenda is the improvement of logistics and other services that support trade. Freight cost differentials among countries often result from inefficiencies in the market structure for transport providers—and from regulations that prevent open competition (Raballand and Teravaninthorn 2008). Trucking in Western and Central

3

Border management modernization and the trade supply chain

African corridors suffers from strict market regulation that depresses transport quality and limits vehicle use: a truck may go as little as 2,000 kilometers a month (compare the United States, where trucks go almost 10 times as far). As a result, fixed costs (gross margin) and transportation costs for these corridors are excessive—up to three times higher than for competitive corridors in Southern Africa, where competition makes transport services better and less expensive and their market more efficient.

Although the problem is recognized, governments and the international development community have limited experience with reforms to improve private logistics services. So the new agenda must focus on providing meaningful incentives for reliable, high quality services—notably by eliminating entry barriers. Yet this mission presents new challenges: in particular, reformers will face political-economic opposition to departures from existing business practices and to changes that limit rentseeking. For example, retired customs officers in many developing countries enjoy customs broker licenses as an unofficial privilege. And informal, fragmented trucking regimes are often maintained in such countries to meet social goals, even when economic harm results in the long term. Even in the least efficient environments, some stakeholders stand to lose from reforms.

Countries and constraints

A supply chain is only as strong as its weakest link. The benefits of progress in one area may not be realized until impediments in other areas are removed.[3] Illustrating this interdependence, a recent typology assigns countries to four broad groups in which logistics performance is largely correlated with country income:

- *Logistics friendly (top quintile)*: high performers, and for the most part high income countries.
- *Consistent logistics performers* (second quintile): typically emerging economies with a strong logistics constituency.
- *Partial logistics performers* (third and fourth quintile): typically low or middle income countries that have not yet consistently addressed all the factors in their poor logistics performance.
- *Logistics unfriendly* (bottom quintile): severely logistically constrained, typically the least developed countries.

Using these four groups, and based on the analysis of various performance factors, one can build a rough intuitive typology of typical constraints faced by countries in each group (table 3.3).

Stepping up implementation

Although the priorities may be set and the initiatives are in place, implementation must still be emphasized if serious progress is to be made. Progress can be ensured in three ways: by focusing on collective aspects of reform, by considering a large portfolio of development assistance programs, and by obtaining technical assistance.

Promoting trade facilitation is a collective effort

Many entities are working to help developing country policymakers and stakeholders carry out trade

Table **3.3**	Typical kinds and degrees of logistics trade constraints, by country logistics performance group and area of logistics impediment				
	Area of logistics impediment				
Country logistics performance group	**Trade related infrastructure**	**Quality and supply of logistics services**	**Core customs modernization**	**Integration of border management**	**Regional facilitation and transit**
Logistics friendly	Few bottlenecks, except rail	Industry leaders	Best practice	Lesser problem	Streamlined
Consistent logistics performer	Capacity bottlenecks to support trade expansion	Emergence of a diversified supply of logistics services	No longer a constraint	Typically the final binding constraint	Depends on the region
Partial logistics performer	Major constraint	Weak market	Potentially a major constraint	Major constraint	Problematic
Logistics unfriendly	Serious constraint	Low development	Often still a major constraint	Major constraint	Main problem for landlocked least developed countries

Source: Logistics performance survey data, 2009.

facilitation reform and modernization (box 3.2). Their activities include projects on the ground—but they also include the promotion of international standards and practices to guide reform.

Key participants at the global level include the World Bank, the United Nations Conference on Trade and Development (UNCTAD), the United Nations Economic Commission for Europe (UNECE), the World Customs Organization (WCO), the World Trade Organization, the Organisation for Economic Co-operation and Development (OECD), and the International Monetary Fund (IMF). Private global groups also help to set priorities, and sometimes are involved in implementation: such groups include the International Chamber of Commerce (ICC), the *International Federation of Freight Forwarders Associations* (FIATA), the Global Express Association (GEA), the International Air Transport Association (IATA), and the

International Road Transport Union (IRU). Also helping to put reforms in place are regional organizations, such as United Nations commissions and regional development banks. Bilateral agencies are the main donors of technical assistance.[4] Finally, the reference forum in trade and transport facilitation is the Global Facilitation Partnership for Transportation and Trade, a network of 250 public and private partners launched in 1999. Its participants work together to design and carry out programs, create knowledge, and support training opportunities.

Several ongoing initiatives have created these partnerships and stimulated implementation in developing countries. Launched in 2005, the World Bank's Trade Facilitation Negotiations Support Project (TFNSP) helps developing countries to negotiate new trade facilitation agreements in the World Trade Organization and to understand their related capacity deficits.

Box **3.2**	Supporters of trade facilitation activities in developing countries

International organizations
- World Trade Organization (WTO)
- World Customs Organization (WCO)
- United Nations Economic Commission for Europe (UNECE)
- United Nations Centre for Trade Facilitation and Electronic Business (UN/CEFACT)
- United Nations Conference on Trade and Development (UNCTAD)
- International Civil Aviation Organization (ICAO)
- International Maritime Organization (IMO)
- The World Bank
- International Monetary Fund (IMF)
- Organisation for Economic Co-operation and Development (OECD)
- Regional international financial institutions

Global business, nongovernmental organizations and institutions, and forums
- International Road Transport Union (IRU)
- International Chamber of Commerce (ICC)
- International Federation of Freight Forwarders Associations (FIATA)
- International Air Transport Association (IATA)
- World Economic Forum (WEF)
- Global Express Association (GEA)
- Global Facilitation Partnership for Transportation and Trade (GFPTT)

Regional and bilateral entities and agreements
- Regional and subregional economic unions
  - Association of Southeast Asian Nations (ASEAN)
  - Common Market for Eastern and Southern Africa (COMESA)
  - East African Community (EAC)
  - Southern African Development Community (SADC)
  - Mercado Común del Sur (Southern Common Market; Mercosur)
  - And others (185 regional agreements were registered with the WTO as being in force at the end of 2005)
- Corridor authorities
- Regional United Nations agencies
- Regional international financial institutions
- Organization for Security and Co-operation in Europe (OSCE)

National entities
- Trade and transport facilitation and coordination committees and task forces, along with trade procedures committees (UNECE currently has 48 registered)
- Customs and other border agencies
- Transport agencies and operators
- Private sector associations (forwarders, shippers, truckers, and so on)

3

Border management modernization and the trade supply chain

A growing portfolio of development assistance: the example of The World Bank

Over the last five years the World Bank and other agencies have increased their stake in trade and transport facilitation. Responding to changing demands and priorities, World Bank projects have grown and diversified—investments and reforms are now complemented by technical assistance and knowledge sharing.

The World Bank's projects in support of trade facilitation totaled about $2.3 billion in commitments for fiscal year 2009, representing approximately 70 percent of the World Bank's total trade related lending (figure 3.3). The most significant projects are for modernizing customs, improving gateway infrastructure (for example, at ports and airports), modernizing trade corridors, improving export promotion, improving trade facilitation and logistics, and modernizing multimodal transport.

The World Bank has made customs modernization a major part of its portfolio, financing over 120 related projects over the past two decades. Such projects at present total $409 million, with an additional $150 million under development. Although improving customs remains a high priority for many countries, the projects increasingly support the modernization of other agencies with border responsibilities—for example, agencies concerned with health, police, quarantine, agriculture, immigration, and product standards.

Corridor projects are increasingly important to the World Bank's trade facilitation work program. Each covers several countries along a single trade corridor, addressing gaps in areas such as infrastructure, border management, and trade transit systems. Recent examples include projects in Central Africa (box 3.3) as well as in Eastern and Western Africa, Central America, and Pakistan and Afghanistan. The share of trade facilitation lending commitments to each World Bank region over fiscal 2004–09 is shown in figure 3.4.

The World Bank continues to support infrastructure projects related to trade, with an emphasis on ports and airports. The most challenging sector has proved to be multimodal transport (railways). Although reform in this sector can reduce freight costs and carbon footprints, its present state makes it marginal to logistics in less developed countries—and even in many middle income countries.

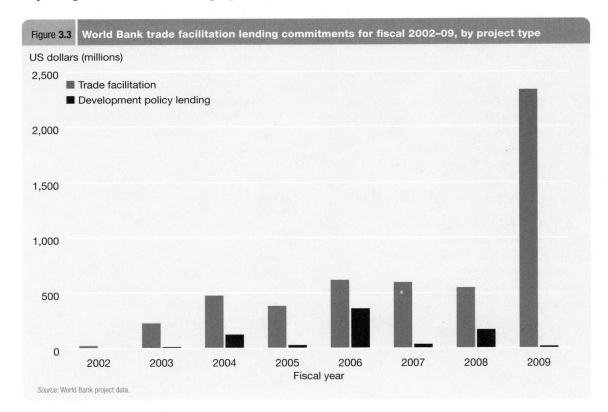

Figure 3.3 World Bank trade facilitation lending commitments for fiscal 2002–09, by project type

US dollars (millions)

■ Trade facilitation
■ Development policy lending

Fiscal year

Source: World Bank project data.

Box **3.3**	**Re-engineering transit regimes: the case of Central Africa**

It is now accepted that regional transit trade arrangements in Asia and Africa should be re-engineered along the lines of systems already working in Europe.[1] For example, both Chad and the Central African Republic are served primarily by a road and rail corridor running through the port of Douala in Cameroon. Goods transit used to take up to six weeks or even more. Seven documents were required, all to be cleared by three separate offices. And there were several checkpoints and controls on the roads to both landlocked countries. Thanks mainly to strong leadership from Cameroonian customs, and as part of a World Bank regional corridor project, agreement was reached on a revised transit system. The main elements of the agreement are:

- The introduction of one common document (modeled on the European Union Single Administrative Document).
- The removal of intermediate checkpoints.
- The use of ICT based on UNCTAD's Automated System for Customs Data (ASYCUDA) system.
- The addition of a bar code to each transit document and container, with optical reading at borders.
- A new bonds system.

Note

1. One such system is the the Transports Internationaux Routiers (TIR), an arrangement now 60 years old that was instrumental in the development of trade across European borders (discussed in chapter 17; see also http://www.iru.org/index/en_iru_about_tir).

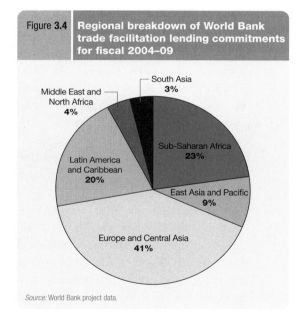

Figure **3.4**	**Regional breakdown of World Bank trade facilitation lending commitments for fiscal 2004–09**

Source: World Bank project data.

The World Bank and other organizations provide technical assistance to developing countries in four ways:

- Making reform toolkits (customs modernization handbooks, port reforms) available.
- Providing data on trade facilitation (such as the LPI and Doing Business Indicators).
- Diagnosing weaknesses, for example through Trade and Transport Facilitation Assessments (TTFAs), which are especially important for project preparation in least developed countries (see World Bank 2010; Raven 2001, 2005).
- Helping domestic or regional institutions to design and carry out reforms.

The recently established Trade Facilitation Facility (TFF; box 3.4) will further expand technical assistance.

Further increasing impact: technical assistance
There is growing demand from developing country governments, not just for reform project investments, but also for advice, knowledge, and technical assistance (with which lending is increasingly linked). Most supply chain reliability gains and logistics cost reductions are likely to result from inexpensive measures such as organizational change and regulatory reform. Still, in many client countries—and especially least developed countries—trade facilitation measures are easier to carry out as parts of larger financial packages than as standalone activities.

Conclusion

The recent economic downturn has made trade facilitation even more relevant than before, while it gives reformers an opportunity to prevail against opposing constituencies. As international shipping costs have dropped dramatically, so the cost of domestic obstacles to trade—as a share of total trade costs—has risen. Changes in demand and in cost structures have led international buyers to favor leaner, shorter, more reliable supply chains (McKinsey & Company 2008a, 2008b).

So countries with poor logistics performance, and countries that depend chiefly on land transport for exporting, are at an even greater disadvantage during the crisis.

Meanwhile, the economic crisis constitutes an opportunity to rethink priorities—even as it leads to the first decline in international trade in 25 years, pushing millions of people back into crippling poverty throughout the developing world. Governments are boosting public investment to counter falling demand. In doing so they should target projects with large economic payoffs, including trade facilitation projects. Similarly, development agencies should counter the impact of the crisis by supporting reforms to reduce trade costs. Large benefits can result for developing countries that depend heavily on trade.

Notes

1. A key message of the World Bank's Logistics Performance Index (see box 3.1).

2. For information on the *Almaty Programme of Action: Addressing the Special Needs of Landlocked Developing Countries within a New Global Framework for Transit Transport Cooperation for Landlocked and Transit Developing Countries,* see the United Nations Office of the High Representative for the Least Developed Countries, Landlocked Developing Countries and Small Island Developing States (UN-OHRLLS), http://www.un.org/special-rep/ohrlls/lldc/default.htm#ALMATY. For the document, see www.un.org/special-rep/ohrlls/lldc/Almaty_PoA.pdf.

3. This is especially true for investments in ICT, which are unlikely to deliver results if they are limited to customs and do not involve other agencies. Investments in corridor infrastructure will not reduce trade costs if they are not complemented by measures to improve the transit systems and the quality of services delivered by truck or multimodal transportation. Likewise, the adoption of modern approaches to risk management by customs simply will not deliver rapid clearance if standards and quarantine agencies continue to require the physical inspection of all imports that fall into any of a large range of tariff headings.

4. For statistics from the World Trade Organization Doha Development Agenda Trade Capacity Building Database (established jointly by the World Trade Organization and the Organisation for Economic Cooperation and Development's Development Assistance Committee), see http://tcbdb.wto.org.

References

Arvis, J., M. Mustra, L. Ojala, B. Shepherd, and D. Saslavsky. 2010. *Connecting to Compete: Trade Logistics in the Global Economy.* Washington, DC: The World Bank.

Arvis, J., M. Mustra, J. Panzer, L. Ojala, and T. Naula. 2007. *Connecting to Compete: Trade Logistics in the Global Economy.* Washington, DC: The World Bank.

Arvis, J., G. Raballand, and J. Marteau. 2007. "The Cost of Being Landlocked: Logistics Costs and Supply Chain Reliability." Policy Research Working Paper 4258, World Bank, Washington, DC.

Eglin, R. 2008. "The Doha Round Negotiations on Trade Facilitation." *The Global Enabling Trade Report 2008*. Geneva: World Economic Forum. 35–9.

Guasch, J., and J.L. Kogan. 2003. "Just in Case Inventories: A Cross Country Analysis." Policy Research Working Paper 3012, World Bank, Washington, DC.

Hoekman, B., and A. Nicita. 2008. "Trade Policy, Trade Costs, and Developing Country Trade." Policy Research Working Paper 4797, World Bank, Washington, DC.

McKinsey & Company, Inc. 2008a. "How Companies Act on Global Trends: A McKinsey Global Survey." *McKinsey Quarterly*. April. http://www.mckinseyquarterly.com.

———. 2008b. "Managing Global Supply Chains: A McKinsey Global Survey." *McKinsey Quarterly*. June. http://www.mckinseyquarterly.com.

Raballand, G., and S. Teravaninthorn. 2008. *Transport Prices and Costs in Africa: A Review of the International Corridors*. Directions in Development Series. Washington, DC: The World Bank.

Raven, J. 2001. *Trade and Transport Facilitation: A Toolkit for Audit, Analysis and Remedial Action*. Washington, DC: The World Bank.

———. 2005. *A Trade and Transport Facilitation Toolkit: Audit, Analysis and Remedial Action*. Washington, DC: The World Bank.

Wilson, J. S., C. L. Mann, and T. Otsuki. 2004. "Assessing the Potential Benefit of Trade Facilitation: A Global Perspective." Policy Research Working Paper 3224, World Bank, Washington, DC.

World Bank. 2006. "Needs, Priorities and Costs Associated with Technical Assistance and Capacity Building for Implementation of a WTO Trade Facilitation Agreement: A Comparative Study Based on Six Developing Countries." Working Paper, International Trade Department, World Bank, Washington, DC.

———. 2008. "Improving Trade and Transport for Landlocked Developing Countries: World Bank Contributions to Implementing the Almaty Program of Action: A Report for the Mid-Term Review." October. Washington, DC: The World Bank.

———. 2010. *Trade and Transport Facilitation Assessment: A Practical Toolkit for Implementation*. Washington, DC: The World Bank.

———. Forthcoming. *Malawi Country Economic Memorandum 2009*. Washington, DC: The World Bank.

4 Borders, their design, and their operation

Michel Zarnowiecki

Governments and the development community have invested significantly in border management reform and modernization. A notable part of that investment has gone to improve border station infrastructure. But experience shows that land border station infrastructure improvement—whatever its architectural or engineering merit—rarely contributes to better border management outcomes unless it is supported by the adoption of modern approaches to managing passenger and cargo flows.

Every border infrastructure investment should follow a comprehensive re-engineering of systems and procedures, and it should be designed specifically to support the adoption of modern border management. Only then can it help to reconcile the two objectives of effective control and trade facilitation. This chapter explores key issues for new investments in border station modernization as part of a wider trade facilitation program.

Definitions and core concepts

Border management means the procedures applied to persons and objects crossing the border to ensure they comply with laws. It also means how different agencies are organized and how they fit into a unified concept of border management. Finally, it means how the physical infrastructure that accommodates the agencies is designed and managed.

Effective border management means ensuring that:
- Everyone and everything that crosses the border is compliant with the laws, regulations, and procedures of the country.
- Users are encouraged to comply. Compliant users are offered facilitated service.
- Offenders are identified and stopped.

To do these three things without disrupting legitimate trade or causing unacceptable queues, delays at the border, or bottlenecks in the adjacent country (or within the country itself), infrastructure and equipment must be adequate to support modern procedures. Even so, procedures are only as good as the legislation governing them. To ensure streamlined operations, every agency at the border must be involved and must cooperate, with appropriate upstream and downstream processes in place.

Borders

What is a border? Where is it? Often these questions can cause confusion, both because of special anomalies (box 4.1) and for other reasons. The concept of a border has changed in recent years: borders need not be at a country's geographic periphery, are not holistic, and can even be outside a country.

Traditionally a border is the limit of two countries' sovereignties—or the

Box **4.1**   **No man's land and border anomalies**

There is no such thing as no man's land (except perhaps the sea beyond territorial waters). A land border is an imaginary line, agreed between two countries and usually defined by geographic features (such as a river, water separation line, or mountain range). Someone moving across the border is always on the territory of one or the other country.

The reason why "no man's land" is a popular expression is that there is sometimes a blank between two border stations. For technical or other reasons, stations are not always erected on the line, so once outgoing travelers have cleared formalities they may still have to travel to the borderline and from the borderline to the adjacent country's border station. Nevertheless, having cleared outgoing formalities, they are still on the country of exit's territory—and subject to that country's sovereignty. Similarly, when they cross into the other country they are instantly under the jurisdiction of that country, even though they have not yet reached the administrative point of entry.

Border anomalies exist. One is the enclave system, where a portion of sovereign territory is surrounded by another country's territory. Territorial continuity may then be ensured by a customs road (as in France between the Spanish enclave of Llivia and mainland Spain, or between the Swiss enclave on French territory at Mulhouse Airport and Switzerland). In other cases the enclave may be totally isolated and its inhabitants may need to cross foreign territory to reach their mainland (a frequent occurrence in Central Asia). There are even enclaves within enclaves. An Uzbek road, for example, crosses a Kazakh enclave located on Uzbek territory. In these cases the enclaves are secured by border stations at points of entry and exit, usually creating difficulties for local populations seeking to travel to their home country.

Another apparent anomaly is the status of juxtaposed or shared border facilities, when two countries operate their border crossing procedures at the same location—which may be well inside the territory of one country. In such cases an international agreement is necessary to define the status of the road to the borderline, to avoid legal and jurisdictional difficulties over incidents involving travelers who have cleared entry formalities but still must travel on the exit country's road to arrive at the country of entry.

limit beyond which the sovereignty of one no longer applies. The border, if on land, separates two countries. Crossing the border means that persons, vehicles, and goods must comply with the laws of the exit country and—if immediately contiguous—the entry country. At sea the border is the limit of territorial waters. Borders usually, but not always, correspond to geographical separation. They may also be drawn or redrawn along ethnic lines or zones of economic influence. The principle of border delineation notably affects border operations.

A border is not necessarily at the geographical periphery of a country. International gateways can be well inside national territory. Airports, railway stations, and river ports on international waterways are treated as border stations, even though air travelers may have been over national territory for hundreds of miles.

Inland clearance facilities are areas where goods are kept before duties and taxes are paid, or before the goods are released for consumption on the domestic market. Similarly, economic zones exist—known as free zones, export processing zones, bonded industrial estates, and the like—where goods are deemed outside national territory and must pass through customs control before entering the main territory. The point of exit from the zone—and its perimeter—is, in practice, a border.

A new tendency is to clear goods on the premises of importers. Among other requirements, the importers must allocate space in their warehouse for uncleared goods. Such space must be materially separated from the rest of the building by what amounts to a border fence or wall.

Borders are not holistic. Different processes can take place at different places. For example, a truck's driver may be cleared by immigration at the border, but the goods transported in the truck may be cleared at an inland location. Borders then essentially become institution-based and are no longer geographic.

The borders between the Soviet Union and its noncommunist neighbors were often doubled. There was not only a borderline, but also a border zone extending far inland. Entry into that zone—whose purpose was to further control cross border movements and possible infiltration by foreign agents—was restricted to its inhabitants and permit holders, and was controlled through checkpoints. Clearance can also be segmented: preclearance may take place in the exit country and final clearance in the entry country. For example, immigration checks on both the French and British sides of the English Channel take place at the ferry ports of embarkation, but final immigration clearance is granted when disembarking.

Borders can be outside a country. Some border stations operate on foreign soil using agreed co-location arrangements. When a station is at a distance from the borderline, travelers cleared for entry must still travel to the geographical border on a road under the sovereignty of the exit country. Entry country authorities cannot act against such travelers should the travelers commit offenses before crossing the borderline.

At some Canadian airports, United States Customs clears passengers for entry. The passengers are technically under United States jurisdiction and can then disembark at domestic terminals. Should a violation be detected, however, the United States authorities cannot prosecute them but must hand over the offenders to their Canadian counterparts.

Crossing a Schengen border means a traveler is cleared for onward travel in other Schengen countries at the first point of entry into the Schengen space. However, entry clearance may not be valid for all countries: Austria admits United Nations Laissez Passer holders with no visa, whereas they need a visa for other Schengen countries. If such a traveler wants to visit a Schengen country that does not accept United Nations Laissez Passer, he is not considered cleared for entrance into that country.

The customs territory

The customs territory usually coincides with national territory—but it does not always perfectly coincide. The customs territory is where customs and other control measures are applicable to goods entering or leaving the country. Some parts of a national territory may not be customs territory (free zones, for example), and some parts of a customs territory may be outside the boundaries of the state (as when parts of co-located border facilities are on foreign territory). Customs and its powers are discussed in box 4.2.

Border crossings

Although a border crossing is any point along the borderline where a country can be physically entered, usually it is a specially established road,

---

Box 4.2   Customs: its zone of competence

Although customs is traditionally associated with borders—and in some countries is restricted to border stations—customs has a more general mandate to prevent smuggling. Smuggling can happen at a border station or across a border outside the station precinct. Smugglers usually reduce their risk (in case they should be caught with large quantities of smuggled items) by storing goods in the vicinity of the borderline, managing their operations from there, and gradually removing the goods onto the domestic market. For this reason western countries and countries traditionally under their influence have often used two notions:

- The *customs territory* is the part of the national territory where customs laws and procedures are applicable.
- A *customs border intervention area* can be at the border station, along the borderline, or inside a specifically designated zone extending inward from the borderline (usually a 20 to 50 kilometer strip of territory).

Customs has comprehensive powers of enforcement throughout the customs territory. However, it has extended powers of control, investigation, search, and arrest within the customs border intervention area. The border station is only an administrative facility for apparently compliant users.

Other countries that have modernized their customs legislation—for example, after transition, in order to align to western standards—often refer (redundantly) to a customs territory totally coinciding with their national territory. Nevertheless, these countries usually restrict normal customs operations to parts of approved border crossings designated customs control zones, and to a few inland locations such as inland clearance stations or bonded warehouses.

Borders, their design, and their operation

bridge, tunnel, or building. There are three kinds of border crossings:

- Any point of access to the national territory, whether authorized to the public or not.
- An unguarded border crossing used by certain inhabitants—usually local residents, whose property might straddle the border, or other people (preapproved or not) who comply with all the rules for it.
- A guarded border crossing, either restricted to some categories of users and traffic or open to all traffic.

Border stations

Border stations are official points of entry into a country, where its national sovereignty is officially and administratively established and where traffic is controlled to ensure compliance with its laws. More narrowly defined than a border crossing, a border station may serve two countries, and—under international best practice—action taken by officials on one side of the border may have legal value in the adjacent country.

Depending on the mode of transport, border stations may have different designs. Rail crossings are usually placed at major junctions or marshalling yards, not necessarily on the border. International airports and seaports have designs of their own. River landing stations are often placed inside cities or close to them. Border stations are marked by standard signs (box 4.3).

A border station is often served by a customs approved road, a compulsory itinerary for reaching the border station of the country of entry after crossing the borderline (sometimes with associated procedures).[1]

Main functions performed at border stations

A border station should accommodate customs, immigration, and other control agencies.

Customs

The role of customs is to ensure that goods and passengers entering the country are accounted for and that they meet national requirements. Yet in western countries, where customs for a long time was the only institution to operate at borders, *customs* is often used as shorthand for all border management functions and agencies. In many countries customs is still the only administration with a permanent presence at the border.

Immigration

Immigration (box 4.4) verifies the identities of people entering or leaving the country and confirms their legal authority to do so, largely by checking passports and visas. Immigration is carried out either by a special department or by customs or another police or military authority (border police, border guards, or border troops).[2] Usually immigration also makes a record of cross border movements. Typically it is not concerned with commercial freight, but only with the legality of the people bringing it. Often immigration follows the blanket control concept, under which increased checking is held to increase security and longer waiting times are considered acceptable.

In this chapter *border police, border guards,* and *border troops* are terms used interchangeably to describe the agency that carries out immigration checks (unless there is a specific immigration service) and that ensures general policing of the border station and borderline (unless this function is also exercised by customs).

Other control agencies

Control agencies often present at border stations include:

- *Transport.* Transport ministry officials are in charge of weighing trucks, collecting road taxes,

Box **4.4** | **Customs and immigration**

In some countries customs handles immigration functions, which is quite logical. Identifying vehicles and individuals is part of customs risk assessment, and customs officials read passports.

In other countries immigration officials replicate customs checks, for various reasons. The police may consider that their primary function is to fight smuggling (sometimes defined as a criminal, not customs, offense). They consider customs prone to corruption, so they want to double check. They look for illegal immigrants, so they will search every commercial vehicle. And in former communist countries, sometimes backed by pretransition legislation, they consider that they should run the border, believe that they are responsible for security, and therefore should know everything that is going on—even if they do not have the tools to analyze the information and commercial data available.

The chosen approach is the prerogative of the country. Yet it should be kept in mind that making customs replicate immigration checks can be expensive and ineffective, can generate conflict, and can be time consuming for cross border traffic, which may be checked twice, sometimes with inconsistent procedures and results.

and enforcing transport permit and licensing requirements.

- *Quarantine.* This includes preventing infectious diseases, disinfecting vehicles, monitoring health regulations, checking health carnets, and the like.
- *Sanitary and phytosanitary.* Their purpose is to ensure that consumers in a country are supplied with food that is safe to eat. Control is based on documentary evidence (certificates) and occasional sampling and testing.
- *Standards and consumer protection.* Industrial products are subject to verification of their conformity with international, regional, and national standards.
- *Radiology.* Detectors at border stations prevent the entry or exit of radioactive material. Atomic energy control bodies intervene when a suspicious consignment is detected, and cooperation with them for risk management is encouraged.
- *Ecological.* In some countries an environmental officer is on duty at the border.
- *Ministry of foreign affairs.* In some countries visas may be issued at the border and a consular officer is on duty.[3]
- *Ministry of commerce.* In countries where the commerce ministry used to play a major role in international trade, it may retain its leading position for cargo reporting and issuing and verifying import and export permits (which is the fundamental element of customs control).

Many other agencies—up to 40 in some countries—may also operate at the border. However,

a distinction should be made between the customs border (wherever goods are cleared) and the physical border station. Most of the other agencies would be present at the customs border and not at the physical station.

The private sector at the border

Private operators at border stations offer various services related to border processing (box 4.5). Such services fall into four main categories:

- *Commercial services* include customs clearing brokers (useful in establishing transit documentation, though not necessary when goods are cleared inland), bank offices (where duties and taxes collected by customs and all other agencies are often paid), and exchange offices (one or several). Differing insurance regulations, or the absence of an international standard (such as the green card for motor vehicle insurance), can also require the presence of insurance brokers.
- *Personal services* include parking lots, fuel stations and mechanical repair shops, catering facilities (restaurants, bars, and sometimes hotels), and occasionally tourist offices.
- *Duty free shops* are licensed and bonded warehouses outside the country's fiscal territory, offering goods on which domestic taxes are not collected (box 4.6).
- *Illegitimate services* are inevitably attracted by crowds staying for long periods at border stations. At some border crossings prostitution is a problem, with its accompaniments (criminals;

Box 4.5 The private sector at the border

There are four reasons why the private sector may want to be present at the border, often supported by the agency that builds or operates the border facility. First, a service is to be provided to travelers. Second, when delays are long, a captive public is good business for restaurants and cafeterias. Third, the agency that runs the border station usually collects a fee for leasing commercial facilities. Fourth, access to the border zone can facilitate informal cross border activities.

However, there is no practical reason why people should be kept waiting at a border station except in cases of fraud or irregularity. Ideally nobody should be kept waiting. Allowing commercial activity at border stations can motivate commercial operators to encourage officials to delay traffic as much as possible, promoting patronage of local facilities. Moreover, commercial activity can cause other problems including:

- Uncontrolled movement across the borderline by people offering and facilitating services.
- Difficulties in controlling people working at the station who use, and sometimes abuse, the commercial facilities.
- Leakages in duty free shops.
- Fiscal difficulties with value added tax (VAT) collection and refunds.
- Criminal gang activity.
- Prostitution.
- Corruption.

Finally, when there are too many catering facilities border officials tend to use them rather than do their work—and the size of the border station can also become unmanageable.

Box 4.6 The case for duty free shops

Travelers are entitled to buy in duty free shops without paying tax. However, when entering the adjacent country they must comply with allowances and pay duty on any excess. Since duty free shops are not for the convenience of officials or local residents who are not genuine travelers, many countries impose a rule such as that the benefit applies only to travelers who remain outside the country for more than 24 hours. Local residents usually have a limited allowance. Duty free shops can take many forms, from floating supermarkets on car ferries (where they bring revenue to the ferry operators) to large scale village markets (common in Central Asia and the Caucasus).

In all cases duty free shops should be kept under control. Otherwise they may open an avenue for smuggling, revenue evasion, and money laundering. Shops must be licensed, preferably by the finance ministry acting on a proposal from customs. Licenses must be revocable in cases of fraud or repeated negligence. The design and layout of shops should be approved by customs. Operators should provide a bond or guarantee.

Shops should be placed between the last control post of the exit country and the first of the entry country. They normally should report to the country on whose geographic territory they are located. Fencing or separators should limit access to traffic entitled to use the shops. Visible, intelligible notices in several languages should explain who is so entitled and what regulations are applicable in both countries. Shopkeepers may be required to ask customers for their passport and note the passport numbers and travelers' names or vehicle registration numbers.

Shop operators should keep the same accounting and inventory books as in bonded warehouses. Customs should carry out regular, unannounced, inventory checks. Border staff and employees should be barred from using the shops, especially when on duty and in uniform. Severe penalties should be instituted for violations.

The legality of duty free shops at land borders has been disputed. Unlike sea travel—where duty free purchases are consumed (in principle) at sea, and can therefore be considered as exported—goods purchased at a land border inevitably will be consumed on another customs territory. They should be taxed on entry—because tourist allowances are based on duty paid items.

HIV and other communicable diseases). Similarly, moneychangers and other runners or intermediaries have been known to extort money from travelers.

Security: new threats and challenges

With border threats mounting in recent years, border stations must provide high security. How stations are designed, organized, and operated directly affects their security performance.

Modern border management bases security on intervention by exception. Its efficient procedures can meet facilitation objectives while ensuring good security. It does not produce zero risk or blanket security.

Border stations should protect

Dramatic increases in border traffic over the past 50 years—and, more recently, fears of terrorism—have forced governments to design new methods of border control and processing, reducing congestion and waiting times. These new methods, widely adapted in market economy countries, were gradually expanded when security became a major issue.

Four of the new methods are:

- Moving customs clearance away from the physical border and nearer to where the goods are stored or consumed (with an effective internal transit control scheme).
- Establishing an inland safety net, allowing undetected border fraud and smuggling to be captured inside the country.
- Developing international cooperation to reduce data discrepancy as much as possible.
- Introducing accreditation and voluntary compliance schemes for both travelers and importers, with expedited formalities for those eligible.

Under this control model the objective is to maintain reasonable security without disrupting cross border movements. The model requires technological solutions (X-ray scanners, other detection equipment, information and communications technology infrastructure). It also requires major innovations in postrelease control and adequate auditing capacity—along with enforcement, interagency cooperation, and an environment that provides a reliable audit trail. These are not all available to some countries, and in some countries they have not been fully internalized.

Security becomes the essential concern

Security is now seen as the main border threat. But the focus is often on terrorism, represented by dangerous individuals or the smuggling of weapons and other dangerous or prohibited goods leading to attacks. This approach has two broad shortcomings.

First, the focus on terrorism ignores other facets of security. Border security is not restricted to preventing the risk of physical attacks on people or property. It also includes revenue collection, consumer protection, and preventing the violation of a country's policies through illicit cross border movement. Compliance is broadly part of the security agenda—as illustrated by various national, regional, and international supply chain security efforts. Another aim of border security is to prevent human and animal health risks. Epidemics spread rapidly with modern transport. The effort to prevent their infiltration at borders includes disinfection and, more recently, scanning travelers on arrival for high temperature and other symptoms of infectious disease.[4]

Second, focusing on terrorism often leads to an institution by institution approach—which is not the best approach to the risks involved. When security is associated with violence there is a tendency to put the police in charge of protecting the country. Trade facilitation then risks becoming an unaffordable luxury. Yet types of irregularity other than illicit movement by terrorists and their weapons may be highly relevant to security. For example, inconsistent trade patterns—which can be detected through customs document control—may conceal terrorist activities, but could be overlooked by police.

Recent experience suggests that trade facilitation does not increase the risk of terrorism. On the contrary, it is designed to identify low risk individuals and businesses. Interagency cooperation, with intelligence sharing, joint task forces, and a team approach to security, is essential to modern border management.

Zero risk is an illusory objective

There is a clear distinction between risks that can be tolerated, as the consequences of failure are not catastrophic (for example, a loss of revenue), and risks that cannot be tolerated, as the consequences of failure may indeed be catastrophic (such as the entry of a terrorist weapon or a highly infectious disease). The fear of such catastrophic consequences often motivates blanket controls and 100 percent physical inspection regimes, irrespective of time and cost.

Yet eliminating all risk is an unattainable objective. An example is the attention to improved airport security in recent years. Although air travelers are submitted to repeated, intrusive, and time consuming checks, audits have identified massive failures in the screening process. In 2007 officials from the United States Government Accountability Office audited security procedures at 19 United States airports by conducting covert tests at security checkpoints. In all cases they passed through undetected with the materials for making improvised explosive and incendiary devices (while bottled shampoo, which they carried as a decoy, was confiscated). Such results support the contention that search methods based on 100 percent inspection are generally ineffective in eliminating risk, though they may create a deterrent (an effect unlikely to discourage hardened terrorists). Blanket screening of all subjects is ineffective, and results can be better with risk based targeting through effective intelligence.

Deciding to establish a border station

As borders shift, new borders appear, and new countries emerge. With diplomatic redrawing of borderlines cutting across communities, where should new border crossings open (box 4.7)? How should borderlines be treated? How should enclaves be dealt with? Decisions to open border stations occasionally have been made without much consideration for the economic benefit to a region or district—and have sometimes resulted literally in dead ends, with roads that stop at the border or are no longer easily passable.

The need for a border station
Establishing a border station is a political decision based on a range of considerations. First, it is a pledge made as part of a diplomatic arrangement. One of the first moves made by adjacent states to establish normal relations is to open a symbolic border crossing. Economic usefulness aside, such a station is a political gesture—how traffic is handled is irrelevant, the crossing being a showcase for both countries. Yet a symbolic station can also have wider consequences. When the Bosnian war ended the Dayton agreements provided that practically every blocked, obstructed, or destroyed road leading from the new state of Bosnia and Herzegovina into the neighboring new state of Croatia should be reopened as a functioning border crossing point. The newly established

Croatian customs agency, with hundreds of border stations that it could not staff permanently, handed the stations over to an inexperienced border police force. For a long time this hindered the evolution of Croatia's customs into a modern border agency compatible with European Union practices. The obvious solution would have been a hierarchy for border facilities: some would be open to local residents, some unguarded—with traffic subject to occasional mobile, inland, and targeted compliance checks—and a few operated as full border stations. But that did not happen, as customs was allowed by law to operate only at approved crossings, with no mobile or inland capability. Changing the law was very difficult, largely because of strong objections from the interior ministry and its border police force.

Second, the opening of a border station has a social dimension. For example, borders in Central Asia were carved under the Soviet Union to cut across ethnic settlements and unify republics in the larger nation. After dissolution, borders that had once been easily crossed—because they were mere administrative divisions—suddenly became closed borders. Opening new border stations was a way for populations divided by such borders to reestablish communication.

Third, establishing a border station is based on economic considerations. The traffic determines the need, and the evolution of traffic patterns is what makes the case for a new station. New border stations are part of infrastructure development, like new motorways, bridges, or tunnels. Opening a new station redirects traffic, but it need not have much local economic impact, as under normal circumstances most goods and travelers are cleared away from the border. Yet closing a border station can have dramatic effects. When the European Union became a single market in 1993 and then expanded the Schengen scheme, customs agencies revisited their border infrastructure policies and the rule became that there should be very few, if any, border controls. Thousands of border officials and their families had to be relocated, in some cases severely affecting local economies that had relied heavily on the government's presence.

Should the border be open or closed?
Under modern border management, borders are considered globally and as bridges connecting

Borders, their design, and their operation

4

Box **4.7** | **Where should border stations be opened?**

Before settling on a location for a new border station, decisionmakers need basic information that—surprisingly—is not always readily available. Such information includes:

- Traffic numbers and—when these are significant—information on any traffic requiring specialized infrastructure (refrigerated cargo, dangerous goods, live animals).
- The shares of travelers that walk across, that drive, and that use taxis.
- The shares of travelers that are seasonal workers, that are local residents, and that are foreigners to both countries.
- Volumes of goods cleared at the border, inland, and in transit.
- The ratio of traffic volumes at peak and off peak periods.
- The average time spent at the border—if possible, broken down by queuing time, agency processing time, clearing agent time (if applicable), and unaccounted time (such as time spent in restaurants and parking lots).
- Present and required staffing (some agencies are reluctant to provide this figure, as it may be classified).

  Second, policies needing clarification include:

- The clearance policy of customs (inland or border clearance, use of nearby inland facilities, transit system type).
- The methods used by customs to deal with traveler allowances (limits, special procedures, or outright commercial clearance).
- The powers and responsibilities of customs. (For example, is control exclusively static, or can customs operate downstream?)
- Relations between agencies, and whether there is a possibility of coordinating or of delegating.
- Major risks at the proposed location (border markets, smuggling routes, cross border criminality, political sensitivity in the adjacent country).

  Third, access infrastructure must be evaluated:

- Are there cross border highways or motorways? Are any planned?
- What infrastructure exists on the other side of the border? (In some cases one country has wanted to open a border station, but there was no road on the other side.)
- What are the width and capacity of access roads? (An overloaded road can cause upstream bottlenecks, with new procedures and infrastructure needed to prevent long backups.)

  Fourth, social behavior must be considered, for three reasons:

- The size of nearby cities may generate new traffic.
- When the border cuts across a single community, there may be numerous back and forth movements, while commuter traffic needs special control and management.
- The degree of compliance within the society affects the control infrastructure.

4

regions and countries—not as walls separating them. To avoid conflicts between security and facilitation, policymakers must reassess border control and surveillance models. There are two main models, open and closed. Each implies different strategic choices. In addition, there are intermediate models.

Open borders. Open borders can be crossed and border stations walked through without checks. Of course conditions vary with circumstances and immediate priorities. Basically a Western European approach, but also practiced in North America, the open border is most fully represented by the Schengen border scheme: nationals of participating countries simply cross the border without any routine check. Another example was Switzerland before it joined the Schengen space: travelers with no more than the tourist allowance in goods, and no need for formalities, could enter or leave the country on unguarded roads. Similarly, farmers with land on both sides of an open border, or pasturing herds along it, can cross it unimpeded (as can their cattle).[5]

Open borders would have proved useful in Dalmatia following the breakup of Yugoslavia, when new borders separated Croatia from Bosnia. Farmers still had land on both sides, but they could no longer move basic supplies—such as fertilizer or cattle fodder—without making detours to lodge export and import declarations at customs houses.

Although open borders mean that some traffic may not need to pass through a border station, such borders do not eliminate control. Rather, open borders presuppose that most border station users—generally people crossing the border—will be compliant, in the first place because compliance is proved to be high throughout the society, and in the second place because people expect the cost of noncompliance to far exceed the benefits from minor fraud. Random or targeted checks, immediate or downstream, are not systematic and do not delay other vehicles.

Where borders are kept open, control over the borderline between two border stations becomes as important as control at the border station. Customs, immigration, and other control agencies have the ability to operate downstream inside a country and to investigate, detect, and prosecute violations related to illegal border crossing.

Although the open border cannot be introduced at once at every border and in every country, it ideally exemplifies modern border management.

Closed borders. Closed borders are usually, but not always, the legacy system of countries that have made a transition from a centrally planned economy. In the previous period borders were closed by default and everyone and everything crossing the borderline was treated with suspicion.[6] The syndrome still exists, with an often overwhelming police or military presence (the border troops or guards) and a heavy focus on screening every person or transaction against potential criminality or irregularity.

Today's security focus has in some ways reinforced the closed border approach. Countries aim to achieve 100 percent compliance and security through systematic controls. They often are not concerned by time lost or by high transaction costs—two effects of closed borders. Indeed, closed borders encourage bribery and other illegality (box 4.8). Despite these drawbacks the closed border approach is gaining ground even in some countries that used to favor open borders, as formal immigration control becomes increasingly zealous and, at airports, security checks become dubiously fussy.

Box 4.8	The closed border between Mozambique and South Africa

The Mozambique–South Africa border has its own iron curtain: cleared land and a tall barbed wire fence, which was once electrified. Yet aerial photography shows well trodden footpaths to the fence, which is regularly cut. Not only smugglers and illegal immigrants, but also local villagers find it more convenient to cross illicitly than to endure a lengthy border process.

A closed border usually can be crossed only at approved stations. Borderline patrolling is done by the army or border police. As anything carried across the border is deemed smuggled, the border patrol need not have any expertise in identifying goods or assessing their value, but is expected simply to hand over to customs whatever was confiscated. (This does not always work well.) Feeder roads, usually fenced off or otherwise secured, funnel all traffic into the border station. An additional feature is sometimes the compulsory transloading of goods from one truck to another.

All closed borders have detailed entry procedures—some of which are replicated, in many cases, at the inland clearance customs facility. The closed border guarantees, in theory, that a country does due diligence for border security. It also can create an opportunity—unfortunately, one that is seldom used—to clear goods at the point of entry, where transloading can facilitate customs inspection (provided it does not mean that everything is inspected).

Intermediate options. When an entirely open border system is not the desirable solution, parts of the model can be adopted. One is self assessment, which allows cars to follow a red or green channel. Introduced by customs many decades ago, this system could also apply to some travelers for immigration control. Selecting the green channel would imply that the driver and passengers do not exceed customs allowances, that they all have valid documentation, and that their vehicle is roadworthy. Driving through the green channel could be accompanied by affixing a special windshield sticker. Occasional random checks are normally a sufficient deterrent to violators. The system can also be reinforced by preauthorization. It is in place at many Western European borders and at parts of the Canada–United States border.

Border area residents can be issued special permits allowing them to cross with expedited immigration checks. Armenia introduced a semiannual import allowance scheme at a border crossing with Georgia where a duty free market operated across the border. Use of the scheme was documented, as passports were scanned by customs and matched against previous movements. Used properly, the scheme enabled genuine travelers to take advantage of the allowance while avoiding long checks.

Preclearance has various scenarios. Many car ferries in the Mediterranean have an on-board immigration officer who preclears incoming passengers. English Channel seaports in both France and the United Kingdom have immigration officials on the opposite side of the channel. In all cases spot checks may be carried out when disembarking. Nevertheless, entering the country is greatly accelerated.

South Africa and Mozambique operate a relief system on peak days (more than 50,000 passengers daily at Christmas and Easter) at the Lebombo–Ressano Garcia border station. When the station is congested all traffic is diverted to a nearby disused airfield on South African territory, where travelers are processed by the customs and immigration authorities of both countries and trucks cleared for export and import. Cleared traffic then moves in batches, under supervision, to the borderline.

Security concerns encourage tightened border controls. The European Union's external borders are now much like closed borders, with new difficulties for people who used to cross over with few or no formalities. Romania's accession to the Schengen space means that Moldovan nationals who used to visit or study in the Romanian province of Moldova now need visas and meet with extensive checks.

Responsible authority

The decision to establish a border station can be made by various authorities. In western countries the initiative often comes from the private sector (chambers of commerce or business associations) or from regional or semipublic authorities. In southern Africa the Maputo Corridor Logistics Initiative is promoting juxtaposed border facilities, also known as one stop border posts, and is contributing to streamlined procedures.

However, opening a border station is usually a decision by the finance ministry or another ministry responsible for customs. Often customs is further consulted—because it is normally considered the lead border agency, and because its knowledge of traffic flows, fraud patterns, and regional economic trends is essential in designing an expensive facility that may affect the country's economy.

In some countries the decision is made by the interior ministry, on the ground that borders are a national security matter. This approach is effective—if all the administrations involved in border processing are adequately consulted. Finally, there are cases where the whole process—from initial design to construction—is handled by the public works ministry, with no consultation of border agencies. This often happened in Central and Eastern Europe, where customs and immigration authorities had to establish their presence in a facility on short notice without providing any design inputs—and sometimes without time to anticipate staffing needs.

International or bilateral agreement

Establishing a border station normally requires international coordination. There can be a formal international treaty with additional protocols (like the Canterbury Channel Tunnel treaty between France and Great Britain), an exchange of diplomatic notes (like those exchanged between Western European countries for establishing juxtaposed border facilities), or, occasionally, a memorandum of understanding (when the border infrastructure needs simple adjustments).

Deciding on a site: in the city or on the highway?

Border stations are placed where they serve a purpose and, sometimes, where they have historical value (as with the barrier gate between Macao SAR, China and mainland China). The placement of a modern border station is subject to three major constraints:

- It should bring traffic but not generate congestion.
- It should be conveniently located.
- It should serve communities and business interests on both sides of the border.

Meeting all these criteria is sometimes difficult.

In cities. Examples of border stations in densely populated urban areas include those between Macao SAR, China and Hong Kong SAR, China and mainland China. These border stations either have existed for a long time, or were erected in a hurry because of political tensions. In 1962 France had a fiscal disagreement with Monaco. Overnight, the French resuscitated a long forgotten border between the two states—placing customs control posts on all major streets into the Principality of Monaco, with a borderline that often cut across buildings. The chaos then created helped motivate the countries to solve the crisis.

In principle urban border stations should improve communication for many people, mainly pedestrians. But such stations can cause major traffic disruption. City border stations were erected along the Bosnia-Croatia border (box 4.9) to maintain historical links between adjoining populations. Geography or longstanding infrastructure can dictate a city route for cross border connections, as in the Detroit-Windsor crossing, which is the busiest commercial entry point from Canada into the United States.

The modern principle is generally to bypass cities and erect border stations outside them, often requiring new road infrastructure. Nevertheless, pedestrian border crossings remain relevant.

On highways and major roads between cities. Highways are ideal for border stations, especially newly built stations. Generally the highway is fenced, so a new station can be built at a distance from the borderline (assuming there is no exit between it and the border). The station can be part of a layby or integrated with an interchange. In the European Union, when new highways are built across single market or Schengen borders, there is usually a contingency infrastructure that allows customs or immigration authorities to establish temporary checkpoints as needed (with electronic signs diverting traffic to specially equipped lanes and inspection areas). Older highways always have border areas, retained even where border station infrastructure was partly dismantled after the emergence of new European Union rules for border control.

The major issue with highway border stations is that they occasionally are distant from major

| Box **4.9** | **The Metkovic-Gabela border crossing** |

The only convenient road between Sarajevo and the Bosnian seaport of Neum, on the Adriatic Sea, now cuts across Croatian territory as a result of new border delineation after the war. The small Croatian city of Metkovic (next to the Bosnian town of Gabela) has become a major border station. Hundreds of trucks crossing every day generated major traffic jams, pollution, and border management issues, for which the city and local road network were not equipped. Although Metkovic had been a border city in Ottoman times, it could not cope with modern traffic conditions. Different options were proposed as temporary measures, including a joint border facility on Bosnian territory and separating commercial from tourist traffic. Yet the only long term solution was to drill a tunnel for a bypass road.

centers, creating housing and communication difficulties for border staff. (However, highway service area staff face similar problems elsewhere.)

Deciding on a function: should each station be specialized by traffic type?

Border stations can be specialized. For example, border crossings between Poland and Belarus in the Brest area are specialized for commercial traffic (Kozlovichi–Biala Podlaska) and for passenger checks (Terespol-Brest). While this requires double infrastructure, it avoids congestion from dual use of access roads and from heavy traffic in built up areas. It also allows the use of specialized equipment and buildings (warehouses, loading docks) and can apply to most transport modes.

Road and pedestrian border stations. These handle traffic that is unpredictable by nature. (Even though traffic statistics provide more or less reliable information on peak and off peak periods, vehicles arrive irregularly and trucks sometimes travel in convoys.) Advance warning schemes—in place in Finland, on roads from Helsinki to the Russian border—let border authorities open new lanes and reinforce shifts ahead of massive vehicle arrivals. Land border operations are based on linear processing, with a tendency to use a first in, first out approach.

When traffic moves on different sides of the road in the two countries, the switchover—which implies enforcement of different highway codes—normally should take place between the two border stations. Yet this can prove inconvenient. On the Mekong Friendship Bridge between the Lao People's Democratic Republic (PDR) and Thailand, the switchover takes place on the Lao PDR side before the entrance to the bridge—meaning that the Lao PDR must apply the Thai Highway Code on its territory. And at border crossings between Afghanistan (right hand) and Pakistan (left hand) the switchover takes place informally between the border stations of the two countries—where, to be sure, only a single lane exists.

Road border stations may be open to all nationalities or restricted to residents of the adjacent countries. Restriction to residents—the approach often used in former Soviet Union countries—is supposed to facilitate control, as special permit or visa exemption systems are often in place. But it is unclear why immigration authorities would have difficulty processing citizens of other countries. Perhaps processing third country nationals can require special computer links that do not exist at all major crossing points in these countries. However, road border stations do serve local border markets—either in two countries (Bagratashen-Sadakhlo between Armenia and Georgia) or one (Kjustendil in Bulgaria, close to the border with Macedonia; Andorra, between France and Spain; and throughout Central Asia)—so the stations may require special infrastructure for controlling large numbers of shoppers.

Rail transport. Railway border stations have, in principle, two major features. First, they are located at major railway stations, junctions, or marshalling yards, not necessarily on the borderline. Second, traffic is normally cleared during a scheduled border stop, which includes technical operations (locomotive change, shunting, maintenance, transboarding, gauge change).

However, some countries impose a first stop at the point of entry, where a first inspection of goods trains takes place pending further inspection at the clearance point (usually the first major stop inside the country). An example is Ukraine. This system duplicates control operations for uncertain benefits, as all the technical operations have either already taken place in the country of origin or will take

place at the first scheduled stop in the destination country.

The traditional control method is to ask passengers to get out with their luggage, walk through a customs and immigration shed (while the train moves along the platform across a symbolic borderline), and reboard. In gauge or train changes the new train waits on the opposite track along the same platform.

Many sleeping car trains, and some international high speed trains, use on-board control.[7] In such cases, the train must not stop in the country of origin after control operations start or in the destination country before they end. On-board control is best adapted to air conditioned trains with automatically locked doors and windows that cannot open during the control. It has proved generally effective, especially when supported with handheld electronic devices for scanning passports or accessing computer records. When an irregularity is detected the control officials always have the right to disembark passengers at the next stop. An international agreement should define the conditions of arrest on foreign territory and the adjudication process. (Some international high speed trains in Europe are equipped for on-board detention.) Border control formalities may also be carried out at the stations of departure and arrival, as for air travel.

A major issue on trains is that carriages offer numerous opportunities for concealing smuggled goods, particularly drugs, which customs officials often detect without being able to identify their owner (who may not even be on board). Illegal immigrants also try to stow away on passenger and freight trains.

Generally border control must fit in a train's scheduled stopping time, though in exceptional cases there can be additional delays. Experience shows that, in most countries, customs and immigration checks take less time than other railway technical operations do.

Air traffic. Crossing a border by airplane has four stages: the first at the departure airport, the second when leaving the departure country's airspace, the third when entering the destination country's airspace, and the fourth at the arrival airport. Even passengers cleared for exit remain under the jurisdiction

4

Borders, their design, and their operation

of the departure country until the moment the plane lands, when they become subject to the laws of the destination country (as for road travel when border stations are at a distance from the physical border-line). This complex process particularly affects duty free shops and other facilities at airports—in some cases duty free purchases are, quite justifiably, delivered to passengers at the boarding gate.[8]

At times an airplane must make an unscheduled landing in a third country. Passengers usually have no visa for that country and may be held, sometimes for long periods in uncomfortable transit facilities.[9] Occasionally travelers have been arrested in the course of such unscheduled landings, often for political reasons.

Some airports serve two countries. For example, at the Geneva airport arriving passengers choose to enter either France or Switzerland.

Airports support joint customs and immigration operations. Some of the immigration controls can take place at the departure airport and are delegated to airline staff. In this case airlines must ensure that passengers have valid entry documents.[10] Advance entry clearance may take place before boarding; for example, United States customs officials preclear passengers at some Canadian departure airports. This practice can raise serious extraterritoriality and administrative issues when an offense is detected.

The Basel-Mulhouse airport is probably the only truly binational airport in the world. Built on French territory, it has a Swiss sector entirely under Swiss jurisdiction and connected to the nearby Swiss city of Basel by a secured three kilometer customs road (though the French highway code applies on that road). There is an international pedestrian border crossing point between the two sectors inside the airport.

Secondary airports at times serve as border crossing points, subject to the filing of flight plans and their screening by customs.[11] But the possibility of using light aircraft for smuggling drugs has led in recent years to the restriction of international light aircraft traffic to approved customs airfields.

River. River border stations may be cross river ferry operations, or they may involve international transport of passengers (mostly) along international waterways (such as the Rhine, Danube, or Mekong rivers). Traffic usually lands within cities at landing piers, but commercial traffic may land outside the cities at river ports (as was the case at the Savannakhet landing pier, outside Vientiane, for traffic coming from Thailand to the Lao PDR before the opening of the Mekong Friendship Bridge).

Seaports. Seaport border operations differ depending on the mode of transport. Car and truck ferry ports normally resemble land border stations, but containerized traffic and shipments requiring reloading demand storage space and major facilities. Either way, a much larger volume of cargo is cleared at the seaport than at a road facility. Procedures for removal in bond to an inland location are rapidly expanding—but they require a reliable, convenient transit system that may not exist in every country.

Deciding on placement details: at the border, away from the border, in several places for several agencies, or nowhere at all?

The location of a border station depends on both geography and politics. Some countries want to assert their sovereignty by placing, if not a border station, then at least a checkpoint on the physical border. For example, when entering Poland from Belarus at Kozlovichi–Biala Podlaska, one meets with a border police checkpoint in the middle of the bridge over the River Bug.

Border stations can be located in four ways: at the physical border, at a distance from the border, in several places for several agencies, and nowhere at all.

At the physical border. Locating a station at the physical border clearly establishes sovereignty and partly simplifies border control, allowing few opportunities to unload goods or travelers before reaching customs and immigration control. But such placement requires space, which is not always available in mountain areas. And the stations can be expensive to build and maintain, physical borders usually being distant from cities. Major telecommunication links may be lacking.

Even a simple checkpoint, if established on the physical border, can generate severe difficulties. Queues can build up in the country of origin, congesting the departure station. If the border is on a river, incoming trucks must wait on the bridge before the checkpoint, threatening to overload the structure—or they must wait at the bridgehead, swelling the queue.

Stations on mountainous borderlines pose similar problems. Access is difficult for staff. Waiting trucks must start up every time they move a few dozen meters. And, if inspection is long and takes place in the open, travelers on foot may endure difficult winter conditions.[12]

When border stations of both countries are co-located, a combined facility can straddle the borderline—each country having a station on its national territory—or it can be entirely on the territory of one country. The facility can be asymmetric, with all functions on one side. Or checks in one direction can take place in one country, checks in the opposite direction in the other. In many bridge and tunnel crossings all controls take place in the country of origin, enabling faster exit at the other end and preventing congestion on the bridge or in the tunnel.

At a distance from the border. Western Europe has long tended to place border stations away from borderlines, usually before roads leading to mountain passes. Sometimes the road must be secured or restricted from there to the border, but often customs relies on road patrols to prevent traffic from bypassing the border station. Borderline patrols are another deterrent. For road bridges and tunnels, border stations usually are at the entrance and exit of the bridge or tunnel.

Even when geography does not dictate station placement at a distance from the border, such placement may be preferred, as the distance between the two border stations can be used as a buffer zone or parking area to reduce congestion at the entrance of the destination country's border facility. The problem with such zones is that there is little control over them unless the border is very precisely delineated. In some countries (as formerly at the border between Benin and Togo) goods, documentation, and license plates may be illegally switched from one truck to another. Shanty settlements may also appear, increasing the risk of smuggling and other crimes.

In several places for several agencies. At some borders various control agencies have various placements.

For example, the border police may be at the physical border and customs away from it—the case in some Baltic states and Central Europe and at several Afghan border stations. This is not a recommended solution, for several reasons. First, when customs is away from the borderline it inevitably loses contact with the movement of goods across the border. Cargo reporting, often delegated to another agency, becomes less reliable. Second, the system can work fairly well only when there is no opportunity for trucks and goods to avoid customs. (At Biala Podlaska, on the border between Poland and Belarus, trucks travel seven kilometers along an entirely fenced and controlled road, and compliance is high.) Third, in countries where noncustoms agencies have little understanding of (or interest in) customs constraints, there is a significant risk that cargo will not be properly reported. In Afghanistan, where both the commerce ministry and border police still resist a real customs presence at the border, stations have been designed for all agencies except customs, and new infrastructure often has tended to relegate customs to a distant location. In such cases fenced roads are not a sufficient deterrent—and they are expensive. The longer they are, the more difficult to control they become, and video surveillance devices are only as good as enforcement response times.

Nowhere. The creation of a customs union, then a single market, in the European Union did not abolish national borders as such—but border stations have disappeared or been downscaled. Occasionally they are known as international observatories with random or targeted customs or immigration checks. However, in most cases the border has become barely noticeable. While national authorities may still stop traffic within the territory, most commercial control takes place at the point of clearance or destination.

Designing border stations

Since border stations are perceived as a country's windows, their layout ideally should allow free flows of traffic. They should act as control points only when there are reasons to stop someone or something. While every border station will have unique characteristics—based on traffic, local mentalities, government priorities, and so on—seven principles need to be followed. They are:

- Flexibility.
- Modularity.
- Adaptability to different control methods.
- Process integration.
- Control by exception and in the lanes.
- Appropriate size.
- Communication of identity.

Flexibility

Designers should keep in mind the need to change configurations easily to accommodate shifting circumstances. For example, though the total number of lanes is fixed, their designation as entry and exit lanes should be allowed to change depending on traffic. Similarly, administrative buildings with changing rooms for men and for women should use mobile partitioning, to adjust to a shifting male-female ratio.

Not all the equipment and infrastructure at very large border stations may be needed at smaller facilities. Initially installing everything that a state of the art facility would require—even when its usefulness is not apparent—is often rhetorically justified on the grounds that the border infrastructure is funded by a foreign donor and it would seem irresponsible not to make the most of the opportunity. But, as experience has repeatedly shown, it can be far better simply to acquire space for a possible future expansion.

For modern single windows and one stop operations it may be worthwhile to plan a joint or co-located facility, even if it cannot be built immediately. The border station between Afghanistan and Pakistan at Towr Kham is ideally placed for joint use by the Afghan and Pakistan authorities (and there is no available space for expansion on the Pakistan side of the border). Co-location cannot be envisioned at present, but the new Afghan facility was designed to enable conversion to binational operations.

Modularity

Flexibility is best with modular design. While the station space and basic infrastructure (power, drainage, stabilized platform for buildings) should exist from the beginning, construction can be gradual.

Some border stations started as containers to which new modules were added as traffic grew.

Too little research has been devoted to specialized border infrastructure modules (control booths, passenger control and search cubicles, staff accommodation and housing, telecommunications and information and communications technology) that could be interconnected and serve as temporary infrastructure. Such modules could be installed in an emergency after a natural or other catastrophic event. War zones, and areas prone to flooding, earthquakes, and the like, would benefit from rapidly deployable contingency facilities providing immediate continuity in border control—as well as offering a cheap alternative in emergencies that require massive foreign aid.

Adaptability to new control methods

Border stations should be designed bearing future control operations in mind. If joint cross border operations are envisioned, the station should designate what will eventually be joint and exclusive control areas, should include lane switches for redirected traffic (for example, green traffic redirected in one country to red control), and should strategically place specialized control buildings (such as scanners) that will be jointly used. If future fast lane processing for some user types is expected, some lanes should bypass the main control infrastructure.

Integration of processes

Control methods are still often based on agency specific procedures even though each agency requires more or less the same infrastructure (at least for booths or windows). Designers should consider single larger booths, housing, for example, customs and immigration officials. Even with a partition in the middle, such booths would better prepare for an integration of processes and possible delegation between administrations—and would immediately reduce vehicle stops.

Control by exception and in the lanes

All traffic should be initially controlled in the traffic lanes, on the ground that cross border movements should be considered legitimate unless there are reasons for doubt. The compliant majority should not be asked to leave their vehicles at border stations.

space, a roundabout design may be envisioned, with the commercial freight building in the middle.

Return loops and escape lanes at strategic locations within the station, and guarded by remote controlled barriers or traffic lights, are necessary for service traffic and for rejected vehicles or those targeted for secondary control. Before the borderline there should always be a layby, where enforcement authorities may carry out final checks or intercept previously cleared vehicles.

Border station operation

Improved border station operation yields improved design, in turn facilitating streamlined processing as described above.

Segmentation by traffic category

In a multipurpose border station various traffic categories are subject to different inspection and control methods. Traffic should be separated as early as possible when reaching the station. Heavy goods vehicles should be taken out of car lanes at some distance from the station and driven or parked on dedicated roads, as width is often a problem for border stations (in mountains or in narrow valleys along rivers). This allows at least light traffic to reach the border normally. If it is not feasible a holding area should be established before the border.

For the rare cases when light vehicles and their trailers carry commercial goods, a policy should be made. Will they be processed under tourist or commercial rules? In which part of the facility?

International transit trucks require much less processing than other trucks, and should be offered special lanes. Likewise, empty trucks should be diverted from main commercial lanes. When two border stations are within a short distance—and if the borderline crossing is wide enough—traffic requiring clearance in the country to be entered could be directed to special lanes in the departure country.

Coaches should have a dedicated lane, which can be next to the car lanes, as car and coach passengers can be processed by the same staff.

Self assessment by red and green channels

Widely used by customs, red and green channel self assessment is not as much used by immigration authorities, who need to examine and possibly stamp every passport. However, full "green" treatment could be tested for travelers not requiring an entry stamp (for example, nationals of the country of entry) and for preauthorized individuals. This type of fast track does not in any circumstances preclude authorities from doing spot checks to verify green channel legitimacy.

When immigration cannot or will not establish a fast track, the customs green channel should be carefully planned.

Control sequencing: which agency should intervene first?

Possible sequences for a single country are:
- First immigration, then customs.
- First customs, then immigration.
  Either sequence can occur on exit or on entry.

Possible sequences for juxtaposed or co-located joint operations are:
- Back to back immigration: first customs exit, then immigration exit, then borderline, then immigration entry, then customs entry.
- Back to back customs: first immigration exit, then customs exit, then borderline, then customs entry, then immigration entry.
- Asymmetrical and separated by country: first customs exit, then immigration exit, then borderline, then customs entry, then immigration entry (both entry-exit sequences may be reversed).
- Asymmetrical and binationally integrated: first customs exit, then customs entry, then immigration exit, then immigration entry, then borderline (customs-immigration and borderline-border control sequences may be reversed).

Each model has benefits and weaknesses.

Back to back immigration. Going through immigration as the last checkpoint in one country and the first in the next—clearly establishes which country has jurisdiction over a traveler at any time (as indicated by the passport stamp). This is a simple and effective model when illegal immigration is a problem: an illegal immigrant can be deported immediately, which is not so simple if the person has already been cleared for entry). The model works best at juxtaposed facilities (where exit and entry immigration officials may share a booth cut by a fictitious border-line). It promotes integration between immigration authorities of both countries, as they work closely together. Such integration is often more difficult to achieve than customs integration. However, back to back immigration prevents full green channel operations. Immigration may want to pull traffic cleared for the green channel by customs back into the main lanes. Furthermore, traffic already cleared for exit by customs with export rebates or refunds, that is refused entry into the other country must be reprocessed and the money reimbursed.

Back to back customs. Making customs the last exit post allows customs green channel operations—as long as customs in the other country adheres to the system and uses similar targeting or selectivity methods.

Asymmetrical methods. Whether separated by country or binational, asymmetrical methods allow preclearance before crossing the borderline. Offences may be awkard to prosecute because of territoriality, unless there is an international agreement.

A combination of all these sequencing models can be used for categories of traffic that require special processing, or to meet other needs depending on the local environment.

Upstream selection

Upstream selection means that each arriving vehicle must select a red or green lane before reaching the facility[27]—reducing congestion, but also requiring that all vehicles drive through immigration. Immigration authorities must staff all the booths in open green lanes. Coordination between customs and immigration is essential. And the fast track green lane must offer a significant benefit to users (box 4.13).

Self selection within the station

With self selection within the station, drivers cleared by immigration choose red or green before reaching customs. Some distance is required for traffic to switch over. That prevents routine joint processing by customs and immigration.

Off lane control

With off lane control examination bays are at an angle from the lane, so that traffic not selected for examination can move straight to the exit of the facility. Each bay accommodates only one vehicle. A targeting officer at the entrance directs some green lane traffic to the bay, the other vehicles proceeding unchecked to the exit. The system works well if customs accept that, once all examination bays are filled, traffic waiting behind should not be held except under very special circumstances.[28]

An Eastern European country introduced a similar design that integrated customs and immigration booths in the inspection bays, which were designed to hold three vehicles at a time. Apparently the system was not well explained to users, because all traffic chose the bays. As drivers had to leave their vehicles for passport control, theirs blocked those waiting behind. The system brought no noticeable benefit.

Field operations and staffing issues

This section mainly concerns border stations that operate 24 hours a day. In cases where border stations

---

| Box **4.13** | **Green channel failures** |

One director general of customs, eager to follow an international advisor's recommendation for red and green channel operations, introduced the system at a major road border station with little or no preparation. The following day the green channel was completely jammed. Why? First, because border police did not participate in the scheme. Second, because every vehicle in the green lane was stopped by customs. When drivers selected the red channel, which was empty, they were turned back if they said they had nothing to declare.

In another country the red and green channel system was introduced at an airport. Passengers with goods to declare who selected the red channel were told simply to walk down the green channel and talk to the first available customs officer (there were dozens of them). But before they could, customs would pounce on them, search them, and confiscate goods the travelers had intended to declare.

In both cases the situation eventually improved.

Borders, their design, and their operation

4

close at night, control staff from customs and the border police should remain on site to ensure that no unreported traffic passes through.

Changes in shift

Shift changes can bring borders to a standstill. The situation is aggravated when agencies have different shift patterns—and, even more, when shift changes happen more or less at the same time on both sides of a border.[29]

The situation is bad in countries where a formal change in shift takes place only between outgoing and incoming shift leaders. Shift cashiers sign off the account sheet and tally it with the cash box. No outgoing officer will ever leave his position without his replacement being there. And control staff members are always eager to finish up. Instructions to staff are distributed throughout the shift or during breaks, rather than during shift changes.

Shift duration

Border staff members often remain on duty for too long. A normal shift is often 24 hours, with an 8 hour break in the middle. No control official can remain alert for so long, especially when bedrooms and a cafeteria are available throughout the shift. The reason for such long periods is financial. Shorter shifts are more expensive because of greater staff rotation, and some officials are paid more for night hours—even when they sleep on site. There has been strong resistance to installing more realistic shifts, even though they would lead immediately to better results.

Shift rotation

With shift rotation, an entire shift reporting for duty is unexpectedly taken to another border station—which in turn sends its staff to the first station. Every time this measure has been applied it has had considerable success. First, the routine was broken, prompting a fresh approach to a new environment. Second, prior arrangements between corrupt officers and importers were disrupted and exposed. Third, truck drivers who routinely would bribe known road, customs, or immigration officials were unpleasantly surprised. The problems with rotation are that it is expensive, it takes a long time to organize, and it is difficult to keep secret for long.

Switching staff among lanes

Moving staff from one lane or position to another is easier than shift rotation. Staff in truck lanes should regularly be switched with those in passenger vehicle lanes.

Shift flexibility

Even the best designed border station will be congested under peak traffic conditions if not enough staff are on duty. So each shift structure should be adapted to the time of day, with fewer staff usually on duty at night than during the day. But this may not always be possible. Many countries have standards for shift composition that cannot be easily altered.[30] Also, there should be more temporary staff posted during busy periods. But with resources limited, plugging one leak may merely open a new one. The best solution is to have cross trained officials from customs and immigration, able to stand in for one another. (The attitude of some countries, that an officer assigned to a specific booth or lane cannot be moved somewhere else within the station, is wrong.)

Handling noncompliance: why detected cases of fraud and irregularity must be monitored

Usually the number of travelers selected for control far exceeds the number of detected cases of fraud and irregularity. On the one hand, customs officials claim that practically all import transactions are irregular in some way or other. On the other hand, that claim is not reflected in annual statistics. The reason is that local case logs are not kept—allegedly because most irregularities are simply overlooked by customs when considered too minor to initiate a case report. If true, this reveals a serious error, as the failure to report encourages secretive behavior, distorts activity reports, and prevents an effective analysis of noncompliance and its causes.

Paper immigration and customs forms: why both are archaic and should be replaced

A majority of countries still insist that arriving—and sometimes departing—travelers should fill paper immigration forms. Such forms require passengers to enter data already in their passports (and, in most cases, machine readable from the passports). In addition, passengers must identify:

- Their flight or vehicle (data already available to immigration officers, or capturable automatically by scanning a boarding pass or vehicle number plate).
- Their entry date (obviously known to the immigration officer).
- The purpose of their visit (essentially statistical data, and unreliable when travelers mean to break labor laws).
- The place of their stay during their visit (useless data, unless to control visitors, for which hotel registration is enough).
- The duration of their visit (data that may be useful, but could be obtained simply by asking).

The immigration forms are then filed and—sometimes—entered into a computer (which is not always online). When the forms are occasionally retrieved and audited many are found to have unreadable or misrepresented data—hardly a surprise, since most are completed in queues, on cramped airplanes, in crowded immigration halls, or in cars while the writer is driving.

Some countries also ask for a customs declaration form on entry.

From a modern border management perspective, both paper immigration forms and paper customs declaration forms are archaic.

Replacing paper immigration forms with other methods. Methods that can and should replace paper immigration forms include:

- A passport scan.
- A very brief interview with the traveler, if necessary.
- When in doubt, a more thorough secondary control.

Replacing paper customs forms with passenger channels. With passenger channels, the traveler's selection of a customs channel is the same as a goods declaration. Travelers with no goods to declare, apart from those included in the allowance, select the green channel. Those with dutiable items—or in doubt—select the red one.

Making a majority of travelers fill a form stating they have nothing to declare is a waste of time and paper. Nevertheless, several countries still use both paper customs declaration forms and customs channel selection—passengers hand their forms to a duty officer in the green channel.

The future of juxtaposed border facilities

Juxtaposed border facilities—also known as joint, co-located, or one stop—are becoming increasingly popular. They have high visibility, denote a strong will to cooperate across borders, and—at least in principle—facilitate cross border movement. Although they are difficult to put into practice—many conditions are required to achieve well integrated functions—they could revolutionize border control.

Background
Co-located border facilities first appeared in the 1920s, in a farm straddling the French-Belgian border—the borderline actually crossed the dining room. Both countries found it more convenient to let interviews occur informally across the dining room table than to use lengthy judicial procedures. That was the first modern infrastructure for cross border cooperation.

Every border station needs to consult with the other side. Sometimes a white flag is hoisted to request a formal meeting, especially when going through national headquarters seems unnecessary. Cross border coordination also occurs at the closing of the border, when both stations stop operating. This can be simple, with border guards from both countries closing a gate and locking it with two keys (one for each country), or it can be colorful, as at the Wagga border crossing between Pakistan and India.

However anecdotal, these examples of cross border relations show the need for regular consultation and cooperation. To further integrate the work of agencies on both sides of the border, juxtaposed facilities are invaluable.

The case for juxtaposed facilities
Juxtaposed facilities are of two types. In the first, two separate border stations are located side by side and treated as one geographical entity. In the second, the border stations of both countries are merged into

Borders, their design, and their operation

4

one station and the full integration of processes is promoted.

Juxtaposed facilities allow economies of scale, better cooperation, simplified formalities, improved control over fraud, and informal data and intelligence exchanges. Moreover, the increasingly apparent economic consequences of long border waiting times argue for joint infrastructure and operations. Well established in western countries for 60 years, and successfully tested in some Central and Eastern European countries before transition, juxtaposed stations have evolved over time. They started as divided stations straddling the border, with each country remaining on its own side. Then they evolved into single stations more on one country's territory. Later still, they embraced the operational integration of border law enforcement agencies. One example is the Schengen Joint Police Stations. Another is the police and customs cooperation centers, or joint Schengen patrols, between the customs administrations and police forces of adjacent countries at some internal borders within the European Union (box 4.14).

Such integration, though probably far in the future for many countries, indicates the possibility and efficiency of cross border integration and coordination. It also reveals the conditions necessary for effective cooperation.

Conditions necessary for juxtaposed or coordinated border operations

The conditions for success are simple, but experience shows that they are sometimes difficult to fulfill. The main problem at juxtaposed stations is how to detect frauds, arrest offenders, and prosecute cases without violating either country's laws.

Understanding what a juxtaposed station means. In some cases heads of state or government become over-enthusiastic about a joint station, thinking it will solve all border issues at a particularly difficult crossing, so they require queues to be drastically reduced by a deadline.[31] In other cases, when opening a juxtaposed facility is meant to demonstrate friendship between two countries, politics and ribbon cutting can matter more than operations. If ministers and heads of state know little about interagency protocols and international operating procedures, still they should be aware of the strong commitment implicit in opening juxtaposed border stations—not only to an architectural design, but also to clarified procedures and streamlined laws and systems of organization.

Binational or international agreement on juxtaposed border facilities. Most international agreements signed now reflect an emerging international standard for juxtaposed border facilities, usually consisting of:

- Placement in the immediate vicinity of the borderline whenever possible.
- Symmetrical arrangement, with one way facilities in each country.
- All checks in the destination country.
- A so called common control area—where officials of both countries carry out their checks—complemented by exclusive control areas for each country.

This template, which has the advantage of simplicity, establishes an apparently novel joint control arrangement. Yet it can have limitations. First, the geography—or the existing infrastructure, when this is to be upgraded—may not be suitable. An example

| Box **4.14** | **Police and customs cooperation centers (Schengen patrols)** |

Police and customs cooperation centers bring together officials from two adjacent countries who have access to their agencies' databases and intelligence networks. Each official is free to share or not share sensitive or confidential data. Centers collect and exchange intelligence, deal with asylum seekers, establish cross border cooperation against illegal immigration (notably through the management of denial of admission procedures and expulsions of illegal aliens), and coordinate the fight against smuggling (drugs in particular).

The centers also coordinate joint surveillance in the border area. Joint patrols consist of officials of both countries whose area of operation is limited to a certain distance from both sides of the border. Law enforcement officials of each country may conduct surveillance and hot pursuit in the opposite country, and may in some cases request a suspect's arrest by its national authorities. Required to operate in uniform, the officials are allowed to carry weapons in the opposite country but to use them only for self defense.

is the Chirundu border station between Zambia and Zimbabwe. The Zambian side is cramped, and the symmetrical arrangement creates traffic difficulties there—whereas the Zimbabwe facility offers large unused spaces that could have been shared by both countries. In other examples juxtaposition has precluded placement of a station at a more convenient location further inside one country.

A second limitation of the emerging international standard is that it subjects all types of traffic to the same rule. In practice heavy traffic might more readily be processed on arriving in a country and on departing the same country, both times in that country—even as light vehicles follow the symmetrical arrangement described above.

A third limitation is the likelihood of traffic buildup. On the one hand, performing all control functions in the destination country seems logical—exit checks are far less stringent, since it is unlikely that departure country authorities will need to prosecute a traveler on foreign territory.[32] At the same time, queues building up in the destination country may spill over into the departure country, jamming cross border infrastructure (such as a bridge). European countries usually perform all checks in the departure country, thus smooth traffic flows in tunnels and on bridges.

International agreements, therefore, should be flexible enough to allow future adjustment to local conditions and circumstances, without the need for new agreements.

Internalizing the agreement for juxtaposed border facilities. International agreements need to be translated into national legislation. This requires often extensive changes to existing texts (unless a provision in the agreement states that it overrides the national legislation of both countries—which is legally possible, but technically unworkable). The needed adjustments can be innumerable, and the process can be delayed by national officials or misinterpreted (leading to inadequate provisions or to a radically different approach in each country). The drafting of supporting laws, regulations, and standard operating procedures—while a national concern—should be coordinated binationally by a technical commission.

Extraterritoriality. Extraterritoriality, in border station operations, means subjection to a sovereignty other than that of the country on whose geographical territory a person or object is currently located. Extraterritorial persons become liable for their acts according to the jurisdiction of one country while on the territory of another, which cannot impose its laws on them. This raises diplomatic problems that binational agreements address in three ways.

First, the border may be redrawn to exclude from the border station's host country all the station areas that fall under the other country's jurisdiction. However, border delineation is a long and complicated process. It implies compensatory retrocession of territory, and it needs to be ratified by both countries. Nor does it allow future flexibility. Finally, the redrawing can create an enclave when a station is too far inland to allow large border modifications.

Second, the border can become a functional and chronological concept, determined by the nationality of the official performing a control. Most such agreements specify the sequence of checks, stipulating that control by the destination country can start only once the departure country has completed its own checks or indicated its intention not to perform them. Travelers and consignments then come under the control of the destination country. For passengers it is fairly easy to establish a well marked turnstile, border gate, or equivalent symbol.

Third, sovereignty can be limited. The authorities of one country operating on the other side of the station are allowed to apply only certain laws, regulations, or parts thereof. The border station's host country retains power over incidents unrelated to the crossing (such as robberies). It is essential to precisely define such cases and the conditions of any intervention. Past issues have led to serious diplomatic incidents.[33]

Fourth, the powers of station staff—particularly to use firearms—should be very clearly defined.

Even while under the jurisdiction of the adjacent country, people can claim the application of the host country's legislation—as when one country but not the other enforces the death penalty. At Canadian airports, United States customs officers who detect drug smugglers have no powers of arrest and must either persuade the smugglers to fly across the border or hand them over to Canadian law enforcement. Similarly, at a juxtaposed border station on Canadian territory a Canadian national has a constitutional right to return home until the official borderline is crossed—even though the Canadian may already be in the United States area.

The powers of control staff. Enforcement agency officials at juxtaposed border stations are allowed to work in uniform within their areas of competence. In principle, firearms can be carried, but their use is usually limited to self defense.[34] Officers are otherwise allowed to perform all the duties within their official mandate. They may, for example, search travelers and consignments (customs), check documents (customs and immigration), document and initiate prosecution (customs and immigration), and arrest offenders (customs, immigration, and police when applicable). They are not subject to border control formalities when crossing into the other country to perform their duties.

Cooperation. To make the most of a juxtaposed border facility, equipment and data should be shared and exchanged as much as possible, for example by:

- Using scanners jointly or sharing them. Legal difficulties over territorial competence can arise if scanners are not operated by officials of the country making the detection—but this is normally solved by following a positive scan with a physical search, during which the detection is officially made.
- Making the results of controls carried out by one country's officials acceptable in the opposite country. Some checks need not be duplicated: customs may accept weight tickets issued in the other country, possibly at a shared weighbridge. Both countries should use the same control protocols, and the calibration and maintenance of control equipment (such as scales for weighing) should be mutually recognized.
- Exchanging computer data on transit procedures and customs declarations, and possibly immigration (or at least passport) data in real time.

Joint operations. Officials of both countries can be encouraged in five ways. First, documents for customs declarations may be processed by customs officials of both countries working side by side. When one country has finished processing an international document, such as a transit form, its officer can pass it to his foreign colleague without the driver or import agent having to lodge it at a new position.

Second, the interface between the two customs computer systems can be used to send messages closing export files (certifying that goods have left a country), entering reliable and standardized data into the declaration processing system of the destination country (with no need to recapture these data), and logging the transaction (establishing the precise time when the virtual border was crossed and the goods handed over from one country to the other—necessary in case of subsequent legal action).

Third, in a back to back arrangement, immigration officers could sit in the same booth, and process the same passport information consecutively and seamlessly. For example, passports would be scanned only once when reaching the immigration booth, and the data would be displayed on the computers of immigration officials of both countries—who would then add whatever additional information they required and check the traveler's status against their agency's specific system.

Fourth, customs officers of both countries can jointly process all fast track commercial traffic, such as empty trucks, in a single booth (since these checks are similar in both countries).

Fifth, when road administrations are present at the border, they could also carry out some controls jointly (weighing, for example).

Joint examinations

Recent initiatives promote joint customs inspections—inspections carried out simultaneously by two countries' customs agencies. The aims are to save time, to avoid fraud, to create synergy between the two agencies, to reduce parking space requirements, and possibly to store temporarily unloaded goods under verification (saving handling costs).

This approach appears unrealistic at this stage, and it is seldom applied. There are four main reasons. First, import and export checks are different. Most data usually verified for imports are not relevant for the majority of exports. Customs agents seldom check export values (never mind whether physical examinations help to ascertain real values), nor are the agents interested in export classification. On rare occasions a risk based targeted control may take place on exported goods—but this is not enough to

Borders, their design, and their operation

justify systematic participation by both countries in a control.

Second, joint examinations may increase the rate of physical examination for no purpose. In a control organization based on risk management, different risk profiles would normally be applied by each country. But joint control encourages each country to participate in physical examinations for declarations that would not normally have been queried by that country. If risk management is a good principle, then joint control is a waste of resources.

Third, joint controls—however integrated—take more time. Two sides inspecting together may delay each other, as they do not have the same objectives and interests.

Fourth, managing violations can be problematic. Binational agreements for juxtaposed border stations usually stipulate that one country can start checks only once the other country has released the goods. But during a joint examination this moment of release is never clearly established. In case of fraud the transporter may validly claim that the control was not carried out in the proper sequence.

Technology at border stations

Borders were efficiently managed long before sophisticated technology appeared. Yet computers, and nonintrusive examination techniques, have revolutionized border controls. Whereas chapter 7 examines information and communications technology in border management reform, this section addresses technology only as it is used at border stations.

Information and communications technology: why the time has come for data sharing
Both customs and immigration can use information and communications technology, including to share data across borders.

Customs. Border delays and inefficiencies are usually blamed on outmoded customs procedures. However, a great majority of customs administrations have now computerized their clearance operations. The chief remaining issues for them are two: installing computer terminals at border stations and developing modules adapted to specific border processes.

Customs computer systems were first designed to automate duty assessment, so they centered on declaration processing, tariff files, and duty calculation algorithms. Only later were additional functions added, such as risk management and transit control. The systems were essentially intended for inland clearance operations, but were sometimes deployed for clearance at border stations. A recent emphasis on border computerization has led to the introduction, in the European Union, of the New Computerised Transit System (NCTS) and the Export Control System (ECS). But in developing countries the existing telecommunications infrastructure may not allow computer connections (nor may the power grid), so computer use may lag behind.

Solving these technical problems entails setting priorities. The speed of customs border processes, or their efficiency, is linked closely to the adequacy of cargo control over entering shipments. Adequacy implies ensuring that all consignments crossing the border are officially reported to customs and that transit control—a mechanism to ensure a true representation of goods at their destination—is in place. Customs also must often enforce additional noncustoms regulations on entering goods.

The best way to prevent fraud (box 4.15) is to rely on data created when a shipment leaves the country of origin—at the very beginning of the transport chain—and to continue using the original transit documentation, or virtual documentation where there is no regional transit system. Computers should be used for capturing upstream data and for transmitting those data to customs points along the route, where the data are matched against vehicles, shipments, and documents. The data should then be fed directly into the destination country's customs computer system. Customs officers at the border thus can conveniently access prereported data using simple access information, such as transit document numbers or vehicle and container registration numbers. For further simplification, scanners can be used to read bar coded data on documents and vehicle license plates.

The Common Market for Eastern and Southern Africa (COMESA), like some other entities, has introduced a regional transit database—the first step towards regional connectivity between customs systems. However, to streamline border processing it will also be necessary to provide customs officials in border

Borders, their design, and their operation

4

At a land border traditional reporting is visual. A customs officer, seeing a vehicle entering the country, notes its registration number. This system lends itself to abuse unless properly audited. First, customs officials can be bribed not to enter a vehicle number in their log, or to enter the wrong number. Second, errors can be made in manually registering vehicles. Third, systems breakdowns—such as power failures (accidental or deliberate)—can prevent proper registration.

Traditional auditing tools are also weak. In their original, manual form they were prone to errors and omission. Customs would manually re-enter in its logs the information in transit documents presented by drivers (assuming an international transit scheme was in operation). The border police would register every commercial vehicle, would sometimes copy the transit documents—about which they had little knowledge, leading to further misunderstanding and errors—and would make occasional reconciliations with customs log books. Down the road checks would then match the documentation presented by drivers with what had been recorded at the border.

Improvements came when the International Road Transport Union (IRU) introduced the Safe TIR arrangement—matching TIR carnets (described in chapter 17) with regular discharge messages sent by customs headquarters to the IRU. Another improvement came when customs introduced inland road patrols, a second level of control independent from border customs authorities.

At seaports problems with the traditional system are less acute. All incoming cargo has a trail of commercial or shipping documentation, which can be tallied against unloading records kept by customs. Similarly, rail transport companies proved reliable partners and had document trails that complemented customs records.

booths with a convenient interface between the national systems and the COMESA database. At present they have none.[35] European Union procedures have made marked progress, with the integration of NCTS and ECS into national customs systems allowing nearly instant discharge of transit shipments.

Another solution, easier to implement, is to connect customs systems across the border. This first step toward more elaborate regional integration is feasible, especially when both countries use ASYCUDA software. Compatibility issues arising when two different versions are used (such as the ASYCUDA++ and ASYCUDA World versions) do not appear insurmountable. The connection can start with messages that a truck or consignment has been released for exit on one side, and it can gradually be extended to complete transit data sharing. Ultimately there can be automatic data input to the destination country's declaration processing system.

Immigration. Computerization is less widespread for immigration checks than for customs control. Rather than keying in all passport data at a control booth, passport scanning (for countries that issue machine readable passports) should be preferred as more reliable. Countries are increasingly testing new electronic gate solutions, such as iris identification (United Kingdom) and digitized fingerprints

(France). These systems rely on preregistering volunteers, and they may be out of reach for most travelers in many parts of the world. Other technologies, including face recognition (Australia's Smartgate project) and biometric data on passports and identification cards, can accept more passengers without requiring preregistration.[36]

In any computer immigration system qualifying travelers should be offered a fast track procedure. Regular border station users, such as truck drivers and local taxi drivers licensed to cross the border, ought to be among the first beneficiaries of electronic identification.

Technically, nothing prevents immigration authorities in one country from sharing data with colleagues on the other side. In the booths, data capture is independent from control so if immigration officers of two countries use a joint boot (box 4.16) they can capture data just once, followed by separate processing in national immigration databases. Wholly automatic control booths, using sophisticated iris and fingerprint scans, can even be programmed to send separate messages to the two countries' systems and release a passenger only after receiving a positive response.

Challenges in establishing data sharing arrangements. The main challenge is to convince agencies that some data can be shared internationally without jeopardizing confidentiality. Passport and biometric data are well known to travelers, who now have no objection to manual data capture. No agency secret is revealed if these data are shared across the border. Transit has been shared across borders manually for decades, so there is no harm in sharing it electronically.

What is important is to ensure that each agency retains full control over its systems and databases. Any joint systems should be designed to insulate agency specific data from shared identification information. A passport can be scanned once and the scan stored in a local community network, and the personal identification data can then be distributed to interested agencies that then check it against their own risk management databases and lookout lists. Similarly, advance transit information can be used for partly generating entry declarations or onward transit documentation.[37]

It is crucial to break the silo mentality. Immigration authorities tend to consider passport control their business and to feel that nobody else should access passport data. But passenger and driver identity is also central to customs risk management (goods and vehicles do not move on their own).

Ensuring data confidentiality implies setting limits on the period for which personal data may be kept and on the ways data may be disclosed. When data are shared across borders, the stricter of the two countries' data confidentiality laws should be enforced. Personal data should be disclosed only to those authorized to ask for it.

Transit monitoring

Computer systems can ensure that a transit operation has been initiated and properly discharged and that documentary requirements are met. That covers operations at administrative processing points, but gives no information on what happens between those points (other than the time consumed by transit). Real time monitoring—or at least a record of all transport incidents—can help identify fraud risks such as partial unloading or load substitution. Various solutions for this problem exist, both after the fact and in real time.

First, tachygraphs or other similar driving recorders can be fitted to trucks and used by the road administration to check on driving and rest times. The recorders also provide customs with valuable information on where a truck has been: a flat line

---

Box 4.16   Examples of joint data collection at border stations

In 2006 Bulgaria introduced an experimental tracking system at the Lesovo border station, with smartcards updated at each workstation during a crossing. Similar systems exist at some Polish border stations. The approach could be expanded through further binational integration, collecting and maintaining a single transaction record for two countries. On one side of the facility a camera with an optical recognition function would read entering license plates and create a unique, date stamped record. At the immigration booth driver and passenger passport data would be scanned and appended to the record. For commercial freight, customs would scan the transit document and the transaction record would be updated when a declaration is lodged. The same would occur at each control position, including automatic weighbridges and the cashier's window. The transaction record would be circulated to all agency systems. When the vehicles leave the facility their transaction records would be automatically discharged by another camera reading.

The approach described above would provide for:

- Reliable capture of identification and procedural data.
- Less fraud and fewer capture errors.
- Detailed records of time spent inside the facility and at each procedural desk, allowing more finely grained performance assessment.
- Precise indications of when vehicles cross the physical or virtual border at juxtaposed border stations.
- Transaction records allow some joint risk management: for example, alerting a particular agency that a vehicle or person it wants to control is inside the border station, or enabling advance consultation of a database. The records can also communicate information or intelligence throughout the border station—or to selected administrations.

indicates long periods of driving at a sustained speed, broken lines denote driving in built up areas, and so forth. Records inconsistent with normal transit itineraries or driving patterns call for a detailed check.[38]

Second, the new generation of customs seals includes chips that keep a record of every manipulation or attempt to break them. True, it is said that no seal, however sophisticated, can resist an experienced smuggler for more than a few minutes. But so called smart seals—connected to transmitters that issue alerts when unauthorized manipulations take place—can validly guarantee that a consignment has not been tampered with. The security provided by such seals is as good as the authorities' speed in responding to the alert. Some countries, such as Kazakhstan, have introduced automatic seal reading gantries at entry and exit points. Each entry reading is automatically sent by satellite link to the exit border station, and when the truck arrives there the seal is scanned again. If the tow records match the transit operation is discharged.

Third, cargo tracking monitors transit trucks fitted with transponders—or radio wave reflective devices—in real time. Available technologies use either satellite tracking or detection loops built into roads at strategic points and major junctions. Attempts have been made to use this system to control every single truck in transit inside a country—an approach known as active tracking, as every truck automatically sends messages at regular points along its route. A spectacular control center in customs headquarters, showing the progress of thousands of trucks daily, is the pride of senior customs managers. However, this is an expensive method of control: it requires many operators to monitor each truck, it uses expensive transponders or smart seals (and transport companies may be reluctant to hire these from customs), and it is vulnerable to fraud (transponders are known to have been neutralized with tinfoil or taken off trucks and reinstalled on decoy vehicles). Moreover, customs must send out a patrol to investigate each anomaly—a resource intensive approach and one that may be ineffective in a very large country.

Passive tracking operates differently: a few volunteer trucks are equipped with transponders at the drivers' expense. Customs pings the transponders whenever a routine check is desired. In exchange, drivers are offered fast track treatment when they reach the border. Drivers therefore are willing to pay for the transponders—apparently a more cost effective system.

Scanners

Border agencies use X-ray scanners for compliance, security, and investigative controls. For best results, the objectives of X-ray scanning policies should be clarified. The way scanners are used can limit their efficiency.

The benefits of scanners are exaggerated
When scanners are planned at a border station, authorities (usually in customs) raise expectations for the equipment and declare an intention to carry out checks for many purposes. Each of the claimed benefits from X-ray scans is discussed in turn below.

"Scanners improve security." They reveal undeclared prohibited and high value goods, including weapons, drugs, cigarettes, and even motor vehicles, that usually are part of wider criminal or terrorist activities. At airports scanners are used for passenger and luggage security. When detection is rare or nonexistent the scanners are said to have a deterrent effect.

"Scanners raise revenue." Many customs administrations claim that scanners help them detect misdeclared items, and reassess revenue on them. However, statistics from before and after the introduction of scanners show that revenue reassessment is rare.

"Scanners have a deterrent effect." Customs administrations also invoke the deterrent effect to justify comprehensive scanning at border stations. But there are many ways to smuggle contraband other than to place it in containers that may be scanned. Weapons are taped to truck bodies, drugs are diluted in innocuous chemicals, and experienced criminals use different densities to shield smuggled goods. Scanning merely encourages smugglers to be more innovative—or to make more bribes to corrupt officials. Finally, although positive scanning results can be spectacular, the worldwide rate of detection through scanners is very low: fraud is revealed by less than one percent of all scans, on average.

Borders, their design, and their operation

How scanners are used

The ways in which scanners are managed and operated also directly affects their efficiency.

Outsourcing. When scanning is outsourced to a private company that charges a fee for every scanned vehicle or container, there is a strong incentive to scan everything that crosses the border. Scanning becomes a routine revenue raiser, with the excuse that it encourages revenue compliance. And fees can be high, hindering trade facilitation. (The only exception is when scanning is mandatory for every container at a seaport, as under the Container Security Initiative.)

Number of scans. The tendency to scan all trucks and containers is sometimes defended with the claim that a scan is not a physical examination. Such claims reflect resistance to the recent pressure on customs administrations to replace 100 percent physical examination policies with a more targeted approach. In fact, scans are physical examinations. Although goods are inspected without unloading, the time taken to direct vehicles to a scanning facility—especially if queue management is poor—often lengthens border processing without improving results. Like manual inspections, routine scans rapidly lead operators and analysts to lose their focus.[39]

Systematic scanning is sometimes used for transit control. The scanned image of an entering truck is attached to the transit documentation and transmitted to the point of exit, where a new scan should reveal if a shipment has been tampered with. Here scanning performs the same function as seals do, and the scan does not necessarily increase transit security.

Modern stations use targeted scans based on risk management and some random selection. In European countries, an increasing number of scans are carried out by mobile or relocatable equipment away from the border on main roads. These downstream checks, which have proved highly effective, are based on prior targeting by mobile inland customs patrols.

Scanning fees. Even when scans are not outsourced, customs may collect a scanning fee. There are four possible fee structures:

- A flat fee is collected—either on scanned vehicles only or on every vehicle, whether scanned or not. This resembles funding airport security through airport taxes.
- A fee is collected only when a fraud is detected. If the fee is made proportional to the value of the detected goods, it becomes part of the penalty.
- The fee is based on the type of vehicle or goods. It becomes a form of customs tariff.
- No fee is collected.

The last solution, fee free scanning, is by far the best. A fee can encourage drivers to pay higher bribes not to be scanned. Fees also add to the cost of transport. Proponents say they are used for maintaining equipment—but the cost of scanning equipment should be included in that of border stations, without the need for an extra fee.

Scanner sharing. Scanning equipment should be shared among agencies. The equipment is expensive, and there is no need to duplicate it except when traffic volumes are extremely high.[40] Agencies have different objectives: for example, the border police may want to check if there are illegal immigrants in a container, when customs are interested only in revenue. Joint use creates synergy and promotes the sharing of intelligence and risk management methods.

Scanners usually are operated by customs. Sharing scanners with the border police can add to customs' relative clout among border agencies. However, this should not mean granting requests by border police to scan all vehicles.

Scanner sharing may raise questions about maintenance, check reliability, and the legal validity of findings when the operator is not the requesting agency. Usually such questions can be resolved through memorandums of understanding and by having analysts from both agencies present during the scan (a policy that also promotes cross-training).

Scanners can also be shared across the border. One country may request another to carry out a scan on its behalf—preferably at juxtaposed border stations, which are governed by agreements on extraterritorial controls—or monitors can be installed in both countries' offices, reducing costs.

Scanners, however promising for detection, are only as good as their operators. The best analysts are usually experienced examining officers, who know what to look for and where. With risk based vehicle and container selection, scanners become an extremely powerful law enforcement tool.

Control equipment

Technology for the control of people, vehicles, and goods is constantly being developed and has boosted the efficiency of border agencies, allowing fewer officials to do better work and to do it more rapidly. But technology cannot replace well trained officers. Efficiency also requires a motivated staff, suitable working principles, adjustments to the environment, and usually new control standards. In many cases, expensive equipment provided by donors—who sometimes did not have it installed on such a scale in their own countries—was rapidly shelved when results did not meet exaggerated expectations.

Future technological improvements cannot be anticipated. When designing a border station it is safest to leave space for traffic flow redesign and additional control areas tailored to new control methods.

Station management

A border station can be a large working place, with a large staff, thousands of users crossing every day, and private employees working inside and around the facility. How can security and maintenance best be ensured?

Security in the station and at its perimeter

Special security needs at border stations concern, first, issues specific to border crossing, and, second, general matters of law and order. Two broad approaches to both concerns are discussed below.

Each major control agency is responsible for its own security and for enforcing laws in its purview. Customs guards and protects its staff and premises, prevents smuggling and related violations, and arrests, detains and charges such violators—in some cases presenting them directly to the appropriate court or prosecutor. (An exception occurs when an offense can be terminated in an administrative or transactional manner.) Customs officers who witness other criminality in the course of duty can act to prevent it—and, under their general law enforcement

powers, they can temporarily arrest offenders until able to hand the offenders over to the appropriate agency. Immigration officers have similar powers.

This independent enforcement model supposes in some countries that officers are armed. It is not transposable to all border control agencies: it does not work for phytosanitary, standards, and transport agencies, for which specific security arrangements must be made if necessary. A temporary or permanent general police assignment may also be necessary when large numbers of people are present at, or travelling through, the border station—to manage crowds, to guide traffic reaching the border, or simply to ensure a uniformed presence. Certain noncriminal issues such as fire and medical emergencies are the responsibility of emergency services, which can be placed at the border or in a nearby center.

Security is provided by the police or armed forces. In this model, whenever a violation is committed the agency that made the detection reports it to the police. The police are then responsible for pursuing the case. The police are also in charge of general law and order at the border station. Under these circumstances immigration may be merged into the border police. But that is a dubious approach, since law and order and immigration control require different forms of organization. Countries that put the police or armed forces in charge of all border station security often are countries with closed borders.

Intermediate options. Afghanistan, which could not arm its customs officers, introduced a customs police—a police officer corps assigned to customs to provide security at border and inland facilities, but reporting and taking orders only from the interior ministry. The arrangement does not work well. The customs police has no loyalty or responsibility to customs, lacks basic skills in customs matters, and occasionally interferes with customs work. Providing adequate customs training to these officers would turn them into a parallel and duplicate customs organization working for the interior ministry.[41]

Other countries have outsourced some border station policing functions to the private sector. For example, at the Chirundu border station in Zambia, private guards marshal trucks and control gates into the country to ensure that all trucks have been released for exit. This additional layer of control—and possible corruption—has no use other than to relieve existing state agencies (which may have limited resources) of general policing duties.

In Israel border station security is handled by the agency in charge of airport security. While technically viable, this solution has led to the fragmentation of border station work and to the duplication of work by security and customs.

International access roads

International access roads pose a problem at juxtaposed border stations distant from the borderline. Vehicles cleared out of such stations by destination country officials must still drive on roads located in the territory of the departure country. During that period the vehicles technically remain in the country out of which they have been cleared. Difficulties may arise in accidents, highway code violations, and cases of customs fraud: which country has judicial responsibility for these cases? Three solutions are possible:

- *The road can be extraterritorialized.* The access road is considered part of the destination country, whose law exclusively applies from the exit of the border station to the borderline. The road should be fenced off to prevent unlawful re-entry into the territory of the departure country.
- *The road can be internationalized.* The access road, though fenced off or otherwise controlled, is under the jurisdiction of the country on which it is located. If the departure country decides to intercept a person or vehicle that has already cleared exit and destination formalities, there could be an international issue: all earlier measures regarding exit and entry procedures would need to be annulled, including penalties already addressed. The traveler could argue that, even though the laws of the departure country were violated, there was no violation of the destination country's laws—and, further, that destination country authorities knew of the violation yet allowed the traveler to proceed.
- *The road can be functionally extraterritorial.* To simplify control, the access road is fenced off and destination country border authorities will undertake no control action along it—but all other national laws apply right up to the borderline, and purely national authorities are competent to

enforce them. A traveler or vehicle leaving the access road for the country on which the road is located is considered as having crossed the border illegally.

Ethics

Corruption is regularly associated with border operations. Examples of petty corruption include payments to a policeman to move up in a long queue, or to a control officer to avoid physical examination or speed a process—not to mention routine goodwill payments to border officials. Other forms of corruption involve more serious criminal activities. Customs is the border agency most vulnerable to corruption allegations. That is not because other agencies are blameless, but because payments to customs appear higher on average than payments to any other agency.

The purpose of this section is not to discuss corruption generally, but simply to envision how it can be dealt with in border infrastructure design. What control mechanisms should be put in place?

Border station design can discourage petty corruption. Shorter queues mean fewer reasons for bribing officials. Green lanes and fast tracks should allow some, ideally most, drivers to pass through without even speaking to an official. Isolated control areas—where there are no witnesses to corruption—should be avoided in planning border stations. Strict monitoring of access roads prevents trucks from waiting for a change of shift before entering stations. Juxtaposed stations allow countries to ensure that similar data are reported on both sides. And hotlines, if well managed, enable drivers who are harassed by control officials to alert customs or another agency immediately.

Corruption cases should not be investigated by the local border police. The border police agency's mandate should not include fighting corruption in customs. Why? Because border police officers may be corrupt. Internal control and investigation, followed eventually by judicial investigation, usually is a more effective approach—and it avoids stigmatizing customs by subjecting it to the agency next door.

Administration of the facility

New border stations are expensive to build, equip, and maintain. In modern, coordinated border management, new and possibly more effective solutions are needed.

Each agency for itself. Traditionally there were a limited number of agencies at a border station, each responsible for its own housing and equipment. In many cases various budgeting and institutional management rules created disparities between the agencies. At juxtaposed border stations such differences can be even more acute: in one example an agency had no budget for telephone calls, or even to heat its buildings in winter. (Conversely, air conditioners in another station's computer room were not turned on, as the management could not afford fuel for the power generator.) Self management and self maintenance at each agency can work well only with coherent resource allocation for all—and the more agencies there are, the more difficult it becomes.

Single management. Having a single management authority usually results in customs (that is, the finance ministry) taking responsibility for all expenses beyond agency specific running costs. But the border police often has ambitions to run border stations. Single management can work, but only with good interagency understanding and coordination.

Management contracts with the private sector. A few African countries have considered private sector management. It would grant the operator a concession to run the station much as an airport authority runs an airport. This system has three disadvantages. First, the operator may increase profits by placing concessions at commercial facilities, with the unwanted result of keeping a captive public in the station even longer than necessary. Second, the operator may collect user fees, limiting freedom of movement (nationals returning penniless may not be allowed to come home). Third, a private operator may gain direct or indirect control over the activities of state agencies.

Local integrated management between agencies. This approach has been tried successfully, in particular at juxtaposed stations. A local management commission, with a rotating presidency, is in charge of all local maintenance issues and reports to a binational committee that supervises the juxtaposed operations. Agency specific operations are outside the mandate of the commission except when they significantly affect the overall efficiency of the station. The commission may appoint an independent station manager to run day to day support services (cleaning, power supply, bill payment, and so on).

Monitoring border station performance

Governments and other stakeholders need to know how border stations are performing. In the case of a new border station they need to know the investment returns for trade facilitation (reduced times), for control (fraud detection, additional revenue collection), and for traffic volumes (how much is generated by the facility?). Performance measurement, and often quantified targets, do the job.

Performance measurement. Agencies' internal systems for monitoring processing times are, too often, based on indicators interpreted in isolation. The systems may not be consistent methodologically. And frequently they ignore what happens before and after the agency's particular control position. For example, immigration officers contend that a passport control takes only 75 seconds—but when there is a queue of over a hundred passengers, the last person in the queue may wait an hour.

A holistic approach to performance measurement has therefore been introduced by various donors and international organizations. It measures average times spent at the border, first overall and then broken down by agency and private operator. In a computerized and integrated work environment, data on these indicators could be collected on a permanent basis and regularly analyzed, prompting new processes to be envisioned when necessary and enabling new local experimental approaches to be validated.

User satisfaction is measurable through user surveys, but also through less formal feedback. The Chinese immigration service introduced a simple and highly effective way of measuring passenger satisfaction before the Beijing Olympics: each immigration booth was fitted with three smiley buttons, which travelers were invited to push depending on how they felt they had been treated by the official. The immediate feedback to management encouraged officers to be professional and courteous.

4

Borders, their design, and their operation

Performance targets. Many countries give customs revenue targets, which can then determine a border station collection objective. Though useful for monitoring assessed revenue, revenue targets also have five perverse effects:

- Staff may care only about transactions with high revenue potential, to the detriment of other control activities.
- Once a monthly target has been met, customs may stop clearing cargo and hold containers until the next month.
- When there is a shortfall in revenue, local customs directors may call importers and ask them for a down payment on future operations (examples are found in some Asian countries).
- Customs directors may encourage importers to clear cargo at their stations by offering discounted duty rates.
- Customs officials may routinely divide the monthly revenue target by the daily number of trucks and containers and charge the result as a flat duty rate.

Revenue targets, therefore—though a useful broad performance indicator—should not be used as a sole performance criterion for staff.

Notes

1. Some countries with older border management systems may also have restricted approved outgoing roads, to prevent access from persons who have no legitimate business at a border station.
2. A recent trend is to demilitarize border control and replace border troops with a civilian border police force—though this has not much changed the organization or the approach to border control.
3. The role of that officer is to issue visas, whereas the control of passports and visas is usually done by an immigration or border police official. It would be possible to merge the two functions, as the issuing of visas at the border can be questioned on security grounds (as well as from a facilitation perspective). The immigration officer might just as well stamp the passport once satisfied that the traveler is legitimate.
4. However, animals can cross borders outside approved border stations, and not all infected travelers are spotted with thermal cameras. Trying to stop an epidemic at the borderline is impossible. Checking the origin of people or animals and their likelihood of being contaminated—assuming that they can be tracked once inside the country—is probably as effective as turning them away at the border.
5. Such preauthorized border crossing originated in Europe in the 18th century, in the mountains between Spain and France: farmers who registered their cattle with customs in both nations obtained free grazing rights. This regime survived until the European Union single market made it irrelevant.
6. The same attitude characterizes some island countries, where control is easier to achieve along the coastline (and where customs has never made great efforts to capture what evades coastal control). Although one island country, the United Kingdom, now has open borders, some of its former colonies in Africa still have closed borders.
7. On the nonstop high speed service between Brussels and London, which goes through Belgian, French, and British territories, passengers are controlled successively by Belgian, French (occasionally), and British customs and immigration officials, irrespective of the territory on which the train is running at the time of the control.
8. This system also weakens the case for arrival duty free shops, since it means that such shops charge no tax for items that—typically—will be consumed in the country to which tax would otherwise be due.
9. One notable exception was Serbia, which in the 1990s—when visas were required to enter the country—issued special visas allowing passengers to continue their journey using any alternative method of transport.
10. Airlines are additionally encouraged to perform these checks, as they may have to repatriate at their own expense passengers denied entry on arrival.

11. In the 1970s French customs introduced an inland air preventive wing, in charge of the control of secondary airports.

12. The Macedonian-Bulgarian border crossing of Deve Bair–Gyueshevo is high in the mountains separating the two countries. As it serves the Bulgarian market city of Kjustendil, many Macedonians used to shop there and walk through the border facilities. Large numbers of people returning from Kjustendil had to wait for customs inspection for long periods—sometimes several hours—without any shelter.

13. Greece also has traditionally dressed Evzone soldiers mounting guard on its northern and eastern borders.

14. With the exception of the country name inside the European Union stars symbol.

15. In Finland the average processing time for exit to Russia is under 5 minutes. According to performance data the average entry time into Russia, at corresponding border stations, is 4–21 minutes for customs processing—but this does not include waiting times, which were estimated a few years ago at six hours, nor does it include processing by other agencies.

16. For example, a customs officer checking one car may become distracted by another waiting car and so hastily dismiss the first. Worse still, by the time the second car reaches the inspection area, the officer may have forgotten why it seemed suspicious.

17. This list assumes that a border station is not the regional headquarters and has only an operational role. (Regional headquarters are very seldom located at the border.)

18. In earlier plans for a border station in Afghanistan, the customs manager had to come out of the building and walk around it to visit border police counterparts because a wall cut the building in two.

19. So-called single windows are sometimes in operation in Eastern European countries, where all documents are submitted in turn to several officials—who may not be interested, but who justify their presence by scrutinizing all forms and manually entering particulars in a register.

20. As a rule, people should not be detained for more than a few hours at the border, and anyone held longer should be transferred as soon as possible to a detention facility inside the country.

21. Such officers need not need be highly placed, as they will report to their managers. But they should have a common understanding of control and traffic flow priorities.

22. In one country in Southeast Europe, when the World Bank funded a building for border police, there was a request for a lecture hall to accommodate the entire regional staff. It was pointed out that the requested room would never be full—as it was unlikely the entire border police force would be simultaneously taken off operational duty.

23. As luggage on coaches is seldom tagged, there may be a problem when unidentified luggage is not claimed.

24. In addition, equipment calibration differences can mean that up to four different weights are indicated for the same truck.

25. Dogs are used for detecting drugs and explosives—principally by customs and border police, but sometimes also by immigration administrations to detect illegal immigrants hidden in containers or trucks. In addition, dogs have recently been trained to detect large amounts of money, belying the myth that money has no odor.

26. An international standard for preventing cruelty to animals.

27. Cars may also have a windshield sticker stating that they are part of an accredited driver scheme.

28. Red lane users select an entirely different route, which takes them to the administrative building or a simplified formalities desk or booth.

29. Albania would close its border with Montenegro for the lunch break, but Montenegro kept its stations open.

30. In addition, trade unions usually object to reductions in shift size.

31. For example, the 2010 deadline for the Lebombo–Ressano Garcia border station,

due to open before the football World Cup in South Africa.

32. A possible exception is immigration exit checks, which can lead to the arrest of wanted criminals.

33. In the 1970s Spanish police arrested Basque separatists in the French part of a juxtaposed border station in Spain—that is, while the police technically were on French territory. And in the 1980s Swiss security services arrested French customs officers for espionage in the French part of the international train station in Basel.

34. There are exceptions. Canada has objected to United States Customs officers carrying firearms while on Canada's territory. French police and customs officers on the British side of the channel tunnel juxtaposed facility have a special, nominative gun permit issued by the British authorities, within a specified limit per shift.

35. In Zambia it is necessary to log out of the ASYCUDA system, log in to the COMESA database, retrieve the data regarding a transit consignment, copy it manually, log back into ASYCUDA, and then enter the data manually. The transaction time, being too long to support fast operations from a booth, prevents the introduction of an effective fast track mechanism.

36. Apart from the initial collection of biometric data when the passport or identification card is issued.

37. On the other hand, some of the full declaration data is confidential and should not be shared with another country, except when provided for under a mutual assistance agreement.

38. French customs officers used tachygraph readings at car ferry ports to identify exiting trucks that had stopped at a motorway layby five kilometers from the port—an unreasonable effort, considering that the trucks had to wait for boarding at the port anyway. Drivers often would pull up at the layby to fill their inner wheels with drugs—and a tire thus filled cannot be driven at more than a low speed for more than a short distance before bursting. Drivers who made it through French customs were similarly quizzed, after reaching Dover, by British customs, who also waited in ambush at the first layby on the road to London.

39. Analysts operating eight hour scanner shifts have been seen sleeping at their posts.

40. At one border station in the Caucasus customs used donor funding to install a scanner. Several months later the local border guards were not aware of its existence. Such outcomes should be avoided.

41. *Customs police* is an oxymoron. Customs are not police, nor are police customs—though each agency has its own policing role. The enforcement role of customs typically is performed by a specialized preventive service, which, though it may have powers and training resembling those of police, consists of customs officers and reports to customs management (for example, the Swiss Border Guard Service is a directorate of the Federal Customs Administration).

References

UNECE (United Nations Economic Commission for Europe) Inland Transport Committee. 1982. "International Convention on the Harmonization of Frontier Controls of Goods." UN document ECE/TRANS/55/Rev.1, United Nations, Geneva.

CHAPTER

5 Building a convincing business case for border management reform

Yue Li, Gerard McLinden, and John S. Wilson

Governments, particularly in developing countries, face many challenges. Competition for limited resources being intense, priorities must be established and difficult decisions made. Gaining genuine commitment to border management reform therefore presents significant hurdles. To secure the necessary political and administrative support for major modernization, a well considered and carefully argued business case—including a robust cost-benefit analysis—must be prepared and sold to key stakeholders.

The business case must appeal to all key stakeholders, and it must include both qualitative (soft) and quantitative (hard) arguments supporting reform. The case must demonstrate that allocating resources to reform is a genuine investment rather than merely a cost. For customs reform alone, a business case and fiscal rationale are relatively easy to prepare. But for the more holistic, comprehensive reform agenda promoted in this book, the business case is more complex and harder to prepare. Yet it is essential if strong internal constituencies supporting the status quo are to be overcome and genuine commitment to reform established and maintained over the long term.

This chapter outlines some of the strong economic evidence in support of border management reform, and it provides practical advice on how to prepare a convincing business case.

A long history of collective trade facilitation initiatives

While trade facilitation and border management modernization are now high on the agenda of the development community and governments throughout the world, the history of international collective efforts to facilitate trade can be traced back at least to the end of World War I. In 1920 the International Chamber of Commerce was founded, and it has since played a major role in promoting the harmonization and simplification of customs procedures. These were the earliest international endeavors to reduce border related trade barriers (Staples 1998).

The end of World War II marked a new era of multilateral effort, and new international coordination initiatives to facilitate trade soon emerged. The General Agreement on Tariffs and Trade (GATT), created in 1947, contained three articles related to border management (articles V, VIII, and X). Those articles, now more than 50 years old, are at the core of the present Doha negotiations on trade facilitation. Signatories to the treaty are still far from full implementation of articles V (on transit issues), VIII (on fees and formalities), and X (on the publication and administration of trade regulations). Later GATT articles on customs valuation, rules of origin, licensing, preshipment inspection, sanitary and phytosanitary controls, and technical barriers to trade (TBTs)—as well as commitments regarding services ancillary to trade, including transport and international finance—further complement articles V, VIII, and X. Collectively these documents represent the World Trade Organization (WTO) disciplines related to trade facilitation.

Other international organizations quickly followed suit. The United Nations Economic Commission for Europe, created in 1947, set up a Working Party on Facilitation of International Trade Procedures. And the World Customs Organization (WCO) has been a key driver of trade facilitation related reform since its founding in 1953. In 1973 it established the International Convention on the Simplification and Harmonization of Customs Procedures (the Kyoto Convention),[1] which was heavily revised in 1999 to reflect major changes in international trade. The WCO's suite of trade facilitation related instruments was further strengthened by its adoption in 2008 of the Framework of Standards to Secure and Facilitate Global Trade (SAFE Framework). The Customs Convention on the International Transport of Goods Under Cover of TIR Carnets (the TIR Convention) was also created in 1959.[2] These initiatives largely defined the concept of modern trade facilitation.

In the mid-1990s nontariff barriers were recognized as a major obstacle to efficient international trade transactions and, ultimately, a drag on national competitiveness. In 2004 trade facilitation was incorporated into the Doha round of multilateral trade negotiations, underlining a strong international consensus on the importance of trade facilitation to economic development and national competitiveness.

Both developed and developing countries in the WTO recognize that trade facilitation represents a win-win for all parties. The present negotiations on trade facilitation aim "to clarify and improve relevant aspects of Articles V, VIII, and X of the GATT 1994 [General Agreement on Tariffs and Trade 1994] with a view to further expediting the movement, release and clearance of goods, including goods in transit" (WTO 2004, annex D).

Potentially large welfare gains from reduced trade costs

The gains from reduced trade costs are best understood by analyzing gains from trade. The analysis here draws on modern trade theories: classic trade theory, factor proportions trade theory, new trade theory, and a new extension from new trade theory that incorporates firm heterogeneities.

In classic trade theory and factor proportions trade theory, gains from trade are rooted in production efficiency achieved through realizing comparative advantage.[3] Both the classic theory, based on technology differences, and the factor proportions theory, relying on endowment differences, predict that international trade allows countries to concentrate more on what they can produce at lower cost—and, at the same time, to consume the same goods at lower prices. The welfare of all will then rise. But because these trade models treat transaction costs somewhat marginally, it is hard to draw direct conclusions from them about how trade costs affect trade patterns. Nevertheless, one essential implication of these theories is that enhancing trade improves welfare internationally through production concentration and greater efficiency. Reducing trade costs can thus potentially help developing economies.

New trade theory, and the closely related new economic geography theory (both pioneered by Paul R. Krugman), expand the category of gains from trade to include efficiency realized through scale economies and greater varieties of welfare improvement. Before new trade theory it was hard to explain why two countries with similar technology, endowment, and tastes would trade with each other in the same type of product. Labeled intra-industry trade, this phenomenon had long been observed and accounted for a large portion of international trade. New trade theory successfully solved the puzzle. In its seminal works (Krugman 1980, Brander and Krugman 1983), new trade theory incorporated the factors of scale economies, product differentiation, and imperfect competition, and demonstrated that two additional types of gains are associated with intra-industry exchanges: production efficiency due to increasing returns to scale, and consumer satisfaction associated with additional varieties from abroad.

Although the new trade theory explicitly incorporated trade costs, its policy lessons regarding trade facilitation were somewhat ambiguous.[4] The general lesson was that developing economies can capitalize various gains from trade through further reductions in trade costs along with their own economic development. The World Bank offers the following assessment: "The main insight from research is that the relationships between transport costs, production locations, and trade patterns are nonlinear. Falling transport costs first led to countries trading more with countries that were distant but dissimilar. When they fell further, they led to more trade with neighboring countries. Similarly, when transport costs fell from moderate levels, production concentrated in and around large markets. When they fell further, some producers could produce more cheaply in smaller markets but still serve large markets" (World Bank 2008).

A recent expansion of new trade theory (represented by Melitz 2003) highlights the importance of trade costs in firm selection and productivity growth. This expansion incorporates firm heterogeneity into the new trade theory framework (Bernard and others 2003; Melitz 2003; Yeaple 2005; Bernard, Redding, and Schott 2007). As many empirical studies have shown, only a small portion of firms in each country actually export. Those that do export tend to be larger, more productive, and more skill and capital intensive. This tendency results from self selection driven by cross border trade costs.[5] The expansion of new trade theory incorporates firm level heterogeneity to account for the new firm level observations, predicting that only the most productive firms can cover the additional cost of exporting and so reap the benefits of a larger market. Less productive ones, which cannot do so, produce only for the domestic market. So falling trade costs affect important firm level decisions: entry and exit decisions, decisions on whether or not to export, decisions on how much to export, technology decisions, and employment decisions.

In essence, the research suggests that reduced trade costs will induce more firms to become exporters while stimulating the growth of existing exporters. These interfirm reallocations may lead to an increase in overall productivity levels and, hence, to overall welfare gains—a new form of gains from trade. Enhancing trade through reducing trade costs thus promises to enhance welfare. In lowering fixed and sunk trading costs one unleashes dynamic gains of comparative advantage, economies of scale, and productivity improvement through resource reallocation.

Trade costs in areas related to border management

Empirical work on barriers to trade has investigated some of the new claims of the new trade theory and assessed the role of constraints not caused by traditional trade policies (such as tariffs and quantitative restrictions). This section will highlight the significance of trade costs and the effectiveness of trade facilitation in areas specifically related to border management.

Trade costs compared with tariff rates

Transport costs, as an important part of transaction costs, can impede trade as severely as high tariff rates can (Finger and Yeats 1976).[6] As tariff rates have declined substantially over the past 20 years, trade costs not related to traditional trade policy have become more visible. One recent study defines trade costs broadly as "all costs incurred in getting a good to a final user other than the marginal cost of producing the good itself" (Anderson and van Wincoop 2004).

Trade costs consist of transportation costs—freight costs, time costs, and policy barriers—plus tariffs and nontariff costs, information costs, contract enforcement costs, costs associated with the use of different currencies, legal and regulatory costs, and local distribution costs. Trade costs are large, and a significant portion of them results from economic policies. More important, the study argues that indirect policies such as transport policy and regulatory policy—rather than direct tariffs and other trade policy instruments—are most important in trade costs. The authors estimate the ad valorem tax equivalent of trade costs for industrialized countries at 170 percent, of which 21 percent falls under transportation costs (including 9 percent for time value in transit), 44 percent under border related barriers, and 55 percent under retail and wholesale distribution costs. They assert that trade barriers in developing countries are higher than those estimated for industrial countries. Furthermore, the same authors argue that the current policy related costs are often worth more than 10 percent of national income (Anderson and van Wincoop 2002).

Other policy interventions also affect transaction costs. One study (Kee, Nicita, and Olarreaga 2009) estimates the magnitude of tariffs and a subcategory of nontariff barriers in ad valorem terms for 91 countries. The results show that nontariff barriers add 70 percent, on average, to the restrictiveness imposed by tariffs alone. In 21 countries nontariff barriers are more restrictive than tariffs.

The time dimension of trade costs

Trade barriers involve both direct financial outlays and costs associated with time delays and uncertainty. The delays and uncertainty encountered in moving goods across borders are among the most vexing impediments for traders in many countries.

The first study to argue the time dimension of trade barriers (Hummels 2001) distinguished two classes of costs: goods depreciation and increased inventory-carrying costs. Each class of costs affects traders in two ways: it affects whether or not a firm will enter foreign markets, and it influences the volume of trade. United States import data was used to show that for each additional day spent in transport, the probability that a country will export to the United States declines by 1–1.5 percent, while the advent of fast transportation between 1950 and 1998 was equivalent to reducing tariffs on manufactured goods from 32 percent to 9 percent. More recently, an ad valorem cost estimate of the time taken to ship goods (Hummels and Schaur 2009) argued that each day saved in shipping time for manufactured goods is worth 0.8 percent of the goods' total value.

The estimates above are based on transport time. Yet time is lost not only because of transport and distance, but also because of inefficient administrative procedures. Using control of corruption as an instrument for delays in export time, one study (Nordas, Pinali, and Grosso 2006) shows that delays will reduce the probability that a country will export to Australia, Japan and the United Kingdom in industries including intermediate inputs, fashion clothing, and electronics—and also that the delays will reduce

the volume of any such exports. Another study (Djankov, Freund, and Pham forthcoming) uses the days it takes to move standard cargo for export in 126 countries to analyze how time delays affect trade volumes.[7] Breaking down the time for export into four components—document preparation, customs clearance, ports and terminal handling, and inland transportation and handling—the study points out that about two-thirds of delays in the sample can be attributed to document preparation and customs clearance. The study also finds remarkable variation in time for export across countries. It takes 116 days to move an export container from Bangui, Central African Republic, to the nearest port and to fulfill the customs, administrative, and port requirements for loading the cargo onto a ship, whereas the same process takes only 5 days from Copenhagen and 6 from Berlin. A delay of one day reduces trade by at least 1 percent—the equivalent of distancing a country from its partners by an additional 70 kilometers.

With global integration and segmented production, many industries depend increasingly on production and supply chain networks. Thus the timeliness and reliability of trade becomes increasingly important. Sectors relying on international supply chain networks are more sensitive to distance, making clusters appealing as a way to avoid time delays (Harrigan and Venables 2004). The United States increasingly imports apparel products from nearby countries, as timeliness matters more for these products because importers and retailers must respond rapidly to fashion and seasonal changes (Evans and Harrigan 2005).

It follows that time delays may also affect the composition of trade, disproportionately reducing trade in time sensitive goods, such as perishable agricultural products (Djankov, Freund, and Pham forthcoming). One day's delay reduces a country's relative exports of time sensitive to time insensitive goods by 6 percent. Investigating the validity of these propositions using firm level data for 64 developing countries, one study finds that, in countries where more time is needed to export, firms in time sensitive industries are less likely to become exporters—and those firms that do export have lower export intensities (Li and Wilson 2009).[8] As an example, if two industries in a country have the same export probability and intensity—but differ in time sensitivity

5

Building a convincing business case for border management reform

by one standard deviation—then cutting time to export by 50 percent opens a 6 percentage point difference between the export probabilities of the two industries, and it increases the difference between their export intensities by 1.9 percentage points. These findings highlight the importance of transaction efficiency in determining comparative advantage.

The effectiveness of trade facilitation

Much recent empirical research on the links between trade and trade costs has thus sought to learn what policies create unnecessary costs and what policies ease those costs. How effective is trade facilitation, and where is it most effective? This subsection reviews recent research on the overall effectiveness of trade facilitation—and, more specifically, of improvements in trade administration, institutional quality, and infrastructure—with some of the findings discussed at firm level. The section also reviews recent evidence on the costs and benefits of aid for trade, which has gained new attention from the international development community.

Overall trade facilitation. A study estimating the trade gains from reforms to reduce trade transaction costs—that is, from trade facilitation—defines such facilitation broadly to include four factors: port efficiency, the customs environment, the regulatory environment, and the infrastructure for electronic business (Wilson, Mann, and Otsuki 2005). Port efficiency covers port facilities, inland waterways, and air transport. The customs environment includes hidden import barriers and irregular extra payments and bribes. The regulatory environment consists of transparency in government policy and success in controlling corruption. The electronic business infrastructure, finally, measures the speed and cost of internet access and the effect of internet on business as a proxy for information and communication services development. Using data from 75 countries over 2000–01, the study shows that improvements in all four areas enhance trade. If the least efficient countries could increase efficiency halfway toward matching the group average, global gains from trades could amount to $377 billion.

Another study (Hertel, Walmsley, and Ikatura 2001) looks at free trade agreements for the streamlining of customs procedures, the harmonization of technical standards, sanitary and phytosanitary regulations, electronic commerce regulations, services trade, and foreign investment rules. Using the example of the Singapore-Japan Free Trade Agreement (FTA) and a modified version of the dynamic Global Trade Analysis Project (GTAP) model, the study estimates the potential gains from automated customs procedures, uniform standards for electronic commerce, and bilateral tariff cuts. The results show that the FTA will substantially increase merchandise trade and boost rates of return in both Japan and Singapore—increasing foreign and domestic investment, as well as gross domestic product, for estimated global gains of more than $9 billion annually.

Trade administration and institutional quality. Empirical work on reforms to customs and other border agencies is scarce—because hard data are lacking, but also because border management issues are intertwined with broader institutional quality issues. One study shows (Wilson, Mann, and Otsuki 2005) that if the least efficient countries could improve their customs environment halfway toward the group average, matching global trade gains of $33 billion could be achieved, while a similar improvement in the regulatory environment could bring an additional $83 billion of gains. From those results it can also be concluded that automating customs is the most important factor in increasing merchandise trade (Hertel, Walmsley, and Ikatura 2001). Another study, based on data from 126 countries, shows that reducing both the number of business registration procedures and the number of signatures required for exporting will lead to trade gains (Sadikov 2007). Each signature eliminated reduces aggregate exports by 4.2 percent—the equivalent of raising import tariffs by 5 percentage points.

A study of transparency in trade, focusing on the Asia-Pacific region (Helble, Shepherd, and Wilson 2007), uses composed measures on transparency that extend beyond border agencies and behind-the-border agencies. Nonetheless, it sheds light on the importance of border reforms and behind-the-border reforms. The study's transparency indicators, both "objective" and based on perception, include uncertainty about import times, the number of agencies an importer must deal with, administrative favoritism, and the prevalence of trade related corruption—indicators that tend to capture the simplicity of administrative procedures and the quality of institutions. The results indicate that transparency, particularly related to the import regime, can be a significant factor in promoting bilateral trade. Increasing import transparency in Asia-Pacific Economic Cooperation member economies to the regional average could have a larger impact than reducing tariffs or nontariff barriers to the same level.

The inhibiting effects of corruption and institutional weakness on trade are well documented. Overall increases in transparency and declines in corruption will spill over to improve border agencies. Weak institutions act as significant barriers to international trade, highlighting the importance of institutional reforms (Anderson and Marcouiller 2002). The insecurity of international exchange in low income countries, arising from corrupt customs practices, unenforceable contracts, and organized crime—all potentially linked to trade facilitation—can be measured rather broadly with indicators of the government's transparency and impartiality and the enforceability of commercial contracts. The result: a 10 percent increase in a country's transparency and impartiality index leads to a 5 percent increase in its import volumes. It is also argued that cross country variation in institutional effectiveness offers an alternative explanation for why high income, capital abundant countries trade disproportionately with each other.

Infrastructure development. Deficient transport infrastructure and poor information and communication services can isolate countries, impeding trade. The issue has received adequate attention only recently. One study links infrastructure development with trade, using a measure that covers the quality of both transport and communication infrastructure (Limão and Venables 2001). The study shows that 40 percent of transport costs in coastal countries, and up to 60 percent in landlocked countries, can be attributed to infrastructure deficiency. If landlocked countries and their transit countries can improve infrastructure from the 25th percentile to the 75th, they can reduce the trade volume disadvantage associated with being landlocked by an estimated one-half.

Motivated by the empirical evidence, the African Development Bank proposed a transcontinental road

network for 42 Sub-Saharan African countries in 2003. A study finds significant overland trade gains from such a network (Buys, Deichmann, and Wheeler 2006)—about $250 billion over 15 years (whereas total expenditure is estimated at $47 billion).

The development of information and communication infrastructure can also stimulate trade flows by reducing initial search costs between international traders and, later, by lowering communication expenses. A study directly investigating communication costs finds (Fink, Mattoo, and Neagu 2005) that cutting the cost of communication between two countries significantly improves bilateral trade flows: a 10 percent drop in bilateral calling prices could lead to 5–9 percent increase in trade between two countries in 1999. Trade in differentiated products responds more to these costs than trade in homogenous products does. Other studies look at specific aspects of information and communications technology development. For instance, expanding telecommunications traffic is associated with greater trade volume (Portes and Rey 2005), and diffusing internet use stimulates both merchandise and services trade (Freund and Weinhold 2002, 2004).

Firm level evidence. The firm is the major player in all international transactions. What enables firms to participate in international trade? Recent developments in trade theory and new available data allow researchers to address this question. The responsiveness of firm export performance to comprehensive trade facilitation reform is highlighted in a study (Dollar, Hallward-Driemeier, and Mengistae 2006) using data from the World Bank Enterprise Surveys, which aim to identify policy constraints on business operation and effectiveness. Covering eight fairly large emerging economies in different continents, the study follows a model (Melitz 2003) in which exporters and nonexporters self select because of fixed export costs. The findings: firms are more likely to export where customs clearance is quick, power losses are low, government services are efficient, and the availability of overdraft facilities is high. And customs clearance, an important part of trade facilitation, is one of the most significant determinants of whether firms export.

A similar model applied to African countries (Clarke 2005) shows that addressing policy related

Building a convincing business case for border management reform

constraints can improve firms' export performance. After controlling for firm characteristics, manufacturing firms are more likely to export where trade and customs regulation is less restrictive and customs administration more efficient. Another study of African countries, again using the Enterprise Surveys (Yoshino 2008), also finds that exporters in countries with more efficient customs agencies send more products abroad. If export intensity (exports as a share of total sales) and export market diversification (number of export destination regions) are used as measures of firms' export performance, then, in addition to firm characteristics, policy related variables including power services and customs administration have an intermediate impact on regional export intensity (Yoshino 2008). A more efficient customs administration is also associated with greater export market diversification.

Aid for trade. Because of the foregoing research, aid for trade—or trade related aid—has drawn new attention from policymakers recently. But the ongoing debate over aid effectiveness points to the complexity of the relations among aid, trade, and growth. Aid could be tied to trade—or induced by an existing trade relationship. Aid could adversely affect the economic growth of recipient countries, in particular through aid induced "Dutch disease." While strong evidence supports the causal relationship from aid to trade—and suggests that well designed aid for trade can mitigate perverse effects on growth—there are few direct cost-benefit analyses of aid for trade.

One study (Helble, Mann, and Wilson 2009) takes a step toward filling this gap by illustrating the cost effectiveness of aid that targets policy and regulatory reform. Using data on aid flows, the responsiveness of trade flows to specific types of aid is estimated. The results confirm that aid targeted to promote trade improves trade performance. Among three types of targeted aid—for trade policy and regulatory reform, for trade development, and for economic infrastructure—aid targeting trade policy and regulatory reform has the highest rate of return: every $1 yields about $697 in additional trade.

Another study, focusing on aid for information technology (del Angel, Li, and Wilson 2009) finds that such aid enhances trade, especially between developing countries. The rate of return is fairly high:

every $1 of assistance is associated with about $647 in additional trade. That is more than 10 percent higher than the comparable rate of return to average aid for trade, $583 (Helble, Mann, and Wilson 2009).

Developing a sound business case

How can the economic arguments supporting border management reform be cast into a form that will capture the imagination and support of key policymakers and decisionmakers? Though dense, economic research is useful both in setting the context for reform and in objectively calculating the benefits from new investments. What is most needed is to contextualize the evidence and demonstrate its concrete relevance to a particular country.

Preparing a business case should start with identifying the key stakeholders and analyzing their needs and ambitions. The case will need to be made in terms that correspond closely to the stakeholders' individual needs.

Special care must be taken to ensure that the initial assumptions made about stakeholders' interests and motivations are correct. Border management reform projects often assume that private sector stakeholders will universally benefit from improved systems and procedures, and that therefore they will all share a positive attitude to the changes proposed. This is frequently incorrect, as all meaningful change creates some winners and some losers. Poor systems and procedures often suit certain stakeholders, who benefit from existing arrangements. For example, complex, opaque, and time consuming border management procedures are an incentive for importers and exporters to use customs brokers and clearing agents. The procedures can create and sustain the need for such services. So customs brokers may not automatically support reform. The degree to which each stakeholder must be involved needs to be determined in advance. Some stakeholders will take a keen interest in the proposed project, while others with a less direct stake may need only to be informed and consulted.

A clear picture of present performance, highlighting both positives and negatives, must be developed and articulated. A comprehensive analysis of strengths, weaknesses, opportunities, and threats can help focus attention on key reform issues and challenges while ensuring that attention is not unnecessarily focused on areas that are performing well. Such an analysis can also help reformers identify likely winners—and losers—and calibrate their business case accordingly. An example is in box 5.1.

In some cases reformers might do well to prepare such an analysis, not only for the project as a whole, but for each key stakeholder. That way the incentives and disincentives for each stakeholder can be better understood—and the project's scope and content presented to appeal to the interests of all. Where stakeholder resistance is likely, the business case can include measures to address particular concerns.

The benefits generally likely to flow from border management reform may include, for government:
- More effective and efficient resource deployment.
- Accurate and improved revenue yield, with less leakage.
- Increased trader compliance.
- Enhanced supply chain security.
- Improved integrity and transparency.

And for the private sector:
- Reduced overall costs from delays and informal payments.
- Faster clearance and release.
- Consistent, predictable application and explanation of rules.
- More effective and efficient resource deployment.
- Improved transparency.
- Reduced numbers of steps in processing.

Once the preliminary analysis has been completed, the business case can be prepared using various templates and formats, many of which are available online. No single template will fit all circumstances, though many countries have established a common format or agreed approach.

The business case must capture the key arguments for a project or activity, its value to key stakeholders, and the human and financial resources necessary for completing it. A sound business case will typically include:
- A clear, concise summary of key issues and any key decisions required.

Box 5.1	Analyzing border management strengths, weaknesses, opportunities, and threats

Possible strengths:
- Technically skilled and competent workforce.
- Strong legislative framework.
- Strong political support.
- Some degree of effective cooperation among various border management agencies.
- Good working relationship with traders.
- Clear and comprehensive diagnosis of key problems already undertaken.

Possible weaknesses:
- High rates of smuggling.
- Alleged corruption.
- Falling revenue.
- Lack of information technology in agencies other than customs.
- Poor customs clearance times compared with neighboring countries.
- Competition and rivalry among border management agencies.

Possible opportunities:
- Regional and international commitments in place, with implementation deadlines established.
- Donor support likely.
- Performance indicators available that clearly identify problems and reform priorities.
- Political pressure already being applied to improve border clearance times and revenue collection.

Possible threats:
- Loss of export opportunities to regional competitors.
- Loss of foreign investment due to poor international reputation.
- Exacerbated revenue loss due to regional integration.
- Huge port infrastructure investments required unless goods clearance can be sped up.

- A clear account of the problems to be solved, with a clear long term vision (the situation expected to be reached if a project goes ahead).
- A clear link between the issues and problems identified and any activities to be agreed on and financed under a project, including possible alternatives and the reasons for their rejection.
- A strong justification for the likely expense, weighing costs against benefits.
- Clear evidence of the proposer's technical capacity to achieve objectives.
- A careful, realistic identification of threats to the success of a project.
- Accurate estimates of required resources.
- Objective performance measures to allow accurate progress monitoring.
- Appropriate governance and supervision mechanisms.

The following sections focus only on those parts of the business case that are most challenging to prepare. Cost estimates, other resource requirements, implementation plans, and the like are not examined.

Describing and contextualizing problems, issues, and consequences

In preparing a clear statement of key issues and problems, care must be taken to put the case in a context understandable to all decisionmakers. Where possible, objective performance indicators—indicators that quantify the scale of problems to be addressed—should be employed. While such information can have various sources, external sources often are considered most credible. For example, in identifying opportunities for improvement in border management it is helpful to draw on external reports and diagnoses by international organizations such as the World Bank, International Monetary Fund, WCO, WTO, United Nations Conference on Trade and Development, and so forth. (Examples include the Diagnostic Trade Integrations Studies conducted as part of the Integrated Framework for Trade Related Technical Assistance and the WCO's Columbus Program diagnostic studies.) Likewise, externally collected performance data—where available—can strengthen the case for reform. In border management, the World Bank's Logistics Performance Indicators are particularly helpful, as are the Doing Business Trading Across Borders dataset[9] and various World Economic Forum rankings. These datasets allow simple comparisons between countries with similar incomes or from the same region—and nothing motivates policymakers more than poor performance rankings compared with those of similar or neighboring countries (or of key competitors).

Early on, the business case should describe existing problems in very clear, unambiguous terms. In addition, it should detail the expected costs or consequences of letting those problems continue—the aim being to make it clear that doing nothing is not a viable option. Where possible, underlying causes should be identified to avoid focusing on secondary symptoms. Also, trends and changes in performance over time should be illustrated. Almost all countries are undertaking some trade facilitation reform. So the business case must demonstrate, empirically if possible (using data sources such as those described above), that reform needs to be faster and deeper to prevent a country's performance from falling—in spite of existing reform efforts—compared with that of neighbors or competitors.

To the statement of issues and problems must be added a close linkage between effects and causes. Also needed is an equally clear long term vision—an account of the situation expected to be reached if the project is endorsed. Often it is useful to specify this situation in a short account of expected outcomes (box 5.2).

Description of proposed solutions—and their capacity to address issues and problems

How will the proposed project solve the problems identified in the first part of the business case? Because resources are always finite, the second part of the case should demonstrate that priorities for project inputs and activities have been set carefully, that the prioritization is based on sensible criteria, and that alternatives to the proposed solutions were considered and were rejected for good reasons. The method used to assess proposed solutions needs to be clearly stated, and all the options explored need to be assessed against each criterion.

To help reformers set priorities for possible reforms in relation to WTO trade facilitation

Box 5.2 **Example of a long term vision for border management reform**

The following long term vision was articulated by one East Asian country's border management reform team:

- A paperless trading environment in which 90–100 percent of documentary requirements and approvals are transmitted to regulatory agencies electronically, where agencies share information and rationalize processes to eliminate duplication and overlapping mandates, and using a system compliant with all regionally and internationally agreed standards.
- A clear, concise, transparent legal framework in which traders know their rights and obligations and have appropriate administrative and legal means to challenge decisions.
- A single window system, allowing traders to discharge all regulatory requirements through one central contact point, adopted in tandem with a review and rationalization of all existing border management agency requirements and mandates.
- A comprehensive risk management and compliance improvement approach, leading to more focused targeting of high risk shipments and to a radically reduced need for routine physical cargo inspections.
- A close cooperation and partnership between government agencies and the private sector in matters related to border management.
- A single, World Trade Organization–compliant service fee, replacing the range of fees previously required by regulatory authorities.
- Organizational structures and human resource management approaches that rationalize and streamline operations and that ensure officials are well trained, appropriately compensated, and well regarded by the public.

commitments, the World Bank and the WCO prepared a simple matrix (figure 5.1). Reformers could agree on criteria for rating each possible activity against two key matrix elements: the benefits to government and traders; and the cost and difficulty of implementation. The stakeholder analysis described above—and the previously construed matrix of strengths, weaknesses, opportunities and threats (see box 5.1)—can be used to inform this process.

The examination in the business case of alternatives to the proposed project need not be exhaustive. What is important is to explain why the alternatives have not been proposed. Also important is to describe how lessons learned from previous reform efforts have been incorporated into the project design. A simple account of what worked, what didn't, and why, will be useful. Lessons based on international experience can add strength and rigor. Here the work of the WCO is particularly helpful. A sample account of rejected alternatives and past lessons (prepared in support of a World Bank border management reform project) is provided in box 5.3.

Figure 5.1 **World Bank–World Customs Organization matrix for setting reform priorities**

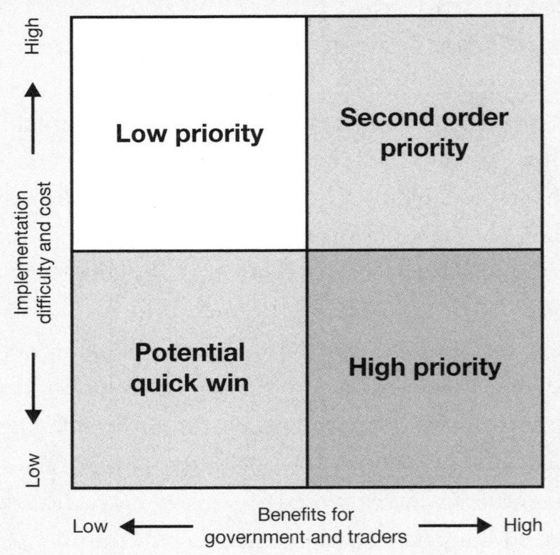

Justifying the project through cost-benefit analysis

Information on costs often is readily available—or can be estimated fairly easily from regulatory change costs, institutional costs, training costs, and equipment and infrastructure requirements. In contrast, it frequently proves difficult to quantify the likely benefits of a reform program and so produce an accurate figure for the expected return on the investment. Many of the benefits are not easy to state accurately in money or value amounts. An information technology program may deliver increased trader compliance, improved staff performance management, increased

Box **5.3**   **A sample account of rejected alternatives and past lessons**

A business case for one World Bank border management reform began with the following paragraphs.

In preparing the reform and modernization project, special attention was paid to examining previous border management reform efforts, both in the country and elsewhere in the world. The lessons learned during this research have been incorporated in the project design and are reflected in the selection of proposed project activities.

First, while the in house development of a new border management information technology system was initially considered, previous experience in the country suggests that such an approach may be beyond the technical competence of the border management agencies at this time. The project will therefore fund the procurement and implementation of an existing commercial off the shelf system customized to fit the specific requirements of the country.

Second, to ensure the long term sustainability of improvements obtained through the project, significant resources will be allocated to developing the capacity of part and full time trainers at the national training academy rather than outsourcing delivery of much of the required technical and administrative training to external providers. This will be accomplished by establishing a training agreement with a suitable international vocational education provider.

Third, a more comprehensive project was considered, but rejected due to a need to obtain immediate results for trade facilitation and revenue collection and prepare for future reform activities by increasing implementation and change absorption capacity of the customs department and other key border management agencies. Limited experience in the management of major change programs precludes a larger scale reform project at this time. Discrete, selected incremental changes will thus have more chance of success and be instrumental in laying the foundations for further and more far reaching future reforms. The more limited project selected provides the largest potential benefit for the resources invested and builds upon and complements work being carried out by a number of donors. It avoids the fate of larger overambitious strengthening projects and profits from the lessons learned in a number of very similar projects being implemented in neighboring countries.

Last, research suggests that one of the most critical success factors associated with the conduct of effective border management projects is the accurate diagnosis of developmental requirements. As such, the project design was based on a comprehensive diagnostic assessment undertaken by a team of World Bank Specialists. To ensure the approach taken during the diagnostic process was robust and comprehensive the World Customs Organization's comprehensive customs Capacity Building Diagnostic Framework was employed. The framework provides a comprehensive template for addressing all key operational and support functions of customs and is based on the application of agreed international standards and best practice approaches.

---

transparency and accountability, and better collaboration with other agencies and stakeholders. But these are difficult to quantify objectively. Rarely can an investment decision for border management reform be made solely from a traditional cost-benefit or return on investment analysis. So a suitable business case should combine an analysis of the investment with a wider view of both quantitative and qualitative benefits. The following points will be useful for reformers attempting to describe and calculate the likely benefits from border management modernization.[10]

Financial and economic analysis

Cost-benefit analyses are a key element of all World Bank project appraisal and approval processes. This section of project documentation—necessary for project approval—summarizes the project's net benefit quantitative to society. Often it is based on a comparison between scenarios with and without the project. Preparing such forecasts in measurable monetary terms, based on calculating the economic rate of return (or net present value) and including sensitivity analysis, can be a complex and sophisticated exercise—but if robustly undertaken it can greatly strengthen the case for reform. According to a comprehensive review of financial and economic analyses in a number of World Bank–financed border management reform projects, several of the business cases shared one major shortcoming: authors stated that projects would be financially and economically feasible, but they did not attempt to quantify the benefits (De Wulf, Le, and Pham 2007).

In revenue management modernization projects—including many border management projects involving customs—financial benefits are reflected in likely budget revenue increases, especially through enhanced control over smuggling and administrative corruption and through more effective administration of special import regimes. Skill development for officials, if a key program element, is also likely to contribute to enhanced management of valuation and tariff classification and reduced revenue leakage. Reformers can use finance ministry data and published economic growth projections to construct a future revenue collection scenario based on these assumptions. Such a scenario will not include productivity or collection efficiency dividends, so it will constitute the "without project" scenario. Having completed and tested it, reformers then can construct one or two "with project" scenarios based on various assumptions about efficiency improvement. In most cases the revenue increases alone—even calculated using very conservative estimates—will be sufficient to demonstrate a strong return on investment and justify resource requirements.

More difficult is to estimate the likely economic benefits. Many border management projects include predictions of reduced costs for traders preparing customs documents and other clearance documents for border management agencies, together with reduced facilitation payments. Many projects also predict that cargo will be cleared faster and more predictably—allowing traders to maintain smaller inventories—and that international trade will expand as the economy becomes more competitive. Little research has been done on the cost of preparing clearance documentation, but an Organisation for Economic Co-operation and Development study (2003)—mentioning survey data from Japan and the European Union—suggests that clearance costs range from 3.5–15 percent of the value of imported cargo. Benefits from faster and more predictable customs clearance include reduced business opportunity loss, lower inventory cost, and lower depreciation of goods delayed in transport. (For savings from reduced shipping time see Hummels 2001.) Improving external competitiveness also expands trade.

To quantify the likely economic benefits from projects related to border management, only basic data on trade volumes and customs clearance times usually are needed. Reductions in administrative and compliance costs from border management projects will depend on local circumstances, but economic research offers a starting point: a reasonable and fairly conservative estimate is a reduction of from 0.1–0.5 percent of cargo value. To calculate the benefits from lower clearance times, the data that can be used include:

- Clearance times.
- The share of imports and exports that enter and leave the country through ports of entry.
- A projection of such imports and exports over the project period.
- A target for reducing the clearance time at each port of entry.

The economic benefits from reduced clearance times can be estimated at 0.5 percent of cargo value for each day by which clearance time is lowered.

Survey data for one East Asian country identified clearance delays that were the responsibility of customs and those that were the responsibility of other agencies at the border. Such data can be used to estimate the benefits both from improved customs operations and from other agencies' reduced clearance delays, justifying extensions of border management reform beyond customs. Numbers of required documents and signatures can be used as proxies for determining likely efficiency gains.

Clearance times should be not only lowered, but also made more predictable. Predictability allows traders to keep only the inventory needed to meet demand. Halving the standard deviation in clearance times is estimated to provide benefits equal to an additional 0.2 percent of cargo value. Where the variability is lower, lower benefits should be assumed. Even when objective data on the variability of clearance times are not available, this likely benefit should be pointed out to policymakers.

Research clearly indicates that better border clearance lowers traders' costs—and that reduced costs in turn enhance external competitiveness, improving export growth. Using conservative estimates, it would be reasonable to add one percentage point to the export growth previously projected for the course of the project. Ranges for such reasonable estimates of benefits, in several categories, are illustrated in table 5.1.

Table 5.1	Estimating potential economic benefits from border management reform		
Type of improvement at border management agencies	**Benefits to government, to traders, and to the country**	**Reasonable range for estimated benefits**
Reducing administrative costs	Reduced costs for government and traders	−0.1–0.5 percent of cargo value
Reducing clearance times	Reduced traders' costs	−0.5–0.8 percent of cargo value
Reducing the variability of clearance time	Reduced inventory levels for traders, leading to reduced traders' costs	For each 50 percent reduction in the standard deviation, −0.2 percent of cargo value
Increasing competitiveness	Increased export growth	+1 percentage point

Demonstrating a capacity to succeed

Many business cases presented to decisionmakers are based on overly optimistic assessments of the reformers' capacity to carry out development projects and achieve meaningful outcomes. Implementation risks are rarely identified and acknowledged, and adequate risk mitigation measures are rarely proposed. Research by the World Bank suggests that it is critical to establish realistic achievable development objectives and to manage expectations based on probable—rather than possible—capacities. Equally important is factoring in likely challenges, including:

- Existing rivalries, competition, and conflicts of interest among ministries and agencies.
- Inadequacies in competence.
- Inadequacies in official remuneration and other incentives.
- Insufficient physical, technical and financial resources.
- Lack of experience in alternative regulatory environments among senior managers.
- Lack of implementation capacity, in government agencies or in the private sector.
- Lack of effective regulatory and nonregulatory frameworks governing customs brokers and other trade related service providers and intermediaries.
- Resistance to change, arising from the threatened removal of unofficial incentives such as bribes.
- Outdated, inadequate organizational structures.
- Lack of public awareness and willingness to support the long term effort needed for meaningful improvement.

To build decisionmakers' confidence that reformers can deliver, it is vital to identify challenges, risks, and risk mitigation strategies. For example, to overcome resistance in government agencies, the agencies should be represented in the governing or advisory group overseeing the project. A realistic assessment of likely winners and losers will identify likely sources of resistance in advance.

Likewise, the project could include a strong consultation and communication strategy. If decisionmakers are likely to be concerned about deadlines, the project may also include strong project implementation and performance metrics. In one recent border management project, progress was periodically assessed through client surveys and objective measures of clearance times at major ports and land border crossings. Such objective indicators and monitoring mechanisms facilitate supervision and establish confidence in the reform team. They also can help reformers to sustain the momentum toward reform among policymakers throughout the project. If resistance to change is anticipated from the private sector, a formal process for consultation, cooperation, and partnership with private sector representatives can be established.

In sum, anticipated risks and challenges should be identified and included in the business case. If they are not, they likely will be identified by the decisionmakers assessing the business case and will harm the reformers' credibility. Understanding the incentives of key players, again, is a must—both in developing the rationale for reform and in learning where resistance is likely to arise.

Conclusion

The business case for trade facilitation through border management reform must be focused on presenting practical solutions to clearly defined problems. It must appeal to all key stakeholders and demonstrate likely benefits, with a cost-benefit analysis to justify the scale of requested investments. To be credible to

Building a convincing business case for border management reform

policymakers it must identify likely barriers to success and appropriate mitigating strategies. Equally important, reformers must demonstrate their capacity to manage the project and meet development objectives.

Economic research overwhelmingly concludes that trade facilitation lowers trade costs, makes countries more competitive, and increases trade. The challenge to reformers seeking support for border management modernization is how to translate that research into a strong, convincing business case. The information and advice in this chapter should help such reformers succeed.

Notes

1. A revised version of the Kyoto Convention came into effect in 2006.
2. For the TIR system see further chapter 17 and "About TIR," International Road Transport Union, http://www.iru.org/index/en_iru_about_tir.
3. For more detailed discussion of the models see Dornbusch, Fischer, and Samuelson (1977); Leamer (1995); Feenstra (2003).
4. For example, the existence of trade costs is one of the key factors giving rise to agglomeration in new economic geography models (Krugman 1991).
5. For example see Bernard and Jensen (1999); Aw, Chen, and Roberts (2001); Eaton, Kortum, and Kramarz (2006); Bernard, Jensen, and others (2007).
6. Estimating transport costs by taking the ratio between cost, insurance, and freight (CIF) and free on board (FOB) values, and calculating the nominal and effective rate of protection, illustrates that transport costs pose a barrier at least equal to that of import tariffs. The conclusion highlights the importance of factoring in barriers that were long excluded in both theoretical and empirical analyses of trade.
7. The data have been incorporated into the "Doing Business Database," The World Bank, http://www.doingbusiness.org.
8. Li and Wilson (2009) use—as do Djankov, Freund, and Pham (forthcoming)—the indicator on export time from the "Doing Business Database," The World Bank, http://www.doingbusiness.org.
9. See "Doing Business: Trading Across Borders," The World Bank, http://www.doingbusiness.org/ExploreTopics/TradingAcrossBorders/.
10. Much of the following is based on De Wulf, Le, and Pham (2007).

References

Anderson, J.E., and D. Marcouiller. 2002. "Insecurity and the Pattern of Trade: An Empirical Investigation." *The Review of Economics and Statistics* 84 (2): 342–52.

Anderson, J., and E. van Wincoop. 2002. "Borders, Trade and Welfare," in *Brookings Trade Forum 2001*, ed. S. Collins and D. Rodrik. Washington, DC: Brookings Institution.

———. 2004. "Trade Costs." *Journal of Economic Literature* 42 (3): 691–751.

Aw, Y. B., X. Chen, and M.J. Roberts. 2001. "Firm-level Evidence on Productivity Differentials and Turnover in Taiwanese Manufacturing." *Journal of Development Economics* 66 (1): 51–86.

Bernard, A.B., J. Eaton, J.B.Jensen, and S.S. Kortum. 2003. "Plants and Productivity in International Trade." *American Economic Review* 93: 1268–90.

Bernard, A.B., and J.B. Jensen. 1999. "Exceptional Exporter Performance: Cause, Effect, or Both?" *Journal of International Economics* 47 (1): 1–26.

Bernard, A.B., J.B. Jensen, S.J. Redding, and P.K. Schott. 2007. "Firms in International Trade." *Journal of Economic Perspectives* 21 (3): 105–30.

Bernard, A.B., S.J. Redding, and P.K. Schott. 2007. "Comparative Advantage and Heterogeneous Firms." *Review of Economic Studies* 74: 31–66.

Brander, J., and P. Krugman. 1983. "A 'Reciprocal Dumping' Model of International Trade." *Journal of International Economics* 15 (3–4): 313–21.

Buys, P., U. Deichmann, and D. Wheeler. 2006. "Road Network Upgrading and Overland Trade Expansion in Sub-Saharan Africa." Policy Research Working Paper 4097, The World Bank, Washington, DC.

Clarke, G.R.G. 2005. "Beyond Tariff and Quotas: Why Don't African Manufacturing Enterprises

Export More?" Policy Research Working Paper 3617, The World Bank, Washington, DC.

del Angel, M.A.M., Y. Li, and J.S. Wilson. 2009. "Information Technology and Telecommunications: Does Aid to Expand Trade Matter?" Mimeo.

De Wulf, L., T.M. Le, and D.M. Pham. 2007. "Estimating Economic Benefits for Revenue Administration Reform Projects," PREM Note 112, The World Bank, Washington, DC, March.

Djankov, S., C. Freund, and C.S. Pham. Forthcoming. "Trading on Time." *Review of Economics and Statistics.*

Dollar, D., M. Hallward-Driemeier, and T. Mengistae. 2006. "Investment Climate and International Integration." *World Development* 34 (9): 1498–1516.

Dornbusch, R., S. Fischer, and P.A. Samuelson. 1977. "Comparative Advantage, Trade, and Payments in a Ricardian Model with a Continuum of Goods." *The American Economic Review* 67 (5): 823–39.

Eaton, J., S. Kortum, and F. Kramarz. 2006. "An Anatomy of International Trade: Evidence from French Firms." NBER Working Paper 14610, National Bureau of Economic Research, Cambridge, MA.

Evans, C.L., and J. Harrigan. 2005. "Distance, Time, and Specialization: Lean Retailing in General Equilibrium." *American Economic Review* 95 (1): 292–313.

Feenstra, R. 2003. *Advanced International Trade: Theory and Evidence.* Princeton NJ: Princeton University Press.

Finger, J. M., and A.J. Yeats. 1976. "Effective Protection by Transportation Costs and Tariffs: A Comparison of Magnitudes." *The Quarterly Journal of Economics* 90 (1): 169–76.

Fink, C., A. Mattoo, and I.C. Neagu. 2005. "Assessing the Impact of Communication Costs on International Trade." *Journal of International Economics* 67 (2): 428–44.

Freund, C.L., and D. Weinhold. 2004. "On the Effect of the Internet on International Trade." *Journal of International Economics* 62 (1): 171–89.

———. 2002. "The Internet and International Trade in Services." *American Economic Review* 92 (2): 236–40.

Harrigan, J., and A. Venables. 2004. "Timeliness, Trade and Agglomeration." NBER Working Paper 10404, National Bureau of Economic Research, Cambridge, MA.

Helble, M., C. Mann, and J.S. Wilson. 2009. "Aid for Trade Facilitation." Policy Research Working Paper 5064, World Bank, Washington, DC.

Helble, M., B. Shepherd, and J.S. Wilson. 2007. "Transparency & Trade Facilitation in the Asia Pacific: Estimating the Gains from Reform." Policy Research Working Paper 41048, The World Bank, Washington, DC.

Hertel, T., T. Walmsley, and K. Ikatura. 2001. "Dynamic Effects of the 'New Age' Free Trade Agreement between Japan and Singapore." *Journal of Economic Integration* 24: 1019–49.

Hummels, D. 2001. "Time as a Trade Barrier," GTAP Working Paper 1152, Center for Global Trade Analysis, Department of Agricultural Economics, Purdue University, West Lafayette, IN.

Hummels, D.L., and G. Schaur. 2009. "Hedging Price Volatility Using Fast Transport." NBER Working Paper 15154, National Bureau of Economic Research, Cambridge, MA.

Kee, H.L., A. Nicita, and M. Olarreaga. 2009. "Estimating Trade Restrictiveness Indices." *Economic Journal,* January.

Krugman, P.R. 1980. "Scale Economies, Product Differentiation and the Pattern of Trade." *American Economic Review* 70 (5): 950–59.

———. 1991. "Increasing Returns and Economic Geography." *Journal of Political Economy* 99 (3): 483–99.

Leamer, E.E. 1995. "The Heckscher-Ohlin Model in Theory and Practice." Princeton Studies in International Finance 77, International Finance Section, Department of Economics, Princeton University, Princeton, NJ, February.

Li, Y., and J.S. Wilson. 2009. "Time as a Determinant of Comparative Advantage." Policy Research Working Paper 5128, The World Bank, Washington, DC.

Limão, N., and A.J. Venables. 2001. "Infrastructure, Geographical Disadvantage, and Transport Costs." *World Bank Economic Review* 15 (3): 451–79.

Melitz, M.J. 2003. "The Impact of Trade on Intra-Industry Reallocations and Aggregate Industry Productivity." *Econometrica* 71 (6): 1695–1725.

Nordas, H., K.E. Pinali, and M.G. Grosso. 2006. "Logistics and Time as a Trade Barrier." OECD

Trade Policy Working Papers 35, OECD Trade Directorate, Paris.

OECD (Organisation for Economic Co-operation and Development). 2003. "Quantitative Assessment of the Benefits of Trade Facilitation." Document TD/TC/WP(2003)31/FINAL, OECD, Paris.

Portes, R., and H. Rey. 2005. "The Determinants of Cross-Border Equity Flows." *Journal of International Economics* 65 (2): 269–96.

Sadikov, A.M. 2007. "Border and Behind-the-Border Trade Barriers and Country Exports." Working Papers 07/292, International Monetary Fund, Washington, DC.

Staples, B.R. 1998. "Trade Facilitation." Mimeo.

Wilson, J.S., K.L. Mann, and T. Otsuki. 2005. "Assessing the Benefits of Trade Facilitation: A Global Perspective." Policy Research Working Paper 3224, The World Bank, Washington, DC.

World Bank. 2008. *World Development Report 2009: Reshaping Economic Geography.* Washington, DC: The World Bank.

Yeaple, S.R. 2005. "A Simple Model of Firm Heterogeneity, International Trade, and Wages." *Journal of International Economics* 65: 1–20.

Yoshino, Y. 2008. "Domestic Constraints, Firm Characteristics, and Geographical Diversification of Firm-Level Manufacturing Exports in Africa." Policy Research Working Paper 4575, The World Bank, Washington, DC.

5

Building a convincing business case
for border management reform

6 Core border management disciplines: risk based compliance management

David Widdowson and Stephen Holloway

Contemporary border management reflects a complex interplay between a variety of actors in international trade, both across government through its public sector agencies and between government and the private sector. The border in many cases is the physical manifestation of the intersection of regulation and commerce. Its proper management is critical to the cost effectiveness of international trade transactions and the smooth flow of legitimate goods and people from both public and private sector perspectives. Any shortcomings in border management tend to highlight weaknesses in a country's regulation of trade and immigration, and their impact is felt in issues such as supply chain security, health, and safety.

The reality of increased trade volumes and passenger traffic—a consequence of globalization and advances in transportation and electronic commerce—poses particular challenges for border agencies, especially as public sector resources have remained relatively stable over the same period. Furthermore, in most countries a number of agencies have some form of regulatory responsibility at the border. Each of these agencies has its own specific mandate from government, and taken together they cover issues as diverse as health, product safety, quarantine, immigration controls, and security, as well as revenue and other customs concerns.

Notwithstanding that there may be several agencies with border management responsibilities, the fundamental nature of the challenge that each confronts is the same. The challenge is to facilitate the legitimate movement of people and goods across increasingly blurred, or even virtual, borders while—at the same time—meeting the government's mandate to maintain the integrity of the border, to protect the community, and to prevent the unlawful or unauthorized movement of people and goods.

The reference to blurred or virtual borders acknowledges that, for security and other reasons, a number of countries are pushing their borders outward in a virtual sense through the mandating of advance information prior to departure of the goods (or person). In this context the United States Department of Homeland Security refers to the global security envelope, a regulatory approach that seeks to establish a chain of trust throughout the supply chain—from manufacture through transport to its ultimate receipt by the consumer. This concept is physically manifested through regulatory initiatives such as the Container

Security Initiative and the Advanced Manifest Rule.

Similarly, at a multilateral level the World Customs Organization (WCO) Framework of Standards to Secure and Facilitate Trade (SAFE Framework) provides a policy framework for pushing borders outward by undertaking export inspections at the point of departure if requested by the country of destination.

The consequence of such policy initiatives has been to highlight a shift in focus on the part of border agencies from one that is essentially transactional, treating the movement of goods and people as a series of individual steps from departure to arrival, to one that is more holistic, using an integrated and interdependent process from the inception of the transaction to its completion and with multiple players intervening at different times and assuming different responsibilities. The broader focus on upstream and downstream elements of the supply chain has the potential to increase trade friction, that is, impede the flow of trade and increase its costs. These considerations increase the complexity of the task confronting modern border agencies and bring issues of control, intervention, and facilitation into stark relief—a point discussed in more detail below when the chapter examines the philosophy of effective border management.

The agreement at the 2001 Doha Ministerial Conference to consider trade facilitation for a World Trade Organization (WTO) rules-based agreement represents another significant input into the equation, highlighting border management as a major component of achieving trade efficiency. The agreement recognizes that an efficient and effective border management regime is critical to the achievement of sustainable growth and development, as is evident in the World Bank's Logistics Performance Index (Arvis and others 2007) and the World Economic Forum's *Global Enabling Trade Report* (WEF 2008).

This chapter examines the core border management disciplines that underpin efficient and effective border management, whether in respect of goods, people, or modes of transport. First, however, the chapter sets the scene for these core border management disciplines by considering why regulatory compliance management has evolved in the way that it has—from what was essentially a gatekeeper approach to one that is now grounded firmly in risk management. That evolution has taken place as a necessary consequence of the increased volume and complexity of international trade and transport.

In relation to goods, the United Nations Conference on Trade and Development (UNCTAD) has estimated that (2006, p. 3):

A trade transaction may easily involve 30 parties, 40 documents, 200 data elements, and require re-coding of 60 to 70 percent of all data at least once. For example, within a port community where the two main actors, namely, the forwarding and the ship's agents, must communicate and coordinate information flows, the exchange of information can amount to about 10 percent of the commercial value of the traded goods. Sources of information that could be involved include the port authority, shippers, banks, insurers, carriers, Customs, etc.

UNCTAD further concluded that about one-third of international trade in goods involves trade in unfinished goods and components that form part of a global supply chain, and that a similar percentage represents trade within the same company. It is likely that those percentages have increased since the UNCTAD report was prepared, and indeed the WCO estimates that the percentage of intracompany trade is now closer to 50 percent (WCO 2008). Most of that trade is moved within an integrated global logistics system in diminishing timeframes, to meet global sourcing and just-in-time business models that emphasize low inventory.

A recent SITPRO[1] study estimated that the United Kingdom's import perishable food supply chain generates one billion pieces of paper annually; duplicate consignment data are keyed in at least 189 million times per annum; the cost of document related administration is estimated to be around 11 percent of the supply chain value per annum; the cost of delayed, incorrect, or missing paperwork is a little over £1 billion per annum for the sectors studied; and the total cost of generating paper documentation for the perishable sectors studied (4.5 million document sets) is estimated at £126 million per annum (SITPRO 2008).

The magnitude of the task for border agencies can be further demonstrated through recent statistics in relation to the movement of people.

The International Organization for Migration has indicated that "there are more than 200 million estimated international migrants in the world today," which is about 3 percent of the global population and, in fact, would constitute the fifth most populous country in the world (IOM 2005, 2008). Furthermore, there are roughly 20 to 30 million unauthorized migrants worldwide, comprising around 10 to 15 percent of the world's immigrants, and by 2007 the global number of refugees reached an estimated 11.4 million persons (Ratha and others 2008).

It is also interesting to note that international tourism is ranked fourth in terms of export income after fuels, chemicals, and automotive products. From 1950 to 2007 international tourist arrivals grew from 25 million to 903 million, with export receipts of almost $3 billion per day, and in 2008 international tourist arrivals reached 924 million according to the United Nations World Tourism Organization, with long term growth estimated at an average of 4 percent a year.[2]

These figures demonstrate the challenges that border agencies confront in fulfilling the objective of facilitating legitimate trade and travel while seeking to identify unlawful transactions and movements. The volumes alone lead to the realization that physically checking every consignment and every person that crosses the border is impossible and that a more sophisticated approach is needed based on intelligence led risk management.

There is another aspect of this that needs to be considered. When most people think of border management or border control they automatically think of uniformed customs officers. However, the fact is that the effective regulation of international trade and travel involves a diverse range of controls that go well beyond frontline customs procedures. If the objective of trade and passenger facilitation is to improve the efficiency of movement of goods and people across borders in order to reduce costs while maintaining national security and ensuring compliance with national policy requirements, then the satisfaction of that objective requires the involvement of a number of government agencies with responsibilities at the border.

A country could have the most efficient and effective customs administration in the world, but if the clearance of goods is also subject to checks and approvals from other regulatory authorities that result in delays in getting the goods to market, it hasn't altered the bottom line for businesses adversely affected by the loss of opportunity and increased costs that result from that delay. Consequently, unless regulatory authorities with border responsibilities coordinate their activities, there is the real danger that such delays will be realized on a regular basis along with unnecessary compliance costs and the associated administrative cost of operation. There is also potential for the unlawful entry of goods or people if border agencies fail to share intelligence, thereby providing a complete risk profile of a particular consignment or individual.

As the World Economic Forum has stated in its *Global Enabling Trade Report 2008* (WEF 2008, chapter 1.5, p. 69):

> Even in developed countries such as the United Kingdom, there are close to 60 or even more distinct regulatory procedures and regimes that affect cross-border operations. These operations fall into the wider categories of revenue collection and fiscal protection, public safety and security, environment and health, consumer protection, and trade policy. Procedures, documentary requirements, inspections, visas, and vehicle regulations, as well as general security issues can all severely hamper the movement of goods across borders.

In the same report there is a telling observation from the perspective of business that highlights the issue of lack of coordination particularly well (WEF 2008, p. 70):

> The private sector can often do no more than comply with the requirements and bear the costs that are associated not only with collecting, producing, transmitting, and processing required information and documents, but also with the expenses of setting up and financing guarantees, laboratory testing, inspection fees, stamp charges, service

Core border management disciplines: risk based compliance management

fees levied by shipping lines and banks, labour and handling charges to deliver goods to inspection facilities and to present goods, storage charges, and possible out-of-hours surcharges . . . Typically such unpredictable circumstances are the result of multiple and contradictory documentation requirements or lengthy inspection procedures by agencies that include customs, immigration, health and sanitary authorities, police and other security agencies, and standardization or conformity assessment agencies.

Similar observations are made in the World Bank's *Logistics Performance Index 2007* and are reiterated in its *Logistics Performance Index 2010,* where the authors conclude (Arvis and others 2010, p. 16):

> Customs is not the only agency involved in border management; collaboration among all border management agencies—including standards, sanitary, phytosanitary, transport, and veterinary agencies—and the introduction of modern approaches to regulatory compliance are especially important.

It is also interesting to note an earlier study (Wilson, Mann, and Otsuki 2005) that examined port efficiency, customs, regulatory transparency, and services sector infrastructure and then quantified the outcomes. It concluded that increasing global capacity in trade facilitation by half, when compared with the global average, would increase world trade by $377 billion, amounting to a 9.7 percent rise in global trade. The study estimated that about $107 billion of the total gains would come from improvements in port efficiency, about $33 billion from improvements in the customs environment, *and $83 billion from improvements in the regulatory environment*. In other words, there is significant scope for improvement outside of customs regulation alone.

Regulatory control, facilitation, and intervention

At this point it is worthwhile to clarify a few concepts. First, border management agencies have an overarching responsibility to maintain control over the cross border movement of goods, people, and conveyances. That is a given. Systems and procedures to achieve control include a range of interventions, including nonintrusive activities such as documentary and physical monitoring, screening, and auditing. They also include more intrusive activities such as documentary checks, physical examinations, scanning, sampling, and testing. Note that the commonly used term *nonintrusive intervention* can be quite confusing, as it suggests a hands off approach to examining goods (such as scanning) but often ignores the fact that such regulatory activities are often highly intrusive in terms of the resultant time delays.

Second, border agencies also have a mandate to provide an appropriate level of facilitation to trade and travel, and consequently they need to maintain regulatory control in a way that reduces the impact of interventionist strategies as much as possible. This implies keeping the amount of intervention or interference to the minimum necessary to achieve the policy outcome and also ensuring that regulatory requirements (red tape) are not unduly onerous or overly prescriptive. In seeking to achieve this balance, border agencies must simultaneously manage two risks—the potential for noncompliance with relevant laws and the potential failure to provide the level of facilitation expected by their government (Widdowson 2006).

Third, some observers take exception to the concept of achieving a balance between intervention and facilitation, claiming that an increase in one necessarily implies a decrease in the other. What is at issue here, however, is not a set of scales with intervention on one side and facilitation on the other. Rather it is akin to the need to achieve a balanced lifestyle in terms of one's work and personal life. In this context it is widely accepted that striking the right balance can produce a more productive and rewarding lifestyle both at work and at home. Similarly, it is possible to achieve optimal levels of both intervention and active facilitation.

Last, it is important to understand that control and facilitation are not mutually exclusive. It is often assumed that as the level of facilitation increases, so the level of control decreases. Similarly, where regulatory controls are tightened, it is commonly assumed that facilitation must suffer as a result. However, as discussed later in this chapter, this should not be the case, as they are equally important contributors to the achievement of a country's policy objectives.

As noted above, maintaining cross border control is nonnegotiable, but the way in which it is achieved should not ignore the need to provide appropriate levels of facilitation. Inevitably, however, policy objectives such as tourism, labor immigration, and economic competitiveness may encourage a more facilitative approach, while other policy objectives such as national security and public health will encourage a more interventionist approach. Border agencies must therefore analyze all such policy objectives to create an effective and efficient system of regulatory control that facilitates legitimate trade and travel while providing a barrier and disincentive to the entry of illegal goods and travelers.

Consequently, while border agencies have a fundamental responsibility to ensure that legal requirements are met, the manner in which this is achieved is often quite flexible. For example, the law may require that certain goods may only be imported under license or that travelers must meet specific criteria in order to be granted an entry visa. However, the manner in which these requirements are implemented by the relevant agency is often open to administrative discretion. A particular law may be administered prescriptively in a one size fits all fashion, or it may be administered with a degree of flexibility that takes account of varying circumstances.

To visualize the various approaches often adopted by border agencies to fulfill their mandate, it is possible to represent the concepts of facilitation and control as two distinct variables within a broader regulatory matrix (figure 6.1).

The top left quadrant in the matrix (high control, low facilitation) represents a high control regime in which regulatory requirements are very stringent, but to the detriment of facilitation. This can be described as a *red tape approach* and is often representative of a risk averse management style. Administrations that fall into this category pride themselves on the fact that everything is done by the book, although their legislative base may not be relevant to today's environment. In most modern societies such an approach is likely to attract a great deal of public criticism and complaint due to the increasing

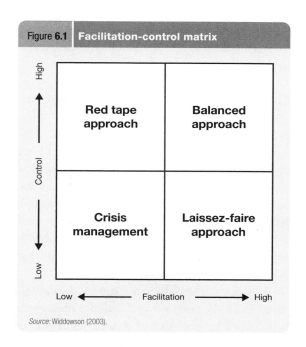

Figure **6.1** | **Facilitation-control matrix**

Red tape approach	**Balanced approach**
Crisis management	**Laissez-faire approach**

Control (High → Low); Facilitation (Low ← → High)

Source: Widdowson (2003).

expectations of the business community that regulatory intervention should be kept to a minimum.

The bottom left quadrant (low control, low facilitation) depicts the approach of an administration that exercises little control and achieves equally little in the way of facilitation. They use copious quantities of red tape, but achieve little in the process. This *crisis management approach* is one that benefits neither government nor the business community.

The bottom right quadrant (low control, high facilitation) represents an approach in which facilitation is the order of the day, but with little in the way of control. This is the easiest situation to achieve for a border agency, as it represents a do nothing approach—but it results in chaos. Such organizations have streamlined their processes to the highest degree; they may have no backlogs, but error rates tend to be very high. This *laissez faire approach* would be an appropriate method for managing compliance in a perfect world—one in which the business community voluntarily complies without any threat or inducement from government. Such an environment would present no risk of noncompliance. But it doesn't bear much resemblance to reality.

Finally, the top right quadrant (high control, high facilitation) represents a *balanced approach* to both control and facilitation, resulting in high levels of both. This approach to compliance management brings the greatest possible benefits to both the

Core border management disciplines: risk based compliance management

border agency and the international trading community. It is this approach that border agencies should be seeking to achieve.

The application of risk management

Effective application of the principles of risk management is the key to achieving high levels of both control and facilitation, and border agencies that are able to achieve this state (the *balanced approach* in figure 6.1) do so through the effective use of risk management. In contrast, agencies in a state of total crisis management (zero facilitation, zero control) are adopting a compliance management strategy that is devoid of risk management.

So what is the risk in the term *risk management*? From the perspective of a border agency it is best defined as the chance of something happening that will have an impact on organizational objectives (see below, where the concept of risk is further discussed). A border management strategy that includes some element of control, however small, essentially represents a method of treating potential noncompliance with border requirements. Equally, a border management strategy that achieves some degree of facilitation essentially represents a method of treating the potential failure to facilitate trade.

As noted previously, border agencies around the world are responsible for managing a broad range of risks as they seek to fulfill their responsibilities in areas such as revenue collection, sanitary and phytosanitary standards, community protection, and the facilitation of trade and travel—and there are the interagency coordination issues implicit in such a multifaceted environment.

Customs often is the lead, or the agency with delegated authority required to manage risks on behalf of other government departments and agencies such as health, immigration, agriculture, trade, environment, and statistics. This is generally achieved through the administration and enforcement of a diverse range of agreed control regimes pursuant to service level agreements between the respective agencies (Widdowson 2007). Risk management activities might include the analysis of internal risks, such as those impacting on public confidence, and external risks, such as declines in economic outlook (a global financial crisis or health risks associated with swine or bird flu).

In recent times border agencies around the world have seen a dramatic increase in workload across all areas of activity, fueled by the technological advances that have revolutionized trade, transport, and transmission of information. At the same time, there is a universal trend toward ensuring that public sector responsibilities are carried out as effectively and efficiently as possible. This often means that border management agencies are required to operate in an environment of static or even decreasing resources (Holloway 2009, p. 14), and it is in this context that agencies have been exploring more structured methods of managing risk.

Risk management is a technique that facilitates the effective allocation of resources. Risk management as a concept is nothing new, and there is no doubt that the vast majority of border agencies have in place some form of risk management procedures or guidelines, either formal or informal. For example, as noted above, no border agency is going to check each and every single passenger, consignment, carrier, or crew member. Nor is it likely to have the resources to do so. So-called nonintrusive detection technologies have improved levels of intervention but still rely on risk management to make their effectiveness as high as possible. In other words, risk management is at the heart of border management efficiency and effectiveness.

Through the use of a variety of risk management techniques, which vary considerably in levels of sophistication and effectiveness, border agencies worldwide seek to identify the risks associated with cross border transactions and activities and to focus their resources where they are likely to achieve the best results. Sustaining the effectiveness of that risk based approach to resource allocation involves the creation of an evaluation and continuous improvement cycle. Such a cycle allows border agencies to learn from the results of the application of particular strategies and to predict future risks, rather than simply react to such risks as they emerge.

Risk as a concept

The concept of risk has two elements:
- The likelihood of something happening.
- The consequences if it happens.

The *level of risk* is the product of the likelihood of a risk occurring and the consequences if it does occur. Action taken to manage a risk needs to address the likelihood of an event occurring, the consequences if it does, or both. Further action is then required to ensure that activities designed to mitigate risk (often referred to as risk treatments) achieve their planned objectives. As previously discussed, ongoing monitoring or evaluation is required in case changes in internal and external factors cause a change in the level of risk.

The next step is to explore how risk is identified and managed in practice by border agencies. The answer is that they do so by following a structured process that is integrated with broader strategic planning activities.

A process framework for risk management

The management of risk is recognized as an integral part of effective border management practice. It involves an iterative process consisting of six steps that, when undertaken in sequence, provide a very effective decisionmaking framework.

Risk management, in a technical sense, is the term applied to the logical and systematic process of establishing the context, identifying the risk, analyzing the risk, evaluating the risk, treating the risk, monitoring the risk, and communicating risks and outcomes. It may be applied to any activity, function, or process in a way that will enable border agencies to reduce losses as much as possible and increase opportunities as much as possible. In fact, risk management is as much about identifying opportunities as it is about avoiding or mitigating undesirable consequences of risks.

Several generic risk management processes developed around the world provide a systematic method of managing risks to achieve organizational objectives. These processes are iterative because risks are not static—they are continually changing. The diagram set out below in figure 6.2 outlines the risk management process quite clearly.

Integrating risk management with border management

While risk management is practiced in some form or another by all border agencies, very few address risks in a systematic way. This is generally because risks tend to be dealt with at an operational or tactical level, rarely at a strategic level.

The management of risk is integral to any management process and, as such, should not be regarded as something that is done in isolation from an organization's management framework. Indeed, many organizations make the mistake of treating risk management as a separate activity that is carried out in ignorance of other functions. By doing this, management and staff of the organization come to view risk management as a necessary but mechanical task that consumes both time and resources.

The ideal way to avoid that mindset is to integrate the management of risk into the agency's everyday management practices so that it becomes second nature. A major part of any management framework is the planning process, and this is the ideal place for the formal and systematic management of risk to begin.

It is important to understand the overall goals and objectives of the border agency or function when considering potential risks because, as stated previously, the risks to be considered—both positive and negative—are those that may hinder the achievement of organizational objectives. Therefore, the central element of any risk management framework should be a clear statement of the

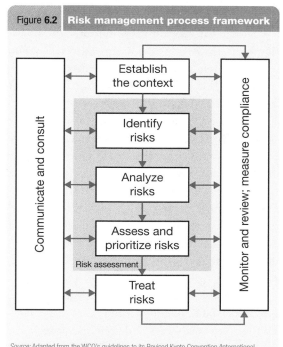

Figure 6.2 **Risk management process framework**

Communicate and consult

Establish the context

Identify risks

Analyze risks

Assess and prioritize risks

Risk assessment

Treat risks

Monitor and review; measure compliance

Source: Adapted from the WCO's guidelines to its Revised Kyoto Convention (International Convention on the Simplification and Harmonization of Customs Procedures, as amended, general annex, chapter 6; available at http://www.wcoomd.org/Kyoto_New/Content/content.html) and the Australian and New Zealand Standard on Risk Management (AZ/NZS 4360: 2004).

Core border management disciplines: risk based compliance management

agency's objectives, together with an identification of risks to be managed.

The actual design of the particular border management system that implements the risk management framework should be based on proper consideration of the variables that can affect its ongoing implementation. For example, some variables are the physical characteristics of the border, the relationship with neighboring countries (as relevant), the infrastructure and technology available, and the volume and characteristics of goods and passengers, to name a few.

A very important aspect of any risk management framework is the need to document the process. Adopting a formal process for managing risk ensures that a border agency is accountable for its decisions and facilitates transparency in decision-making processes. The various components of the risk management process as illustrated in figure 6.2 are as follows.

Establishing the context. This is probably the most vital step in the risk management cycle because it provides the foundation on which the remainder of the risk management process is based. It should therefore be as comprehensive as possible.

As previously discussed, a risk may be defined as any factor that may adversely impact an organization's objectives. It is therefore critical to review and refine the agency's objectives until they are clearly established. They then become the reference point for the other risk management processes.

Having established and clearly articulated the agency's objectives, it is important to consider the environmental factors that could have an impact on the area of concern, since any decisions about risk need to be made in the context of the environment in which they occur. It is therefore important to look at the big picture and identify relevant aspects of both the internal and external environment associated with the process or activity being examined.

An important part of establishing that context is to understand the interdependencies of the organization, key capabilities, and decisions made. What impact do those decisions have on the organization as a whole, other agencies, or the movement of goods and persons across the border?

Consideration of the *internal environment* should include such things as:

- Demographics of the organization, including the number and levels of staff.
- Staff competencies and knowledge base.
- Organizational structure.
- Hours of operation and location of offices.
- Responsibilities and accountabilities.
- Communication and reporting mechanisms.
- Operating procedures.
- Systems and technology.
- Reference to relevant documents, such as the strategic plan, action plans, operational instructions, codes of conduct, and other policy documents.

In examining the *external environment*, it will be necessary to consider issues such as:

- Relevant treaties and international obligations.
- Government legislation and policy.
- Interagency agreements.
- The nature and volume of international trade and transport flows.
- Socioeconomic issues.

A useful technique to adopt in relation to establishing the context for risk management purposes is what is called an environmental scan, in which the following (nonexhaustive) aspects of both the internal and external environment are examined:

- Organizational.
- Operational.
- Policy.
- Legislative.
- Political.
- Geographic.
- Economic.
- Commercial.
- Technological.

Capturing relevant issues under these headings helps an agency obtain an overall perspective on factors that may adversely impact the achievement of its objectives.

Risk identification. Risk identification is a matter of asking (and answering) two questions:

- What can happen (that will have an impact on the agency's objectives)?
- How and why could it happen?

The first question identifies the risks and the second question provides valuable information about potential causes. This exercise is further assisted by asking some additional questions:

- What can happen?
- What are the key drivers?
- What are the existing controls or treatments?
- What is the likely impact?
- What are the operational influences?
- What might be the causal factors (such as inadequacy in existing controls)?
- Who is involved?
- Who is affected?
- How does the risk occur (for example, as a result of system failures or poor planning)?
- Is it likely that the risk will occur immediately, in the short term, or in the longer term?

There can be many sources of risk, some reasonably capable of being managed by a border agency and some less susceptible to management. However, it is important to consider all such risks as part of an effective risk management process.

Risk analysis. The principal purpose of the risk analysis stage is to establish the significance of each risk previously identified, so that informed decisions can be taken with respect to the strategies to adopt and the resources that will be needed to manage them. This is achieved by analyzing the relationship between the likelihood of the risk occurring and the consequences if the risk does occur. The combination of these factors provides a level of risk for each identified risk, allowing an agency to compare and prioritize those risks.

There are essentially three methods that can be used to analyze risk—quantitative, semiquantitative, and qualitative. In situations where risks can be expressed in quantitative terms with a reasonable degree of accuracy, quantitative methods can be used. These generally require access to reliable data as well as technical input from a statistics specialist, who provides an accurate determination of probability. The approach most commonly used by organizations, particularly at the more strategic level, is the qualitative approach, where managers use experience, intuition, and judgment to make decisions.

It should be noted, however, that there will always be a degree of subjectivity when using qualitative risk analysis methods, and some margin of uncertainty should therefore be taken into account.

It is common practice to assess the potential consequences and likelihood by using a sliding scale. How an agency defines such a scale and its attributes will partly be influenced by the kind of risks the particular agency is dealing with, its legal and policy context, and the mechanisms it already has in place to deal with those risks.

By way of illustration, the most basic form of risk assessment scale utilizes three definitions of *likelihood* and three definitions of *consequence*. When represented in a matrix format, this enables the level of risk to be identified. A risk assessment scale matrix then enables the level of a risk to be determined from its factors.

The definitions used for *likelihood, consequence,* and *level* should reflect the agency's particular context and parameters. Generally, however, *likelihood* is best understood as answering the question: "What is the probability that the event will happen?" The meaning of each answer is as follows:

- *High likelihood* means the event is expected.
- *Medium likelihood* means the event could be expected.
- *Low likelihood* means the event may occur, but only infrequently.

Similarly, *consequence* is best understood as answering the question: "If it happens, then what adverse effects will result?" The meaning of each answer is as follows:

- *High consequence* means significant adverse effects.
- *Medium consequence* means moderate adverse effects.
- *Low consequence* means a minimum of adverse effects.

With the levels of likelihood and consequence assessed for each identified risk, the level of each risk can be determined using the matrix (table 6.1). To use the matrix:

- Determine the likelihood and consequence for each risk—for example, high consequence and medium likelihood (lightly shaded in table 6.1).
- Plot the intersection—for example, that of high consequence and medium likelihood (more heavily shaded in table 6.1).

To interpret the resulting level of risk, refer to the definitions:

- *High risk* means highly likely to cause serious disruption.

- *Medium risk* means likely to cause some disruption.
- *Low risk* means unlikely to cause any disruption.

In the example in table 6.1, the level of risk is medium (the more heavily shaded cell), meaning that the risk event is likely to cause some disruption to the agency objective.

While a three by three matrix is often used to measure the scale of risk, it should be recognized that three levels of risk represents a fairly simplistic scale. If a more precise measurement of risk is required, more levels can be used. For example, a five level matrix examines likelihood as almost certain, likely, moderate, unlikely, and rare and uses a measurement of consequence with descriptions such as catastrophic, major, moderate, minor, and insignificant. Of course there are even more complex models—suffice to say that the concept itself is relatively straightforward.

It may be that many of the risks identified by a border agency will already have controls in place to address them. Some controls might be designed to decrease the likelihood of the risk occurring; others will be intended to reduce the consequences of the event if it does occur. In either case it is important to ensure that the assessment of existing controls includes some level of verification that those controls are, in fact, in place and operating as intended. In most cases this will require some form of audit or testing. Such an evaluation enables the agency to determine whether the controls are sufficient to address the identified risks or whether they need to be strengthened or supplemented in some way. It is also possible that the evaluation highlights the fact that some controls are excessive for the risks identified and, therefore, are consuming resources that would be better allocated to a different area of risk within or outside the organization.

Risk assessment and prioritizing. Risk assessment and prioritizing involves determining whether each risk in question is acceptable or unacceptable, and, among those risks deemed unacceptable, which of them are the most important to manage.

As mentioned at the beginning of this chapter, border agencies are confronted with a multiplicity of risks and responsibilities but only have limited resources to acquit those responsibilities. In the context of the present discussion, it is axiomatic that border agencies will not be able to control all the risks that confront them. For this reason, an agency will need to decide which risks it is willing (and able) to accept, and which risks it will elect to devote resources toward treating. In this way a border agency is able to allocate valuable resources towards those issues that are going to have the greatest consequences if left unmanaged, that have the potential for the greatest results, or that have the best cost-benefit ratio.

Any identified risks deemed as unacceptable by the agency should be managed through a formal treatment plan, but even risks that are considered acceptable should be monitored and reviewed periodically to ensure that the assumptions about their acceptability remain valid. Over time a risk initially regarded as acceptable may, for any number of reasons, become unacceptable and require a treatment plan.

The reasons why a risk may be regarded as acceptable by an agency may include:
- The threat posed by the risk in question is so low that its treatment is not warranted in the context of available resources.
- The cost of treating that risk may be so high that there is no option but to accept it.
- The opportunity cost of accepting the risk may outweigh the threats posed by that risk.
- Controlling the risk is beyond the capabilities or resources of the organization.

In terms of the risk matrix approach discussed above, in most cases, risks that have a moderate or higher risk rating would normally be regarded as unacceptable, although that need not always be the case. It will always depend on the particular objectives and circumstances of the agency in question—and this statement applies equally to the opposite situation of a low risk that would normally be regarded

Table **6.1**	Risk level matrix (risk level determined by likelihood and consequence)		
	Likelihood		
Consequence	**High**	**Medium**	**Low**
High	High risk	Medium risk	Medium risk
Medium	Medium risk	Medium risk	Low risk
Low	Medium risk	Low risk	Low risk

Source: Authors' depiction.

as acceptable but, in certain cases, will have a risk treatment applied to it notwithstanding its lower ranking.

Once an agency has conducted its risk assessment process and decided which risks it must manage, the next question is which of the unacceptable risks should have higher priority given limited resources. Generally speaking, the priority ranking of a specific risk will reflect its rating within the risk matrix. However, it is not uncommon for two risks to be rated equally. If the agency has insufficient resources to address all the unacceptable risks, a decision must be made as to which of the equally rated risks is of relatively higher priority and should be addressed first.

The application of risk management to cross border issues addresses many of the concerns outlined in this chapter, but it can be further leveraged to improve border efficiency and achieve facilitation and security objectives. That is what the chapter will now discuss, before it concludes with a discussion on how the concepts are integrated into a compliance approach.

A case study of risk management appears in box 6.1.

Improving border efficiency: prearrival clearance and postclearance audit

As an adjunct to national security, border agencies are increasingly requiring the submission of advance information in respect to goods and passengers entering the country. This is about adopting a more sophisticated approach to risk management and pushing the borders further out, to create time and space within which to make a risk based decision in relation to the goods or person in question (as previously discussed).

Prearrival clearance is a process that allows a trader to submit data to a border agency early in the transport of goods, for advance processing by the border agency and immediate release of the goods once they arrive at the destination port. This release can even take place prior to the arrival of the goods if such an action is deemed appropriate by the border agency. The prearrival clearance process is particularly important for certain types of goods that are highly perishable or in some other way require prompt handling upon arrival.

Prearrival clearance is not just about facilitation, however; it is also particularly useful for the

| Box 6.1 | Case study: risk management in Cambodia |

Cambodian importers of raw materials for garment manufacture and subsequent export "are subjected to as many as 64 documentary inspections, physical goods inspections . . . [and] a requirement for over 70 signatures and 12 separate payments . . . . [and] exporters who are exporting ready-made garments . . . have to fulfil as many as 90 documentary inspections, possibly 100 signatures and 17 different formal payments, in addition to informal payments they have to make in order to get the thing done."[1]

The Royal Government of Cambodia has since introduced a comprehensive risk management approach to border management. The approach has consolidated and rationalized the requirements of government agencies involved in the inspection and clearance of goods at the border through:[2]

- Raising the level of understanding of all stakeholders—particularly the implementing agencies involved in inspection and audit—of the principles of risk management, compliance management, and information management, and assisting them in the achievement of a strategic approach to risk management and compliance management.
- Providing a framework for risk management whereby the inspection of import and export consignments is focused on high risk shipments and maintains a balance between facilitation and control.
- Developing an understanding of specific risks.

Notes

1. Penn Sovicheat, Cambodia Ministry of Commerce, speaking at the Consultative Meeting on Trade Facilitation and Regional Integration, Bangkok, August 17–18, 2006.

2. Adapted from the Inter-ministerial Prakas No. 995 on Implementation of Trade Facilitation through Risk Management, dated November 6, 2009 (legislation can be ordered through the BNGLaw Web site, http://www.bnglaw.net).

early identification of goods or persons that may pose a health or security risk to the country. Border agencies use risk profiles to aid them in assessing and analyzing the risk posed by goods or persons. A risk profile consists of a set of risk indicators, such as the type of goods, the value of goods, the origin of the goods or person, whether there has been any third country transit or transhipment, the mode of transportation, the payment type, and so on. Risk profiles are developed from data and intelligence obtained by the border agency and other law enforcement agencies and build on information obtained from previous unlawful consignments (or passengers). From a resource perspective, border agencies are establishing cargo analysis units or passenger analysis units to undertake this activity on an ongoing basis.

If these risk profiles can be applied to information obtained by the border agency at an early point in the movement of the goods or person to the destination country, an assessment of the risk posed by the goods or person can be made earlier and an intervention strategy devised accordingly. In other words, there is a benefit to government and business from the use of prearrival information, and consequently there is a more efficient overall border clearance process.

The effectiveness of this screening process is of course dependent on the receipt of advance information. In relation to goods, the emphasis is on obtaining the information as far back in the supply chain as possible in the circumstances, as noted in the discussion on some of the current supply chain security initiatives that have been implemented and the reference to the WCO SAFE Framework. In relation to passengers, the same intention applies with respect to visa processes.

The advance information process is generally supported by sophisticated database technology that makes it possible for agencies to link information from a variety of sources for subsequent analysis, and for the identification of risk flags or alerts in those data. This further speeds the risk assessment and clearance process, provided that the data quality and data management issues are managed effectively. Further discussion of border technology is beyond the scope of this chapter but appears in other chapters of this book.

Since the basis of prearrival clearance is early provision of information for immediate clearance, prearrival clearance must be combined with a capacity for the border agency to undertake more detailed analysis of the information and supporting documentation after the goods have arrived in the country. This is where the concept of postclearance audit comes into play. Audits undertaken by specialists within the relevant border agency can take a variety of forms—from random audits, for verifying compliance with regulatory requirements, to planned or leverage exercises targeting individuals or industry sectors. What they all have in common is a legislative base that provides border officers with powers to enter premises and inspect documents (physically or electronically) in relation to the border transaction, and with trained auditors to undertake those tasks.

Such audits provide border agencies with a clear picture of the transactions in question and an indication of the overall compliance rate within an industry sector. They also highlight or confirm areas of risk where additional compliance or enforcement activity may need to take place, and therefore they complete the risk management loop by producing data that can be fed back into the risk management process (including the updating of risk profiles).

The results of postclearance audits also allow for industry segmentation; in other words, they allow a border agency not only to identify potential unlawful conduct but also to identify highly compliant—and therefore low risk—traders and travelers. Such entities can then be granted fast track permissions or simplified procedures (or both) that contribute to facilitation outcomes while reducing the costs to government that are associated with border congestion. This concept has been given the label of authorized trader programs with respect to goods, and in relation to passenger traffic it is reflected in initiatives (such as Smartgate in Australia) that allow expedited clearance at airports linked to biometric passports.

A case study of information sharing for border security and law enforcement is in box 6.2.

Implementing risk based compliance management

As discussed, a risk management approach to border management is characterized by the early

---

identification of potential risks, with resources being directed towards high risk areas and as little intervention as possible in similarly identified low risk areas. Such an approach permits immediate clearance or even prearrival clearance of goods and the rapid movement of goods and people through ports and airports, thereby providing an effectively controlled environment that supports an appropriate balance between facilitation and regulatory intervention.

The integration of these core border management disciplines into a broader risk based compliance framework, however, requires an understanding and application of several other components additional to risk management. These components (including risk management) can be broadly grouped as follows (Widdowson 2003):

- Legislative framework.
- Administrative framework.
- Risk management framework.
- Technology framework.

Collectively the four components represent key determinants of the manner in which the movement of goods and people may be expedited across a country's borders and the way in which border controls can be implemented with respect to that movement.

This chapter has already discussed risk management frameworks at some length, and other chapters discuss the issue of border technology, so this chapter does not propose to deal with those areas. Yet it is important to discuss some of the issues that arise with respect to legal and administrative frameworks underpinning a risk based compliance approach to border management.

The risk based compliance management pyramid (figure 6.3) illustrates a structured approach to the management of compliance at the border. It provides a logical framework for demonstrating the way in which various types of risk based strategies, including nonenforcement strategies such as self assessment, can be used to effectively manage compliance.

Legislative framework

The charter of any border agency is to ensure compliance with the law. Consequently, the foundation for any effective border management regime must be the establishment of an appropriate legislative framework. This framework must provide the necessary basis in law for the achievement of the range of administrative and risk management strategies that the border agency has chosen to adopt. For example, an appropriate basis in law must exist to enable the agency to allow an importer to self assess its compliance with border regulations.

A transparent and predictable legal framework is essential to ensure that those who are the subject of regulation know what the rules are. If they don't know what the rules are, how can they be expected to comply? While ignorance of the law may be no excuse, poorly drafted or unpublicized laws explain many instances of noncompliance, and therefore various regulatory authorities, including border agencies, are increasingly realizing the need to provide meaningful advice to those who are being regulated. The result, often referred to as a policy of *informed compliance*, involves the use of a range of client service initiatives that are designed to ensure that regulatory requirements are properly understood by the regulated community.

Most theories of compliance, particularly those that can be described as normative theories, adopt a

---

The Schengen Information System is a secure government database that contains information related to border security and law enforcement. The information is shared among the participating countries: France, Belgium, Germany, the Netherlands, Luxembourg, Spain, Portugal, Italy, Austria, Greece, Finland, Sweden, Switzerland, Denmark, Iceland, Norway, Estonia, the Czech Republic, Hungary, Latvia, Lithuania, Malta, Poland, Slovakia, and Slovenia. Ireland and the United Kingdom also have access for law enforcement purposes despite not being signatories to the Schengen Agreement Application Convention, which underpins the system.

Information is stored in the database in accordance with the legislation of each country and is legally recognized by each participant country. It is permanently connected to the various national databases to facilitate real time updating.

Source: Adapted from "Schengen Information System II," European Union, http://europa.eu/legislation_summaries/other/l33183_en.htm.

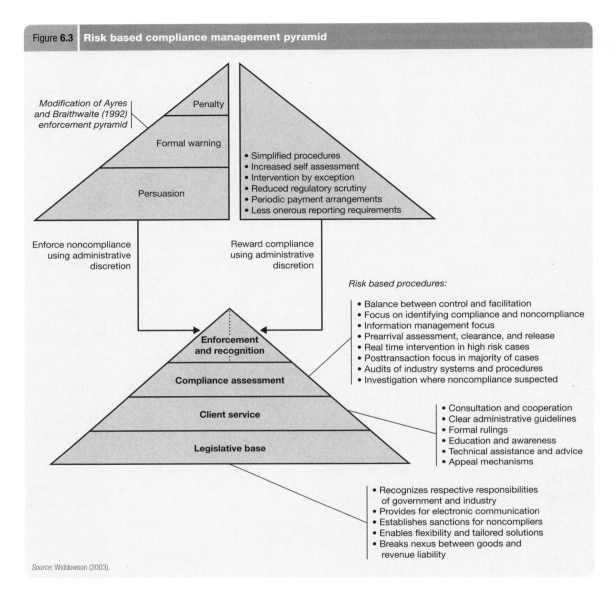

Figure **6.3** Risk based compliance management pyramid

Modification of Ayres and Braithwaite (1992) enforcement pyramid

Penalty

Formal warning

Persuasion

- Simplified procedures
- Increased self assessment
- Intervention by exception
- Reduced regulatory scrutiny
- Periodic payment arrangements
- Less onerous reporting requirements

Enforce noncompliance using administrative discretion

Reward compliance using administrative discretion

Risk based procedures:

- Balance between control and facilitation
- Focus on identifying compliance and noncompliance
- Information management focus
- Prearrival assessment, clearance, and release
- Real time intervention in high risk cases
- Posttransaction focus in majority of cases
- Audits of industry systems and procedures
- Investigation where noncompliance suspected

Enforcement and recognition

Compliance assessment

Client service

Legislative base

- Consultation and cooperation
- Clear administrative guidelines
- Formal rulings
- Education and awareness
- Technical assistance and advice
- Appeal mechanisms

- Recognizes respective responsibilities of government and industry
- Provides for electronic communication
- Establishes sanctions for noncompliers
- Enables flexibility and tailored solutions
- Breaks nexus between goods and revenue liability

Source: Widdowson (2003).

philosophy of appropriateness: that is, the subjects of regulation are assumed to act in good faith and to want to obey the law. Such theories will state as their assumption that compliance or noncompliance is affected principally by the capacity of the entity being regulated, in terms of its knowledge of the laws and its financial and technological ability to comply. For that reason, the best approach is a cooperative one.

Strategies that follow that theory will provide members of the public with the means to achieve certainty and clarity, identify their rights and responsibilities, and assess their liabilities and entitlements. Such strategies include:

- Consultation and cooperation.
- Clear administrative guidelines.

- Formal rulings.
- Education and awareness.
- Technical assistance and advice.
- Appeal mechanisms.

In contrast, a more rationalist theory of compliance tends to encourage more prescriptive approaches to issues of compliance and noncompliance, with the greater focus being on noncompliance and the imposition of penalties as the key mechanism for deterrence. The two competing approaches are discussed in greater detail below with respect to the administrative frameworks for border compliance.

In practice the approach adopted by most modern border agencies is a mix of both normative and rationalist approaches; in other words, it is the implementation of a compliance management system that encourages voluntary compliance while maintaining a foundation or fallback position of enforcement.

Administrative framework

There are various options available to border agencies to enable them to determine whether laws are being complied with. Those agencies that adopt the recommended risk based approach to compliance management will be selective in their use of the broad range of controls available to them, depending on the circumstances and operational objectives. In exercising this selectivity the border agency is recognizing that members of the regulated community present varying levels of risk in terms of potential noncompliance with relevant laws. For example, those with a good record of compliance are unlikely to require the same level of scrutiny as those with a history of poor compliance, as was discussed previously in the context of risk profiling.

Consequently, where an individual or company is judged by the agency to represent a relatively low risk, the level of regulatory scrutiny may be reduced, with greater reliance being placed on that person's self assessment of his or her obligations. This is a commonly used method of recognition (the right half of the peak of the compliance management pyramid in figure 6.3).

In contrast, companies and individuals considered to represent a high risk and transactions or entities for which no risk assessment has been undertaken are more likely to be selected for higher levels of intervention and control. Such intervention can take a variety of forms, but it commonly includes such activities as:

- Documentary checks.
- Physical examinations.
- Audit activity.
- Investigations.

In a high risk situation this intervention will take place at the destination border, but—as discussed—it is increasingly the case that such intervention is pushed out to the departure border. However, it is important to appreciate that in all cases the level and type of intervention should be based on the level of identified risk. As the saying goes, you don't use a sledgehammer to crack a walnut.

As highlighted above, the best practice in compliance assessment is to use advance information coupled with a postclearance audit. The options touched on earlier can now be discussed in a little more detail. There are a number of different audit approaches available to a border agency. They include desk audits, transaction based audits, and system based audits. The nature of the potential risk identified by the agency when the agency selects an individual or company for audit generally will dictate the specific approach that is adopted.

Desk audits are generally used to further examine an unusual transaction, which may fall outside established parameters or normal patterns for a particular type of company or transaction. The desk audit approach may simply involve contacting the company concerned and asking them to provide additional information to support the data declared in the transaction. For example, the auditor may call for any commercial documentation—such as invoices, contracts, and trade catalogs—to support a declared description of goods and their value.

Transaction based auditing involves testing transactions that have been identified as a potential risk. This audit approach is often suitable for use in relation to individuals or small and medium size enterprises (SMEs), where a large proportion of the company's transactions are often considered to be high risk because of the lack of volume and lack of experience in relation to border regulation of international trade. Such entities often lack the resources to maintain a dedicated compliance group to oversee border transactions and are therefore more susceptible to documentary errors and misunderstandings of the regulatory requirements. This susceptibility to errors and misunderstandings should be recognized by a border agency contemplating its approach to noncompliance, because education and outreach programs are often more effective and less costly for both regulators and the regulated than the automatic imposition of a penalty is.

There are of course situations where the volume of transactions undertaken by an individual or SME justifies a different approach, and the same can be said with respect to larger companies depending on their transaction profile.

Transaction based auditing is also justified in circumstances where a specific risk area has been identified, either as part of a company's or individual's transactions or as a specific industry or goods segment, and therefore a detailed focus on transactions is required to address the risk in question.

System based audits are a step up from transaction testing. They are used to gauge compliance levels by seeking assurance with respect to the underlying systems that are used to create those transactions. The systems based audit involves understanding an entity's business systems and, more important, testing the internal controls in those systems that have been developed to manage compliance. Compliance management systems are a modern inclusion in many enterprise systems run by larger companies, and can be quite sophisticated but are less common in SMEs— a fact that emphasizes the previous point that the particular audit or compliance approach adopted by border agencies should be tailored to the nature and circumstances of the company being audited.

As discussed previously, a corollary of modern compliance management is the importance of identifying compliant companies as well as noncompliant companies. In the past agencies have tended to ignore compliant entities or acknowledge them only in a peripheral fashion, preferring an enforcement focus on noncompliance. They have regarded numbers of prosecutions or of investigations as the only significant performance statistics, rather than asking and seeking to answer the more substantive question: "Have we improved the overall level of compliance?" In other words, the focus was on outputs rather than outcomes. While some border agencies still pursue that approach, most recognize that it is shortsighted and does not provide an effective measure for the government for the success of a particular policy objective.

This issue can be considered in a very practical way as follows: For every instance of good compliance that is identified, the population of noncompliance necessarily declines by one. When extrapolated, this principle will provide a very useful picture of where scarce resources should be concentrated and what areas can be left to their own devices (such as self assessment or coregulation programs). If the risk matrix discussed above is applied to this scenario, the conclusion can be drawn that if a significant company (such as a major importer with high transaction volumes and values) is identified as being

highly compliant, the *consequence* of potential noncompliance will reduce significantly. That is why some administrations focus their compliance assessment efforts on their top 100 companies (in terms of duty payment or volume of trade) in order to get a clearer picture of compliance levels and, in turn, of the potential impact of noncompliance.

The best practice in compliance management in the border context, or any other regulatory context, requires (in the oft quoted metaphor) both carrots and sticks. The enforcement and recognition strategies (the peak of the risk based compliance management pyramid in figure 6.3) are designed to address identified noncompliance and good compliance. Strategies for noncompliance may include a range of enforcement strategies including criminal and civil penalties or name and shame lists, while those for recognized compliers include such things as increased levels of self assessment, reduced regulatory scrutiny, less onerous reporting requirements, periodic payment arrangements, simplified procedures, and increased levels of facilitation.

This approach is reflective of what is described as a compliance improvement approach, the principal focus of which is the achievement of future compliance and ensuring that an appropriate balance exists between incentives for compliance and sanctions for noncompliance.

As previously stated, in the process of assessing the level of compliance, border agencies are going to encounter two situations—either compliance or noncompliance. In relation to noncompliance the instances of noncompliance will range from entirely innocent mistakes to blatant fraud or other intentional illegality. For those persons that are intent on breaking or circumventing the law, some form of sanction will need to apply, such as administrative penalties or, in the more severe cases, criminal prosecution and fines or imprisonment.

This sliding scale should be recognized in the tools that are used by a border agency in the management of noncompliance. In 1992 Ayres and Braithwaite illustrated a range of compliance management options by presenting them in an enforcement pyramid model (Widdowson 2003, p. 45). A copy of this pyramid, on which the upper left hand triangle of the compliance pyramid in figure 6.3 is based, is shown in figure 6.4 below.

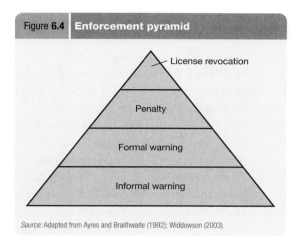

| Figure **6.4** | **Enforcement pyramid** |

License revocation

Penalty

Formal warning

Informal warning

Source: Adapted from Ayres and Braithwaite (1992); Widdowson (2003).

Ayres and Braithwaite contended that the softer style at the base of the pyramid was likely to be used most frequently by regulatory authorities, with the incidence of usage higher in the pyramid decreasing as the sanction increases in severity. It should be noted that Braithwaite developed this model in the context of mine safety and its occupational health and safety concerns. He found that in many of the serious coal mine accidents the law had been broken, either causing the accident or making the accident worse. He saw that improving compliance was an effective method of reducing the risk of accidents (Sparrow 2000, p. 41).

There are many border agencies that do not follow this noncompliance treatment model. They rarely use persuasion or warning letters as a means of dealing with noncompliance, and they focus on more substantial sanctions. Some agencies use civil or administrative penalties—such as goods seizures or infringement notices—for supposedly inadvertent errors, but this is by no means a universal practice.

Those who are tempted to engage in noncompliance on an intentional basis will temper their behaviors according to the probability of detection and the severity of punishment if detected and convicted. Therefore, deterrence of noncompliance can be increased by either raising sanctions (increasing the quantum of penalties or adding imprisonment as a possible sanction) or increasing monitoring activities (postclearance audits) to raise the likelihood that noncompliance will be detected and the offender caught and prosecuted. Theories of deterrence postulate that deterrence is successful where there is a credible likelihood of detecting violations; swift,

certain, and appropriate sanctions upon detection; and a perception among those who are being regulated that these detection and sanction elements are present in the applicable compliance regime.

Again, it must be emphasized that the strategy adopted to deal with noncompliance and to encourage future compliance should depend on the particular circumstances pertaining to that noncompliance and the associated risks. For example, unless an error in a declaration is found to be intentional, it may be more appropriate and cost effective to address the error as systemic; to provide the individual, company, or industry sector with advice and assistance on compliance issues; or to provide formal clarification of the law through government notices, binding rulings, or some other means. This acknowledges that a different treatment will be needed to deal with honest mistakes on the one hand and deliberate cases of noncompliance on the other. Industry familiarization seminars and information brochures may adequately address errors that result from a lack of understanding of the relevant regulatory provisions. However, if someone is actively seeking to commit fraud, seminars and information brochures will have absolutely no impact on their activities. Indeed, such members of the trading community are likely to have a very good understanding of their obligations and entitlements. To treat the risks posed by such individuals (or organizations for that matter), a rigorous enforcement approach is likely to be required, as stated above.

From a border agency perspective, deciding on the right mix of compliance assistance and enforcement strategies is one of the major challenges in a rapidly evolving trade and travel environment that represents varied industry sectors and demographics. How much financial and human resource should be invested in particular strategies, and what will be the most cost effective means of ensuring compliance? Once again, this is where risk management provides significant value added, allowing border agencies to see what are the greatest risks and consequences.

Future trends and conclusions

Contemporary border agencies have now evolved well beyond their historical image as gatekeepers, becoming organizations that are versatile and focused on outcomes (Widdowson 2006). They are rapidly moving away from an approach that manages transactions to one that takes a customer based (account management) view and extends that view as far upstream and downstream in the transport and supply chain as is possible with available data. Through better understanding of customer segments and the risks they represent to effective border management, agencies can be more transparent and predictable in their decisionmaking and in turn can make the best and most productive use of their scarce resources by allocating them to high risk issues while facilitating low risk transactions through the adoption of authorized trader programs and equivalent value added services. Risk management, supported by advances in information and communications technology, is the mechanism by which border agencies are able to have this broader perspective concerning their customers, whether the customers are individuals or companies.

The authors predict that there will continue to be a shift away from more direct regulation to a catalog of alternative strategies, and that these alternative strategies, as far as possible, will emphasize voluntary compliance and self assessment and working with other border agencies and the private sector to achieve border regulation objectives—collaborative border management—while underpinning these strategies with robust enforcement mechanisms.[3] In this context it is worth noting findings in OECD studies that indicate that many tax administrations allocate more than 40 percent of their staffing budgets to enforcement activities (OECD 2008)—meaning that direct and prescriptive regulation comes at a considerable cost, as opposed to achieving voluntary compliance.

At the end of the day, border agencies and the trading and traveling communities are seeking greater certainty when it comes to risk and compliance management, and approaches that can produce such an outcome will garner broad support from governments, the private sector, and the public at large.

Notes

1. SITPRO Limited (its initials derived initially from Simpler Trade Procedures Board) is a United Kingdom nondepartmental public body focused on the removal of barriers to international trade through the simplification and harmonization of trade procedures. See "About SITPRO: The Premier Trade Facilitation Agency," SITPRO, http://www. sitpro.org.uk/about/index.html.

2. See "World Tourism Barometer," United Nations World Tourism Organization, http:// www.unwto.org/facts/eng/barometer.htm.

3. As an example, albeit in relation to environmental policy, the Minnesota Environmental Improvement Act 1995 encourages SMEs to self inspect and report results to the state regulator by offering (limited) statutory protection from enforcement action. Similar voluntary disclosure approaches have been adopted by some border agencies and are a characteristic of United States export control laws.

References

Arvis, J., M. Mustra, J. Panzer, L. Ojala, and T. Naula. 2007. *Connecting to Compete 2007: Trade Logistics in the Global Economy.* Washington, DC: The World Bank.

Arvis, J., M. Mustra, L. Ojala, B. Shepherd, and D. Saslavsky. 2010. *Connecting to Compete 2010: Trade Logistics in the Global Economy.* Washington, DC: The World Bank.

Ayres, I., and J. Braithwaite. 1992. *Responsive Regulation: Transcending the Deregulation Debate.* New York: Oxford University Press.

Holloway, S. 2009. "The Transition from eCustoms to eBorder Management." *World Customs Journal* 3 (1): 13–25.

IOM (International Organization for Migration). 2005. *World Migration 2005: Costs and Benefits of International Migration.* Washington, DC: IOM.

———. 2008. *World Migration Report 2008: Managing Labour Mobility in the Evolving Global Economy.* Washington, DC: IOM.

OECD (Organisation for Economic Co-operation and Development). 2008. "Management-based Regulation: Implications for Public Policy." Document GOV/PGC/REG(2008)5, OECD, Paris.

Core border management disciplines: risk based compliance management

6

Ratha, D., S. Mohapatra, K.M. Vijayalakshmi, and Z. Xu. 2008. "Revisions to Remittance Trends 2007." Migration and Development Brief 5, Migration and Remittances Team, Development Prospects Group, The World Bank, Washington, DC, July 10. Available at http://siteresources.worldbank.org/INTPROSPECTS/Resources/334934-1110315015165/MD_Brief5.pdf.

SITPRO. 2008. "The Cost of Paper in the Supply Chain: 'Project Hermes' Perishable Goods Sector Research." London: SITPRO.

Sparrow, M.K. 2000. *The Regulatory Craft: Controlling Risks, Solving Problems, and Managing Compliance.* Washington, DC: Brookings Institution Press.

UNCTAD (United Nations Conference on Trade and Development). 2006. "ICT Solutions to Facilitate Trade at Border Crossings and in Ports." Document TD/B/COM.3/EM.27/2, UNCTAD, Geneva.

WCO (World Customs Organization). 2008. *Customs in the 21st Century: Enhancing Growth and Development through Trade Facilitation and Border Security.* Brussels: WCO.

WEF (World Economic Forum). 2008. *The Global Enabling Trade Report.* Davos: WEF.

Widdowson, D. 2003. "Intervention by Exception: A Study of the Use of Risk Management by Customs Authorities in the International Trading Environment." University of Canberra, Canberra.

———. 2006. "Raising the Portcullis." Paper presented at the WCO Conference on Developing the Relationship between WCO, Universities and Research Establishments, Brussels, March.

———. 2007. "The Changing Role of Customs: Evolution or Revolution?" *World Customs Journal* 1 (1): 31–37.

Wilson, J.S., C.L. Mann, and T. Otsuki. 2005. "Assessing the Benefits of Trade Facilitation: A Global Perspective." *The World Economy* 28 (6): 841–71.

6

Core border management disciplines: risk based compliance management

CHAPTER 7

Information and communications technology and modern border management

Tom Doyle

Effective information and communications technology (ICT) can help achieve business objectives and drive world class border agency performance. However, ICT alone offers no magic modernization solutions. Successful ICT merely enables modernization and improved performance. The most effective modernization programs address policy, process, and people issues—and then use ICT as an enabler to achieve the agency's mission and vision.

This chapter, focusing on the importance of ICT to modern border management, is not a technical manual for ICT professionals. Rather, it presents:

- An overview of the role of ICT in border management reform and modernization.
- A discussion of lessons learned and critical success factors.
- An outline of five steps to successful implementation.

Background

Border management agencies have long been seen as the collective stewards of the nations' trade and borders. Today, however, these agencies are experiencing unprecedented pressure, with a simultaneous impact on many fronts. Border management agencies are required to perform at the highest levels of efficiency and effectiveness—to collect revenues due to the state, to protect the safety of the community, to facilitate legitimate trade, and to encourage economic development.

Today the trading community uses just-in-time supply chains to maximize competitive advantage, and it demands that border management agencies do not disrupt those chains. Likewise, governments look to border management agencies to lower the cost of doing business and to enable firms to compete globally. In an environment where lowering trader costs can make the difference between success and failure, even the smallest process driven ICT improvement can give traders a competitive edge over firms in other countries.

The focus of border management reform is almost always on enabling border management agencies to fulfill their regulatory roles and responsibilities in ways that are more transparent and friendly to business. Agencies look to ICT for tools to maximize performance and to provide the high assurance demanded by private and public stakeholders.

To put new ICT in place successfully, a border management agency must:

- Secure the political and financial commitment to develop its vision and transformation program.
- Realistically assess its administrative capacity for delivering the vision.

- Select the right partners to support change.
- Continue to evolve and align business and technical strategies in a way that demonstrates the value of collaborative border management to their stakeholders.

The good news is that border management agencies in both the developed and developing world can take advantage of existing and emerging strategies and can access and share experience and good practice approaches. There should be few incentives to reinvent the ICT wheel when information is available about what works, what doesn't, and why. The challenge is to learn from current best practice and create solutions that are innovative, flexible, and scalable. All reformers and policymakers need to understand what these terms mean and how they affect a choice of ICT solutions.

This chapter should be read in conjunction with chapter 8 on national single window systems, chapter 9 on ICT procurement, and chapter 15 on the evolution of customs ICT regionally (with the European Union as a case study).

Information and communications technology for border agencies: past and future

The following section overviews the ICT used by border management agencies since the 1980s and considers its likely evolution through 2020. Agencies can use this information to assess their ICT maturity against past developments and probable future trends. Concomitant changes in the direction of border management agencies are shown in figure 7.1.[1]

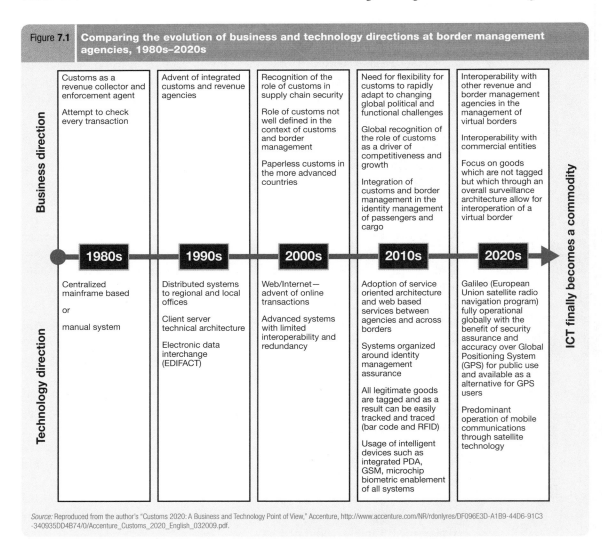

Figure 7.1   Comparing the evolution of business and technology directions at border management agencies, 1980s–2020s

Business direction

1980s
Customs as a revenue collector and enforcement agent

Attempt to check every transaction

1990s
Advent of integrated customs and revenue agencies

2000s
Recognition of the role of customs in supply chain security

Role of customs not well defined in the context of customs and border management

Paperless customs in the more advanced countries

2010s
Need for flexibility for customs to rapidly adapt to changing global political and functional challenges

Global recognition of the role of customs as a driver of competitiveness and growth

Integration of customs and border management in the identity management of passengers and cargo

2020s
Interoperability with other revenue and border management agencies in the management of virtual borders

Interoperability with commercial entities

Focus on goods which are not tagged but which through an overall surveillance architecture allow for interoperation of a virtual border

ICT finally becomes a commodity

Technology direction

1980s
Centralized mainframe based

or

manual system

1990s
Distributed systems to regional and local offices

Client server technical architecture

Electronic data interchange (EDIFACT)

2000s
Web/Internet— advent of online transactions

Advanced systems with limited interoperability and redundancy

2010s
Adoption of service oriented architecture and web based services between agencies and across borders

Systems organized around identity management assurance

All legitimate goods are tagged and as a result can be easily tracked and traced (bar code and RFID)

Usage of intelligent devices such as integrated PDA, GSM, microchip biometric enablement of all systems

2020s
Galileo (European Union satellite radio navigation program) fully operational globally with the benefit of security assurance and accuracy over Global Positioning System (GPS) for public use and available as a alternative for GPS users

Predominant operation of mobile communications through satellite technology

Source: Reproduced from the author's "Customs 2020: A Business and Technology Point of View," Accenture, http://www.accenture.com/NR/rdonlyres/DF096E3D-A1B9-44D6-91C3 -340935DD4B74/0/Accenture_Customs_2020_English_032009.pdf.

In the 1980s business ICT systems—including many used by border management agencies—were primarily silo based, running on centralized mainframes and with business applications and databases housed in a central data center. The hardware and programming skills required were beyond the reach of many developing countries, so smaller border management systems were developed for standalone personal computers. In the 1990s an improved ability to link systems and applications allowed capabilities originally available only on mainframe applications to be made available over faster networks in regional and local offices—a considerable step forward. There were improvements to technical architectures and significant improvements in electronic data interchange, allowing information sharing, which sped up the processing of people and cargo.

In the 2000s further developments in electronic data interchange—and the Internet—allowed customs and border agencies to move more transactions online. Web technologies improved information sharing, typically within agencies, easing data access. Agencies could now more effectively gather and share intelligence. However, many of the systems developed were agency specific and not often interoperable with other agencies' systems. In addition, though systems allowed for the collection of huge amounts of data, agencies' ability to manage and analyze this data for better border management was limited, in part because of their silo based mentality. Collaborative border management (chapter 2) requires a radically different approach.

The 2010s will bring an increasing amount of activity online. Equally important, developments in technology will allow system interoperability, promoting greater sharing of information and intelligence not just within agencies, but across a wide range of stakeholders (for example, other national government departments, border management agencies in other countries, and traders and their agents). Border management agencies will adopt web based services and service oriented architecture[2] to make services interoperable for various business domains. Identity management, remaining a key common component, will include biometric identification and identity verification. Barcode and radio frequency identification (RFID) tags will be further developed to track and trace legitimate goods.

Intelligent and mobile devices, such as integrated personal digital assistants, global systems for mobile communications (GSM), and global positioning services (GPS) will further new applications. Business system processes, supporting services, and ICT applications will be more responsive to changes in the global economy. State of the art ICT will be key to achieving required growth and competitiveness nationally, regionally, and internationally. Also noteworthy will be the emerging ICT and systems requirements for dangerous goods and supply chain security initiatives.

Thanks to the latest technological evolutions, such as service orientation architectures,[3] services orchestration within a coordinated process map has become more accessible. Improved services and new ones have become faster and easier to deliver. Collaboration across departments has become technically more feasible. In summary, sharing of effort across different agencies, countries, regions, and around the world on common processes is now constrained only by the need for prior agreement and genuine goodwill.

One of the key lessons learned over 1980–2010 concerns the decision whether to develop a bespoke or custom build solution or to adopt a commercial off the shelf solution. (Hybrid approaches also exist.) The choice depends mainly on the business context and on an agency's confidence and competence in ICT systems management.

- A bespoke (custom build) solution is more likely for a nonstandard or highly specialized business environment, or for an agency with confidence in its ICT capacity—or, all too often, because of national pride or national security considerations.
- A commercial off the shelf solution—modeled after other similar systems and based on widely agreed standard procedural models—is likely for a standard business environment or for an agency with less confidence in its ICT capacity. A standard business environment allows more reuse of ICT solutions, offers greater fit, and it favors the application of ICT standards and international agreed procedures. Commercial off the shelf solutions are more likely if confidence in the agency's ICT capacity is low, if its in-house ICT competence is limited, or if its history with ICT is thin.

In the end the choice is likely to be governed by the agency's procurement policy—and by the availability of proven commercial off the shelf solutions.

Other considerations in the choice between bespoke and commercial off the shelf solutions include, first, the difficulty and complexity of interface development, and, second, commercial considerations (such as a license fee) for commercial off the shelf products. A determining factor may be the presence of development constraints, such as local demands to comply with existing operating systems, current applications, development methods, or vendors. A proper application of standards and interoperability principles can help to overcome such technical concerns, which are becoming less valid with time.

Often a strong belief in the uniqueness of national border management operations gives rise to the view that a commercial off the shelf solution cannot fit a country's border environment. Border management agencies may be unwilling to make the procedural adjustments required by a commercial off the shelf product. Such objections may be weighed against the benefits to international operators: without commercial off the shelf solutions, operators must adjust their documentation to many countries' needs. Ultimately the choice of solution, however critical, is primarily a decision about procurement (see chapter 9) and not deployment.

Making information and communications technology work for border management: critical success factors

The experiences of border agencies with ICT programs since the 1980s reveal 12 critical success factors. They are:

- *An aligned legal and regulatory framework.* A modern legal and regulatory basis needs to be in place before any ICT design or implementation. The time needed for regulatory or legislative change can easily exceed the time needed to develop new systems, so it is important make the two overlap: for example, time used to prepare amendments to laws may also be used for prototyping and testing ICT prior to system design or even procurement. Because regulatory change may have unforeseen outcomes that then require new processes, a close relationship between

regulators and technologists during this process is desirable (though in practice uncommon).

- *Clarity about business outcomes.* Business outcomes are not always well described before or during ICT program design, which can result in poor service delivery. Service level agreements with key dependent partners and stakeholders should be defined and agreed on as early as possible in ICT program planning. It is important to align the envisioned business outcomes with overall outcomes in the agency's vision and strategy.
- *Effective governance.* A governance model, setting out the roles and responsibilities of stakeholders, must be established. If the decisionmaking process and procedures for issue escalation are not established and rigorously followed, a loss of direction can ensue—wasting time, raising costs, and delaying the delivery of required benefits.
- *Specific ICT policy issues.* Further ICT policy issues arise with newer border management systems because the systems often involve more than one government agency, each silo based and each with different policies (if any) for such things as security and identity management. Policies might need to be mutually agreed on for issues including:
  - Privacy.
  - Identity management.
  - Security.
  - Accessibility and digital inclusion.
  - Intellectual property rights.
  - Standards and interoperability.
  - Governance, architecture, and procurement.
  - Green computing.
  - Social networking.
- *A robust business case.* A robust business case is often essential to securing the necessary political backing, investment, and resources for an ICT development. Business cases for ICT investments often have relied on a traditional cost-benefit analysis (see chapter 5). Information on cost is often readily available. More difficult is to quantify the benefits and project an accurate return on the investment—many benefits are not quantifiable in monetary terms. An ICT program may increase trader education and

compliance, improve performance management for staff, and enhance collaboration with other agencies and stakeholders. A suitable business case will combine an analysis of the investment required with a wider view of both quantitative and qualitative benefits.

- *Operational aspects.* Who does what? How is it financed? Though critical, the answers to these questions are not always well articulated and agreed on before a program starts. If the lead time necessary for a complete analysis of delivery model and procurement options is not allowed, unplanned financial and time constraints can result, making deployment, operation, and the cost of delivery problematic.
- *Business process efficiency.* An important factor in the most successful ICT programs is the link to business process efficiency. Experience suggests that any program lacking a complementary project to review and align the processes in an organization will generally fail, requiring users to work around incompatibilities to operate a shadow or backup system. Without exception, an initial review of existing business processes should inform the design of required business processes, so that the new ICT system will in turn be designed to enable the new processes.
- *Change management.* A retrospective view of ICT program deployment reveals that most project managers, if they were starting their program again, would have invested more in change management. A change management program should consider required changes in behavior, support the required training and learning, and help with role and job design and restructuring.
- *Organization performance.* The design and implementation of any new ICT program requires competent and skilled support resources. Organization and human resource management are critical. Success metrics (generally referred to as key performance indicators), which measure operational efficiencies and improvements, need to be determined at the start of a program and then gathered and monitored during implementation and operation. Regular progress reporting, using concise and accurate measures, must ensure that both the client management and those who put

the program in place have the right information to make decisions on intervention.

- *Interoperability.* As effective border management increasingly relies on sharing information and intelligence among varied stakeholders (including those based outside the home nation), interoperability is increasingly required. Developments such as systems oriented architecture improve the ability to link existing systems. Future ICT systems must allow secure links to other national and international systems.
- *Data privacy and protection.* Privacy and protection become even more important as the demand grows for more data sharing, data reuse, and adherence to national and international data protection legislation.
- *Standards and frameworks.* Success requires the application of standards to ICT system design, development, and implementation approach and methodology. All too often ICT developments, particularly when custom built, result in poor service and high costs because process, data and interchange standards were not applied.

Expected benefits

The benefits from border management ICT are achieved over time, as features are introduced and as the agency and its partners adapt to the change. Developing nations especially need to keep a close eye on benefits' realization. Foreseen benefits should be reviewed at set intervals.

Typically the expected benefits for a nation moving toward collaborative border management (chapter 2) are, first, increased efficiency from increased control, and, second, improved administration of the border management value chain. Benefits need to be understood quantitatively and qualitatively— the qualitative ones being most essential.

The key goals of the agency must be aligned to the ICT strategy design principles and desired end state. The ICT initiative must tie into the agency's modernization objectives—for example, national community and economy protection and the facilitation of legitimate trade. The categories of people, process, and technology can be used to classify some of the main benefits that a border

Information and communications technology and modern border management

management ICT program might be expected to bring (table 7.1).

Not all benefits realized from an implementation will be tangible or measurable. Agency leadership must buy into the intangible benefits and understand that they will not hurt the traditionally paramount bottom line. Particularly relevant to customs, these intangible benefits will be felt on both small and large economic scales (for example, through a decrease in the smuggling of scarce natural resources). While the intangible benefits are not as easily classified as the tangible ones are (see table 7.1), they can be glimpsed in the following list (which is not exhaustive):

- Improved confidence in the agency's border control and safety.
- Improved consumer safety and protection.
- Increased foreign direct investment.
- Reduced circulation of narcotics, dangerous, counterfeit, contraband, and prohibited goods.

Clearly the benefits will vary from agency to agency and with national priorities. Developing nations typically will aim to achieve process stability and efficiency, whereas organizations with mature ICT will fine tune their solutions to further realize the intangible benefits. However, the expected benefits should not drive system design, but should flow naturally from it as its end product.

Steps to modernization

An ICT modernization program has six key aspects. To deliver on all six, high level steps are required.

Those steps are set out in table 7.2, with a summary of typical activities at each step and a set of the outcomes expected from each.

Step 1. Vision, mandate, and desired outcomes

The starting point for any border management ICT program should be a definition of how the program contributes to the future vision of the agency. Policy documents explain how the government understands user needs and requirements and how it proposes to address them. A multiannual strategic plan (3–5 years) explains how the vision can be achieved over one or several successive plans. These documents, agreed at the board level within agencies, provide the program direction and mandate. The strategic plan should be reviewed annually (or at the discretion of the executive committee), and it should be further developed in annual work programs—programs that proposed an approach to putting common building blocks, common services, or specific service delivery capabilities in place.

The definition of desired outcomes, also important at the beginning, should align to the agency's desired overall outcomes, including:

- *Efficiency.* Making the best use of agency resources and continually ensuring that people, processes, and technology are aligned to provide cost effective services to customers and citizens.
- *Transparency.* Being trusted by all agency stakeholders, adopting processes and technology to eliminate corruption, instilling transparency

Table **7.1**	Benefits that might be expected from a border management ICT program	
Category	**Qualitative benefits**	**Quantitative benefits**
People	• Ability to cope with increasing trade volumes • Improved performance management capability • Increased capacity to partake in value adding work functions • Buy-in to a realizable career model • Increased trader trust and education	• Percentage increase in redeployment opportunities • Percentage increase in trusted traders
Process	• Reduction in manual administration and non value adding activities • Faster transaction turnaround times • Reduction in compliance control activities and processes that are not intelligence based • Decreased fraud inherent to the incumbent systems	• Percentage of automated activities • Monetary benefit realized through implementation of more efficient methodologies
Technology	• Ability to build on a scalable border management solution • Accurate performance metrics and reporting • Improved collaboration and interoperability with other border agencies and related organizations	• Reduced cost for future development, thanks to consolidated development platform • Return on investment due to benefits attributed to technology

Source: Author's construction.

Table 7.2 **Six aspects of ICT modernization: steps, typical activities, and expected outcomes**

Aspect of modernization (high level step)	Typical activities	Expected outcomes
1. Vision, mandate, and desired outcomes	• Construct a robust business case • Define green paper • Conduct information technology diagnostic	• Communication of vision and mission • Buy-in • Policy documents
2. Blueprint	• Analyze challenges and constraints faced by the program • Produce a high level, functional solution design • Draft an overall roadmap for the program	• Business process, training, application, and technology blueprint
3. Operating model	• Agree on the business areas to be affected • Define the key business capabilities required for the solution • Define and set out the required operating model	• Logical operating model
4. Business architecture	• Produce the business process design • Do a capability assessment • Conduct change management	• Logical business process model
5. Technical architecture	• Define the key technical areas linked to the business processes and system requirements	• ICT diagnostic of current baseline • Business and system requirements • Business and system processes • Organization design
6. Deployment	• Deploy the program in phases	• On time delivery of program, with required outcomes achieved • Functional design documents • System interface design • Technical specification documentation (such as an application service oriented architecture definition) • Technical architecture • Systems implementation blueprint • Testing approach

Source: Author's construction.

and integrity in staff through a world class human capital program.

• *Accuracy.* Supporting a culture of getting things right the first time—with processes and technologies that enable precise decisions related to examination, tariff, investigation, payments, and so forth.

• *Integration.* Working effectively with internal and external agencies to deliver efficient, transparent, and accurate services to customers and citizens, with a focus on interoperability, partnering, and joint outcomes.

Step 2. Blueprint

The blueprint step includes most diagnostic work, planning (including milestone planning), and resource scoping. Typically used to determine the inefficiencies in the present state and the value added future state, a blueprint ordinarily involves:

• Obtaining a high level understanding of present and future business and ICT needs.

• Confirming high level business requirements with business stakeholders.

• Mapping the present organizational structure.

• Confirming the present technology infrastructure.

• Documenting the present situation, including business capabilities, the high level technology architecture, the high level technology infrastructure, and organization model requirements.

• Developing a model of the future state, defining the high level business capabilities to be supported, a support service delivery model, an organization and resource model, and the high level technology development, architecture, and infrastructure.

Step 3. Operating model

An operating model schematizes the relationship between all program areas, showing how the program is organized and how it operates across both business and technology aspects. An effective operating model enables an ICT program to deliver the required benefits—ensuring the ICT components are working effectively with the rest of the organization—and it shows the interfaces with external stakeholders. The clear link from the operating model to the process flows used to run and deliver the program is discussed further under step 4.

An important mechanism for dialogue between business and ICT, the operating model is critical in creating the basis for ICT projects that support the overall goals of the organization.

Step 4. Business architecture

The business (or enterprise) architecture must include detailed processes—captured in an overall process model—and a clear view of required roles, responsibilities, and capabilities. The process model is key to business communication. A clear understanding of all processes in the proposed architecture is critical to identifying independencies among processes and data requirements, and it can provide a strong basis for rationalizing particular business processes and data requirements. A process model can be further detailed as a matrix, with a column for each area process and a row for each process across areas. Such a matrix displays,

for example, the relationship that trader management (a horizontal process across areas) would have on risk assessment at the border (a vertical area process). Process models can be further detailed and strengthened through close collaboration with the consulting and software industries, which also have process models based on many clients' specific experiences.

Required roles, responsibilities, and capabilities can be represented partially in a diagram of principal players.

The business architecture also must specify capabilities and business processes required to give the program the highest possible value and impact.

Step 5. Technical architecture

A first layer of system functional rollout represents the logical order in which functionalities will be introduced. Technical preparation includes analysis, system design, and system build or configuration. Every technical delivery should be tested according to a solid testing methodology, from component testing to product testing, integration testing, performance testing, and finally user acceptance testing. A technical architecture is mapped in figure 7.2.

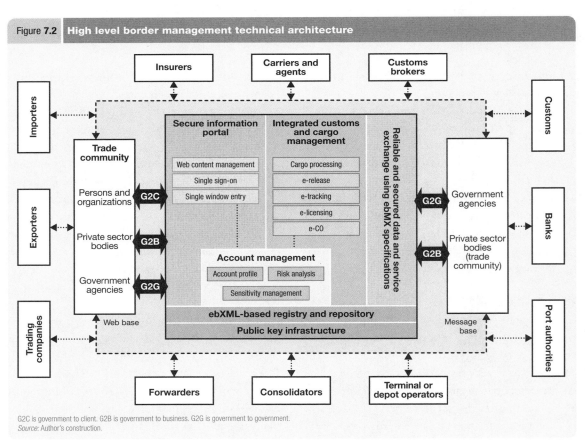

Figure **7.2** **High level border management technical architecture**

G2C is government to client. G2B is government to business. G2G is government to government.
Source: Author's construction.

Information and communications technology and modern border management

Step 6. Deployment

Deployment is planned in phases, one for each functional group and activity area defined on the transformation roadmap (chapter 2). Principles for the phased plan are:

- Each phase of deployment must deliver value to the operational environment as well as to trade.
- Operational deployment need not be tied or linked to system functional rollout.
- Organizational change capacity and capability are key success factors for a large, complex collaborative system.

A typical deployment plan used in ICT programs for border management agencies is set out in figure 7.3.

Conclusion

This chapter, in discussing successful ICT modernization for border management agencies, has emphasized that ICT is not in itself a solution but an enabler for wider agency modernization.

Effective governance, organization, and alignment of ICT programs must be ensured. Effective implementation does not start with system or vendor selection, but with a view of how ICT can enable an agency to better achieve its vision and required outcomes. The end of effective implementation is not pressing the button to go live, but being able to ensure that the program is consistently working to meet agency goals.

Notes

1. It should be noted, however, that the table reflects customs experience rather than that of other agencies, based on the fact that in most countries customs agencies were the first to automate.

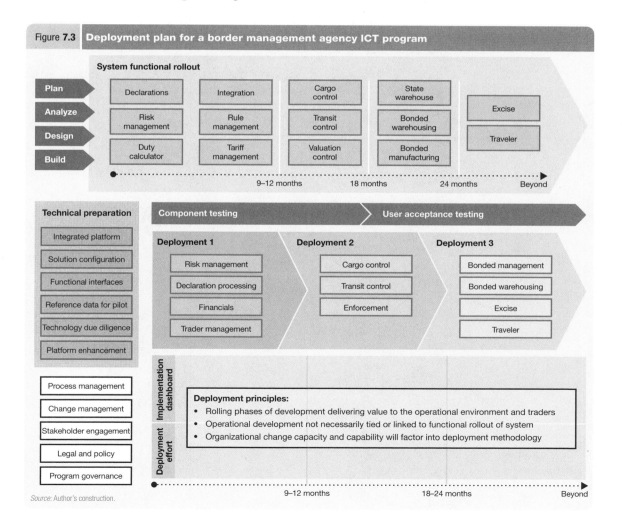

Figure 7.3 Deployment plan for a border management agency ICT program

Source: Author's construction.

Information and communications technology and modern border management

7

2. For more information see "Web Services and Service-Oriented Architectures," Barry and Associates, http://www.service-architecture.com/.

3. For more information see "The Four Tenets of Service Orientation," John Evdemon, http://www.bpminstitute.org/articles/article/article/the-four-tenets-of-service-orientation.html.

Developing a national single window: implementation issues and considerations

Ramesh Siva

At present there are no known implementations of comprehensive collaborative border management. Therefore, careful attention should be paid to the broad similarities between features of the collaborative model—its actors, processes, stakeholders, incentives, and disincentives—and those of national single window systems for trade. Such a comparison will indicate close parallels in a number of areas.

Countries in recent decades have made serious, systematic efforts to add efficiencies to trade by creating national single windows. Those that have succeeded have greatly improved their ability to compete for foreign direct investment. Other countries, especially in the developing world, have noted this correlation and have sought single windows of their own. And regional initiatives have encouraged the development of national single windows as a prerequisite to joining the regional systems (the Association of Southeast Asian Nations Single Window is an example).

Emerging knowledge and experience are beginning to identify interlinked areas that ultimately determine the success or failure of national single windows. Those same areas are critical for any effort to extend the single window concept to that of collaborative border management.

What is a national single window?

The term *national single window* is increasingly used to denote coordinated national electronic information exchanges with a focus on legislation, procedures, and information and communications technology (ICT). Such systems focus on paperless trading—for customs clearance, for license and permit approval by government agencies, and (in a few cases) for transport and logistics activities associated with cargo import, export, transit, transshipment, and border management.

National single windows have been mandated by the Association of Southeast Asian Nations, as a first step toward a regional single window to be used by all 10 of the association's member countries. The European Union plans to open its single window for all member countries by 2012. And the Asia-Pacific Economic Cooperation—which shares many members with the Association of Southeast Asian Nations—plans to open its single window for all country members around 2012–13. Other, similar intraregional (but not yet interregional) initiatives are at the planning stage.

Each of the single windows has a slightly different emphasis. The Association of Southeast Asian Nations is adopting a "your export is my import" philosophy. Europe is aiming for improved movement of goods across national borders. And the Asia-Pacific Economic Cooperation is now concentrating chiefly on supply chain security. No doubt the objectives of all these single windows—and of various followup initiatives—will converge in time.

The single window concept has broad implications for electronic government. The trade single windows mentioned above are essentially government to government, government to business, and business to business exchanges. Other single windows are aimed at a wider constituent set. For example, vehicle licensing initiatives enable citizens to renew and pay for vehicle licenses online. The major players in this type of single window may include central government agencies, commercial organizations, and local, state, or provincial organizations and companies—ministries of transport, police, insurance companies, banks and finance companies, motor dealers, and citizens—covering the business to government, business to business and business to consumer categories. Another common type of single window is the tax lodgment initiative, involving (for example) citizens, tax accountants, tax authorities, ministries of finance and treasury, and a range of social service, pension, and health authorities.

Each of these types of single window shares the collaborative features (interagency and organizational) of multiparty initiatives, linked together for a single set of objectives and covered by common policies, regulation, and legislation.

Published definitions of single windows so far have been rather vague. The most commonly quoted definition for a trade process single window, Recommendation 33 from the United Nations Centre for Trade Facilitation and Electronic Business (UN/ CEFACT 2005), is skewed toward developed countries and is considered by many practitioners to be somewhat Eurocentric. For example, it calls for the single window to be the vehicle for collecting all fees and charges levied by government agencies. Since many developing countries fund individual agencies through their trade process revenue collection mandates, the agencies' loss of control over the source of their income is unwelcome, to say the least. To succeed, collaborative systems need incentives—not disincentives.

A broadly conceived single window will cover the activities of all trade processing organizations and agencies. This starts with customs and with government licensing, inspection, and approval agencies, such as the ministries of trade, industry, economics, agriculture, health, defense, and finance—and with the subsidiary permit issuing agencies—such as those for animals, plants, and drugs. In some countries the number of separate agencies exercising inspection and approval responsibilities may exceed 20. These agencies may be considered the front office, or formalities process for trade.

The organizations involved in the physical movement of goods may then be considered the back office. These include airports, maritime ports, container terminals, road and rail terminals, and transport, logistics, and storage for goods moved by air, road, rail, and shipping (maritime, river, and waterway). Also in the back office are trade professionals, such as freight forwarders, customs brokers and shipping agents, together with the amorphous category of messengers.

Other major agencies and organizations in a national single window community include postal authorities, messenger and courier companies, nongovernment organizations, statistics organizations, trade promotion bodies, consolidators, container owners, bulk and liquid terminal and storage operators, pilots, stevedores, and, finally, importers and exporters.

With this scope, a single window must focus on organization, governance, regulation and legislation, project management, process reengineering, and change management, funding, and planning. Clearly ICT is important—but it is subsidiary to many of these other aspects. Success can take years, and change often outpaces progress. Nevertheless, putting the single window in place is an unavoidable national imperative. To try and fail is better than to fail to try.

It should now be apparent that the ideal approach to ICT for single windows is not through a single computer or closely coupled central host configuration. A centralized facility of some type is, of course, required. But the philosophy of a particular single window needs to be well thought out before any procurement is even considered. A detailed process flow analysis is needed, leading to an understanding of all major and minor trade related agencies, organizations, and processes. Then, an approach to re-engineering and change management is needed that embraces simplification, standardization, and single entry of data along with data reusability. The application of ICT to this re-engineered design will match the notional architecture, which evolves from the business process and the objectives of the single window designers.

The window design must use existing ICT assets, databases, programs, and systems as much as possible. The best designs are the most flexible—designs that limit touchpoints between the single window and other trade processing systems to the exchange of required data elements, with no redundancy in any information delivered or received.

An emerging debate in the design of ICT for single windows concerns the central facility: should it be a portal, a data switch, or a data repository? If a repository, does it have added functionality such as a customer relationship management (CRM) tool for trading partner communications? Or does it have a structured query language, or data base management system, which facilitates data mining—and if it has data mining capabilities, does it allow retrospective investigations into specific clearances and approvals (enabling a sort of cold case squad)? It has even been suggested that every single window needs a data or information ombudsman, so that systems users can become self regulating.

Design philosophy dictates governance. Single window operations traditionally have been led by customs authorities, since they are—at an early stage—the only ones to have the funds, the repository, and the data capture ability needed to establish a single window. And such efforts have normally been limited in practice to data capture by customs, for customs purposes. They have been aimed only at obtaining clean declarations. Government agency licensing and approval details normally comprise very few data elements—in some cases resulting from exhaustive processes and inspections.

Many government agencies have broader national objectives: to protect the health and welfare of the nation, to prevent the spread of dangerous diseases, to ensure the protection of national culture and wealth. To be sure, the major objective of customs—protecting the government's trade revenues—is extremely important. Nevertheless, as a nation becomes more developed, the revenue it

collects through customs will gradually decline as a proportion of its gross domestic product. Moreover, traditional roles of customs agencies are now becoming subsumed by their growing border protection duties. And government agencies' responsibilities are becoming ever more onerous, a result of the proliferation of trade and free trade agreements (some generated by the World Trade Organization, others regionally).

These developments are causing the ownership, governance, and management of single windows to move gradually toward location in a collaborative, neutral body—not under the sway of a single major trade community player. This is a controversial tendency. But recent stakeholder debates about single window governance lead inescapably to the conclusion that a successful, fully functional single window needs an autonomous, neutral, objective body to represent and to mediate among government agencies and other public and private organizations.

The ultimate objectives of a single window are:
- To increase efficiency.
- To provide an infrastructure for handling increasing trade flows.
- To support modern supply chain management techniques.
- To reduce the costs involved in international trade.

The single window aims to provide all trade related parties in a country—government agencies, commercial actors, and individuals either directly or indirectly concerned in an import or export process—with an increasingly paperless environment that reduces processing costs, improves revenue collection, and boosts compliance with regulations and laws. At the same time, the window aims to facilitate trade by keeping delays in goods receipt and delivery as low as possible.

The ability to pre-enter and preclear goods before the arrival of the ship or aircraft carrying them—including the finalization of all licensing requirements and the payment of all government fees and duties—is merely the first step in more efficient commercial cargo handling. The second and more crucial step is often described as value added services, or, as mentioned earlier, the back office function. Value added services are provided by linking or integrating the government's computerized processing system with

Developing a national single window: implementation issues and considerations

the commercial cargo handling, storage, and transport systems. No environment can be absolutely paperless—there will always be a need for original documents. Still, paper documents should represent a rare exception. For example, the personal effects of a ship's crew need to be declared on arrival in port, and the declarations are usually presented as paper documents. It would be too cumbersome to create a wholly automated system for this exception (even though, someday, a web based system is sure to emerge).

In addition to centralized computer processing and goods pre-entry and preclearance, another innovation that improves enforcement through better, more focused targeting is the risk based selection of imports and exports for document examination and physical cargo examination. Postclearance audits conducted at an importer's premises—where not only the standard documentation required by government agencies, but also all other commercial information, including banking details, should be available—can confirm the integrity of the system. In some more advanced countries such postclearance audits are carried out as close as possible to the point of sale, especially for food items. Since one of the main goals of inspection is consumer safety, postclearance audits can even be delegated to local consumer protection agencies.

Centralized computer processing and, more broadly, an electronic processing environment brings savings to government agencies, reducing the staff required to handle and file every transaction and store of documentation. It also brings savings to commercial operators, eliminating—to a great extent—multiple handling of goods and documents. That is not to say that government agencies simply reduce staff; some officers can be assigned to new functions, such as postclearance audits.

Why a single window?

Already adopted in varying degrees around the world, the single window concept is essential to modernizing import and export processes, increasing compliance with laws, more closely harmonizing the governmental and business interests in importing and exporting, and breaking down international trade barriers. In most countries companies engaged in international trade must regularly submit large volumes of information and documents to government authorities to comply with import, export, and transit regulations. Often this information and documentation must be submitted to several agencies, each with its own manual or automated system and its own paper forms. These requirements, with associated compliance costs, burden both governments and businesses. They can be a major barrier to the growth of international trade, particularly in developing countries.

A single window can make information more available, improve its handling, and simplify and expedite information flows between trade and government. It can lead to more harmonizing and sharing of data across government systems, bringing great gains to all parties involved in cross border trade. Finally, it can make official controls more efficient and effective, reducing costs for both governments and traders through better resource use.

Single windows for trade

As specified by UN/CEFACT (2005) in its Recommendation 33, a single window allows parties involved in trade and transport to lodge standardized information and documents through a single entry point to fulfill all import, export, and transit related regulatory requirements. For electronic information, each individual datum should be submitted only once. However, a single window need not necessarily use advanced ICT—even though such technology often can greatly enhance a single window.

For single windows that emphasize ICT, two complementary models are emerging.[1] One, here termed *single window lite,* limits itself to formalities or front office functions. The other, with fuller functionality, is here termed a *trade facilitation single window.* Whereas a single window lite facilitates the lodging of standardized information once to fulfill all import, export, and transit related regulatory requirements, a trade facilitation single window does so for all import, export, and transit related regulatory and commercial logistics requirements. Thus a trade facilitation single window is a more generalized data and information interchange facility, supporting not just business to government transactions but also business to business logistics related transactions. In practice such single window applications often have been called *trade nets* (for example, Singapore's TradeNet) or *trade exchanges*. Also useful in implementation is a distinction between *trade processes* and *regulatory processes*.

Alas, the creation of either type of national single window inevitably meets with policy obstacles and bureaucratic turf challenges that often compromise the window's chances of success.

Critical areas, typical impediments, and key factors in success

National single windows face many challenges beyond those typical of large and costly ICT systems. Eight critical areas for such windows can be distinguished:[2]

- The national legal and regulatory framework for trade.
- The governance model for the national single window.
- The operational model for the national single window.
- The fee structure for the national single window.
- Service level agreements for the national single window.
- Business process re-engineering and continuous change management.
- Organizational and human resource ICT management in border management agencies.
- Functional and technical architecture for the national single window.

The national legal and regulatory framework for trade

A review and analysis of the current national legal and regulatory framework for trade, and of related areas that will govern the functions and operations of the electronic national service window, is the first critical area. The legal basis for accepting electronic transactions, the legal admissibility of these transactions, and the legal ability of agencies to accept and process electronic transactions should be clearly established. The analysis should then focus on identifying gaps and impediments in laws, as well as regulations that would hamper the national single window. If gaps or other impediments are identified,

recommendations for corrective actions—including new amendments to laws and regulations, or new regulations—should be prepared, in consultation with government and other stakeholders as needed.

The legal framework for processing shipments into and out of any country is large and complex. The rules that guide or constrain different agencies are often interlinked—at times they have even been proven contradictory. Here more than in any other area, a complex and possibly confused legal and regulatory environment is the perfect cover for bureaucrats and reticent government agencies unwilling to reform or modernize.

In addition, approaches to interpreting legal frameworks for agencies vary situationally. Such interpretations may be used at times as levers for agencies getting their way. Incorporating business rules into a system is likely to show that interpretations of rules can vary regionally as well, as they do in most countries.

A common characteristic with the experience of modern public services is that a given agency will closely guard its mandate, not to execute government policy, but to preserve procedure and artifacts of procedure. The procedures' correct execution can loom large in the value system of government employees, leading them to resist change. The policy purposes of a given procedure, regulation, or law may be obscure, with desired outcomes not expressed or the link between outputs and outcomes unclear. Is the link between import processing delays and national economic performance apparent to all? Officials may cling to procedure. Such resistance is often found in moving from reliance on high rates of physical cargo examination to risk based selection for examination.

The import of goods ideally should be a single process. So should their export. The trader at present must pass through a number of agencies, each with a narrow and vertical focus resembling a stovepipe. Each agency may require complete documentation of all the steps already taken. In principle, recognizing that all prerequisites will be completed before the shipment is released—or simply acquiring the ability to verify completion of each step online—should allow all agencies to work in parallel, avoiding the need for a sequential progression through each stovepipe.

The governance model for the national single window

An operational national single window presents many public service delivery challenges. Foremost is the need to safeguard the government's ongoing policy interests in trade. Operationally, the national single window presents a highly visible, public collaboration by multiple government agencies to deliver a critical government service and so enable efficient trade. A clear governance mechanism is needed to:

- Oversee the operating entity for the national single window.
- Provide policy oversight for the national single window operating entity.
- Protect the government's policy interests in the national single window.
- Oversee the success of the national single window in meeting government policy objectives.

In addition, this governance mechanism needs to handle the following coordinating functions:

- Providing a common framework of agency regulations to achieve key needs for efficient and effective border processing of goods declared using the national single window.
- Coordinating an ongoing interagency review of regulations to ensure effectiveness, consistency, and support for modernized procedures.
- Coordinating the promulgation of agency regulations to put the framework into practice and conduct the review.
- Ensuring adequate stakeholder consultation, including in agencies and in the national single window operating entity.
- Developing a framework for monitoring new regulations to ensure consistent application of the regulatory framework and review results.
- Funding expert assistance for the regulatory review.
- Guiding agencies unable to resolve disagreements related to processing cross border shipments.

Ideally, all agencies involved in the national single window should have some representation in the governance mechanism. Similarly, various key user stakeholders (traders, shipping companies, customs brokers, freight forwarders and other private sector entities) should have some representation or advisory capability in the governance of the national single window.

The operational model for the national single window

The implementation of a national single window requires typically unprecedented cooperation and collaboration by multiple government ministries, agencies, and other statutory bodies. Every bureaucrat's instinct is to control this new beast.

The government should define potential operational models for the national single window in discussions, both internally and also with other identified stakeholders (including those in the private sector). The operational model should include everything from obtaining and establishing technology and infrastructure platforms to the management, operation, and provision of services through the national single window. Options, such as establishing public-private partnerships, state owned enterprises, or a specialized government agency—as well as other arrangements or combinations of arrangements—should be explored. International experience in such operational models, as well as comparable experiences from other sectors in the country, should be taken into account. A roster of these options should be prepared for decisionmakers' consideration. The strengths, weaknesses, and risks of each option, specifically within the national environment, should be identified.

International experience illustrates various approaches to introducing a national single window, and it is difficult to distill the best. However, strong messages emerge from the critical success factors and greatest hurdles that are presented for eight single windows in annex 8A. The success factors include commitment by all stakeholders, cooperation between agencies, government support, and information sharing. Changes in procedures and processes are also highlighted. For the service provider there are government ownership, private ownership, and public-private partnerships. The deciding factor is what works best with a country's local laws, intergovernmental relationships, and within a given trading environment.

Fee structure for the national single window

The government must define an appropriate user fee structure in consultation with individual government agencies and other stakeholders, including private sector stakeholders. International experience should be taken into account along with existing World Trade

Organization rules and disciplines (for example, under the General Agreement on Tariffs and Trade) and others that are likely to emerge. The user fee is expected to cover at least the costs of operation and maintenance, plus any incremental costs to government agencies participating in the national single window. Determining and gaining agreement on a revenue sharing model—to ensure that all participating stakeholders are reimbursed for administrative expenses incurred through participation—is key.

Service level agreements for the national single window

Critical to efficient functioning are agreed service levels. To meet the timeliness and predictability objective, a generalized framework of service levels and overall service level for the national single window need to be prepared in consultation with the window operator, participating government agencies, and other stakeholders (including in the private sector). The service level agreements developed should take into account international practices in other national single windows as well as any other interagency service level agreements for similar activities.

Service level agreements have most value when they can be monitored. A monitoring framework and methodology, to ensure that service levels are kept and bottlenecks identified, should be simultaneously developed and implemented. Monitoring and enforcement of service level agreements are critical to national single window governance.

Business process re-engineering and continual change management

One should not think of automation projects. One should think instead of modernization projects. Automation is often a given—but calling any particular improvement automation wrongly signals that the driving force will be technology and that its drivers will be the technology people. The real issue is a business issue: what needs to be done, not how. So the driving force should be business process efficiency. And the drivers should be business experts with a keen awareness of the possibilities of automation for end users.

If the leaders of business process automation are technical experts with some knowledge of the business—instead of business experts with some technical knowledge—then, in too many cases, obsolete procedures are automated; international best practices are ignored; and little or no attention is paid to management, control, human resources, and training. To avoid that outcome, business experts must first identify their requirements and desired outcomes through a diagnostic exercise, producing a scoping document that takes into account best practices. Such a document helps ICT experts design a solution, and it helps suppliers propose a delivery approach and outcomes.

The business change approach should:

- Describe the main change phases and activities for the modernization program.
- Identify key performance indicators to measure the impact of reforms.
- Outline times for each phase, including key deliverables and milestones.
- Identify dependencies among modernization program tasks.
- Estimate resources required.
- Continually communicate—to agency staff and to external stakeholders—the reform program's management expectations, present status, and successful outcomes to date.

The resulting business change management plan should mirror timescales, milestones, and deliverables in the technology plan. It should be revised, at intervals, to reflect business process definition changes and ongoing impact assessments.

Organizational and human resource management for ICT in border management agencies

Border agencies will continue to need more technically proficient ICT staff, but the nature and level of needed skills will change. As technology becomes more complex and agencies more dependent on its various types, it will no longer make sense to group all technical people under one organizational umbrella.

For traditional ICT management, two groups remain critical:

- A strategy, planning, and contracts management group—intensely business oriented and determining policy, strategy, planning, and project design—residing in the agency's planning department or reporting to the agency head (not the ICT department).

Developing a national single window: implementation issues and considerations

- A training and operational support group of systems analysts and programmers, supporting and maintaining the agencies' ICT infrastructure (software and hardware operational support may be outsourced).

The career paths of these two groups are different. The first shares the career path of high management. The second includes a subset of ICT experts, properly speaking, who are continually poached by the private sector. Unless government offers comparable salaries (an unlikely occurrence), the ICT unit must expect high rotation and offer ongoing training for new staff. Not all technical staff members will depart to the private sector. Some, such as systems analysts, project managers, and knowledge workers, will be poached by business units within the agency because working in ICT has made them understand how a business process works.

Increasingly, as ICT becomes more deeply embedded within the agency and core business functions are enabled for it, the agency will need to adjust its staffing profiles for it, with innovative recruiting, retention, and reinvigoration and training. Human resources management will need to grow to support full career personnel development across the organization while also recruiting and retaining specialized experts, such as forensic computer specialists, internal auditors, website managers, security specialists, and ICT people with customs expertise (rather than generalists).

Functional and technical architecture for the national single window

For efficiency and effectiveness in border management reform, ICT is critical. Border management agencies are challenged to ensure national security and safety, revenue collection, and trade facilitation with increasing efficiency. ICT does this by reducing as much as possible the cost, number, and duration of operations and transactions. Some border management agencies are joining forces, integrating processes, and improving the processes through automation. It is imperative that the integrity and security of the process not be sacrificed to efficiency.

Governments and their border management agencies are information consumers and information factories. There are at least five reasons why ICT will keep spreading into all aspects of border management processes:

- Governments are increasingly promoting paperless offices.
- Computers are increasingly powerful.
- Internet based technology is increasing, greatly facilitating communication.
- Software and hardware are becoming commoditized.
- Public expectations for efficient government are increasing.

On the one hand, ICT can greatly boost the effectiveness of business processes, increase control over operations, make operations more transparent, and help to block decision leakages and improve efficiency. On the other hand, ICT can discourage corruption—by reducing face to face interaction between users and government officials, by reducing arbitrary decision-making, and by increasing accountability.

What ICT cannot do is compensate for a lack of discipline, management, or control. By itself, ICT cannot improve the business process. It must be accompanied by appropriate delivery services.

National single window implementation requires an ICT platform to function seamlessly and efficiently. A clear, functional blueprint should first be developed that takes into account the needs and requirements of all stakeholders, and that becomes the primary basis for the technical architecture and system specifications. Additionally to be taken into account (as appropriate) are:

- International practices in other national single windows.
- Regional (such as the Association of Southeast Asian Nations') single window requirements.
- Industry trends in technology and infrastructure platforms.
- Technology and infrastructure environments in participating government agencies and in the country more generally.

A generalized functional specification and technical architecture are further detailed later in this chapter.

Good practice models

Which existing single windows present good practice models? Here the benchmark is whether a model comes close to meeting the definition of a single window adopted by most countries—the one proposed by UN/CEFACT (2005) and the Association of Southeast Asian Nations. It has three pillars:

- Single submission of data and information.
- Single and synchronous processing of data and information.
- Single decisionmaking for customs release and cargo clearance.

While a number of countries claim to have a national single window, very few have one as defined above—though many have programs to attain it. In many cases, especially in more advanced economies, the process involves building integration layers among agencies' existing legacy systems, which have provided electronic submission facilities to the trading community for some time. In some cases this integration involves creating seamless interfaces among existing trading and port community networks.

Thus, countries are moving toward common objectives, but in different ways dictated by their legacy systems and constraints. In the following brief summary two models have been singled out as best representing the accepted definition of a single window. Singapore's is well established. New Zealand's, which has been conceived and is being submitted for government approval, illustrates the analysis and consultation required to build the business case for a national single window.

The best model now in operation: Singapore TradeNet

Singapore's TradeNet 4.0, the current version, has become more simple, with fewer fields required to submit a permit application. Other new features include integration with TradeXchange, an electronic platform for information exchange between traders and logistics operators both in the country and internationally. TradeNet and TradeXchange are operated by CrimsonLogic PTE through a public-private partnership.

A good practice model with a business case: New Zealand's Trade Single Window project

UN/CEFACT (2005) Recommendation No. 33 guides New Zealand's Trade Single Window project, now merged with the Joint Border Management Project involving government agencies including customs and the agriculture and forestry ministry. A business analysis has been completed and possible functional and operating models evaluated. Preferred options, with a business case, were submitted to the government in October 2009. Further action depends on government funding and approval for the selected model.

Other models

Most of the countries said to have introduced, or to be introducing, a single window are well documented in case studies (UN/CEFACT 2006). But the term *single window* is loosely used to describe varying degrees of electronic data interchange, ranging from direct trader input to a single portal—one giving access to different subsystems—to simple download from a portal of forms that are then filled in and presented manually. A number of electronic facilities are still backed up by paper document submission. In most of the usually cited examples, the single window is still a goal to be attained and a work in progress.

The following brief case studies represent work in other countries by comparison with the two models above, which come closest to best practice as defined in World Customs Organization and United Nations recommendations (UN/CEFACT 2005). The examples show the incremental process of building on earlier legacy systems.

United Kingdom. The United Kingdom International Trade Single Window, launched in November 2007 to provide a single submission point for importers and exporters, does not yet do so. Customs submissions are still through the customs agency system, Customs Handling of Import/Export Freight (CHIEF). At present the International Trade Single Window gives traders a separate portal for help with import and export processes and regulations, and it contains an online tariff to assist with classification. The first online processing facility will be Automatic License Verification, allowing electronic applications for export and import licenses issued by the Department of Business, Enterprise and Regulatory Reform. The license will be sent electronically to CHIEF and the need to submit paper documents to customs will vanish. Future work will aim at single submission.

United States. The United States single window initiative is being coordinated by the International Trade Data System project, aimed at helping participating government agencies integrate with the Automated Commercial Environment (the new trade system of Customs and Border Protection). About 30 agencies are now involved. The Automated Commercial Environment provides a single entry access portal for both trade and the participating agencies. The ultimate aim is single submission but implemented at present are account management, online report requests (tracking), periodic monthly statements, and electronic manifest submission.

Australia. Australia's TradeGate provides an environment for trade and logistics operator message exchange. Importers and exporters can submit customs declarations through TradeGate's ImportNet and ExportNet modules.

In 2005 Australia implemented the Integrated Cargo System, which replaced a number of legacy systems for reporting all cargo movements to customs, expanded and strengthened automated data feeds between customs and other agencies, and now performs some verification of other government agencies' permits. A Customs Connect Facility, developed to provide a secure gateway to customs applications, performs customs public key infrastructure functions such as validation and authentication of digital certificates, and it houses an engine that transforms incoming messages from the United Nations Electronic Data Interchange for Administration, Commerce, and Transport (UN/EDIFACT) into XML. The electronic data interchange (EDI) messages used by customs in the Customs Connect Facility and Integrated Cargo System are developed from the UN/EDIFACT 99b Message Implementation Guidelines produced by UN/CEFACT. Data in the messages are aligned to the United Nations Trade Data Element Directory (UNTDED).

Australia, as part of a commitment to the Asia-Pacific Economic Cooperation, is moving toward an integrated cargo processing and single window environment. It has created an international trade single window project led by customs, which has produced a strategic plan.

Canada. The Canada Border Service Agency has been exchanging data electronically with other government departments since the late 1990s, when proofs of several model concepts were implemented. During 2006–07 consultations with government departments and analyses of business processes led to the development and design of harmonized datasets and interface options. These interfaces, in place since 2007–08, are subject to ongoing monitoring.

Ghana. The Ghana Community Network, a public-private partnership enterprise, reflects the desire of the government to modernize customs through physical infrastructure work, communication networks, upgraded customs facilities, and electric generators in remote border stations. A joint venture company was formed with a 10 year mandate to operate customs, using customs staff. Customs has a 20 percent share, while the total public share is 35 percent (including two other public shareholders) and two private shareholders hold the remaining 65 percent. The main private shareholder, a Geneva based inspection company, holds a 60 percent share. Operation is funded, and dividends to shareholders paid, through a levy on imports of 0.4 percent of the free on board (FOB) price. The underlying technologies are provided by CrimsonLogic, the company that operates Singapore's TradeNet.

The Ghana Community Network started as a value added network (VAN) service for electronic declaration submission and clearance. It was expanded to provide online access for other modules, such as electronic manifest submission, final customs valuation reporting e-Permits, e-Exemptions, electronic valuation of used vehicles, and e-tracking. Access to these facilities is through a single portal, but the processes are not consolidated through single submission, and customs declarations are submitted electronically through the Ghana Customs Management System.

Generalized functional and technical architectures for a national single window

Functional requirements in any sector are primarily driven by system users. In developing the functional and technical requirements and specification for a national single window system, all stakeholders need to be taken into account.

Targeting functional requirements to users and their needs

A national single window has a broad array of users, from traders to oversight agencies.

Trade users. The main targeted users of the national single window are importers, exporters, brokers, and the like—trade users—throughout the country at ports involved in import, export, transshipment, transit, and other customs regimes within the country (either directly using their own facilities or through their brokers and agents). Their anticipated uses are:

- Lodging each trade submission securely as a single electronic message.
- Using business to government messaging, where the trader's (or broker's) in-house system directly permits this without further re-entry; or using a business to government client; or using a web based interface to be provided by the national single window.

For payments of taxes, nontax revenues, and other fees, trade users could either authorize direct debit (under a standing order) or pay separately and provide receipt details (of business to business banking instructions, internet banking, over the counter payments, and the like). Through their single submission they can:

- Track the progress of lodgments they are authorized to view.
- Receive electronic responses to their lodgments, either as government to business messages or by web based lookup.
- Rely on the electronic responses to the lodgments to clear goods for import or export, either requiring no further interaction with government or—if the goods are selected under risk management principles—involving further document or physical inspections.

These uses are illustrated in figures 8.1 and 8.2.

In many countries the trade user is also required to retain all original documents related to a trade submission in an identifiable, locatable, collated folder. The folder may be physical, electronic, or a combination. All such folders are to be held securely and be readily available for audit by government agencies. Severe penalties may be applied for breaches of security and irretrievability.

A registration process is required, usually using a national taxpayer identification number or the equivalent. Generally the national single window does not perform registration alone, but relies on the registration processes of government agencies where trade users substantiate their credentials.

Figure 8.1 | **Business to government service: the Indonesia National Single Window**

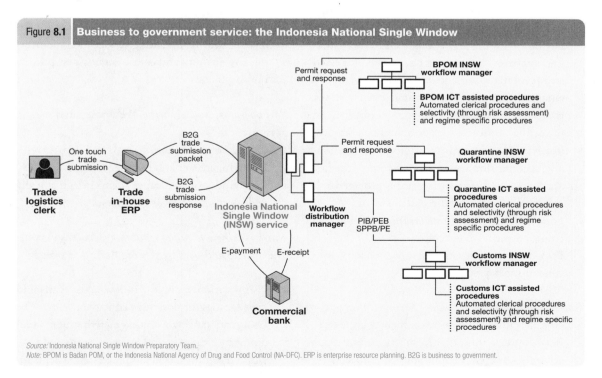

Source: Indonesia National Single Window Preparatory Team.
Note: BPOM is Badan POM, or the Indonesia National Agency of Drug and Food Control (NA-DFC). ERP is enterprise resource planning. B2G is business to government.

Figure **8.2** | Web service: the Indonesia National Single Window

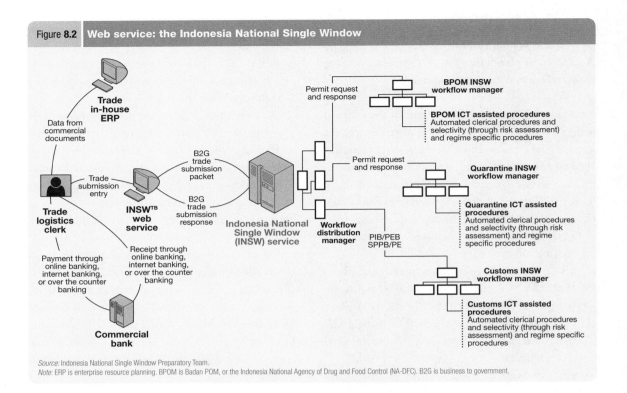

Source: Indonesia National Single Window Preparatory Team.
Note: ERP is enterprise resource planning. BPOM is Badan POM, or the Indonesia National Agency of Drug and Food Control (NA-DFC). B2G is business to government.

Commercial banks. The anticipated uses for trade submissions at commercial banks are:

- Accepting and processing instructions for electronic transfer: from trade users' accounts to government accounts as payment (for taxes, nontax revenues, and other fees under standing orders for direct debit, as well as for business to business banking arrangements, internet banking, and over the counter payments). For fixed and regulated payments the trade user can calculate and pay in advance at the time of the trade submission. For payments depending on particular services—such as quarantine services involving laboratory inspections and, occasionally, classification services for customs—the fees are determined after the service is provided and would entail a second direct debit.
- Forwarding reports of electronic and nonelectronic payments as e-receipts.
- Providing information for any investigations concerning payments.

Government agencies, including permit issuing agencies. The anticipated uses at government agencies are:

- Receiving electronic data from trade submissions according to agency regulations and procedures.

- Processing permit applications according to agencies' internal business processes and within agreed service levels.
- Responding electronically to the trade users.
- Using national single window audit trails and message logs for postentry control.
- Using national single window metering for internal auditing, including service level monitoring and analyses and continual business process improvement.

Port operators and agencies. The anticipated uses at ports are:

- Giving notice of vessel arrivals and departures.
- Receiving master and house manifests.
- Receiving goods clearance permits electronically and accepting them as gate passes.

National single window regulator or oversight body. The anticipated uses by the regulating or oversight body are:

- Using national single window audit trails and message logs for postentry control.
- Using national single window metering internal auditing, including service level monitoring and analyses and continual business process improvement.

National statistics body and central bank. The anticipated use by national statistics bodies and banks is to receive periodic trade related statistics based on trade sanitized transactional data.

Commercial auditors. The national single window operator would be subject to normal requirements for tax administration reporting and for the company registrar. It would also be required to provide commercial access, in confidence, to all records within the national single window for commercial auditing.

Law enforcement agencies. Law enforcement agencies, such as the national police, need unrestricted access to the national single window—and to the oversight body's internal records, detailing audit trails of transactions and other data on traders—for national security matters and for criminal investigations.

Business process functional requirements

Three main business processes flow through the national single window:

- Registration. This process assigns an importer, exporter, or customs agent a unique and secure identification that will grant access to facilities within the national single window as authorized.
- Submission and clearance (all customs regimes). All information for permits, licenses, declarations, and the like—to clear goods for import, export and other customs regimes—is submitted only once, preferably in a single message.
- Customer service. Traders retrieve account status information, track submissions, obtain support for inquiries (on tariffs, regulations, permit requirements, and the like), and access help desk facilities.

Other related requirements

While some criteria are not strictly functional requirements, they need to be taken fully into account in system design and development (a list appears in table 8.1 at the end of the chapter).

Technical architecture

The technical infrastructure for the national single window required at various locations will typically comprise server equipment, network equipment, and system software (operating system, database,

application integration, business process management and message handling, session and transaction management). By nature the national single window is generally a highly centralized system that links and communicates with systems owned and operated by many entities. Such implementations need to be highly scalable and fully redundant. The national single window central data center should have a fully redundant disaster recovery center in a geographically remote location. Network communications channels, similarly, should be established with redundancy in mind. For example, in connecting with its public telecommunications carrier, each channel should be connected to a distinct exchange or switch—and that exchange or switch, in a net, to at least two other switches.

Topology and features

A typical national single window, diagrammed in figure 8.3, has architecture that anticipates facilities for:

- Access and usage security architecture (identification, authorization, encryption, nonrepudiation, audit trails).
- Physical security architecture (transaction logging, restart journals, backup sets, restart methods, recovery methods).
- Performance monitoring model (data logging and analysis).
- Infrastructure resilience features (data storage, data access controllers, servers, processors, communications channels) and identification of single points of failure.
- Scalability policy, plans, and features.
- Software architecture.
- Data quality controls (field validation, referential integrity).
- Data standards (United Nations electronic Trade Documents [UNeDocs], national trade data element dictionary, World Trade Organization reference tables).
- Message standards (XML, other standards).
- Internationalization (language requirements in messages, all traded currencies for World Trade Organization members).
- Harmonized Commodity Description and Coding System codes (may require agency data set harmonization).

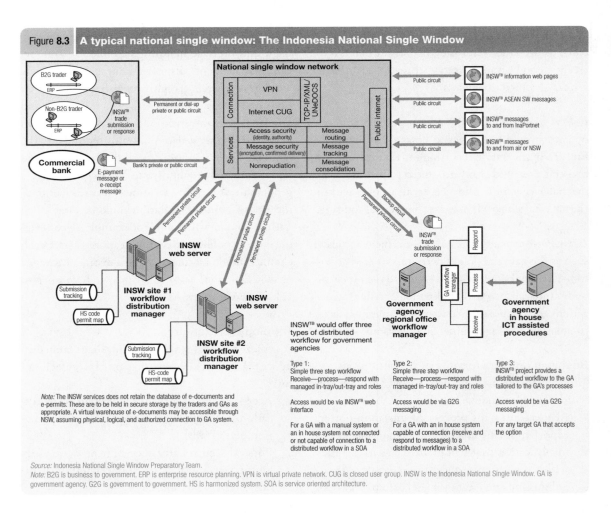

Figure 8.3 A typical national single window: The Indonesia National Single Window

Note: The INSW services does not retain the database of e-documents and e-permits. These are to be held in secure storage by the traders and GAs as appropriate. A virtual warehouse of e-documents may be accessible through NSW, assuming physical, logical, and authorized connection to GA system.

Source: Indonesia National Single Window Preparatory Team.
Note: B2G is business to government. ERP is enterprise resource planning. VPN is virtual private network. CUG is closed user group. INSW is the Indonesia National Single Window. GA is government agency. G2G is government to government. HS is harmonized system. SOA is service oriented architecture.

- Implementation support (usage manuals, training, help desk).
- Commercial infrastructure (server equipment providers, communications equipment providers, other hardware providers, infrastructure software providers, support and maintenance providers).
- Software development toolset.
- Software development method.
- Software development artifacts (requirements specification, design specifications, source code, configuration tables, testing plans and results).
- Version control and configuration control methods.
- Development plans (anticipated rollout, functional expansion, ongoing work and time scales).

Conclusion

This chapter has discussed the critical areas that need to be taken into consideration before, during, and after the creation of a national single window. Clearly a national single window, with its many stakeholders in government and the trade community, is probably one of the most complex public sector reform and modernization initiatives.

Information and communications technology (ICT) is not a solution—it enables solutions. Developments since the 1980s have helped border management agencies learn lessons that need to be considered for future programs. In particular, ICT programs need effective governance, organization, and alignment.

The key steps in creating a national single window do not begin and end with system and vendor selection. A view of how ICT can enable agencies to better achieve a collective vision—and required outcomes—is indispensable. The end of effective ICT implementation is not pressing the button to go live, but ensuring that the program is consistently working to meet agencies' goals.

Table **8.1**

General criteria for required national single window functions

Requirement	General criteria
Presentation language	• All languages that need to be supported by the system should be identified. • For printed media, multiple language types may be required. The design would include markers on client records to indicate language preference, with the language used on notices selected accordingly.
Message languages	XML, UNeDocs components, or other international standards.
Field validation	For all defined messages—whether originating from a terminal operator as data input or another system—fields are required to undergo the field type validation consistent with the field and, where appropriate, referential checks.
Currency support	• The software is required to support amounts in all trading currencies. • The length of fields for accounts must support decimal numbers with integer parts of at least 12 digits and decimal parts of 2 digits.
De minimis amounts	The system should have the capability of recording and handling de minimis amounts if applicable.
Print and display	Throughout the functional requirements the term *print* may be used to describe subfunctions that may result in hard copy output. For low volume output the term print should be taken to mean having the corresponding output either printed to hardcopy or displayed to the terminal device.
Printing on paper	• Paper documentation from the system is expected to be minimal. • Where required, stationery types to be supported must include cutsheet A4 stationery and cutsheet letter. The stationery may be preprinted. The minimum technical infrastructure specifications must include printers with characteristics that match the stationery characteristics proposed.
Reference tables maintenance	Online maintenance of reference tables is required to implement a table driven system. The ability to create, edit, delete, and inquire upon reference tables is required.
Configuration table maintenance	Screen maintenance of configuration table is used for setting software switches and environment settings.
User menu	• Web style, hierarchical menu access to functions will be provided. • User permissions will allow only available options to be accessed. • Administration messages will be broadcast through the menu.
Access security	• Provide a secure means of controlling access to each function and subfunction for authorized users. • Allow specific user to access specified functions, including change password. • Provide username and password check to link to default first webpage after login. • Store password using one way encryption. • Provide mandatory renewal of password after a definable number of days, tracking passwords so that previous passwords cannot be reused. • Prohibit users from accessing the underlying server and client operating system other than through function calls controlled by the application software. • Provide message security though public key infrastructure, verifiable digital certificates, and encryption. • Provide database security through encryption, with administrator functions limited to very few personnel. • Administer confidentiality requirements for all administration personnel.
Audit	• The system should provide a trail of interactions—message originating, users or officer originating, and system generated—and of all changes to data, with date and time stamps, message contents, and before and after images. • This should include login logs and function-access logging. • A scheme for data access tracking is also required, for functions that do not modify. • Audit trails must be searchable by date and time range, message origin, accessed data type, and identifier.
Metering	• The business processes will be implemented through a workflow based architecture. • Each workflow will be triggered by a business event and accordingly date and time stamped, with the stamp also recorded in a metering database. • Each subsequent process step through the various workflows will likewise be date and time stamped. For real world processes, date and time stamps will also be kept for the arrival of the workflow item at the step, the commencement of real world actions (observation of a workflow item's arrival), and the final response to the workflow item. • The meters are used in the service level agreement reporting and the dashboard.
Service level agreement reporting	• Reports may be prepared for any meters and at any level within the workflow, with selection by data and time range, workflow subset or element ranges, trader, government agency, government agency role, government agency user, and other ranges to be defined. • Such reports are to be available to authorized users at the national single window operator, national single window oversight body, government agencies (restricted to meters pertinent to them), and traders (restricted to workflows initiated by them).

(continued)

8

Developing a national single window:
implementation issues and considerations

Requirement	General criteria
Business process dashboard	• A near real time display will provide the performance status of key indicators drawn from the workflow meters, including at least the arrival rate of trade submissions, average time to handle message routing of trade submission within the national single window, queue length at each government agency, average process time within each government agency, and average overall process time until the clearance response to the trader. • The users of the dashboard are the national single window operator and national single window oversight body. • From the dashboard indicators the user can drill down to other meters.
Transactional integrity	Message based integrity requires that the designed effects of a single message are either entirely retained or entirely discarded, with the status clearly identifiable by the message originator.
Database integrity checks	The database storage must check for the logical internal consistency of the database.
Data relationship integrity check	Purpose built checks ensure that referential integrity is built by design knowledge rather than database constraints.
Online help	Online help facility is context sensitive, at least to the page and field level.
Data retention	Data and all audit logs are to be retained and accessible in a practical manner for at least 5 years in primary storage, 10 years in archival storage.
Data archiving	Data can be moved from highly available disk storage to less accessible storage or, after 10 years, purged entirely.
Operational simplicity	The system must exhibit simplicity of use, operation and maintenance, features most readily demonstrated by describing the operating and support environment (including the number of user, operating, and support staff at installed sites).
Ad hoc inquiry	In addition to the inquiry and report features described throughout, the system should support and facilitate other inquiries by authorized, trained officers from the client terminal.
Data export	The system should support, and there should be no impediment to, the selective extraction of data by statistical modeling and reporting tools.
Design constraints—server operating system	Operating system is desired for servers (Windows server, UNIX, or the like).
Design constraints—server database	Recognized, fully functional, ANSI SQL compliant product, with commercial warranty and widely installed customer base, and which supports the scalability, transactional integrity, and resilience requirements.
Design constraints—client operating system	Not constrained. Need to allow for a broad range of users.
Design constraints—service oriented architecture (SOA) toolset	Not constrained.
Design constraints—framework product	A framework product approach, based on an operated service for UN/CEFACT style single windows with customization by modification by reference tables and configuration tables preferred, but customization by software development permissible. The delivery approach needs to be specified comprehensively.

Design constraints—workflow toolset	Commercially available workflow management toolset, with commercial warranty and widely installed user base. Provides definition and management facilities for:
	• Workflow definition (creating and editing):
	  • Graphically defined and modified, with version control and configuration control.
	  • Event driven.
	  • Hierarchy of workflow subsets and steps.
	  • Automated and manual steps.
	  • Automated logical processing including database interaction through service requests.
	  • Role based manual steps with acknowledgment (automatic when observed in role's in-tray) and response actions.
	  • Showing sequence, logical branching, repetition, and parallelism.
	  • Workflow instance persistence.
	• Workflow manager:
	  • Accepts and responds to business events (initiating messages).
	  • Utilizes workflow definitions to administer the status of any workflow instance and route the steps in any active workflow instance over any length of time, through to completion of the workflow.
	  • Maintains workflow integrity and transaction integrity (including database integrity) for any and all workflow instances.
	  • Automatically captures and records date and time data pertaining to the start, stop, and idle periods of a workflow and its workflow steps.
	  • Enforces access control.
	  • Provides facilities for workflow instance monitoring, diagnosis, and repair.

Requirement	General criteria
Design constraints—client application languages	No constraints other than compatibility with technical infrastructure.
Design constraints—system engineering	• The implemented products for the national single window must be underpinned by a published architecture encompassing requirements specification, high level design specification, detailed design specification, technical infrastructure specifications, and implementation specification including message schema, database schema, service schema, source code, and presentation layer definitions. • A widely used, commercially available and supported system engineering tool must be the repository for the published architecture.
Design constraints—system management configuration, version control	• The implemented products for the national single window will be administered through a widely used, commercially available, and supported system management toolset for the configuration tables and reference tables of the software application at various versions, plus the configuration and installation definitions for technical infrastructure components, also at various versions. • The system management approach and toolsets will support at least environments for live service at dual redundant sites, a transition-to-live environment for pre-live acceptance testing, system test environment, development environment, and training environment. • The architecture will be based on message dissemination and distributed workflows, with the scheduling of any system changes to be negotiated with affected users.
Design constraints—escrow	All system engineering definitions and all system management definitions for all products placed in any environment other than development will also be placed in escrow.
Service requirements—training	• Training of traders and government agencies will be necessary. • Training would be performed as an initial burst and then periodically. • Seminar style and small group hands on training would be provided on dedicated training configurations. • Web based tutorials would be provided.
Service requirements—support	• Short term on site support for government agencies is required for initial implementation of any distributed workflow systems. • On call support is required for government agencies when any new versions of the services are planned—possibly including changes for type 1 or type 3 distributed workflows, as shown in the technical architecture or assistance, with any necessary changes in type 2 workflows where the government agency has a connected in house system.
Service requirements—data conversion	• An initial conversion of registered traders and other control information will be required. • A switchover plan from the current operational system or systems to the national single window is required (so that no declarations or requests for permits are lost). Conversion is a computerized process for extracting records from an electronic database, manipulating that data as required, and loading it into the national single window data structures.
Service requirements—data take-on	The solution may require data take-on for proper service operation. Take-on is a computerized process for capturing data from various sources, manipulating the data as required, and loading the data into national single window data structures.
Service requirements—warranty, support, and maintenance	• Help desk, customer service, fix on fail and preventative maintenance for application software and technical infrastructure, and technical advisory services for all users are required.

Source: Indonesia National Single Window Preparatory Team.

Notes

1. This discussion draws on presentations by the author and Gerard McLinden in 2007.
2. The content of this chapter draws from technical assistance work for the Indonesia National Single Window.

Annex 8A
International single window border management implementation, by country

United States

Details	• The International Trade Data System (ITDS), established in 1996 for import and export and integrated government oversight of international trade, is owned and operated by the United States government with customs as the lead agency.
	• The United States Department of Homeland Security Customs and Border Protection (CBP) is redesigning its system and developing the new Automated Commercial Environment (ACE). The main clients are international trade agencies and government agencies involved in imports and exports. Besides federal trade agencies, trade community participants include exporters, carriers, importers, customs brokers, freight forwarders, and so on.
Operational model	A facility for integrated government oversight of overseas trade.
Funding	The ITDS is funded through appropriations as part of the development of the ACE and the new CBP system. The United States government has no profit motivation. A cost-benefit analysis reveals savings, not profits, through ACE.
User fees	No user fees are collected to finance the ITDS or ACE.
Critical success factors	• Leadership—commitment at the highest level.
	• Budget—commitment to long term funding.
	• Technical—must respond to the needs of participating agencies and the trade community.
	• Operational—buy-in, cooperation, operational vision.
Greatest hurdles	The critical success factors are also the greatest hurdles.

Malaysia

Details	In 2002 Malaysia started developing its system, now about halfway through development. Electronic logistics and electronic permits are running. A cross border exchange service is in the pilot stage. Other upstream and downstream data and processes will continue to be developed. System development was initiated by Dagang Net—a private company—with the establishment of a single point where data from one application to an authority or recipient can be reused for other applications to subsequent authorities and recipients.
Operational model	The current model allows the user to file an application and reuse the information for submission to other authorities.
Funding	The cost to Dagang Net when it revamped its operation in 2004 was US$3.5 million.
User fees	The cost of operating the electronic logistics service is borne by the government. There is a fixed price for each electronic permit. Under the cross border exchange service there will be a fixed price for each message received.
Critical success factors	• Support from the government and policymakers.
	• Government agencies' involvement.
	• Demonstrated user benefits.
	• Standardization and harmonization of information parameters among government agencies including customs.
Greatest hurdles	• Making users willing to change.
	• Harmonizing information.
	• Citing paper documents.
	• Changing procedures and processes.

Finland

Details	The first electronic system, set up in 1993–94, was replaced in 2000 by the PortNet system—likewise replaced in 2007 by PortNet 2. Operated by the Finnish Maritime Administration, PortNet encompasses all maritime requirements, customs processes, and terminal notifications regarding containers.
Operational model	A national maritime traffic database, accessed with username and password. User access is restricted to users' own information, but government agencies have access to all information.
Funding	The system is financed at present by the Maritime Administration, the customs office, and the 21 largest ports, some privately owned. Thus, it could be called a public-private partnership. But with the recent emphasis on security it is thought the system should be state owned.
User fees	There have been no user charges so far. It has been considered inappropriate to charge for the mandatory supply of information. But a charge on users who still provide information on paper—a paper handling charge—has been discussed.
[crit]ical success factors	• Cooperation between the parties responsible for maritime safety, maritime security, cargo logistics and environmental issues.
	• A system that generally works well.
[greatest] hurdles	• Difficulty of establishing cooperation between authorities.
	• Reluctance to share information.
	• Need for active authority—who will take the lead?
	• Dispersal of authorities under different ministries and uncertainty about responsibility for an application covering a large jurisdictional area.

Sweden

Details	Swedish Customs—the only public service at Sweden's borders—performs several tasks for other public services, such as the National Board of Trade and the Swedish Board of Agriculture. All such partner agencies were involved in the design and development of information and communications technology (ICT) supporting foreign trade. The first true single window, established in 1989 and focusing solely on the export system, was later enhanced to cover transit and (later still) imports. The single window now includes electronic funds transfer and functions for some agencies not related to imports or exports (for example, hunters and gun registration).
Operational model	Customer submits information to Swedish Customs. Information required for a specific procedure (for example, issuing a license) is forwarded to the public service responsible. For other information, a customs declaration is submitted electronically and selected information extracted and forwarded to the public service responsible (for example, trade statistics are forwarded to Statistics Sweden).
Funding	The system initially was financed with dedicated funds from the Swedish government. New services, designed and implemented today, are financed under existing budgets allocated to each government agency. Automated processes allow Swedish Customs to allocate resources with special emphasis on enforcement or more complex matters. Some initiatives are ongoing, and consideration is being given to using public-private partnerships for developing new systems of greater complexity.
User fees	Free of charge, except for more advanced services such as submitting electronic customs declarations using the United Nations Electronic Data Interchange For Administration, Commerce, and Transport (UN/EDIFACT). With no revenue, costs are not covered.
Critical success factors	• Identifying and offering efficient solutions for processes and procedures used by several customers, creating critical mass. • Listening to end users' requirements and demands.
Greatest hurdles	The challenge of providing a technical framework suitable for the electronic submission of information by small and medium-size enterprises. The solution: web technology (whereas major companies that submit numerous customs declarations are offered solutions enabling them to use existing business systems).

Hong Kong SAR, China

Details	The single window for Hong Kong SAR, China began operations in 1997, operated by Tradelink Electronic Commerce Limited (appointed by the Hong Kong SAR, China government). Processes government trade documents, including trade declarations, dutiable commodities permits, certificates of origin, production notifications, restrained textile export licenses, and electronic manifests. In 2004 an expanded single window initiative was introduced, called the Digital Trade and Transportation Network (DTTN), with Tradelink again the successful bidder for development and operation. DTTN is seen as the vehicle for Hong Kong SAR, China's aspiration to become the preferred international and regional transportation and logistics hub.
Operational model	DTTN is an information platform interconnecting the trade, logistics and finance industries to enhance efficiency, facilitate the business process interconnect requirements of industry, and promote new business opportunity development. A common and shared user platform with defined standards and protocols, it will attract existing suppliers and foster new businesses—such as logistics software development—as well as value added services that will contribute to economic development.
Funding	DTTN Limited is a private entity jointly owned by Tradelink, the Hong Kong SAR, China government, and industry associations.
User fees	There is a DTTN document fee of no more than HK$2.50 (US$0.32) for each document successfully delivered. There are also an initial connectivity fee, a training fee, an annual fee, and customization fees for specific document transformations and the like. Any value added services from application service providers may be charged by the providers separately and additionally.
Critical success factors	• Neutrality—DTTN provides a level playing field for all stakeholders without undue bias toward particular players or industry sectors. • Nonexclusivity—fair access to all industry stakeholders. • Transparent, accountable, and responsible operations—DTTN will be strictly scrutinized, while confidential or mission critical information will not be misused. • Least possible interference with internal business processes—DTTN will only provide data interchange facilities, not require organizations to change their own processes. • Respect for market forces—DTTN is designed to complement businesses, not compete with private initiatives (except when a need for value added services is not being met in the private sector). • Ease of access and use—DTTN is user friendly, intuitive, and centered on the participant.
Greatest hurdles	• None reported.

Developing a national single window: implementation issues and considerations

Singapore

Details	The first national electronic trade document processing system, introduced in Singapore in 1989, involved several government agencies. Today Singapore's TradeNet allows the trading community to submit trade documentation to all relevant government authorities through a single electronic window. TradeNet's key objectives are to: • Reduce the cost of trade documentation. • Reduce turnaround times for trade documentation. • Provide authorities with more efficient streamlined processing. • Attract foreign direct investment through efficiency and transparency. Recognized for its large contribution to Singapore's probusiness environment, TradeNet has increased efficiency and lowered business costs for the Singapore trading community.
Operational model	A member of the shipping and trade community submits trade declaration using any TradeNet front end software from an approved provider, with data submission methods including web applications, client based input, and host-to-host connections. The front end system sends trade declarations using the TradeNet single electronic window for automated processing by various authorities. A permit processing submodule uses an intelligent routing agent to determine work required for each permit application and route it to relevant authorities for processing according to specific rules for each controlling agency involved. With automated processing, 90 percent of declarations do not require manual intervention, and users can receive and print cargo clearance permits within 10 minutes. Options also exist for declarants to transmit data directly using their host systems in any format. A Web portal lets traders process their permits, check transaction status, make billing enquiries, and download code tables (port, country, harmonized system, and the like). The portal also lets authorities process the declarations and make inquiries.
Funding	Initial S$24M (about US$14.3 million) in shareholder capital invested in CrimsonLogic, a private company (formerly known as Singapore Network Services). Thus, the government need not pay for the network. Instead, the beneficiaries—trading companies—pay for services, without incurring development or maintenance costs.
User fees	CrimsonLogic charges declarant fees on a pay per use model. A use fee is charged for each permit processed. Users also pay one time registration and subscription fees, plus monthly fees to maintain system accounts.
Critical success factors	• Government's foresight in identifying problems, finding a solution, and championing implementation. • Cohesiveness of all stakeholders. • Systematic planning, with phased implementation strategy. • Adoption and use of appropriate technology.
Greatest hurdles	Difficulty of the initial change.

Senegal

Details	Senegal's ORBUS, started in 1996 by the Ministry of Commerce and fully operative in March 2005 under the Ministry of Finance, is now managed by the Customs Department. Stakeholders who previously had their own systems (banks, insurance companies, inspection, customs) were provided with an open interface that they could use either on its own—manually feeding data into their systems—or by creating a 100 percent electronic link from their systems. Other stakeholders were provided with ORBUS as their new system (hardware and software supplied to public stakeholders, software alone to private stakeholders). ORBUS is connected to banks, insurance companies, the Livestock Department, Plant Protection Office, and the Currency and Credit Department (in charge of controlling exchange permits).
Operational model	Designed to facilitate foreign trade procedures through electronic exchanges among stakeholders, ORBUS 2000 has as its key point a Facilitation Centre that coordinates operations and monitors system performance.
Funding	Government mainly financed the pilot. After the project's transfer to customs it was financed by a committee, including private sector and government, that collects US$10 per customs declaration to maintain and improve the system.
User fees	• There is a one time US$200 subscription fee. • There is a fixed US$10 price per transaction, with an additional US$2 price per document. • Stakeholders who are not connected pay no subscription fees but must pay an additional US$10 service charge for each transaction. • The single window was self sustaining after one year, with fees determined to cover all operating costs plus research and development. Since the central servers are hosted by customs, ORBUS and the customs system (Trade X) share the same central infrastructure, with maintenance supported by customs.
Critical success factors	• Strong government involvement. • Customs leadership. • Public-private partnership. • Creation of an autonomous entity to develop and operate the single window. • Regular information meetings with stakeholders.
Greatest hurdles	• Resistance to change. • Power migration or reduction with the introduction of ICT.

Mauritius

Details	Mauritius, a small island economy, is extremely open and highly dependent on the outside world for consumables and equipment. Phase 1 of its TradeNet single window system began in July 1994, and the system was fully operative in December 2000. Designed from scratch by Singapore Network Services Limited and Mauritius Network Services Limited, it is the first electronic data interchange network on the island and is modeled on Singapore's TradeNet (with local needs taken into account). Mauritius Customs adopted its single goods declaration form following a World Customs Organization recommendation. In 2001 the system integrated a program for electronic declarations submission by operators of bonded warehouses in the port area (for goods in transit). It is now providing for the electronic payment of customs duties and taxes.
Operational model	A value added network system, based on mailboxes, with no integrated participant systems. The network operator allows transmission of electronic documents between various parties. Operated as a public-private partnership.
Funding	Equipment, software, and staff costs were incurred in establishing a company as the value added network operator. There were also equipment purchasing expenses for customs.
User fees	One time user costs include registration fees and the price of software. Further pricing is set for each transaction element and applied on a current basis.
Critical success factors	• Commitment from all stakeholders, with participation by both government and the private sector in the operating company. • Implementation in phases, making the project more manageable and acceptable.
Greatest hurdles	• Difficulty replacing the existing system of the United Nations Conference on Trade and Development (UNCTAD)—ASYCUDA—at Mauritius Customs. Without any possibility of getting a new version of ASYCUDA that could link to TradeNet, the need to develop a local customs management system with the help of international consultants set back the launch of phase 3 by almost two years.

References

UN/CEFACT (United Nations Centre for Trade Facilitation and Electronic Business). 2005. "Recommendation and Guidelines on Establishing a Single Window to Enhance the Efficient Exchange of Information between Trade and Government: Recommendation No. 33." United Nations Publication ECE/TRADE/352, United Nations Economic Commission for Europe (UNECE), Geneva.

———. 2006. "Case Studies on Implementing a Single Window to Enhance the Efficient Exchange of Information Between Trade and Government." UNECE, Geneva.

Information and communications technology procurement for border management

Tom Doyle

Information and communications technology (ICT) is central to all aspects of border management reform and modernization. And its importance will grow—for several reasons:

- The public increasingly expects more efficient, effective government.
- Governments are striving to improve the overall regulatory control and trade facilitation environment through increased transparency and partnership.
- Governments and the business community increasingly emphasize paperless transactions using digitized information.
- Border management agencies are seeking to expedite merchandise release and delivery timeframes and to improve the interchange of information within and among agencies and private sector operators.
- Computers are increasing in power and functionality, becoming easier to use for more complex business processes.
- Internet based technology is becoming ubiquitous, greatly facilitating communication.
- Software and hardware are becoming commoditized.

Well designed, built, tested and deployed ICT solutions have been proven to make business processes more effective and improve both control and transparency in border management. Such solutions help block decision leakages and improve efficiency, effectively discourage corruption (by reducing face to face interaction between users and government officials), and help to reduce arbitrary decisionmaking and increase accountability.

But ICT is only a facilitator, an enabler, an efficiency booster. It cannot compensate for lack of discipline, management, and control. Accordingly,

ICT alone cannot improve border management.

The role of ICT procurement in border management reform and modernization

As is highlighted in chapter 8, business process automation has all too often been led by technical ICT experts with some knowledge of the business. It should instead be led by business experts with some knowledge of technical ICT issues. When technical rather than business experts have led, the result frequently has been that obsolete procedures are automated and best business practices ignored, with little or no attention to management, control, human resources, and training.

This chapter's underlying assumption is that business experts must first identify their requirements and desired outcomes. They should do so by using a diagnostic exercise to produce a scoping document that takes into account best practices in domain experience. Such a document helps ICT experts design a solution and helps suppliers propose an appropriate delivery approach and outcomes.

The key factors affecting ICT modernization at border management agencies are of three main types: external, technological, and institutional. Each is discussed in turn below.

External factors

Four external factors affect the use of ICT for border management modernization. All four increasingly demand attention. They are:

- *Population growth and increasing development.* These drive trade and passenger traffic volumes and patterns to become more complex, creating more work for border agencies and reducing their ability to focus on individual and transaction based merchandise and passenger processing. More attention must then be focused on preclearance programs and intelligent risk management—approaches that require enhanced data exchange, both within and among trading and neighboring countries, and better management of border crossings and ports of entry.
- *Trade agreements and international cooperation.* These drive, and will continue to drive, an increasing demand for more and better exchanges of regulatory and trade facilitation information. Such improvements require increased computer power and more complex applications, such as higher security and multilingual data translation. The business communities involved in international trade (trucking companies, air cargo, forwarders, traders, and so forth) will continue to want ICT at the basis of business transactions, including regulatory control and logistics processing systems that use electronic documentation. The increased sophistication of port community systems represents an opportunity for border management agencies to

harness the data for improved control and trade facilitation.
- *Rising public expectations.* The demand for speed, safety, and security are the main drivers of public expectations. Border management agencies will be further pressed to increase efficiency while remaining effective. More complex and intelligent ICT support for business processes will be demanded. Transparency and governance will continue to be public priorities. So will improved, but less intrusive, border security.
- *Sophisticated international crime.* Increased data sharing, improved international cooperation, and more extensive computer power and elaborate applications are needed to fight crime. Border management agencies will continue to become more involved with offshore fraud and cybercrime investigations, and they will need to develop electronic forensic skills for investigating and presenting electronic evidence in courts.

Technological factors

The continuing rapid evolution of technology is both an opportunity and a threat for border management agencies and the trading community. Key considerations include:

- *Computers and devices.* Computational devices are constantly becoming smarter, smaller, and more complex—leading not only to increased computer use, but also to an increased use of mobile phones and other handheld devices, all using ever larger bandwidths and ever more powerful wireless technology.
- *Paperlessness.* More and more information will be digitized, with consequences for security, legal admissibility, certification, and archiving.
- *Open standards.* Standards will continue to emerge and be agreed internationally for data, software, and hardware. Such standards will allow for modular, scalable application development and will enable seamless data exchange between connected systems.
- *Flexibility in packaged software.* Commercial off the shelf software provides options for modernizing business processes without commissioning custom built software— speeding up and reducing the cost of ICT implementation.

- *Ease of data exchange.* The wide use of a small number of formats for holding and transmitting data (for example, XML) has made data exchanges between government agencies very simple, leading to increased demand for more data exchange.
- *Compatibility.* Software and internet compatibility among different devices will continue to improve.

Institutional factors

Relationships among stakeholders inside and outside of border management agencies are increasing the demand for overarching, national and international standards and guidelines. Such partnerships are creating a greater need for local and international cooperation and an increasing necessity for easily modifiable, scalable systems such as national and regional single windows. Particular institutional considerations include:

- *Collaboration among agencies.* Interagency coordination and collaboration will allow faster ICT development, implementation, and operation.
- *Modernization and efficiency.* The need for greater efficiency will require the development of front office systems, such as single windows, and the modernization of back office processing systems. Enterprise resource management systems will be increasingly adopted.
- *Out of port processing.* Out of port processing, en route or inland, will continue to expand, reducing agencies' home based work. This expansion will require agencies to network more and more—politically as well as technologically—with national and international organizations.
- *Data collection, storage, and analysis.* Border management agencies will continue to collect, store, analyze, and report on trade import and export data, along with other data. Such data will need to be validated and certified before transmission to businesses and other government agencies. Agencies will need to introduce quality assurance mechanisms, performance audits, and other integrity mechanisms—and, eventually, performance based management and incentive systems.
- *Internal ICT and human resource capacity.* Should ICT solutions be tailored to the ICT management and human resource capacity of border management agencies? Or should the adoption of an ICT solution dictate what capacity is needed?
- *Outsourcing and third party support.* Governments and their border management agencies traditionally have not been very good at maintaining and updating systems and equipment or at hiring and retaining sufficiently capable ICT staff. Border management agencies will turn increasingly to outsourcing and third party support for application software development and for technological infrastructure provision. Agencies will rely more on the private sector for their infrastructure—their computer power and telecommunications—and thus will not need to buy and maintain expensive equipment.

As border management agencies continue to evolve and innovate in response to growing international external pressures, changing technology, and increased demand for institutional cooperation, public sector procurement processes will need to do the same.

Public sector ICT procurement processes

In public sector procurement, government organizations engage with third parties (typically from the private sector, but sometimes from other public sector areas) to procure goods and services. Such procurement ranges from simple purchases, such as office stationery, to complex transactions, such as major state investments in construction and major modernization initiatives. Increasingly, however, public services are also provided by private companies.

Procurement is one of the largest costs in business—it can be 60 percent of total costs for the average private company. However, few people or businesses have a grasp of the true cost of procurement beyond the price at which a product or service is purchased (Degraeve and Roodhooft 2001). Public sector procurement processes tend to be systematic yet bureaucratic, methodical yet lengthy, detailed yet vague, objective yet difficult to navigate. They focus heavily on inputs and processes rather than on outcomes. Today most public sector entities have a procurement strategy, standard contract formats, and financial rules that govern how they procure. Though necessary and prudent, such constraints often limit the creativity of public sector procurement decisionmakers, including at border management agencies.

Typical ICT procurement processes for the public sector

Today's public sector ICT procurement processes have limitations and constraints.[1] But new best practices are emerging. The choice and application of a procurement approach will need to be aligned with legislation and with agencies' existing procurement policies, strategies, and organizational capabilities.

A typical procurement process approach comprises the following steps:[2]

- Define the purchasing process and procedure to be used.
- Ensure that the process complies with all relevant legislation.
- Ensure that accepted tendering organizations:
  - Are compliant with relevant corporate legislation.
  - Are financially sound.
  - Represent minimal business risk.
- Contract for procurement.

Every country, region, and worldwide institution broadly follows the approach above. For example, here is the European Union tendering process:

- *Advertisement.* An expression of interest is made and tender documents are issued to respondents.
- *Selection.* Prequalification questionnaires are submitted and scored.
- *Award.* The award takes place in four steps:
  - Prequalified applicants (based on the questionnaire) are notified.
  - Invitations to tender are made.
  - Tender documents, probably including method statements, are submitted.
  - Tender documents are scored.
- *Contract.* Either the contract is awarded, or shortlisted applicants are invited to make a presentation and then the contract is awarded.

Another example of ICT procurement is described in box 9.1.

Typically the approach adopted is governed by a procurement policy or set of regulations. Thus, European Union procurement processes are governed by the European Union Procurement Directives[3]—though they also are affected by European case law, based on decisions made by the European Court of Justice. In a developing country procurement is governed by national law, but is also to be applied strictly according to any donor agency requirements.

Typical procurement approaches include public tendering, competitive dialogue, selective tendering, and tendering by invitation. Each is described below:

- *Public tendering.* Notices sent through national or international media announce that any interested party can respond to the public sector entity's tender request. Public tendering is equitable in that it imposes no prerequisites. Most suitable for smaller, less complex projects for which it is difficult to ascertain the availability of suppliers with the required expertise, public tenders often result in lengthy procurement cycles—because of the vast array of respondents, the varied solutions they propose, and the work of assessing their responses.
- *Competitive dialogue.* Relatively new and innovative—and now being adopted across the European Union—this variation on public tendering allows altering the tender during the process based on respondent feedback. Respondents may have one on one discussions with the prospective client during the procurement cycle, benefiting both sides through a better mutual understanding of client requirements and supplier solutions. Success is highly dependent on the ability of clients and suppliers to interact in a workshop format and to avoid drawing out the procurement cycle.
- *Selective tendering.* A form of tendering similar to public tendering, but with prequalification criteria to limit respondents to those who meet minimum requirements. Often the requirements are based on financial soundness, insurance requirements, and quality standards. Because entrepreneurial startup companies (normally indigenous) are likely to be eliminated for not meeting prerequisites, selective tendering restricts innovation and discourages fresh responses.
- *Tendering by invitation.* In a drawdown, a shortlist of companies is prequalified by a framework or panel. An example was the CataList framework adopted in the United Kingdom.[4] Once

Recognizing the complexity inherent in the procurement of information systems, The World Bank introduced its two stage procurement process for the supply and installation of information systems in March 2003. In the first stage the purchaser solicits nonpriced technical proposals to address functional requirements. In a direct and structured dialogue (the clarification process), the purchaser and each competent bidder reach a clear and documented understanding of aspects of the bid that meet the purchaser's requirements, aspects that do not meet the requirements, and aspects that are missing. Based on this bidder specific, documented understanding (and additionally based on possible amendments to the bidding documents), each bidder with a sufficiently responsive first stage bid is then requested by the purchaser to submit a second stage bid that is complete, final, and priced. These second stage bids are then handled and evaluated in essentially the same manner as a single stage bid is.

The two stage process maintains openness in technological and implementation approaches. It permits interaction between the purchaser and bidders during the first bidding stage. It can save the purchaser time in formally translating its business and functional requirements into detailed technical specifications. Such time savings, however, are somewhat offset by the additional time required to conduct the first stage bid. The two stage process also requires the purchaser to be fully prepared to undertake a detailed technical dialogue with bidders, which likely will be necessary—and it will also require the purchaser to diligently record individual results from the first stage.

Two stage bidding has been used extensively in World Bank financed projects for complex information systems procurement. While it often has been used very successfully, in a troubling number of instances it has gone completely awry. Anecdotal evidence suggests that the main cause of problems is the purchaser's misunderstanding of the principles of the process. Too often the first stage is treated, for example, as a short-listing process, with the objective of eliminating as many bidders as possible—rather than as an exercise in leveling the floor by ensuring that as many bidders as possible can provide at minimum a technically acceptable solution. Typical World Bank borrower countries have no equivalent in public sector procurement to the two stage procurement process, further aggravating the situation.

Two stage bidding is an extremely flexible and powerful tool, both for the traditional purpose of procuring hardware, software, and integration services, and also for pursuing newer approaches such as outcome based procurement. Standard bidding documents for the two stage supply and installation of information systems already incorporate total cost of ownership into the evaluation methodology. Greater care must be taken, however, to ensure that the underlying philosophy and principles of the process are well understood by the purchaser.

—Ramesh Siva

companies are on the framework—from which public sector entities are not obliged to choose— the companies must then tender again, case by case, with no guarantee that they will get any contracts.

Limitations of the typical public sector procurement processes described above

Six constraints and limitations are inherent in all the public procurement process types described above:

- *Separation of design and build.* Preventing the company that designed a project from participating in the project build restricts procurement. Although the separation adds transparency and competition, accountability is lost—no one party is responsible for the overall solution— and skill is lost as the design supplier is replaced by the delivery supplier, increasing overall costs

and extending timelines. The loss of overall accountability reduces the likelihood of an innovative outcome.

- *High sale cost.* The duration of the procurement stage for complex solutions can be more than 24 months, increasing the sale cost to the private sector. The increase can mean that the public sector is less strategically important to service providers. It can also result in a higher price to the client.

- *Radio silence.* Strict procedures governing client contact during public procurement processes often mean that potential suppliers cannot garner all the information they need to respond precisely.

- *Poor uptake of e-tendering.* More and more government entities are adding e-tendering, but many e-tendering sites have limited functionality, acting as little more than message boards for announcing new tenders. In many cases the failure to use sites more results from the complexity of the tenders and the need for significant manual intervention. Nevertheless e-tendering should be harnessed more, to streamline procurement regardless of the content of tender responses.

- *Low personnel retention.* The length of procurement processes adds significantly to public and private sector costs. One reason is that it hinders both the public sector and private sector suppliers from ensuring that skilled staff are retained throughout a procurement. In particular, the availability of skilled public sector staff is often key to procurement decisions. The government must ensure that personnel are trained in the latest ICT service concepts—and must then be able to earn a return on its investment in those personnel.

- *Lowest cost wins.* The key driver or award criterion in most public sector procurement processes emphasizes value for money—a term widely used and understood by suppliers to mean the lower the cost, the better. So public procurements start a race to the bottom for suppliers, resulting in tender responses riddled with caveats and assumptions. The government's reason for making value for money the central criterion is to assure taxpayers that their money is prudently spent.

Other tendering processes include design contests, precommercial procurement, forward commitment procurement, alternative procurement practices, standing offers, strategic sourcing, and processes to deal with unsolicited proposals.[5] The choice of a procurement process depends on the requirements and abilities of the procuring entity (United Kingdom Office of Government Commerce 2007).

Best practices in ICT procurement for the public sector

Developing and realizing best practices in ICT procurement is not easy. It involves breaking down barriers between internal groups, and it demands a new supplier approach. It also requires significant investments in people, training, analysis, measurement, and technology. Yet it offers benefits including improved third party responses, more realistic expectations by all stakeholders, and increased collaboration among all parties.

Some best practices now being adopted—but not yet as widely practiced within the public sector as they could be—are the following:

- *Cooperative supplier relations.* Strategic suppliers offer value that is not available in the procuring entity, so such suppliers should be integrated into procurement strategies and frameworks. The procuring entity must understand that the supplier needs to make an adequate profit.

- *A culture of continuous improvement.* Do not stand still, even when procurement procedures are yielding the required outcomes. Continually collaborate with other procurement entities. The market's responses to tenders change, and what it can offer changes—so the procurement process must also continually improve.

- *A cross functional approach.* Procurement should not be the sole responsibility of the procurement or supplier management function. Collaboration among all stakeholders ensures a smooth and responsive procurement body (Fitzgerald 2002).

- *Evaluation expertise.* It is critical that the procuring entity exploit all available market information and intelligence. The evaluation committee should have the competencies necessary to evaluate technical, operational, economic, and social criteria. The standard practice is to entrust this evaluation to a multidisciplinary team that represents all stakeholders (Fraunhofer ISI 2005).

- *The senior buy-in.* Success for many ICT projects will depend on a buy-in by senior client stakeholders. Critical at all stages of delivery, this buy-in is just as critical during procurement.

- *Change management.* Far more than just a design, a build, and a run, ICT projects can also involve changes to working practices, changes to communications, changes in responsibility, and changes in interactions with the outside world. The system end user must be involved at all stages of procurement—a key feature of carefully structured change management.

- *Technology evolutions.* The use of e-tendering sites can streamline the entire procurement process—and can make it easier to access tendering materials, ensure security of sensitive information, provide governments with consistency in tendering, and allows searches of relevant tenders by prospective providers (Kajewski and Weippert 2004).

Case study in ICT procurement

This section describes one example of an innovative public sector ICT procurement process—that of the Australian Taxation Office, illustrating outcomes based procurement. (Other examples that could have been included include the State of California, illustrating benefits based procurement.)

Outcomes based procurement: the Australian Taxation Office

The Australian Taxation Office (ATO) reformed and modernized procurement by making it outcomes based. According to the office commissioner (Carmody 2005):

> After an initial strategy work, the ATO contracted an international consulting and technology company to carry out the design and planning of the modernization program including the procurement of new enterprise-wide systems. This involved the development of a more detailed solution blueprint and transition plan, revised business case, program plan for implementation, and project definitions, including requirements and design. A variety of other program deliverables were created during the high level program design including stakeholder management, project and risk management, and program and functional specifications. Overall program costs, benefits and business outcomes measures, and other benchmarks were clarified. Key program risks and mitigation strategies were identified in assessing the proposed replacement systems release plan and contingencies. In parallel with this work, the procurement of commercial software and the contracting of program implementation was prepared.
>
> Two independent international consultancy companies were engaged during the design and planning phase to carry out a quality assurance of the business process design and technology directions. The program outcomes and measured definitions, strategies, management, and development approaches and resulting contracts were examined and adjusted. Notably, in assessing the achievability of the original three-year program, a key issue was the availability of skilled resources. On analysis, it became clear that the concentration of skills required could not be sustained for the duration of the program. By extending the program to four years, and rescheduling some deliverables, a more achievable skill base and demand profile was achieved.
>
> The significance of the procurement activities required the establishment of a full time procurement unit seconded to the program backed up by legal advisors, an independent probity advisor, and a probity auditor.
>
> The procurement strategy—based on "using commercial software, a transfer solution based on systems deployed from other revenue agencies for core processing systems and working with a prime contractor and program integrator"—provided "a basis for driving the business outcomes and managing the risks."
>
> The same prime contractor was retained during the program implementation, where "the nature of the partnership" was "fundamentally grounded in the achievement of eight critical program outcomes:"
>
> 1. "An integrated processing system (people/process/technology) for all [ATO] products."
> 2. "An effective active compliance and advice capability."
> 3. "Effective, improved client service."
> 4. "Improved enterprise-wide outcome management of work."
> 5. "Uninterrupted delivery of [ATO] business."
> 6. "A system with integrity and performance."
> 7. "Productivity and sustainability benefits."
> 8. "The program delivered effectively and professionally."

The program implementation contract contained three key features of outcomes based procurement:

- "A mutual focus on delivery of solutions that achieve outcomes rather than the delivery of a system that has highly detailed pre-determined specifications." The prime contractor's remuneration "is tied to the delivery of these outcomes progressively through the program," with additional contract fees possible if the agreed outcomes are achieved and reduced fees if the agreed outcomes are not.
- "Price certainty for the ATO" through a fixed price contract. Within this fixed price, the prime contractor has:
  - "Fixed the fees it will receive, contingent on the delivery of the agreed outcomes."
  - "With appropriate contingencies, underwritten significant elements of other costs, such as ATO work effort, and hardware and software costs, which [the prime contractor] will have a significant role in managing."
- A single point of accountability for outcomes. "The roles and responsibilities of client and supplier are clearly defined, with staff from both sides working together in joint teams, and with the overall effective management and delivery of the program being the responsibility of the prime contractor."

A proposed approach to public sector ICT procurement

While the systematic approach and egalitarian principles of public procurement must be followed, the process should not be constrained by overregulation.

Processes should be allowed to evolve in response to the ever changing services offered by the private sector. Innovation is best developed through best practice sharing among public sector bodies. Generally ICT procurement needs to become more than an operational activity with operational decision criteria—it must be a part in the strategy of the procuring entity, especially given the amount of taxpayers' money allocated through procurement processes. In short, a new mindset is needed within government institutions. Outlined below are six suggested features of such a new mindset. They are not meant to be prescriptive, but to open a debate on the most appropriate procurement process given the particular mission of the public sector entity:

- *Treating procurement as a demand measure.* In some developed countries public sector requirements can drive the private sector to innovate. In the United Kingdom, for example, it is believed "that Government should act as a lead user of innovation demonstrating new technologies and providing innovative solutions to public services and societal challenges . . . and giving the public long term value for money" (United Kingdom Department for Innovation, Universities and Skills 2008). Because governments have considerations that transcend the private sector principles of profit and market share, governments should collaborate more in specific areas (such as border management) to develop common understandings of their needs—creating an incentive for private sector companies to continually innovate to meet those needs.
- *Orienting procurement toward outcomes.* Border management, like other government activities, must be oriented toward outcomes—social outcomes, economic outcomes, and the like. Government makes policies to promote the outcomes. But it should engage the private sector to deliver solutions and, in some cases, to operate them (United Kingdom Office of Government Commerce 2008).
- *Demanding ethical standards.* Given recent corporate scandals, governments need to increase incentives for service providers to meet the highest ethical standards, including for antibribery compliance, export compliance, data protection, accounting (as in the United States' Generally Accepted Accounting Principles),[6] employee protection, and so forth.
- *Adopting a broader value for money approach.* Buy cheap, buy twice. Often the cheapest solution does not succeed, being only minimally compliant with requirements—and then becomes expensive as its scope (initially narrow) requires broadening after the contract is awarded.

(This necessity tends to come to light in the detailed design of the solution.) A broader value for money approach should be defined and agreed, one that considers total cost of ownership, risk and reward, social considerations, and overall benefits—not just purchase price. Cultural fit between the two working partners should be a key criterion, as should flexibility and expandability, especially for ICT solutions (figure 9.1).

- *Allowing flexibility and evolution.* Procurement procedures and conditions often are rigid and bureaucratic. While it is necessary to ensure fair competition and compliance with the law, it is also important not to prevent the procuring entity from finding the best solution—and not to prevent providers (such as systems integrators) from generating it. In a collaborative procurement process each provider can continually probe client requirements, allowing the client to modify the requirements while giving all parties a clear understanding of them. The procuring entity would be sure of comparing apples with apples, and competition would be fairer as assumptions would be clarified for all.

- *Managing expectations.* When public sector ICT procurement processes are lengthy and delayed, market expectations are not met. Delays can cause the solutions proposed to become invalid, as technology quickly changes. Managing expectations for timelines and decisionmaking criteria at the outset of a procurement process is critical. And externalities—such as budget allocations and the political impacts of elections—should be prevented, as much as possible, from affecting the process.

Conclusion

Collaborative border management aims to transform the way border agencies do their business, through intergovernmental and interagency networking arrangements and through partnerships with customers (chapter 2). The ICT procurement process is central to these aims. The principle of ICT procurement for border management modernization should be that strengthening a partner's capacity reduces pressure on a border management agency's own capacity.

To make ICT procurement processes more efficient and effective, public sector entities should develop more outcome based procurement processes. The government entity should define its end state outcomes—not a series of inputs that private sector providers must interpret. Border management solutions come with especially sensitive and stringent social, political, economic, and technological prerequisites, all of which must be assessed with care and precision to arrive at successful solutions. Also, better understanding of private sector drivers can allow public sector entities to enter into procurement processes with their eyes open. And the procurement process should no longer be a barrier to coordination. Collaborative border management creates a basis for collaborative procurement, where several agencies join forces to seek a single solution—avoiding the procurement of separate solutions that overlap or conflict and are not interoperable.

Outcome based procurement creates a client-supplier partnership with a common focus and shared risk. Its principles are:

- Strategic partnerships.
- Business driven solutions.
- Best value evaluation.
- Performance based payments.

Business risk management can be significantly improved through risk sharing, alleviating an agency's fiscal constraints.

Crisis situations can make the argument for a change of procurement approach easier to

Figure **9.1** | Value for money assessment factors: a broader approach

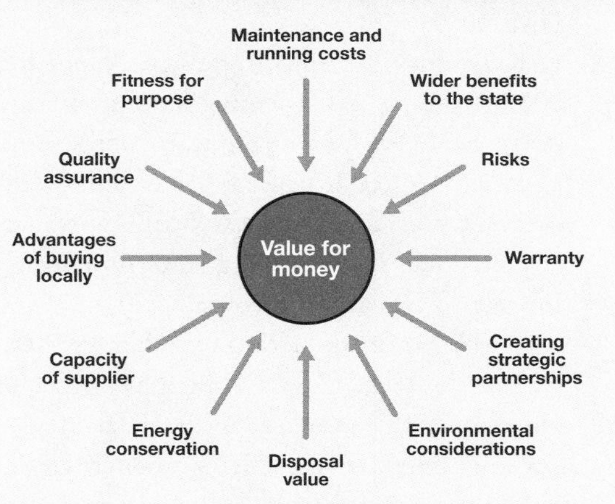

Source: Adapted from "Purchasing Principles," Tasmania [Australia] Department of Treasury and Finance, Procurement and Property Branch, http://147.109.254.182/winninggovernmentbusiness/getpage.jsp?uid=C528898C7747AF92CA2574AA0018DC02.

Information and communications technology procurement for border management justify—but continuous improvement should be attempted in ICT procurement processes, whatever an agency's situation. As a result, all stakeholders—especially citizens and members of the trading community—will benefit through improved services and reduced compliance and administrative costs.

It is additionally important to marry the style and experience of the contracting team to the desired contract approach. Many public agencies have pursued public-private partnership arrangements—in some cases requiring the private sector to fund an entire program—only to revert to traditional, adversarial negotiations at the time of contracting. At that time it is critical that the client and vendor teams understand the relationship being contracted and have experience in the corresponding form of negotiation. Otherwise the long term relationship is jeopardized and the form of the resulting contract is not ideal for either party.

Notes

1. See "Overview of the Agreement on Government Procurement," World Trade Organization, http://www.wto.org/english/tratop_E/gproc_e/gpa_overview_e.htm.
2. See "Procurement and Tendering: Processes and Regulation," Finance Hub, http://www.financehub.org.uk/selling_goods_and_services/default.aspa.
3. See "Public Procurement Legislation," European Commission, http://ec.europa.eu/internal_market/publicprocurement/legislation_en.htm.
4. See now "Buying Solutions: The National Procurement Partner for UK Public Services," Buying Solutions, http://www.buyingsolutions.gov.uk/.
5. See "Province of Nova Scotia Sustainable Procurement Policy," Nova Scotia Procurement Services, https://www.gov.ns.ca/tenders/policy/pdf_files/procurementpolicy.pdf.
6. See "Generally Accepted Accounting Principles," United States Federal Accounting

Standards Advisory Board, http://www.fasab.gov/accepted.html.

References

Carmody, M. 2005. "Revitalising the Tax Administration System: The Australian Experience." Australian Taxation Office, Canberra, Australia. http://ato.gov.au/content/downloads/oecd.pdf.

Degraeve, Z., and F. Roodhooft. 2001. "A Smarter Way to Buy." *Harvard Business Review* 79(6): 22–23.

Fitzgerald, K.R. 2002. "Best Practices in Procurement." *ASCET—Achieving Supply Chain Excellence through Technology* 4. Available at http://www.ascet.com/chapters.asp?chapterID=7732&n=2&t=Procurement.

Fraunhofer ISI (Fraunhofer Institute Systems and Innovation Research). 2005. "Innovation and Public Procurement: Review of Issues at Stake." Study for the European Commission ENTR/03/24, Fraunhofer-Institut für System- und Innovationsforschung, Karlsruhe, Germany.

Kajewski, S., and A. Weippert. 2004. "E-tendering: Benefits, Challenges and Recommendations for Practice." *Proceedings CRCCI International Conference: Clients Driving Innovation*. http://eprints.qut.edu.au/4056/1/4056_1.pdf.

United Kingdom Department for Innovation, Universities and Skills. 2008. *Innovation Nation*. Norwich, United Kingdom: Information Policy Division.

United Kingdom Office of Government Commerce. 2007. "Finding and Procuring Innovative Solutions: Evidence-Based Practical Approaches." Norwich, United Kingdom: Office of Government Commerce. Available at http://www.ogc.gov.uk/documents/Finding_and_Procuring_Innovative_Solutions_%283%29.pdf.

———. 2008. "An Introduction to Public Procurement." Norwich, United Kingdom: Office of Government Commerce. Available at http://www.ogc.gov.uk/documents/Introduction_to_Public_Procurement.pdf.

Information and communications technology procurement for border management

9

10

The role of the private sector in border management reform

Andrew Grainger

International trade is an activity largely conducted by private sector businesses. Consequently, private sector concerns are a key feature in any border management reform initiative. An important role of border agencies—especially where trade is important to a country's economy—should be to ensure that trade controls and procedures are applied in such a manner as not to needlessly disrupt business operations. Where well administered, trade facilitation can be achieved without any compromise on the level of control.

The private sector plays a major role in border management reform: as stakeholder, as partner, and as service provider. In particular, private sector involvement can benefit border agencies through:

- *Consultation*. Border management agencies can develop tools and mechanisms to consult with private sector stakeholders about reform needs and initiatives.
- *Collaboration*. Border management agencies can partner with the private sector to encourage compliance with trade controls and procedures, through collaborative arrangements that motivate traders to internalize—and take responsibility for meeting—border control objectives.
- *Contracting*. Border management agencies can (and increasingly do) rely on private sector services to complement or augment government resources and capabilities.

Private sector concerns—and possible contributions to reform

Much of the demand for border management reform has its roots in the frustration of private sector stakeholders—buyers, sellers, and the various intermediaries and service providers who enable the movement of goods. All these business stakeholders are directly affected by how the public sector stakeholders—all the administrative and regulatory agencies with border management responsibilities—apply and enforce their controls (box 10.1).

The potential list of private sector concerns can be long. Such concerns often refer to the complexity of rules and procedures and to the lack of accurate, up to date information on requirements. Frustration can also arise from poorly drafted rules and procedures that clash with operational practices. The numbers of forms and approvals required for particular operations can be another source of frustration. Traders may also find themselves caught out by changes in rules and procedures, such as new document requirements and new control measures introduced without sufficient publicity. Another issue might be a lack of information and guidance material, forcing traders to rely on the advice of professionals such as lawyers and customs brokers—or to

Private sector stakeholders:
- Traders
  - Small and medium size enterprises
  - Large and multinational enterprises
  - Foreign firms and investors
  - Exporters and importers: operating within one industry
  - Exporters and importers: operating across industries
  - Distributors and retailers
  - Buyers' and sellers' agents
  - Importing foreign companies from developed countries
  - Importing foreign companies from less developed countries
- Transport and related services
  - Shipping lines
  - Ferry operators
  - Airlines
  - Trucking and haulage companies
  - Railway companies: operating international routes
  - Logistics service providers
  - Freight forwarders
  - Customs brokers
  - Banks and finance companies
  - Insurance companies
- Facilities and infrastructure
  - Seaports
  - Ferry ports
  - Airports
  - International rail terminals
- Inland container ports
- Port operators and stevedores
- Cargo handlers and handling agents
- Warehouse operators
- Transit shed operators
- Port community system providers
- Information and communications technology (ICT) service providers
- ICT systems developers

Public sector stakeholders:
- Revenue and customs
- Port health authorities
- Food standards agency
- Marketing boards
- Trading standards bodies
- Department for trade and industry
- Civil aviation authority
- Health and safety executive
- Border and immigration service
- Treasury
- Maritime coastguard agency
- Home office
- Quarantine inspection service
- Plant health inspectorate
- Police
- Highway agency
- Third country representatives from the executive (customs officers, for example) and from consulates (to authenticate documents)

Source: Adapted from SITPRO and Grainger (2008).

---

identify current requirements through costly trial and error.

Traders may also find procedures applied differently from one location to the next, with inconsistencies ranging from different document formats to divergent interpretations of control requirements and objectives. Such variations in the enforcement of controls and procedures can easily lead traders to make inadvertent errors. They can also result in market distortions, as businesses redirect their traffic along otherwise inferior transport routes.

The considerable overlap and duplication of control—for example, between customs and other border agencies and licensing authorities—is yet another concern. So is the overlap between regulators'

controls and procedures and those that companies maintain for commercial purposes. For example, many companies with brands and reputations to protect operate quality control systems that are considerably more stringent than any procedures specified by regulators.

Businesses may also find that regulatory requirements conflict with established commercial practices. For example, the electronic systems used by regulatory agencies may fail to adequately accommodate the prevailing industry standards for the sharing of electronic data. A further example is the reluctance of some businesses to disclose information that enables customers or competitors to estimate profit margins or learn details about cheap supply sources.

As a consequence of this reluctance, even in developed countries, businesses often forgo preferential or simplified customs procedures for fear of disclosing such commercially sensitive information. Another example is the fact that many countries allow practices favoring narrow private sector interest groups at the possible cost of creating wider implications for the supply chain. For example, some countries mandate that traders must employ publicly licensed customs brokers whenever the traders deal with customs. Similarly, in some countries trade may only be permitted if conducted through the agency of an officially licensed trading company.

Important to note is that many trader frustrations about cross border trade are shared by border agencies. Inefficient procedures not only inflate business costs, they also inhibit a border agency's ability to meet its control objectives. For example, a country's inspection efforts are severely impeded if its laws make it difficult for government officials to use risk management principles (chapter 6). And onerous regulations encourage traders to illegally circumvent costly, time consuming procedures by finding ways to shortcut regulatory requirements or by entering the shadow economy.

Good border management reform practice takes into account the frustrations experienced by traders. Ongoing review of controls and procedures as well as the frustrations experienced by private sector stakeholders ensures that optimal trade facilitation solutions are found and adequately implemented (figure 10.1). In fact, many concerns first expressed and remedied at the country level have been used by international organizations—such as the United Nations Centre for Trade Facilitation and Electronic Business and the United Nations Conference on Trade and Development—as a basis for trade facilitation recommendations.[1] For background, some of the trade facilitation concepts and ideas associated with border management reform—and echoed in wider trade facilitation discussions such as those at the World Trade Organization (WTO 2009)—are listed in box 10.2.

Dialogue between the private and public sectors can identify opportunities for reform, but it also brings other benefits. It encourages a climate of shared responsibility and ownership. It helps to set reform priorities, leading to initiatives that focus

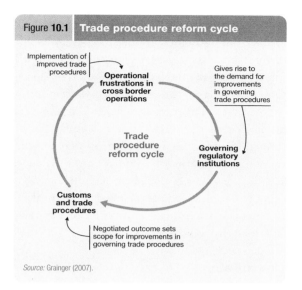

Figure **10.1** **Trade procedure reform cycle**

Implementation of improved trade procedures

Operational frustrations in cross border operations

Gives rise to the demand for improvements in governing trade procedures

Trade procedure reform cycle

Governing regulatory institutions

Customs and trade procedures

Negotiated outcome sets scope for improvements in governing trade procedures

Source: Grainger (2007).

Box **10.2** **Trade facilitation concepts derived from traders' frustrations**

The following 18 trade facilitation concepts are derived directly from traders' accounts of their operational frustrations.

Concepts for improving regulation
- Simple rules and procedures
- Avoidance of duplication
- Memorandums of understanding
- Alignment of procedures and adherence to international conventions
- Trade consultation
- Transparent and operable rules and procedures
- Accommodation of business practices
- Operational flexibility
- Customer service provisions for government administrations
- Mechanisms for corrections and appeals
- Fair and consistent enforcement
- Proportionality of legislation and control to risk
- Time release measures
- Risk management and trader authorizations

Concepts for improving the use of information and communications technology (ICT)
- Standardization of documents and electronic data requirements
- Automation
- International electronic exchange of trade data
- Single window

Source: Grainger (2008b).

on the most desired outcomes. Finally, a structured approach to interactions among private and public sector stakeholders can be used to gain a systemwide understanding of complex international trade operations extending beyond individual organizations.

Regular public-private exchange can also yield a collective vision for reform. Such a vision may be formally specified (in a published vision statement, for example), or it may be implicit in the dialogue. Finally, the alliances forged through dialogue—if suitable—can lead to joint lobbying for political patronage, and to a consequent investment in sustainable, long term border reform.

Consultation

Consultation with private sector stakeholders is one of the main methods for governments to identify operational issues, untangle operational complexities, agree on remedies, and carry out reform. One approach is for private and public sector representatives to share their concerns in national, departmental, and local collaborative forums, where they can then jointly explore border reform options and approaches. Other mechanisms include arm's length approaches, such as open consultation letters inviting interested parties to express views on a given issue, and approaches driven by assessment and research, such as the investigation of private sector trade facilitation reform requirements using surveys, toolkits, and commissioned studies. Such private-public consultation often escalates from the local and national policy levels to the regional and international.

Collaborative consultation
Vehicles for collaborative consultation vary with the focus, objectives, and requirements of their sponsors and members. Some are national, others specific to departments and to localities.

National trade facilitation bodies. A common model for collaborative consultation follows Recommendation 4 of the United Nations Centre for Trade Facilitation and Electronic Business (UNECE 2001), which proposed national trade facilitation bodies often called transport and trade facilitation committees or trade procedures committees (PRO

committees). Driving the creation of such national consultation vehicles is the recognition that all the groups directly involved in trade and border reform—government agencies, trade and transport service users, and trade and transport service providers—must be represented on any committee for border reform or other trade facilitation reform (box 10.3).

National trade facilitation bodies—listed on the UNECE-UN/CEFACT Web site[2]—can be organized in various ways. For example, the guidelines for UN/CEFACT Recommendation 4 propose a model including a committee, a permanent commission, and a secretariat. The committee, representing the various stakeholder groups, meets three or four times each year. The commission, consisting of a small number of representatives elected by the committee, meets more often to follow up on actions specified by the committee. The committee and its permanent commission are supported by a full time secretariat with suitable technical experience, and by consultants when required. It is acknowledged, however, that arrangements and funding can differ greatly with each country's national administrative conditions (UNECE 2000).

Among other models for trade facilitation bodies, the following three are common:

- National bodies, funded by governments but operating independently.

Box **10.3**	**"The needs of all parties . . . must be identified": extract from Recommendation 4 of the United Nations Centre for Trade Facilitation and Electronic Business (2001)**

22. Facilitation activities must be approached in a coordinated manner to ensure that problems are not created in one part of the transaction chain by introducing solutions to another part. The needs of all parties, both private and public sectors, must be identified before solutions can be found and those best placed to explain their needs are those directly involved in the transaction chain. This requires an effective forum where private-sector managers, public-sector administrators and policy makers can work together towards the effective implementation of jointly-agreed facilitation measures.

Source: UNECE (2001).

- National committees, funded by governments and under government departments.
- Private sector organizations, independent from governments.

How well each model will work—for various purposes—can depend on a country's institutional environment. Accordingly, in establishing a vehicle for collaborative consultation, the pragmatic course is to consider how power, resources, authority, and legitimacy can best be mobilized. Examples of the three models listed above are described in box 10.4.

Box 10.4   Examples of three models for trade facilitation bodies

Models for trade facilitation bodies vary. Because the results of each depend on the institutional environment, each should be recommended only with caution. Examples of three common models appear below.

SITPRO (United Kingdom)
Originally known as The Simpler Trade Procedures Board, SITPRO was set up in 1970 as the United Kingdom's trade facilitation agency. It was reconstituted as a company limited by guarantee in April 2001. SITPRO is a Non-Departmental Public Body and primarily funded by the Department for Business, Enterprise and Regulatory Reform (BERR). SITPRO's mission is to "simplify international trade" and to actively participate at the domestic, European, and international policy levels.

SITPRO's work is guided by a Board of five Directors plus two Ex-Officio Board Members representing UK Customs and BERR, an Advisory Council, and a large network of Strategic Advisory Groups. At any time there are about 100 executives and specialists taking part in the work of Advisory Groups. These groups help identify trade barriers, make recommendations for improvement, and define the Executive's work program. Advisory Groups include representatives from a cross section of United Kingdom business and government. Meetings for most groups take place several times per year. The Executive has nine fulltime staff members and is headed by a fulltime Chief Executive.

SWEPRO (Sweden)
SWEPRO (the Swedish Trade Procedures Council) is the Swedish forum for trade facilitation, where Sweden's central stakeholders gather to discuss and exchange views on national and international work. Its roots date back to the mid-1950s. SWEPRO's mission is also to spread knowledge about the benefits of trade facilitation and to participate actively in international processes in the area. SWEPRO is fully financed by the Swedish government

SWEPRO includes representatives of business and public authorities through the Swedish Bankers' Association, The Swedish Network for Electronic Affairs (NEA), the National Board of Trade, Swedish Trade Federation, ICC Sweden, the Swedish International Freight Association, Swedish Association of Local Authorities and Regions, Swedish Customs, and the Swedish Ministry for Foreign Affairs. The full forum meets four times annually. The forum may also decide to form project related working groups, which, depending on issue, participation, and scope, will meet more frequently.

The SWEPRO secretariat is administered by the National Board of Trade and participates actively in international work on trade facilitation, as well as initiating its own projects and providing the government with analysis and reports about Sweden's national trade facilitation work in all areas (EU, UN, WTO, OECD, and so forth). The secretariat has three staff members who are also trade facilitation analysts at the National Board of Trade.

ODASCE (France—Office de Développement par l'Automatisation et la Simplification du Commerce Extérieur)
ODASCE, the French International Trade Facilitation and Simplification Body, was created in 1972 by executives from private industries with the backing of the French Directorate General for Customs and Excise. It is funded by membership subscriptions plus income generated through training activities. 120 companies, ranging from multinational organizations to one man operations, subscribe to ODASCE membership. Over 1,500 companies take part in ODASCE training courses. The Board (Conseil d'Administration) is made up of up to twenty members, elected by the annual General Assembly. Appointments are unremunerated and rotate every four years. The Board also appoints the Bureau—which includes a President, two Vice-Presidents, Treasurer, and Secretary—to support the day to day operations and to give policy direction to the three permanent staff based in Paris.

ODASCE regularly produces trade facilitation related position papers, organizes a range of seminars and conferences, and makes direct representations to the French Administrations on behalf of its members.

Source: Personal communication from SITPRO, SWEPRO, and ODASCE (see further the ODASCE Web site, http://www.odasce.asso.fr; the SWEPRO Web site, http://www.swepro.org; and the SITPRO Web site, http://www.sitpro.org.uk).

10

The role of the private sector in border management reform

Department specific consultation vehicles. Often a border reform issue will pertain to just one government border agency (such as customs). Nevertheless, a prudent government department will recognize the significance of private sector stakeholders in any border management initiative and will consult widely when initiating reform. It may set up a dedicated consultation vehicle—a pragmatic and efficient approach to enable face to face discussion with key representatives (an example appears in box 10.5). Such a vehicle should complement national trade facilitation rather than compete with it. In countries with active private sector consultation, the national trade facilitation body may refer some matters to the dedicated consultation vehicles of particular departments.

Local consultation vehicles. Many border management improvements can be made apart from national initiatives. For example, larger port operators concerned about border management issues often host regular meetings between private and public sector stakeholders to raise local issues—issues that are often operational and independent from procedures defined by regulation. Topics of concern might include operating hours at customs stations, local submission procedures for paper documents, technical specifications for the port's electronic infrastructure and customs interfaces, the coordination of inspection with the port's stevedore, queuing procedures at the port gate, staff identification checks and port access, health and safety awareness, and coordination mechanisms among government executives within the port.

Similar to the national or department specific level, local consultation initiatives also enable representatives to recommend practical reform measures. Pragmatic improvements at the local level need not be expensive. Seemingly simple actions can achieve meaningful gains: examples include providing a notice board, posting estimated ship and aircraft arrival times on a Web site, updating contact details for staff members in a handbook or database, and enabling joint inspections by notifying noncustoms agencies whenever customs opens a consignment.

Arm's length consultation approaches

Unlike face to face collaborative efforts among representatives of specific interests, an arm's length consultation approach seeks contributions from the wider business population, including individual firms, experts, and professionals who may disagree with their own professional bodies or trade associations. An open letter or consultation call is published, outlining a project or issue and inviting interested parties to respond. The written responses are collated and summarized in a report, which often includes a catalog of respondents' recommendations. A good practice is to give respondents enough time to prepare their responses—especially important for business interest associations, which may take time to identify the views common to their members. Another good practice is to publish an interim draft report, allowing respondents to confirm whether their views and recommendations have been captured accurately.

Although the arm's length approach to consultation is not face to face, it ensures that anyone with an opinion can offer it. It also can show whether participants at national trade facilitation committees or in departmental consultation vehicles are expressing their constituents' views.

Since consultation calls usually are published in newspapers, government gazettes, or public Web sites, critics point out that the calls can easily escape the notice of interested parties and possible contributors. Some progressive administrations use a central consultation database to register interested parties, who are notified of all published consultation calls.

Some consultation calls may seek information that is commercially sensitive, such as data on costs. And responses can be sensitive for other reasons—as when views are expressed that could upset relationships with staff, unions, or government officials. The confidentiality of responses must be assured when individuals or business interest associations request it.

Consultation approaches based on assessment and research

Policymakers concerned about private sector views increasingly apply standardized assessment methods and tools to gather and assess information on private sector reform needs. For example, tools available to examine trade facilitation include the Trade Facilitation Framework from the United Nations Economic and Social Commission for Asia and the Pacific (UN ESCAP 2004), the Trade and Transport Facilitation

The JCCC was established in 1969 to exchange views on and discuss proposed changes to Customs procedures and documentation relating to the entry and clearance of goods. It gives the opportunity for HMRC to consider representations from over 20 member organisations on a face to face basis. There are four scheduled meetings per year, chaired by the Director of Customs and International Directorate. A number of smaller subgroups are used to discuss in-depth technical issues. These groups are set up if required and disbanded once their purpose is achieved.

Private sector representatives:
- Airline Operators Committee Cargo United Kingdom (AOCC UK)
- Association of International Courier and Express (AICES)
- Automated Customs and International Trade Association (ACITA)
- British Chambers of Commerce (BCC)
- British International Freight Association (BIFA)
- British Ports Association (BPA)
- British Retails Consortium (BRC)
- Chamber of Shipping (COS)
- Chartered Institute of Logistics and Transport (CILT)
- Community System Providers (CSPs)
- Confederation of British Industry (CBI)
- Customs Air Transport Consultative Group (CATICG)
- Customs Practitioners Group (CPG)
- Food and Drink Federation (FDF)
- Freight Transport Association (FTA)
- Institute of Chartered Shipbrokers (ICSB)
- Railway Industry
- Road Haulage Association (RHA)
- Royal Mail
- SITPRO
- United Kingdom Aerospace Industry Customs Group (UKAICG)
- United Kingdom Major Ports Group (UKMPG)
- United Kingdom Warehousing Association (UKWA)

Membership:
The aim of the JCCC and its subgroups is to consult with the widest possible spectrum of trade interests and to achieve the highest standards of interests from them. To achieve this, the following criteria for membership are applied. A trade body must:
- Be a national organisation with a primary interest in the movement of goods and/or people.
- Not represent particular (air)ports.
- Not solely represent individual company business interests.

JCCC subgroups active in 2008 include:
- Customs Civil Penalties Subgroup
- National Clearance Hub (NCH) Subgroup
- International Trade Operating Systems Working Group
- New Community Transit System (NCTS) Subgroup
- Impex [Import-Export] Subgroup
- Export Control System/Import Control System (ECS/ICS) Subgroup
- Customs Procedures with Economic Impact, End Use and Free Zones Subgroup

Staffing:
- Secretariat support from the HMRC communication team. They also arrange the meetings, minutes, and agenda.
- All subgroups are chaired by a senior policy officer from customs
- Depending on the topic of discussion other policy officers from across HMRC are likely to be invited to the JCCC and its subgroups as required.
- Minutes and record are produced by customs staff. Private sector members are given the opportunity to correct or amend minutes before publication.

All JCCC and subgroup activities are published at http://www.hmrc.gov.uk/consultations/jccc.htm and include:
- Information Papers.
- Minutes for the main JCCC.
- Minutes for the JCCC subgroups.
- Newsletters.

Source: Personal communication with HM Revenue and Customs (see further "Joint Customs Consultative Committee," http://www.hmrc.gov.uk/consultations/jccc.htm).

Assessment (World Bank 2010; see also Raven 2001, 2005), and a self assessment guide on articles V, VIII, and X of the General Agreement on Tariffs and Trade (World Bank and Widdowson 2007).

Similarly reliant on data provided by private sector stakeholders are robust cost-benefit analyses, regulatory impact assessments, and postimplementation reviews—all key components of good project management practice (for example, Prince2; see OGC 2005). The data gathered may be quantitative or qualitative. Quantitative data may include border clearance times, estimates of the cost for a particular type of compliance operation, and reports on the numbers of documents and data transactions required for a particular declaration. Qualitative data may include the perceived impact of operational requirements, the outcomes expected from reform programs, and perspectives on matters of ongoing concern.

Surveys and questionnaires are commonly used to gather data from large numbers of respondents in the private sector. Low in cost, they are easily attached to consultation calls. Web based survey tools can also be efficient in distributing surveys and collecting data. But any qualified analysis of survey and questionnaire data must consider the survey respondents. For example, views of the cross border environment among shippers may differ from those of freight forwarders, and both may differ from the views of transport and infrastructure service providers. The views of occasional traders, who deal with an issue only intermittently, may differ from the views of traders who deal with it every day. Also, when surveys are attached to consultation calls there is a risk that respondents may deliberately misreport data to promote a desired outcome.

Because of the diversity of private sector organizations and the range of their interests, the design of surveys and questionnaires presents methodological difficulties. Data must be interpreted in the context within which the data were given. So it is good practice to use additional, alternative data gathering methods. Such alternative methods include:

- Querying national trade facilitation committee representatives (a quick way to obtain indicative data).
- Observations and site visits.
- Case studies.
- Visibility studies.
- Interview series.
- Pilot studies.
- Structured research—for example, conducted by universities or consultants—to address specific border management problems.

Informal consultation

Informal consultation—also common in border management reform—can help policymakers maintain a good relationship with the private sector. Frequent policymaker meetings with key stakeholder groups can ensure that concerns are identified as early as possible, before problems escalate. One possibility is regular breakfast or lunch meetings. Roundtables and workshops can be useful for larger numbers of participants.

Should meetings be formally documented? Policymakers should consider this question carefully. On the one hand, taking minutes can ensure that the meetings are transparent. On the other hand, using the Chatham House Rule usually results in freer and less inhibited discussions.[3] Both administrators and private sector representatives may fear to have their words quoted publicly. In cases where past meetings have produced conflict, it may be a good idea to ask an independent outsider to chair the meeting and keep it focused on shared objectives.

Consultation at multiple policy levels

Because many procedures applied to cross border trade are embedded in wider international regulatory regimes, reforms in one country often must be coordinated with reforms in others. Such coordination takes place at the bilateral, regional, and international policy levels, but it often is initiated by specific operational concerns raised at local or national policy levels.

For example, the private-public interactions that affect the reform of United Kingdom customs procedures are outlined in figure 10.2. Traders are likely to seek change first at the local level, then at the national level when local actions cannot resolve the problem—perhaps because the procedures that hamper the traders' operations are based on national laws. This escalation from local to national efforts may take place through the agency of the local customs office, through local trade associations, or through both (for example, in a coordinated lobbying campaign launched after a local port user group meeting). At the national level the issue is likely to be aired in the United Kingdom Joint Customs Consultative Committee (JCCC) or in SITPRO (see box 10.5). But if reforms are dependent partly on third country trading partners, such as the United States,

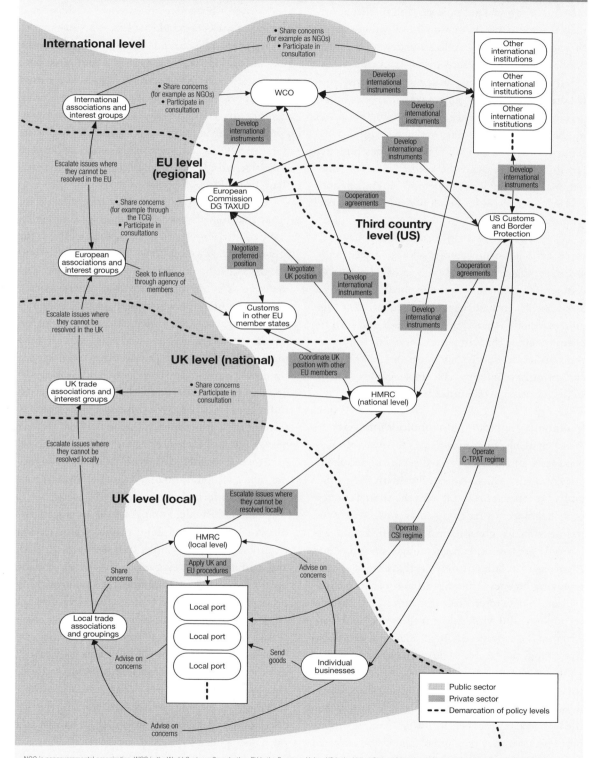

Figure 10.2 Consultation at several policy levels: public-private dialogues in the reform of United Kingdom customs procedures

International level

• Share concerns (for example as NGOs)
• Participate in consultation

Other international institutions

Other international institutions

Other international institutions

Develop international instruments

WCO

Develop international instruments

Develop international instruments

International associations and interest groups

• Share concerns (for example as NGOs)
• Participate in consultation

Develop international instruments

Develop international instruments

Escalate issues where they cannot be resolved in the EU

EU level (regional)

European Commission DG TAXUD

Cooperation agreements

Develop international instruments

US Customs and Border Protection

• Share concerns (for example through the TCG)
• Participate in consultations

Third country level (US)

Negotiate preferred position

Negotiate UK position

Develop international instruments

Cooperation agreements

European associations and interest groups

Seek to influence through agency of members

Customs in other EU member states

Develop international instruments

Escalate issues where they cannot be resolved in the UK

UK level (national)

Coordinate UK position with other EU members

UK trade associations and interest groups

• Share concerns
• Participate in consultation

HMRC (national level)

Operate C-TPAT regime

Escalate issues where they cannot be resolved locally

Operate CSI regime

UK level (local)

Escalate issues where they cannot be resolved locally

HMRC (local level)

Apply UK and EU procedures

Share concerns

Advise on concerns

Local port

Local port

Local port

Local trade associations and groupings

Advise on concerns

Send goods

Individual businesses

Public sector

Private sector

Demarcation of policy levels

Advise on concerns

NGO is nongovernmental organization. WCO is the World Customs Organization. EU is the European Union. US is the United States of America. UK is the United Kingdom. DG TAXUD is the Directorate-General of the EU Taxation and Customs Union. TCG is the TAXUD Trade Contact Group. HMRC is HM Revenue and Customs (the UK customs agency). C-TPAT is US Customs and Border Protection's Customs-Trade Partnership Against Terrorism. CSI is US Customs and Border Protection's Container Security Initiative.
Source: Author's construction.

or are embedded in regional European Union legislation, then efforts may be escalated further to the bilateral or regional policy level. And further efforts may be made at the international level—for example, through sharing best practices and developing international recommendations and instruments.

The interplay among policy levels can also contribute to border management reform. For example, private sector experience in developing countries might help determine whether a given initiative is likely to work, helping to establish a best practice recommendation. And the use of perceived international best practices can help in obtaining funds and other resources for development aid and capacity building.[4]

Coordination mechanisms at various policy levels can contribute to joint reform efforts—for example, shared standards and the alignment of rules and procedures. Coordination at the regional and bilateral levels can also include shared reform deliverables. Examples include a shared electronic trade and customs environment in the European Union's electronic customs initiative (European Commission 2007) and a commitment to interoperable single window systems in the Association of Southeast Asian Nations.[5]

Managing conflicting stakeholder interests

A key challenge for policymakers trying to evaluate private sector concerns is the diversity of stakeholders' concerns, which can conflict with each other and so hamper reform. Despite the shared interest of stakeholders in reducing costs, some will stand to lose from any given reform. Simplified trade and customs procedures can encourage importers and exporters to handle customs clearance on their own, removing business from agents and brokers. Modernization may force firms to invest heavily in new technology, and while larger traders may soon benefit from the upgrade, smaller traders and occasional traders may not be able to offset the costs as quickly.

Interests can also conflict between participants in two different operating environments when reform initiatives are applied indiscriminately to both. When the United Kingdom began customs X-ray scanning, port operators were required to bring goods selected for scanning to the X-ray facilities. This requirement created few difficulties at container ports where port operators owned cargo handling equipment. But at

roll on–roll off (RORO) ports, which mostly lack such equipment, it proved more problematic. The truck drivers who used to drive straight off ships could no longer do so—nor could haulers,[6] who used to pick up cargo deposited quayside off ships, simply leave the port. Instead, drivers and haulers whose cargo have been selected for X-ray scanning are now required to transport their cargo to the new X-ray scanning facilities first, causing delays—an issue further compounded by maximum working and driving hours (Grainger 2008a). Unsurprisingly, container port operators perceived the new scanning policy differently than the RORO port operators did.

The public sector, too, may foster conflicts of interest that impede border reform. For example, in many countries—especially those subscribing to the Revised Kyoto Convention—customs agencies will acknowledge the important role of the private sector in cross border operations. But other agencies, always assuming the worst (perhaps in accordance with a cultural norm), may tend to be more aggressive about enforcement and may resist aligning themselves closely with private firms. Such aggressiveness is often counterproductive. Even in developed countries traders admit that they have diverted traffic because of perceived variations in the enforcement of trade procedures (Grainger 2008a). Where heavyhanded enforcement is not needed, it can lead in the worst of cases to a loss of trade—or to an exodus of less scrupulous traders from the formal economy to the informal one.

Some stakeholder groups may not be able to participate in a dialogue about private sector reform requirements. For example, staff members at small and medium size enterprises, as they focus on daily operations, may have little time for a policymaking process—unless they see an immediate effect on operations. Similarly, overseas business interests, even if they have a vital role in border reform, may not be able to participate in consultations as regularly as national organizations do. Consultation methods that policymakers can use to engage less accessible stakeholders include conferences, training events, telephone help lines, and informal exchanges and open door policies.

A major challenge for reformers is to identify and pursue a reform program that aims to improve the economy as a whole—not to further the interests of particular sectors. In areas where there is considerable consensus among stakeholders, reform recommendations can quickly be agreed on. In contrast, wherever policymakers lack full knowledge about stakeholder interests and about the implications of change, frequent formal and informal meetings with key stakeholders—often complemented with substantiated research—are essential to meaningful border management reform.

Collaboration between the private and public sectors

The private sector not only shapes much of the demand for border management reform—it also bears the greatest responsibility for meeting regulatory control requirements. Yet efforts by the government to enforce rules and procedures across the board are costly, and they are also likely to inhibit trade significantly.

In contrast, a more efficient approach to control and enforcement encourages traders to internalize control objectives, making the private sector a collaborator with the public sector in the pursuit of border management goals. Successful collaboration strategies also make enforcement far more efficient, and they can reduce trade compliance costs—expanding revenue while shrinking the shadow economy.

To give one example, the so-called 20:80 principle—whereby 20 percent of the trade population is responsible for 80 percent of customs declarations—often applies. In fact, the ratio can be far higher in trade intensive economies (published research is scarce, but anecdotal evidence suggests that ratios of 5:95 or even 3:97 are not unusual). Consequently, a smart collaborative enforcement strategy is to encourage those traders with the highest volumes to internalize regulatory control objectives, freeing border agency inspection resources for use in controlling riskier movements. Commonly applied vehicles for the encouragement of good compliance records include preferential treatment and risk management, formal partnership agreements, licensing regimes, and assurance based controls. Specific incentives might include permission to use simplified trade and customs procedures as well as access to operational privileges, express treatment, exemptions, and fiscal benefits. The World Customs

Organization's concept of authorized economic operators (WCO 2007) is much discussed at present.

Preferential treatment for authorized traders

Under most preferential cross border control arrangements, traders who meet certain requirements are authorized to receive operational or fiscal benefits. The requirements can vary but normally include a good compliance record and an assessment of the trader's compliance capabilities and systems. Operationally, such arrangements allow border agencies to shift administrative responsibilities onto authorized traders—usually through an audit based control regime—rather than require declarations for every cross border transaction.

Commonly employed by customs agencies (especially those subscribing to the Revised Kyoto Convention), conditional authorizations for preferential treatment let authorized businesses:

- Benefit from simplified import clearance procedures.
- Clear goods at premises located outside ports and away from borders.
- Make declarations periodically, rather than for each consignment.
- Pay duties periodically, using self assessments to do so (box 10.6).

Customs conducts occasional checks to verify traders' compliance with the conditions of their authorization. Breaches lead to sanctions such as fines, criminal proceedings, and deauthorization. Deauthorization puts traders at a disadvantage, and the fear of it can be a powerful incentive for traders to keep compliance capabilities high.

Preferential customs treatment may include not only simplifications that are largely operational, but also procedures that confer fiscal benefits—the main purpose being to ensure that national taxes do not put businesses operating in export markets at an unfair disadvantage. Such fiscally beneficial procedures govern areas including (WCO 1999):

- The temporary storage of goods.
- Customs warehouses and free zones.
- Transit and transshipment.
- Processing under customs control.
- Inward processing relief, including suspension and drawback.
- Outward processing relief.

Authorization usually is conditional on maintaining a good compliance record and on meeting set requirements for systems and administration. Much of the compliance is monitored through audits held periodically (for example, every one to three years), rather than through control of each consignment.

Once control is internalized by the private sector, traders as well as border agencies benefit. The reason is that traders can reduce or eliminate customs and other border agency transaction costs. For example, the cost of paperwork is reduced when traders are authorized to declare goods periodically rather than for each consignment. Similarly, paperwork and its cost can be reduced by granting authorizations that allow electronic trade data to be exchanged between private sector information and communications technology (ICT) systems and those of the public sector. Such authorization ensures that data already captured by electronic systems—for example, the electronic port inventory systems, express carrier booking systems, and broker and agent systems—can be automatically passed on to the regulatory authorities.

Of course, systems of preferential treatment for authorized traders can work only where robust recordkeeping requirements are enforceable.

Assurance based controls

The principle of audit based control is often extended to ensure product safety and compliance with product standards. For example, since it is not feasible to test every imported electrical appliance for safety, most countries appoint special agencies or private sector inspection bodies (sometimes called notified bodies) to ensure that goods comply with product standards. Such standards usually are based on international norms, while variation from those norms and the use of recertification requirements are treated as nontariff barriers.

Assurance usually requires companies to use management systems—often embedded in the quality control systems of manufacturers—to ensure that final products comply with standards. Compliant companies with good manufacturing practices receive a certificate, and they may also mark their goods with required kite marks (for example, electrical consumer goods brought into the European Union may be marked *CE).* Authorities need not test or intercept goods, but can quickly assure themselves that goods are safe by referring to the kite mark and accompanying documentation. Similar control practices exist in many areas where border checks are not feasible. Assurance regimes range from safety standards for toys to strict hygiene requirements for the handling of food.

By making private firms fully responsible for managing compliance, assurance based controls free companies to manage compliance in ways that suit their own operations. They also lighten the operational burden on border agencies. Finally, they allow the free movement of goods that carry proper kite marks and documentation.

Risk management

Risk management for border agencies sets control levels according to perceived degrees of risk. It distinguishes between trusted and less trusted traders, and among shipments with higher and lower compliance risk, rather than enforcing blanket controls at set quotas (for example, 100, 50, or 5 percent of all traffic). Reducing inspections for traders with good compliance records, and giving businesses a strong incentive to boost compliance capabilities, risk management—like audit based control—can free up government resources. It also can cut the indirect transaction costs that traders incur because of delays at the border and the resulting loss of business. (Risk management is discussed further in chapter 6.)

Licensing trade in restricted goods

Restricted goods may be highly sensitive (military equipment, national treasures). They may require special control to prevent diversion for unregulated use (medicines, ingredients in illegal drugs). Or they may be prohibited entirely, with the exception of certain legal uses (narcotics, waste). By licensing trade in restricted goods, government agencies can set strict conditions on traders—and can hold traders accountable for meeting them.

Licensed traders normally are required to invest heavily in their control and compliance capabilities. A well managed licensing regime also allows regulators to access sensitive control information as early as possible. And licensing that is supported by formal or informal partnership arrangements gives regulators access to further information about parties up or down the supply chain from the licensed trader—effectively extending control beyond the border.

Licensing conditions normally are specific to the type of goods and trade. For example, licenses for firms trading in medicines could include very stringent requirements that the distribution of the goods be controlled by medical professionals. Companies supplying military equipment, or equipment with military applications, could be compelled to seek special permission from the defense or trade ministry and provide assurances that goods do not fall into the wrong hands. And companies dealing in waste could be required to conduct checks verifying that the recipients of the waste are suitably qualified to dispose of it safely and ethically.

Partnerships

Partnerships in border management usually arise when border agencies seek to extend control beyond their authority or competence. Well designed voluntary partnerships—being less expensive than more prescriptive, legislative enforcement—can benefit traders and border agencies alike.

For example, voluntary partnerships are common in supply chain security, where agencies seek to identify security risks before goods are shipped. Countries adopt supply chain security programs that impose conditions on firms seeking certification—in practice also imposing conditions on firms that seek to do business with certified companies. Such partnerships seek to extend security and control across the supply chain in exchange for operational or commercial incentives—for example, in simplified procedures, fast track border clearance, and reduced operational interference at the border.

Examples of security driven partnership programs include the United States Customs-Trade Partnership Against Terrorism (US CBP 2004) and the European Union's security amendment introducing the authorized economic operator concept into its customs code (European Parliament and Council of the European Union 2005). The underlying principles of these programs are echoed in the World Customs Organization's Framework of Standards to Secure and Facilitate Global Trade (the SAFE Framework; see WCO 2007) and are partly captured in the International Organization for Standardization's specifications for supply chain security management systems (ISO 28000).[7]

A less formal partnership vehicle, the memorandum of understanding, gives some structure to business-government arrangements while avoiding the expense of writing and defining laws. It also allows greater operational flexibility than narrowly defined legislation does. Memorandums of understanding between border agencies and key private sector actors—such as carriers and port operators—can govern issues as diverse as safety procedures (for example, when inspection staff must wear hard hats and high visibility jackets), codes of conduct (for example, agencies will inspect vehicles where they will disrupt operations as little as possible), and information sharing for criminal investigations (for example, businesses will give customs officers necessary access to computer systems). Memorandums of understanding also can be used to engage trade associations—for example, to provide tipoff procedures in campaigns against crime, ensuring that whistleblowers can speak anonymously through such associations and that their information reaches the right people.

Private sector organizations often choose to self regulate or to develop their own standardized procedures. The public sector, rather than developing new controls and procedures, can aim to draw on synergies. For example, security measures developed with the insurance industry or with a sector specific trade association often reflect the same motives that have driven officially developed controls and procedures to prevent crime. Similarly, commercial document standards developed to help share information between contracting businesses—such as for transport and shipping documents—can also be used to collate information for official control purposes. Other areas in which synergies between private sector practice and regulatory requirements can be found include quality standards, security seals, commercial contracts (such as the Incoterms; see ICC 1999), and electronic data standards (such as XML and Electronic Data Interchange [EDI]).

Contracting

The private sector is not merely a stakeholder with an interest in operational efficiency. Some private sector companies specialize in supplying their services to border agencies. For example, private sector companies may be used to run offices and facilities, support operational tasks, and cater to an agency's need for more specialist tasks (box 10.7). The extent to which they are so used will vary by country and by agency.

Private companies that are stimulated by competition and by innovations in technology and

---

Box 10.7 Services supplied by private sector businesses to border management agencies

Types of service that the private sector can supply to border agencies include the provision of offices and facilities, the completion of operational tasks, and the supply of specialist services. Examples of each type are listed below.

Providing offices and facilities:
- Land, buildings, inspection facilities
- Utilities (water, electricity, and other energy supply).
- Electronic infrastructure, office equipment, information and communications technology (ICT) equipment
- Other equipment and tools (cars, uniforms, telephones, office stationery, inspection equipment)

Completing operational tasks:
- Preshipment inspection
- Destination inspections
- Independent certification and verification
- Moving cargo to and from inspection facilities
- Unpacking and repackaging inspected cargo
- Managing and maintaining electronic infrastructure
- Independent analysis and testing (laboratory services)
- Supplying permanent and temporary support staff (skilled and unskilled)

Supplying specialist services:
- Staff training
- Printing and publication services
- Catering and hospitality services
- Electronic infrastructure development
- Staff insurance, pension, and health services
- Building, equipment, and infrastructure maintenance
- Donor funded capacity building projects delivered by private contractors

management can complement evolving border agency requirements. Used well, vendor services enable border agencies to focus on core functions such as control and enforcement. The private sector can also help introduce new skills and capabilities, overcome temporary resource limitations, and offer service enhancements that benefit the wider trade community.

To ensure that control and enforcement objectives are served as well as possible, activities should be reviewed continually—to identify core and noncore activities, and to distinguish those that should be outsourced from those that are best conducted in-house. The best choices for organizational performance are seldom easy to identify. Sound cost-benefit analyses are needed.

To illustrate the decisions about private sector suppliers that a border agency may have to make, consider the dissemination of customs tariff information. Traditionally such information is printed by in-house publishers, often reaching several hundred pages, and then sold to traders. Yet private publishers—and specialist government publishers—usually have better economies of scale for printing and distribution. If such third parties can disseminate the information at a lower cost, outsourcing the job to them makes good business sense (contractual arrangements aside). Online publication is even more cost effective, radically reducing distribution costs: traders can print only the pages they need. And if customs administrations lack the ability to host and update online publications, they can procure commercial off the shelf solutions, which may be much cheaper than in-house solutions.

Carefully procured private services can also improve a border agency's technological capacity. When agencies adopt new technology, simply purchasing new equipment usually is not enough. Staff require instruction in its use, and management practices need adjustment to ensure that it is applied in the best manner possible. For example, a procurement strategy for modern X-ray scanners should include operations research, advisory services, and training. If these are managed well, the agency will internalize the new skills. Another example of vendor services is the help that private sector companies can provide to border agencies recovering from civil conflict. Services can range from initial requirement gathering exercises to assistance with operations, active management of border controls, the implementation of good governance practices, and long term training commitments.

Less comprehensive arrangements between agencies and commercial suppliers include the maintenance of pools of experts, consultants, and contractors who can be brought in at short notice. Their expertise is usually specialized—for example, in training, research, development, ICT systems, and regulatory impact assessment. Such pools enable border agencies to ensure access to critical expertise when it is needed, without incurring the expense of permanent staffing. And reform projects often do require expertise beyond that of regular staff.

Governments occasionally contract private services for frontline control and enforcement. For example, in many countries governments contract preshipment inspection companies to increase revenue—and as a stopgap measure where border management integrity problems arise. Under preshipment inspection contracts, the contractor:

- Inspects cargo for export before shipment.
- Verifies relevant commercial documents for accuracy.
- Instructs the importer through an inspection certificate or a report of finding on correct duties and taxes—on which basis the importer pays duties.

Using preshipment inspection companies for clearance is controversial, however. It introduces an additional layer of control—often with significant operational disruptions—which the more developed countries (with good border management practices) do not require.

Vehicles for contracting with private organizations

There are three principal contracting vehicles for bringing in private sector services: through public procurement, through regulated fee structures or revenue sharing models, and through conditions specified in business authorizations.

Public procurement rules and procedures, which vary by country, are often set by a dedicated public procurement office or specified by departmental procedures and public auditors. When funds are provided by donor agencies further criteria are likely to apply.[8] Any large expense will

The role of the private sector in border management reform

usually require a cost-benefit evaluation—though practices vary with institutional arrangements and with the amounts at issue. In addition, good practice normally dictates that private service procurement is subject to tender, ensuring that the government—and the economy at large—receives the best value for its money.

Contractual arrangements governed by regulated fee structures—for example, to conduct a laboratory test—normally are also put to tender and are subject to similar procurement rules. The same is true for contractual arrangements governed by revenue sharing models—for example, where companies that help collect duties and taxes take a percentage (as some preshipment inspection companies and providers of electronic customs infrastructure do). The defining feature of regulated fee structures and revenue sharing models is that the expense for investment is recovered from the traders rather than from the border agencies. This approach to contracting can be attractive where agency resources are tight—but, if inefficiently managed, it risks becoming a tax on trade.

Finally, business authorizations may set conditions for the provision of services to border agencies wherever certain private operators are required by law to be authorized by the government. In the United Kingdom, for example, the customs authorization for port and airport operators handling overseas cargo includes conditions that specify requirements for suitable offices and inspection facilities as well as provision for working inventory systems. Similarly, veterinary and quarantine authorities can set their own conditions for dedicated border inspection posts, while further conditions frequently apply to the handling of dangerous and hazardous goods.

Management challenges in engaging private sector suppliers

Private vendors can complement efficient border agency operations. They can crucially support reform by supplementing available resources and capabilities. In return, however, they expect to be able to make a profit. The fact that their interests are primarily commercial need not conflict with reform objectives—so long as those interests are well managed.

The poor management of private commercial interests can enable private rentseeking. For example, if a procurement contract for ICT does not specify international standards, the vendor may build a system using its own standards, forcing traders to procure special software. Some less scrupulous vendors may even make heavily discounted offers to government, expecting to recover the resulting losses through excessive profits from traders' purchases of additional products or services.

Another challenge can be the fragmentation of border institutions in many countries. The many government stakeholders with an interest in border management and operations (see box 10.1) are likely to have diverse spending criteria and different preferred vendors. Those criteria and preferences can clash severely when services must be procured jointly, as for a single window system. Customs may be authorized to spend money only on private services to improve customs procedures—not on services to improve the trade environment more generally. And conservative customs officers may hesitate to approve spending on services that benefit other agencies. Even when such interdepartmental tensions can be resolved, differing supplier preferences can pose further obstacles. Major political support may be needed to meet such institutional challenges.

Despite the great benefits that private suppliers can offer border agencies, procurement officers must approach each decision critically, asking whether particular suppliers have the skills and capabilities they need. Damage from failed projects can be severe, especially when it affects the wider trading community—likely causing severe losses, not just to certain firms, but throughout the economy. The cost of fixing what has failed adds to total border management costs.

Conclusion

The private sector has two roles in border management, as a stakeholder and as a service supplier. As a stakeholder it generates a demand for reform and can help border agencies ensure that control objectives are met. As a service supplier it can help border agencies focus on core activities while providing access to new skills and capabilities. Both roles put private companies at the heart of any border management reform program—as drivers, as partners, and as suppliers.

Policymakers should recognize the private sector's diversity, and they should carefully consider how and when to approach particular communities within it. The interests of such communities vary and are not always aligned. Balancing them can be difficult for policymakers pursuing border management reform. Guidance from dedicated trade facilitation committees, often with government sponsorship, can help identify the best solutions and help put them in place. And better substantiated research—surveys, questionnaires, case studies, pilot programs, interview series, open consultations, and cost-benefit analyses—can further help to fine tune reform programs.

Notes

1. See "United Nations Centre for Trade Facilitation and Electronic Business Trade Facilitation Recommendations," United Nations Economic Commission for Europe, http://www.unece.org/cefact/recommendations/rec_index.htm.

2. See "United Nations Centre for Trade Facilitation and Electronic Business: List of National Trade Facilitation Bodies/Committees," United Nations Economic Commission for Europe, http://www.unece.org/cefact/nat_bodies.htm.

3. For the rule see "Chatham House Rule," Royal Institute of International Affairs, http://www.chathamhouse.org.uk/about/chathamhouserule/.

4. Between 2002 and 2005 donors committed an average $21 billion annually to narrowly defined aid for trade projects (OECD and WTO 2007). From 2001 through 2006 grants and loans to trade facilitation projects increased from $101 million to $391 million (http://tcbdb.wto.org/category_project.aspx?cat=33121).

5. See "Agreement to Establish and Implement the ASEAN Single Window, Kuala Lumpur, 9 December 2005," Association of Southeast Asian Nations (ASEAN), http://www.aseansec.org/18005.htm.

6. Also known as hauliers.

7. See "ISO 28000:2007," International Organization for Standardization, http://www.iso.org/iso/iso_catalogue/catalogue_ics/catalogue_detail_ics.htm?csnumber=44641.

8. See for example "Procurement Policies and Procedures," The World Bank, http://go.worldbank.org/YZVQ9VQ490.

References

European Commission. 2007. "Electronic Customs Multi-Annual Strategic Plan, 2007 Yearly Revision (MASP Rev 8)." Working document TAXUD/477/2004–Rev. 8–EN, European Commission, Brussels.

European Parliament and Council of the European Union. 2005. "Regulation (EC) No 648/2005 of the European Parliament and of the Council of 13 April 2005 amending Council Regulation (EEC) No 2913/92 establishing the Community Customs Code." *Official Journal of the European Union,* April 5: L 117/13–19.

Grainger, A. 2007. "Trade Facilitation and Supply Chain Management: A Case Study at the Interface Between Business and Government." PhD diss., Birkbeck, University of London.

———. 2008a. "Customs and Trade Facilitation: From Concepts to Implementation." *World Customs Journal* 2 (1): 17–30.

———. 2008b. "Trade Facilitation and Import-Export Procedures in the EU: Striking the Right Balance for International Trade." Briefing paper EP/EXPO/B/INTA/2008/06, European Parliament, Brussels.

ICC (International Chamber of Commerce). 1999. *Incoterms 2000: ICC Official Rules for the Interpretation of Trade Terms.* Paris: International Chamber of Commerce.

OECD (Organisation for Economic Co-operation and Development) and WTO (World Trade Organization). 2007. *Aid for Trade at a Glance 2007: 1st Global Review.* N.p.: OECD and WTO..

OGC (United Kingdom Office of Government Commerce). 2005. *Managing Successful Projects With Prince2.* London: TSO.

Raven, J. 2001. *Trade and Transport Facilitation: A Toolkit for Audit, Analysis and Remedial Action.* Washington, DC: The World Bank.

———. 2005. *A Trade and Transport Facilitation Toolkit: Audit, Analysis and Remedial Action.* Washington, DC: The World Bank.

SITPRO and A. Grainger. 2008. *A UK Review of Security Initiatives in International Trade.* London: SITPRO. http://www.sitpro.org.uk/policy/security/initiatives0108.pdf.

UNECE (United Nations Economic Commission for Europe). 2000. "Creating an Efficient Environment for Trade and Transport: Guidelines to Recommendation No. 4—National Trade Facilitation Bodies." Publication ECE/TRADE/256, United Nations, Geneva.

———. 2001. "National Trade Facilitation Bodies: Recommendation No. 4, Second Edition, Adopted by the United Nations Centre for Trade Facilitation and Electronic Business (UN/CEFACT)." Publication ECE/TRADE/242, United Nations, Geneva.

UN ESCAP (United Nations Economic and Social Commission for Asia and the Pacific). 2004. *ESCAP Trade Facilitation Framework: A Guiding Tool.* New York: United Nations.

US CBP (United States Customs and Border Protection). 2004. *Securing the Global Supply Chain: Customs-Trade Partnership Against Terrorism (C-TPAT) Strategic Plan.* US CBP, Washington, DC.

WCO (World Customs Organization). 1999. *International Convention on the Simplification and Harmonisation of Customs Procedures (As Amended).* Brussels: WCO. http://www.wcoomd.org/Kyoto_New/Content/Body_Gen%20Annex%20and%20Specific%20Annexes.pdf.

———. 2007. *SAFE Framework of Standards to Secure and Facilitate Global Trade.* Brussels: WCO.

World Bank. 2010. *Trade and Transport Facilitation Assessment: A Practical Toolkit for Implementation.* Washington, DC: The World Bank.

World Bank and D. Widdowson. 2007. "WTO Negotiations on Trade Facilitation Self Assessment Guide." World Trade Organization Document TN/TF/W/143, World Trade Organization, Geneva.

WTO (World Trade Organization) 2009. "WTO Negotiations on Trade Facilitation: Compilation of members' textual proposals." Document TN/TF/W/43/Rev.19, Negotiating Group on Trade Facilitation, WTO, Geneva.

10

The role of the private sector in border management reform

11

Reform instruments, tools, and best practice approaches

Robert Ireland and Tadatsugu Matsudaira

In addition to the critical considerations for border management modernization discussed in other chapters of this book, three dimensions of modernization should be addressed: sector specific modernization, interagency coordination, and cross border harmonization. Looking at these three dimensions, this chapter explains how international instruments, tools, and best practice approaches—hereafter referred to collectively as international instruments—can be most useful to countries. The chapter presents a typology of the international instruments and discusses how countries can work toward adopting each. An annex briefly describes many of the key international instruments, tools and best practice approaches currently available to reformers.

Three dimensions of reform

Discussed in this section are three dimensions of border management reform: sector specific modernization, interagency coordination, and cross border harmonization.

Sector specific modernization

As border agencies face the continuous challenge of improving their business processes, either to identify efficiencies in the traditional operational and procedural fields or to meet a changing policy or global environment, sector specific modernization is commonly observed in border reform efforts. Because the regulatory framework of a sector is often formulated on an agency basis, a sector specific approach is often seen as an agency specific approach. For example, a customs administration can improve its own risk management system without consideration of other border agencies'

mandates or trading partners' practices, and equally, other border agencies can also improve their own risk management systems in isolation. While this may create definite improvements at the agency level, it will not deliver an optimized process for the end user.

Interagency coordination

To deliver an optimal industry level solution, alignment and cooperation with other national stakeholders is necessary. Forms of interagency coordination vary widely in scope and include activities such as increased data sharing, harmonization of data requirements and coding, delegation of authority, joint operational activity (such as joint customs and quarantine inspections), and the use of a single window for border clearance processes. Interagency coordination may enable multiple agencies to share a single noncompliance database or see one agency conduct risk

Reform instruments, tools, and best practice approaches

management activities on behalf of other border agencies. A true interagency approach will enable the development of a single access point for the border clearance process (a single window) rather than a sector specific approach that, while improving individual processes, will still require the trading community to deal with multiple points of access to complete regulatory requirements.

Cross border harmonization

The third dimension of border management reform is cross border harmonization. The need to consider cross border harmonization comes directly from the fact that international trade is, by definition, a cross border transaction. Cross border harmonization increasingly draws policymakers' attention because of evolving regional integration initiatives and is of great interest particularly to landlocked countries, whose competitiveness is partly governed by the performance of neighboring countries. The export process in one country relates directly to an import process in another country and, with increased integration of trade supply chains, opportunities exist to create efficiencies through harmonization efforts that can treat both the import and export procedures as part of the same clearance process. Targeted areas could include harmonization of data requirements and procedures, coding harmonization, delegation of authority, synchronization of working hours, joint inspection processes, sharing of facilities (juxtaposed offices, one stop border posts), and regional single windows.

The need for coordination

Interagency coordination and cross border harmonization will require modification in one or more agency's systems, and this raises issues of jurisdiction and demarcation. A regulatory framework is traditionally based upon an individual agency's requirements within a sovereign country. For example, customs laws may prescribe how a customs administration operates—but not how other agencies should undertake their regulatory responsibilities. Equally, one country's customs laws cannot dictate the roles and responsibilities performed by another country's customs administration.

The impact of an interagency approach may be significant. Regulatory requirements on data and documents, including formatting and coding, may need to be consolidated between agencies, and information and communications technology (ICT) systems may require extensive modification or complete redevelopment to enable integration and systems compatibility—raising the questions of who changes what and who pays. In addition to these technical issues, the question of who leads the changes and who bears the burden can result in a situation where individual agencies may agree with the concept of an interagency approach, but gaining consensus on how these changes should be implemented becomes problematic. For example, consider the situation where all key border agencies have their own ICT systems which are not interoperable and they discuss implementation of a single window. In such a situation, when one agency states that the single window should be based on its system, it is not difficult to imagine that the other agencies would counterargue and prefer a single window based on their own agency specific systems. Sustainable high level political commitments, such as decisions at the ministerial or cabinet level, would help to resolve such issues—but ministers need an appropriate guide.

The role of international instruments

International instruments can range from legally binding requirements, such as those incorporated in World Trade Organization (WTO) agreements, through to recommended best practices and guidelines. Usually they are developed and negotiated by countries in specialized multilateral organizations. As international instruments are generally agreed and ratified at the political level, they can be a persuasive driver of change—with high level political commitment, interagency conflicts over leadership and ownership can be managed across agencies.

Change based on international instruments can also bring clarity to overall change objectives, thus increasing engagement with industry stakeholders (including donor community stakeholders, private sector stakeholders, and government employees). International instruments are not generally standalone texts, and usually they are supported by implementation guidelines to help countries make the necessary changes to their systems and procedures. Furthermore, certain international instruments function

11

Reform instruments, tools, and best practice approaches

as benchmarks of change by providing monitoring indices (discussed further in the following sections).

Because international instruments are international public goods, countries and agencies can expect more expert assistance to be available through specialized international agencies and developed countries that have already adopted such instruments. Also, with international experience and lessons learned from other countries (including developing countries facing similar situations—for example, landlocked countries), donor assistance may be more achievable when a country places emphasis on international instruments rather than on its own unique solutions.

Finally, adherence to international instruments, when it is announced to stakeholders and the general public, provides higher predictability and transparency for the trading community and investors. It creates a favorable environment for international trade and direct investment, and it shows the clear willingness of the country to adopt international standards and provide services and a regulatory framework at the global level.

Sponsors of international instruments

Numerous specialized international bodies develop and maintain trade related instruments. Some of the more widely known organizations and associations are listed in box 11.1. The list is indicative only—it should not be regarded as exhaustive. For example, WTO agreements also provide an international harmonization framework in certain areas of trade formalities, and ongoing multilateral negotiations on trade facilitation[1] will likely produce a new WTO agreement following the completion of the negotiations.

Typology of international instruments

Countries might use and refer to international instruments in their border management modernization efforts. These instruments may be categorized in the following areas:

1. Standardized cataloging of commodities crossing borders.
2. Standardized cataloging of identifiers of consignments crossing borders.
3. Standardized methods of transmitting information related to the consignments.

| Box 11.1 | Sponsors of international instruments |

Intergovernmental organizations

- CODEX: Codex Alimentarius Commission (a joint subsidiary body of the Food and Agriculture Organization of the United Nations [FAO] and the World Health Organization [WHO])
- ICAO: International Civil Aviation Organization
- IMO: International Maritime Organization
- OIE: Office International des Epizooties (officially the World Organization for Animal Health)
- UN/CEFACT: United Nations Centre for Trade Facilitation and Electronic Business (a subsidiary body of the United Nations Economic Commission for Europe [UNECE])
- UNECE: United Nations Economic Commission for Europe (a regional body of the United Nations)
- WCO: World Customs Organization (officially the Customs Co-operation Council)
- The World Bank (officially the International Bank for Reconstruction and Development [IBRD])

Others (not intergovernmental bodies)

- IATA: International Air Transport Association
- ISO: International Organization for Standardization

---

4. Standardized regulatory procedures for consignments crossing borders.
5. Border agency information management systems for consignment data processing.
6. Needs assessment to identify the gaps between current border management practices and anticipated levels.
7. Performance indicators to measure modernization progress and to identify bottlenecks.

This section will give a detailed explanation of each type of instrument. It will also refer to a number of specific international instruments. These instruments are discussed in more detail in annex 11A. (For the full names of concepts, instruments, and organizations to which this section refers using only initials, acronyms, or other abbreviations, see notes to table 11A.1, in the annex to this chapter.)

Standardized cataloging of commodities crossing borders means a harmonized description of the commodity and its sharing among stakeholders. As duty rates and many regulations are based on commodity type, it is imperative to have a coding system for

Reform instruments, tools, and best practice approaches

identifying and describing goods. In reality the goods classification system of one agency could be different from that of another agency: for example, if the customs goods classification system is different from the quarantine goods classification system, such a difference undermines interagency coordination. Another example is in a single window environment, where the trader needs to input data only once for multiple regulatory purposes. If the customs and quarantine goods classification systems are different, the trader would need two goods description data inputs to satisfy both regulatory requirements. The internationally adopted instrument for goods classification is the WCO's Harmonized Commodity Description and Coding System (HS Convention; see annex).

Standardized cataloging of identifiers of consignments crossing borders enables multiple stakeholders to identify specific consignments within the supply chain and create linkages between the physical consignment and its associated information. The ability to track and trace individual consignments supports trade facilitation and security as well as food and product safety and logistics quality. Illustrative cataloging references are the Unique Consignment Reference (UCR) and Unique Shipment Reference (USR): for example, ISO 17364 and ISO 17365.

Standardized methods of transmitting information related to the consignments enables seamless data sharing and data flow among the stakeholders within a country and across a border. Traditionally this was done in the form of paper, but increasingly it is done electronically. In a paper format, the UN Layout Key provides a base format for multiregulatory purposes. The concept of Single Administrative Document (SAD), originally developed in the EU and based on the UN Layout Key, is now in wide use. These instruments not only standardize the paper format but also prescribe what sort of information is required for the formalities. UNTDED provides countries with standardized definition of such data requirements. Added to this, certain international instruments provide standardized description of data requirements besides goods description. Such areas include coding on location, country name, and means of transport. For electronic data transmission the UN has developed UN/EDIFACT and the

United Nations electronic Trade Documents Project (UNeDocs). In the customs domain, the WCO's Data Model guides standardized data requirements and their definition and the application of codes for electronic transmission. IATA's standardized electronic messages on air cargo operations (for example, freight manifest) are widely used in the industry.

Standardized regulatory procedures for consignments crossing borders are provided by specialized international organizations. They are developed through a series of consultations and negotiations focusing on achieving both trade facilitation objectives and appropriate levels of control. In the customs arena the key instrument is the WCO's *International Convention on the Harmonization and Simplification of Customs Procedures,* also known as the Revised Kyoto Convention (WCO 1999). This convention and its associated guidelines provide customs administrations with guiding principles on managing an internationally harmonized border clearance process. Similar guidelines are provided by conventions in the areas of road traffic, ship and port management, and air transportation.[2] In addition, certificate and technical conformity procedures for the importation of certain types of goods are provided by instruments of CODEX (for foods) and OIE (for animals and animal products).

Border agency information management systems for consignment data processing guide countries on how to construct the ICT platform for their clearance processes. In the WCO's Revised Kyoto Convention (WCO 1999), chapter 7—titled "Application of Information Technology"—and its associated guidelines provide valuable information to countries introducing a customs ICT system. UN/CEFACT Recommendation 33 (UNECE 2005) gives guidance on establishing a single window. Also, its Single Window Repository (UNECE 2006) provides information on other countries' single window systems.

Needs assessment to identify the gaps between current border management practices and anticipated levels is increasingly used when a country or agency would like to modify its systems in order to meet certain targeted situations. Originally developed as a model to measure the difference between expected service

11

Reform instruments, tools, and best practice approaches

levels and delivered or perceived service levels, gap analysis is a method useful in comparing an organization's existing performance with its desired performance based on recognized norms (Parasuraman, Zeithaml, and Berry 1985). The World Bank's Trade and Transport Facilitation Audit (TTFA), for initial diagnosis, has been used in more than 40 countries (see Raven 2005; the recently revised version, retitled Trade and Transport Facilitation Assessment, is now available in World Bank 2010). The World Bank, together with the IMF, OECD, UNCTAD, and WCO, has also produced a needs assessment guide (World Bank 2008) for the WTO Trade Facilitation Negotiations, which has been used by more than 80 WTO members. The WCO also developed the Customs Capacity Building Diagnostic Framework and has used it to identify customs needs in more than 100 countries.

Performance indicators to measure modernization progress and to identify bottlenecks are valuable tools to monitor the modification and, in certain cases, to fine tune modernization efforts. In many instances, border management modernization emphasizes streamlined procedures and the reduction of dwell and processing times. The WCO's Time Release Study (WCO 2002a) is one such tool, providing stakeholders with data and information to identify the current situation, identify bottlenecks, and to monitor the effects of modernization. Any national effort also needs to be reflected in the behavior of international traders and investors. The World Bank's Logistics Performance Index (LPI) reflects private sector perceptions of the country's performance in trade facilitation and modernization (Arvis and others 2007; Arvis and others 2010).

The hierarchy of international instruments

This section describes four legal categories of international instruments, from those with binding force to those with a strictly informational function.[3] It provides a general overview of these four categories.

Conventions are instruments with legal binding force on the contracting parties.[4] To become a contracting party, a national ratification process is often necessary

(for the party to indicate high level commitment to adherence to the convention provisions). The accession instrument has to be deposited at the depository. Contracting parties are given incentives to eliminate noncompliance situations—for example, by peer pressure, by the driving force of the market, with technical assistance and capacity building support, through a dispute settlement mechanism, and, in a few cases, through sanctions. Examples are WTO agreements, the WCO's HS Convention (WCO 1999, 2008b), and the IMO's FAL Convention (IMO 1965).

Recommendations are unilateral acts with no binding legal force—they simply propose a given behavior to countries. The purpose of such recommendations is to examine the technical aspects of national systems, as well as related economic factors, with a view to proposing to the countries practical means of attaining the highest possible degree of harmonization and uniformity. No penalty is incurred in case of nonconformity by the sponsoring party. Nevertheless, to increase international accountability, certain recommendations contain an acceptance procedure. In such cases a country needs to deposit its acceptance instrument at the repository. Examples are UN/CEFACT recommendations.

Guidelines and guides are nonbinding instruments and tools whose purpose is to provide interested national agencies with information on a particular technical matter and to encourage them to take the appropriate measures as an aid to decisionmaking. They frequently follow intentions of political will and include declarations such as the WCO's revised Arusha Declaration on integrity in customs (WCO 2003b). There is no acceptance mechanism for them. Examples are the WCO's Time Release Study (WCO 2002a) and the World Bank's Trade and Transport Facilitation Audit approach (Raven 2005).

Compilations, case studies, and best practices are compilations of foreign experiences whose purpose is to provide interested national agencies with cases for a particular technical matter and to deepen understanding of the issues as an aid to decisionmaking. Examples are UN/CEFACT's Single Window Repository (UNECE 2006) and the World Bank's Customs Modernization Initiatives.

Reform instruments, tools, and best practice approaches

A suggested way to work towards the adoption of international instruments

If a country or agency is interested in adopting or complying with an international instrument, the following steps should be considered:[5]

- *Institutional agreement to adopt or comply with the instruments always needs change management.* In developing agreement, both the pros and cons of adopting the instrument need to be examined. Depending on the result of this preliminary examination, the country or agency might have a general idea whether to adopt or comply with it entirely or partially, and over what time period.

- *Translation of the instrument into the local official language is important* to enable the instrument to be incorporated or reflected in the local regulatory framework. By doing the translation, questions on the interpretation of terms and phrases may arise for which clarification is needed.

- *Consultation with stakeholders is needed* to highlight its importance in the case of interagency coordination and cross border harmonization. For the purpose of reducing the conflict costs and seeking synergies, when reforming regulations, parties and regulators sponsoring similar regulations should be consulted. Often regulators are cognizant of their own sector but fail to look at flows of goods, means of transport, and people and their associated information. Private sector entities and the ministry in charge of competitiveness might well be in a position to look at the issues from the perspective of overall trade flows.

- *Situation analysis, or gap analysis,* is the practice of identifying the current situation and assessing gaps vis-à-vis the anticipated models. It is advisable to conduct this practice with the stakeholders in order to let them share their views. Gap analysis is conducted not only to identify gaps between the current situations and the anticipated models, but also to identify obstacles that might prevent the country or agency from adopting or complying with the international instruments. Remedial actions are also agreed in this way. Here, attention needs to be paid to several different aspects including, for example, strategic management, the legal and regulatory framework, administrative guidelines, resources (budget, human, equipment, and infrastructure), human development, and communication.

- In order to implement the actions identified in the situation or gap analysis, if necessary, *budget arrangements* can be addressed. In the case of a lack of capacity, *dialogue with donors and experts* should be carried out on specified objectives and actions.

- *A formulation of reform packages* needs to be set up along with the identified actions. In this stage the responsible organizations, tangible objectives, timeframe, list of stakeholders to be consulted, project management body, and key performance indicators need to be specifically described in order to produce actionable plans.

- If the identified actions require it, *reform in legislation, regulations and organizations* should be carried out. For a smooth change management implementation process, an inclusive approach in cooperation with the other stakeholders is advisable.

- If necessary, *tendering for experts, procurement of equipment, and infrastructure* are also addressed. If the country or agency does not have an adequate number of trained staff, *appropriate training* should be delivered to identified staff. The objectives of modernization should be well shared with the stakeholders—staff in particular—through *good communication.*

- In the case of international agreements, *accession work* is necessary. In many countries, the accession work belongs to the ministry of foreign affairs, which is not necessarily familiar with the substance of the international convention in question. The agency responsible for substantive matters should help the ministry ensure smooth and accurate work. In certain countries the agency responsible may second its staff to the ministry of foreign affairs for the accession work.

- *Monitoring the progress* of modernization work is essential for sustainable project management. If any implementation difficulties are encountered the cause of the difficulties should be identified and addressed—whether by modifying the actions, timeframe, resources, or management, or by some other method. In this process attention should be paid to the formulation of a governing monitoring body. It is also advisable to have representatives of stakeholders in the governing body who can share all the information with their organizations and counterparts. Regular monitoring is imperative to allow them to receive early warning. The earlier corrective measures are taken, the lower the conflict costs and wasted resources.

- *Feedback to the international organization sponsoring the instrument* is highly recommended. For a smoother path on or toward an international instrument it is advisable for the country to participate in standard setting and maintenance work within the sponsoring organization. There are several benefits from this, the most important being that the country may be able to reflect its interest and any concern in the international instrument. At the very least it could register and share its interest and concerns, which could facilitate a subsequent provision of assistance and support.

Another important aspect of participation is that the standard setting and maintenance body is the place where national experts meet and is the best place to receive accurate information, answers, and details on foreign experiences. Through participation in the work, national delegates avail themselves of knowledge and can develop a network of experts. They will also have a sense of ownership of the international instruments.

Tables 11.1 and 11.2, for example, show attendance at the WCO's Permanent Technical Committee and HS Committee—both technical experts' meetings. The former discusses customs procedures, the latter the classification of goods. The two tables show regular participation by developing country WCO members in both technical committees.

Conclusion

International instruments provide a valuable tool for modernizing border management processes. To enjoy the greatest possible advantage from international instruments, reformers need to be aware of these instruments and familiarize themselves with them. Stakeholder consultations and an inclusive approach remain the key to success. Governments should consider encouraging their national experts to participate in the international standard setting and maintenance work at the sponsoring international organizations. This constitutes an essential part of capacity building.

As crucial messages to the sponsoring international organizations, continued maintenance of the

---

Table 11.1 Attendance at the WCO's Permanent Technical Committee meetings, 2002–06

Attendee information	Year of meeting				
	2002	2003	2004	2005	2006
Number of members attending the meeting	59	60	60	53	60
Percentage of all WCO members attending	36	37	37	32	36
Percentage of non–EU, non–OECD members among members attending	54	60	53	50	62

EU is European Union. OECD is Organisation for Economic Co-operation and Development. WCO is World Customs Organization. To maintain consistency across years, calculations assume that all EU and OECD members are the same to 2006, though in fact some members joined during the period examined.
Source: Matsudaira (2007).

Table 11.2 Attendance at the WCO's HS Committee meetings, 2004–06

Attendee information	Month and year of meeting				
	May 2004	October 2004	March 2005	September 2005	May 2006
Number of members attending the meeting	62	69	66	76	68
Percentage of all WCO members attending	38	43	40	46	40
Percentage of non–EU, non–OECD members among members attending	66	71	68	70	71

EU is European Union. HS Committee is Harmonized System Committee. OECD is Organisation for Economic Co-operation and Development. WCO is World Customs Organization. To maintain consistency across years, calculations assume that all EU and OECD members are the same to 2006, though in fact some members joined during the period examined.
Source: Matsudaira (2007).

instruments and accumulation of cases for the instruments should be carried out, and advocacy outreach and promotion activities, as well as pooling of experts, are desirable. In addition, sponsoring international organizations should consider working more with their counterparts to widen the scope and application of current agency specific international instruments.

Border management modernization is a crucial endeavor for governments seeking to improve their international trade policy objectives. Whether the primary objective is trade facilitation, revenue collection, security, societal protection, or a mixture of these, improving the effectiveness and efficiency of border agency operations will contribute to achieving these objectives. This is particularly relevant now with the global financial crisis that began in 2007 and intensified in 2008–09, and which has led to plunging international trade volumes.

In the past, many governments have focused on modernization of customs administrations without recognizing the impact on other border agencies. Thus, national leaders should now take a more comprehensive and holistic approach to border management. This chapter has attempted to introduce the reader to the major instruments and tools developed by international organizations and available for countries interested in strengthening their border management, especially in the context of trade facilitation and collaborative border management. For those readers already well versed on the items, the chapter provides an extensive list of references to the leading literature on the topics and technical information from international organizations.

11

Reform instruments, tools, and best practice approaches

Annex 11A
Key international instruments for border management modernization

The universe of border management modernization is immense. For example, a *Compendium of Trade Facilitation Recommendations* (UNECE and UNCTAD 2001) contains over 200 trade facilitation instruments and recommendations (see Butterly 2003, p. 34). Therefore, this annex concentrates on cornerstones that international organizations and associations have developed and that are accessible to all countries. Instruments developed by national administrations or customs unions (such as the EU) are not highlighted. Because this chapter has focused on trade facilitation, the annex will primarily consider goods rather than persons—but it is

worth mentioning here that several organizations, such as the International Organization for Migration (IOM) and the Organization for Security and Co-operation in Europe (OSCE), have developed strategies for controlling people crossing borders.

The instruments covered below are listed in annex table 11A.1. They fall into the seven categories of border management modernization instruments listed earlier (in the main text of the chapter), and they are presented here basically in the order of the seven categories (some instruments cover more than one category). The technical complexity of each instrument means that only a snapshot of each can be provided. Accordingly, reference is made to sources (in some cases Web pages) that describe the instruments in more detail for practitioners or researchers.

Table **11A.1** International instruments and tools for border management modernization			
Name of instrument or tool	Type	Contribution to trade facilitation	Primary sponsor
HS Convention	International convention	Standardized commodity description for nomenclature	WCO
WCO Recommendation on UCR and guidelines	Recommendations and guidelines	Standardized unique consignment reference	WCO
ISO Standards on UCR and USR	Guide	Standardized unique consignment reference and unique shipment reference	ISO
UN Layout Key	Guide	Standardized trade document format	UNECE and ISO
UNTDED	Guide	Standardized consignment data elements	UN/CEFACT
UN/EDIFACT	Electronic data interchange standard	Standardized process for the electronic exchange of trade data	UN/CEFACT
WCO Data Model	Electronic transmission tool	Trade data elements and mechanism for transmission; also a single window tool	WCO
Cargo-IMP	Guidelines	Standardized air cargo document format	IATA
Revised Kyoto Convention and Guidelines	International convention	Standardized customs procedures	WCO
SAFE Framework of Standards	Guidelines	Standardized customs security and trade facilitation best practices	WCO
TIR Convention	International convention	Standardized road trade facilitation measures	UNECE
FAL Convention	International convention	Standardized maritime trade facilitation measures	IMO
Annex 9 to Chicago Convention	International convention	Standardized air transport trade facilitation measures	ICAO
Principles for Food Import and Export Inspections and Certifications and associated Guidelines	Guidelines	Standardized food safety certification and conformity procedures	CODEX
Terrestrial Code	International convention	Standardized animal quarantine procedures	OIE
Customs ICT Guidelines	Guidelines	Standardized approach on use and application of ICT to customs operations	WCO
UN/CEFACT Recommendation 33	Recommendation	Standardized approach to establishing a single window	UN/CEFACT
Single Window Repository	Compilation	Online compilation of national single window experiences	UN/CEFACT
Trade and Transport Facilitation Assessment	Guiding tools	Needs assessment tools for preliminary trade and logistics facilitation diagnostic	The World Bank
Diagnostic Framework	Guiding tools	Needs assessment of customs organizational and operational capacity	WCO

(continued)

11

Reform instruments, tools, and best practice approaches

Name of instrument or tool	Type	Contribution to trade facilitation	Primary sponsor
WTO Trade Facilitation National Self-Assessment of Needs and Priorities	Guiding tools	Needs assessment tools to identify gaps and actions necessary to comply with proposed WTO trade facilitation measures	The World Bank in cooperation with the IMF, OECD, UNCTAD, and WCO
Time Release Study	Guiding tools	Performance indicators to measure time from goods arrival to release and to identify bottlenecks	WCO
Logistics Performance Index	Guiding tools	Performance index to measure private sector's perception of logistics performance	The World Bank
Other UN/CEFACT recommendations	Recommendations	Variety of trade facilitation measures	UN/CEFACT

Cargo-IMP is Cargo Interchange Message Procedures. Chicago Convention is the Convention on International Civil Aviation. CODEX is the Codex Alimentarius Commission. Customs ICT Guidelines is the Kyoto Information and Communications Technology Guidelines. FAL Convention is the Convention on Facilitation of International Maritime Traffic. HS Convention is the Harmonized System Convention. IATA is the International Air Transport Association. ICAO is the International Civil Aviation Organization. ICT is information and communications technology. IMF is the International Monetary Fund. IMO is the International Maritime Organization. ISO is the International Organization for Standardization. OECD is the Organisation for Economic Co-operation and Development. OIE is the Office International des Epizooties. SAFE Framework is the Framework of Standards to Secure and Facilitate Global Trade. Terrestrial Code is the Terrestrial Animal Health Code. TIR is Transports Internationaux Routiers. TIR Convention is the Convention on the International Transport of Goods under cover of TIR Carnets. UCR is Unique Consignment Reference. UN is the United Nations. UN/CEFACT is the United Nations Centre for Trade Facilitation and Electronic Business. UN/EDIFACT is the United Nations Electronic Data Interchange For Administration, Commerce and Transport. UNCTAD is the United Nations Conference on Trade and Development. UNECE is the United Nations Economic Commission for Europe. UNTDED is the United Nations Trade Data Elements Directory. USR is Unique Shipment Reference. WCO is the World Customs Organization. WTO is the World Trade Organization.
Source: Authors' compilation of information presented in the text.

HS Convention

The International Convention on the Harmonized Commodity Description and Coding System, also known as the HS Convention, Harmonized System, or HS, was adopted in 1983 at the WCO in Brussels and came into force in 1988. The HS Convention provides for standardized goods classification as well as a maintenance body and revision procedures. As of February 2009, 135 countries plus the European Community had signed the HS Convention and over 200 countries claimed to apply the HS nomenclature in practice. This means that more than 98 percent of merchandise crossing borders was classified based on the HS classification.

HS goods classification consists of approximately 5,000 commodity groups organized in 96 chapters beginning with live animals and ending with works of art, collectors' pieces and antiques. Each item is uniquely identified with a six digit code. To reflect the diverse interests of countries, countries are allowed to add a further suffix to the internationally harmonized 6 digits for more detailed classification. Although HS classification was developed by customs experts, its objectives are not limited to customs purposes. Indeed, the HS Convention is widely used in, for example, trade statistics, monitoring of controlled goods, rules of origin, internal taxes, and international trade negotiations—as well as in the trading community, for purposes such as commercial sales contracts and freight tariffs.

The WCO's Harmonized System Committee is in charge of maintaining the Convention and meets twice a year to clarify classification issues and to negotiate amendments to the HS nomenclature. The HS is formally amended every 4–6 years to reflect actual trade patterns and social or regulatory interests; the most recent amendment will enter into force on January 1, 2012.

Reference: http://www.wcoomd.org/home_wco_topics_hsoverviewboxes.htm

WCO recommendation for Unique Consignment Reference (UCR) and guidelines

The WCO adopted a recommendation for UCR in 2001 and modified it in 2004. The purpose of UCR is to assist multiple stakeholders seamlessly track and trace the flows of the consignment and its associated information. The instrument recommends that UCR should be structured at a consignment level in accordance with ISO 15459 and its updated versions (see below), or other relevant standards or industry specific reference numbers not exceeding 35 alphanumeric characters, enabling a unique origin-to-destination information and documentation trail for the entire international trade transaction. It also recommends that the UCR should be unique nationally and internationally, lasting for a sufficient period of time (at least 10 years according to the guidelines). The instrument also recommends the importance of determining the issuing party and the party responsible for maintenance.

Reform instruments, tools, and best practice approaches

11

Reference for recommendation: http://www.wcoomd.org/pftoolsucrrecomm.htm

Reference for guidelines: http://www.wcoomd.org/files/1.%20Public%20files/PDFand Documents/Procedures%20and%20Facilitation/UCR_new_e.pdf

ISO standards on UCR and USR

ISO 15459 was adopted in 1990 as a unique identifier specifying a particular transport unit (such as container and pallet) used in international supply chain. As international trade and logistics transactions have become complex, and the need to track and trace a shipment has become more important, it became obvious that a single standard was no longer enough to identify a particular shipment. Accordingly, ISO 15459 was modified as a multipart standard that includes transport units, registration procedures, common rules, individual items, returnable transport items, product groupings, product packaging, and groupings of transport units. These standards are quite pertinent after recent developments in radio frequency identification devices (RFID). Relevant ISO standards on supply chain application for RFID include the following standards: ISO 17363 (freight containers), ISO 17364 (returnable transport units), ISO 17365 (transport units), ISO 17366 (product packaging), ISO 17367 (product tagging).

Reference: http://www.iso.org/iso/iso_catalogue/catalogue_tc/catalogue_detail.htm?csnumber =43347

(ISO publication of the contents of ISO standards is fee-based.)

UN Layout Key

The UN Layout Key is a set of model forms for trade documents (paper based). It was developed and adopted by UNECE in 1963. A number of international organizations responsible for banking, customs, freight forwarders and postal services, and transport by sea, rail, and road made a decision and recommendation to align their internationally established document formats to the Layout Key. UN/CEFACT adopted a recommendation inviting the governments and interested organizations to pursue their efforts to align all document formats in international trade with that Layout Key. It has been registered as ISO 6422.

The Layout Key covers the commercial transaction sector, the payment sector, transport and related services, and official formalities. It provides not only for the size, design, and format of the forms, but also for data elements and their definition. Guidelines for application adopted in 2002 provide practical information on the Layout Key.

Reference: http://www.unece.org/cefact/recommendations/rec01/ece_trade_270_E.pdf

UNTDED

In recognizing the need for a standardized listing of consignment data elements, UNECE and UNCTAD developed UNTDED as a comprehensive directory of standard trade data elements and codes. UNTDED provides for data element name, definition, tag number, attributes, and element use and location in relevant documents. As it provides universal definitions, it could be used as a common terminology to convert one country's data element to the other country's data element, as in communications between Chinese and Japanese (with English as the common language). The application is not limited to international trade; it could be used in any e-commerce, including health, insurance, and medical. UNTDED is maintained by UN/CEFACT. The ISO adopted UNTDED in 1993 (not necessarily the latest one) as the ISO standard, ISO 7372 (UNECE and UNCTAD 2001, p. 63).

Reference: http://www.unece.org/trade/untdid/UNTDED2005.pdf

UN/EDIFACT

Recognizing the importance of a standardized approach to the electronic transmission of trade data, the UN/ECE developed the United Nations/Electronic Data Interchange For Administration, Commerce, and Transport (UN/EDIFACT)—the international standard for electronic data exchange of trade information (Butterly 2003, p. 54). It incorporates an electronic version of UN/TDED .

UN/EDIFACT provides for a set of internationally agreed standards, directories and guidelines for the electronic interchange of structured data—in particular those related to trade in goods and services between independent, computerized information systems (UNECE 1994). By using UN/EDIFACT, several standard electronic

Reform instruments, tools, and best practice approaches

messages for international trade transactions and operations are developed. Such messages include CUSDEC (declaration to customs), CASCAR (cargo report to customs), and CUSREP (response from customs).

UN/EDIFACT and the messages based on it are maintained by UN/CEFACT. The ISO adopted UN/EDIFACT syntax rule as ISO 9735.

A UNeDocs project to provide an XML based electronic message for more interoperability than EDI based messages "has been suspended by the UN/CEFACT Bureau and is currently under review."[6]

Reference: http://www.unece.org/trade/untdid/d08a/d08a.zip

WCO Data Model

The concept of harmonized customs data began life in 1996 when the Group of Seven (G7) launched the Customs Data Harmonization Initiative. In its 1996 Communiqué, issued from Lyon, the G7 stated: "[I]n order to facilitate the free flow of trade, we will initiate an effort to further standardize and simplify customs procedures among our countries. Uniform documentation and electronic transmission standards would reduce costs for business and government, complement efforts in the WTO by eliminating barriers to trade and development, and so promote growth." (G7 1996, paragraph 25). The G7 made this decision because of concern that the confusing, duplicative, and nonstandard systems of data were a significant nontariff barrier to trade. By 1998, G7 Customs experts had developed a simplified and harmonized data set for import and export procedures. As a result, over 800 data elements requested for import declaration by G7 countries in 1996 were reduced to 128 data elements in 2005 (WCO 2006).

In 2002 the WCO took over management of the G7 data sets and UN/EDIFACT message specifications, which became known as Version 1 of the WCO Data Model. Version 1 included the G7 data sets for cargo reporting and goods declarations for both imports and exports; message implementation guidelines based on the UN/EDIFACT customs messages CUSCAR and CUSDEC; the code sets (international and G7), used for the coded data elements; and the revised Kyoto Convention Customs Data Principles (WCO 2002b). Version 2 was expanded to include other border agencies, the transit procedure, and conveyance reporting (WCO 2004a, paragraph 12). The current Version 3 includes requirements for customs and for other border agencies such as agriculture, human health, environmental protection (Basel Convention), and marine safety (WCO 2008a, paragraph 7). The WCO Data Model is consistent with UN/CEFACT work and is expected to be widely used. For example, UNCTAD's customs processing ICT system, the Automatic System for Customs Data (ASYCUDA), which has been introduced in over 80 countries, is compatible with the WCO Data Model.[7]

Reference: http://www.wcoomd.org/home_wco_topics_pfoverviewboxes_tools_and_instruments_pftoolsdatamodel.htm

(Details are copyright protected. For more detail please contact the WCO.)

Cargo-IMP

IATA developed and maintains Cargo Interchange Message Procedures (Cargo-IMP), which is designed for use between airlines and other parties as an electronic message source for specifications concerning space allocation in the aircraft, air waybill, flight manifest, accounting, status, discrepancy, embargo, customs, Cargo Accounts Settlement Systems (CASS) billing,[8] dangerous goods, allotments, and surface transportation. For example, FWB is a standardized electronic message format for master air waybill, FHL is that for house air waybill. IATA is promoting paperless air cargo processing (e-Freight) for which these electronic messages are the keys to realization.

Reference: http://www.iata.org/ps/publications/cimp.htm

Revised Kyoto Convention and Guidelines

The WCO's Revised Kyoto Convention is the international trade facilitation convention for customs (WCO 1999). The first iteration of the *International Convention on the Simplification and Harmonization of Customs Procedures* was adopted in 1973 at the WCO Council sessions in Kyoto and entered into force in 1974. The revised convention was adopted in 1999 and came into force in 2006 with 40 contracting parties. It had 64 contracting parties as of June 2010.

The Revised Kyoto Convention has a main body comprised of administrative provisions, accompanied by a general annex and specific annexes. The general annex, which is obligatory to accept in the accession to the Revised Kyoto Convention, provides for basic trade facilitation measures generally applicable to any customs regime. The specific annexes, which are optional for accession, provide for measures for specific customs regimes (such as inward processing and temporary admission). Each annex or annex chapter is accompanied by guidelines that essentially provide interpretation and a collection of customs best practices. The contents of the general annex and specific annexes are (WCO 1999):

General annex
- Chapter 1: General principles
- Chapter 2: Definition
- Chapter 3: Clearance and other customs formalities
- Chapter 4: Duties and taxes
- Chapter 5: Security
- Chapter 6: Customs control
- Chapter 7: Application of information technology
- Chapter 8: Relationship between the customs and third parties
- Chapter 9: Information, decision and rulings supplied by the customs
- Chapter 10: Appeals in customs matters

Specific annexes
- A1: Formalities prior to the lodgment of the goods declaration
- A2: Temporary storage of goods
- B1: Clearance for home use
- B2: Re-importation in the same state
- B3: Relief from import duties and taxes
- C1: Outright exportation
- D1: Customs warehouses
- D2: Free zones
- E1: Customs transit
- E2: Transshipment
- E3: Carriage of goods coastwise
- F1: Inward processing
- F2: Outward processing
- F3: Drawback
- F4: Processing of goods for home use
- G1: Temporary admission
- H1: Customs offences

- J1: Travelers
- J2: Postal traffic
- J3: Means of transport for commercial use
- J4: Stores
- J5: Relief consignments

While the Revised Kyoto Convention is focused on customs procedures, it recognizes the importance of other border agencies to trade facilitation and the crucial need for cooperation. For example, the Revised Kyoto Convention contains a binding transitional standard on coordinated border management: "[I]f the goods must be inspected by other competent authorities and the Customs also schedules an examination, the Customs shall ensure that the inspections are coordinated and, if possible, carried out at the same time" (WCO 1999).

Reference: http://www.wcoomd.org/home_wco_topics_pfoverviewboxes_tools_and_instruments_pfrevisedkyotoconv.htm

SAFE Framework of Standards

Following the September 11, 2001 attacks in the United States, the WCO membership considered an instrument of security standards that would emphasize four core features: (1) receipt of advance data in electronic form for all cargo, (2) the use of risk assessment to analyze the data to determine high risk cargo, (3) the use of nonintrusive inspection equipment (NII) such as X-ray machines to inspect high risk cargo, and (4) the use of an authorized economic operator (AEO) system that would grant benefits, such as faster clearance time, to businesses that the government validated as low risk. This initiative culminated in the adoption of the WCO Framework of Standards to Secure and Facilitate Global Trade (SAFE) in 2005 (WCO 2007b). SAFE comprises two pillars: relationships between customs administrations and relationships between customs and the trade community. Not being an international convention, SAFE is nonbinding. Yet most WCO members have signed a pledge that they will work to implement SAFE, with the qualification that many would need capacity building assistance to do so.

As its title shows, although security (which is the focus of chapter 18) was the primary basis for the creation of SAFE, it is striking that its architects designed an instrument that strives for a balance between security and facilitation—one based on the

11

Reform instruments, tools, and best practice approaches

assumption that a border agency can apply appropriate controls for purposes of security while still facilitating trade. Indeed, SAFE's emphasis on risk assessment in order to avoid customs intervention in every consignment—for example, inspection or scanning—is also at the heart of the Revised Kyoto Convention.

Reference: http://www.wcoomd.org/home_wco_topics_epoverviewboxes_tools_and_instruments_epsafeframework.htm

TIR Convention

One of the more complex set of procedures at the border relates not to imports and exports, but to goods in transit. Indeed, GATT Article V is devoted to issues of transit. While not relevant to all countries, transit is especially important to landlocked countries that are at the mercy of bordering countries for their participation in international trade. The need for coordination between border agencies of landlocked countries and their neighbors engenders the need for standardized mechanisms for border procedures.

The Convention on the International Transport of Goods under cover of TIR Carnets (TIR Convention) focuses on the international transit system during road transportation and is a crucial trade facilitation tool.[9] Under the auspices of the UNECE it was adopted in 1959 and entered into force in 1960. It was revised in 1975. While the TIR Convention was founded by European countries, it can be ratified and used by any country. Currently there are over 65 contracting parties covering all of Europe and several countries in North Africa, the Middle East, and North and South America. While originally intended for road transport, it can also be applied to other forms of transport such as container ship. The TIR Convention provides for a guarantee network in cooperation with the International Road Transport Union (IRU), through which it is issued (UNECE 2007).

The TIR Convention is intended to cover the movement of goods under seal. In the past it was common for border agencies to physically inspect goods in transit, to ensure there were not violations of laws related to customs duties and to guard against reimportation. The TIR system involves the use of one transit document, a TIR Carnet, and a

system of seals. Customs at the border of the transit country can inspect the TIR Carnet and confirm that the seal is secured rather than conducting a full blown physical inspection (UNECE 2007). The five pillars of the TRI Convention are (UNECE 2007, pp. 6–7):

1. Goods should travel in customs secure vehicles or containers.
2. Throughout the journey, duties and taxes at risk should be covered by an internationally valid guarantee.
3. Goods should be accompanied by an internationally accepted customs document (TIR Carnet), opened in the country of departure and serving as a customs control document in the countries of departure, transit, and destination.
4. Customs control measures taken in the country of departure should be accepted by all countries of transit and destination.
5. Access to the TIR procedure for national associations to issue TIR Carnets and natural and legal persons to utilize TIR Carnets shall be authorized by competent national authorities.

Reference: http://www.unece.org/tir/convention/bases.htm

FAL Convention

The International Maritime Organization (IMO) is an intergovernmental organization based in London that provides a regulatory framework and cooperation forum for shipping. On the issue of trade facilitation at borders, the IMO has a role because it has developed some instruments that relate to cargo vessels traveling between ports. In 1965 the IMO adopted the Convention on Facilitation of International Maritime Traffic (FAL Convention), which states that its primary purpose is "to facilitate maritime traffic by simplifying and reducing to a minimum the formalities, documentary requirements and procedures on the arrival, stay and departure of ships engaged in international voyages."[10] The purpose of the FAL convention is to prevent delays in maritime traffic, foster cooperation between governments on maritime issues, and to promote standardization of maritime formalities. The FAL Convention Annex contains standards and recommended practices on formalities, documentary requirements, and procedures. The annex also contains eight standardized forms for the arrival of both goods and persons at seaports. The annex promotes the use of EDI to transmit forms between ports and ships. As of 31 January 2009 the FAL Convention had 114 ratifications (the IMO has 168 member states and three associate members), covering about 90 percent of global shipping tonnage.[11]

Reference: http://www.imo.org/Conventions/contents.asp?topic_id=259&doc_id=684

Annex 9, Chicago Convention

The Convention on International Civil Aviation, known as the Chicago Convention, was adopted in 1944. Article 37 of the Chicago Convention requires contracting states to committed "to collaborate in securing the highest practicable degree of uniformity in regulations, standards, procedures, and organization in relation to aircraft, personnel, airways and auxiliary services in all matters in which such uniformity will facilitate and improve air navigation" (ICAO 1944). In 1949 the ICAO Council adopted "Standards and Recommended Practices" on facilitation, which became Annex 9 to the Chicago Convention. Originally Annex 9 dealt primarily with simplifying procedures for the clearance of aircraft and its cargo and passengers, standardizing required documents, and reducing paperwork. In the 11th edition of Annex 9 the scope expanded to include issues such as using risk management during inspections, security, and enforcement (ICAO 2002). There is now a 12th edition (ICAO 2005). There were 190 contracting parties to the Chicago Convention as of January 2009.

Reference: http://www.icao.int/icao/en/atb/fal/

Principles for Food Import and Export Inspections and Certifications and associated Guidelines

Codex Alimentarius is a compilation of standards, codes of practice, guidelines, and other recommendations related to foods. It is maintained by the Codex Alimentarius Commission, which was established in joint collaboration between the Food and Agriculture Organization of the United Nations (FAO) and the World Health Organization (WHO). Its "Principles for Food Import and Export Inspection and Certification" provides principles for governments with the aim of ensuring an optimal outcome consistent with consumer protection and the facilitation of trade. Its associated guidelines provide a framework for the development of import and export inspections and a certification system consistent with these principles.

References:
- www.codexalimentarius.net/download/standards/37/CXG_020e.pdf
- www.codexalimentarius.net/download/standards/354/CXG_026e.pdf

Terrestrial Code

The Terrestrial Animal Health Code (Terrestrial Code) is a set of standards and recommendations maintained by OIE; the objective of the latest version, Terrestrial Code 2009, is to assure the sanitary safety of international trade in terrestrial animals and their products. Standards and recommendations include a user guide, animal health surveillance, import risk analysis, animal health measures applicable before and at departure, border posts and quarantine stations in the importing country, design and implementation of identification systems to achieve animal traceability, zoning, and compartmentalization. In particular, section 5 deals with trade measures, import and export procedures, and veterinary certification.

Reference: www.oie.int/eng/normes/mcode/en_sommaire.htm

Customs ICT Guidelines

These Guidelines, derived from the guidelines for Chapter 7 of the General Annex to the Revised Kyoto Convention, are maintained by the WCO (WCO 2004b). They are designed to help customs make decisions on improvements in services to clients through the use of ICT, which the guidelines call information and communications technologies (ICT). The Customs ICT Guidelines identify the principal areas of customs program delivery where the application of ICT may be viable. In addition, the guidelines identify and suggest possible trading partner interfaces and attempt to outline a number of issues that customs administrations will encounter if they choose to develop ICT systems. Such issues include legal issues and requirements, security, client consultation, and a brief explanation of various communication protocols.

Reference: http://www.wcoomd.org/home_wco_topics_pfoverviewboxes_tools_and_instruments_pftoolsict.htm

UN/CEFACT Recommendation 33

UN/CEFACT Recommendation 33 is a recommendation on establishing a single window. It defines a single window as "a facility that allows parties involved in trade and transport to lodge standardized information and documents with single entry point to fulfill all import, export, and transit related regulatory requirements. If information is electronic, then individual data elements should only be submitted once" (UNECE 2005). Thus the recommendation does not exclude a possibility of a nonelectronic single window. The recommendation is supplemented by guidelines that illustrate three basic models for a single window: a single authority, a single automated system for the collection and dissemination of information, and an automated information transaction system. It also provides guidelines on practical steps in planning and implementing a single window, with a compilation of national experiences.

Reference: www.unece.org/cefact/recommendations/rec33/rec33_trd352e.pdf

Single Window Repository

The Single Window Repository is an online compilation of countries' single window experiences. As of November 2009, 14 cases were available on the UN/CEFACT Web site: Finland, Germany, Ghana, Guatemala, Hong Kong SAR, China, Japan, Korea, Malaysia, Mauritius, Senegal, Singapore, Sweden, the United States, and the former Yugoslav Republic of Macedonia. According to UN/CEFACT, 30 single windows are in operation in the world and the repository intends to cover all of them. Following UN/CEFACT Recommendation 33, the repository has a standardized approach where all the national experiences in the repository provide information on background of the introduction of single window, establishment, services, operational model, business model, technology, promotion and communication, judicial aspects, standards, benefits, lessons learned, future plan, and contact information.

Reference: http://www.unece.org/cefact/single_window/welcome.htm

Trade and Transport Facilitation Assessment

The World Bank developed the Trade and Transport Facilitation Audit (Raven 2005) as guidelines to help countries and reformers conduct an accurate initial diagnosis of constraints for trade and transport facilitation, and to help them design corrective trade activities. The approach has been implemented in more than 40 countries over the past 5 years. This toolkit has recently been updated to reflect lessons learned in World Bank operations, and the revised version—retitled Trade and Transport Facilitation Assessment—is now available (World Bank 2010).

References:
- http://www-wds.worldbank.org/external/default/WDSContentServer/WDSP/IB/2002/01/18/000094946_0201040949053/Rendered/PDF/multi0page.pdf
- http://siteresources.worldbank.org/EXTTLF/Resources/Trade&Transport_Facilitation_Assessment_Practical_Toolkit.pdf

WCO Diagnostic Framework

The WCO Customs Capacity Building Diagnostic Framework (WCO 2005) emerged from the philosophy that was enshrined in the Customs Capacity Building Strategy adopted by the WCO in June 2003 (WCO 2003a). The strategy posits that it is difficult to reform a customs administration if there is not a comprehensive and accurate understanding of its capacity building needs. Hence, the WCO advocates that a diagnostic or needs assessment be conducted to gain a clear view of an administration's operations and organization by comparing its characteristics and performance with internationally accepted standards.

Because the WCO's strategy contends that customs modernization must include a holistic and comprehensive approach, its Diagnostic Framework is organized under seven clusters that cover every aspect of a customs administration: strategic management, human and financial resources, legal framework, customs systems and procedures, information and communications technology, external cooperation, and good governance. For each cluster the Diagnostic Framework lists a series of diagnostic questions, common weaknesses, potential solutions and improvement options, and useful resource material.

At the conclusion of a diagnostic mission the diagnosticians prepare a report that summarizes the current capacity of a customs administration and what needs to be done to raise that capacity. The Diagnostic Framework can be used for purposes of needs assessment by both external experts or by internal staff. It is a key component of the WCO's Columbus Program, which has been carried out in more than 100 WCO Member countries.

Reference: http://www.gfptt.org/Entities/ReferenceReadingProfile.aspx?id=d32b7bd3-0b5f-40a5-a045-00d320153cf0

Trade Facilitation Self-Assessment of Needs and Priorities

The WTO Trade Facilitation National Self-Assessment of Needs and Priorities (WTO 2009) was developed by the World Bank in cooperation with the IMF, OECD, UNCTAD, and WCO as a response to concerns from developing countries about the potential obligations of a final trade facilitation agreement. The tool, which has been used by over 85 WTO member countries, presents a comprehensive list of all the trade measures currently being negotiated in Geneva and outlines a strategy for identifying whether or not a country is in compliance with the measures. If a country determines it is not in compliance with a particular proposed measure, the tool is helpful in ascertaining what needs to be done to reach compliance—for example, through the application of local remedies, through capacity building, or through technical assistance. In practice the tool is used at a workshop that brings together stakeholders from all border agencies and the trade community to conduct a gap analysis. The purpose is that with all the relevant stakeholders in one venue analyzing the measures, the combination of the appropriate expertise and a checks and balances verification process will lead to a more accurate assessment of the status of compliance, needs, and priorities.

Reference: http://www.wcoomd.org/files/1.%20Public%20files/PDFandDocuments/Procedures%20and%20Facilitation/WTO_Documents_E/tnTFW143R3.pdf

Time Release Study

The WCO developed the Guide to Measure the Time Required for the Release of Goods, or Time Release Study (TRS), as a performance measurement tool in the trade facilitation modernization arsenal (WCO 2002a). The TRS can be used for imports, exports, and goods in transit and all modes of transport. While the TRS was originally developed for use by customs administrations, it is applicable to all border agencies involved in the release process. Indeed, it is crucial to success that all border agencies, along with all trade stakeholders, be involved in the study (so that differentiations can be identified). To be useful, the TRS goes beyond measuring time—a study must also consider the commodities being traded, the mode of transport, the location, what government agencies were involved, and the inspection channel (green, yellow, or red; WCO 2007c). More important, the TRS identifies causes and attributes of the delay by soliciting feedback from the stakeholders, especially private sector service providers.

The TRS is helpful in identifying obstacles to the release process, including a lack of skilled or knowledgeable resources; poor or unused ICT; fragmented or confusing legislation; deficient coordination amongst border agencies; inadequate communication between border agencies and the trade community; inefficient payment mechanisms or weak banking systems; a deficient infrastructure; a substandard or delayed declarations submission; excessive numbers of required supporting documents; a lack of simplified procedures; and customer delays in removing goods (WCO 2007c).

The WCO has developed a Web based application for creating a database for the TRS. Countries can use the TRS software to generate reports indicating the average times and standard deviation for each step in the process of releasing goods. The software is on the WCO server, and use is password protected to ensure the confidentiality of the data (WCO 2007a).

The tool is becoming widely recognized. For example, a proposal under consideration in the WTO Trade Facilitation negotiations would require that "(WTO) Members shall measure and publish their own average time for the release of goods in a consistent manner on a periodic basis, using such tools as the WCO Time Release Study" (WTO 2008).

Reference: http://www.wcoomd.org/files/1.%20Public%20files/PDFandDocuments/Procedures

%20and%20Facilitation/Time_Release%20_
Study_ENG.pdf

Logistics Performance Index

The Logistics Performance Index (LPI) was developed by the World Bank and is based on results of the survey of international logistics service providers (global freight forwarders and express carriers) with respect to their perception of logistics friendliness in the countries where they are operating and those with which they are trading. The combined survey results are supplemented with objective data on the performance of key components of the logistics chain in the home country—data collected for 100 countries, from which the LPI is produced.

The LPI consists therefore of both perception and objective measures. It measures performance along the logistics supply chain within a country and has three parts: perceptions of the logistics environment of trading partner countries, information on the logistics environment in the home country of operation, and real time-cost performance data for the home country of operation. It is increasingly quoted by policymakers and reformers in referring to their countries' logistics performance and capacity building needs.

Reference: www.worldbank.org/lpi

UN/CEFACT Recommendations

UN/CEFACT produced and maintains a number of trade facilitation recommendations, including the UN Layout Key for Trade Documents and the most recent on the single window concept (Recommendation 33). The numbered recommendations are:

1. United Nations Layout Key for Trade Documents
2. ISO Country Code for Representation of Names of Countries
3. National Trade Facilitation Organs: Arrangements at the national level to coordinate work on facilitation of trade procedures
4. Abbreviations of INCOTERMS: Alphabetic code for INCOTERMS 1990
5. Aligned Invoice Layout Key for International Trade
6. Numerical Representation of Dates, Time and Periods of Time
7. Unique Identification Code Methodology
8. Alphabetic Code for the Representation of Currencies
9. Codes for Ships' Names
10. Documentary Aspects of the International Transport of Dangerous Goods
11. Measures to Facilitate Maritime Transport Documents Procedures
12. Facilitation of Identified Legal Problems in Import Clearance Procedures
13. Authentication of Trade Documents by Means other than Signature
14. Simpler Shipping Marks
15. Code for Ports and Other Locations (UN/LOCODE)
16. PAYTERMS: Abbreviations for Terms of Payment
17. Facilitation Measures related to International Trade Procedures
18. Code for Modes of Transport
19. Codes for Units of Measurement used in International Trade
20. Codes for Types of Cargo, Packages and Packing Materials with Complementary Codes for Package Names
21. Layout Key for Standard Consignment Instructions
22. Freight Cost Code
23. Harmonization of Transport Status Code
24. Use of the United Nations Electronic Data Interchange For Administration, Commerce and Transport (UN/EDIFACT)
25. The Commercial Use of Interchange Agreements for Electronic Data Interchange
26. Pre-Shipment Inspection
27. Codes for Types of Means of Transport
30. Electronic Commerce Agreement
31. E-Commerce Self-Regulatory Instruments (codes of conduct)
32. Compendium of Trade Facilitation Recommendations
33. Establishing a Single Window (with guidelines) (Recommendations 28 and 29 have been removed.)

The following numbered and unnumbered recommendations are under development:

34. Single Window Data Harmonization (also Guidelines)
35. Legal Framework for International Trade Single Window

Online (Alternative) Dispute Resolution
Cross Border Recognition of Digital Signature
Reference: http://www.unece.org/cefact/
recommendations/rec_index.htm

Notes

1. Negotiations on a review of, and possible improvements in, the General Agreement on Tariffs and Trade (GATT) Articles V, VIII and X, on customs cooperation and on technical assistance and capacity building support in these areas. See WTO (2004), annex D.
2. UN/ECE's TIR Convention, IMO's FAL Convention, and ICAO's Chicago Convention (annex 9), all introduced in the annex to this chapter.
3. The section is inspired by Matsudaira (2007).
4. Legal binding force differs from the "enforceability" of sanctions against a noncompliant contracting party. Certain conventions provide a transition period, a grace period, or reservation rights on specific provisions. Generally countries have discretion to ratify or not to ratify the convention.
5. The proposed approach is inspired by Mikuriya (2004), WCO (2006), and World Bank (2008).
6. See the online notice from UN/CEFACT, http://www.unece.org/cefact/unedocs.html.
7. See further the ASYCUDA Web site, http://www.asycuda.org/aboutas.asp.
8. CASS is an IATA program designed to simplify the billing and settling of accounts between airlines and freight forwarders. See further "Publications and Interactive Tools: Cargo Interchange Message Procedures (Cargo-IMP)," IATA, http://www.iata.org/ps/publications/cimp.htm.
9. See further "TIR—TIR Convention," UNECE, http://www.unece.org/tir/convention/bases.htm.
10. See IMO (1965) and, for the convention as amended through 2005, "Convention on Facilitation of International Maritime Traffic, 1965," IMO, http://www.imo.org/Conventions/contents.asp?topic_id=259&doc_id=684.

11. See further "Facilitation Section (FAL)," ICAO, http://www.icao.int/icao/en/atb/fal/.

References

Arvis, J., M. Mustra, L. Ojala, B. Shepherd, and D. Saslavsky. 2010. *Connecting to Compete 2010: Trade Logistics in the Global Economy.* Washington, DC: The World Bank.

Arvis, J., M. Mustra, J. Panzer, L. Ojala, and T. Naula. 2007. *Connecting to Compete 2007: Trade Logistics in the Global Economy.* Washington, DC: The World Bank.

Butterly, T. 2003. "Trade Facilitation in a Global Trade Environment." Part 2 of *Trade Facilitation: The Challenges for Growth and Development,* ed. C. Cosgrove-Sacks and M. Apostolov. New York: United Nations.

G7 (Group of Seven). 1996. *Economic Communiqué: Making a Success of Globalization for the Benefit of All.* Lyon: G7.

ICAO (International Civil Aviation Organization). 1944. *The Convention on International Civil Aviation.* Chicago: ICAO.

———. 2002. *Annex 9 to the Convention on International Civil Aviation: International Standards and Recommended Practices—Facilitation.* 11th ed. Montréal: ICAO.

———. 2005. *Annex 9 to the Convention on International Civil Aviation: International Standards and Recommended Practices—Facilitation.* 12th ed. Montréal: ICAO.

IMO (International Maritime Organization). 1965. *Convention on Facilitation of International Maritime Traffic.* London: International Maritime Organization.

Matsudaira, T. 2007. "Trade Facilitation, Customs and the World Customs Organization: Introduction to the WCO Trade Facilitation Instruments." *Global Customs and Trade Journal* 2 (6): 243–54.

Mikuriya, K. 2004. "Legal Framework for Customs Operations and Enforcement Issues." In *Customs Modernization Handbook,* ed. L. de Wolf and J.B. Sokol. Washington, DC: The World Bank. 51–66.

Parasuraman, A., V. Zeithaml, and L. Berry. 1985. "A Conceptual Model of Service Quality and

Reform instruments, tools, and best practice approaches

Its Implications for Future Research." *Journal of Marketing* 49 (4): 41–50.

Raven, J. 2005. *A Trade and Transport Facilitation Toolkit: Audit, Analysis and Remedial Action.* Washington, DC: The World Bank.

UNCTAD (United Nations Conference on Trade and Development). 2008. *"Border Agency Co-ordination/Cooperation."* Technical Note 14, UNCTAD Trust Fund for Trade Facilitation Negotiations, UNCTAD, Geneva.

UNECE (United Nations Economic Commission for Europe). 1990. *UN/EDIFACT Draft Directory: Introduction and Rules.* Available at http://www.unece.org/trade/untdid/texts/d100_d.htm.

———. 1994. "Design of UN/EDIFACT Messages, Guidelines and Rules Submitted by the Message Design Guidelines (MDG) ad hoc Group." Document TRADE/WP.4/R.840/Rev.2, UNECE, Geneva.

———. 2005. "Recommendation and Guidelines on Establishing a Single Window to Enhance the Efficient Exchange of Information Between Trade and Government." UN/CEFACT Recommendation No. 33, United Nations, New York and Geneva.

———. 2006. *Case Studies on Implementing a Single Window.*

———. 2007. *TIR Convention Handbook.*

UNECE (United Nations Economic Commission for Europe) and UNCTAD (United Nations Conference on Trade and Development). 2001. *Compendium of Trade Facilitation Recommendations.* Geneva: United Nations.

WCO (World Customs Organization). 1999. *International Convention on the Simplification and Harmonisation of Customs Procedures (As Amended).* Brussels: WCO.

———. 2002a. *Guide to Measure the Time Required for the Release of Goods.* Brussels: WCO.

———. 2002b. "WCO Customs Data Model." Internal document PC0090E1, WCO, Brussels.

———. 2003a. "Capacity Building in Customs: A Customs Capacity Building Strategy Prepared by the World Customs Organization on Behalf of the International Customs Community." World Trade Organization (WTO) document GCW467, WTO, Geneva.

———. 2003b. "The Revised Arusha Declaration: Declaration of the Customs Co-operation Council Concerning Good Governance and Integrity in Customs." Customs Co-operation Council, WCO, Brussels.

———. 2004a. "Issues Arising from the 46th IMSC Meeting." Internal document PM0130E1, WCO, Brussels.

———. 2004b. *Kyoto Convention Guidelines on the Application of Information and Communications Technology.* Brussels: WCO.

———. 2005. *Customs Capacity Building Diagnostic Framework.* Brussels: WCO.

———. 2006. "Fact Sheet: The WCO Customs Data Model—Version 2.0." WCO, Brussels. Available at http://www.wcoomd.org/files/1.%20Public%20files/PDFandDocuments/Procedures%20and%20Facilitation/CustomsData_Model_ENG.pdf.

———. 2007a. *Internet Software for the Time Release Study: User Manual.* Brussels: WCO. Available to WCO members at http://www.wcoomd.org/members/files/Members%20PDF%20EN/FacilitationProced_PDF/TRS%20user%20manual-updated.pdf.

———. 2007b. *WCO SAFE Framework of Standards.* Brussels: WCO.

———. 2007c. "Time Release Study." Internal document PC0179E1a, Permanent Technical Committee, WCO, Brussels.

———. 2008a. "Current Status of the WCO Data Model." Internal document PC0214E1a, WCO, Brussels.

———. 2008b. "Position Regarding Contracting Parties to the HS Convention and Related Matters." Internal document NC1314E1a, WCO, Brussels.

World Bank. 2008. "Self Assessment Guide for Technical Assistance and Capacity Building Support Needs and Priorities." Document TN/TF/W/143/Rev.2, WTO (World Trade Organization), Geneva.

———. 2010. *Trade and Transport Facilitation Assessment: A Practical Toolkit for Implementation.* Washington, DC: The World Bank.

WTO (World Trade Organization). 2004. "Doha Work Programme: Decision Adopted by the General Council on 1 August 2004."

11

Reform instruments, tools, and best practice approaches

WTO draft document WT/L579, WTO, Geneva.

———. 2008. "WTO Negotiations on Trade Facilitation Self Assessment Guide," document TN/TF/W/139/Rev.1 and TN/TF/W/139/Rev.1/Add.1, Negotiating Group on Trade Facilitation, WTO, Geneva.

———. 2009. "WTO Negotiations on Trade Facilitation Self Assessment Guide," Trade Facilitation Negotiating Group meeting document TN/TF/W/143/Rev.3, WTO, Geneva.

11

Reform instruments, tools, and best practice approaches

12 Managing organizational change in border management reform

Darryn Jenkins and Gerard McLinden

Managing change successfully in a complex institutional environment requires a strong sense of direction and purpose, widespread organizational ownership, perseverance, access to advice and support when needed, and a committed and stable leadership team. It must be planned and executed in concert with all key stakeholders, adequately resourced, and based on a realistic timeframe. Managers must build a strong organization to gather internal and external support while coping with the expectations created by the process. The managers must develop a clear strategy with performance measures calibrated to the situation.

Unfortunately, many reform programs establish new organizational structures or deploy new technology rather than make more basic human and procedural changes. However important new procedures, structures, and technology may be, meaningful and sustainable change is unlikely unless there are appropriate incentives that can persuade employees to support and contribute to reform. Some broad change management principles are set forth in table 12.1.

Border management extends beyond the role of any single agency—even one created by merging functions formerly assigned to various organizations (such as customs and immigration). Even after such a merger, there will be several agencies with border management responsibilities. So integrated and efficient institutional arrangements are needed, arrangements that delegate tasks and introduce embedded procedures for both policy and operational coordination. The parts of a comprehensive reform plan are listed in box 12.1 (their practical applications were detailed in chapter 2).

The external dimension of border management reform

The list of external stakeholders in border management is long. It includes the government, other public sector agencies, the private sector, and the international trading community. Each of these groups will have its own interests and, thus, its own perspective on the advantages and disadvantages of whatever reforms are considered.

Even within groups, interests will differ. In the private sector, for example, procedural improvements favored by traders who find the current system complex and opaque may be opposed by customs brokers who fear the changes will reduce traders' need for their services. For reform to succeed in the long term, key stakeholders must be persuaded that changes are necessary, well conceived, and directed. Unanimity is not required—but any changes resisted by key constituencies will take a long time to succeed, perhaps longer than any administration can endure.

Table **12.1**	**Key organizational change management principles**	
Principle	**Objective**	**Challenge**
Managerial focus and leadership	Maintaining focus on the reform program	A key challenge facing senior management in the reform program is that they already have very demanding day to day responsibilities but will need to commit their time increasingly toward the reform.
	Empowering the senior management team	The effectiveness and credibility of senior management is a prerequisite for driving the change management program, particularly in leading and directing middle management and staff.
	Considering the effect on morale	A balance will need to be struck between sensitivity to staff concerns during the change process and avoiding distraction from the principal tasks of reform. It is important to assess the opinions of staff through regular consultations to strengthen their voice. At the same time, a steering committee and senior management must make the necessary decisions.
Setting the change agenda	Developing action plans and targets early on	A sense of purpose will be instrumental in driving change. It is management's task to establish reform objectives and targets and to communicate them to staff in clear terms. This will help to align efforts to common goals, while engendering a sense of success as results are achieved.
	Monitoring and communicating progress	Success on performance targets can help to counter low staff morale during change. Management should identify operational and administrative reforms that can be easily and objectively measured and keep these goals visible to staff.
Communication and coordination	Ensuring adequate communication mechanisms	A complex organization demands robust mechanisms for disseminating accurate, timely, and precise information. This is particularly important when roles, responsibilities, reporting structures, and processes will be undergoing change.
	The need for regular consultation	Regular consultations with management teams and employees are important. In addition to improving information flows, such consultations will help staff to accept ownership of the change process, help overcome stakeholder resistance, and identify implementation risks and constraints before progress is hindered.
Human resource issues	Auditing and monitoring personnel resources	Senior management needs to be fully aware of the availability of skills to meet core objectives and reformulated job descriptions.
	Using training to support the change management program	Change management relies on human skills. Existing staff capacity often is insufficient to make reforms successful. The change management agenda needs to include staffing and training plans.
	Ensuring valued staff are retained	Valued staff must be retained despite the uncertainty that change can produce. Usually the best staff are the most employable elsewhere. Senior management must show it is aware of, and values, their contribution.
	Establishing clear staff roles and responsibilities	Throughout the reform process, a continuing staff communication program must explain changing roles and responsibilities. This can help maintain staff accountability, productivity, morale, and direction during the disruption.
	Maintaining staff motivation and discipline	During change programs, staff can lose motivation and discipline can break down. Systems to monitor and maintain high levels of performance and discipline among officials must be in place. So-called soft rewards, such as complimenting staff on performance, providing sincere thanks for effort, and celebrating small victories, can be effective in affirming the worth of individuals to the organization and maintaining their motivation.

12

Managing organizational change in border management reform

Accordingly, reformers must develop a broad commitment to reform and its overall direction across the political spectrum.

International experience over the past two decades has shown that political will is the largest factor in the success—or failure—of public sector reform. Change will not happen without clear, sustained government support. At the same time, government support rests on industry and popular support. In seeking political support reformers must work toward widely shared objectives, particularly if strong and easily mobilized domestic constituencies are likely to oppose the changes. While building

expectations is an important part of selling reform, those expectations, to be credible, must accommodate reality and the change capacities of the actors involved. The various and sometimes contradictory interests of stakeholders make mobilizing support a complex and difficult task. Border management reform requires many government agencies to be committed to change. Clearly establishing what each agency is expected to do—and how its fulfillment of its responsibilities will be measured and reported—is crucial.

Promoting the reforms to partner agencies as early as possible will pay off when it comes time to

Objectives and role

Relate wider government and ministry objectives and goals to the agency:

- Define the agency's role in contributing to these goals.
- Define the agency's short and medium term objectives.

Functions and work program

Review and assess government needs and translate these into specific deliverables:

- Define the functions of the agency.
- Identify key tasks required to accomplish goals.
- Review appropriate methodologies and define appropriate work practices for each task.
- Prepare annual and five year work programs.
- Set out performance targets and deliverables.
- Develop a reporting and monitoring system.

Management and organization

Develop an appropriate management system to deliver specified products, covering:

- Management resources.
- Performance monitoring and evaluation procedures.
- Incorporation of monitoring feedback in to work programs.
- Planning and budgeting systems and processes.
- Information and accounting systems.
- Simplification of procedures.
- Organizational and departmental improvements.
- Reporting hierarchies.
- Harmonization of practices, formats, and standards.

Resource requirements

Determine resource requirements associated with the work programs, including:

- Finance, logistics and staffing requirements.
- Human resource requirements.
- Staff training and development.
- Sources for finance.
- Information and communications technology requirements.

initiate a dialogue with government decisionmakers. Such an approach will ensure that other interested agencies are full partners rather than possible critics. Genuine interagency reform is unlikely if there appear to be clear winners and losers among participating agencies. To be successful, proposed reforms will need to accommodate the legitimate concerns and operational needs of all key agencies—reforms should be built on a shared vision for the future and joint ownership of the reform program. (The various interests and concerns of participating agencies are discussed in chapter 5.)

Genuine consultation and willingness to compromise will make the change program more credible. A complicating factor in many developing countries is that border management agencies often are at various stages of development. Customs, typically, already has an automated system and a good grasp of aspects of the modern approach to border management, such as risk management. Other border management agencies often do not—and therefore may feel at a disadvantage in negotiations.

While the value of accommodating all border agencies' interests is generally recognized, the need for interagency coordination during change is often neglected or considered only as an afterthought. Public sector agencies often compete for power, influence, and resources and are therefore not natural partners in such endeavors. Longstanding animosities and suspicions may need to be overcome—a prospect that often can seem all but impossible. In such cases senior government officials must step in and, if necessary, make personnel changes to demonstrate genuine commitment to reform. Yet since even ministers may champion the interests of their own agencies over those of the nation, reformers should have hard data to encourage agreement—at least on the problems, if not on the solutions. To show how individual border agencies contribute to clearance delays, data from comprehensive time for release studies can be useful. Without such data agencies may simply blame customs or poor trade infrastructure for any and all delays.

Informal approaches at the senior level are often a means of softening resistance. Managers should always be willing to share information—even when it seems like a one way street—to allay suspicion and establish sound communication and cooperation channels. This approach can be smoothed by engaging stakeholder agencies as early as possible, preferably well before particular solutions are identified. Seeking contributions from all players during development can also do much to allay fears and suspicions.

A useful starting point in discussions is to establish firm ground rules and criteria for determining success. Some possible rules—for example, no participating agency will be abolished or incorporated into another, no staff will be declared redundant, and no policy options will be taken to the government until unanimously approved—may all prove useful in generating broad support across agencies. Without such rules agencies may participate primarily to protect their own budgets. Collaborative border management (the model outlined in chapter 2) is based on increasing effectiveness without making radical organizational and structural changes.

Senior managers, in seeking closer relations with other agencies, should identify the officials best equipped to lead dialogue with stakeholders. They should be selected for merit (including personal qualities) and not simply for the organizational positions they occupy—though of course some hierarchical sensitivities will need to be observed.

Border agencies must also develop their external relations with the trading community they serve through a balanced and comprehensive program of consultation, public relations, and education. Public support is vital to regulatory reform, so the public must be assured that its views will be heard, valued, and acted on. Management must sell the reforms, not only emphasizing good outcomes, but also being candid about possible negative consequences. Strategies should be developed to overcome likely objections. In short, an effective communications strategy should include various media and include regular face to face interaction with stakeholder groups (briefing members of parliament, for example, before annual budget debates). Standing meetings with stakeholders (quarterly with closely involved clients, or even monthly if a new program or major policy change consultation is involved) are a good source of feedback on how well the program is being received—and are a valuable experience for managers, who will be required to explain where the program is heading. Likewise, such standing meetings offer a sound basis for dialogue on unforeseen problems as they emerge. The steps in a general communications and awareness plan are laid out in box 12.2.

Box 12.2	Communications and awareness plan

- Identify and define awareness raising objectives and strategies.
- Prioritize messages to be conveyed to recipients, including the public and the media.
- Undertake a cost-benefit analysis of different communications and awareness raising strategies.
- Undertake a comparative analysis of the effectiveness of communications media.
- Identify the different stakeholder groups and analyze their needs and capacities.
- Design communications and information materials, including manuals, communications guidelines, fact sheets, press relations packs, and a communications toolkit.

Border management organization structures

Changes of government often bring changes in organizations' responsibilities, mandates, and reporting relationships. Even when such changes are needed, they are often undertaken without any coherent reform strategy to address underlying problems. In that case structural changes may give the impression of progress yet result in little—if any—improvement to performance.

To be sure, outside stakeholders may welcome what they see as a shakeup of troubled agencies about which they have been complaining—justifiably or otherwise—and these reactions alone may be reason enough to restructure. The perception of change can, in turn, drive reform.

Nevertheless, care must be taken throughout the reform process to ensure that daily operations continue to meet government standards. Maintaining effectiveness must take the highest priority, higher even than achieving short term modernization goals. For example, a large restructuring of government border management responsibilities must neither reduce revenue collection nor delay the processing and clearance of goods.

Reformers, as they sift through organizational options, must therefore consider how easy or how difficult it will be to achieve desired outcomes. To do so requires a thorough analysis of both the work and the disruption entailed by a given strategy, as well as any likely impact on operational effectiveness. Once reformers have weighed these factors they may prefer a lengthier and more pragmatic process—with less organizational disruption—to a more rapid and disruptive one.

Current trends in border management organization

The world today presents a bewildering array of border management arrangements. Rather than address every option, it will be more useful here to classify the major ones and comment on them—and, in particular, to explain the recent trend of merging various government agencies into single overarching organizations with a focus on achieving broader policy objectives.

Revenue authorities were formed in a number of developed countries to improve effectiveness and efficiency. However, in developing countries revenue authorities were established through direct pressure from multilateral institutions and bilateral donors. Developing countries, where it is important to reward staff for results while quarantining salary increases from the wider civil service, found it expedient to move away from rigid civil service processes and outmoded terms and conditions of service. The revenue administration model was seen as a vehicle for this aim.[1]

Similarly, in the last few years, and in direct response to the heightened international security environment, authorities—notably in the United States—have moved toward forming border control agencies. The structural design of these amalgamations has varied, though the motivation has commonly been driven by changing political priorities.

Some border management changes have not succeeded, often because serious problems in the organization were simply passed on to a new agency: issues such as failing management, poorly conceived reform strategies, disagreement on the direction of reform, and inadequate funds and human resources. Reform has failed in other cases because the change lacked political will and managerial direction. In some cases there was never a strong intention to succeed, and reform was intended to go no further than to a presentational level. And often different organizational cultures, working methods, and staff competencies have made genuine integration difficult.

The effect such arrangements have had on border management is important, given the conflicting mandates and priorities of border management agencies (chapter 1). In the developed world revenue from trade taxes collected at the border is less crucial to national budgets, and border enforcement need not seriously impair revenue collection. But in the developing world revenue from trade flows is a critical part of national budgets. Decisionmakers must recognize revenue agencies' competing objectives and must not copy inappropriate models—however great the perceived pressure to do so. In these circumstances conservative models of organization retain their value, though added resources may be needed to deal with new and emerging priorities.

Single revenue agencies. Over the last 20 years numerous governments have opted to collect revenue through a single agency. Such agencies range from a fully integrated revenue authority, outside the civil service and acting under discrete legislation, to a loose collection of bodies that nominally report to a director general of revenue and exist within the civil service (while retaining legally separate—if effectively constrained—individual identities and operational independence).[2]

Zambia, for example, established a revenue agency that successfully built on the experience of Uganda. In Zambia the existing customs and tax departments of the civil service were brought together under a commissioner general. Later a value added tax division was added. Each of the three divisions was headed by a commissioner, as was the common management services area responsible for corporate functions such as human resources, finance, information technology, and office services. Together with the commissioner general, the commissioners form the senior management group of the revenue agency, while a board of directors, appointed by the minister and comprising senior government and private sector representatives, oversees the agency. This structure has continued, and arrangements similar to it have been instituted elsewhere—notably in Africa and Latin America, where it is now the most common form of organization.

In the United Kingdom and Canada customs and tax agencies were amalgamated. Canada experimented with common technical units in audit and program evaluation, areas in which it had been an international leader for some time. Its experience underscores the need to foresee how cultural differences in the two agencies can create tensions in the amalgamated agency. The United Kingdom experimented with common units in enforcement. Estimates of its success have been clouded by the government's later move to form a border agency that combines elements of customs and immigration, traditionally seen as culturally nonaligned organizations.

Mergers of tax and customs into one agency are often resisted by staff and managers. Some argue that an easier way to increase efficiency would be to invest more in both agencies—others that merging them will result only in a new, larger dysfunctional organization. Yet it was found that a single revenue agency could use resources more effectively (through the combination of common services, for example) and more effective operations (through information sharing and through combined audits and investigations against common corporate targets). In theory these more effective operations are achievable through interagency cooperation, but in practice such cooperation has rarely been successful—in either the developing or the developed world. Also, the united front that top revenue agency management can present is a powerful tool for improving compliance and building a strong organization within the government.

The integration of tax and customs compliance audits has not always succeeded. Different technical areas require different knowledge and skills, and small management efficiency gains often are outweighed by the stresses of forced amalgamation. Yet joint audits can be useful in dealing with a specific corporate target. Experience suggests that agencies should retain separate compliance audit capacities, but also that joint audits should be mounted whenever appropriate. The lack of integrated compliance audits, however, can lead clients to complain about a lack of coordination among the audit units and about the disruption of business by auditors' separate visits to their premises. To reduce inconvenience to clients, agencies should ensure that their audit units coordinate their programs.

The integration of tax and customs investigation units has an equally mixed record of success.

Whether to merge these units seems to be a matter of choice. On the one hand, such mergers seem to work better for investigation units than for audit units, perhaps because investigators are closer to sharing a single mindset. On the other hand, the technical skills needed to identify and secure evidence for particular kinds of revenue fraud mean that investigators from each technical area still must be included. Sharing a location can be helpful for such joint investigations, though it is not necessary.

The integration of intelligence units, once again, has not been consistently successful. Some argue that intelligence should not be too closely linked with investigation because intelligence spans all operational areas. Linking intelligence very closely to investigation has sometimes caused intelligence to suffer (in border enforcement, for example). The other approach is treating intelligence as a support function shared equally by all users—leading some managers to locate it in the support side of the functional structure. Wherever the intelligence unit is located, it must be well managed by knowledgeable people who can ensure that its operational needs are met and that its focus remains on clients.

One clear result of integrating tax and customs into a single revenue agency is that, within the new agency, the part responsible for border management—the customs part—tends to focus chiefly on revenue collection, even though that is just one of its many responsibilities.[3] This tendency can hamper the customs part of the revenue agency in developing partnerships with the private sector and with other border management agencies. And that in turn can mean that key government priorities, such as trade facilitation, take second place.

Single border protection agencies. In recent years governments have increasingly emphasized protecting communities by sharing intelligence and controlling the movement of goods and persons. One result of this emphasis has been the creation of border protection agencies.

However, there is a danger that such agencies may be created—and others dissolved—without a coherent underlying strategy. Such cases can create difficulties, as structural change is substituted for real management reform.

Often the best course is to fix problems without setting up new structures. As an Australian review argues, "to create new organizations or merge existing ones . . . raises several risks" (Smith 2008):

It could disrupt unduly the successful and effective work of the agencies concerned and create significant new costs. Large organizations tend to be inward looking, siloed and slow to adapt, and thus ill suited to the dynamic security environment. For a number of the agencies concerned national security considerations are embedded with a broad range of other service delivery, policy, program and regulatory functions which could be jeopardized by restructuring them around their security roles.

An alternative course, the review continues, is "to recognize and build on the strengths of existing institutions but to identify weaknesses and address them" (Smith 2008).

Even having a cogent strategy for the new agency does not guarantee success. For example, the United States has concentrated on physical security at the border. Under a community protection principle, the government has created a homeland security agency that incorporates any and all activities possibly related to border control. The agency's size makes management complex, and this in turn makes it more difficult to achieve underlying objectives, such as coordinating efforts across border functions. Thus the Department of Homeland Security contains:

- A customs and border protection agency.
- An immigration and customs enforcement body.
- A transportation security administration.
- A directorate of citizenship and immigration services.

And that is not all—the department includes other organizational units with overlapping mandates.

In the United Kingdom the government has set up a border agency incorporating certain functions of the previous Border and Immigration Agency, the United Kingdom Visas Agency, and customs border control (including verification of goods). Policy for these activities remains scattered among the Home Office, HM Revenue and Customs, and the Foreign Office.

Canada has formed a border services agency that combines the operational functions of customs, quarantine, and immigration, while leaving policy to the relevant ministries and agencies (for example, Citizenship and Immigration Canada and the Canada Revenue Agency). The new agency looks much like a traditional customs agency—it has all the responsibilities that customs would have, plus immigration and quarantine checking at the border.

The management implications of border agency organization

The organization of border agencies is dictated by government priorities. No model is equally appropriate for every situation; all have advantages and disadvantages.

Existing arrangements vary widely. Some governments have one border agency with separate policy and operational arms (the United States). Others maintain several ministries with policy functions, plus a single operational agency within one of those ministries (Canada, the United Kingdom). Still others have the traditional arrangement: several agencies, each including both policy and operational functions.

On the one hand, a single border agency can cut costs through the sharing of corporate services (training, human resources, information technology, finance and administration). It also may reduce the cost of coordination. And it can improve risk identification and client segmentation.

On the other hand, interagency cooperation can be secured in less disruptive ways than through creating a single border agency—an underlying principle of collaborative border management (chapter 2). And yet reformers who favor collaboration over integration must weigh the benefits of coordination against its costs: for example, that of maintaining separate systems and that of stretched communication lines. Furthermore, change across multiple organizations requires long lead times, affecting how functions develop.

In the end the choice of a given structure for border management will depend on a country's circumstances, on its history of public administration, and on the likelihood of securing political will for the effort. Often the choice is also directed by international factors—and complicated by the move toward

Managing organizational change in border management reform

national single windows for processing goods across borders (chapter 8; briefly discussed below). Executives in border management agencies may have little ability to influence the choice.

Whatever structure is chosen, achieving government objectives is key to success. Yet experience shows that government objectives for border management often are undefined or ambiguous. So it is of paramount importance to forge a clear, widely shared vision. Without such a vision, it is extremely difficult to articulate reform strategies and to choose appropriate organizational forms.

A consistent theme: separating border policy from border service delivery. One theme is clear in the present approach of governments to border management. As more countries seek to increase border management capacity and to collaborate effectively, governments increasingly tend to make small border policy units set the agenda for the larger operating agencies. Known in France as a cabinet scheme of administration, this feature of border management organization is also seen in the United Kingdom's division of functions between commissioning agents (the policy departments, such as the Home Office and the treasury) and service providers (border agencies, now the single border agency).

Separating border policy from border service delivery sits comfortably within the collaborative border management model (chapter 2) and can be less organizationally disruptive. Still, such a separation must be formalized through framework agreements defining work principles—for program accountability, for delegation to service delivery agencies, and for the functional split in roles and responsibilities between policy agencies and service delivery agencies. To make the separation work, the government must clearly identify obligations, accountabilities, and performance measures. It must develop incentives to full participation and disincentives to nonparticipation. And it must establish means of verification.

In policy agencies, the heads of each corporate function should be responsible for ensuring that frameworks are regularly reviewed to reflect any changes to the operating model or to delivery standards. And in the service delivery agencies, business plans should set out how objectives will be delivered, resources deployed, and performance levels met, while any information sharing responsibilities must be clearly articulated and enforced. Similarly, the relationships of service delivery agencies with delivery partners should be clear, well structured, and based on a shared understanding of accountabilities. There should be a process for regularly reporting performance issues and risks. Operating performance should be reviewed regularly through a structured process—both within each service delivery agency and with the policy agency—that focuses on present and long term achievements. And there should be an unbiased process for dispute escalation and resolution.

Policy agencies must resist the temptation to micromanage service delivery agencies. There should be a mechanism for airing concerns. For this purpose some administrations have an overarching management board, including the heads of policy agencies and of service delivery agencies—an internal body operating at the same level, and in the same way, as regular top management meetings in any organization.

Management implications for individual agencies. At the agency level several approaches to organizational structure have shown varying degrees of commitment to functional control lines. Other issues—with the system of government, with the devolution of authority, and with integrity—have in many cases been influenced by both history and geography. In countries with strong provincial government, autonomy hinders the pursuit of national control and consistency. For example, Afghanistan and the Lao People's Democratic Republic share a desire to centralize customs policy and regulations as part of border management reform, but both national governments' plans for greater centralization face entrenched provincial networks, structures, and attitudes.

Where centralization encounters these obstacles, management may prefer a phased approach as more prudent. Successful reform uses the energy of the people most affected to drive change: they must adopt reform and own it. To do so they must be convinced to accept the substance of change and its timing—the reason why change management is now so much discussed by prospective reformers.

Often individual organizational structures can be changed to show that priorities have changed—or to overcome particular problems. For example, any

12

Managing organizational change in border management reform

effort to increase central control over regional offices should be based in headquarters. And any effort to increase attention to value added border management functions—such as risk management, intelligence, and information and communications technology—will have a stronger organizational form if divisions are created for these activities, each headed by a senior official.

Human resources management

Human resources management is critical to border management reform. Change is about people—and grand visions for reform can mean little to people who have more immediate concerns, such as providing food, shelter, and education for their families.[4]

A change program must look at human resources early on. If changes to terms and conditions are needed, agency staff will accept delay. But they will do so less gracefully if real problems are ignored. During change, management should:

- Listen to staff members' perspectives.
- Equip staff to do the job—while dealing with staff members whose performance does not meet agency standards.

The starting point is to review the human resources regime, looking at—but also beyond—its normal functions of recruitment, selection, mobility, remuneration, and separation. (A full list of elements to be reviewed appears in box 12.3.)

At one border management agency, senior managers expressed skepticism when a major reform program introduced—as its first change—a requirement that all staff selection be based on merit (whether for hiring, for training, or for attendance at external training and development events). The agency was notoriously nepotistic. But the managers also asked why priority would be given to a seemingly minor matter when the agency had major problems with structure and operating efficiency. In reality, the agency's integrity problems resulted partly from the way the agency's staff had been transferred in from existing civil service departments—removing them

---

Box 12.3   Human resources development plan

Staffing elements:
- Identify obsolete staff positions.
- Identify outdated positions requiring reformulation and skills upgrading.
- Identify options for reducing unnecessary positions and model budgetary implications.
- Recommend options for recruitment to new and remodeled positions.

Job descriptions:
- Create new and revised positions.
- Integrate new tasks into existing positions.
- Modify existing job descriptions to enhance focus and increase consistency with core objectives.

Training elements:
- Identify training objectives and targets.
- Identify training priorities by staff position and function, target audience, and modes of delivery.
- Set requirements for staff trainers to ensure training skills are transferred.
- Identify procedures for the selection of training candidates.
- Establish exchange programs and internships with other administrations.
- Establish options for skills development training.

Increased professionalism:
- Analyze legislation and internal procedures to identify areas where officials have insufficient or excessive discretionary powers.
- Interview officials and other stakeholders to identify gaps.
- Review past and pending disciplinary cases, if any.
- Review integrity strategies to identify lessons.
- Identify principal human resources transparency implications and integrity strategies.
- Identify options for transparency training, drawing on international best practices.
- Advise on mechanisms for integrity testing of potential recruits and staff.
- Review and comment on the code of conduct.
- Propose modifications to the mission statement and core values based on assessments.
- Advise on internal disciplinary proceedings and staff sanction mechanisms related to transparency and integrity.
- Develop proposals for strengthening internal audit procedures.
- Disseminate mechanisms for circulating information and guidelines to operational staff.

Managing organizational change in border management reform

from the civil service pension scheme and so depriving them of a safety net. Also contributing to the integrity problems was the absence of any way for staff to get loans for housing or other personal purposes. Recruitment lead times are fairly long, and the agency needed new, energetic staff members to drive reform. So human resources management was, in fact, essential to reform.

Leadership

What makes leadership effective? What are the characteristics of a good leader? Such questions about leadership stir academic debate. What they rarely acknowledge is that an organization requires various types of leadership at various times. During reform, inspirational leadership will encourage staff to help make changes. But during consolidation a more transactional style will help cement the changes, making them sustainable.

Reform requires leadership that is not only strong but visible. Leaders lead from the front—they must be visible, persuasive, and able to articulate their vision in terms understood by all key stakeholders, particularly the officials who will put the changes into effect.

Leadership during change must also demonstrate the values that leaders espouse. Typically the leaders of a reform create its long term vision, and they oversee the development and implementation of a coherent transformation strategy. To be effective a leader's vision should be simple, credible, and focused on overcoming current problems, bridging the gap between the present and a better future. A vision that stakeholders accept will energize reform. Such a vision must have emotional, as well as intellectual, appeal.

A good leader encourages supervisors and managers to take some risks, to reward innovation, and to accept error (up to a point) as an inevitable effect of delegating responsibility. A special challenge for senior management is the need to build officials' confidence in themselves. Strong, affirmative leadership can conduce to such confidence, which is a prerequisite for real change.

Leaders are spokespersons: they represent the organization to external constituencies. While such communication is demanded by stakeholders, it also—when effective—can motivate and satisfy staff.

Much literature on organization change focuses on the importance of reform champions in driving reform initiatives. While the personal commitment of one or two individual leaders often can make a major difference to the success or failure of reform programs, it is equally important to build a broad team of leaders all committed to achieving the same reform goals. Experience suggests that leaders often change and that reform programs based only on the personal commitment of one or two individuals are unlikely to succeed in the longer term.

Management group

A comprehensive reform strategy involves the participation of managers and supervisors at all organizational levels. Early on, therefore, a reform must develop managers—ideally through both formal coursework and practical training, either internal or external (or both). Managers demonstrating a commitment to change must be recognized for their contribution.

Since candidates are likely to be scarce, and since managing reform puts stress on organizations, finding suitable managers requires planning and incurs some risk. Once the structure is established, reformers can begin determining which existing managers are suitable and where it may be necessary to fill gaps in competence from the outside. If a group of promising managers is immediately below the organizational level required, their qualifications for advancement—formal education, technical barriers, and desired personal qualities—should be assessed against the official job description and position requirements (which should be updated as part of restructuring, discussed below). If officials have the required qualifications the organization should consider advancing them, even those who lack seniority. For those with the required personal qualities, but without a particular qualification or experience, individual development plans should be drawn up and discussed with them, and a projection should be made about when they will be ready for advancement.

The process described above should be used to make staffing plans for all management positions, either to fill immediately from within, to fill externally by transfer or appointment, or to leave vacant for a short time to qualify an internal candidate. A structured managerial succession plan will result,

Managing organizational change in border management reform

identifying likely candidates and transparently outlining a competency development process that is calibrated to the projected management vacancies. By showing all immediate and forthcoming management recruitment needs, this plan will enable recruitment to meet needs as they arise, rather than lag behind to the detriment of operations.

Existing cultural and administrative norms often give merit second place to seniority. Those norms may be violated when younger, better qualified officials are identified for management positions. So be it: advancements based on merit will clearly signal that times have changed.

Resistance to change

Resistance to change will not evaporate overnight, no matter what steps are taken to overcome it. But once a core group of staff has been convinced that management is serious and committed about a reform—and that the reform will be supported politically and bureaucratically in the long term—that group will support and work for change. To make that happen, senior management must be visible, trustworthy, and persuasive about the new vision.

In many cases resistance is passive. Where there is pressure to conform, and particularly where there is nepotism or corruption, it may be difficult for an individual to support reforms led by senior management. In such cases leaders must be fair, consistent, and persistent in conveying the values that drive change.

Finally, leaders must recognize the effect of poor infrastructure on staff morale. Officials will not work and make sacrifices for reform if management cannot adequately accommodate them in a professional environment. To ask officials to work harder and better, to preach pride and self esteem, to assure them of their importance to the national effort, and then to let them work in appalling conditions is unconscionable. If the officials are to take responsibility for change, the management must also assume responsibility. The officials must be persuaded that management is doing its best to improve working conditions and, where possible, living conditions.

Merit selection

Managing a comprehensive change program often involves large staffing changes, to ensure that the best people are in place to drive the process. Early on, it can be useful to introduce or reinforce the principle that recruitment and selection are based exclusively on merit. Such an approach powerfully signals to officials that they have opportunities to contribute and that longstanding inequities will no longer be tolerated. Apart from the benefit of having better qualified and motivated officials in key positions, merit selection gives staff early warning that informal and customary networks are no longer effective. In some administrations management should expect considerable resistance to such a change, both inside and outside, as established relationships lose their influence over staff advancement.

Merit selection should apply not just to recruitment and promotion but to specialized training and development opportunities. Some basic technical training should be given to all staff. But selection for external attachments, overseas placements, and attendance at workshops and conferences should be used to develop promising employees and to reward performance. People selected for specialized training should be those best suited to applying the training at work. Such training opportunities—especially those that involve travel (which in practice often go to the most senior or most favored, rather than to the best qualified or to those making the greatest contribution to corporate objectives)—can be offered to selected lower level officers to broaden their horizons, promote their long term development, and keep them motivated. During change these officials will be relied on to carry the vision forward, and management should recognize the burden that their exposure places on them.

Remuneration and reward

Many border agencies operate within the constraints of civil service terms and conditions. The constraints vary by country and agency. But they are greatest in developing nations, where civil servants' salaries and work conditions often are less favorable than they are in the industrialized world. Many border agencies in the developing world must find ways to reward staff adequately, financially and otherwise. If officials are required to carry out changes that reduce their informal income—a requirement of many reform programs—they must be compensated. Unfortunately, reformers often overlook this need because they lack the resources to give officials incentives for participating in reform. One novel approach to salary supplementation for border management, a formality service fee, is discussed in box 12.4.

For officials who must use special skills, and who can demonstrate through special training requirements that they have those skills, it may be possible to persuade central agencies to create a separate job category with a higher salary range than the standard one. The approach may be limited by disparities across agencies, but it offers possibilities. A variation is to place the special category higher within the job category. This solution sometimes gains more support from central agencies because the disparities are

quarantined within one agency without touching the central agencies. Another variation is to add skill and responsibility loadings on top of ordinary salaries. Such loadings might be available to specialists, to staff on special task forces and projects, or to staff with difficult or dangerous assignments. Many further variations on this general approach can be identified by senior managers with some imagination.

Bonus schemes are another way to reward outstanding performance. But care must be taken to ensure that bonus schemes do not reward only officials deployed to certain positions—and that they reflect government objectives. For example, in countries where customs is part of a revenue authority,

---

Box 12.4 **The introduction of a formality service fee by Thai Customs**

International studies have identified and discussed the problem of corruption in government agencies operating at the border. Of all government agencies, customs is often cited as being among the most corrupt. To battle such corruption, most commentators highlight the importance of establishing appropriate human resource management strategies—strategies contributing to an environment that fosters integrity and offers staff appropriate incentives to perform in a professional and ethical manner.

One key element of this approach to combating corruption in border management requires government agencies to ensure that remuneration levels afford a reasonable standard of living for officials. Unfortunately, while commentators recognize the issue, few have offered any practical means for increasing remuneration in environments with limited financial resources and where it is difficult to quarantine public sector pay increases to border management officials. The novel approach adopted by Thailand's customs agency is an interesting attempt to address the issue in a practical way.

Thai Customs has been attempting to tackle the problem of corruption for many years. It initiated reforms aimed at simplifying formalities and modernizing systems and procedures, both to limit corruption opportunities and to eliminate incentives for traders to offer bribes to officials. While these efforts were partly successful, it became clear that the very low wages paid to customs officials posed a significant barrier to meaningful progress in eliminating corruption.

After exploring a number of options, Thai authorities decided to pilot the collection of a formality service fee (FSF), with the proceeds used to supplement

salaries (95 percent) and to finance the introduction of new technology (5 percent). A fee of 200 Baht (approximately $6.20) is applied to each import or export entry, with an additional fee of 70 Baht (approximately $2.20) per entry for recording data in the customs electronic clearance system.

The Thai FSF was introduced following extensive consultations with all key stakeholders, including relevant ministries and the private sector. It is tied to a series of other reform and modernization initiatives. Since its introduction it has been subject to regular, independent evaluation. The results so far appear very positive, with reported complaints regarding misconduct by customs officials falling from 92 in 2006 to 69 in 2007 and just 36 in 2008.

Traders, though required to pay the FSF, are generally positive about its introduction as it is predictable, nonnegotiable, and subject to a formal receipt—thus eliminating the time and costs incurred in negotiating the informal arrangements that previously applied. According to a survey conducted in August 2008 by Associate Professor Dr. Ratana Sursakdis Amorn in association with Thai Customs, 85.7 percent of economic operators agreed with the continuation of the FSF provided that the modest fee amounts were maintained.

Introduced as a pilot in 2004, the FSF is now being reviewed to determine whether it should be continued. The positive feedback from the private sector so far indicates that the pilot has been successful in tackling one of the most difficult anticorruption issues facing border management reformers.

Source: Personal communication with Thai Customs officials.

Managing organizational change in border management reform

12

bonuses are typically paid for meeting revenue targets—a practice that gives officials an incentive to raise revenue without concern for the needs of traders. In such countries customs officials understandably make governments' trade facilitation objectives a secondary priority.

Rewards other than money can motivate officials to participate in reform. The recognition of effort can take many forms: officials may be invited to join senior officers at public hearings or important meetings, to brief senior officers or ministers, to represent the agency at functions, to attend interagency committees. All are ways to reward good performance and to show that the organization values an individual's contribution. A similar effect can be realized for the work unit as a whole simply by seeking staff views on performance improvements—and by acting on those views.

In agencies where staff lack access to pension schemes, housing funds, or small loans to assist families during domestic and seasonal crises, a good employer will try to fill the gap—not to become a social welfare agency, but to patch holes in the safety net for staff. Such efforts are not entirely altruistic. The organization benefits when officials are happier, more motivated, and less likely to be tempted by rentseeking opportunities. For example, a retirement benefit scheme may be based on insurance and staff contributions. Or a fairly small government contribution, and loans by ballot, may be used to seed a staff housing scheme until a sizable fund emerges. Other solutions to the difficulties sometimes faced by developing country staff include relieving their greatest financial burdens by paying annual bonuses during the most difficult season of the year, rather than at the end. In short, management can do much to help and reward its staff without breaking the bank.

Rotation and job mobility

Regular rotation can build confidence, cultivate skills and experience, and foster a better understanding of how an organization's disparate parts fit together. Even if initially expensive, rotation is justifiable for staff members who may come under outside pressure. It reduces the risk that they will commit rentseeking by making them less closely identified with particular clients. It motivates them

by varying their work environment. That said, some specialists should remain in their work units for longer periods: for example, investigators and laboratory technicians must stay at their posts longer, to ensure that the investment in their training yields a return. But staff in positions where extra pay is regularly available—from overtime or shift work, for example—may be moved more often to avoid inequities in pay across job levels.

The argument that rotation has a negative effect on expertise, because people shift just as they are learning their jobs, is not convincing. A workforce that is trained, committed, and motivated can combine rotation with effectiveness.

Staff rotation can also be used to address problems that arise where staff selections have not been made on merit. A change of position can help a staff member who has not performed well, though it should not be used as a means of letting people—or their managers—off the hook. Any problems should be relayed to the receiving work unit, which can determine a course of action.

For rotation to succeed it must be well planned, transparent, and consistent. All staff must know the outline of the scheme and how it applies to their jobs. The dates of moves should be known well in advance. Only in extreme circumstances should a rotation be delayed: discomfort felt by management is not a valid reason. Rotation should have a high priority, with adequate funding set aside for it.

The rotation of managers can be handled separately, but should be included in the policy—staff cannot be expected to accept rotation when managers are exempt. Managers should be expected to experience all aspects of the work of the organization. A set rotation period should be adhered to (in some countries, for example, managers are moved every two or three years). Managers should be shifted if their performance is poor, perhaps to be replaced by people with lower rank but with good performance records. Managers need to accept this arrangement as the price of their status.

Clients must know of the rotation policy and the reasons for it. Not all will agree with it—and some may attempt to derail it—but that should not affect implementation. Clients will have to accept lower quality service in the period immediately before and after a series of transfers, but this inconvenience will

Managing organizational change in border management reform

be balanced by the gains from breaking unhealthy relationships that have become too close.

Integrity programs

An extensive body of literature addresses corruption in border management agencies, yet often it simply reports and describes the problem. There is little practical information on how to deal with corruption effectively where junior officials have large discretionary powers and work closely with the private sector, and where close supervision is difficult—precisely the situation of many border management officials. The role of management is to transparently reduce financial and social stresses, to encourage adherence to corporate values, and to punish breaches of published codes of conduct that staff members have agreed to follow.

Corporate values can be instilled starting with the induction process, which should be revisited in all training activities. Integrity workshops can be run back to back with short technical training sessions. Another technique is to dedicate one session in each training course to an integrity case study.

At the corporate level, the first priority is to have a comprehensive integrity policy statement and action plan that clearly define how each staff member is responsible for preventing corruption. Such responsibilities begin with self assessment. First, senior management—say, tiers two and three—should identify vulnerabilities and mitigation strategies at a diagnostic workshop. The results will help refine a comprehensive integrity action plan in a framework developed by top management. Second, work unit staff should assess systems and controls to pinpoint areas most vulnerable to corruption. This two step process makes management's position clear to all, with no room left for corporate values to be misunderstood. The World Customs Organization's comprehensive integrity development framework, comprising initiatives designed to encourage opportunity and incentive, was initially developed for customs but is equally applicable to all border management officials.[5]

Clients should not be forgotten. Clear, unambiguous standards of behavior for private sector representatives should be framed through a similar process guided by both industry bodies and nongovernmental organizations. Key to any integrity and anticorruption strategy is the principle that corruption has two sides—border officials rarely bribe other border officials. A citizens' charter, setting out what the private sector can expect from border management, can be useful.

Codes of conduct and disciplinary codes

Over the past decade many border management agencies have put in place codes of conduct that spell out the behavior expected of officials and prescribe sanctions for those who fall short. Sanctions that raise the moral cost of inappropriate behavior need support from leadership. Such sanctions are more likely to be accepted in a climate that rewards ethical behavior, where values espoused by senior management are genuine and expressed in actions. Just as a code of conduct should go beyond integrity and cover behavior in the workplace and beyond, it should reflect the values an organization expects staff to demonstrate.

Disciplinary codes set forth detailed procedures for extreme and persistent poor performance. A disciplinary code should distinguish between minor offences, such as repeated lateness or failing to carry out a lawful order, and more serious ones, such as lying about qualifications, failing to arrive at work for an extended period, or being found guilty of a serious criminal offence. The code should specify a range of applicable penalties: examples include warnings, official reprimands, fines, salary reductions, and dismissal.

Managing performance

At the beginning of each reporting period—usually a calendar year—each staff member should agree with a supervisor about tasks and standards. The agreement should be put in writing (many organizations have forms for the purpose). The staff member's progress should then be reviewed at regular intervals of no more than six months. If any adjustments are agreed on during these regular reviews, either to the tasks (because they have changed) or to the standards (because the initial ones were unrealistic), such adjustments should be recorded.

During the regular reviews, any poor performance by the staff member should be discussed openly. Its causes and possible solutions should be identified and recorded. A date should then be set for a followup review, usually on an accelerated schedule (say, after three months rather than six). If at the followup review the poor performance has persisted, the staff member should get a warning that disciplinary action may follow unless improvements are made—and another followup review should be scheduled. If nothing changes after the second followup review the manager should take disciplinary action, with sanctions possibly including dismissal.

Managers who notice a staff member's continued poor performance between reviews should not wait until the next regular review, but should accelerate the staff member's review schedule. To wait for the next regular review will be unfair to the staff member and unhelpful to the work unit.

In some cases it might be appropriate to establish formal performance contracts with key officials. Such an approach has been piloted by customs authorities in Cameroon, where it has given a strong boost to the overall reform program (box 12.5).

Training and staff development

Successful management demands a training and staff development policy that systematically sets out types and levels of training—covering a career progression through the ranks, and including specialist and management training and development. Training programs should be based on assessed organizational need and on future staff needs. A training master plan should be adopted to ensure that all staff members, including new recruits, are equipped with the basic technical skills their jobs demand—including further training and education to prepare them for advancement and specialized tasks (box 12.6). The plan can identify courses appropriate to staff members at each level; staff members may then enroll in further courses on their own initiative.

A fully effective training system must allow all staff members equal opportunity to participate—a point often overlooked, especially in remote

| Box **12.5** | **Cameroon Customs Integrity Initiative** |

Within the Cameroonian context, customs is perceived as one of the institutions with the most important problems of transparency. A new program financed by the World Bank and introduced in 2006 was designed to strengthen the chain of command by holding each link accountable—with the assistance of activity, performance, control, and risk indicators—in an effort to improve understanding of activities on the ground, to provide an effective decisionmaking tool, and to reduce corruption in customs. (Lessons of the first phase of the reform were published in Libom Li Likeng, Cantens, and Bilangna 2009.)

Cameroon Customs had already carried out steps to strengthen accountability. They included the regular publication of revenue collection data, increased contacts with the business community, automation through the use of ASYCUDA software, and reduced information asymmetry through the use of individual performance indicators. Still, the Head of Customs wanted to initiate a second wave of reforms—to change the behaviors of frontline officials, and to reduce corruption and increase performance. Accordingly, she commissioned the development of an integrity action plan with a specific focus on human resources policies through a monitoring and incentive framework.

A pilot was set up and performance contracts for the two largest customs stations were designed. In early February 2010—following a dialogue among frontline officers and senior management—individual and team performance contracts with measurable indicators were signed. Each inspector's performance was to be assessed through eight indicators: four related to trade facilitation, four related to the customs clearance process and fines. For each indicator a maximum or minimum value was set based on median monthly values in the three preceding years. An inspector achieved his or her contract if he or she improved performance by 15 percent on all indicators after the six month pilot period.

For inspectors below 100 percent contract performance, a system was established that begins with warnings and interviews and can lead to the inspector's transfer to another customs station. For the best performing inspectors a limited financial bonus is granted, along with nonfinancial recognition.

Frontline officers, as well as middle management, supported the initiative because they wished to have their performance assessed on the basis of objective criteria. Early results show that performance contracts have led to decreased clearance times and reduced poor practices, with revenues maintained at the same level as before. Moreover, the contracts have contributed to increased information flow from inspectors to the Head of Customs.

For further information contact Gael Raballand (graballand@worldbank.org).

Managing organizational change in border management reform

A training master plan should do ten things:
- Identify training objectives and targets (based on a needs review and human resources capacity assessments).
- Classify training priorities by subject area, target audience, and means of delivery.
- Propose training courses or programs, indicating those that exist already and those that will need to be developed.
- Set requirements for internal staff trainers, to ensure that training skills are transferred.
- Set procedures for trainee and internal trainer selection.
- Create manuals and documentation for training courses, conferences, and workshops.
- Outline terms of reference and contracts for trainees.
- Create a strategic training framework showing how the plans will be met, including a training timetable for course participants and trainers.
- Set up a quality control monitoring program, including continual reviews (for example, feedback questionnaires and informal discussions).
- Set up a program for the long term monitoring and upgrading of training capacities.

locations. Such equality of opportunity can be ensured by developing course materials in a modular form and by making them available to staff everywhere (as in distance learning). Technical training, for example, can be broken into three or four difficulty levels, and a set of modules for each can be distributed in whatever way is most convenient for offices. Staff members can then complete each module in sequence, as far as their various development paths may lead them. To enhance training with face to face tutoring, expert officers can become mentors for a region. The system described here can be applied to materials such as those made available through the World Customs Organization e-learning scheme.

Management must support these broad training approaches by developing and putting in place individual plans for each officer. These plans should be reviewed and adjusted each year as part of performance management. Supervisors have a responsibility to counsel staff on their individual development—to remedy any deficiencies, and to help staff members realize their potential. Such counseling can be part of a planned transfer or promotion regime for staff.

Interagency arrangements

Border management needs to focus on developing practical interagency arrangements. In some cases this means the amalgamation, or full integration, of agencies. In other cases it means major policy and operational coordination in resource use—for example, in information and intelligence.

Some customs agencies already have a longstanding responsibility to conduct primary health and immigration checks on persons entering the country, with support from secondary referral desks staffed by the agencies mainly responsible for those areas. A government's reasons for assigning these tasks to customs may include resource constraints and a desire to further national interests (for example, by promoting tourism). Underpinning the arrangements may be extensive service level agreements linked to agreements between ministers and departmental chief executives—the departments agree to reach certain service levels, and government in turn agrees to provide extra resources. This approach offers a best practice model for interagency arrangements.

Customs, since it is at the crossroads of trade, is ideally placed to act on behalf of other agencies with border management roles. National single windows for international trade are increasingly being established for this purpose. A national single window is generally described as providing:
- A single point where all the data required by regulation to clear goods across a border can be lodged.
- A single point where parties can be notified of a decision to release goods from border control.

The national single window can take various forms, but most involve electronic links and messaging among government agencies and the trading community. A national single window will provide for the payment of duties, taxes, and any applicable fees and charges. The payments generally are to be made electronically to the accounts of the government agencies concerned.

Care must be exercised in using the term *single window*. Some arrangements provide a single window for lodging documents at each border point.[6] Others are comprehensive, enabling data to be lodged electronically in a system that links all relevant border agencies (chapter 8).

A comprehensive national single window can extend to peripheral agencies, such as the registrar of companies (depending on the system for registering clients). To ensure control it is preferable to have one identifier across all government activity—for example, by requiring that a taxpayer identification number be quoted in all dealings with government. It is surprising that this simple but effective policy has not been widely adopted. Instead, some single window designs now give each participating agency its own identifier, allocated only to clients who can first show that they have taxpayer identifiers. Such duplication undermines trade facilitation and regulatory control.

As border operations become more integrated, the place of value added services in interagency arrangements arises as a crucial issue. At stake here are the larger questions about structural change examined earlier in this chapter: what are the concerns that mainly drive border reform, and what form of organization best reflects these concerns? The easiest form to attain might be one based on traditional customs functions, but with added health, quarantine, and immigration tasks. Assuming that policy is set by a central cabinet, the border organization's only remaining role would be to establish procedures for operational liaison with outside agencies that also have interests at the border (police, security, intelligence). Such procedures are already in place at well functioning agencies: perhaps the best example is the Canada Border Services Agency.

With the advent of single window systems, however, customs commercial clearances are being linked to value added trade services. Such linkages add complexity to an already difficult mix at the border. In countries where the value added services are available they generally are provided by trade portals linked to government agencies and banks, as well as to customs brokers and freight logistics operators. Such portals already exist in some countries, and as more administrations look toward single window arrangements the lines between the portals and border control are becoming blurred. Some models, such as Australia's and Singapore's, have trade portals outside the government with limited links to government agencies. Australia's trade portal is a

nongovernmental nonprofit sponsored by its members, but Singapore's portal is private and for profit (chapter 8). Other, technically complex systems are being designed elsewhere to mix border controls with business operations in a more encompassing fashion. In some cases public-private partnership arrangements are being considered—arrangements that would bring public policy into play, since policy and regulatory functions cannot properly lie outside government control and thus should not be vested in public-private partnerships (though some have suggested they might be).

Wherever an administration locates itself in this spectrum, increasing interagency cooperation and integration at the border requires a gradual approach. Reform proponents often lose sight of the time and resources needed to re-engineer processes. Usually such re-engineering requires the creation of new electronic links across agencies, followed by a cleansing and uploading of data. Issues of funding and timing are involved, as are issues of priority setting (for allocating scarce national resources) and of development assistance funding.

Any integrated approach to border reform—whatever its sophistication—will rest on a set of agreed control regimes for streamlined, yet comprehensive operations covering the interests of all agencies concerned. Where there is a single focal point, interagency arrangements must be formally recorded. Depending on each client agency and its role at the border, the arrangements may range from statements of broad operational principles to detailed service level agreements.

Conclusion

Without detailing all that is required for managing change, this chapter has offered a framework for reform. It has suggested specific actions, and it has looked at the strategies and philosophies that have guided successfully reformed organizations. It has attempted to identify what worked and what did not—as officials, despite their good intentions, may fall into traps. Organizations will have various problems according to their circumstances. But for reformers wondering what to do next, the foregoing outline should point toward a path to workable solutions.

12

Notes

1. The discussion of revenue authorities and their formation in De Wulf (2005) remains useful and accessible, other than in a few matters of detail.

2. See the readings referenced in De Wulf (2005) and Taliercio (2003).

3. In all the arrangements described here for integrating tax and customs into a single revenue agency, the customs part of the new agency continues to be involved in both revenue collection and border management—the two functions not having been separated during the merger. Arguments can be made for and against this continuation of customs' twofold function based on its implications for the revenue collection (some focusing on efficiency, others on effectiveness). However, none of those arguments is relevant to border management or to perceptions of border management.

4. Maslow's familiar theory is sound: people look to their primary needs first.

5. All WCO tools related to integrity are available on the WCO Web site, www.wcoomd.org.

6. Ukraine began its modernization moves with this change in its Odessa port operation. Clients appreciated having all agency representatives co-located and not having to go from one agency to another.

References

De Wulf, L. 2005. "Human Resources and Organizational Issues in Customs." In *Customs Modernization Handbook*, ed. L. De Wulf and J.B. Sokol. Washington, DC: The World Bank. 31–50.

Libom Li Likeng, M., T. Cantens, and S. Bilangna. 2009. "Gazing into the Mirror: Operational Internal Control in Cameroon Customs." Discussion Paper 8, Sub-Saharan Africa Transport Policy Program (SSATP), The World Bank, Washington, DC. Available at http://siteresources.worldbank.org/EXTAFRSUBSAHTRA/Resources/DP08-Cameroon-Full.pdf.

Smith, R. 2008. *Report of the Review of Homeland and Border Security*. Canberra: Australian Government.

Taliercio, R.R., Jr. 2003. "Administrative Reform as Credible Commitment: The Impact of Autonomy on Revenue Authority Performance in Latin America." World Bank, Washington, DC.

12

Managing organizational change in border management reform

13 Nontariff measures: impact, regulation, and trade facilitation

Olivier Cadot, Maryla Maliszewska, and Sebastián Sáez

Like the ebbing tide uncovering rocks on the sea bottom, the progressive reduction of tariffs (currently around 5 percent for industrial countries and 10–20 percent for most developing countries) has revealed the importance of other barriers to trade. Some of those barriers are inherent to doing business across borders: informational costs, dealing in foreign currencies and languages, and so on. These "natural" trade costs are very large: Anderson and van Wincoop (2004) estimate their combined ad valorem equivalent at 36 percent.[1] Some others, however, are inflicted by policy. These policy induced nontariff barriers (NTBs) are very diverse in nature, from regulations that ostensibly address domestic issues (say, public health)—but have an incidental impact on trade—to specific border procedures, such as customs clearance, that may raise trade costs because of the way they are implemented on the ground.

Reducing these NTBs is part of a broader trade facilitation agenda aimed at the reduction of overall trade costs. This agenda—and the linkage between trade facilitation and NTBs—gained prominence with the 2001 Shanghai Accord of the Asia-Pacific Economic Cooperation (APEC), which pledged to reduce trade costs by 5 percent over the following five years. It is now very much at the core of the Doha Round's agenda as well.

In spite of a voluminous literature, the definition of NTBs, their identification, and the measurement of their effects on trade are still very much a fuzzy science. Early attempts at measuring the effect of nontariff barriers focused on easily identified policy instruments such as quantitative restrictions and prohibitions. However, use of these old style measures has largely receded, thanks in large part to negotiated phaseouts and strengthened multilateral disciplines. New generation measures are much broader in scope, including rules of origin, traceability requirements, sanitary and product standards, and regulations of all sorts. They have proliferated for a variety of reasons, most often to increase consumer safety, and often—though not always—without explicit protectionist intent. The term *nontariff measures* (NTMs) has gained acceptance to designate these measures without the pejorative (protectionist) connotation associated with the term NTB.

Naming is one thing, measuring another. Analysts of NTMs, seeking to identify NTMs and to measure their effects on trade, have proposed a range of approaches briefly reviewed below. None is flawless, and numerous difficulties remain.

Managing organizational change in border management reform

To make progress on the NTM streamlining agenda, policymakers need a reasonably clear picture of how prevalent NTMs are, how NTMs' effect on trade can be assessed quantitatively, and what multilateral, regional, and national disciplines are already available to contain the trade inhibiting effects of NTMs. These three issues interact, in the sense that data on NTMs can be important in enforcing the existing disciplines and targeting negotiations to open trade. This chapter takes stock of present knowledge with respect to these questions. Its conclusions may be previewed here:

- Between one-third and two-thirds of traded goods are affected by one or more nontariff measures, with technical standards appearing in surveys as both the most prevalent and the most difficult to comply with.

- Estimates of the ad valorem equivalents (AVEs) of NTMs suggest levels roughly comparable to tariffs—5 percent to 10 percent on average, with very substantial peaks. Estimates of the effect of NTMs on trade flows suggest that harmonization and mutual recognition agreements can provide substantial gains in trade, particularly for smaller firms with substantial compliance and information costs.

- The rules of the World Trade Organization (WTO) provide an agreed benchmark for NTMs' acceptability, help governments persuade their trading partners to bring NTMs into rule compliance, and provide a basis and setting to negotiate further market opening. Substantively these rules require nondiscriminatory treatment and permit member governments to maintain whatever level of protection they desire—but require them to meet certain conditions. Regulations must be necessary to achieve a legitimate policy objective, not disguised barriers to trade or unnecessarily restrictive of trade. Where the WTO rules stop, negotiations begin; governments have undertaken higher than WTO levels of discipline in regional trade agreements and through bilateral arrangements, and they have unilaterally liberalized NTMs when they view this action as being in the national economic interest.

The chapter is organized in three main sections. The first section below discusses the definition and identification of NTMs and methods to quantify their effects. Following is a section that examines WTO disciplines as well as efforts to streamline NTMs at regional and national levels. A final section provides conclusions and policy recommendations.

Defining nontariff measures and measuring their inhibiting effects on trade

We seek out and catalog NTMs for a specific reason: to understand better the measures that are displacing or replacing tariffs and to understand where discipline on NTMs would be beneficial. Tariffs are obvious, directly observable, and unambiguously intended to affect trade—but NTMs are regulatory measures that may affect trade even unintentionally, whatever their primary purpose. Thus, whether a regulatory text qualifies as an NTM or not depends on its trade effects—and NTMs accordingly can be defined as regulatory texts that either create a wedge between domestic and foreign prices or affect trade flows.

Baldwin (1970) added a normative dimension by defining nontariff measures as "any measure (private or public) that causes internationally traded goods and services to be allocated in such a way as to reduce potential real income." However, introducing normative considerations is a source of complication rather than clarification. For instance, NTMs may be used to correct market failures that would otherwise reduce welfare but not income; so focusing on their income reducing effects may wrongly suggest that they are undesirable. Definitions based on price or quantity are less conducive to misinterpretations.

For want of a universally acceptable definition, ad hoc taxonomies have flourished. Baldwin (1970, for example) as well as Laird and Vossenaar (1991) took intent and impact as their key defining criteria. The WTO has also developed an NTM nomenclature for negotiation purposes. The WTO nomenclature, reproduced at the broadest level, is shown in box 13.1.

The scope of NTMs captured by the WTO nomenclature is fairly wide and includes numerous behind-the-border measures. For instance, "Government participation in trade" (category I) includes a broad range of measures, including the presence of

<table>
<tr><td>Box **13.1**</td><td>**Classification of nontariff measures by the World Trade Organization's Non-Agricultural Market Access (NAMA)**</td></tr>
</table>

I.   Government participation in trade
II. Customs and administrative entry procedures
III. barriers to trade
IV. Sanitary and phytosanitary measures
V.   Specific limitations and quantitative restrictions
VI. Import charges and levies
VII. Other (intellectual property and safeguards)

Source: Adapted from WTO (2003b).

<table>
<tr><td>Box **13.2**</td><td>**Classification of nontariff measures according to the United Nations Conference on Trade and Development (UNCTAD) in 2009**</td></tr>
</table>

The nomenclature adopted for nontariff measures in 2009 by the United Nations Conference on Trade and Development (UNCTAD) contains the following categories, at the broadest level of aggregation (the first letter in the code for each category):

A000 Sanitary and phytosanitary measures
B000 Technical barriers to trade
C000 Preshipment inspection and other formalities
D000 Price control measures
E000 Licences, quotas, prohibitions and other quantity control measures
F000 Charges, taxes and other paratariff measures
G000 Finance measures
H000 Anticompetitive measures
I000 Trade related investment measures
J000 Distribution restrictions
K000 Restriction on postsales services
L000 Subsidies (excluding certain export subsidies classified under P000, below)
M000 Government procurement restrictions
N000 Intellectual property
O000 Rules of origin
P000 Export related measures

Source: Authors.

state owned enterprises, single channel marketing arrangements, and so on.

In 1994 UNCTAD created a classification that has been widely used since because it underlies coding in the Trade Analysis and Information System (TRAINS), which records data on tariffs and NTMs into the statistical system of the United Nations Statistical Division (UNSD). However, UNCTAD's 1994 coding has become obsolete, for two reasons. First, it featured old style measures—quantitative restrictions and the like—that have largely been phased out. Second, it grouped into catchall categories many measures important now, such as product standards.

In 2006 UNCTAD's Group of Eminent Persons on Non-Tariff Barriers (GNTB) started working on a new classification, more appropriate to record the new forms taken by NTMs (and closer to the WTO's). The new classification, adopted in July 2009, is shown at the broadest level of aggregation (one letter) in box 13.2.

The new nomenclature provides better disaggregation of NTMS, at one letter and one digit (64 categories), one letter and two digits (121 categories), or even one letter and three digits (special cases). It covers a wide range of measures, some of which are clearly behind the border (an example is anticompetitive measures, which include arcane measures like compulsory national insurance). The new nomenclature has not been widely used yet, and some ambiguities will need to be dealt with. Nevertheless, it will provide the basis for the new wave of NTM data collection to replace TRAINS.

Work by the Organisation for Economic Co-operation and Development (OECD) has also

conducted work on the issue, leading to a separate classification set out in an influential paper by Deardorff and Stern (1998). This OECD classification is fairly similar to that of UNCTAD, but the OECD classification also includes investment measures and lumps together import surcharges of all sorts with contingent protection measures (antidumping, countervailing duties, and safeguards).

Data sources

The primary source of data on NTMs is UNCTAD's TRAINS database, which is managed by a multi-agency consortium of the IMF, ITC, FAO, OECD, World Bank, UNCTAD, UNIDO, and WTO. The TRAINS database draws on information provided by governments, combined with the WTO's NTM database and information collected by regional secretariats (for example, ALADI, SIECA, and SAARC) along with some regional development banks, such as the Inter-American Development Bank.

Coverage in TRAINS has never been complete. Its classification focused on a relatively narrow set of measures, and implicitly limited the instruments it covered—and government reporting has always been haphazard (see de Melo and Carrère 2009 for details). Out of 165 countries for which trade statistics are available on the COMTRADE database, only about 100 have NTM entries—and the entries are essentially for 2000–01, though some updating has recently taken place. A major effort, led by an UNCTAD Multi-Agency Support Team (MAST), is underway to seek up-to-date data from an expanding number of countries. The data collection effort is based on UNCTAD's new classification. Instead of relying on government reporting, UNCTAD commissions consultants to seek NTM information from national authorities, regional secretariats, importers' associations, chambers of commerce, and other private sector sources. It is expected that capacity building will lead, over time, to self sustaining data collection systems at the national and regional levels.

Exporter and importer surveys provide a source for more qualitative data on NTMs. For instance, the World Bank (2008a) carried out interviews of exporters and government officials in 13 countries in Asia and Latin America and carried out similar interviews in East Africa (World Bank 2008b). Coverage varies substantially across countries, as does the balance between private sector and public sector information.

Finally, the World Bank has developed two indicators for specific components of trade costs:

- The Doing Business project (see http://www. doingbusiness.org/) measures the cost of fees for importing or exporting a 20 foot container (World Bank 2009, p. 49; Djankov, Freund, and Pham 2006).
- The Logistics Performance Index (LPI; see http://www.worldbank.org/lpi) measures the infrastructure and regulatory environment in which logistics chains operate, based on survey data from global freight forwarders and express carriers, with direct measurement of some quantitative indicators.

These indices are designed chiefly to raise political awareness on trade facilitation issues. Caution should be exercised in using them for rigorous statistical analysis.

Measurements of incidence and impact

It is an understatement to say that coverage ratios, AVEs and, more broadly, estimates of the impact of NTMs on trade vary substantially across studies, making it difficult to draw sweeping conclusions. Nevertheless, a number of observations can be made.

First, NTMs affect a very large share of imports, while standards and technical regulations are now the major form of NTM. The studies reviewed show coverage ratios ranging between one-third and two-thirds of imports (34 percent for industrial country imports from developing countries according to Nogues, Olechowski, and Winters 1986; 57 percent in the sample of Kee, Nicita, and Olarreaga 2009). Moreover, one of the most striking results to come out of recent work (see for example Disdier, Fontagné, and Mimouni 2008) is the prevalence of product standards in agrifood trade. Subject to caveats discussed in the previous section, International Trade Centre survey results suggest that technical barriers (essentially standards) are just as prevalent for a wide range of products and destinations. Thus, standards and technical regulations seem to have superseded quantitative restrictions as the major form of NTMs.

Second, as for the severity of NTMs, estimated AVEs show overall averages of 5 percent to 10 percent, with substantial peaks—higher than tariff peaks. Kee, Nicita, and Olarreaga (2009) find averages of 9.2 percent (simple) and 7.8 percent (trade weighted) across 4,545 product specific regressions. These estimates are somewhat lower than those of Bradford (2003), who finds average AVEs ranging from 7.8 percent (Canada) to 28 percent (the United Kingdom) to 52 percent (Japan). If products with no NTMs are eliminated, AVEs climb to 39.8 percent and 22.7 percent respectively in Kee, Nicita, and Olarreaga (2009). These higher orders of magnitude are comparable to those obtained using price based methodologies by Andriamananjara and others (2004), although individual estimates vary substantially: for instance, Andriamananjara and others (2004) find a 73 percent average AVE for apparel, against only 20 percent in Kee, Nicita, and Olarreaga (2009). Kee, Nicita, and Olarreaga (2009) also observe that NTM AVEs, unlike tariffs, tend to rise with income levels, reflecting stiff agricultural NTMs in rich countries.[2] A reality check is provided by a recent survey on nontariff trade costs between Arab countries that returned AVEs ranging between 2 percent and 11 percent, with an average of 6 percent (Hoekman and Zarrouk 2009).

Estimates of the trade reducing effect of NTMs are largely consistent with these AVEs. Using a gravity equation, Hoekman and Nicita (2008) find an elasticity of trade to NTMs around one-half, implying that cutting the AVE of NTMs in half—from around 10 percent to around 5 percent—would boost trade by 2–3 percent.

The studies examined find that standards and technical regulations have a particularly significant impact on trade. Chen, Otsuki, and Wilson (2006), using a gravity equation, find that standards have a stronger impact on developing country exports and that testing and inspection procedures reduce exports by 9 percent and 3 percent respectively. Access to relevant information about standards seems key, as informational barriers by themselves reduce trade by 18 percent while firms with foreign capital—typically larger ones with better access to information—are less affected. Finally, nonharmonized standards cause diseconomies of scale for exporters, reducing the likelihood of entry in foreign markets (in addition to reducing volumes conditional on entry). Czubala, Shepherd, and Wilson (2007) also find that the trade inhibiting effect of standards is reduced when they are harmonized. These results are confirmed by Baller (2007), who found that mutual recognition agreements had a strong positive effect both on the probability that bilateral trade takes place and on its volume.

The policy implications emerging from this body of work are thus fairly clear: standards related NTMs have a real impact on trade, compliance costs matter, and harmonization and mutual recognition agreements that reduce those compliance costs—without necessarily watering down the substance of the measures—can have a positive impact on trade flows.

The conclusions are similar for trade facilitation. Djankov, Freund, and Pham (2006) estimate that a one day delay in shipment for exports means a reduction in trade of at least 1 percent—and 7 percent if the exports are agricultural products. Wilson, Mann, and Otsuki (2003) simulated changes in trade flows among APEC member economies to improve efficiency in the use of ports, the customs environment,

the use of e-business tools, and certain regulatory harmonization measures at the border (regulatory environment). They estimated that the combination of these measures would yield a remarkable 21 percent rise in trade ($254 billion) in the APEC region. The measures with highest impact were those related to port efficiency and the regulatory environment. Indeed, Francois, Van Meijl, and van Tongeren (2003) noted that trade facilitation measures typically bring higher benefits than most measures now under discussion in the Doha Round's market access negotiations.

World Trade Organization disciplines on nontariff measures

NTMs exist within a framework established by the rules of the trading system, including the multilateral rules of the WTO Agreement, the rules in regional trade agreements, and even rules agreed in bilateral or plurilateral negotiations. The following section discusses these rules and their connection to the empirical analysis of NTMs and their effects.

Legal rules provide an agreed normative benchmark for NTMs' acceptability. By characterizing some NTMs as illegal they define which NTMs a government is obligated to address and which its trading partners have a right to complain about. Conversely, where an NTM is not characterized as illegal under the rules, trading partners and their stakeholders who seek action to reduce its trade reducing effects can only obtain it if the importing country agrees. Thus, the rules draw the line between actions that trading partners can expect for free and actions for which they must negotiate and pay in some form.

Substantively, these rules require nondiscriminatory treatment and permit member governments to maintain whatever level of protection they desire, but they do not stop at nondiscrimination. They require that regulations be necessary to achieve a legitimate policy objective and not be disguised barriers to trade or unnecessarily restrictive of trade. Where the WTO rules stop, negotiations begin; governments have undertaken higher than WTO levels of discipline in regional trade agreements and through bilateral arrangements, and they have unilaterally liberalized NTMs when they view this action as being in the national economic interest.

Nontariff measures: impact, regulation, and trade facilitation

WTO disciplines. Until 1979 the General Agreement on Tariff and Trade (GATT) limited its basic rules for regulation to two requirements—not to discriminate and not to ban or restrict imports. But the drafters recognized a short list of policies that would trump trade liberalization, some of them highly relevant to NTMs. The 1979 Agreement on Technical Barriers to Trade (TBT Agreement; WTO 1994c) expanded GATT disciplines on regulation with a plurilateral code that added rules affecting even nondiscriminatory regulations. Finally, after the Uruguay Round, the WTO Agreement included an amended TBT Agreement as well as a new Agreement on the Application of Sanitary and Phytosanitary Measures (SPS Agreement). Going far beyond nondiscrimination, these two agreements provide additional discipline on NTMs.

Nondiscrimination and the GATT. The principle of nondiscrimination is central to the GATT. A multilateral tariff agreement, the GATT also includes nontariff obligations designed to secure the value of the agreed tariff concessions and to generalize their benefit to all GATT members on a most favored nation basis. These nontariff obligations now apply to all WTO members through the GATT's incorporation into the WTO Agreement.

Because a discriminatory internal tax or regulation can eliminate any benefit of a tariff binding, GATT article III:1 recognizes the principle that internal taxes, charges, and regulations should not be applied to imported or domestic products to protect domestic production. Article III:2 prohibits imposing on imported products internal taxes or charges higher than those imposed on like domestic products. And article III:4 requires that imported products be accorded "treatment no less favorable than that accorded to like products of domestic origin in respect of all laws, regulations and requirements affecting their internal sale, offering for sale, purchase, transportation or use" (WTO 1986, p. 6).

As a GATT panel described it in 1958 when writing about article III:4, "the intention of the drafters of the Agreement was clearly to treat the imported products in the same way as the like domestic products once they had been cleared through Customs. Otherwise indirect protection could be given" (GATT 1959, p. 60).[3] Moreover—since the GATT's most favored nation clause for border charges (article I:1) also applies to internal taxes and regulations—a WTO member must apply the same regulations to like products from any WTO source.

In dispute settlement decisions interpreting article III:4, GATT panels clarified that the scope of this provision is very broad indeed. According to the panel in 1958, "the drafters of the Article intended to cover in paragraph 4 not only the laws and regulations which directly governed the conditions of sale or purchase but also any laws or regulations which might adversely affect modify the conditions of competition between the domestic and imported products on the domestic market" (GATT 1959, p. 60).[4] In later decisions panels clarified that this nondiscrimination requirement has a very broad scope—applying, for instance, to technical regulations, government benefits, sales practices of state owned enterprises, regulations on product quality or ingredients, measures discouraging the use of certain products, labeling regulations, and shipping charges of government run railways or postal services.

In principle, the trade effects of an NTM are of no importance in determining whether an NTM violates the GATT's nondiscrimination principle—trade effects from the NTM should be considered irrelevant. Since 1949 it has been recognized that any higher taxation of imported products violates article III, even if no damage is shown and even if there is no tariff binding on the product in question. As a GATT panel found in 1987, the prohibition on tax discrimination between like products does not protect expectations of any particular trade volume but only expectations about the competitive relationship between imported and domestic products (WTO 1995, p. 128).

But what if a regulation or tax treats imports less favorably without any explicit discrimination between like products? Disputes over such de facto discrimination have confronted the WTO dispute settlement system with the task of distinguishing between on the one hand, domestic regulatory or tax schemes that were clearly set up so as to discriminate, and, on the other, domestic schemes set up for some other purpose that have an unintended negative effect on imported products.

WTO panels and the WTO Appellate Body have solved this conundrum by drawing on the the principle in article III:1 that taxes and regulations

Nontariff measures: impact, regulation, and trade facilitation

should not be applied so as to protect domestic production. They have agreed that the provisions on national treatment in articles III:2 and III:4 must be interpreted in the light of this principle. Thus, in judging dissimilar taxation of two products that compete with each other, WTO panels will only find a violation of article III:2 if "the design, the architecture, and the revealing structure" of the tax measure show that it is applied so as to protect domestic production (WTO 1996, paragraph 29).[5]

The WTO's approach to de facto discrimination does not amount to letting in trade effects through the back door. The orthodox doctrine that, even if there is no trade, discrimination violates the rules remains as valid now as in 1949. The decisions referred to above have simply shown that, when a regulation or tax does not explicitly discriminate against imports, more flexibility will be shown if its demonstrable purpose was to advance some nontrade objective.

Exceptions. The GATT also includes a short list of exceptions in article XX that permit a government to maintain measures that would otherwise violate the positive rules of the GATT—for instance, measures that discriminate against or between imports or that ban importation of a good. The article XX exceptions permit measures necessary to, or related to, certain named policies—for instance, measures "necessary to protect human, animal or plant life or health," measures "necessary to protect public morals," measures "necessary to secure compliance" with otherwise GATT-consistent laws and regulations, and measures "relating to the conservation of natural resources if such measures are made effective in conjunction with restrictions on domestic production or consumption" (WTO 1986, pp. 37–38). A proviso to the list requires that the measures in question not be "applied in a manner which would constitute a means of arbitrary or unjustifiable discrimination between countries where the same conditions prevail, or a disguised restriction on international trade." In any dispute the complaining party bears the burden of proof as to whether the positive rules have been violated; however, exceptions are an affirmative defense, for which the burden shifts to the defending party (WTO 1986, p. 37).

Accordingly, for an NTM, a trading partner must demonstrate a rule violation (such as denial of national treatment). The importing country then must show that the measure:

- Falls within the policy objectives listed in article XX.
- Does not discriminate arbitrarily between countries where relevant conditions are the same, and also takes into account relevant differences.
- Is not a form of disguised protectionism.

Three of the exceptions in article XX refer to measures "that are necessary." But what is necessary? To analyze necessity panels have used a balancing approach. In the leading WTO case on this issue, concerning a Korean discriminatory regime for imported beef, the WTO Appellate Body noted that necessity claims must be evaluated in relation to circumstances. It further noted that such evaluations always involve weighing and balancing a series of factors, prominently including (WTO 2001, paragraph 164):[6]

- The actual contribution made by the measure to achieving the stated objective within article XX.
- The importance of the common interests or values protected.
- The measure's restrictive impact on trade.

In this case and others the WTO Appellate Body has looked for a relation between the measure and the end pursued that is not just a contribution to accomplishing the objective, but closer to being indispensable to accomplishing that objective. The party seeking to demonstrate that its measures are necessary must establish this through evidence or data establishing that the measures actually contribute to the achievement of the objectives pursued. Evaluation of a measure's necessity also requires an evaluation of its restrictive effect on trade (or on the sale or distribution of imports behind the border, if the issue is justifying behind-the-border discriminatory regulations). The less restrictive an NTM is, the more likely it is to be justifiable as "necessary" (WTO 2009, paragraphs 305–10).

But it cannot really be necessary for an NTM to violate GATT rules if there is some reasonably available, GATT-consistent way for the government to accomplish the same goal. A GATT panel pointed this out in the *United States–Section 337* case in 1988 (GATT 1989), and other WTO panels have repeatedly recognized the essential truth of this proposition.[7] In the *Korea–Beef* (WTO 2001)[8] and *United States–Gambling* (WTO 2005)[9] cases the Appellate Body clarified that, as a panel evaluates necessity, it must examine whether the defending party could reasonably be expected to employ an alternative measure that is WTO-consistent (or less WTO-inconsistent) and that would achieve the objectives pursued by the measure at issue. An alternative measure may be not "reasonably available" if it is merely theoretical in nature or imposes on a member an undue burden, such as prohibitive costs or technical difficulties in its implementation. Moreover, an alternative measure that is "reasonably available" must preserve the defending party's right to achieve its desired level of protection with respect to the objective pursued under article XX (Sáez 2005). Where the complaining party identifies an alternative measure the defending party has the burden of demonstrating that its GATT-inconsistent measure is "necessary" (WTO 2009, paragraph 319).

To determine whether such an alternative measure exists, then, the panel must evaluate three things:

- Whether the alternative measure is economically and technically feasible.
- Whether the alternative measure would achieve the same objectives as the original measure.
- Whether the alternative measure is less trade restrictive than the original measure.

If any of these elements is not met, the alternative measure is deemed to be not compatible with WTO obligations. Here, as well, economic information on the NTM at issue is directly useful.

Beyond nondiscrimination: the SPS and TBT Agreements

While the GATT bans discrimination in internal taxes or regulations, GATT rules impose no limitations whatsoever on a nondiscriminatory measure's objectives, subject, policy focus, or methodology. Government regulatory sovereignty remains supreme. A government could even impose a nondiscriminatory regulation that burdens all trade—such as a requirement that all goods offered for sale must be labeled only in the language of the importing country, or must be shipped in containers that have been painted pink.

The SPS Agreement and the TBT Agreement go beyond GATT rules to address the impact of NTMs on trade, even in cases where the NTMs are nondiscriminatory. The SPS Agreement—developed as part of the Uruguay Round agricultural trade package—specifically tackles typical NTMs affecting food trade and applies only to sanitary and phytosanitary measures, which are typical NTMs affecting food. The TBT Agreement provides related but separate disciplines that apply to all other standards, technical regulations, and conformity assessment procedures for all products.[10]

The SPS Agreement (WTO 1994b) presents the tradeoff between free trade and regulatory sovereignty most explicitly. It states that WTO members have the right to take SPS measures—but it requires that such measures must be applied only to the extent necessary to protect human, animal, or plant life or health, and that the measures must be based on scientific principles and not maintained without sufficient scientific evidence (articles 2.1, 2.2). Whether scientific evidence supports a measure is an element of whether the measure is necessary and proportional. A member has the right to set its desired "appropriate level of sanitary or phytosanitary protection," but in doing so it must take into account the objective of minimizing negative trade effects (article 5.4).

Article 2.2 of the TBT Agreement confronts the same tradeoff in similar terms. It requires that members ensure that technical regulations are not prepared, adopted, or applied with a view to, or with the effect of, creating unnecessary obstacles to trade. It further clarifies that technical regulations must not be more trade restrictive than necessary to fulfill a legitimate objective, taking into account the risks of nonfulfilment. Unlike GATT article XX, which is limited to a short list of acceptable excuses such as public morality and public health, TBT article 2.2 provides an open illustrative list of acceptable "legitimate objectives."

These SPS and TBT necessity requirements encourage members to address nontrade problems, such as product safety, through less trade reducing and more efficient measures. Thus, the costs in terms of trade inherent in the regulations should be clearly lower than the benefits obtained. These agreements promote a more efficient use of instruments that create fewer distortions from an economic standpoint.

The analysis of necessity under the SPS and TBT Agreements rolls together the same combination of themes as the analysis of necessity in article XX:

- A measure's contribution toward a policy objective.
- The legitimacy and importance of the objective pursued.
- The measure's restrictive impact on trade—including the government's choice not to employ reasonably available alternatives that would have been less restrictive.

There is an essential difference, however. In any dispute applying SPS article 2.2, 5.4, or 5.6 (or any combination of these) to a (nondiscriminatory) SPS measure—and in any dispute applying TBT article 2.2 to any other measure—the complaining party bears the burden of proving there is a lack of necessity. On the other hand, in a GATT dispute where the defending party invokes an affirmative defense under article XX, the defending party bears the burden of proof on all the issues in article XX (including necessity, and nondiscriminatory, nonprotectionist application). This difference can make a substantial difference in the outcome of the dispute.[11]

Panels in SPS disputes have not had difficulty applying the three part test outlined above, relying on objective expert evidence on the risks combated by a measure—for example, fish diseases in the *Australia–Salmon* dispute (WTO 1998)[12] or plant diseases in the *Japan–Apples* dispute (WTO 2003a).[13] Since the alternative measures proposed by exporting countries will always be significantly less restrictive than the disputed measures are, the only questions are whether the proposed alternative is technically and economically feasible and whether it would deliver the importing country's designated appropriate level of protection. As the WTO Appellate Body noted, the SPS Agreement does not explicitly require a member to define appropriate levels of protection routinely for all products—but in a dispute the panel must use some benchmark for SPS obligations, and if the defending party does not supply a defined appropriate level of protection the panel must infer such a definition from the level of protection in the defending party's SPS measures (WTO 1998, paragraphs 205–07).[14] In the compliance phase of the *Salmon* and *Apples* disputes each panel relied on its experts and quickly concluded that the importing country's amended import regime failed the three part test.

No panel has yet applied the necessity and proportionality test in TBT Agreement article 2.2 (although claims under article 2.2 are at issue in at least two pending disputes).

Regionalism and other preferential trade agreements

Governments have also addressed NTMs—especially those arising from standards, technical regulations, and conformity assessments—through preferential trade agreements (PTAs). The communication channels created in setting a preferential trade agreement can build mutual trust and confidence in the judgment of other regulators, creating a basis for agreements on the harmonization of standards, on the mutual recognition of test data, or on the mutual recognition of conformity assessment.

Similar benefits can arise from other, similar agreements made within an established bilateral or plurilateral relationship. Examples include mutual recognition agreements between the European Union and the United States and agreements related to standards among members of APEC.

SPS and TBT provisions in preferential trade agreements. Preferential trade agreements made by the European Union, and those made by the United States, contain measures to reduce or eliminate NTMs. Horn, Mavroidis, and Sapir (2009) review measures in 28 such agreements with developed and developing countries. The authors distinguish among 52 policy areas, which they divide into two types of commitments:

- Commitments going beyond the WTO, but in areas already covered by commitments agreed at the multilateral level—reconfirming existing WTO commitments or providing further obligations (WTO+).
- Commitments related to areas or policy instruments that are qualitatively new—not previously regulated by the WTO (WTO-X).

The SPS and TBT measures are examples of WTO+. In contrast, labor laws, environmental measures, and measures on the movement of capital—among others—are examples of WTO-X.

Preferential trade agreements made by the European Union and those made by the United States cover WTO+ areas to a very large extent. The TBT provisions in European Union agreements typically not only reinforce the commitments from the WTO TBT Agreement, but also establish forums to promote unilateral or mutual recognition of standards and of conformity assessment. In contrast, the agreements made by the United States are less deep in their commitments, typically reconfirming the WTO obligations of preferential partners. However, most TBT provisions in United States agreements are legally enforceable—in contrast to European Union agreements.[15]

The coverage of SPS provisions by preferential trade agreements is less common, and rarely are the provisions legally enforceable.[16] Most of the United States agreements contain exemptions from dispute settlement for SPS measures—dispute settlement is allowed for only by the two agreements that contain legally enforceable SPS provisions.

For TBT provisions the most common approach taken in a number of agreements signed between developed and developing countries is the mutual recognition of conformity assessment results (Lesser 2007; Permartini and Budetta 2009).[17] Such mutual recognition is considered to be less costly than the harmonization of regulations, standards, or conformity assessment procedures. The next most common approach is to increase transparency requirements—urging members to notify each other about new and modified regulations and procedures.

Other approaches that are often adopted in PTAs include harmonizing technical regulations, harmonizing standards, harmonizing conformity assessment procedures, and—the least common—accepting other parties' technical regulations as equivalent to one's own (despite differing technical specifications). All these approaches are compatible with each other. Often a preferential trade agreement includes a range of measures based on various approaches.

For TBT commitments most preferential trade agreements do not include provisions more stringent than those in the WTO TBT Agreement—yet many include provisions resembling those in the WTO+ category. The farther reaching commitments concern the acceptance of technical regulations as equivalent and the mutual recognition of conformity assessment procedures and bodies (bodies where parties must explain nonequivalence to other parties' conformity assessment procedures and nonrecognition of those procedures). In addition, a few developed countries—European Union members and more developed members of APEC and the Association of Southeast Asian Nations—have arrangements for the mutual recognition of conformity assessment results in certain sectors (for example, in telecommunications and in electrical, electronic, and medical equipment).

The depth of TBT liberalizations depends on several factors. The first is the degree of the parties' development. Provisions on the harmonization of standards and, most important, the recognition of conformity assessment results are included in preferential trade agreements among countries with similar degrees of development. The second factor is the degree of integration. Deeper and more comprehensive agreements, such as customs unions and economic association agreements, most often go beyond the WTO TBT commitments. The third factor is whether the European Union or the United States is involved. In preferential trade agreements involving the United States liberalization related to TBT can take several forms: for example, the acceptance of the partner's technical regulations as equivalent, alignment toward international standards, and the mutual recognition of conformity assessment results. In contrast, preferential trade agreements between the European Union and European Neighborhood Policy countries are based on harmonization toward European Union regulations, standards, and conformity assessment procedures—while in European Union preferential trade agreements with more remote countries (such as Chile) convergence towards international standards is preferred.

Unilateral reform: lessons from two decades of reform

More than other areas of trade policy, NTMs are intimately linked to national regulatory structures. Unlike tariff reductions, NTM reforms affect not just industry structures but also how public agencies work and interact with the private sector.

Nontariff measures: impact, regulation, and trade facilitation

Accordingly, streamlining NTMs should be viewed as part of a broader regulatory reform agenda such as that embraced by industrial countries in the 1990s. And regulatory reform requires strategic thinking. This section summarizes some lessons from international experience—in particular, six case studies from the World Bank's Doing Business project and its Foreign Investment Advisory Service program, recently studied by the Investment Climate Advisory Services of the World Bank Group (FIAS 2009). The six countries were Australia, Hungary, Italy, the Republic of Korea, Mexico, and the United Kingdom.

Improving the substance and improving the process—two complementary objectives. Streamlining NTMs involves two distinct, though complementary, policy objectives. One is to improve the substance of existing NTMs. The other is to improve the process through which new NTMs and regulations are issued and put into practice.

In the short run, when regulations are too many and too harmful, a cleanup process is the first step—and possibly the one that yields the highest immediate returns. Improving the substance of existing NTMs means reviewing them in light of existing evidence about their effects. Transparency is critical. Often it is fairly easy to spot regulations and NTMs that are redundant, harmful, and unnecessarily complicated—and sometimes such NTMs are known to competent ministries. To eliminate harmful NTMs all that is needed is to expose and shame the responsible ministries in roundtables with the private sector (as was done in Mexico; see FIAS 2008a)—or to create registries, such as single windows, where the ministries are asked to justify all measures.

In the long run, though, what matters is the regulatory process. Any modern society requires a constant stream of new product standards and regulations as technology and societal preferences change. To slow that stream, in 2004 Mexico imposed a regulatory moratorium. This, however, could only be a temporary fix. What is needed is not just to prevent regulatory proliferation, but, more broadly, to improve how regulations are issued and enforced. And that requires putting in place procedures that have clear, consistent requirements for transparency, impartiality, and economic rationality. Here the

international best practice is to impose mandatory regulatory impact assessments.

A need for leadership. Change often occurs when a crisis makes it impossible to do business as usual—provided that leadership can seize the opportunity. "A crisis is a terrible thing to waste," wrote Thomas Friedman (2005, quoted in World Bank 2009, p. 19).

Mexico's regulatory reform gathered momentum immediately after the so-called Tequila Crisis of 1994–95. The impetus for reform came from recognizing that the private sector—hard hit by the crisis—could no longer hope for help from trade protection after Mexico had joined the GATT (now WTO) and the North American Free Trade Agreement (NAFTA). Under the new constraints, improving national competitiveness by cutting red tape suddenly appeared as the only option. Similarly, Korea launched its regulatory reform in response to the 1997 crisis, which exposed the vulnerability of a development model based on state intervention and widespread nontransparency (FIAS 2008b).

But a crisis is not enough: leadership is needed to seize the opportunity and transform it into political momentum. The governments of both Korea and Mexico could read the signals correctly, draw the right conclusions, and get into action—because minds were ready. For instance, in Korea, the wave of reforms of the late 1990s built upon partly successful efforts that stretched back to 1981.

Reform is often driven by a surprisingly small group of technocrats. Mexico's regulatory reform was top down. Driving it was a small group of 15 to 20 economists and lawyers, many of them trained abroad and sharing a vision that placed markets, not the state, at the center of Mexico's growth strategy. Korea's regulatory reform was also very much top down—so much so that the lower ranks of the administration ultimately did not own it.

Support at the highest level is crucial when reformers take on powerful vested interests, but it is not enough in democracies with separation of powers. The Mexican technocrats had full support from Presidents Salinas (1988–94) and Zedillo (1994–2000), and in particular from their legal counsels. But such presidential support became less decisive after the Institutional Revolutionary Party (PRI) lost control of Mexico's Congress in 1997. In the long run there is no alternative equal to building coalitions and strong institutions.

Start small—even when aiming high. NTMs are distortionary, typically benefiting a few at the expense of many, so building coalitions to get rid of them should not be a problem. Yet in heavily distorted economies many groups benefit from one rent generating policy or another, and each fears it will be next. Uncertainty about the distributional impact of reforms adds to inertia.

In order to overcome fear and inertia losers must be visibly compensated. The art of reform is to find compensations that are less distortionary than the measures being eliminated. For instance, in the Democratic Republic of Congo (DRC), overstaffed parastatals (companies owned or sponsored by the state) impose myriad border taxes to cover their payrolls without providing much service in return. Those taxes, which typically go with complicated procedures, raise trade costs and slow down the movement of goods. But restructuring parastatals involved in transit procedures and infrastructure—and downsizing their bloated workforces—would set a precedent for many other, equally inefficient parastatals in other sectors of the economy. Setting such a precedent is, understandably, loathed. In such a case, building viable coalitions for restructuring would involve not only reaching out to importers penalized by high trade costs, but also neutralizing losers by offering credible social plans. Inasmuch as those social plans could be financed out of well designed taxes, they would be less costly to the economy than the parastatals' present stranglehold on trade.

The interaction between parastatal restructuring, social liabilities, and tax reform illustrates another key principle: synergies between reforms. Once domestic taxes are adequately designed and collected, border taxes are easier to dispense with. Other areas of synergies include procedural changes and technology upgrading in customs administrations as well as investments in infrastructure, regulatory simplifications, and changes of behavior on the ground. For instance, better roads cannot reduce transit times as long as redundant checkpoints and blockades are maintained by police, paramilitary forces, and bureaucracies, as is often the case in Africa.

Regulatory reforms should aim high, but they should also start small. Reform processes often have little credibility or goodwill at the outset. They need to assert themselves by picking low hanging fruit and winning easy battles. This is the strategy that was successfully followed by Mexico's early reformers. A good entry point for NTM reform is the creation of a registry of existing NTMs and regulations, based on compulsory notification by competent ministries. A guillotine approach can also be used—mandating the elimination of a set number of (generally redundant or obsolete) regulations. For instance, in 1998 Korea's President Kim Dae Jung instructed all ministers to eliminate half their regulations by year end (FIAS 2008b).

Lock in reforms through legislation. However well designed and needed, reforms are always at risk of reversal. When Mexican elections returned a majority in Congress that was hostile to the president, partisan politics greatly slowed reform. By 2000 general reform fatigue in the face of disappointing growth (though Mexico's disappointing performance was due to a variety of factors that had little to do with the reforms) had eroded political support for further regulatory reform. In 2003 the newly created regulatory oversight commission lost a key battle against the telecommunications sector, waiving its right to issue an opinion on a draft regulation for the sector that was favored by incumbent operators. The same year its head was abruptly replaced, and in 2009 the agency found itself without direction for several months in a row.

Reforms need to be locked in through legal reform—so they become legally enforceable—and through the creation of sufficiently powerful institutions. Mexico's federal regulatory oversight body, the Comisión Federal de Mejora Regulatoria, proved too weak to maintain momentum, having failed to secure for itself a prestigious role like that of the Comisión Federal de Competencia responsible for enforcement of competition law. Korea's Regulatory Reform Committee also lacked clout because its expertise was insufficient (FIAS 2008b).

When domestic commitment is not enough, international agreements can serve as anchors, as discussed earlier in this chapter. NAFTA provided a strong anchor for the Mexican reform process because the political cost of breaking away from it would have been prohibitive—and Mexico's NAFTA partners also had regulatory reform agendas of their own, generating policy coherence in the bloc. The prospect of European Union accession provided the strongest possible anchor to Hungarian reforms because of its reliance on mutual recognition and because of the single market's very ambitious regulatory reform agenda. However, the degree of commitment provided by trading agreements varies—and so does the substance of their NTM reform agendas. For instance, the East African Community (EAC) has an agenda of NTM elimination, but so far its implementation on the ground still lacks force.

To ensure that reforms are carried out, engage middle management. Reforming alone is hard. Mexico's experience shows the critical need for international support. Its regulatory oversight bodies drew heavily on support from peer agencies, international experts, and stakeholders most affected by NTMs. Product standards, in particular, are increasingly complex—yet regulatory needs do not differ radically by country. There is no need for a national agency to expend scarce resources duplicating work (expert review, standard setting) that has already been done elsewhere. But fruitful contact and cooperation with foreign agencies requires that national agency staff have enough training to communicate with foreign peers. Economists, engineers, and lawyers in Mexico's regulatory oversight bodies who had been trained in the United States felt at ease communicating with counterparts there, as well as in Canada and the United Kingdom. This ability to exchange ideas and bring home best practices made the economists, engineers, and lawyers efficient and highly motivated—showing the value of selecting agency staff carefully at the outset.

Engaging middle-ranking administration levels in the reform process is crucial. Whatever high level pronouncements may say about NTM streamlining and regulatory reform, not all agencies will march in step—and the pace often is set by those that are slowest to cooperate. In Mauritius, as part of a thorough modernization of customs, online application procedures are being put in place to speed requests for permits delivered by other ministries. Some of those ministries apparently remain unaware that the point

is to speed clearance, since they still require trips to their offices in downtown Port Louis. Similarly, risk management techniques introduced by customs agencies in several countries are incompletely understood by other agencies.

Works on corporate change management often observe that the strongest resistance to changes in rules and procedures typically comes from middle management. The same is true in public agencies. A change mandated from the top is only as good as division heads and lower ranking officials make it—and they may be uncertain about the effect of regulatory reform on their own status and position. When regulatory improvement comes as part of an aggressive agenda of state retrenchment and privatization it can easily be perceived as hostile and threatening, leading to inertia or passive resistance. In Mexico a spoils system made it possible to change public agency staff down to the middle ranks in key areas (FIAS 2008a). But such a system creates a risk of politically motivated reversal later on—and it does not help make reforms viable in the long term. Far better is the use of training and communication to gain the support of a stable, competent administration. Indeed, Mexico's regulatory oversight body sought such support through capacity building seminars—but its means were too small.

In the end, NTMs are and will remain an important component of trade regulations. What is needed is a clear understanding of the policy objectives sought and a constant review of their impact and appropriateness. When they are needed, and often they are needed, policymakers need to constantly strive to reduce their trade distorting impact and seek ways to ensure effective administration at least cost to legitimate traders.

Notes

The authors would like to thank Amelia Porges for her comments and suggestions, particularly on World Trade Organization law—though as usual the authors are solely responsible for any errors.

1. They estimate the "representative" ad valorem equivalent of trade cost between two industrialized countries at a whopping 170 percent. Of this 21 percent is transportation,

13

Nontariff measures: impact, regulation, and trade facilitation

44 percent is border related trade barriers, and 55 percent is retail and wholesale distribution costs. Of the 44 percent of border related costs 8 percent is tariff and nontariff measures and 36 percent is nonpolicy trade costs, of which 7 percent is the language barrier, 14 percent the currency barrier, 6 percent information costs, and 3 percent a "security barrier." Note that percentages do not add up because they compound (so the total is more than the sum).

2. The methodology of Kee, Nicita, and Olarreaga (2009) makes it possible to estimate different AVEs for the same product depending on the importing country's factor endowment.

3. The panel that wrote the report, titled "Italian Discrimination Against Imported Agricultural Machinery" (quoted here at paragraph 11), comprised trade officials who had participated in negotiating the GATT in 1946–48.

4. Panel titled "Italian Discrimination Against Imported Agricultural Machinery" (quoted here at paragraph 12).

5. In WTO (1996–2008) at DSR 1996:I, 97.

6. In WTO (1996–2008) at DSR 2001:I, 5.

7. Available online at http://www.wto.org/gatt_docs/English/SULPDF/91390261.pdf (GATT *Basic Instruments and Selected Documents* reference number BISD 36S/345).

8. In WTO (1996–2008) at DSR 2001:I, 5.

9. In WTO (1996–2008) at DSR 2005:XII, 5663 (and see Corr.1 at DSR 2006:XII, 5475).

10. Chapter 16 addresses SPS measures extensively; this chapter's analysis is limited to the essential principles of the agreements. SPS article 1.1 provides that the SPS Agreement applies to all SPS measures that may, directly or indirectly, affect international trade; annex A defines the scope of SPS measures subject to the agreement (health protection measures, principally to protect against risks arising from the entry, establishment, or spread of pests or diseases or from additives, contaminants, or toxins in food, beverages or feedstuffs). The TBT Agreement applies to all technical regulations, standards, and

conformity assessment schemes except SPS measures—for instance, food regulations imposed for other reasons.

11. A "necessity test" (a requirement that a measure must be necessary to achieve stated nontrade policy objectives) also appears in GATT articles XI:2, XII:2, and XII:3(c), (i), and (d), and in corresponding provisions of article XVIII; GATS articles VI:4, XIII:2(d), and XIV; the GATS Annex on Telecommunications, paragraph 5(e); TRIPS articles 8.2 and 27.2; and GPA article XXIII:2 (see for example WTO 2003b).

12. In WTO (1996–2008) at DSR 1998:VIII, 3327 (and see Corr.1 at DSR 1998:VIII, 3407).

13. In WTO (1996–2008) at DSR 2003:IX, 4481.

14. In WTO (1996–2008) at DSR 1998:VIII, 3327 (and see Corr.1 at DSR 1998:VIII, 3407).

15. Horn, Mavroidis, and Sapir (2009) found that 12 out of 14 United States and 5 out of 14 European Union agreements under review had legally enforceable TBT provisions.

16. Only 8 European Union agreements cover SPS measures, with only 3 containing legally enforceable provisions. Out of 12 United States agreements with SPS provisions, only 2 include legally enforceable commitments.

17. Lesser (2007) reviews 28 PTAs signed by Chile, Mexico, and Singapore. Piermartini and Budetta (2009) review 70 signed agreements representing regions, all levels of development, and all degrees of depth in the trade among the parties.

References

Anderson, J., and E. van Wincoop. 2004. "Trade Costs." *Journal of Economic Literature* 42: 691–751.

Andriamananjara, S., J. Dean, R. Feinberg, M. Ferrantino, R. Ludema, and M. Tsigas. 2004. "The Effects of Nontariff Measures on Prices, Trade, and Welfare: CGE Implementation of Policy-Based Price Comparisons." Working Paper 15863, Office of Economics, United States

International Trade Commission, Washington, DC.

Baldwin, R. 1970. "Non-Tariff Distortions in International Trade." Washington, DC: Brookings Institution.

Baller, S. 2007. "Trade Effects of Regional Standards Liberalization." Policy Research Working Paper 4124, The World Bank, Washington, DC.

Bradford, S. 2003. "Paying the price: final goods protection in OECD countries." *Review of Economic and Statistics* 85: 24–37.

Chen, M.X., T. Otsuki, and J.S. Wilson, 2006. "Do Standards Matter for Export Success?" Policy Research Working Paper 3809, The World Bank, Washington, DC.

Czubala, W., B. Shepherd, and J. Wilson. 2007. "Help or Hindrance? The Impact of Harmonized Standards on African Exports." Policy Research Working Paper 4400, The World Bank, Washington, DC.

Deardorff, A., and R. Stern. 1998. "Measurement of Non-Tariff Barriers." Studies in International Economics, The University of Michigan Press.

de Melo, J., and C. Carrère. 2009. "Non-Tariff Measures: What Do We Know, What Should Be Done?" Working Paper 200933, Centre d'Études et de Recherches sur le Développement International (CERDI), Clermont-Ferrand.

Disdier, A.-C., L. Fontagné, and M. Mimouni. 2008. "The Impact of Regulations on Agricultural Trade : Evidence from the SPS and TBT Agreements." *American Journal of Agricultural Economics* 90: 336–50.

Djankov, S., C. Freund, and C. Pham. 2006. "Trading on Time." World Bank Policy Research Working Paper 3909, The World Bank, Washington, DC.

FIAS (Investment Climate Advisory Services of the World Bank Group). 2008a. *Regulatory Transformation in Mexico, 1988–2000: Case Studies on Reform Implementation Experience.* Washington, DC: The World Bank.

———. 2008b. *Regulatory Transformation in the Republic of Korea: Case Studies on Reform Implementation Experience.* Washington, DC: The World Bank.

———. 2009. *Lessons for Reformers: How to Launch, Implement, and Sustain Regulatory Reform.* Washington, DC: The World Bank.

Francois, J., H. Van Meijl, and F. van Tongeren, 2003. "Trade Liberalization and Developing Countries Under the Doha Round." CEPR Discussion Papers 4032, Centre for Economic Policy Research, London.

Friedman, T. 2005. *The World Is Flat: A Brief History of the Twenty-First Century.* New York: Farrar, Straus and Giroux.

GATT (General Agreement on Tariffs and Trade). 1959. GATT *Basic Instruments and Selected Documents, 7th Supplement.* Geneva: GATT.

———. 1989. "United States: Section 337 of the Tariff Act of 1930, Report by the Panel." GATT document L/6439, GATT, Geneva.

Hoekman, B., and A. Nicita. 2008. "Trade Policy, Trade Costs, and Developing Country Trade." World Bank Policy Research Working Paper 4797, The World Bank, Washington, DC.

Hoekman, B., and J. Zarrouk. 2009. "Changes in Cross-Border Trade Costs in the Pan-Arab Free Trade Area, 2001–2008." World Bank Policy Research Working Paper 5031, The World Bank, Washington, DC.

Horn, H., P.Mavroidis, and A. Sapir. 2009. "Beyond the WTO? An Anatomy of EU and US Preferential Trade Agreements." Blueprint Series 7, Bruegel, Brussels.

Kee, H., A. Nicita, and M. Olarreaga. 2009. "Estimating Trade Restrictiveness Indices." *Economic Journal* 119, 172–99.

Laird, S., and R. Vossenaar. 1991. "Porque nos preocupan las barreras no arancelarias?" *Información Comercial Española.* Special Issue on Non-Tariff Barriers. 31–54.

Lesser, C. 2007. "Do Bilateral and Regional Approaches for Reducing Technical Barriers to Trade Converge towards the Multilateral Trade System?" Trade Working Paper No. 58, TAD/TC/WP(2007)12/FINAL, OECD, Paris.

Nogués, J., A. Olechowski, and L. Winters. 1986. "Extent of Non-Tariff Barriers to Industrial Country Imports." *World Bank Economic Review* 1: 181–99.

Piermartini, R., and M. Budetta. 2009. "A Mapping of Regional Rules on Technical Barriers to Trade." In *Regional Rules in the Global Trading System,* ed. A. Estevadeordal, K. Suominen, and R. Teh. Cambridge: Cambridge University Press. 250–315.

13

Nontariff measures: impact, regulation, and trade facilitation

Sáez, S. 2005. "El Comercio de Servicios en el Marco del Sistema de Solución de Controversias de la Organización Mundial del Comercio." Serie de Comercio Internacional 60, División de Comercio Internacional, Comisión Económica de para América Latina y el Caribe (CEPAL), Santiago de Chile.

Wilson, J., C. Mann, and T. Otsuki. 2003. "Assessing the Potential Benefit of Trade Facilitation: A Global Perspective." World Bank Policy Research Working Paper 3224, World Bank, Washington, DC.

World Bank. 2008a. "A Survey of Non-Tariff Measures in the East Asia and Pacific Region." Policy Research Report 42853, The World Bank, Washington, DC.

———. 2008b. "Non-Tariff Measures on Goods Trade in the East African Community: Synthesis Report." Report 45708-AFR, The World Bank, Washington, DC.

———. 2009. *Doing Business 2010: Reforming Through Difficult Times—Comparing Regulation in 183 Economies*. Washington, DC: The World Bank.

WTO (World Trade Organization). 1986. "The Text of the General Agreement on Tariffs and Trade." Geneva: WTO. Available online at http://www.wto.org/english/docs_e/legal_e/gatt47_e.pdf.

———. 1994a. "Agreement Establishing the World Trade Organization." Geneva: WTO. Available online at http://www.wto.org/english/docs_e/legal_e/04-wto.pdf.

———. 1994b. "Agreement on the Application of Sanitary and Phytosanitary Measures." Geneva: WTO. Available online at http://www.wto.org/english/docs_e/legal_e/15-sps.pdf.

———. 1994c. "Agreement on Technical Barriers to Trade." Geneva: WTO. Available online at http://www.wto.org/english/docs_e/legal_e/17-tbt.pdf.

———. 1995. *Guide to GATT Law and Practice: Analytical Index*. Updated 6th ed. 2 vols. Geneva: WTO and Bernan Press.

———. 1996–2008. *Dispute Settlement Reports*. 43 vols. Cambridge: Cambridge University Press.

———. 1996. "Japan—Taxes on Alcoholic Beverages." WTO internal documents WT/DS8/AB/R, WT/DS10/AB/R, WT/DS11/AB/R, WTO, Geneva.

———. 1998. "Australia—Measures Affecting Importation of Salmon." WTO internal documents WT/DS18/R, WT/DS18/AB/R, WTO, Geneva.

———. 2001. "Korea—Measures Affecting Imports of Fresh, Chilled and Frozen Beef." WTO internal documents WT/DS161/AB/R, WT/DS169/AB/R, WTO, Geneva.

———. 2003a. "Japan—Measures Affecting the Importation of Apples." WTO internal documents WT/DS245/R, WT/DS245/AB/R, WTO, Geneva.

———. 2003b. "Table of Contents of the Inventory of Nontariff Measures." WTO document TN/MA/S/5/Rev.1, WTO, Geneva.

———. 2005. "United States—Measures Affecting the Cross Border Supply of Gambling and Betting Services." WTO internal document WT/DS285/AB/R, WTO, Geneva.

———. 2009. "China—Measures Affecting Trading Rights and Distribution Services for Certain Publications and Audiovisual Entertainment Products." WTO internal document WT/DS363/AB/R, WTO, Geneva.

14 Regional integration and customs unions

Erich Kieck and Jean-Christophe Maur

When a customs union is formed, states have an opportunity to improve the management of national and regional borders. Yet customs unions have not fully exploited this opportunity. Most efforts—with the exception of the European Union—have focused simply on facilitating the movement of goods across borders, not on integrating border management more broadly. Even so, customs unions provide some examples of the most advanced forms of regional integration and cooperation in border management.

This chapter surveys the border management issues facing both regional trade agreements (RTAs) and customs unions.

The rise of preferential liberalization: a changing landscape for border management

Customs unions are still less common than other, lighter forms of regional integration such as free trade agreements (FTAs). Yet customs unions face many of the same challenges—while pushing customs and border cooperation much further, yielding some of the most advanced and sophisticated forms of regional border cooperation and border policy management.

Apart from customs unions, many RTAs have been formed in recent years as a result of trade liberalization initiatives. Preferential trade agreements are being negotiated, in addition to the multilateral negotiations now underway as part of the World Trade Organization (WTO) Doha Development Round. From 1948 through 1994 there were 144 notifications of RTAs to the General Agreement on Tariffs and Trade (GATT). In contrast, since 1995 there have been 240 such notifications to the WTO.[1] More than 90 percent of notifications concerned FTAs.

The unprecedented rate of growth in RTAs—especially during the last decade—has been driven in part by increased WTO membership and by new notification obligations. All WTO members are today party to at least one RTA, with one exception (Mongolia). The average African country belongs to four RTAs, the average Latin American country to seven.

A 2006 study notes other patterns in RTAs (Fiorentino, Verdeja, and Toqueboeuf 2007):

- Bilateral RTAs account for 80 percent of all RTAs.
- There has been a shift from using RTAs to achieve regional integration toward gaining strategic market access.

- Europe has the largest number of RTAs, accounting for almost 50 percent of RTA notifications to the GATT and WTO.
- African RTAs come closest to the traditional concept of regional integration based on geographic proximity.
- All the customs unions of which the WTO has been notified are among geographically contiguous countries.

Among regional integration's various forms, or stages (box 14.1), the most common is the FTA. (Regional transit regimes and trade corridor arrangements are discussed in chapter 17.) Partial scope agreements are limited to developing countries—since developed countries are constrained by WTO article XXIV, which mostly precludes such agreements, and also since such agreements eventually are likely to form a path toward FTAs (Fiorentino, Verdeja, and Toqueboeuf 2007). The main reason why FTAs are much more common than the other three forms of preferential market integration (customs union, common market, and economic and monetary union) is that the onus of coordinating policies—particularly border policies—is much lighter on FTAs. Parties to a customs union must develop a common external tariff (CET), which presupposes common tariff and industrial policies. Customs unions also require a higher degree of political convergence and trust than FTAs do. Similarly, the two more advanced forms of integration—common markets, where provisions for the free flow of goods are extended to labor and capital, and economic and monetary unions, where parties share a common currency and macroeconomic policies—are least common because they require the greatest policy coordination, political convergence, and trust among parties.

An FTA requires the parties merely to negotiate rules of origin and agree to tariff reduction schedules.[2] They need not achieve the deeper policy convergence required by customs unions. In contrast with customs unions, FTAs enable the contracting parties to maintain their own external tariffs on goods imported from third parties. Preferential rules of origin are used to determine whether goods imported from one contracting party to another are entitled to preferential tariff treatment. So FTAs are simpler, and therefore faster to negotiate, than customs union agreements

| Box **14.1** | **The five stages of regional integration** |

- *Partial scope agreement:* Two or more customs territories extend preferential market access to each other on a fixed (usually limited) number of goods.
- *Free trade agreement:* Two or more customs territories extend preferential market access to each other on goods, services, or both.
- *Customs union:* The members apply a common external tariff on trade with third parties, while they allow goods to move among the members' territories free of customs duty.
- *Common market:* A customs union without cross border controls on flows of labor and capital.
- *Economic and monetary union:* A common market with a common currency and macroeconomic policies.

Source: Adapted from Balassa (1961).

are. Finally, most FTAs are bilateral (Do and Watson 2007, p. 8). In contrast, most customs unions of which the WTO is notified are truly regional (among neighboring countries) and involve more than two parties.

One result of the proliferation of RTAs (mostly in the form of FTAs) is an increasingly complex global trading regulatory system. Access to markets is governed by various rules and procedures. The Director-General of the WTO, Pascal Lamy, has observed:[3]

The proliferation of regional trade agreements can greatly complicate the trading environment, creating a web of incoherent rules, and intricate rules of origin. An increasing number of WTO Members are party to ten or more regional trade agreements, most of which for a given Member, contain agreement-specific rules of origin. This . . . complicates life for customs officials who are obliged to assess the same product differently depending on its origin, thus compromising the transparency of the trading regime. Borrowing the expression used by Professor Bhagwati—this is where we begin to have a real "spaghetti bowl" of twisted rules of origin.

Regional integration and customs unions

Article XXIV of the GATT and the Enabling Clause: WTO legal requirements

The overall goal of the WTO is to support international trade and development. Its five constitutional principles are trade without discrimination, the removal of barriers to trade, predictability (through transparency and binding trade rules), the promotion of fair competition, and encouraging development and economic reform.

The WTO constitutional principle of trade without discrimination is, in turn, supported by two principles: that of the most favored nation and that of national treatment. The most favored nation principle prohibits a WTO member from discriminating among its trading partners. It is found in WTO legal texts such as the GATT 1994, the General Agreement on Trade in Services (GATS), and the Agreement on Trade-Related Aspects of Intellectual Property Rights. In article I of the GATT 1947 (and accordingly under GATT 1994) the WTO members undertake to extend "any advantage, favour, privilege or immunity" to all members "immediately and unconditionally" with respect to—among other matters—"customs duties and charges of any kind imposed on or in connection with importation or exportation"; "the method of levying such duties and charges"; and "all rules and formalities in connection with importation or exportation" (GATT 1986, p. 2).

The rules of the multilateral trading system create exceptions to the nondiscrimination and most favored nation principles. These exceptions include the 1971 waiver to enable the Generalized System of Preferences (GSP), the 1979 Enabling Clause, article XXIV of GATT 1994, and article V of GATS. GATT article XXIV provides for customs unions, FTAs, and interim agreements resulting in the formation of customs unions or FTAs. Where WTO members have entered into customs union, FTA, or interim agreements, they are in effect exempted from the most favored nation principle in their trade with the other parties to these agreements—for both granting and receiving privileges.

By 15 December 2008, the GATT and WTO had been notified of 13 customs union agreements and 6 customs union accession agreements (table 14.1). All the accession agreements pertained to the expansion of the European Economic Community. Of the 13 customs union agreements, 2 pertained to customs unions between the European Economic Community and other parties (Andorra and Turkey). All these agreements were notified to the GATT and WTO in terms of either GATT article XXIV or the Enabling Clause.[4]

Article XXIV of the GATT contains the specific and general requirements for the formation of customs unions and FTAs. The main objectives are to:

• Prevent an adverse impact on third parties by prohibiting the establishment of additional or

Table **14.1**	Customs unions notifications to the World Trade Organization by 15 December 2008 (excluding the European Community accession agreements)		
Agreement		**Basis for notification**	**Date of notification**
Andean Community		Enabling Clause	October 1, 1990
Caribbean Common Market (CARICOM)		Article XXIV	October 14, 1974
Central American Common Market		Article XXIV	February 24, 1964
East African Community		Enabling Clause	October 9, 2000
European Community–Andorra		Article XXIV	February 23, 1998
European Community–Turkey		Article XXIV	December 22, 1995
EC Treaty		Article XXIV	April 24, 1957
Economic and Monetary Community of Central Africa		Enabling Clause	July 21, 1999
Eurasian Economic Community		Article XXIV	April 21, 1999
Gulf Cooperation Council		Enabling Clause	November 19, 2007
Mercado Común del Sur (Mercosur)		Enabling Clause	February 17, 1991
Southern African Customs Union		Article XXIV	June 25, 2007
West African Economic and Monetary Union		Enabling Clause	October 27, 1999

Source: Authors' compilation.

higher external trade barriers (the "external" requirement).

- Ensure the creation of "genuine" RTAs by removing tariffs and other regulations of commerce on substantially all intra-RTA trade (the "internal" requirement).
- Article XXIV:4 also requires that the aim of these agreements should be to facilitate trade between the participants and not to raise barriers to the trade of third parties.

GATT article XXIV:8(a) provides that the key elements for a customs union are:

- The substitution of a single customs territory for two or more customs territories. A customs territory is defined as a territory that maintains separate tariffs or other regulations of commerce for a substantial part of the trade of the territory with other territories.
- The duties and other restrictive regulations of commerce are eliminated with respect to substantially all the trade between the constituent territories of the union, or at least with respect to substantially all the trade in products originating in such territories.
- Substantially the same duties and other regulations of commerce are applied by the members of the customs union with respect to trade with territories that are not part of the union.

The definition of a customs union and the external requirement (on trade with territories not part of the union) are specific to customs unions and relate to the standing of the common external tariff, which GATT article XXIV: 8(a)(ii) defines as being "substantially the same duties and other regulations of commerce" in WTO law. The term *substantially* was interpreted in a WTO dispute as having "substantially the same duties and other regulations of commerce" as for third parties. This ruling implied that a common external trade regime by customs unions means "sameness," and that flexibility is limited (Devuyst and Serdarevic 2007).

Motives for signing regional trade agreements and links with border management

States enter into RTAs for various reasons. The most obvious economic reason is the need to secure better market access for products, especially compared with other countries that produce the same goods. Yet in reality the agreements usually form part of a broader political and economic program informed by international, regional, and national issues.[5] These issues are reflected in the policies included in the agreements with a bearing on how border management policies are affected by regional integration. Discussed below are some of the reasons for forming RTAs that may have implications for border management.[6]

Market access. True market access would require the rationalization of border management policies to facilitate trade, as liberalization and good border governance are complementary policies. However, the use of less transparent forms of protection—which may include administrative policies such as standards regulations implementation or customs procedures—could be used to deny some of the benefits granted by reducing trade barriers.

Harmonization and regulatory cooperation. Related to market access, regulatory cooperation and the harmonization of policies and procedures are becoming important in modern RTAs. The broad scope for regulatory alignment in border management includes the harmonization of documentation and procedures, the mutual recognition of procedures and standards, the exchange of information, and more. Access to the better practices of trade partners may be a supplementary incentive for poor countries with low capacity.

Foreign policy. Facilitating trade clearly helps to deepen trade relations. Cooperation on policies related to borders—a highly sensitive area—helps build trust. So a customs union may have a supplementary foreign policy role, deepening cooperation and making shared policies necessary (to set up and run the union). The most famous RTA, the European Economic Community, was created largely for political reasons and specifically regarded as an instrument to prevent further conflict among European economies through increased trade and economic integration. It went on to become a customs union, then a common market, and finally a monetary union.

New security dimensions. Both RTAs and increased cooperation among regions are used to develop common responses to emerging challenges. Some new economic and noneconomic challenges include preventing terrorism, protecting the environment, promoting labor standards, and ensuring economic security. Border management has an important role here. Part of the response to the terrorist attacks in the United States, for instance, was to create a single Department of Homeland Security in charge of all border policies. Common border security initiatives may be mooted in RTAs—while it often happens that bigger, more developed countries conclude RTAs to reward political allies.[7]

Policy lock-in. Participation in trade agreements enables states to lock in domestic economic reform measures in the medium to long term by preventing changes. An international legal commitment makes it more difficult to reverse painful but necessary short term commitments without incurring retaliation or a loss of confidence from other states and investors. Trade facilitation reforms are not necessarily easy, as powerful interests (tax revenue administrations and some private sector providers of clearance, transport, and logistics services) are linked with border processes.

Economies of scale. Some RTAs between African economies with small domestic markets can benefit the countries by creating economies of scale. Examples exist for private and public services that are integral to border management: the RTAs allow reducing border management's costs as well as improving its quality by expanding the scale of operations, making more sophisticated border and logistics services feasible. Higher value added services, certain types of infrastructure and equipment, and viable bond systems may similarly become feasible. Finally, forming an RTA can enable cost sharing with trade partners.

Critical size. Another scale effect is to provide some global bargaining or market power to countries as a group. One economic rationale for countries to form a customs union by adopting a common external tariff might be to set optimal tariffs.[8] Forming an RTA, countries may also seek to join ranks in international

forums such as the WCO and the WTO to express a common position and increase their influence.

Regional market failures. Regional market failures can be seen in the lack of the scale effects described above. But other aspects of failures can be seen when border management challenges require policy coordination among trade partners. For instance, modern border management requires modern information and communications technology (ICT) and financial tools (such as guarantees) and thus requires regional networks and interconnections.

Being landlocked. The most urgent regional market failures are seen in landlocked countries, which depend on cooperation with neighbors to manage international transit. Forming an RTA with neighboring countries that have coastal access can provide a solid institutional framework for addressing transit.

Clearly integration motives run much deeper and broader in customs unions than in RTAs. In customs unions such motives generally go beyond merely economic reasons and span the foreign policy dimensions described above. Countries in customs unions are ready to share more in common than countries in FTAs are, and customs unions are often a first step toward deeper integration. The defining characteristic of customs unions is to create large commonalities for border policy through a common external tariff.

Managing a customs union's external border and common external tariff

This section and the following one more closely examine customs unions and their implications for border management.[9] Customs unions are a very advanced and sophisticated form of regional integration in border management. Features that are unique to customs unions, but also characteristic of FTAs, will be signaled as such.

Factors in the choice of any particular regional integration options will include:
- The overall aims of the FTA or union.
- The scope and depth in which member states are willing to share national sovereignty.
- The perceived benefits and costs of FTA or union membership.

- The need to maintain national control for economic, fiscal, or security reasons.
- The institutional trust between member states.

In most customs unions (and by implication in FTAs), all internal borders remain for the purposes of moving goods between members. Here most FTAs and customs unions have focused facilitation efforts largely on goods, services, and transport, and much less on people. Exceptions include the European Union, which in 1990 adopted the Schengen Convention and in 2005 established the European Agency for the Management of Operational Cooperation at the External Borders of the Member States of the European Union (FRONTEX), and—to a lesser extent—the Economic Community of West African States.[10]

Cross border flows—of goods, services, transport, and people—are still very much managed using a silo approach. Not all management is informed by broader policy issues such as migration or security. Sectoral strategies, or strategies specific to border agencies, are used without a single overarching strategy.

The exception (again) is the European Union. Following the September 11, 2001 attacks on the United States, various reviews examined ways to improve the management of the external border. A 2003 communication from the European Commission referred to the "complementary and intertwined nature" of roles played by customs and border agencies (2003, p. 37). In 2004 the commission also submitted a communication on proposals to improve police and customs cooperation (European Commission 2004).

Defining the border in a customs union

What does *border* mean in a customs union? Customs union policymakers must help to determine the answer. The WTO defines a customs union as—among other things—"The substitution of a single customs territory for two or more customs territories." For border management and trade facilitation this means more than the replacement of two or more sets of tariffs with a common external tariff. Decisionmakers face various architectural options:

- Where will goods be cleared—at the first point of entry into the union, or in the country of final destination?

- Does the revenue from customs duties deriving from the application of the common external tariff belong to the union or to members?
- If the revenue accrues to the members, does each country retain what it collects or will the revenue be shared according to a formula?
- How will value added tax and sales tax on goods traded between member states be dealt with?
- Will common prohibitions and restrictions be agreed, or will each country enforce its own?
- Will provision be made for the mutual recognition of standards and controls?
- Should provision be made only for trade in goods across borders, or also for trade in services and movements of people?

Answers will prompt additional design considerations. For example, if it is decided that clearance should take place in the country of final destination or that revenue be shared according to trade within the union, provision should be made for controls to track movements of goods among union members. Additional provisions will need to be agreed, increasing complexity and the cost of doing business. Still, these disadvantages could be outweighed by other considerations.

The common external tariff

To define the CET, countries must first categorize goods into a common tariff nomenclature and then agree on a tariff that will apply to all countries in the customs union for each nomenclature band. In agreeing on the CET countries must find consensus on why a tariff should be applied at all. This is a challenging task since tariffs, particularly in developing countries, are designed to further important national policy objectives. Most commonly the primary objective is to raise government revenue. Depending on the structure of consumption in each country, different products will generate different revenue streams—so members of a customs union will not necessarily have similar interests in maintaining a given tariff for a given sector. A secondary objective of tariff policies is to protect domestic industries (including on a temporary basis, as with safeguard measures) or to provide space for infant industries. Here too, the sectoral objectives of union members will vary. For instance, Mercado Común del Sur does not maintain a CET for all sectors but excepts sensitive industries, such as sugar and automobiles. Despite such complications, negotiating a CET is an opportunity to simplify the tariff structure and even to proceed to some external liberalization (DNA 2007).

Putting CET procedures into practice also requires some harmonization among members. In the customs unions surveyed, one issue with the CET was the gap between commitment and implementation—a gap consisting specifically of exceptions and derogations to the CET. In this sense most customs union CETs can be described as imperfect. Administratively, common customs procedures and close interagency cooperation are required to maintain the integrity of a CET, including a common basis for the valuation of goods. In the Southern Africa Customs Union, for example, all member states apply the WTO valuation rules—but both free on board (FOB) values and cost, insurance and freight (CIF) values are used, so the effect of the tariff is not uniform.

Revenue administration

Revenue administration is the second key feature of customs unions. The CET is not an end but a means to an end. Changing tariff policy is the first objective, simplifying intraregional trade by abolishing internal restrictions the second. And the choice of a revenue collection and retention regime for CET revenues—as well as for other duties and taxes imposed on cross border movements of goods—has important implications for the simplification of intraregional trade.

The final destination principle. The most common customs union practice is for member states to apply the final destination principle, whereby revenues are collected and retained by the country of final consumption. In the East African Community, the final destination option is applied, though it will be reviewed in 2011. In the interim arrangement of the Gulf Cooperation Council,[11] revenues are collected at the external border of the customs union and then transferred to the member where the cleared goods will be finally consumed—but efforts are underway to review this arrangement.

The final destination principle is fair—customs duties are accrued by the customs union member in which the goods will be consumed—but it is

administratively complex, and it also raises issues about the meaning of customs unions. Applying the principle requires a control mechanism (a transit regime, bonding processes, even rules of origin)—firstly to enable members to account for and collect duties on goods imported into their territories, and secondly to prevent diversion, that is, the entry and exit of goods moved through the territory of one member into that of another under suspension of duties.

The origin principle. Exceptions to the final destination principle are the European Union and Southern Africa Customs Union, where the origin principle is applied. A great advantage of the origin regime is that it removes any need to control the movement of goods within the union for revenue collection, offering both a simpler administrative solution and more freedom for the movement of goods within the union.

A formula for revenue redistribution must be agreed, and may also incorporate a common pool of resources to be disbursed on regional projects. In the European Union, customs duties collected[12] are for the union's budget and fund its common policies, member states keeping only a percentage to cover the administrative cost of collection. In the Southern Africa Customs Union (SACU) customs duties are paid into a revenue pool and shared through a formula.[13] Studies have been undertaken in Mercosur on a customs revenue distribution mechanism, but this mechanism has not been finalized.

The origin regime presupposes great trust among member administrations in the capability and integrity of their partners—since revenues are collected on behalf of the union and then redistributed among its members. When customs unions include landlocked countries, coastal countries necessarily will collect revenues on behalf of their neighbors.

Fiscal borders and internal controls

Fiscal borders and internal controls serve four aims:

- They are monitoring devices in the administration of all indirect taxes levied on the destination principle—that is, by zero rating exports for value added tax (VAT).
- Fiscal or national borders provide a backstop against roundtripping for indirect taxes, and a

trigger point for VAT refunds for honest exporters and importers.

- For excise duties, fiscal frontiers are the detection point for smuggling—they enable authorities to monitor both duty paid and tax free items crossing the border.

- National borders also serve nonfiscal purposes, such as immigration control, health standards, maintenance, security, and drug enforcement.

The aim of FTAs and customs unions is to abolish tariffs and other trade barriers on goods traded among members (the "internal" requirement of the WTO). But elimination of duties on goods moving among members' territories is problematic for developing countries that rely on such duties for state income. Therefore, some customs unions have not yet entirely liberalized their regional markets. In the East African Community an asymmetrical approach is followed, to attain the elimination of duties within the union while allowing space for adjustment: Kenya does not impose duties on goods from other members, but until 2010 they can impose duties on goods imported from Kenya. In the Southern Africa Customs Union a special clause allows member states to impose duties on goods produced in other member states for the protection of infant industries. However, apparently only two members impose these duties, each on one product.

The transactional imposition of VAT or sales tax on goods traded between customs union members is one of the key reasons preventing the removal of internal controls. Pressure to reduce tax compliance burdens for business makes it an attractive option to scrap or reduce fiscal frontiers in customs unions. Goods would be cleared, and international trade taxes (customs duties and VAT or sales tax) paid, at the point of first entry into the customs union. But such an approach is problematic, since in most customs unions different countries impose VAT and sales tax at different rates.[14] Trade liberalization has reduced the importance of customs duties as a source of income for most developed, and some developing, countries—yet VAT and sales tax on imported goods remains an important source of government income, and its importance has grown with the growth in international trade and the increase in VAT and sales tax collections on imported goods. Furthermore, VAT and sales tax are of interest not only for imports but also for exports. Most countries refund or zero rate VAT and sales tax on exported goods. Illegal activities, such as so-called ghost exports and roundtripping, compel countries to control the exportation of goods from their territories to prevent fiscal fraud.[15]

In most customs unions measures related to indirect taxes affecting the importation, transit movement, and exportation of goods are dealt with nationally—not regulated regionally. The exception, again, is the European Union, where controls between member states were abolished with the introduction of the single market in 1993. A new VAT control system, including a VAT Information Exchange System, catered to trade between member states. Challenges arose, and the European Union is still grappling with VAT leakage through schemes such as the so-called carousel fraud (box 14.2).

Internal controls, however, are required not only for fiscal purposes but also to enforce national prohibitions and restrictions. Such prohibitions and restrictions can give effect to international commitments, such as the Convention on Trade in Endangered Species. They can protect society, for example by requiring a permit to import firearms. And they can protect industry, for example, by banning the importation of all or certain types of secondhand goods. In the Gulf Cooperation Council, Saudi Arabia enforces controls aimed at preventing the importation of pork products and alcohol for religious reasons. Ideally, customs unions would try to standardize prohibitions and restrictions. Such standardization is, of course, necessary when a union decides to abolish internal controls or to clear goods at the first point of entry into the union.

Putting the common external tariff into practice: duty relief and suspensions schemes

One important practical consideration for a CET is to reduce the risk of trade deflection—importers choosing entry points into the union that are likely to grant them more favorable treatment. The deflection risk can be reduced through internal border controls, which tend to remain in place where revenues are collected on the final destination principle. But for unions using the origin principle internal controls are much weaker, so the burden is on the border at the point of entry. Accordingly, it is

In removing customs control at its border the European Union had to devise a new solution for collecting value added tax (VAT). Since rates vary by member state, the European Union system has to be able to tax goods depending on where the value added is generated. Until 1993 the destination principle was applied: the VAT paid on all inputs was rebated to exporters and applied on the full value of the good for importers, effectively detaxing goods when they left one country and retaxing them when they entered another.

Under the transitional system agreed in the borderless European Union, pending a definitive system, the destination principle was retained. It still applies today—with the major difference that no customs officers are charged with verifying that goods are actually exported. Instead, exporting firms must supply the VAT number of their customers in the destination country, allowing authorities to verify that the exports indeed qualify for an export rebate—and ensuring that importers cannot claim a VAT credit for imported purchases.

In theory the VAT number allows tracing the movement of goods and thus administering VAT. But in practice the incentives for fraud are considerably increased under the transitional system. The reason is that a good's importer is responsible for collecting the VAT on its full value when reselling it (not just for the seller's share of value added, as would be the case if the good had been sourced domestically)—making fraud much more profitable. The simplest such fraud occurs when the importing company goes bankrupt—"missing"—before the VAT is collected. More sophisticated, and harder to detect, is the carousel fraud: goods are resold to buffer companies, sometimes several times, before being re-exported to the country of origin (when the exporter additionally receives a fraudulent VAT rebate).

Three options have been considered for a definitive system to reduce VAT fraud—said to cost as much as 2–4 percent of total VAT receipts, or about half the union's budget. The options are: a harmonized VAT plus national sales tax system (called VIVAT), a reverse charge system, and collection on the origin principle.

Source: Adapted from Baldwin (2007).

also necessary to reduce the incentives for traders to circumvent duties. To do so member countries must closely harmonize tariff collection policies and procedures.

In particular, duty exemption and suspension policies must be closely harmonized. Exemption policies—partial or full—apply to certain categories of goods. Such policies need to be managed carefully, as they can be a source of fiscal leakage. Generally the categories of product exempt from duties are similar—goods destined for display and exhibition, goods for diplomatic use, and so on—yet there are differences across countries. For instance, some countries exempt goods consumed by the government. It is important to harmonize the categories of exempt goods.

Duty suspension policies also can be a source of fiscal leakage. Such policies are an important aspect of export promotion—their objective being to avoid indirectly taxing imports by taxing imported inputs, or to avoid taxing goods that will not be consumed in the country (transit trade, exhibition goods). Administrative methods depend on the circumstances requiring duty suspension: temporary admission for re-exportation, temporary admission for inward processing, manufacture under bond, customs warehousing, export processing zones, and transit. The East African Community has plans to harmonize duty suspensions, but until recently had not done so, and national policies continued to prevail (DNA 2007).

How regional trade agreements and customs unions are ushering in a new operating model for border management

In customs unions, and even more in RTAs, reform efforts have mostly been focused on trade facilitation—not border management. One reason is that the main objectives of such arrangements are trade related. Another is that since "public opinion would easily accept the transfer of sovereignty rights in the economic field, but not so in judicial and law enforcement matters," therefore "no strong lobbying group . . . would have pushed for the abolition of law enforcement borders as business and trade had done since the 1950s regarding the free movement of goods and services" (Hobbing 2005). Regional

14

Regional integration and customs unions

initiatives have ventured beyond trade facilitation, for example by liberalizing movements of persons—as in the European Union, but also in the Common Market for Eastern and Southern Africa and the Economic Community of West African States, which give nationals from the region the rights to enter member countries without visas and to access local labor markets.

Most customs unions have undertaken some trade facilitation—modernizing and simplifying procedures, expediting the movement of goods—yet there is a striking gap between good proposals and commitments, on the one hand, and implementation on the other. The challenge is to balance continuous improvements while working toward regional and national implementation. Developments in trade facilitation also appear to be driven by particular issues, not anchored in a holistic vision and strategy with political and technical support.

The trade facilitation provisions of customs unions and RTAs—usually underpinned by institutional mechanisms, such as working groups and committees[16]—focus mostly on customs issues. In particular, they include commitments to:

- Apply GATT article VII as the basis for the valuation of goods.
- Accede to and implement the WCO's Revised Kyoto Convention (WCO 1999).
- Apply modern procedures and techniques, such as risk management and automation.
- Make the amendment, application, and interpretation of customs laws and procedures more transparent.

Strategic issues

The common border management policy for a customs union should have trade facilitation at its center. Many elements of such a common policy are, in theory, applicable to RTAs as well—but the common border management policy may prove more challenging without the strong incentives created by a common tariff policy.

As the strategic starting point for a common policy, a shared policy blueprint and operating model should outline the future approach for applying regulatory controls. The blueprint and model should be both forward looking and aspirational, but at the same time should address real challenges, bottlenecks,

and other concerns. Finally, it must canvassed, politically supported, resourced, and understood.

Beyond the WTO customs union minimum requirements—and the best practice of first movers such as the European Union—customs unions have ample latitude in setting a strategic direction and charting new approaches to border management. The close integration implied by a customs union can call forth a vision and working methods that go beyond national borders and horizons and beyond traditional customs union cooperation.

The blueprint and operating model should be anchored in a comprehensive strategy that links goals with specific actions. It should identify timeframes, responsible parties, and interdependencies. And it should have a monitoring mechanism that will alert decisionmaking bodies in case of delay or technical deadlock, allowing the bodies to propose remedies.

In customs unions, as in countries, movements of people and goods across borders should be subject to modern controls following international standards and best practice. Elements in a new border management operating model for customs unions could include:

- Managing risk.
- Simplifying and harmonizing policies and procedures.
- Eliminating duplication;
- An integrated business solution.
- Traveler, trader, and third party management.
- Enhanced mutual administrative assistance.
- Mutual recognition.
- An enabling legal framework.
- Strengthening policymaking and delivery institutions.

The selective review below focuses on elements for which RTAs (FTAs and customs unions) offer new border management solutions. Other elements also matter, but do not necessarily differ much from modern border management policies that could be put into practice outside a trade agreement.

Risk management: toward a common customs union strategy

Risk management in customs and border operation responds to various needs, including the need to facilitate legitimate trade and travel while coping with an increasing workload. It recognizes that resources should be targeted on high risk people, goods, and activities. In a customs union it is difficult to move toward a common understanding of border management if member states take divergent approaches to risk identification and management.

Risk management is therefore central to the aims of uniformity across a customs union and coordination among border agencies. It should inform the union's border management blueprint and operating model. Risk management can help customs unions that are resource strapped—and it can sharpen strategic objectives and identify impediments, ensuring proper priorities and allocation.

A common risk management strategy allows all border agencies initially to share information on goals, strategies, priorities, and methods used against noncompliance. In the European Union a proposal was made to establish a common external border practitioners unit to oversee and plan operations for the common risk strategy (European Commission 2003, p. 46). The Andean Community has also started work on regional risk criteria, units of risk, and information exchange formats.

Some supporting tools for a customs union common risk management strategy are discussed below. One is the common application of authorized economic operator and trusted traveler schemes. Another is the exchange of information through interconnected systems.

Simplifying and harmonizing policies and procedures

Border related procedures in RTAs often are outdated and based on paper documents. Existing procedures should be reviewed against international conventions (such as the WCO's Revised Kyoto Convention) and international best practice, to ensure that procedures are radically simplified and that they incorporate modern techniques including risk analysis and the extensive use of ICT. Generally RTAs offer a good anchoring point for initiating such reform, providing useful forums for experts to exchange views, access best practices, and devise solutions to common problems.

Transaction costs for traders crossing borders can be reduced by harmonizing procedures and documentation requirements. Customs unions have strong incentives to harmonize, not only customs policies and procedures (such as revenue collection on the origin principle), but also policies promoting transparency and information exchange, which build trust.

In most African regional formations and customs unions that include several landlocked countries, transit policies and procedures at present are not successful.

The international standards developed by the WCO for goods can be adjusted for managing movements of people across FTAs and customs union borders. Procedures already followed in customs unions, such as the European Union, should be examined and emulated where feasible.

Adopting a single common customs declaration for the importation, exportation, and transit movement of goods facilitates their processing. It also enables regionally standardized clearance and common transit procedures (box 14.3), and it facilitates the transition to a national or regional single window (chapter 8). Similar standardized documents can be developed for controlling movements of people. In Mercosur the Technical Committee on Customs Affairs was tasked to develop the Mercosur Single Customs Document and the 1999 Asunción Program. In the South Africa Customs Union the member states adopted and implemented the Single Administrative Document, covering all customs transactions, in 2006. The members of the Andean Community have developed a common customs document and apply common rules on customs inspections through the Integrated Manual of Procedures for Regional Inspection.

Eliminating duplication: rationalizing controls through one stop approaches

Harmonizing rules and procedures is one aspect of eliminating duplication costs. Joint border operation is another. In FTAs, and where decisionmakers decide to maintain all or most internal customs union controls, joint border controls—or one stop border posts—can reduce delays, duplication, and red tape (chapter 4) while also improving controls and reducing the risks of smuggling and of false declarations.

Regional integration and customs unions

The New Computerised Transit System (NCTS) is a paperless electronic system extending to 23 countries—19 European Union countries, the European Free Trade Association countries, and Liechtenstein—and linking over 3,000 customs offices. It covers transit procedures based on the European Union Single Administrative Document, mainly for road transport. Since 1 July 2005, transit declarations must, as a general rule, be lodged electronically. A subsequent phase, completed in January 2006, included computerized handling of guarantees and enquiries. European Commission statistics show a rise in the number of NCTS transit movements, from around 5.5 million in 2004 to more than 7.5 million in 2005.

To realize the electronic network, the European Commission took the lead by developing a standard NCTS software application—the minimum common core (MCC)—and ensuring its maintenance. Adopted by 15 out of 25 members states (the others have developed their own application), the MCC was funded by the Customs 2000 program budget (23 percent of the total budget). This harmonization of the basic software architecture has been challenging, encountering compatibility problems with most national customs ICT systems.

A second part of the NCTS reform is the codification of transit procedures in a manual, published in 2001, and offering guidelines for aligning the implementation of transit policies. However, the European Court of Auditors finds widespread divergence in implementation. Similarly, simplified measures for transit (authorized consignor and consignee status, comprehensive guarantee) were not demonstrably in place in a majority of member states.

The European Court of Auditors found that the European Commission had successfully assumed its coordination role for the implementation of the NCTS—but it outlined shortcomings in the lack of operational agreement between the European Union and member states, and in the fact that monitoring of implementation was yet to be done and had been left to the member states. Numerous discrepancies were found in the application of legal provisions at the country level, and implementation has been defective in several areas:

- The status of authorized consignors was not properly checked in several countries.
- Enquiries in case of nonarrival were conducted with delays and subject to imperfect communication between customs agencies.
- Recovery proceedings were slow (in case of nonarrival, debt can be recovered from the country which had to collect the duties).
- The accounting of noncollected duties was also slow and inconsistent because of divergent interpretations.

Another general issue noted by the European Court of Auditors was unsatisfactory data collection. Finally, automated risk analysis using information generated by the NCTS was only applied in a few member states surveyed—and in most member states checks on transiting goods were nearly nonexistent, because they were not considered a priority.

Source: Adapted from the European Court of Auditors (2007).

One stop posts have proved challenging, for several reasons. First, joint controls are incorrectly perceived to reduce the efficacy of enforcement. Second, concern arises around sovereignty and jurisdictional issues when two countries' border officers work together in the territory of one. Third, there is likely no common vision for joint operation at the various agencies that conduct border controls.

One stop posts bring various border functions—immigration, customs, and other border controls—closer together. For example, customs officers from two bordering states conduct import and export procedures in adjacent offices or rooms. The country on whose territory this occurs must give foreign customs officers jurisdiction on its territory—a requirement that can raise sensitive issues of national sovereignty. However, international experience has demonstrated that these issues are easily solved through bilateral negotiation and national enactment.[17] Issues requiring attention in the establishment of one stop border posts include:

- The legal framework.
- Mapping current controls, procedures, and documentation.
- Agreeing on the one stop controls, procedures, and documentation.
- A traffic flow system.
- Facilities and infrastructure ICT issues.
- Human resources.
- Monitoring.

The Mercosur countries, in the Recife Agreement, reached consensus on 16 border points where integrated controls should be applied. The South Africa Customs Union identified the establishment of one stop border posts as a high priority trade facilitation issue, but little progress has since been made. The East African Community has made progress in establishing a one stop border post between Kenya and Uganda at Malaba. The Andean Community aims to have single controls in place at all common border posts, according to the Community Policy for Border Integration and Development, and a pilot is in place for the single control of goods at the Pedro de Alvarado and La Hachadura border posts between Guatemala and El Salvador.

An interesting arrangement of the mutual recognition type is in place between Norway and Sweden: one country handles border procedures and enforcement on the other's behalf. In other words, at one border post Norway will undertake its own controls and controls on behalf of Sweden, while at another border post Sweden does the same.[18] Preconditions for such cooperation include a high level of trust.

New trade facilitation and international security measures demand that travelers and cargo spend time at ports of entry. This demand can be met by using nonintrusive baggage and cargo examination equipment, such as scanners. Joint controls and one stop border posts allow the joint acquisition, or joint use, of such equipment. Adequate infrastructure—including, for example, inspection and detention facilities—is also needed (chapter 4).

Integrated business solution: automation and managing interconnections

Simplified procedures, and common or harmonized procedures, pave the way for developing integrated business solutions and interconnectivity. Technological advances can enable greater integration of the ICT solutions used by administrations to link databases, enabling the real time sharing of information and the application of more sophisticated risk management and intelligence. This reduces paperwork and congestion at ports of entry, expedites the admission of people and goods, fast tracks clearance, and reduces opportunities for corruption in filing goods and cargo declarations and in presenting travel documents. Related to interconnectivity is the introduction of a common single administrative document (examples given above).

The ideal for customs unions is to have a common ICT system. Where this is not a goal, then systems should at least be interconnected to exchange data seamlessly and electronically. When used with other arrangements, such as an authorized economic operator system or trusted traveler scheme, interconnection can avoid duplication in the submission of information and so make the arrangements most effective. In the Andean Community a pilot for the electronic transmission of customs declarations has received support from draft regulations.

Mutual administrative assistance: sharing information and intelligence

The real time exchange of data between national agencies, and the existence of interconnected systems, have other benefits. As long as internal controls are in place, the exchange of information helps national agencies ensure compliance. In developing countries it is especially beneficial to have mutual administrative assistance provisions, which combat underinvoicing by enabling export and import administrations to share declared values. Interconnected systems enable agencies not only to share transactional data, but also to cooperate in establishing a common valuation database for the customs union.

A Mercosur mutual administrative assistance agreement in 1997 aimed at preventing and suppressing customs offenses, provides for (among other things) the exchange of data. In 2000 the Mercosur Committee of Customs Directors approved an action plan to counter customs infringements, with a list of practical measures to fight smuggling (Lopes de Lima n.d., p. 10). An annex to the Southern Africa Customs Union Agreement has been developed that provides for customs mutual administrative assistance. The Andean community also has a mutual administrative assistance framework in place.

Mutual assistance does not require an RTA. Standalone international customs cooperation and mutual administrative assistance agreements have been signed. For instance, South Africa has agreements with 16 countries and is currently negotiating with 10 others, including several African neighbors.[19]

The United States has bilateral agreements with 62 countries.[20] The European Union has such individual agreements with 7 countries, and it has included provisions for mutual assistance in its RTAs.

Useful benchmarks for preparing new texts—or updating existing ones—include the WCO model agreement on mutual administrative assistance, the WCO Johannesburg Convention, and recent customs union mutual administrative assistance texts. A new trend is to include agreements of mutual assistance in the text of RTAs—likely offering a better framework to guarantee effective cooperation, and also ensuring coherence in various aspects of bilateral cooperation on customs issues.

Mutual recognition

Another mechanism to eliminate duplication is mutual recognition. In a customs union context this can include mutual recognition of valuation, classification, and origin rulings; of the registration and licensing of client types (traders, brokers, bonded warehouses, and so forth); of regulatory permissions, such as certificates; and of travelers, through the cross border operation of trusted traveler schemes. Mutual recognition requires high degrees of trust and standardization, with seamless communication and information exchange channels.

Mutual recognition schemes do not require an RTA. For instance, the European Union and the United States are negotiating mutual recognition of authorized economic operators—and the United States already has such agreements with Canada, New Zealand, and Jordan. Japan and New Zealand also signed such an agreement in 2008. However, RTAs offer a good conduit for the negotiation of mutual recognition. In particular, customs unions make mutual recognition agreements easier by pushing countries to harmonize.

Creating an enabling legal framework

Agreed customs union designs, principles, policies, and procedures must be anchored in a legal instrument. One goal of a customs union is to ensure the uniform and consistent application of union rules. A common enabling framework promotes this goal's attainment.

Customs codes must provide a good framework for modern and efficient operations—and they must be aligned. The customs code establishes the competence of the customs authorities, provides overall coherence in customs procedures, helps make procedures more predictable and transparent, encourages cooperation with the private sector, and provides a framework for appeal procedures (de Wulf 2005).

One option for customs unions is to develop a common customs code, as the European Union did in 1992, the West African Economic and Monetary Union did in 2003, and the Gulf Cooperation Council did in 2003. The process of adopting a common legal infrastructure can serve as vehicle for harmonization, simplification, and modernization in accordance with international WCO principles.

Yet this process can be challenging. Mercosur adopted a customs code to deal with both substantive and procedural issues in 1994, but the code has not yet entered into force, for reasons allegedly including "overstretch" (Vervaele 2005, p. 13). In 1997 the Mercosur Customs Affairs Technical Committee was instructed to conclude an additional protocol to the customs code to address, among other issues, free zones and the CET. Other examples of regional initiatives include the Andean Community's Community Customs Rules, adopted in 2003, and the South Africa Customs Union Agreement's provision that the legislation of member states on customs duties shall be similar (further provision is made for the adoption of annexes to regulate customs matters).

The design and status of a legal framework, and its relation to national laws, will be informed by the union's legal regime and practice as well as by the constitutional practices of member states. The framework can take the form of a customs code—either self executing or requiring national action—and can be included in annexes or protocols to agreements. In a customs union the principles of transparency and access to information require that the legal framework should be published, easily accessed, and regularly updated.

Strengthening institutions: capacity building, coordination, and enforcement

Coordinated border management demands capable regional and national agencies, while such capable agencies also promote institutional trust: agencies are willing to cooperate on cross border solutions

Regional integration and customs unions

14

if they have similar capacities. Capacity and trust are also integral to customs union viability and to removing internal trade barriers, as both put pressure on members to achieve similar and acceptable border regulation and enforcement.

Most RTAs and customs unions have established institutions, such as committees, to coordinate their sectoral activities. In most cases coordinating mechanisms are in place for trade in goods, but not for border issues. For the goal of coordinated border management, consideration needs to be given to establishing a mechanism representing all the border agencies active in the region—in addition to sector specific mechanisms.

Beyond creating regional and national governance structures, regional and national agencies also need capacity building. Some can come from regional and international partners such as the WCO, which is setting the tone for customs capacity building with its Columbus program.[21] Its approach could be applied to other border agencies. For example, the WCO's Time Release Study approach (chapter 11) could be used by customs unions to measure flows across their external and internal borders and identify improvements.

Regional trade partners can also be important allies for capacity building. In some instances—arguably in developed country–developing country RTAs, but also in RTAs involving middle and low income countries—regional partners will have more advanced border management policies and greater expertise. The South Africa Revenue Service, for instance, provides technical assistance to regional partners.[22]

Even where capacity is more evenly distributed across a region, cooperation requires coordination and global capacity. For instance, since a minority of noncompliant traders will use every possible opportunity to bypass controls, agencies must combine static controls with mobile operations against criminals. Joint operations, while significantly limiting the options of those criminals, can familiarize agencies within and between countries with each other's working methods and feed into a common risk management approach. Similarly, common training standards and joint training programs—sectorally as well as for bordering countries—can build much institutional trust. This training should be not only for operational staff but also for border managers

and for agency leadership. Integrity training should be considered, since controls are only as good as the people enforcing them.

Customs unions can set up regional funds to fund regional capacity and coordination and national capacity building projects. In theory regional funds could be financed directly from CET revenues, but—in all existing cases except the European Union—revenues remain treated as accruing to national members.

Finally, new institutional configurations for customs unions should be considered.[23] These include:

- A regional customs executive agency to manage and execute all customs activities for the union.
- A regional customs executive agency to develop operational policy and standards (with implementation by member states).
- An integrated external customs and border management agency to bring together all border agencies.

These options can improve coordination and add efficiencies. They can also concentrate resources in a union with a capacity deficit.

Conclusion: enabling delivery to work toward results

Regional economic integration outcomes for customs unions offer much potential but frequently have not met expectations. Some of the reasons are:

- *Political unwillingness.* Governments may hesitate to part with certain sovereign decision-making powers. Customs unions require much collective trade and tariff policy development, including the joint negotiation of trade agreements with third parties. Tensions between regional and national interests force national governments and their stakeholders to weigh the perceived loss of sovereignty against the benefits of regional cooperation. This is especially true for developing countries whose independence is relatively recent.
- *Fiscal concerns.* Putting a customs union agreement into practice entails reducing or eliminating of duties and necessitates fiscal adjustment. Sometimes this is very difficult for developing countries that rely on customs duties for fiscal purposes.[24]

- *Gaps in capacity and skills.* Such gaps delay implementation and frustrate progress. Developing countries, and especially their national administrations, often lack the capacity and skills to participate in or actively work toward regional integration arrangements.
- *Lack of alignment.* Putting a customs union agreement into effect requires the whole of government. Usually it is driven by or involves the ministries or departments of foreign relations, international trade, finance, and agriculture, as well as customs administrations. Interagency cooperation within and between countries must be secured through the design and implementation of agreements and initiatives.

Good practice dictates that the policy objectives should be underpinned by clear actions and timeframes and a clear allocation of responsibilities and resources, with political and administrative buy-in to the strategic framework and with institutional focus and support. All this is more difficult for unions and national administrations faced with skills shortages. Nevertheless, the aims are to allocate responsibility and ensure accountability, both of which require action by both national administrations and customs union secretariats. Among possible accountability measures, one is the requirement of regular reporting to political heads or senior officials on progress made and challenges faced.

Further principles for regional integration and customs unions include:

- To make needed implementation actions possible, national administrations and customs union secretariats must work to build institutional capacity and to overcome distrust between national agencies (in the same country and in different countries).
- Political leaders and senior officials are responsible for setting the tone and pace—generating a sense of urgency and creating the necessary enabling frameworks.
- To create incentives for cooperation between officials, customs union activities can be linked to organizational and individual performance contracts (other methods are also possible).
- Implementation also requires that the movement from policy to execution be supported by a structured program management approach.

This means, for one thing, that initiatives should be properly scoped, broken down into delivery chunks, prioritized, sequenced, and attached to milestones. It also requires that the best and brightest should be tasked with delivery.

- Resource allocation can be supported by a common vision and action plans, which should make it easier to quantify the needed resources and motivate their provision. Customs unions with resource constraints should make the most of scarce resources by giving critical activities the highest priority and by reaching out to international cooperating partners. For example, both the East African Community and the Southern Africa Customs Union have started engaging the WCO Capacity Building Directorate to help develop a common trade facilitation vision, to ensure the vision is aligned with WCO and other international instruments and best practices, to develop action plans, and to reach out for financial and technical support donors.

Generally, RTAs—and customs unions as a specific advanced case—provide an ideal basis for transnational coordinated border management. The member states of customs unions share a common goal of promoting economic integration through applying a common external tariff, removing duties on goods traded between their territories, and harmonizing their policies in related areas. As a corollary, they are also committed to removing nontariff barriers and simplifying movements of people and goods through the union. Most customs unions so far have not focused systematically on coordinated border management; most reform efforts have focused on measures to facilitate trade, usually from a customs perspective. Furthermore, most customs unions still have some internal controls—for fiscal reasons, for security, or for other reasons.

The increasing complexity of managing ever larger movements of people and goods across borders, combined with the number of regulatory role players involved, is compelling customs union policymakers to adopt a coordinated border management approach and to consider unionwide approaches to risk management, mutual recognition, joint or one stop controls, trusted traveler and trader schemes, and real time information exchange within and between countries. A comprehensive approach involving strategy, policy, process, people, and technology is required—while high level commitment and implementation also remain critical.

Notes

1. The WTO Web site contains a chart and graph of new and cumulative RTAs, by year, from 1949–2009. See "Regional trade agreements: facts and figures," WTO, http://www.wto.org/english/tratop_e/region_e/regfac_e.htm.
2. As do partial scope agreements.
3. Quoted from "Multilateral and Bilateral Trade Agreements: Friends or Foes?", Annual Memorial Silver Lecture (31 October 2006), Columbia University, New York, in, "Lamy warns bilateral agreements are not 'the easy way out' from the suspended talks," WTO, http://www.wto.org/english/news_e/sppl_e/sppl46_e.htm.
4. Most of the agreements (13) were notified in terms of article XXIV. Fewer (6) were notified in terms of the Enabling Clause.
5. For a review of rationales behind the formation of RTAs, see for example Schiff and Winters (2003).
6. See also Maur (2008).
7. Fiorentino, Verdeja, and Toqueboeuf (2007), paragraph 24.
8. An optimal tariff is a way for large countries to create positive terms of trade effects—that is, to force suppliers to lower their prices—in the large countries' favor. Because large countries represent an important share of the world market, they can influence world prices.
9. This section limits most examples to current customs unions—unions of which the GATT or WTO has been notified—thus excluding other regional groupings that aspire to a customs union, such as the Common Market for Eastern and Southern Africa (COMESA), the Economic Community Of West African States (ECOWAS), and the South African Development Community (SADC).
10. The Schengen area excludes five EU members and includes three non-EU countries.

11. The Gulf Cooperation Council consists of Bahrain, Kuwait, Oman, Qatar, Saudi Arabia, and the United Arab Emirates.
12. Tariff revenues in the EU constitute only a very small share of revenues collected at the border.
13. Interestingly, the SACU pool consists of customs duties but also excise duties. Customs duties are shared on the basis of the level of intra-SACU trade—and this requires reliable trade statistics, especially on goods moved between member states. The SACU formula also provides for a development component into which a percentage of excise duties is paid and shared on the basis of developmental indicators.
14. In practice VAT is a consumption tax, since firms are reimbursed for the inputs they buy even when the inputs are for their own consumption.
15. Ghost exports are transactions where customs clearance documents are presented for the exportation of goods without the actual goods being exported. Roundtripping takes place where goods are exported but then smuggled back into the export country.
16. For example, the SADC Protocol on Trade establishes the Sub-Committee on Customs Cooperation, and the North American Free Trade Agreement (NAFTA) establishes the Trilateral Heads of Customs Conference.
17. This has been done successfully in countries such as Austria, the Czech Republic, Estonia, France, Latvia, Germany, Hungary, Poland, Switzerland, and the United States.
18. A motivation for Norway, Sweden, and Finland to sign cross border cooperation agreements (starting in 1960) was "division of labor"—that is, sharing the cost of manning the 1,630 kilometer border between Norway and Sweden and the 739 kilometer border between Norway and Finland (see Maur 2008).
19. A list can be downloaded at "Customs Agreements on Mutual Administrative Assistance," South African Revenue Service, http://www.sars.gov.za/home.asp?pid=946.
20. See "Customs Mutual Assistance Agreements (CMAA) by Country," United States Department of Homeland Security,

http://www.cbp.gov/xp/cgov/border_security/international_operations/international_agreements/cmaa.xml.

21. The WCO Columbus program provides for—among other things—undertaking diagnostic missions to pinpoint pressure points and challenges, developing project plans, and delivering tailor made solutions.

22. The South African Revenue Service reports assistance to other African administrations in four forms of capacity building: "providing policy, legal and operational assistance," "hosting study visits to share best practices with other administrations," "providing training interventions either at the SARS Academy or in other countries," and "seconding SARS officials to other administrations and hosting officials seconded by other administrations" (Maur 2008).

23. See pp. 18–19 in "Customs 2020: A Business and Technology Point of View," Accenture, http://www.accenture.com/NR/rdonlyres/DF096E3D-A1B9-44D6-91C3-340935DD4B74/0/Accenture_Customs_2020_English_032009.pdf.

24. For example, trade taxes account for approximately 25 percent of state revenues in Sub-Saharan Africa (Baunsgaard and Keen 2005, p. 3).

References

Balassa, B. 1961. *The Theory of Economic Integration.* Homewood, Illinois: R.D. Irwin.

Baldwin, R. 2007. "EU VAT Fraud." *Vox: Research-based Policy Analysis and Commentary from Leading Economists,* June 14–22. Available at http://www.voxeu.com.

Baunsgaard, T., and M. Keen. 2005. "Tax Revenue and (or?) Trade Liberalization." Working Paper WP/05/112, International Monetary Fund, Washington, DC.

Devuyst, Y., and A. Serdarevic. 2007. *The World Trade Organization and Regional Trade Agreements: Bridging the Constitutional Credibility Gap. Duke Journal of Comparative & International Law* 18(1): 1–75.

De Wulf, L. 2005. "Regional Integration and Customs Integration." Mimeo., World Bank Institute, The World Bank, Washington, DC.

DNA (Development Network Africa). 2007. "Evaluation of an Appropriate Model for a SADC Customs Union." Report Commissioned by the South African Development Community Secretariat, DNA, Pretoria.

Do, V.D., and Watson, W. 2007. "Economic Analysis of Regional Trade Agreements." In *Regional Trade Agreements and the WTO Legal System,* ed. L.Bartels and F. Ortino. Oxford: Oxford University Press. 7–22.

European Commission (Commission of the European Communities). 2003. "Communication from the Commission to the Council, European Parliament and the European Economic and Social Committee on the Role of Customs in the Integrated Management of External Borders." Document COM (2003) 452 final, Commission of the European Communities, Brussels.

———. 2004. "Communication from the Commission to the European Council and the Council on Enhancing Police and Customs Co-operation in the European Union." Document COM (2004) 376 final, Commission of the European Communities, Brussels.

European Court of Auditors. 2007. "Special Report No 11/2006 on the Community Transit System, with the Commission's Replies." Notice 2007/C 44/01, European Union, Brussels. Available online at http://eur-lex.europa.eu/LexUriServ/LexUriServ.do?uri=OJ:C:2007:044:0001:0019:EN:PDF.

Fiorentino, R.V., L. Verdeja, and C. Toqueboeuf. 2007. "The Changing Landscape of Regional Trade Agreements: 2006 update." Discussion Paper 12, Regional Trade Agreements Section, Trade Policies Review Division, World Trade Organization Secretariat, Geneva.

GATT (General Agreement on Tariffs and Trade). 1986. "The Text of the General Agreement on Tariffs and Trade." Geneva: GATT. Available at http://www.wto.org/english/docs_e/legal_e/gatt47_e.pdf.

Hobbing, P. 2005. "Integrated Border Management at the EU Level." CEPS Working Documents no. 227, Centre for European Policy Studies, Brussels.

Lopes de Lima, J.A.F. n.d. "International Co-operation in Mercosur : Is the 'Third Pillar' More Advanced Than the 'First Pillar'?" Mimeo. Available
at http://www.asser.nl/default.aspx?site_id=
8&level1=10790&level2=10865&level3=&
textid=29424.

Maur, J.-C. 2008. "Regionalism and Trade Facilitation: A Primer." *Journal of World Trade* 42(6):
979–1012.

Schiff, M., and L.A. Winters. 2003. *Regional Integration and Development.* Washington, DC: The
World Bank.

Vervaele, J. 2005. "Mercosur and regional integration
in South America." *International and Comparative Law Quarterly* 54 (2): 387–410.

WCO (World Customs Organization). 1999. *International Convention on the Simplification
and Harmonisation of Customs Procedures (As
Amended).* Brussels: WCO.

14

Regional integration and customs unions

CHAPTER

15

Information and communications technology in support of customs unions: a case study of the European Union

Tom Doyle and Frank Janssens

This chapter provides a case study on the use of information and communications technology (ICT) to support the customs union now in place at the European Union (EU). The customs union is a pillar of the EU, essential to the functioning of its single market. Such a market can function properly only with common application of common rules at its external borders. The customs union has made the EU better able today to combine efforts toward two goals: facilitating trade and protecting the interests of citizens.

The chapter looks both at broad developments in customs ICT at the EU and at a specific case, the creation of the New Computerised Transit System (NCTS). It is hoped that the lessons drawn here—both from the broad developments and from the NCTS case study—will usefully guide other customs unions pursuing economic integration.

The EU customs union

In June 2008 the EU celebrated the 40th anniversary of its customs union, inscribed as a political objective in the 1957 Treaty of Rome. On that occasion the European Parliament adopted a resolution[1] highlighting major achievements of the EU customs union and also offering a prospect for the future.

The mandate of the customs union is to act as a single customs territory applying a single legislation in a uniform way. The goals are to facilitate legitimate trade, to apply a single commercial policy effectively, and to protect society by fighting fraud, terrorism, and organized crime. From the outset the major

principles of the EU customs union have been:

- No customs duties at internal borders between EU member states.
- Common customs duties on imports from outside the EU.
- Common rules of origin for products from outside the EU.
- A common definition of customs value.

Two key achievements of the EU customs union are the creation of a Common Customs Tariff and a Community Customs Code. The tariff applies to goods imported across the EU's external borders. The legal framework for the code was established in 1992.[2] With the completion of the internal market, goods now circulate freely between EU member states.

The division of responsibilities between the European Commission and EU member states is based on a subsidiarity principle.[3] This principle is intended to ensure that decisions are taken as closely as possible to the citizen, and that constant checks are made to determine whether action at the community level is justified (in view of alternative possibilities at the national, regional, and local levels). Specifically, the commission will not take action outside areas that fall within its exclusive competence, except in cases where EU action would be more effective than action taken nationally, regionally, or locally.

The subsidiarity principle is closely bound up with the principles of proportionality and necessity, which require that any action taken by the EU should not go beyond what is necessary to achieve the Treaty of Rome's objectives. In practice the EU's legislation, international agreements, and overall coherence are managed by the European Commission through cooperation among European institutions and EU member states, with operational responsibilities remaining at the national level. The EU's legislation is directly applicable in its member states, and national administrations are required to align their national legislation and implementing provisions accordingly.

The EU's 27 national customs services now work together to act as a common customs service by applying common legislation and working methods. A work program, Customs 2013, has been created to reach this important goal—as well as to reinforce security (within the EU and at its external border) and to strengthen the fight against fraud. Other objectives have been added: for example, to make European business more competitive by reducing transaction costs through automation and simplification.

The use of ICT for customs at the EU: the situation today

Embedded in the provisions of the EU's new customs code[4] is an enhanced mission for EU customs. The use of ICT is essential to this enhanced mission, which includes the integration and interconnection of new and modernized customs procedures throughout the EU.

Mandate and governance

Developments in ICT are closely linked with the evolution of policy, legislation, and procedures in the EU customs union. Initially ICT was a purely national competence—systems were designed for the operational responsibilities of individual member states. Later, to replace paper based trans-European procedures, solutions known as customs trans-European electronic systems were developed. For the EU's economy to continue competing globally, it was essential to be able to exchange electronic information with the trade through various interfaces based on commonly used technology.

The mandate to create and operate trans-European customs systems required a legal basis for the possible—or even obligatory—use of electronic declarations.[5] A major initiative for the EU customs union, Electronic Customs has its direction and content governed by regulation,[6] joint decision,[7] and a common code of practice.[8]

Under the Customs 2013 work program, ICT developments are governed by a detailed work program and priorities for investments made from the EU budget. Such investments must be approved by the EU's member states and monitored through regular meetings of its Customs 2013 Committee. All project documentation is maintained by the European Commission and published on secure Web sites to guarantee its availability to all concerned parties.

Organization

The typical approach to customs ICT developments begins with the European Commission preparing a project proposal, which is then reviewed by national delegates of the Electronic Customs Group. A common position—taking into account the views of the EU member states—is established. The European Commission then takes responsibility for the design, development, and implementation of the agreed position.

At the start of each new project a project plan and user requirements are prepared by the European Commission and reviewed and agreed by the Electronic Customs Group. Business process models are then prepared. The models are incorporated into the system functional specifications. Once the specifications are adopted, the system technical specifications become the basis for software development. All software must undergo detailed testing before its acceptance and deployment.

Before ICT solutions can be allowed to enter into production, EU member states must subject the solutions to conformance tests. The European Commission typically operates the test tools, reference data systems, and statistical tools. It also may

Information and communications technology in support of customs unions: a case study of the European Union operate a central repository for information destined for a nonoperational use that is not time critical (for example, statistics).

Business architecture

The business architecture—including the implementing provisions and operating guidelines—is in principle based on EU legislation. Until recently visual representations of each business process were improvised, with accompanying descriptions. Now, as part of a modernization effort, new methods to represent business processes are being tested (described below).

The business architecture reflects the reality that the EU member states perform operational tasks while the agreed regulatory framework is managed by the European Commission. All business processes linked to the operational environment are managed at the national level. But for all ICT systems where interactions are required between national administrations, or between the national administrations and the European Commission, common specifications must be developed. These specifications refer generally to three distinct domains (figure 15.1):

- *Common domain:* where customs to customs information exchanges happen—between national administrations, between the national administrations and the European Commission, or both.
- *National domain:* where customs to customs information exchanges happen between customs entities of the same national administration.
- *External domain:* where customs to business information happens—mainly the declarations

provided by trade to customs administrations, with the resulting followup traffic.

In the common domain—to ensure its sound functioning as part of a decentralized system—almost all features of the functional specifications must be *mandatory* requirements: that is, they must be implemented as described in the specifications.

The features of the national domain are also described in the functional specifications. However, these features are *optional* or *recommended,* meaning that national administrations are in principle free to follow them or not. Recently the customs agencies of EU member states—supported by trade representatives—have shown a willingness to avoid drafting 27 discrete versions of specifications for the national domain.

Traditionally the specifications in the external domain have remained *recommended* or *strongly recommended,* meaning that national administrations are not obliged to follow them. As a result, interfaces between trade and various national administrations in the EU are heterogeneous and often technically incompatible.

Internal research at the European Commission is suggesting the establishment of a collaborative environment: the European Commission would propose functional specifications for the common and external domains, while national administrations would complete the environment with the national domain.

In the future a business process modeling tool (available online for authorized users) will be used to make system specifications. Tool and functional

Information and communications technology in support of customs unions: a case study of the European Union

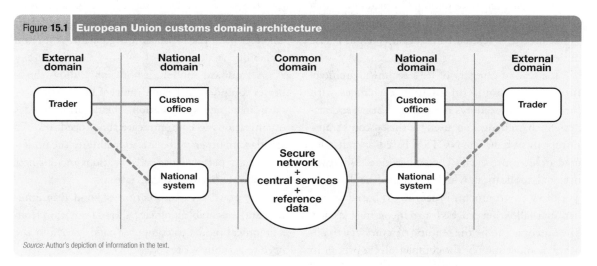

Figure **15.1** **European Union customs domain architecture**

Source: Author's depiction of information in the text.

specifications will gradually be completed, reviewed, agreed, and aligned. The final product will visualize business processes, with textual descriptions for more comprehensive understanding. The tool is also intended to maintain the business logic, both in rules and in associated conditions needed for future operations. The end product will then be used to obtain system process models, which will be the basis for further technical specifications. The goal is to automate the process as far as possible, drawing upon this work for software development and for automating all activities related to ICT (including testing) as far as possible in the European Commission and in EU member states.

Technical architecture

The first category of ICT technical architecture is centralized. A cluster of databases located centrally, at the European Commission, holds reference information necessary for the functioning of the EU customs union. These centralized systems make the required information available throughout the EU, to ensure that all administrations and all customs offices are synchronized and are using correct and updated reference information.

An example of these centralized systems is the electronic integrated customs tariff, which holds the tariff nomenclature, tariff rates, and additional tariff related information (such as antidumping measures). An electronic file transmission update—in practice a daily file—updates the national tariff databases of EU member states. The national tariff system contains the information received from the European Commission along with national information (such as national prohibitions and restrictions) and national measures related to taxation (such as excise duties).

The second category of ICT technical architecture uses electronic information exchanges with formats and procedures harmonized between partners. Such exchanges are used for the customs trans-European system. The NCTS is based on a distributed architecture: each EU member state has its own national application, which processes the data in a workflow environment. Processing is based on the national validation process for an incoming message. The outcome can be the sending of a message to another member state or the completion (in part or in full) of the workflow. The European Commission operates no central business application, but it operates central services such as monitoring, the maintenance of common reference data, and the coordination and compiling of statistics on the overall system.

Both categories of systems use a secure common systems interface network for data transmission. The network provides telecommunications services as well as the monitoring and support services that enable the interface among various technologies.

Methods and tools

A specialized methodology for ICT system development and operations—Tempo—is based on industry best practice for systems development and project management. Closely following the recommendations of the world's most widely accepted ICT service management approach,[9] Tempo includes a set of guidelines and document templates. The quality assurance team working for the European Commission keeps Tempo up to date, taking into account factors such as experience, technical evolutions, and state of the art methods elsewhere. The use of Tempo is mandatory for the European Commission but available as an option for EU member states.

For tools—in systems development, operations testing, and management reporting—the European Commission has a policy of using commercial off the shelf (COTS) solutions as much as possible.

Research is being done on tools to draft business process models with the help of computers. Such models can be used by vendors to develop solutions with their products using compliant Web service interfaces.[10] A standard executable language allows users to deploy mission critical processes on a reliable technical platform, assuring performance and scalability.

A standard modeling notation[11] allows businesses to understand their internal business procedures in a graphical notation. The notation enables organizations to communicate the procedures in a standard manner, while it also facilitates the understanding of performance collaborations and business transactions between organizations.

The powerful combination of modeling notation and executable language allows migration from a graphical model to computer code—without the need to actually write code.

Business processes change regularly with changing business requirements. The ideal approach is to:

- Draw the updated processes.
- Ensure that all data mappings are completed, that the business rules and conditions are defined, and that workflow parameters are defined.
- Finally (through the tool used), get the process deployed in a test or production environment.

Services have recently been added to make information exchange tools more accessible. One such service is a light client facility, comparable to a Web browser and providing direct access to central information. Web services allow automated online consultation of centralized systems.

Combinations of centralized and decentralized systems, as described above, have recently been created to make available a new type of single trans-European system that provides more functions and limits the costs for EU member states.

The Economic Operators System (EOS) of the EU is a combination of:

- Centrally stored information distributed for national operations.
- Information exchanged by countries after processing at the national level.

Workflows at the central and national levels thus exist in combination in the EOS. In case of desynchronization, the central repository takes precedence and national databases will be resynchronized automatically.

To facilitate trade, at the central level the European Commission has created a data dissemination system[12] that provides economic operators and the general public with online information. The information includes the complete customs office list, customs tariff information, a tracking facility for export and transit movements, and so forth.

Lessons from the EU experience

Nine lessons may be drawn from the EU experience with customs ICT development.

First, technical heterogeneity makes interoperability technically challenging. The current ICT environment is characterized by heterogeneous technical architectures (hardware, systems software, database and middleware, application software, and communication infrastructure and software). The inability to create a more homogenous environment has resulted in a costly systems integration effort, requiring much development, operation, and maintenance.

Second, meeting legislative deadlines can be challenging. It has been particularly challenging for the EU because each member state must draft a national project plan and align it with those of all other EU member states and of the European Commission.

Third, for satisfactory results all partners must complete development and testing on the same timetable. Without such alignment, countries ready by an agreed date cannot benefit from their investments. Getting the EU countries to agree on a single start date for operations has been a major challenge.

Fourth, conformance testing for ICT solutions must be mandatory, to prevent newcomers from endangering the customs operations of countries already in production. The EU approach to the delivery of system upgrades has been to give countries a time window for starting operations. Letting operations start gradually—one country at a time—leaves time for sound analysis and corrective actions.

Fifth, long transition periods should be avoided—to minimize technical risks and problems arising from the need to support old and new functionalities in parallel.

Sixth, budgetary restrictions and competing national priorities make it difficult to plan for new systems and for modifications to existing solutions. For the NCTS the European Commission funded the development of a startup national system, which was then made available to EU member states free of charge.

Seventh, the management of centralized ICT solutions entails meeting certain demands—for versions in several languages, for specific changes requested by individual partners, and for operational support tailored to each partner's software platform (as for the various platforms used by EU member states).

Eighth, responsibility may be transferred to the partners through training and procurement support for system maintenance. In the EU the need to support more and more branched software (a result of countries' needs to individualize the software) persuaded the European Commission to launch an initiative for certain member states to take over the management, maintenance and evolution of their applications. The initiative was a joint effort. A similar effort for collective software development was launched—though it ran afoul of diverging national requirements, legal differences in public procurement processes, and so forth. Other efforts likely will follow, to promote economies of scale and faster progress in automating customs functions.

Ninth, to overcome shortfalls, labor must be redistributed so that tasks are carried out where resources are available. Countries with the resources to keep building on the agreed path must make their specifications, software, test tools, and other ICT features available to those without such resources. Here the central authority's aim should be to promote progress through increased cooperation without pushing for shifts in competence. In the EU the present financial crisis has meant that there are fewer resources for investments to develop new ICT solutions, or even to add functionality to existing systems. Overall modernization in the EU may slow as a result of some countries' resource constraints. The European Commission assumes a vital role in organizing, coordinating, and making available environments for joint use—virtual or conference meetings and joint documentation storage—along with specifications and software.

What aspects of ICT for customs are transferable from the EU to other customs unions?

This section begins by suggesting overarching principles for ICT development by customs unions other than the EU customs union, based on the EU customs union's experience. It then looks at the advantages, disadvantages, and risks of a single standard system—or centralized system—compared with those of national systems. It concludes with a list of recommended actions.

Overarching principles for ICT at other customs unions

The way forward suggested here for customs unions outside the EU is to create a strategic plan setting out the vision, objectives, and business, technical, and organizational frameworks needed for sustainable interoperable systems. The strategic plan should lead to the delivery of essential services, ensuring that all national and regional policies and procedures related to electronic customs (e-customs) and to trade facilitation are coherent.

In a customs union whose partners remain in charge of operations at the national level, creating and operating ICT systems requires trust, goodwill, and much coordination. It further requires a clear mandate, a governance structure, and a clear and adequately resourced work program—along with the constant coordination efforts.

The first hurdle is to create a common vision and measurable, outcome based deliverables for projects agreed on in advance by all partners. A realistic work timetable should be adhered to, functional and technical system specifications agreed to. If some countries correctly apply the timetable and have systems ready by the agreed deadline while other countries encounter delays and miss the deadline (for sound reasons or otherwise), it is very difficult economically for the countries that meet the deadline.

Regional interoperability must be assured to allow a seamless data flow between member states of a customs union that is building a common transnational ICT system. Business processes throughout the union must benefit regulatory authorities, supply chain partners, and traders. The processes should render risk analysis more effective, allowing for efficient monitoring of trade flows and the appropriate selection of consignments to be checked. Furthermore, the processes should reduce business operating costs in the region, speed the movement of goods across regional borders, and reduce paper based formalities as much as possible.

A centralized system or several systems?

Given the overarching principles set forth above—and taking into account present financial constraints, which can affect the development and maintainance of ICT systems—a comparison can be made between two approaches to systems development for customs unions. First, having a centralized system (or single standard system) comes with certain advantages, disadvantages, and risks. Second, having several discrete national systems (or a distributed system) brings other advantages, disadvantages and risks.

A centralized (or single standard) system—one used by all countries in the customs union—is more feasible the greater the alignment of rules and legislation. The appropriateness of such a system will be determined largely by the customs union's integration capability and by the political will of its members.

A centralized (or single standard) system brings the following benefits:

- Significant economies of scale, reducing system development and maintenance cost and the extent of development and operations efforts.
- An ability to build the system on international best practices in this business domain, starting with fresh technology building blocks and basing development on a technical platform that uses open standards (for example, services oriented architecture).
- An ability for traders to use—or interface with—only one system.
- The better equipping of regional management for regional trade, external tariff management, and national self determination in revenue collection.

In addition, the following specific features are possible using a centralized (or single standard) system:

- Any installations serving multiple countries can be deployed in a way that ensures the data of any country are secure—accessible only to the officials of that country.
- A central suite of reference data can be set up (for example, for the common external tariff, for value and classification information, for origin certificates, for transit guarantee management, and for other reference material such as stamps or an office list).
- The system can be configurable in various sizes, from a small installation to a very large one.
- The system can be enabled to permit extensive timely and remote operations support.
- Business continuity can be assured, utilizing a load balanced infrastructure.

However, experience suggests that it is difficult for a customs union to develop and operate a centralized (or single standard) system. The reasons for this difficulty are mainly political rather than technical. An alternative is to have several systems (or a distributed system). The price of having several systems is a need for greater coordination and higher investments in human and financial resources, both for systems development and for systems operations.

The customs union must develop a strategic plan to deliver the requirements for further regional convergence. In many areas common legal and procedural rules do not, by themselves, ensure a level playing field for economic operators. So, beyond the necessary regulatory changes, common guidelines and working methods may be required. The strategic plan should match the legal and business integration with an appropriate technical approach, to be completed in accordance with an agreed multiannual timetable.

Under the strategic plan, economic operators should be able to access unionwide information related to import and export requirements through an information portal. The portal should also contain information about rules on the movement of goods across borders (for example, agricultural, environmental, and other regulatory legislation). The first step is for the customs union member states to agree on a common standard. Such a common standard will, in turn, facilitate the interlinking and harmonization of national information portals.

For risk to be managed efficiently, the exchange of intelligence information is essential. So is risk analysis, conducted according to common criteria and standards. To allow a rapid, direct, and secure exchange of control information (to counteract national and regional threats), a secure electronic system is needed—one that allows the dissemination and exchange of intelligence information across all regulatory control points in the region.

National risk systems must allow interconnectivity and interoperability. The development of a risk management framework requires, among other things, common functional and technical specifications for national risk analysis systems—to ensure that regional profiles can be readily incorporated into the national systems. The successful regional application of risk management depends on parallel developments in authorized economic operator schemes, audit controls, standardized customs controls, and technical interconnectivity capabilities.

A regional valuation database could be developed—containing import and export values for genuine trade in the region, and accessible by all customs offices throughout the region. The values would be accessible by customs code heading, commodity description, manufacturer, quantity, country of origin, or destination. Valuation data could be obtained (wherever this is cost effective) from sources including recently used invoices, catalogs, vendor price lists and offers, questionnaires, and third party service providers such as preshipment inspection companies.

A regional legislation database could be developed to provide details on prohibitions and preferential rate regulations. Such a database would simplify the management and validation of documents and enable economic operators to benefit from exoneration or exemption on certain products. The database could also provide for recording details of regulations on restricted, exonerated, and exempted goods on import and export.

Implementation strategy

The following actions are recommended for existing or emerging customs unions.

- Prepare a document describing the customs union's *ICT strategic objectives* (goals to be achieved), to be approved by all member countries after discussion and review of the text.
- Put in place a suitable *governance structure,* supported at the highest political level. The structure should establish clear agreements for the distribution of labor among participating countries—including the creation of a central secretariat—and for their provision of suitable human and financial resources, both for the management of the central secretariat and for the resulting work program. The governance structure should also establish a steering committee to provide guidance, make strategic decisions, and resolve issues escalated from the operational level.
- Establish a *scope document* and a *multiannual strategic plan* (including a *timetable*)—documents that together yield a clear *implementation strategy.* The scope document should set implementation priorities (top, middle, and lower), leading to the establishment of several project phases. The multiannual strategic plan should provide a clear overview of all major tasks, with the timetable for their execution.
- Based on the objectives, establish detailed *user requirements* for the system—a list to include

both functional (customs) and nonfunctional (mainly technical) requirements.
- Establish a *coordinating body* that will ensure the full information of all parties concerned, provide them with an opportunity to discuss issues in establishing ICT systems, ensure that operational decisions are proposed for decision—or (if no decision can be reached) sent to the steering committee—and, finally, keep a risk register and ensure that a security policy is established. The coordinating body should drive progress by making proposals and suggestions, without threatening national competences.
- Establish a *monitoring and reporting policy.* Monitoring will provide correct and objective information. Reporting will ensure that national and central authorities are duly informed. The regular provision of appropriate information will greatly help to secure resources for future initiatives—as well as support for any remedial actions.
- It is recommended to use a *project management tool* in defining a program plan that encompasses the various ICT projects. Such a tool can help track progress and the use of resources—like a GPS, it guides the customs union toward its goal of functioning well.
- Organize regular (annual) *evaluation exercises,* to learn from experience and to keep the spirit of cooperation high. Such exercises should yield operational improvements and create a mechanism for continuous improvement.

A case study: creating the New Computerised Transit System

Since the introduction of ICT in customs systems across Europe, the creation of an electronic European transit system has been an ambition for the EU. Initially this ambition was thwarted by processing power limitations, by the high price of memory capacity, and by limited bandwidth—but also, and perhaps most importantly, by the lack of any real political will or determination to develop a pan-European system.

Even as progress toward the development of a pan-European system was being frustrated, the existing common and Community transit systems—which were paper based—became more prone to fraud. Increasing numbers of movements were not closed in their allowed timeframes, mainly for the simple reason that highly taxable goods had disappeared from official records during transit. These cases were time consuming and difficult to close. Often the fraud could not be traced to its perpetrators, leaving the principal (the person accepting responsibility for the consignment) or the guarantor with little option other than to pay the duties and taxes at stake.

Because rising fraud threatened the existing European transit system, the European Parliament created the Enquiry Committee to investigate. A key finding of the committee was that the existing paper based system was no longer fit to support trade in Europe, particularly given the increasing demands of global commerce. The committee recommended that the transit system be automated—as soon as possible.

Business objectives and challenges

The main objective in creating a new European transit system was to replace the paper based system with a reliable, automated one that would enable customs authorities to identify open movements online. Under the paper based system most movements took several weeks to close, as postal services were used to return papers from destination offices to departure offices. In contrast, the new electronic system should provide information immediately, enabling inquiries from the moment when the time period expired for performing a transit.

Other objectives included covering all the territory covered by the paper based system; requiring the trade to submit transit declarations electronically to customs; and having the new system perform several logical checks prior to validation (to keep mistakes to a minimum).

There were two major challenges. The first was convincing the trade to switch from a paper based system to an electronic one—bringing benefits for the system (in quality and in reduced vulnerability to fraud and irregularities), but also for the trade (mainly in reduced transaction costs, as there would no longer be a need to fill out paper forms and bring them to customs offices).

The second major challenge was coordinating all the countries involved and getting them to cooperate. When the system was created 20 countries were involved. Now there are more than 30. The success of the project depends on the will to succeed among all countries involved—and on the existence of a coordinating authority able to orchestrate all the actions needed for progress. For the NCTS the European Commission agreed to assume the role of coordinator and to host all international meetings required for the project.

The European Union's approach to NCTS transformation

The NCTS project was the largest ever undertaken in the EU customs and trade domain. It also mounted a major challenge to the status quo, prompting some resistance and skepticism from the start. The parties affected were concerned about the scale of changes and about the long NCTS development cycle.

To manage these concerns, a gradual transformation approach was adopted. Initially the systems development was scoped. In the first major work phase only essential functionality was developed. In the next phase automated guarantee management was introduced. The third phase focused on introducing the automated enquiry procedure for nonclosed movements.

The phased approach enabled a quick start in the first phase, restricting participation to limited numbers of countries and of traders—to test the NCTS system's functionality and efficiency. Only after the system had proved itself over several months, without any major problems, were more countries able to join. And only in the following phase were all countries obliged to participate. At that time it became mandatory for the trade to use the new system, with the old paper based system surviving only as a fallback option.

The solution blueprint adopted for the NCTS

The NCTS project was ambitious from the outset, as the first major international scale automation project in the EU customs and trade sector. The countries involved were not on a common platform, and their progress towards automation varied.

To avoid major delays from debates and negotiations, it was decided that the NCTS would be built largely on the basis of the existing paper based system. Existing business processes and legal frameworks would thus need only slight adjustment to allow the replacement of paper by electronic messages. The data elements to be exchanged could be simply taken from paper documents. The only matters requiring agreement would be message definition and format. When the system was conceived there was no real alternative to the UN/EDIFACT format—which was well documented in the international field—so agreement on it was quite rapid.

Driving the adoption of the NCTS

As the NCTS was being developed in parallel to the existing paper based system, countries initially could volunteer to take part as early adopters. The Czech Republic, Germany, Italy, Spain, the Netherlands, and Switzerland were the first countries to use the NCTS in its first phase. Where countries opted to join, traders too could learn and use the system voluntarily.

The countries that volunteered in the first phase of the NCTS cited several reasons for joining, including:

- A realization that the paper based system was in crisis, and that urgent solutions were needed to offset the growing financial risks linked to highly taxable goods.
- A belief that once the new system achieved critical mass, it would increase efficiency and so reduce costs for both agencies and private parties.

The countries that did not volunteer initially cited:

- A desire to wait until the new system was stabilized.
- Worries about the extra cost and effort of acting as test cases.
- Some skepticism about the implementation timeframe—and general uncertainty about the long term prospects for project success.

The companies and traders that became early adopters generally were large and medium size enterprises. Smaller companies questioned the return on the investment (joining costs). They needed more proof that the eventual benefits would justify upfront costs, time, and efforts.

After an initial period of development and use, the NCTS received a positive evaluation and was opened up to all countries using the common and Community transit systems. This second development phase emphasized achieving interconnectivity among all user countries. Traders still had the option of migrating to NCTS and using the paper based system as a backup.

In the third phase the whole NCTS system became mandatory, not only for national agencies, but also for traders. Every transit declaration now had to be electronic. Also, the international guarantee management system was introduced, ensuring that NCTS movements validated at any point in the customs territory of participating countries are covered with an international guarantee valid throughout the whole territory.

Whenever an evolution from one phase to the next involved changes in the international part of the system, the evolution was covered by extensive conformance testing. This meant that the customs agency concerned had to evaluate its national application against an automated test tool and successfully execute a number of business scenarios.

Transformation outcomes

With the NCTS developing over several carefully planned phases, transformation outcomes have been gradual. The volume of transactions has steadily grown over the years, as countries have joined the NCTS and as it has replaced the previous paper based system.

Using the NCTS today are 27 EU member states plus Switzerland, Norway and Iceland. In addition, a growing number of countries in East and Southeast Europe have official observer status while preparing national NCTS applications, with a view of joining in upcoming years. In 2008 the system was used for about 20 million transit movements throughout Europe (figure 15.2).

The NCTS now enables European customs services to start an enquiry procedure at any moment. For sensitive (high duty) consignments, agencies no longer need to wait weeks for a paper copy to return before starting an enquiry. In practice the enquiry is started as soon as the validity period for the NCTS movement ends. This period can be set in the system, taking the distance of the movement and other circumstances into account.

No real cost-benefit analysis of the NCTS has been done. However, questions asked of the trade community have yielded the estimate that, for each transit movement, the NCTS has obtained a

15

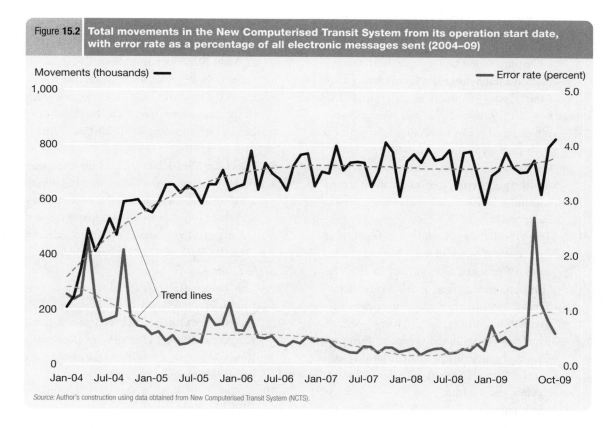

Figure **15.2** **Total movements in the New Computerised Transit System from its operation start date, with error rate as a percentage of all electronic messages sent (2004–09)**

Movements (thousands) ▬   ▬ Error rate (percent)

1,000   5.0

800   4.0

600   3.0

400   2.0

        Trend lines

200   1.0

0   0.0
Jan-04 Jul-04 Jan-05 Jul-05 Jan-06 Jul-06 Jan-07 Jul-07 Jan-08 Jul-08 Jan-09   Oct-09

Source: Author's construction using data obtained from New Computerised Transit System (NCTS).

productivity gain of about 30 minutes. With labor costs gross billed at €30 an hour, the 8,800,000 movements in 2008 would then achieve annual cost savings of €132,000,000. Although labor may cost less for customs brokers in some areas, the cost savings remain impressive—suggesting that the NCTS investment repays itself annually several times over.

Lessons learned from the NCTS project
Three critical success factors have enabled the development of NCTS to its present state:
- Strong political will and support.
- A mandated coordinating body providing direction, momentum, and the required flow of information to all parties involved—to communicate progress, and to ensure the correct implementation of commonly agreed rules (since the system can only function well when all parties have delivered what is required in their domains).
- Quick agreement on systems architecture—particularly on which aspects are to be centralized and which decentralized.

There is general acknowledgment between the European Commission and its member states that the NCTS project was set up and organized successfully. The main changes, if the work were redone, would be technological: choice of systems architecture, more use of XML (rather than UN/EDIFACT), better tools to manage central system reference data and statistical information.

The NCTS project has succeeded so far. Its major achievement has been making it possible to follow up on nonclosed movements, halting the fraudulent use of the previous system—a use that undermined that system's financial stability. The NCTS has also brought financial benefits to both public and private users by increasing their productivity.

Notes

1. "European Parliament resolution of 19 June 2008 on the fortieth anniversary of the Customs Union," P6_TA(2008)0305, European Parliament, http://www.europarl.europa.eu/sides/getDoc.do?pubRef=-//EP//TEXT+TA+P6-TA-2008-0305+0+DOC+XML+V0//en.

15

Information and communications technology in support of customs unions: a case study of the European Union

2. Implementing powers are conferred on the European Commission, which is assisted by a Customs Code Committee. Both the regulation establishing the Community Customs Code—Council Regulation (EEC) No 2913/92—and the code's implementing provisions can be accessed through the Web page "Taxation and Customs Union: Customs Legislation," European Commission, http://ec.europa.eu/taxation_customs/common/legislation/legislation/customs/index_en.htm.

3. The subsidiarity principle is defined in article 5 of the treaty that established the European Economic Community in 1957. See "Europa: summaries of EU legislation—Treaty establishing the European Economic Community, EEC Treaty—original text (non-consolidated version)," European Union, http://europa.eu/legislation_summaries/institutional_affairs/treaties/treaties_eec_en.htm.

4. "Regulation (EC) No 450/2008 of the European Parliament and of the Council of 23 April 2008 laying down the Community Customs Code (Modernized Customs Code)," European Union, http://eur-lex.europa.eu/LexUriServ/LexUriServ.do?uri=OJ:L:2008:145:0001:01:EN:HTML.

5. "Decision No 624/2007/EC of the European Parliament and of the Council of 23 May 2007 establishing an action program for customs in the Community (Customs 2013)," European Union, http://eur-lex.europa.eu/LexUriServ/LexUriServ.do?uri=OJ:L:2007:154:0025:01:EN:HTML.

6. "Regulation (EC) No 648/2005 of the European Parliament and of the Council of 13 April 2005 amending Council Regulation (EEC) No 2913/92 establishing the Community Customs Code," European Union, http://eur-lex.europa.eu/LexUriServ/LexUriServ.do?uri=OJ:L:2005:117:0013:01:EN:HTML.

7. "Decision No 70/2008/EC of the European Parliament and of the Council of 15 January 2008 on a paperless environment for customs and trade," European Union, http://eur-lex.europa.eu/LexUriServ/LexUriServ.do?uri=OJ:L:2008:023:0021:01:EN:HTML.

8. See note 4.

9. The Information Technology Infrastructure Library, known as ITIL. See "Welcome to the Official ITIL Website," United Kingdom Office of Government Commerce (OGC), http://www.itil-officialsite.com/home/home.asp.

10. Business Process Execution Language (BPEL), short for Web Services Business Process Execution Language (WS-BPEL) is an OASIS standard executable language for specifying interactions with Web Services.

11. The notation is known as BPMN. See "Object Management Group/ Business Process Management Initiative," OMG, www.bpmn.org.

12. Electronic databases accessible through the European Commission's Web site are listed at "Taxation and Customs Union: Electronic Databases," European Commission, http://ec.europa.eu/taxation_customs/common/databases/index_en.htm.

16 Sanitary and phytosanitary measures and border management

Kees van der Meer and Laura Ignacio

In addition to customs processing, all agricultural food and forestry products face sanitary and phytosanitary (SPS) measures as part of the border release process. Since these products are important to many developing countries—and shipments are relatively small—much of their trade faces SPS procedures.

This chapter starts with a discussion of the nature of SPS management and the role of the World Trade Organization (WTO) Agreement on the Application of Sanitary and Phytosanitary Measures (SPS Agreement), followed by a discussion of characteristics of agricultural product markets and SPS agencies. The segmentation of the food market poses special challenges for safety management and trade promotion.

The chapter discusses the general pattern of limited cooperation between SPS services and customs. The performance of SPS border management can be improved by promoting cooperation with other border agencies, the private sector, and sister organizations in other trading countries. Involving SPS agencies in cooperative border management can benefit governments and the private sector. Unfortunately this cooperative aspect of SPS has received little attention from international agencies.

The SPS clearance process differs from the customs clearance process: a major aim of SPS services is export promotion (market access), and work volume away from the border may be much larger than at the border. In developing countries, SPS agencies face great challenges in performing their roles in ways that comply with international principles, adequately protect health, and promote market access.

SPS controls and their management

Governments have long been concerned about the potential for economic damage caused by the introduction and spread of plant pests and animal diseases, since individuals can do little against such hazards. Government measures can include trade bans, movement controls, quarantine, disinfection, and destruction of infected products and animals. Pests and diseases can spread easily over borders, so control measures are an area of cooperation among countries. The focal points of such cooperation are the Office International des Epizooties (OIE, called in English the World Organization of Animal Health) and the International Plant Protection Convention.[1]

Governments set rules against unsafe food, as individual consumers have only a limited ability to verify themselves the safety of what they eat. The Codex Alimentarius Commission is the international framework for food safety, operated by the Food and Agriculture Organization of the United

Nations (FAO) and the World Health Organization.[2] Two bodies cooperate in standard setting for animal food product safety: OIE leads on zoonotic threats in food (threats pertaining to diseases that can be spread from animals to humans), the Codex Alimentarius Commission on hygiene and other aspects. Since food chains may also be contaminated by unsafe agricultural inputs and the unsafe use of inputs, governments also control the quality and safety of pesticides, veterinary drugs, animal feed, and fertilizers in import, trade, marketing, and use.

WTO principles for SPS control. While there are clear justifications for importing countries controlling the safety of imported plants and animals and the products thereof, countries may be tempted to use SPS measures as disguised protectionist measures. Therefore, the use of SPS measures has been brought under the discipline of the WTO trading regime. Members of the WTO must sign its SPS Agreement (WTO 1994a) as well as its Technical Barriers to Trade (TBT) Agreement (WTO 1994b). The agreements stipulate that an importing country has the right to refuse market entry and control imports—provided that it justifies such measures under the principles of the agreements, including:

- *Transparency.* Information on SPS measures is easily accessible. There are set procedures for notification in cases of new or amended measures.
- *Nondiscrimination.* Measures are equally applied to importers as well as domestic producers. Similarly, all trading partners are subject to the same requirements.
- *Proportionality.* Interventions are proportional to the health risks to be controlled.
- *Equivalence.* There is mutual recognition among trading partners of different measures that achieve the same level of protection.
- *Science based measures.* Measures to protect plant, animal, and human health are based on scientific principles and sufficient scientific evidence. Generally this requires the assessment of risks involved and the definition of an acceptable level of risk.
- *Regionalization.* Recognition of the possibility that disease or pest affected countries may have areas or regions that are disease or pest free, and allowing exports from such areas or regions.

In addition, countries are encouraged to harmonize their policies with international SPS standards and measures—such as those espoused by the Codex Alimentarius Commission on food safety, the International Plant Protection Convention on plant health, and OIE on animal health—but are allowed to apply stricter requirements as long as the requirements are based on scientific justifications that include an assessment of risks. Countries may also apply fewer and less stringent standards or opt not to apply international SPS standards and measures, provided that this does not affect the rights of other countries under multilateral trade rules.

Capacities needed. Implementing these principles is complex and demands many capacities in which developing countries generally are lacking. Countries first need an extensive legal and regulatory framework for food safety and plant and animal health, with transparency, the rule of law, and the capacity to implement measures. In substance, a country must be able to:

- Monitor its status on plant pests, animal diseases, and food safety.
- Operate testing and diagnostic laboratories.
- Certify the safety of plants, animals, and products.
- Carry out inspections at borders and behind them.
- Conduct risk analysis and risk management.
- Report any plant and animal pests and diseases and any food hazards to trading partners and international organizations.
- Participate in bilateral and international negotiations on market access and trade agreements.

A minimum requirement for international recognition of these services is the use of international standards. Some of the services may be delegated to nongovernment entities, but the government competent authority[3] should provide proper supervision.

Developing countries' limited capacities mean that such countries face difficult choices about priorities in carrying out SPS control measures—specifically, in three areas:

- Putting in place import requirements that protect sufficiently against health hazards and comply with WTO principles.
- Complying with demands from neighboring countries and importing countries that hazards

be prevented from spilling over to their territories, and providing information about any pest and disease situations.

- Putting in place nondiscriminatory measures for the domestic market, in synergy with the export and import controls.

Market access. Exporting countries confront a range of requirements imposed by importing countries. Market access requests are decided on the basis of risk assessment procedures, for which the Codex Alimentarius Commission, the International Plant Protection Convention, and OIE—among others—have provided standards. Requirements include product and process standards and may also address producers and production facilities, production methods, storage and transport facilities, disinfection treatment, required certificates, and capacities of competent authorities.

Importing countries commonly require certificates affirming product health and safety. They include veterinary health certificates for nearly all animals, animal products, and animal production inputs; phytosanitary certificates for nearly all plants, plant products, and plant production inputs; and, in many cases, food safety certificates for fresh and processed food.

First time exports of most agricultural and food products to a country usually must be approved. Exporting countries usually are required to provide data on their pest and disease situations based on international standards (especially International Plant Protection Convention and OIE standards). Not providing such information may result in product bans based on the precautionary principle.[4] Importing countries, however, may not ban imports of goods from countries with pests and diseases that are also widespread in the importing countries' own territories and for which the importing countries have no control programs. International standards allow for establishing pest free or disease free zones that, in principle, can divide a country into different zones for export and import requirements. However, establishing such zones demands much capacity, and getting them recognized by trading partners is difficult.

For animal products (including fishery products), many countries require preapprovals for imports, preapprovals that are given only if hygienic and structural conditions in the food processing plants are acceptable. Such preapprovals may also depend on the ability of competent authorities to control the safety of exported products. Inspection teams from the importing country may visit the exporting country to verify—before market access is granted—that production, processing, and transport facilities, and the capacities of the competent authority, comply with importing country standards.[5]

Agricultural inputs—such as seed, feed, pesticides, and veterinary drugs—present high risks. Seed, other propagation materials, and live animals can carry new pests and diseases into a country. Importation therefore usually requires formal quarantine or post entry quarantine measures, and trade from countries with certain pests and diseases may be forbidden. Feed may contain pathogens (the pathogen responsible for bovine spongiform encephalopathy, or mad cow disease, is a notorious example) and may be tainted with dangerous pollutants and toxins. Once these undesirable contaminants enter the food chain they cannot be removed, resulting in food products that are dangerous to consumers and possibly leading to export bans—so feed warrants intensive controls. The same applies to forbidden pesticides and veterinary drugs, or forbidden formulations of these substances.

For animal and plant health issues, the capacity of public agencies and the relations between governments are crucial to gaining and maintaining market access. Private capacities play a less important role in market access for these issues—except for enterprises that deal with breeding stock or with seed and planting material.[6] In contrast, for food safety, once market access has been obtained, responsibility lies mainly in the private sector—unless frequent noncompliance by an exporter triggers public intervention in the importing country.[7]

Most countries waive the risk assessment requirement for products that have long been imported without problems. But if noncompliance with import standards is frequent, if there is a case of a food hazard, if a plant or animal disease breaks out in the country of origin, or if quarantined pests and diseases are detected, then trade may be suspended until a risk assessment is conducted and special measures are agreed. Examples of suspensions include:

- The European Commission's ban on seafood products from China, Thailand, and Vietnam when forbidden antibiotics were detected.

- Japan's ban of spinach from China when residues of forbidden pesticides were detected.
- The ban in many countries of bovine and poultry products from countries where bovine spongiform encephalopathy and avian flu were detected.
- Bans of milk products from China during the melamine crisis.
- The banning by the United States of raspberry imports from Guatemala after cyclospora contamination was found.

Requirements for food and agricultural products usually identify three import categories: prohibited articles, restricted articles, and nonprohibited articles. Prohibited articles are banned from import, except perhaps with special permits for research purposes. Restricted articles can only be imported if special requirements (permits, certificates, disinfection) are met. Nonprohibited articles generally can be imported with no requirements, or with simple routine ones (such as phytosanitary certificates).

Market differentiation

Developing countries can be characterized according to a three tier market structure for food products, with different food safety management issues in each tier (Van der Meer and Ignacio 2007).

Tier 1 is the demanding export market segment, mainly selling in Organisation for Economic Co-operation and Development (OECD) countries. Demand for safety assurances, including traceability, is high in this market segment. Buyers exclude noncompliant suppliers. Supply chain controls are mainly carried out by private companies. Generally the buyer pays a price premium for compliance and traceability. In this segment governments play a facilitating and supervising role.

Tier 2 is the emerging domestic modern market segment, consisting mainly of supermarkets, tourist restaurants, and international fast food chains. In this segment market demand for safety assurances is still weak—the main factor in competition and in market access is still product price. Private enterprises struggle to recover the cost of supply chain coordination. Here the government can help by supporting good hygiene practice, good agriculture practice, good manufacturing practice, and safety and quality management systems based on hazard

analysis and critical control points (HACCP). The government can also control the safety and quality of agrochemicals and feed, and it can work to prevent environmental hazards. This segment is growing in all developing countries, driven by urbanization and growing modern food retail chains, but it still represents a small share of food sales.

Tier 3 is the traditional food market segment. It is operated by mainly small informal players without supply chain coordination, and it remains dominant (by trade volume) in all developing countries. Generally there is no price incentive for safety assurance systems that promote good agriculture, hygiene, and manufacturing practices, or for systems based on HACCP. The main role for government in this segment is to prevent supply chains from becoming tainted by pathogens, banned pesticides and veterinary drugs, and other dangerous chemicals, and to ensure that no unsafe or substandard food enters the market. Given the weakness of public capacity, the complexity of these markets, and the large number of small enterprises involved, most governments can effectively control only a limited number of hazards.

Market segmentation has implications for border management. Goods in tier 1 require few checks by the public sector, since private enterprises manage controls throughout the supply chain. Tier 2 companies will conduct some controls, though less comprehensively. Tier 3—including bulk shipments without known producers and ultimate buyers—poses the most risks and requires the most control. Still, not all tier 3 shipments are the same. Often there is much small, local, and informal agricultural and food trade, especially along land borders in developing countries. Such trade is especially difficult to control—and usually does not require intensive controls, because food production and consumption practices are generally the same on both sides of the border. Although some controls are needed to prevent the smuggling of unsafe foods—and to respond in the event of food safety incidents—burdensome checks on small traders at international border crossings only create incentives for illegal trade. Even less necessary for informal local trade are phytosanitary and veterinary controls, since pests and diseases are often the same on both sides of the border. Such controls are needed only during outbreaks of contagious animal diseases, such as avian flu or foot and mouth disease.

As the distance from a product's origin to its destination increases, SPS risks also increase (since pest and disease situations are more likely to differ in two places the greater their physical separation). In addition, such risks are higher wherever traceability is lacking and producers and traders are anonymous—not unusual conditions in developing countries.

Accordingly, the formal trade segment requires an adequate SPS control system, and government trade promotion programs are targeted at this part of trade—the part for which the cost of border clearance is an important factor in competitiveness.

SPS control clearance

Border processing by SPS agencies is preferably guided by recommendations of the standard setting bodies—the Codex Alimentarius Commission, the International Plant Protection Convention, and OIE (annex 16A).

Border post SPS clearance is only part of the total SPS clearance process. The process starts with an application for import licenses and permits. For many products, sanitary or phytosanitary certificates are needed from the origin country. Obtaining the required permits, licenses, and certificates can be time consuming (filing applications in advance, waiting for approvals) and costly (fees and unofficial payments).

At the border, quarantine officers check required papers, collect statistical and other information, and check whether goods conform to the papers. The officers do partial or full physical inspections, take samples, and perform simple tests or send samples to a laboratory. Finally they decide on destruction,[8] quarantine, or treatment—and on release or rejection. Animals may be quarantined in the exit country under that country's competent authority. Fresh products and live animals usually need to be checked and released at the border post. Other quarantined goods may be sent to bonded private or government warehouses, where inspections can be carried out and from which the goods are released after all diagnostic and other requirements are met.

Controls should depend on the risks associated with goods. Even if no formal risk management is in place, controls will differ by goods, shippers, and perhaps informal payments. Import permits and health certificates need not result in faster clearance at the border.

Many SPS agencies perform their role in sequence with customs.[9] In some countries—such as the People's Republic of China—customs decides which goods need SPS clearance. After a customs declaration is filed, the applicant may be directed to the SPS agencies for further clearance before returning to customs. In contrast, in Cambodia a general inspection agency—Camcontrol—has, among its other duties, that of checking at the border for product identity and food safety in all incoming shipments. That results in more duplication of data and paperwork than is found in the People's Republic of China.

Rentseeking. Rentseeking can affect SPS agencies in many ways. Public funding for inspection services and laboratories is often very low, and the focus is on regulatory inspections rather than food safety risks. Unofficial policies encourage agencies to conduct more inspections and laboratory tests than are needed. Inspections are biased toward selecting formal enterprises, from which a fee can be collected—not toward selecting high risk producers. Some countries require health certificates for all exports (even if the importing countries do not require such certificates) and collect samples to test food safety. Some countries also test imports extensively. Finally, even if these problems are absent and administrative processing is efficient, inspectors may prefer to deal with goods owners or their agents in person to allow for the collection of informal payments. In sum, existing incentives in many countries tend to drive inspectors away from risk based inspection and toward practices that increase transaction costs—both contrary to the SPS and TBT principles of the WTO.

Market access role. The capacities of SPS agencies play an important role in gaining and maintaining market access. Increasingly, to gain market access, countries must be able to provide basic data on their plant pest, animal disease, and—less frequently—food safety situations. Some developing countries spend more time and effort assuring market access and complying with importing countries' requirements than on import control.

Transit. Customs transit systems are subject to SPS controls, provided there is a reason to believe that allowing the transit shipment presents a risk.

For processed food there is generally no ground for assuming a risk. But the situation differs if plants, plant materials, animals, and animal products are involved (see annex 16A). If any pests are present in transited goods and could enter the country, shipments are subject to normal phytosanitary controls. Traders can avoid these controls by using sealed trucks or containers, provided the seals are not broken (for transloading or otherwise). A more stringent regime applies to animal diseases: any suspicion that diseased animals are present, even in a sealed truck or container, can block entry.

Common weaknesses in SPS control procedures. SPS control measures in most developing countries are far from satisfactory.[10] They do not adequately protect against trade related health hazards, do not sufficiently ensure market access, and are too costly for traders. Health protection weaknesses often include:

- The inability to identify (diagnose) health hazards as a result of weak staff qualifications at both inspectorates and border posts, insufficient diagnostic and testing capacities to verify animal health and product safety, and an insufficient operating budget.
- Lack of systematic data gathering and an absence of risk profiles.
- Little guidance for inspectors about priority health hazards.
- The absence of inspection manuals.
- A bias in interventions toward revenue generation from fees and informal payments.

Market access weaknesses often include:

- Inadequate data collecting and processing, leading to an inability to provide needed information to trading partners for obtaining market access.
- Inadequate expertise to challenge adverse decisions by importing countries.
- The nonrecognition of a country's competent authority by its trading partners—because of weaknesses in its institutional framework, in its control capacities, or in its technical expertise.

Costs of doing business often include:

- Separate declarations for SPS control and customs.
- Duplication of tasks and data gathering at the border by customs, quarantine agencies, and border police (immigration).
- Poor coordination of border processes and time consuming sequential processes.
- Inadequate information technology, making electronic lodging impossible.
- Inefficient and redundant bureaucratic procedures.
- Higher inspection rates than necessary because of poor risk management.
- Unnecessary duplicative administrative requirements for private and public safety (quality) assurance schemes and transport documentation.
- Rentseeking and corruption.
- Unnecessary testing, inspection, and disinfestation treatment costs.

Priorities in developing countries. Most developing countries seem to give the highest priority to promoting market access by meeting importing countries' requirements. Health protection also receives attention, yet health controls are often ineffective and driven partly by rentseeking (fees and informal payments). Developing countries generally give much less attention to the cost of doing business, at least at the agencies responsible for conducting controls. The incentive structure for developing country quarantine agencies, for example, often prompts many inspections, tests, certifications, and permits—with little emphasis on risk management and reducing inspection rates. International support from donors and international organizations (such as FAO and OIE) usually targets SPS control capacities for improving market access and health protection, while it gives less attention to the transaction costs borne by the private sector.

Performance measurement. Measuring the performance of SPS agencies is very difficult. No performance indicators exist. Virtually no efforts are made to assess performance, other than through specialists' subjective judgments. Time release studies (chapter 11) could capture some of the time spent on SPS controls at the border—but such data are not used in SPS services. One reason for not using time release study data is the preoccupation with market access and health protection. Another may be that the cost of SPS procedures is generally higher away from the border than at the border. Moreover, the individual contribution of each SPS service (plant health, animal health, and food safety) in time release studies may be too small to be measured precisely, so the results may be less useful for reforming policy.

Institutional issues for coordinated border management

In a coordinated border management approach it is necessary to address the relations among SPS agencies, other border agencies, and private stakeholders.

SPS agencies and customs agencies. It may be cost effective for customs agencies to perform certain general tasks for SPS agencies—tasks such as checking conformity between goods and documents, deciding whether goods should be checked by quarantine officers on referral, and checking expiration dates on food labels. Indeed, some countries formally delegate these powers to customs.

Yet SPS agencies generally see such cooperation with customs as a mixed blessing, if not as a direct threat. Regularly heard from SPS agencies are the complaints that customs is interested only in taxation, not in health protection; that customs officials have no expertise in SPS issues; and that delegating SPS tasks to customs results (allegedly) in the release of goods that need SPS checking.

Accordingly, SPS agencies frequently expend much political energy protecting their existing mandates and administrative competence. (It is also fair to say that many customs agencies are not eager to take on additional tasks.) Similar arguments arose in turf struggles between customs and immigration authorities. But the successful delegation models used for many years by customs and immigration in Australia—and more recently in the United States—suggest that customs can perform routine tasks, such as immigration processing, without lowering standards.

With effective information technology, and with a dataset based on harmonized system codes, it should be possible for customs to ensure that goods subject to SPS inspection are sent to the proper quarantine officials. However, the experience of one middle income country with extensive international trade shows that, despite many years of talks, customs and SPS agencies have not been able to agree on information sharing procedures for control and risk management. That is why many SPS agencies still collect their own information—failing to make

progress in e-commerce and to establish a national single window (chapter 8).

To be sure, more product and process information may be required for SPS control than for customs control. For SPS there may be more product details, as well as seasonality information, so a shared database using harmonized system codes might require additions beyond those codes. The problem is not insurmountable with effectively deployed information technology, developed in cooperation with all users. At present SPS agencies typically are behind in their adoption of such technology.

The typical SPS agency is also behind in using risk management techniques effectively. One reason why cooperation between customs and SPS agencies may be difficult is that risk assessment generally seems more complex for SPS than for customs. Causes of complexity include:

- The range of products, hazards, and ecological conditions related to SPS.
- The cost of collecting data on health hazards.
- The varying SPS control requirements imposed by importing and exporting countries.

Because of this technical complexity and the gap in capacities, involving SPS agencies actively in collaborative border management will require prolonged capacity building as a precondition. At present there is apparently little understanding of the differences between customs agencies and SPS agencies in risk parameters, risk assessment, and risk management. This lack of understanding can lead to the mistaken belief that the goal is to establish a single integrated risk management system for both agencies. In fact, the most that is possible is some coordination in selecting shipments for physical inspections.

What is needed is not one risk management system but, instead, one comprehensive risk management framework. Such a framework should use proven disciplines to meet the risks faced by both customs and SPS agencies.

Coordination among SPS agencies. Overlapping jurisdictions and rivalry among SPS agencies are common—especially between agencies in agriculture ministries and public health ministries. Overlapping responsibilities may be functional (animal product safety and human health), or they may arise from agency responsibilities for different parts of the overall supply chain (agricultural inputs, production, primary processing, transport, and wholesale and retail markets). Some countries have tried to solve coordination problems by merging the various services into a single agency.

After recent changes, the United States has only one border inspection agency (the Department of Homeland Security). China has one organization responsible for inspection and market access policies (the General Administration of Quality Supervision, Inspection and Quarantine). And other countries have only a single agency for food safety.[11] No solution is perfect—a single agency may struggle to acquire the necessary competence in policymaking, data collection, standard setting, risk management, and control over domestic production and markets.

Having a single quarantine agency on the border gives some advantages in efficiency and in cooperation with customs and other border agencies. But these advantages may be reduced by additional coordination issues and by strife among SPS agencies behind the border. The collaborative border management model, discussed in chapter 2, offers some hope of overcoming such obstacles without a disruptive process of organizational amalgamation (see also chapter 12).

SPS agencies and the private sector. A particular challenge in modernizing border clearance for agricultural and food products—especially in tier 1, but increasingly in tier 2—is the extensive use of private sector certification and traceability of goods through the supply chain. Such certification and traceability requires much administrative work, so it would be best for the private sector if the required information were integrated in formats that could also be used for SPS, customs, and other agencies. The same information could then be used for other private sector administrative requirements—for example, in transport and logistics service providers and in financial institutions. Several countries are making efforts to develop such public-private data models to increase competitiveness and promote trade.

The international framework and support for modernization

Customs modernization is strategically important for SPS agencies. As discussed in chapter 11, many

international organizations (such as the World Customs Organization) have produced strategy and guidance documents for customs modernization. In addition, some donor agencies have helped to modernize customs in regional cooperation and economic integration projects.

Within SPS agencies, however, there is little awareness of these international efforts at customs modernization. Nor is there any similar international drive to modernize SPS agencies. Although the United Nations Centre for Trade Facilitation and Electronic Business has recommendations for national single windows that cover all agencies with border functions, no international organization seems to pursue interagency border cooperation. The World Customs Organization deals only with customs agencies and has no projects with other border agencies (though its good practice recommendations call for cooperation among such agencies).

The international framework for SPS comprises the Codex Alimentarius Commission, the International Plant Protection Convention, and OIE. This framework differs from the international customs framework, despite some similarities. The most important role of the international SPS framework is to set standards, as mandated by the WTO in its SPS Agreement. That mandate has led to efforts at increasing the number of international science based standards. The constituencies of the three standard setting organizations within member states—food safety authorities for the Codex Alimentarius Commission, national plant protection organizations for the International Plant Protection Convention, and veterinary organizations for OIE—are all mainly technical in their expertise and mandate.

While OIE is a membership organization similar to the World Customs Organization, the Codex Alimentarius Commission is formally a cooperative arrangement between the World Health Organization and the FAO, located in the FAO. The International Plant Protection Convention is a convention deposited with and facilitated by the FAO. All three have limited resources. Work on good practices and training for food safety, plant health, and animal health depends mainly on the FAO and donor funding and, to a lesser extent, on the World Health Organization and OIE.

At international organizations, work on good practices for SPS system development focuses mainly on international standards and on compliance with the SPS principles of the WTO, sector by sector (for food safety, for plant health, and for animal health). Both the FAO and OIE have noted the importance of coordination between SPS agencies and customs. But no work on good practice has resulted, and the nod to coordination has not been reflected in the border management modernization agenda. Although the SPS principles of the WTO require that measures be science based and proportional to the risks they address, these principles do not explicitly formulate a goal of promoting trade by reducing transaction costs as much as possible. Generally the work that is being done on good practices for SPS control does not contribute much toward coordinated border management in goods clearance. There is no comprehensive body of recommendations on how to harmonize the work of SPS agencies with that of customs—whether in product codes, in information technology and database systems, in electronic commerce, or in national single windows.

Individual OECD countries are leading in the development of new systems. New Zealand has developed E-cert, allowing information exchange on SPS certification through web based XML data files that can be used in preclearance.[12] And the Netherlands, adapting E-cert principles, has developed CLIENT for preparing and issuing all certificates and planning any related inspections. As an e-commerce system through which exporters can do all applications and lodging online, CLIENT could considerably reduce steps and requirements.

Exporters of some goods destined to the Netherlands, and competent authorities in exporting countries, can use the CLIENT system.[13] Yet most developing countries will be far from able to adopt such systems until they receive extensive support. No international agencies are actively supporting this kind of border modernization improvement.

Conclusions and recommendations

Customs and SPS agencies differ in many ways. Much smaller than customs, SPS agencies are behind in modernization, particularly for information technology and risk management. Costs related to SPS control generally are higher behind the border than at the border. And SPS agencies—unlike customs—have important roles in gaining and maintaining market access by providing information to importing countries and meeting their requirements. Although no broad assessments are available, it is fair to say that in several developing countries more resources seem to go into this role than into controlling imports.

There are no system performance measurement tools for SPS agencies (such as time release studies for customs). Rentseeking often biases the development and implementation of SPS systems, jeopardizing compliance with the SPS principles of the WTO.

In most developing countries customs and SPS agencies cooperate very little. Duties are separately performed and guided by agency mandates. Frequently the relationship is adversarial. Although the World Customs Organization and other international organizations have established recommendations for a coordinated customs approach, until recently they have had virtually no capacity building projects for achieving cooperation between customs and SPS agencies.

The work of international organizations—the FAO and, to a lesser extent, the World Health Organization and OIE—on good practice for SPS systems development is based on the principles and recommendations of the WTO's framework for SPS and for TBT. While emphasizing cooperation with customs, the framework has no recommendations for achieving it.

There is little available empirical information on practical issues affecting coordination between SPS and customs agencies in using product code systems, or in mandating and delegating SPS control tasks to customs. Work is needed to bring a cooperative border management perspective to good practice recommendations for SPS systems development and implementation. Special attention should be given to:

- Reducing SPS control transaction costs.
- Exploring ways to reduce the duplication of SPS control tasks—through the delegation of administrative tasks and simple SPS control tasks to customs—and using the results to create good practice recommendations.

Sanitary and phytosanitary measures and border management

- Harmonizing product codes for customs and SPS control, to enable information exchange and—where appropriate—the delegation of tasks.
- Improving the exchange of information between SPS agencies in exporting and importing countries.
- Evaluating future directions in the development of information technology for SPS control—to improve risk management and (eventually) to link SPS agency systems with those of customs, the private sector, and other border management stakeholders.
- Developing performance measurement for SPS agencies.
- Developing a vision for SPS systems development in relation to goods clearance systems that reflects customs modernization, e-customs systems, national single windows, and a collaborative border management approach.

Annex 16A
Guidelines on the entry of imported food products and agricultural goods

This annex summarizes the guidance on border management that is provided by SPS standard setting bodies—the Codex Alimentarius Commission, the International Plant Protection Convention, and OIE.

Food products

Legislation should establish a country's competent authority over the food import control system and should clearly define the procedures necessary to verify that imported foods conform to the importing country's food safety requirements. Procedures at the border may include:

- Checking documentation.
- Verifying product identity against documents.
- Examining food and packaging.
- Collecting and testing samples.
- Rejecting or destroying shipments that do not comply with requirements.

The nature and frequency of inspecting, sampling, and testing imported foods should be based on the risk to human health the product presents. Risk is determined using available scientific information in relation to the consumption of the food. Risk may depend on the product, the country or region of origin, the exporter's or the exporting country's history of compliance (or noncompliance), and other relevant information. Thus, consignments of high risk foods (for example, meat and fish products) may have to undergo 100 percent inspection until a defined number of consecutive consignments meet requirements, establishing a compliance history. Sampling frequency may be higher for consignments for products, exporters, or importers with no, or poor, compliance history.

Sampling should be based on Codex Alimentarius Commission sampling plans or internationally accepted or scientifically based sampling plans. Analytical tests should be conducted using validated analytical methods.

Alternatively, the importing country can use memorandums of understanding, mutual recognition agreements, or certification arrangements with competent authorities of exporting countries to recognize controls put in place by the exporting country to facilitate the entry of goods. Thus, the importing country may decide to release without inspection foods that are accompanied by an official certification. These agreements are useful for importing countries that have limited capacities for diagnostic testing or tracking systems. Authorities may also decide to reduce routine inspections if the importers have controls over suppliers and means to verify their compliance.

For goods being re-exported, the destination country's requirements should be specified in the accompanying certificate of re-exportation, and inspections should be made accordingly.

The importing country's competent authority should set forth the criteria to determine whether consignments are:

- Accepted.
- Allowed entry, if cleared upon inspection or verification of conformance.
- Released after reconditioning or other corrective measures, if the product was originally nonconforming.
- Rejected, but with the option of redirecting the product for uses other than human consumption.
- Rejected, but with an option to re-export or return to the country of export at the exporter's expense.
- Rejected with a destruction order.

For more on food safety controls see "Appendix: Principles and Guidelines for Imported Food Inspection Based on Risk," in Codex Alimentarius Commission (2003).

Animals and animal products

Countries and their veterinary authorities are encouraged to adopt sanitary measures to ensure the safe trade of animals and animal products.[14] A country's import requirements should take into account the health situations in exporting, importing, and transit countries and may require prior consultation. Members of the OIE should use OIE standards to harmonize their requirements. Stricter standards should be adopted based on import risk analysis.

Certification can ensure that commodities comply with OIE standards. The certificate should not allow the exclusion of pathogens or animal diseases already present in the importing country and not

16

subject to an official control program, nor should it allow the exclusion of pathogens or diseases not listed by OIE (unless justified by an import risk analysis).

The veterinary authority of the exporting country is responsible for veterinary certifications in international trade. It gives authorization to certifying veterinarians, provides instructions and training, and monitors activities to guarantee integrity and impartiality.

At border posts and quarantine stations, veterinary services should provide adequate personnel, facilities, and equipment to implement measures justified by the amount of international trade and by the epidemiological situation. Such measures include:

- Clinically examining and obtaining specimens of material for diagnostic purposes from live animals or carcasses of animals affected or suspected of being affected by an epizootic disease, and obtaining specimens of animal products suspected of contamination.
- Detecting and isolating animals affected by, or suspected of being affected by, an epizootic disease.
- Disinfecting, and possibly disinfesting, vehicles used to transport animals and animal products.

In addition, border posts and quarantine stations should have facilities for feeding and watering animals. Importing countries should make available to the public a list of border posts equipped to conduct import controls.

An importing country should accept only animals that have been examined by an official veterinarian of the exporting country, as attested by an accompanying international veterinary certificate issued by the exporting country's veterinary authority.[15] Similarly, an importing country should require an international veterinary certificate before accepting semen, embryos, ova, hatching eggs, and broodcombs of bees; meat and products of animal origin intended for human consumption; and products of animal origin intended for use in animal feeding or for pharmaceutical, surgical, agricultural, or industrial use.

For aquatic animals and products, the importing country should accept raw, uneviscerated fish of species susceptible to a disease listed by OIE and destined for introduction into an aquatic environment or for human consumption only if the fish have been examined by the competent authority of the exporting country, as attested by an accompanying international aquatic animal health certificate.

The importing country may refuse entry to:
- Animals found to be affected by, suspected of being affected by, or infected with a disease capable of being transmitted to animals in its territory.
- Aquatic animals found to be affected by a disease listed by OIE and of concern to the importing country.
- Semen, embryos, ova, hatching eggs, and broodcombs of bees, and products of animal origin intended for use in animal feeding, or for pharmaceutical, surgical, agricultural, or industrial use—if certain diseases in the exporting country, or in transit countries that preceded the importing country, are capable of being introduced by these products into its territory.
- Meat or products of animal origin intended for human consumption, if inspection shows that these might be a danger to the health of persons or animals.
- Animals, semen, embryos, ova, hatching eggs, and broodcombs of bees that are not accompanied by an international veterinary certificate, and aquatic animals that are not accompanied by an international aquatic animal health certificate.

If international veterinary certificates are not correct or do not apply to the products, the veterinary authority of the importing country may either return the products to the exporting country or, alternatively, subject them to adequate treatment to make them safe.

For animals, the importing country may choose to quarantine them for clinical observation and biological examinations to establish a diagnosis. If the diagnosis confirms the presence of an epizootic disease, the importing country may return the animals to the exporting country or slaughter them if return to the exporting country is not practical or would pose a danger.

Countries are encouraged to apply risk management in dealing with hazards arising from trade in animals and animal products, to implement objective, scientific, defensible, and transparent measures to achieve protection appropriate to the risk.

Sanitary and phytosanitary measures and border management

Transit. A transit country may require an international veterinary certificate; it may also examine the health of animals in transit unless the animals are transported in sealed vehicles[16] or containers. A transit country may refuse passage if:

- Exams show that the animal or consignment of animals in transit are affected by or infected with any epizootic diseases listed by OIE.
- The international veterinary certificate is inaccurate or unsigned.
- The transit country considers that certain diseases in the exporting country, or in a transit country preceding it in the itinerary, are capable of being transmitted to its own animals.

For more information on veterinary controls see OIE (2009a, 2009b).

Plants and plant products

The national plant protection organization[17] of a country is responsible for the phytosanitary import regulatory system, which prevents the introduction of quarantine pests[18] or minimizes the entry of regulated nonquarantine pests[19] with imported commodities and other regulated articles.[20] A regulated article is any material capable of harboring or spreading pests and deemed to require phytosanitary measures, particularly where international transportation is involved. They include plants and plant products used for planting, consumption, or processing; packaging materials, including dunnage; soil, organic fertilizers, and related materials; potentially contaminated equipment, such as used agricultural and earth moving equipment; travelers' personal effects; and international mail.[21] The national plant protection organization should make public lists of regulated articles.

Phytosanitary measures, such as prohibitions, restrictions, and other import requirements, may only be applied if necessary based on phytosanitary considerations, scientific justifications, international standards, and other relevant requirements and considerations of the International Plant Protection Convention. Import prohibitions apply only to quarantine pests, while regulated nonquarantine pests are subject to established pest tolerance levels.

Border measures may include documentation checks, consignment integrity checks, verification of treatment during shipment, and phytosanitary inspection, testing, and treatment. Phytosanitary inspection of entire consignments is often not practical and should be based on sampling.

Depending on the inspection results, consignments may be detained in a postentry quarantine station for inspection, testing, or treatment—or its distribution or use may be restricted. Tests following internationally agreed protocols may be required to identify or confirm a visually detected pest, to check for infestations not detectable by inspection (if part of a requirement), and to check for latent infections.

The primary document in the international trade of plant and plant products is the phytosanitary certificate attesting that consignments of plants, plant products, or other regulated articles have been inspected or tested by the exporting country's national plant protection organization and have been found compliant with specified phytosanitary import requirements of importing countries. Importing countries should require phytosanitary certificates only for regulated articles such as, but not limited to, plants, bulbs and tubers, seeds for propagation; fruits and vegetables; cut flowers and branches; grain; and growing medium. Phytosanitary certificates should not be required for processed plant products that have no potential for introducing regulated pests, or for other articles that do not require phytosanitary measures. However, phytosanitary certificates may also be required for:

- Plant products that have been processed but have a potential for introducing regulated pests (for example, wood and cotton).
- Regulated articles for which phytosanitary measures are technically justified (for example, empty containers, vehicles, and organisms).

In cases of noncompliance, such as the detection of a listed quarantine pest or a regulated nonquarantine pest in a consignment of plants for planting, measures such as detention, treatment, reshipment, or destruction may be taken. Administrative noncompliance, such as erroneous or incomplete phytosanitary certificates, may be resolved with the exporting country's national plant protection organization.

Transit. For goods in transit, consignments that are transported and remain in sealed containers throughout the passage do not present a phytosanitary risk and will not require phytosanitary measures. Possibilities

16

of risk occur when consignments are transported in open containers, are held for a period of storage, or are split up, combined, or repackaged, or if the means of transport changes (for example, from ship to railway). In such cases phytosanitary measures may be needed.

For more information on phytosanitary controls see FAO (1997, 2001, 2004, 2005b, 2006, 2009).

Notes

1. The Office International des Epizooties was established in 1924. The International Plant Protection Convention was established in 1952—with roots in a five country agreement of 1881 and in the Convention for the Protection of Plants of 1929—and its secretariat is under the Food and Agriculture Organization of the United Nations.

2. In 1963 the FAO and the World Health Assembly established the Codex Alimentarius Commission. It has its roots in the late 19th century Austro-Hungarian Empire.

3. In general, a "competent authority" is an office legally charged to supervise and enforce safety measures.

4. The precautionary principle, in article 5.7 of the SPS Agreement (WTO 1994a), supports taking protective measures even without complete scientific evidence of risk.

5. The use of inspection teams is established practice at the European Commission (Directorate General for Health and Consumer Affairs) and in OECD countries. The practice is now also followed by the People's Republic of China.

6. Producers for export, however, may have to follow protective measures, such as nettings for preventing insects in fruit and vegetable production.

7. There are, however, cases where private enterprises have been leading and supporting the public sector to meet conditions required for obtaining market access. This can go as far as helping a government formulate legislation based on what works in an exporting country.

8. In some countries quarantine staff, having no authority to seize goods, must call on customs or border police if goods need to be seized and destroyed.

9. The 2004 Cross Border Transit Agreement of the Greater Mekong Subregion recommends simultaneous inspection and joint processing by customs and other agencies, but the operational implications have never been fully worked out on the ground.

10. An illustration can be found in an assessment for Lao People's Democratic Republic (World Bank 2009).

11. See World Bank (2007), pp. 36–39, for some examples.

12. E-cert of New Zealand is compatible with The United Nations Centre for Trade Facilitation and Electronic Business. See "E-Cert—Value for the Regulator (Prepared by New Zealand)," Second FAO and WHO Global Forum of Food Safety Regulators (Bangkok, Thailand, 12–14 October 2004) Conference Room Document 38, at http://www.fao.org/docrep/meeting/008/ae150e/ae150e00.htm.

13. Other countries are interested in participating in the New Zealand and Netherlands initiatives, and some are making efforts to adopt the systems.

14. This information generally applies to aquatic animals as well.

15. For aquatic animals the required document is an international aquatic animal health certificate.

16. *Sealed* means that an attached seal attests to the vehicles having undergone actions such as cleaning, disinfection, and inspection.

17. Each country that ratifies the International Plant Protection Convention is required to have a national plant protection organization, which is the competent authority.

18. A quarantine pest is a pest of potential economic importance to the area it endangers and not yet present there—or present there, but not widely distributed there and being officially controlled.

19. A regulated nonquarantine pest's presence in plants for planting affects the intended use of those plants with an economically unacceptable impact. The pest is therefore regulated

within the territory of the importing contracting party.

20. A regulated article is any plant, plant product, storage place, packaging, conveyance, container, or soil—or any other organism, object, or material capable of harboring or spreading pests—deemed to require phytosanitary measures, particularly where international transportation is involved.

21. Special provisions govern the import of pests, biological control agents, and other regulated articles for scientific research and education (FAO 2005a).

References

Codex Alimentarius Commission. 2003. "Guidelines for Food Import Control Systems." Document CAC/GL 47-2003, Codex Alimentarius Commission, Rome.

FAO (Food and Agriculture Organization of the United Nations). 1997. "International Standards for Phytosanitary Measures: Export Certification System." Publication 7, International Plant Protection Convention, FAO, Rome.

———. 2001. "International Standards for Phytosanitary Measures: Guidelines for Phytosanitary Certificates." Publication 12, International Plant Protection Convention, FAO, Rome.

———. 2004. "International Standards for Phytosanitary Measures: Guidelines for a Phytosanitary Import Regulatory System." Publication 20, International Plant Protection Convention, FAO, Rome.

———. 2005a. "International Standards for Phytosanitary Measures: Guidelines for the Export, Shipment, Import and Release of Biological Control Agents and Other Beneficial Organisms." Publication 3, International Plant Protection Convention, FAO, Rome.

———. 2005b. "International Standards for Phytosanitary Measures: Guidelines for Inspection." Publication 23, International Plant Protection Convention, FAO, Rome.

———. 2006. "International Standards for Phytosanitary Measures: Consignments in Transit." Publication 25, International Plant Protection Convention, FAO, Rome.

———. 2009. *International Standards for Phytosanitary Measures: Glossary of Phytosanitary Terms.* Publication 5, International Plant Protection Convention, FAO, Rome.

OIE (Office International des Epizooties). 2009a. *Terrestrial Animal Health Code 2009.* OIE, Paris.

———. 2009b. *Aquatic Animal Health Code 2009.* OIE, Paris.

Van Der Meer, K., and L. Ignacio. 2007. "Standards and Supply-Chain Coordination—Impact on Small-Scale Producers." In *FAO Commodities and Trade Proceedings 2: Governance, Coordination and Distribution Along Commodity Value Chains,* Rome, 4–5 April 2006. Rome: FAO Trade and Markets Division. 85–94.

World Bank. 2007. "Food Safety and Agricultural Health Management in CIS Countries: Completing the Transition." Report 40069-RU, The World Bank, Washington, DC.

———. 2009. "Lao People's Democratic Republic – Sanitary and Phytosanitary Measures: Enhancing Trade, Food Safety and Agricultural Health." Report No. 48802, Rural Development, Natural Resources and Environment Department, East Asia and Pacific Region, The World Bank, Washington DC.

WTO (World Trade Organization). 1994a. "Agreement on the Application of Sanitary and Phytosanitary Measures." WTO, Geneva. Available online at http://www.wto.org/english/docs_e/legal_e/15-sps.pdf.

———. 1994b. "Agreement on Technical Barriers to Trade." WTO, Geneva. Available online at http://www.wto.org/english/docs_e/legal_e/17-tbt.pdf.

17 Transit regimes

Jean-François Arvis

This chapter looks at transit regimes: specifically, the case of goods moving into a customs territory but not cleared for consumption, and with no payment or delayed payment of import duties, domestic consumption taxes, or other charges normally due on imports. In such cases transit regimes are intended to protect the revenues of the country through which goods are moving (the transit country) to avoid their leakage into its domestic market.

Transit regimes cover the movement of goods on land trade corridors. Landlocked countries depend totally on transit corridors passing through their neighbors. Yet transit often takes place between coastal countries—in fact, the most active transit corridors are between such countries. Admittedly, transit can also take place when goods entering a country pass through part of the same country before being cleared inland.

Transit procedures should be simple to avoid generating excessive delays and costs. Poorly designed and implemented transit regimes are a major obstacle to trade. According to many international organizations and transport facilitation forums, dysfunctional transit procedures are a major factor in higher trade costs for landlocked developing countries. Various global and regional initiatives have sought to improve transit regimes. Generally, developing countries are increasingly doing this in the context of regional trade agreements.

The regional transit regime is key to implementing regional trade, customs, and transport agreements. The subject raises complex questions, especially given the entanglement of domestic and regional policies in areas including transportation, services, and trade. A full analysis of regional transit regimes—or of the economics of transit supply chains and the political economy of corridors serving landlocked countries—would expand the policy focus far beyond the scope of customs reforms and border management. The World Bank has published several updates providing comprehensive coverage (Arvis and others 2007; World Bank 2008; Arvis, Mustra, and others 2010; Arvis, Marteau, and Raballand 2010; Arvis 2010; World Bank 2010).

The following overview of transit regimes and their implementation at the national and regional levels overhauls the chapter by the same author in the *Customs Modernization Handbook* published by the World Bank (De Wulf and Sokol 2005). More extensive information, including analysis of transit systems and regimes, is available in a working paper to which the author contributed (Arvis 2010).

The chapter develops its main messages (box 17.1) in five sections, of which the first introduces the concepts, and the second the basic principles of a transit

- Transit regimes are based on three universal components: bonds, manifests, and the process for authorizing transit operations. Inefficiency can be traced to the deviant implementation of one or more of these principles—due to a lack of trust, due to weak compliance, or to accommodate local interests.
- Chaining transit regimes across borders into door to door carnet systems—such as the TIR or common transit in Europe—has obvious advantages. Although regional agreement posits the existence of carnet systems, no working examples exist other than the two mentioned.
- A weak case can be made for localized carnet systems (as opposed to TIR implementation)—and a strong case for localized common transit where there is sufficient regional integration.
- Policymakers need a comprehensive approach to transit related policies beyond the customs transit regime: associated transport policies, infrastructure policies, and corridor cooperation policies.
- A transit regime does not need a heavy information and communications technology (ICT) infrastructure, nor one that is distinct from the pre-existing customs ICT module. Transit requires the tracing of manifests and carnets, for which real time technologies—such as e-seals using the global positioning system (GPS)—are neither essential nor always desirable.

Note: TIR, as it is now known, stood initially for Transports Internationaux Routiers (International Road Transport). The TIR Convention is the only extant global transit regime (detailed later in this chapter).

regime and its procedures. The third looks at the contribution of legal treaties, the fourth at regional systems (using the cases of the only two working examples, TIR and common transit in Europe). The fifth provides an overview of a central topic: implementation. The sixth and seventh cover facilitation issues and enabling measures.

Types of transit

In discussions of transit regimes, transit most often—but not always—refers to road and rail transportation between landlocked and nonlandlocked countries. In some cases transit is from a country of origin to a destination country, and borders are crossed only once. In other cases a transit shipment crosses several borders—for example, a shipment from the Netherlands to Russia crosses Germany and Poland.[1]

It is useful to distinguish between international and national transit. International transit procedures are used when national borders are crossed. National transit is when goods are transferred within national borders, from the point of first entry into a country to another location in the same country where customs procedures are conducted (dry ports are an example). Both types of transit can be combined—a typical situation in many landlocked developing countries where imported goods arrive at national borders from other transit countries and then are most often shipped under national transit to main economic centers. In both cases the basic customs mechanisms are similar. However, implementation is easier for national transit.

A third category is door to door transit, where only one procedure covers international and national transit for all the countries on a trade corridor. This procedure dispenses with the usual renewal of international or national transit at each border. Developed initially with the TIR (see box 17.1, note 1; detailed below), door to door transit will be referred to in this chapter as a *carnet* system (after the TIR instrument).

Transit systems and transit regimes

Transit systems here mean the infrastructure, legal framework, institutions, and procedures serving trade corridors (seen as a whole). Every transit system must have six components:

- The political commitment to allow transit trade—formalized in bilateral, regional, or multilateral treaties.
- The physical infrastructure for transit, including border checkpoint facilities.
- Public and private institutions and people with certain capacities and competences related to the movement of goods along a trade corridor. These institutions and people comprise:
  - Public agencies in the transit country supervising the flow—mainly customs and other agencies involved in controlling international trade and transportation.

- Transportation services, including the trucking industry, customs brokers, and freight forwarders.
- Trust building mechanisms, partnerships, and cooperative initiatives that bring together the many participants in the transit and corridor operations.
- An enabling environment for movements of vehicles and people—including vehicle regulations, the provision of trade in freight services across countries, allocation visas for drivers, mutual insurance recognition, a financial sector integrated across countries, and law enforcement.
- The provisions and procedures applicable to shipments in transit and to the carriers or traders of the goods.

The sixth and last component listed, transit provisions and procedures, is the subject of this chapter. Hereafter it will be referred to as the *transit regime*—a narrower concept than the transit system.

All six transit system components are essential. Corridor infrastructure and agreements to move vehicles and goods across borders are preconditions for trade. But the heart of the transit system is the transit regime, which governs and makes possible the movement of goods from their origin (often a seaport) to their destination (such as a clearance center in the destination country). The efficiency of the transit supply chain depends on the design of the transit regime and, above all, on its implementation.

The basics of customs transit

A transit regime is, in essence, a public private partnership by which operators are authorized for transit when they meet a set of criteria and provide financial guarantees. In exchange, customs allows unimpeded transit for trucks or trains. The key requirements for a well functioning transit system, developed over centuries, are universal and include:
- Customs should make sure the cargo is secure by sealing appropriately designed vehicles (closed trailers or containers).
- The principal of the transit operation—the owner of the goods, or, more often, his agent (a freight forwarder or trucker)—should deposit a guarantee (or a bond) covering the value of taxes and duties that would be due in the transit country. The guarantee may depend on the fiscal risk of

the operation: for instance, some products (such as alcohol) are considered high risk. The guarantee may be set according to the transit operator, and in some cases (such as railways) it may be waived.
- The regulation of transit operators is needed from both a customs and transport perspective, since the transit operator provides a service that includes both brokerage and transport.
- Customs should properly manage the information on goods in transit and, specifically, should reconcile information on entries into and exits from the customs territory (or during clearance in the case of national transit). This is necessary to identify violations and potential leakages.

The typical transit procedure, depicted in figure 17.1, is implemented as follows:
- At the initiation of transit (at the entry post), customs verifies the transit manifest and affixes the seals against a guarantee provided by the principal.
- At the termination of transit (at exit post or an inland clearance destination), customs checks the seals and manifest and discharges the guarantee after reconciling information on entries into and exits from the customs territory (inbound and outbound manifest information).
- When the cargo is high risk—or when not enough security is offered by the seals and the guarantee—goods may move in convoys guarded by customs officers.
- It is common and acceptable practice to impose (reasonable) specified routes and impose a maximum transit time.

Thus, associated with the physical movement of goods are two types of flows: information (manifest) flows and financial (guarantee) flows. A functional transit regime ensures that the physical movements, information flows, and financial flows are effectively synchronous. Otherwise, for instance, a delay in the information associated with transit manifests may postpone the discharge of bonds and increase costs.

Key concepts and definitions
Key to a discussion of transit regimes are the following concepts:
- Seals.
- Documentation flow.
- Principal and guarantor.
- Guarantees.

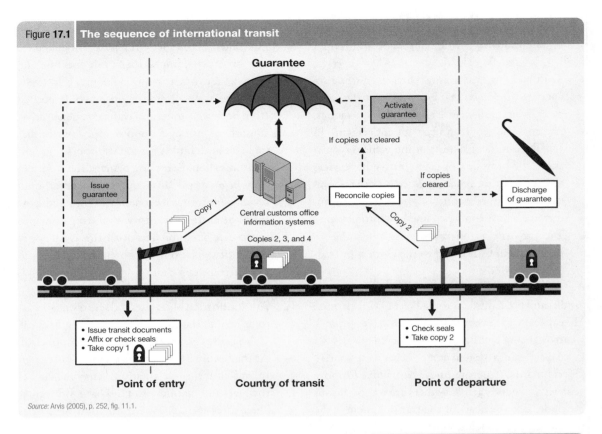

Figure 17.1 The sequence of international transit

Guarantee

Issue guarantee

Activate guarantee

If copies not cleared

If copies cleared

Copy 1

Central customs office information systems

Copies 2, 3, and 4

Reconcile copies

Copy 2

Discharge of guarantee

• Issue transit documents
• Affix or check seals
• Take copy 1

• Check seals
• Take copy 2

Point of entry   **Country of transit**   **Point of departure**

Source: Arvis (2005), p. 252, fig. 11.1.

Seals. There should be a physically secure mechanism so that goods present at the start of the transit operation will leave the transit country in the same quantities, form, and status. The easiest and best way for customs to guarantee this is by sealing the truck,[2] to ensure that goods cannot be removed from or added to the loading space of the truck without either breaking this seal or leaving visible marks on the loading space. Seals and trucks approved for use in the transit operation therefore must conform to well specified criteria that ensure their effective and secure operation (box 17.2). New transport seals are being studied; prototypes already in use include a microchip that is activated when broken, transmitting a signal that is picked up by satellite and sends information to the organization or principal of the sealed container (including information on its location). Although the prices of such automated seals are high at present, they are expected to fall in the coming years.

Documentation flow. To control the start and completion of a transit procedure, a system for monitoring the movement of goods is needed. This system could

be based on paper documentation shipped from the customs post at the exit from the transit country—after validation of the valid transit transaction—and issued by the customs post that controls the origin of the transit shipment. Increasingly, however, such documents are sent electronically. When the copies of the documents match, the transit operation is completed and the guarantee released. When they do not match, the transit procedure is not completed satisfactorily, and import duties, taxes, and other charges are increased by a stipulated fine.

Principal and guarantor. The *principal* is the owner of the goods—or more often, the owner's representative (such as the carrier). The principal initiates the transit procedure and is responsible for following that procedure—providing guarantees and the necessary documentation. To act as the principal (or agent) companies must be registered, must obtain a guarantee to cover the transit operations, must use a transit customs document and bill of lading, must present the goods and declaration at the relevant customs offices (of departure, transit, and destination), and must accept responsibility for the sealing of the transit vehicle.

A *guarantor* is a private or legal person who undertakes to pay jointly and separately with the debtor (in most cases the principal) the duties and taxes that will be due if a transit document is not discharged properly. A guarantor may be an individual, firm, or other body eligible to contract as a legal third person. Normally it is a bank or insurance company. Guarantors must be authorized by customs, which—as a rule—publishes a list of financial institutions authorized to act as guarantors.

Guarantees. The guarantees acceptable by customs are defined by the regulations of the transit country. Within the open options of financial securities, the choice is the exclusive responsibility of the principal. A guarantee can be provided as a bond by a bank or as a form of insurance by a guarantor, who can be reinsured internationally by well known and reliable insurance companies (this is the case with the TIR). Nonguarantee forms of security, such as deposits, may still be in place in some transit countries although they cannot be recommended. At times the principal is also the guarantor—a common practice for rail transport, which grants customs access to more direct recourse mechanisms.

There are two categories of transit guarantee:
- An individual guarantee covers only a single transit operation effected by the principal

concerned, covering the full amount of duties, taxes and other charges for which the goods are liable.
- A comprehensive guarantee covers several transit operations up to a given reference amount, set to equal the total amount of duties and other charges that may be incurred for goods under the principal's transit operations over a period of at least one week.

In general the calculation of a transit guarantee is based on the highest rates of duties and other charges applicable to the goods, and it depends on the customs classification of the goods. The amount covered by the comprehensive guarantee is 100 percent of the reference amount. If the principal complies with a certain criterion of reliability, the amount of the guarantee to be specified to the guarantors may be reduced by customs. For high risk goods, customs can be allowed to calculate the guarantee at a percentage related to the risk of nonclearance.

An international transit regime such as the TIR allows for further savings. For individual guarantees many countries avoid potentially complex valuation procedures by offering vouchers based on ranges for the value of goods that transit operators carry. Although this system may cost more on average, it is much simpler at initiation. The TIR guarantees attached to the TIR carnet are effectively vouchers. (The costs of guarantees are discussed later in the chapter.)

Transit and border management: specific but limited requirements

There are essential conceptual and operational differences between transiting goods through the transit country and their final clearance in the destination country. These differences are not always recognized, including by government decisionmakers. As a result the design and implementation of transit systems in developing countries often depart from good practice.

Transit is a transport operation under customs control—not a clearance or series of clearances. To this extent, it is not conceptually different from international shipping.

The agent for a transit operation is the carrier or the freight forwarder, not the owner of the goods. The agent furnishes the guarantee and lodges the transit declaration (manifest) with customs. This agent is normally (but not always) different from the declarant making the final declaration.

The transit declaration is a simplified document, such as a road or rail manifest, and should be processed in an entirely distinct way from clearance at the border. The transit manifest and final declaration are separate documents serving separate purposes. For instance, a transit manifest might not carry information about the harmonized system (HS) classification of the cargo. Customs does not need to value the goods for each vessel precisely—it needs only to be sure that a proper guarantee is issued by the transit operator for all its goods currently in transit.

For transit traffic, the due diligence expected of customs is limited to affixing or checking the seals and verifying the guarantee instrument. As a general rule no inspection of the goods is required. Other border agencies, such as standards or quarantine, are not parties to transit operations.

The transit manifest relates to the container or trailer, which between origin and destination may be hauled by various vehicles (there may be a change of tractor—or there may be multimodal transport, such as by ship or rail and then by road).

Transit in international law

Over the years transit provisions have been codified by a number of international conventions—the most important being the agreements on transit in the General Agreement on Tariffs and Trade (GATT),[3] the World Customs Organization's amended International Convention on the Simplification and Harmonization of Customs Procedures, or Revised Kyoto Convention (WCO 1999), and the 1982 International Convention on the Harmonization of Frontier Control of Goods (sometimes called the Geneva Convention; UNECE Inland Transport Committee 1982). Key principles derived from these international instruments are summarized in box 17.3.

Box 17.3   **General provisions applicable to customs transit as codified by international conventions**

1. *General*
- Freedom of transit.
- Normally no technical standards control.
- No distinction based on flag or owner origin.
- No unnecessary delays or restriction.

2. *Customs diligences in transit*
- Limitation of inspection (especially if covered by an international transit regime—such as the TIR, described later in this chapter).
- Exemption from customs duties.
- Normally no escort of goods or itinerary.
- No duty on accidentally lost merchandise.
- No unnecessary delays or restriction.
   In addition, under an international transit regime such as the TIR:
- The transit regime applies to multimodal transport when part of the journey is by road.
- Flat rate bonds are used for transit goods.

3. *Health and safety*
- No sanitary, veterinary, or phytosanitary inspections for goods in transit if no contamination risk.

4. *Security offered by the carrier*
- Declarant to choose the form of security, within the framework afforded by legislation.
- Customs should accept a general security from declarants who regularly declare goods in transit in their territory.
- On completion of the transit operation, the security should be discharged without delay.

Source: Authors.

The actual customs transit regime varies widely across countries. In many countries and regions the basic transit arrangements, such as guarantees, are poorly implemented and greatly penalize land-locked countries. In other countries and regions national transit provisions have evolved into harmonized and regionally integrated transit regimes (the best working example is the TIR, detailed later in the chapter).

In the GATT agreements on transit, article V provides for freedom of transit. It states that: "There shall be freedom of transit through the territory of each Contracting Party, via the routes most convenient for international transit, for traffic in transit to or from the territory of other Contracting Parties." Further, it affirms that:

> . . . except in cases of failure to comply with applicable customs laws and regulations, such traffic coming from or going to the territory of other contracting parties shall not be subject to any unnecessary delays or restrictions and shall be exempt from customs duties and from all transit duties or other charges imposed in respect of transit, except charges for transportation or those commensurate with administrative expenses entailed by transit or with the cost of services.

The Kyoto Convention came into force in 1974 and was revised in 1999 (WCO 1999). While the convention is worded very broadly, its annexes define customs terms and recommend certain practices. An annex section in the amended convention (WCO 1999, Specific Annex E, chapter 1), focusing on applicable customs formalities and seals, informs the discussion of these topics later in this chapter.

The 1982 International Convention on the Harmonization of Frontier Control of Goods (or Geneva Convention) is very much about transit facilitation, recognizing the importance of transit for countries' economic development. It promotes joint customs processing through the simplification of customs procedures and the harmonization of border controls, drawing heavily on the European experience. Article 10 applies to goods in transit: "contracting parties are bound to provide simple and speedy treatment of goods in transit, especially for those traveling under an international transit procedure," and parties should also "facilitate to the utmost the transit of goods carried in containers or other loads units affording adequate security." Articles 4 to 9 promote the harmonization of control and procedures. Contracting parties are bound to:

- Provide staff and facilities that are compatible with the traffic requirement (article 5).
- Organize joint border processing to ease controls (article 7).
- Harmonize documentation (article 9).

Regionally integrated transit systems

There are obvious advantages to integrating transit across borders in a region or along a trade corridor—eventually linking countries, or even regions. No one doubts that a unified international regime is superior to a chain of national procedures.

International transit calls for the cross country harmonization of procedures and documentation. It requires an internationally accepted guarantee system and stipulates mutual control of transit operations. Authorities in each customs territory along a trade corridor are ultimately responsible for transit in that territory, and they can set their own rules. Legally, the chain is a sequence of independent transit procedures. However, large gains are possible with cross border cooperation and with the creation of framework to integrate transit across territories into a single seamless procedure. A key element of the framework is a single document that accompanies the shipment along the transit chain and allows officials to verify the shipment's compliance with the transit regime. Such a document is commonly known by its French term, *carnet.*

A major development in transit systems, the carnet allows for a single transit procedure throughout several territories. Operators gain greatly from:

- The elimination of duplicated or reinitialized procedures (documentation, seals, guarantees) at borders.
- Reductions in complexity and in administrative costs, since operators can use a single transit manifest and a single guarantee.

A carnet transit regime, or regional single procedure regime, must include the following ingredients to ensure cross border comparability and an effective chaining of transit procedures in each country:

- Harmonized documentation.
- Common standards for transit operators.
- Common enforcement standards.
- A regionally integrated system to ensure interoperability in bonds across countries and consistency in manifest reconciliation (to discharge or call guarantees consistently, customs in country B should be able to call a bond issued by a guarantor in country A).

The most difficult element in a carnet transit regime is regional integration. The only fully developed regional systems to date are the TIR and the European common transit system. Each represents the most logical solution to the bond and manifest problem, but at a different degree of regional integration. The many attempts to copy the TIR and the common transit system in developing regions have not succeeded (Arvis, Marteau, and Raballand 2010; Arvis 2010).

The TIR convention, under the United Nations Economic Commission for Europe (UNECE), is the only global transit system. Created in the 1940s in Europe, it was instrumental in boosting trade according to the objectives of the Marshall Plan. The TIR is the main instrument for trade from Europe to distant trading destinations in Eastern Europe, Central Asia, Northern Africa, and the Middle East.

The common transit system streamlined some features of the TIR in the 1980s, taking advantage of greater economic and financial integration within European Union and European Free Trade Association countries. For a group of countries, the common transit system is now conceptually very similar to the national transit system.

The TIR

The international transit regime initially known in French as Transports Internationaux Routiers (International Road Transport) is now referred to in documentation and legal texts only as TIR. The Customs Convention on the International Transport of Goods under Cover of TIR Carnets, or TIR Convention (UNECE 2002, section 2, pp. 31–231)—adopted in 1960 and revised in 1975—is not only one of the most successful international transport conventions but also the only existing global transit regime (though it is still Eurocentric). So far the TIR

Convention has 68 parties, primarily in Europe, the Middle East, North Africa, and Central Asia. It is not yet implemented in the Americas or East Asia regions, where TIR membership is spotty. There are parties to the convention in Sub-Saharan Africa.

Widely seen as the best practice for international transit regimes, the TIR system is a model for any future regional transit frameworks. Many developing countries want either to join the TIR system or to design regional equivalents replicating its essential factors. These factors—more fully explained in the UN Economic Commission for Europe's TIR manual (UNECE 2010) and in the International Road Transport Union (IRU) website[4]—include five main pillars:

- *Secure vehicles.* The goods are to be transported in containers, or compartments of road vehicles, constructed so as not to allow access to the interior or the goods removal or addition of goods during the transit procedure—ensuring that any tampering will be clearly visible.
- *International guarantee valid throughout the journey.* Wherever the transport operator cannot (or does not wish to) pay the customs duties and taxes due, the international guarantee system ensures that the amounts at risk are covered by the national guarantee system of the operator.
- *National associations of transport operators.* National associations control their members' access to the TIR regime, issue the appropriate documents, and manage the national guarantee system.
- *TIR carnets.* The standard international customs documents accepted and recognized by all signatories of the TIR Convention.
- *International and mutual recognition of customs control measures.* The transit and destination countries accept control measures taken in the country of origin.

In essence, TIR operations can be carried out in participating countries by a truck operator who is a member of a national association, with the network of national associations acting as guarantor. Both the national associations and the IRU, which issues the carnets, are private. In this respect the TIR system embodies a win-win working partnership between public and private entities.

The TIR system has been a success, the number of carnets issued rising from 3,000 in 1952 to 3.1 million in 2007. The main reason is that all parties involved (customs agencies, other legal bodies, transport operators, and insurance companies) recognize that the system saves time and money through its efficiency and reliability. The TIR Convention is simple, it is flexible, it reduces costs, and it ensures the payment of customs duties and taxes that are due with the international transport of goods. Furthermore, the convention is constantly updated in accordance with the latest developments, mainly in fraud and smuggling. The TIR is used mostly between European Union countries and trading partners outside the union—but it is also used in transit operations in Central Asia, the Caucasus, the Maghreb, and parts of the Middle East.

In countries that use the TIR system the national guaranteeing association is recognized by the country's customs agency. The association, in most cases representing the transporters, guarantees payment within the country of any duties and taxes that may become due because of any irregularity in the course of the TIR transport operation (depicted in figure 17.2). Because the national guaranteeing association is not a financial organization, its obligations are usually backed by insurance policies provided by the market. The IRU arranges for a large international insurance company to provide a guarantee of last resort. The guarantee is for a fixed amount—it covers taxes and duties up to US$50,000.

The TIR carnet is a physical document with several copies, or *vouchers*. At each border one copy is removed and retained. The cover itself is sent back to the IRU once the TIR transport has been terminated at the destination's customs office. The carnet is printed by the IRU and distributed by national associations. Its price depends on the national association and the number of sheets or vouchers, based on the number of borders to be crossed.

The IRU plays several essential roles in the TIR system:

- It certifies national associations and audits their capacity to regulate the entry of trucking companies.
- It sells carnets to national associations to cover the cost and management of the carnets, as well as the cost of reinsurance between national associations.
- It functions as a clearing house for guarantees and information—essentially reconciling

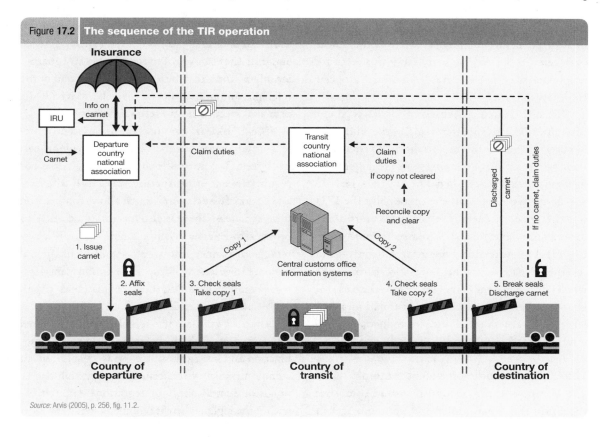

Figure **17.2** **The sequence of the TIR operation**

Source: Arvis (2005), p. 256, fig. 11.2.

manifest information and checking the validity of customs claims to allow transfers. According to the IRU only 3 percent of customs claims are fraudulent, while the rest are spurious claims resulting from customs' loss of carnet information.

To qualify for TIR, each trucking firm (or other transporter) must make a contract with the national guarantee association that includes three obligations: to meet all requirements set out in the TIR Convention, to return each used TIR carnet after completion of the TIR transport, and to pay any amount of duties, taxes, and other charges on demand by the national guarantee association. Companies participating in the system must meet the criteria of the convention to become members of the national association, and they must make a fixed one-time payment of about US$8,000. Again, the TIR system is applicable only to containers or road vehicles with load compartments to which there is no interior access after a customs seal has secured it.

At present the TIR carnet is still a paper document—a serious handicap. However, steps are being taken to make it electronic. The IRU has developed an Internet based application allowing TIR carnet holders to send their carnet information electronically to the relevant border control agencies in advance, before the holders arrive at the offices of departure or entry. In early 2009 this software was being tried out in several Central European countries.

The TIR system is criticized for its apparent centralization, a feature that explains the reluctance of developing countries to join the TIR system and their preference for developing purely regional alternatives (such as the so-called *TIR lite*). For the IRU the carnet system is a private monopoly. The IRU sets the price for entry into the system—the cost for operators and for national associations to satisfy TIR professional and financial standards—and sets the price for each transit operation through the wholesale price of the carnet (its cost to the national guarantee association, which adds a markup when setting the carnet's retail price for individual transport operators).

The European common transit system

The European common transit system comprises the European Community and common transit systems—systems that apply to goods imported into any of the 27 European Union member states and 4 European Free Trade Association countries[5] from outside that area, as well as to exports in the reverse direction. The Community transit system applies to trade between European Union members and third countries, while the common transit system (in the more restricted sense) to trade between European Union and European Free Trade Association countries under essentially the same rules. Imports are subject to duty in the destination country in accordance with the European Union's common external tariff, and to value added tax (VAT) in accordance with national tax rates. The recently implemented New Computerised Transit System (NCTS) has made the European common transit system even friendlier (chapter 15).

Guarantees can be of three kinds: a cash deposit, guarantee by a guarantor (who vouches for the trader), or a guarantee voucher (a multiple of the standard €7,000) valid for up to one year. For a regular procedure the guarantee must apply specifically to an individual trip. Authorized transporters (and other principals) may present comprehensive guarantees valid for multiple trips and longer periods, but covering only the total duty expected to be at risk in an average week—the so-called reference amount. The coverage of the comprehensive guarantee or guarantees can be less than 100 percent of the reference amount, and it can even be waived if the principal meets conditions that imply low risk.

The European common transit system represents a very streamlined evolution of a regional carnet system. It is now fully computerized, it does not require the soft infrastructure of the TIR (the IRU and national associations), and it allows competition for guarantees. There is also less intermediation by brokers. In essence it is like a national transit system, but expanded into an economically integrated region. However, the European common transit system is more demanding than the TIR, and its preconditions are less easily met.

The TIR was designed to help connect national transit systems without the preconditions of harmonization and integration. In contrast, the European common transit system requires a very high degree of customs and financial integration—and trust—within the region where it is implemented. The most binding requirement is that a bank in one country must be willing to routinely issue bonds that another country's customs can confidently call. That requires a high degree of integration—yet it may be possible within small, or very homogeneous, groups of developing countries. The same standards should be applied to authorized operators. Finally, common transit should be backed by harmonized transport policies.

Common implementation issues for transit regimes

This section discusses implementation issues in four categories:

- Issues for developing country transit regimes.
- Differences between transit facilitation and trade facilitation, with related misconceptions.
- Technological requirements (tracing, not tracking, is needed).
- Things that are unnecessary, undesirable, or unworkable.

Common implementation issues in developing countries

Even when a trade corridor crosses several countries, the basic transit procedure is implemented at the country level. In most cases—especially in low income economies and corridors serving landlocked least developed countries—there are too many deviations from core transit principles for the transit regime to support efficient supply chains.

Weak information systems and poor guarantee management are major problems. Unlike clearance, which happens in one place, transit requires an exchange of information from at least three places: that of transit initiation, that of transit termination, and that of the guarantor (to validate and discharge the bonds). The management and tracing of the manifest is not always properly and rigorously implemented and, in many cases, is not automated, causing major errors and delays (such as in the discharge of bonds). Moreover, the tracing and reconciliation of manifests can be very imperfect. According to the IRU, 95 percent of reported TIR related customs claims arise from the loss of carnet pages in customs systems—not from fraudulent behavior.

Bonds and guarantees are basic financial products—available from the local banking and, ultimately, insurance industries. Regular transit operators have a comprehensive guarantee, equivalent to a standing line of credit, which among other benefits should make the guarantee available at the time when the transit declaration is introduced. Pricing may vary, but fundamentally the cost of the guarantee is proportional to the time between its initiation and its discharge. Hence, inefficient information exchange and delayed discharge entail significant costs. The author of this chapter has even observed instances where the logistics companies had to arrange for the return of validated manifests (for example, from Chad to the Central African Republic)—an obvious conflict of interest.

On African corridors the comprehensive guarantee may cost as much as 0.25 percent or even 0.5 percent of the value of the goods for each country crossed. Voucher guarantees, adequate for occasional operators, avoid this problem, as they are not time sensitive—but typically they cost more. Contrary to a widespread opinion, the TIR carnet (a voucher by nature) is fairly cheap in such circumstances, since on average it is priced at 0.2 percent of taxes and duties (or typically 0.1 percent of value of the goods) for the basic guarantee. In any case, the cost of the guarantee is much less than transportation costs.

The initiation of transit is often lengthy, especially in ports. Along virtually all the developing country corridors visited by the author, the time to initiate transit in a port is similar to the time to clear goods for local consumption in a coastal country. In some instances it can take even longer—in 2008, for instance, it took four weeks in the Dar es Salaam corridor in Tanzania and two in the Beira corridor in Mozambique. There is no simple or single explanation for this problem, which affects both large and small transit operators. However, it seems that in many cases customs does not clearly separate clearance from transit procedures but applies the same process to both.

In reality, transit goods should not be subject to the same risk management and control as locally cleared goods. Document checking, classification, and valuation should not be sticking points for transit goods. In theory, transit can be initiated in a port using the information already available in the shipping manifest.

Lax regulation of entry may not encourage high quality and compliance. Of particular importance are the regulations applicable to transit operators (truckers and freight forwarders) and customs brokers. Better services may be encouraged by creating thresholds for the operators authorized to participate in transit operations—for instance, in company size (number of trucks, equity), professional requirements, and deposits (for brokerage operations). Although the aim often is to keep requirements low and the market open for small operators, the problem is that lax regulations encourage the development of low quality services—services that cannot cover the full transit supply chain and undermine the development of good, comprehensive services.

Lax regulation of entry generates rents. In most Commonwealth countries liberal regulations make customs brokers *de jure* or *de facto* mandatory intermediaries for customs operations, resulting in an overly intermediated supply chain. According to recent research transit cargo from Durban (South Africa) to clearance in Blantyre (Malawi) had to use eight different brokers—one on each side of every border—essentially to fill and submit the same information on the same document used by the Common Market for Eastern and Southern Africa and Southern African Development Community. In addition, different domestic banks were covering the transit in each of the four countries on the corridor.

Queueing systems for trucks, or *tours de rôle* for individual truckers, are still very prevalent in francophone Africa and in some countries in the Middle East. They bring costs up, lower service quality, and prevent the emergence of organized companies having long term commercial relationships with shippers and freight forwarders.

Conversely, transit regimes in developing countries today rarely provide incentives for compliant transit operators offering the best services with minimal fiscal risk. In Syria a guarantee ceiling limits the number of trucks in transit that a company can operate to two or three. The European common transit system relies largely on the concept of authorized economic operators, with specific incentives—such as reduction or even a waiver of the comprehensive guarantee—for their operations. On most corridors in developing countries the same principle of incentives (lower guarantee, fast track) could be applied, since much of the trade is managed by large global and regional companies delivering comprehensive logistics services.

Control mentality and convoys. As already exemplified by the problem of initiation in ports, customs agencies often are suspicious with transit. They may resort to the use of convoys during the transit trip, where the transit vehicle is escorted by policemen and a customs official. Convoys need time to be created (up to four days' wait) and are slow. Additional delays—and costs—are borne by the principal, and do not eliminate all risk of fraud and corruption. Illogically, convoys do not exempt principals from the need for guarantees. Though convoys tend to be less prevalent nowadays, they still exist, notably in Western and Eastern Africa and Western Asia. In the absence of convoys control points and checkpoints may be imposed.

Regional carnet systems have not succeeded, apart from the TIR and the European common transit system. Typically transit takes place over at least two territories: one or more transit countries plus national transit in the destination country. The value of integrating the transit systems and regime over the corridor, or even a subregion covering several corridors, has been recognized for a long time. So has been the fact that the TIR and European common transit system are the natural references for transit at the regional level. However, no other regions have succeeded so far at passing beyond harmonization to the integration of national transit.

With the enormous success of the TIR system, the same concept has been made the basis for attempts to establish bilateral and multilateral agreements among countries elsewhere: for example, in Asia, Africa, and South America. In South America, despite the soundness of the legal framework[6] and transit trade growth in the Mercado Común del Sur (Mercosur) countries, the spirit of the rules is not fully reflected in procedures. Among the Andean countries integration is significantly lower than in Mercosur, even though an Andean Manifest is in use. Eastern Asia has several agreements, such as the Greater Mekong Subregion (GMS) Agreement for

Facilitation of Cross-Border Transport of Goods and People (CBTA), which has similarities with the TIR. Implementation efforts, though steady, have not yet fully materialized.

Africa's geography and the number of its land-locked countries make it highly dependent on transit corridors. It hosts several transit agreements on paper—but implementation has faced various challenges. There are four different regions with separate problematics: Western Africa (the West African Economic and Monetary Union, or UEMOA, plus Ghana), Central Africa (the Douala Corridor), Eastern Africa (the Kenyan and Tanzanian corridors), and Southern Africa. In many ways the integration of transport and customs policies is most advanced in Africa, at least within the main regional groupings—in Western Africa, UEMOA and the Economic Community of West African States (UEMOA–ECOWAS); in Central Africa, the Economic and Monetary Community of Central Africa (CEMAC); in Eastern Africa, the East African Community (EAC) and the Common Market for Eastern and Southern Africa (COMESA); and, in Southern Africa, the Southern African Development Community (SADC). There are few restrictions on the movement of people and vehicles, and there are common vehicle insurance systems (yellow and brown cards in ECOWAS and COMESA). Furthermore, UEMOA and CEMAC are a monetary union where residents can cross borders with simple identification documents. Unfortunately, all this has not yet created an efficient transit regime.

Western Africa has chosen as its common transit system the Transit Routier Inter État (TRIE), based on the TIR. Unfortunately, the TRIE has not succeeded so far, as implementation has departed from an important principle: the regulation of entry, and incentives for quality services, have been jeopardized by using queueing systems for truckers in the application of protectionist and interventionist bilateral agreements. Also, excessive overloading has made it impossible to seal cargo. The situation is better in Southern Africa, but—as mentioned above—the traditional role of customs brokers and the fragmentation of guarantees prevent the emergence of a regional system.

Three lessons emerge from a review of implementation problems and the lack of success in creating

regional systems (Arvis, Marteau, and Raballand 2010; Arvis 2010). First, an efficient transit regime depends on the other components of the transit system, including institutional capacities, private sector capacity, and other political-economic constraints. Second, misconceptions in transit design and implementation have appeared even in conducive environments for a successful transit regime. Third, the conceptual differences between the TIR and the European common transit system are complex and are not always fully understood.

Most regional experiments such as the TRIE have been implicitly based on two principles—principles that clearly depart from the experience of the efficient regimes in Europe. One is that transit should be as open as possible to small scale operators. The other is that regional systems should be adapted to meet those operators' needs. The resulting approach waters down key design principles and implementation mechanisms (such as guarantees and their management), as is known from history and from the European experience.

The main conclusion is that there is no strong business case for regional TIR lite. Instead, common transit may be implemented within a subregion in the very few cases where regional integration—in transport and financial services, trade, and customs—makes it possible. Between regions, or within regions with limited integration, TIR should be seriously considered as a global transit regime.

Transit facilitation and trade facilitation: differences and misconceptions

Transit trade usually is small compared with imports and exports, and usually it requires less oversight, capacity building, and investments. Transit facilitation measures may differ from, or they may complement, the trade facilitation measures proposed in this handbook.

Transit facilitation relies on components in four categories, listed below.

- *Building national capacities,* including:
  - The implementation in the customs code of a real national transit system, with the provision for a transit manifest different in form and substance from the customs clearance declaration.

- The creation of a service specialized in transit.
- The training of border officers in border posts accredited for transit.
- *Improvement in the information system:* customs should implement a rigorous paper or ICT based documentation cycle that reconciles entry and exit documents.
- *Regulation of entry* for operators involved in transit.
- *International cooperation:* this should address issues such as the harmonization of documentation, the mutual recognition of controls and guarantees, and the exchange of information.

A little help from technology: tracing, not tracking, is needed

Customs agencies must properly manage the information on transit manifests or carnets in order to do three things:

- Trace the goods entering and exiting the country, with adequate management of transit manifests or carnets.
- Discharge the bonds.
- Communicate with other participants, or with an overseeing body (such as the IRU) in the case of a carnet system. An ICT system can be of great practical help. Within customs in the transit country, the system electronically tells the exit post to expect the arrival of a shipment within a plausible timeframe. When closed by the exit post, the transit information is input and the guarantee is automatically released.

The automation of customs documentation is widespread. Several applications have modules for national transit. For instance, the United Nations Conference on Trade and Development (UNCTAD) has already developed transit add-ons to ASYCUDA++. The national transit module is already built in new generation systems such as ASYCUDA World and its competitors.[7] So far these systems have not been adapted to carnet systems.

The interconnection of national customs is desirable and practically indispensable for a truly regionally integrated system, such as the NCTS in Europe. It allows for a seamless exchange of information on a transit manifest or the initiation and termination of a bond. At that stage NCTS is the only fully functional application for regional transit.

The e-TIR, which has a different concept, is in its pilot phase. In e-TIR the carnet barcode or Safe-TIR number helps validate a page of the carnet at one of the border crossings, and this information is sent into a central database to which each participating country has access. Radio frequency identification device (RFID) technology applied to vehicles or trailers may also facilitate the tracing of cargo on a corridor and speed up controls at entry and exit checkpoints. As of mid-2010 there are no full scale examples.

Tracking as opposed to tracing: Transit goods can be traced through the automation of carnet or transit manifest. Tracking, in contrast, involves localizing the merchandise. The prices of global positioning system (GPS) tracking devices are falling, and they are ever more popular with large trucking firms that want to know where their vehicles are at all times (so they can alert consignees if delivery is likely to be delayed). Drivers who have breakdowns also want their companies to know where to find them, and GPS devices have become important management tools for logistics operators.

Such tracking for the benefit of cargo owners should not be confused with tracking by customs or other border agencies, which may be done with or without the trucker's knowledge. Suppliers recommend electronic devices to customs authorities, and products such as e-seals with GPS tracking have their appeal. However, for a transit system to work, there is absolutely no practical need for real time tracking. There are serious disadvantages as well, including the reinforcement of the control mentality (with the potential for abuse) in place of a partnership approach with incentives for compliant operators offering guarantees. In addition, there is no established best practice or clear guidance for how customs can use tracking information—nor has any developed country implemented it.

Recent experience suggests that the eventual contribution of e-seals and tracking may be less to improve procedures than to help rebuild confidence between customs and transit operators, leading to the disuse of unfriendly control solutions such as convoys. For instance, in Jordan e-seals have been implemented recently to dispense with convoys. Kenya and Ghana are doing the same with the support of trucking companies.

Those examples show that technology is unlikely to change the principles of transit regimes, which are universal and predate the industrial revolution. While the automation of information and of financial flows is very desirable, much clarification is needed on how to do it, especially between countries.

What is not needed, not desirable, and does not work: some common misconceptions corrected

The perception of a need for real time tracking and GPS, or for heavy ICT, is not the only misconception commonly encountered in corridor transit facilitation projects. Other misconceptions are rectified below.

- *Freedom of transit does **not** mean:*
  - *Freedom to choose routes in transit countries.* It is perfectly acceptable for a transit country to impose certain routes for transit traffic, as long as it does not discriminate by trade type or by carrier nationality. For instance, environmental reasons or infrastructure load capacities may justify the concentration of heavy vehicles on certain routes. Customs may also impose routes for transit traffic to prevent trucks from wandering.
  - *Transit services open to everybody.* The regulation of entry to favor compliant operators is desirable. A major problem is that many developing countries have pushed for transit to be as open as possible to the local trucking sector.
- *Transit does **not** require a heavy border infrastructure.*
  - Since the process at the border should be limited to fairly simple diligence—check the manifest and the seals, no inspection—there is no need for a large transit infrastructure.
  - Transit does not require specific border post arrangements.
  - Transit flows should be separated from the flows cleared at the border: for example, there may be a separate fast lane at a border post with substantial activity (100 trucks a day).

- Transit facilitation in fact reduces the need for border infrastructure.
- *Needs for ICT are very limited, and overreliance on ICT solutions may be counterproductive.*
- *Bonds are not expensive, and transit cannot do without bonds.* The costliness of bonds is an argument commonly used against joining the TIR, or for developing an idiosyncratic solution. But even when bonds are fairly expensive (for example, up to 1 percent of value), their cost is much less than that of other logistics needs—such as transportation—or than the impact on production and distribution of an inefficient transit supply chain (Arvis, Mustra, and others 2010). In fact, the cost and low availability of bonds are a consequence—not a cause—of inefficiency in transit regime implementation. In many developing countries, it is true, small transit brokers cannot easily mobilize bonds from commercial banks—but with proper regulation of entry, or in a regional system, those brokers should not be in the market. The cost of bonds is also increased by the time taken to discharge transit and by a lack of competition for their offering (for example, in Western Africa a monopoly is given to chambers of commerce, for which bonds are an important source of revenue).
- *Some simple ideas on where and how to clear— though apparently common sense propositions— simply **do not work**.* Among such ideas, some of the ones most found in reports and project proposals at present are:
  - *For landlocked countries, clearance at the port of entry in the gateway country.* Beyond the obvious issues of territorial jurisdiction, the main problem with this idea is that the transit country, to prevent fraud or fiscal loss, still needs a system to make sure that goods are consumed in the destination country. At best there can be preclearance, with the risk of adding a layer of procedures. In rare instances this is feasible: for example, where there is a very short transit corridor and a dominance of transit trade over domestic trade at the port of entry.[8]
  - *For a customs union to dispense with transit procedures entirely.* In fact, since VAT or sales taxes are collected in the country of

consumption, some transit mechanism must be maintained—even if a collective mechanism is agreed for the collection of extra-union duty (as in the EU and SACU).

Enabling policies for transit facilitation, apart from those related to customs

Transit system implementation relies not only on customs related measures but also on policies related to transport, infrastructure, and services. Such policies have been comprehensively treated (World Bank 2008; Arvis 2010). Nevertheless, here are a few of the more important.

Harnessing open markets for transport and logistics services

Liberalizing access to markets. Countries that still closely regulate their trucking industry should take a second look at restrictions on entry into the industry and at restrictive arrangements that have the effect of reducing truck capacity utilization or service quality. Transit countries that reform their trucking regulations—first for domestic traffic, and second, for bilateral traffic and transit traffic to landlocked neighbors—stand to benefit.

In many instances, restrictions (such as quotas) for transit truck operation comes from the desire of landlocked least developed countries to secure a certain share of the transit traffic for their own truckers. However, experience in both Central Africa and the Greater Mekong Sub-region shows the drawbacks of bilateral negotiations that restrict the numbers of operators and the market shares of certain other countries. Protectionism of this sort generally is at the cost of the trading community, through lower productivity and through higher tariffs.

The inefficiencies of a *tour de role* system are many. Having to wait in line is the most obvious but not necessarily the most damaging. A greater ill is the barrier introduced between the freight owner and the trucker, preventing them from negotiating their contracts directly. Much is to be gained if these parties can get to know each other through regular service, so that the freight owner knows who is carrying his goods and what risk he runs of pilferage or late delivery. The trucker also benefits by coming to understand the freight owner's quality requirements: punctuality, special handling, and other concerns.

Regulating for quality instead of quantity. License restrictions often applied include limitations on where a carrier may operate (defined regions or routes), on truck types, and on the kinds of commodities to be carried, as well as the rigid separation of for hire services from own account operations. Governments practicing such restrictions are encouraged to consider replacing them with quality licensing. Quality licensing tests and recognizes an operator's ability to perform—its technical skills, its bookkeeping and financial capacity. As an adjunct to the TIR, the IRU offers an internationally recognized certificate of professional competence for trucking firm managers and their drivers. Quality licensing does not set a prior limit on the number of carriers to be certified, but it raises the professional standards of the industry. It can empower carriers to charge higher rates for superior services, and it can qualify them for entry into the TIR system.

Rewarding reliable transporters. Border control agencies that introduce selective inspection on the basis of risk analysis are likely to favor the higher standard carriers, those who maintain a consistent pattern of operations that can be recognized in a customs risk analysis database. Such carriers can be rewarded with green channel treatment, reducing delays to a minimum.

Avoiding the repeated weighing of trucks in transit. Multi-axle trucks involved in international trade are rarely the worst overloading offenders. Nevertheless, in some corridors they are considered easy targets for informal payments and are repeatedly stopped and weighed. As an alternative—for consistency with the goal of developing a premium class of international freight movements—containers moving overland should be weighed before departure from the port of entry in the transit country (or from the point of origin in a landlocked country) and at border crossings. They should be provided there with official weight certificates exempting them from further weight checks in the same country, provided that seals remain unbroken.

Enhancing the role of integrators (freight forwarders). With the intensified focus on source to destination supply chains, there is now a premium on good forwarding services. Delivery that is reliable and on time is highly valued. Shippers are increasingly willing to pay specialist agencies—multimodal operators—to assume full responsibility for the entire supply chain. By means of a through bill of lading, the shipper enters into a single transport contract with the freight forwarder—who in turn makes separate contracts with trucking firms, railways, or shipping lines to cover each leg of the multimodal journey.

Shrinking the role of customs brokers. Even as freight forwarders are increasingly used, the demand for customs brokers is being reduced by the focus on integration and by the trend toward shifting clearance from border crossings to destination points (consignees' premises). Declarations can now be prepared by the shipper and filed electronically. The introduction of true regional transit systems will also reduce the need for intermediaries at the border.

Inland container depots. In recent years these have grown in number, as they offer a convenient intermediate solution between clearance at the border and clearance on the buyer's premises. Similar to dry ports, inland container depots often are located in the outskirts of hub cities, where the price of land is moderate and where arterial highways and railways give good access while avoiding interference with urban traffic. The core functions of such depots are the unloading of containers from long distance trucks (and trains) into short term bonded storage; the inspection of the containers; the payment of duty and obtaining of customs clearance; and the reloading of the containers onto local trucks for delivery in and around the city. A secondary function that may be added is warehousing, where containers—after being cleared by customs—can be unstuffed and their contents delivered to multiple destinations, or even broken down, processed, and repackaged for multiple final buyers (as with pharmaceuticals or auto parts).

Managing trade corridors

The main practical reason for looking at trade corridors in a policy perspective is to focus not only on improving the routes used by transport and other logistics services in the corridor, but also on increasing the quality of those services. The right management framework can give a landlocked country a say in the provision of infrastructure and services on routes that, though important to its trade competitiveness, lie outside its borders. Six points are important here:

- Corridor management agencies are another way of building trust between partners (and have performed well in this respect, at least in Eastern Africa).
- Corridor groups need to have clear development objectives, with a mandate for problem solving.
- Corridor issues, by their nature, are often solved through interactions among many public and private entities.
- Corridor management requires a strong and enthusiastic champion.
- Corridors can pilot reforms.
- Funding for corridor management is a special challenge.

Monitoring, measuring, and benchmarking corridor performance

Monitoring the performance of corridors is important if interventions are to be targeted. Most corridor performance measurements have included cost and time, but not all have specified the unit of transport: per ton, per consignment, per truck, or per twenty foot equivalent unit (TEU). This complicates comparison across corridors. Reliability and safety are also important, but they are hard to specify consistently. An international consensus needs to be developed on these definitions.

A promising contender is the method that the United Nations Economic and Social Commission for Asia and the Pacific (UNESCAP) has developed, using a graphical method to show corridor performance (cost and time). It is now widely used throughout Central and Eastern Asia. Another example is the FastPath software, developed for the United States Agency for International Development (USAID) to help identify and evaluate potential improvements in developing countries with port and logistics chain inefficiencies.

To generate indicators of a corridor's performance, a monitoring method should be used that incorporates the best characteristics of both the

UNESCAP and FastPath models and that is compatible with both of them. Among the advantages of such a method are that it differentiates between exports and imports, that it specifies the overseas origin or destination of freight movements, and that it includes maritime segments. It also provides readily understood specifications of minimum cost and time, including the shipment size to which the specifications refer and how variations above the minimum should be estimated. Finally, it generates an estimate of the total transport cost using the corridor and so offers a basis for assessing the importance of proposed improvements.

Notes

1. Still, in a few cases cargo originates and ends up in the same territory but transits through a second country. For instance, commodities destined for the Northeastern part of India and originating from other parts of India transit through Bangladesh, as all alternative Indian routes are much longer.

2. For illustrative purposes we focus on trucks; however, the same applies for other modes of transport, such as wagons, barges, and so forth. In practice the procedures may be simplified for trains.

3. See "WTO Legal Texts," World Trade Organization, http://www.wto.org/english/docs_e/legal_e/legal_e.htm.

4. See "IRU: International Road Transport Union," IRU, http://www.iru.org.

5. Norway, Iceland, Switzerland, and Liechtenstein.

6. Acuerdo sobre Transporte Internacional Terrestre (ATIT).

7. CGnet in Ghana, Gainde in Senegal, Simba in Kenya.

8. The best known example is the Ethiopian transit trade cleared in Djibouti.

References

Arvis, J.F. 2005. "Transit and the Special Case of Landlocked Countries." In *Customs Modernization Handbook,* ed. L. De Wulf and J.B. Sokol. Washington, DC: The World Bank. 243–64.

———. 2010. *Connecting Landlocked Developing Countries to Markets: Trade Corridors in the 21st Century.* Washington, DC: The World Bank.

Arvis, J., J. Marteau, and G. Raballand. 2010. *The Cost of Being Landlocked: Logistics Costs and Supply Chain Reliability.* Washington, DC: The World Bank.

Arvis, J., M. Mustra, L. Ojala, B. Shepherd, and D. Saslavsky. 2010. *Connecting to Compete: Trade Logistics in the Global Economy.* Washington, DC: World Bank.

Arvis, J., M. Mustra, J. Panzer, L. Ojala, and T. Naula. 2007. *Connecting to Compete: Trade Logistics in the Global Economy.* Washington, DC: World Bank.

De Wulf, L., and J.B. Sokol, eds. 2005. *Customs Modernization Handbook.* Washington, DC: The World Bank.

UNECE (United Nations Economic Commission for Europe). 2010. "TIR Handbook: Customs Convention on the International Transport of Goods Under Cover of TIR Carnets (TIR Convention, 1975)." UNECE document ECE/TRANS/TIR/6, United Nations, New York and Geneva. Available at http://www.unece.org/tir/tir-hb.html.

UNECE Inland Transport Committee. 1982. "International Convention on the Harmonization of Frontier Controls of Goods." UNECE document ECE/TRANS/55/Rev.1, United Nations, Geneva.

UNECE (United Nations Economic Commission for Europe) and UNCTAD (United Nations Conference on Trade and Development). 2001. *Compendium of Trade Facilitation Recommendations.* Geneva: UN.

WCO (World Customs Organization). 1999. *International Convention on the Simplification and Harmonization of Customs Procedures (As Amended).* Brussels: WCO.

World Bank. 2008. *Improving Trade and Transport for Landlocked Developing Countries: World Bank Contributions to Implementing the Almaty Programme of Action.* Washington, DC: The World Bank.

———. 2010. "A Global Review of Transit Regimes." Mimeo., International Trade Department, The World Bank, Washington, DC.

18 The national security environment: strategic context

David Widdowson and Stephen Holloway

The radically changed nature of the international trading environment since the September 11, 2001 attacks on the United States has had a significant impact on border operations. In many cases the regulatory burden on the international trading community has increased considerably. Indeed, while no doubt well intentioned, a number of government responses to the international security threat may do little more than increase the regulatory burden on honest traders and achieve little in the way of enhancing the ability to identify potentially high risk individuals or consignments. Well designed national security requirements can, however, be incorporated seamlessly into border operations in a way that can enhance national security without compromising trade facilitation objectives.

This chapter explores ways in which this can be achieved—with specific commentary on recent developments in regulatory supply chain security initiatives, and on the appropriateness of various regulatory responses from the perspective of risk management and commercial practicality. The chapter identifies key elements of a contemporary compliance management strategy and their application in mitigating risk. It then identifies specific risks to the security of the international supply chain and analyzes a range of compliance management strategies intended to address such risks. Based on that analysis, it provides policymakers and administrators with a range of recommended policy responses and operational strategies.

Regulation of the international supply chain since September 11, 2001

The regulatory focus on the international supply chain changed after September 11, 2001 from one that was generally facilitative to one that placed the security of the supply chain at the center of border management policy. Border control—of which supply chain security is but one element—has always formed part of the regulatory continuum, and since the 1980s there has been a global effort on the part of regulators to achieve an appropriate balance between facilitation and regulatory intervention. There is, however, clear evidence indicating that the balance has been tilted heavily towards intervention following the 2001 attacks (Widdowson 2006), at least as far as many developed countries are concerned.

More significantly, whereas customs border control issues have traditionally centered on commercial illegality (for example, duty evasion) and general community protection (for example, against harmful products and biological threats), the 2001 attacks highlighted the potential for the supply chain itself to be utilized by terrorists to cause physical and economic damage. A proliferation of security focused control regimes ensued. Indeed, supply chain security promptly became the priority issue, and with the three day closure of the United States borders, the economic impact of any breakdown in the supply chain became obvious to everyone involved in international trade. A number of initiatives, introduced to improve the security of the supply chain, were developed and implemented, first by the United States and subsequently by other countries and international organizations. Understandably, the United States initiatives have tended to lead the supply chain security agenda, and that continues to be the case, although with increasing controversy and some resistance from other countries and the private sector. Cases in point are the controversial Importer Security Filing and Additional Carrier Requirements for cargo arriving in the United States by ocean vessels—commonly called the 10+2 rule[1]—and the practice of 100 percent maritime cargo container scanning under the Secure Freight International Container Security project.[2]

Such controversy serves to challenge the appropriateness of certain approaches to supply chain regulation, and it questions whether the supply chain is becoming regulated and controlled to the detriment of the efficiency and effectiveness of both government and business. In analyzing the appropriateness of the diverse regulatory regimes from the perspective of risk management and commercial practicality, it is first necessary to briefly examine the principal elements of a contemporary compliance management strategy.

Elements of modern compliance management

Models for managing regulatory compliance essentially fall into two broad categories: normative and rationalist (INECE 2009). The normative model advocates the encouragement of voluntary compliance through cooperation, support, and the positive reinforcement of compliant behavior. The rationalist model, on the other hand, advocates an enforcement approach, the focus of which is the deterrence of noncompliant behavior by punitive means.

In practice regulatory agencies will generally adopt compliance management strategies that incorporate both normative and rationalist elements. These elements effectively represent opposite ends of a compliance management continuum that seeks, firstly, to encourage voluntary compliance, but also includes a range of punitive measures that may be applied in the event of noncompliance.

A number of issues need to be considered when determining the best mix of elements that should be present in a regulatory framework. These include the need to achieve a cost effective outcome consistent with the desired policy outcome; the nature of the operational environment that is being regulated including the commercial practices that apply; and the extent to which the regulatory requirements are likely to impact on the operational effectiveness of the activity being regulated.

Consequently, most compliance management regimes will comprise a combination of regulatory approaches, with the specific components of a particular scheme being dependent on the scope of the risk that is to be treated and the demographics of the regulated population. Moreover, the selection of individual strategies to be employed will depend not only on the risk that noncompliance might present but also on the consequences that might ensue from failure.

Regardless of the strategy adopted, the rule of law must remain at the core of any regulatory regime, bearing in mind the fact that the fundamental role of the regulator is to ensure compliance with the law. Achievement of government objectives (in this case ensuring security of the supply chain) relies first and foremost on well constructed rules, and it is therefore incumbent upon regulators to continually question the validity of the rules that have been established in order to ensure their ongoing relevance to the policy aim. In the political climate since the 2001 attacks, however, it takes a very brave person to question the validity of rules that have ostensibly been designed to mitigate supply chain security risks. This issue will be addressed later.

The national security environment: strategic context

Several models have been developed to identify better practice in regulatory compliance management, all of which emphasize the need for an effective legislative base. The model shown in figure 18.1 illustrates the need for a sound legal basis on which to build the range of administrative and risk management strategies which the border agency chooses to adopt (see for example Widdowson 2005b).

Informing the international trading community

An appropriate range of client service strategies, including effective consultation arrangements and clear administrative guidelines, is necessary to provide the commercial sector with the means to achieve certainty and clarity in assessing their liabilities and entitlements (reflected in the second tier of the pyramid in figure 18.1). In 1997, when calling for an urgent international process of regulatory reform, the Organisation for Economic Co-operation and Development (OECD) stated that such reform should include more flexible approaches to regulatory compliance management, with the longer term goal of shifting governments "from a culture of control to a culture of client service" (OECD 1997).

Such a cultural shift has required government agencies to accept the view that strategies other than enforcement activities represent legitimate means of mitigating the risk of noncompliance and are critical to achieving an effective balance between facilitation and regulatory intervention. Indeed, it is of critical importance to ensure that the commercial sector is provided with the ability to comply with regulatory requirements. They need to know the rules. If they don't know, then how can they be expected to comply? While ignorance of the law may be no excuse, it explains many instances of noncompliance and, consequently, the need to provide meaningful advice to those who are being regulated is essential.

Compliance assessment

The elements of compliance assessment in the border management context generally include data and physical screening, documentary checks, and risk based scanning and physical examinations as well as preshipment and postshipment audits and investigations (reflected in the third tier of the pyramid in figure 18.1).

Effective compliance assessment includes strategies that are designed to identify both compliance and noncompliance. This does not sit well with those who favor a focus on noncompliance and who argue that the only recognized result of compliance assessment activities is the identification of noncompliance, together with associated enforcement actions such as prosecution and monetary sanctions (Widdowson 2006). The saying "If it isn't counted, it won't get done" applies aptly to this situation. In other words, if the management focus is solely on the identification of noncompliers, staff will fail to see the relevance of identifying compliant traders. This is a particular problem in much of the developing world where traders, regardless of their compliance record, face almost exactly the same regulatory controls as noncompliant traders—so frequently there are few positive incentives associated with maintaining a strong compliance record.

In recent times, there has been an increased emphasis on a partnership approach to assessing and achieving regulatory compliance, and some such strategies that have been introduced in the supply chain security environment are discussed later. The government and industry partnership concept is based on the premise that companies with a good record of compliance require less, or different, regulatory scrutiny than those with a history of poor compliance or about which little is known. The partnership approach to security has been adopted across a range of sectors—examples include the United States Department of Homeland Security Transport Security Administration's Known Shipper Database (commonly called the Known Shipper program) for

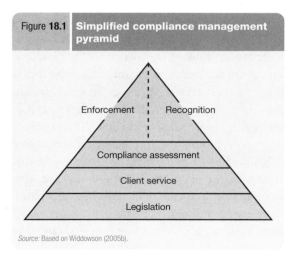

Figure **18.1**   **Simplified compliance management pyramid**

Enforcement | Recognition

Compliance assessment

Client service

Legislation

Source: Based on Widdowson (2005b).

The national security environment: strategic context

the air transport industry[3]—and its potential application to air passengers is also a topic for debate.

Recognition

A key element of the partnership strategy seeks to provide highly compliant companies with benefits such as facilitated clearance arrangements, an entitlement to self assess, and reduced regulatory scrutiny—benefits that provide compliant companies with the incentive to demonstrate their commitment to comply with regulatory requirements. The effectiveness of such arrangements hinges on a healthy working relationship between government and industry, based on partnership and trust: that is, a relationship that reflects a mutual commitment to accountability and improving compliance.

Later in this chapter we examine a number of partnership arrangements that seek to mitigate risk by:

- Identifying compliant businesses, including those that are dedicated to ensuring the security of their supply chains.

- Encouraging participation in such partnership arrangements by providing a range of benefits that formally recognize the compliant nature of participating businesses.

- Enabling regulatory agencies to place a greater focus on the trade transactions of higher risk businesses.

Such partnerships must be a two way proposition with clearly identified costs, benefits, and responsibilities for both parties. Consistent with the cooperative, consultative approach that a partnership program is intended to achieve, industry should be invited to play a major role in identifying the range of incentives that may be made available under such an arrangement. Signing up to such partnership programs is not, however, a cost free decision, and therefore the benefits offered through such programs need to be tangible and meaningful.

Provided such programs can achieve mutual benefit for both government and industry, the partnership approach is destined to succeed. However, if the anticipated benefits fail to materialize for either of the parties, the relationship is likely to be less than successful, particularly when would-be participants have made a significant investment in the initiative. Given that one of the parties to such a partnership is a regulatory authority, it is hardly surprising to learn that the benefits that fail to materialize are generally to the detriment of industry (Widdowson 2005a).

Enforcement

Naturally, in the process of assessing the level of compliance with border regulations, agencies encounter two situations: compliance and noncompliance. The noncompliance spectrum will range from innocent mistakes to blatant fraud. If the error nears the fraudulent end of the spectrum some form of sanction will need to apply, such as administrative penalties or—in the more severe cases—prosecution, license revocation, or possible criminal prosecution.

Before determining the need for or nature of a sanction, however, it is important for regulators to identify the true nature of the risk by establishing why the error has occurred. For example, it may result from a control problem within a company due to flawed systems and procedures, or it may be the result of a deliberate act of noncompliance. In such situations the most appropriate mitigation strategy will depend on the nature of the identified risk and, unless the act is found to be intentional, it may be appropriate to address systemic problems within the entity or to provide the company (or perhaps an entire industry sector) with advice on particular compliance issues or provide formal clarification of the law through binding rulings or other means (Widdowson 1998). In all cases the severity of the measures applied should appropriately reflect the level of noncompliance—in other words, "let the punishment fit the crime."

Management based regulation

The concept of management based regulation seeks to leverage business knowledge, experience, and practice to achieve the regulatory objective. Thus it has the potential to be far more cost effective than prescriptive regulation, and it certainly is less disruptive of those business processes. It is also more likely to encourage innovation in managing compliance risk, since businesses are more likely to comply with their own internal rules and procedures than with those imposed externally by government. Indeed, there is empirical evidence to suggest that management based regulation can lead businesses to make risk related behavioral changes (Bennear 2007).

Using this approach, regulated entities are often expected to develop plans or management systems that comply with criteria prescribed by the regulatory authority—for example, security plans under the International Ship and Port Security (ISPS) Code, or physical security and access restrictions under the various customs authorized economic operator and related programs. The regulatory approach may include a requirement for certification by government regulators or third party auditors of the plans and management practices, together with evidence of compliance (OECD 2008). The OECD has recognized the importance of compliance measurement with this regulatory approach, as with compliance oriented regulation generally (OECD 2008, p. 10):

> Performance standards focus attention on desired outcomes and provide flexibility to find less costly or better solutions but making them work depends on being able to measure and monitor performance. Sometimes it is difficult to operationalize the desired outcome into an enforceable regulatory standard, or sometimes it is prohibitively costly for the regulator to monitor outcomes.

This is an important issue with respect to regulation of the international supply chain, because it is particularly difficult to monitor or measure supply chain security risk in a way that is meaningful to business—keeping that risk below a specified level. There is no such thing as zero risk in the international supply chain, and (at least at an operational level) businesses are often better positioned to identify risk in their supply chain than are regulators—although that changes as the focus moves to broader strategic risk.

This then leads to a discussion of risk management in the context of supply chain security and, in particular, whether that risk can be identified in a way that facilitates the design of cost effective and efficient regulatory approaches to supply chain security that meet both government and private sector concerns.

The nature of supply chain security risk

The changed nature of maritime transport security risk is in many ways, despite the 2001 attacks, reflective of the increase in the volume and complexity of international trade itself. Technological innovation, leading to the twin benefits of vast improvements in the speed of transportation and communications and the lowering of costs, has resulted in better access to overseas markets and a much greater diversity among entities involved in international trade. It has also resulted in exponential growth in the use of containers for maritime transport.

The changing nature of trade is also highlighted by a 2006 UNCTAD report, which estimates that about one third of international trade in goods involves trade in unfinished goods and components and a similar percentage represents trade within the same company (UNCTAD 2006). It is likely that these percentages have increased since the time the UNCTAD report was prepared. Indeed, the WCO estimates that the percentage of intracompany trade is now closer to 50 percent (WCO 2008).

The majority of such trade occurs within an integrated global logistics system in diminishing timeframes, to meet global sourcing and just-in-time business models that emphasize low inventory. Companies manage a continuous flow of goods that are transported as part of an intricate logistics and supply chain management system that ensures delivery at precisely the moment they are required for use as an input in production.

The benefits in cost savings and efficiency are significant, but so are the commercial risks considering that even a short disruption to that supply chain can have considerable financial consequences (Kommerskollegium 2008).

Global sourcing is becoming an increasingly common trend in modern supply chains. An example, the sourcing for production of the Apple iPod nano (box 18.1), highlights not only the complexity of today's international supply chains but also the difficulties in managing the associated risks—both from a commercial perspective in ensuring just-in-time delivery of components, and from a business and government perspective with respect to securing the supply chain from potential security threats.

The reality is that there is a convergence of interest between business and government in maintaining a secure supply chain. It requires cooperation and coordination to function effectively and to minimize the risks of disruption to, or abuse of, the legitimate flow of goods. This collective benefit in

The Apple iPod nano is a small mobile MP3 device to which users can download their preferred music using a personal computer connected to the Internet. The central microchip of iPod nano is provided by a US company (PortalPlayer). The core technology of the chip is licensed from a British company (ARM) and is modified by PortalPlayer's programmers in California, Washington State, and Hyderabad.

PortalPlayer works with microchip design companies in California, which provide the finished design to a company in Chinese Taipei that produces wafers imprinted with hundreds of thousands of chips. These wafers are then cut up into individual disks and sent to another facility in Chinese Taipei, where they are individually tested.

The chips are then encased in plastic and readied for assembly by Silicon-Ware in Chinese Taipei and Amkor in the Republic of Korea. The finished microchip is then warehoused in Hong Kong SAR, China before being transported to mainland China, where the iPod is assembled.

Source: Adapted from "Stark Reality" (2006).

supply chain security is recognized in the study undertaken by the Swedish National Board of Trade (Kommerskollegium 2008).

The development and implementation of strategies to mitigate supply chain security risks is therefore complicated and frustrated by the high degree of interdependence and associated network characteristics exhibited by modern global supply chains. This has created great uncertainty as to where the risks actually begin and end, since what at first may look like a minor event can quickly turn into a fullblown crisis (OECD 2009b). An often quoted example is the fire at a single source supplier used by Ericsson that resulted in $400 million in lost sales for Ericsson, a drop in stock price of 11 percent, and the eventual exit of that business line. The principle is illustrated on a global scale when one considers that the current financial crisis resulted from regulatory approaches that were adopted with relative confidence but that failed to identify the potential global ramifications of a seemingly isolated risk in one sector of a particular economy.

Up to this point the discussion has been mainly about generic risks that flow from the complex and interdependent nature of modern supply chains, but the focus on counterterrorism since the 2001 attacks has required the international community to seriously consider the ephemeral characteristics of terrorist risk. Unlike other risks (such as accident risk) where the events are unintentional and their likelihood can be reasonably estimated from empirical observations, the probabilities associated with a terrorist attack are much harder to quantify. The OECD suggests two reasons for this (2009a, p. 6):

First, terrorist attacks are relatively infrequent. This is especially true of attacks that belong to the class of extreme events, with low probabilities, major consequences, and possibly spillovers into connected systems. For such infrequent events, past events carry little information on future probabilities.

Second, attaching probabilities to intentional acts is particularly problematic because of the possibility of strategic behavior: terrorists adapt their strategy to changes in the security environment in which they operate. Since little is known about how they will respond (because the set of available strategies is very large), it is not clear how security policies or other relevant changes affect probabilities. In sum, terrorist attacks are not characterized by risk but by uncertainty, meaning that no credible objective probability can be assigned to their occurrence.

What can be said with some degree of certainty is that the nature of risk in the international trading environment requires flexibility and resilience to be engineered into regulatory initiatives to ensure their effectiveness, and that this notion of flexibility and resilience requires cooperation between and across business and government rather than a parallel and self centered (silo) approach. It also requires both national and international perspectives that acknowledge the increased connections and interdependencies between and among economies. It requires, in other words, the practical application of the collaborative border management concept outlined in chapter 2.

As the OECD points out in its studies of country risk management when discussing the necessity for collaboration between government agencies, there may be an exposure "to unforeseen vulnerabilities when risks arise that do not fit neatly within the remit of one particular department . . . Indeed efficient risk management may be compromised by the inability to deal effectively with bottlenecks in the exchange and analysis of information or to set priorities informed by the entirety of a country's risk portfolio" (OECD 2009b). Furthermore, the risk management efforts of one company can be nullified by the inattention or inadequacy of a single supply chain partner (Closs and others 2008). In other words, the security of the entire trade supply chain is only as good as its weakest link.

If it is accepted that container cargo is one of the unique features of modern international cargo transportation and that there is potential for it to be utilized by terrorists or by organized crime, then one of the critical supply chain security risks to be analyzed relates to the international movement of containers and, more specifically, to what is inside those containers.

The specific stuffing location is paramount from a security perspective because it represents the last point in the container transport chain where the physical contents of the container can be visually identified and reconciled with the commercial invoice and/or bill of lading. After the doors are shut and sealed and until they are re-opened by Customs or by the consignee at the final destination, all information regarding the contents of the container (such as the manifest, the bill of lading and even the commercial invoice) are necessarily unverified. Thus the originating shipper has a critical role to play in the container security by generating a clear, accurate and complete inventory of the physical contents of the container. Proper site security, stuffing procedures and oversight of the stuffing process are necessary for this important link in the chain to be secure (OECD 2005, p. 29).

It is axiomatic that cargo containers are at their most vulnerable in terms of having unlawful cargo introduced into the supply chain when they are at rest and least vulnerable when they are in motion (see OECD 2005). This has driven a great deal of the regulatory design thinking around supply chain security measures and placed particular emphasis on those nodes in the network where the container is handled or stored.

The OECD makes another important point when it notes that most international container trade passes through one or several ports. In this context it is important to note that none of the small, feeder ports that transship cargo through the world's major hubs can be ignored as a potential risk node in the broader supply chain dynamic. It is true that it is incumbent on such ports to put in place security measures in accordance with the requirements of (for example) the ISPS code, but the effectiveness of those measures is in turn dependent on the commitment to supply chain security of the governments that are responsible for them and the quality of the relevant regulatory framework and its enforcement.

A common thread that can be discerned from the various risk characteristics of the modern supply chain is the importance of supply chain visibility. Visibility represents the key to early risk identification and response and is a precondition for supply chain resiliency. It must therefore be considered to be of equal significance to both government and business.

At present most supply chain security initiatives have as their foundation a concept of layered security. This concept attempts to design redundancy into the system so that security breaches at one level can be guarded against at a subsequent level. Such initiatives acknowledge that an insecure supply chain has adverse effects on both business and government—and that all, to a greater or lesser degree, require public and private sector participation to be embodied in the proposed regulatory measures. However, it is suggested that a number of these initiatives are less efficient and effective in their design than others because they fail to contribute to supply chain visibility.

Supply chain visibility: a business perspective

A Global Supply Chain Benchmark Report, published by the Aberdeen Group in June 2006, emphasized the importance of supply chain visibility to business. It found that a lack of supply chain visibility—coupled with poor automation—impacts a company's bottom line through longer lead times, larger inventory buffers, budget overruns, and demand-supply imbalances. In particular, large multinationals are of a scale where poor visibility and uncoordinated multitier processes result in significant just-in-case inventory carrying costs, premium freight expenses, and extended cycle times (Aberdeen Group 2006). Some particularly relevant findings from the report include:

- Some 79 percent of the companies included in the report said that the lack of supply chain process visibility is their top concern.
- Among the companies included, 82 percent were concerned about supply chain resiliency—but just 11 percent were actively managing this risk.
- The top five gap areas relating to supply chain risk were risk profiles of vendors (56 percent), supply chain security (51 percent), logistics capacity and congestion (47 percent), risk profiles of countries (46 percent), and weather disruptions and natural disasters (44 percent).
- In addition, 47 percent wanted to improve the data quality of the event messages, including for timeliness, completeness, and accuracy.
- According to 91 percent of companies, unexpected supply chain costs were eroding their anticipated low cost country sourcing savings, with transportation budget overruns being the top culprit.

The Aberdeen Group's report reveals that improvements in supply chain risk management are being achieved through the adoption of two core strategies: first through "increasing logistics and supply agility by ensuring alternate suppliers, carriers, routes, and the like are arranged," and second by "improving visibility and automation of supply chain activity" both upstream and downstream in the supply chain.

Bearing in mind the importance of compliance (performance) measurement, multinational businesses are increasingly measuring the performance of their supply chains via the concept of total landed cost. The Aberdeen Group's research shows that the best performers are those companies that have been most successful in reducing their total landed costs and documentation. These companies are "twice as likely to have current budgeted trade compliance projects as their peers." It is further noted that "as regulatory oversight intensifies, enterprises are finding increased value in moving to a single trade compliance platform for the entire company that enables consistency of product classifications and restricted party screenings and provides a common view of compliance activity and trade costs" (Aberdeen Group 2006).

In this context it can be argued that supply chain visibility and resilience are critical characteristics of an international compliance strategy, and that a focus on trade compliance is as important to business as it is to regulators. Both are seeking to maintain security across the supply chain, although motivated perhaps by different objectives. As the Aberdeen Group's report (2006) states:

> Managing international logistics is not like managing an extended domestic supply chain; it's fundamentally a multi-party process fraught with greater unpredictability in quality, lead times, costs, and risks. Rather than create the absolute-lowest-cost fixed network, leaders are building into their logistics networks more points of flexibility. This helps them continually scan their environment for bottleneck symptoms or spikes in demand and take action.

Supply chain visibility: a government perspective

Supply chain visibility is of equal importance to governments, since greater visibility provides regulatory authorities with the information they need to analyze risks, identify high risk or suspect shipments, and target potential security threats. The critical element here is information, since the regulator's ability to identify and treat risk is dependent on the timeliness and quality of information. If the information that is provided to commercial operators and regulators is inaccurate or intentionally false, the best regulatory scheme in the world will be unable to achieve its objectives in the absence of other sources of intelligence. This theme is further explored later in this chapter.

Supply chain visibility in real time allows a rapid response to emerging risks, and if this is combined with effective risk management systems that include proactive event and exception management,[4] the whole process of supply chain security is significantly enhanced. End-to-end supply chain visibility, although difficult to achieve, improves responsiveness for business (production rates and shipment lead times) and government (early risk identification).

The international movement of cargo is far from being fully visible, because there is no single regulatory agency with end-to-end supply chain responsibility. As the OECD has previously observed, the most vulnerable period for the container is at the time of its stuffing, before the shipper seals it. The system relies on the trusted shipper, and the majority of stock is presumed to be safe. However, the bill of lading represents a weak point in the chain: how do the authorities or downstream industry players know what is actually packed in the container? The bill of lading is rarely verified through inspection of the containers after packing or during transport; and road transport, where the container is in the hands of a single person for a lengthy period of time over large distances, is especially problematic (OECD 2005).

The ideal visibility outcome for both government and business is visibility on demand. This can only be achieved through close integration of relevant government and business logistics systems. This concept has been discussed at length among border management agencies as best practice with respect to achieving seamlessness in cross border transactions, and it is predicated on government having direct and secure access to commercial data for risk assessment purposes.

Although some may claim that this ideal has been achieved in the context of single window initiatives (see chapter 8), a true single window with on-demand access to existing commercial data by government and other stakeholders—such as port authorities and freight forwarders—has yet to become a reality. While some of the more progressive port community systems may be presented as role models in the port environment (see for example Long 2009), a similar solution in the broader supply chain is far from being a reality. Indeed, there may be a degree of resistance among participants in international trade to share with government what in most cases represents valuable commercial information, for fear of competitors gaining access to price sensitive and competitive information. As Dahlman and others (2005) state:

> Large shipping companies have information on the containers they transport and where they are at any given time. Smaller feeder companies are usually less organized. The information systems are unique to each company and do not interact with those of harbors or customs authorities. This information is of commercial value, and it is unclear how much information shipping companies are willing to share, and with whom and under what conditions.

While there is no doubt that a lack of timely and accurate data reduces supply chain visibility, the major barrier to end-to-end supply chain visibility remains this lack of integration and its surrounding challenges—including the technology and infrastructure limitations of the various stakeholders up and down the supply chain, which in many cases include government.

The OECD recognizes such shortcomings in its identification of common challenges to effective risk management, which include "misinterpretation or misrepresentation of data, communication bottlenecks and logistics breakdowns, which may increase with every step taken between a source of information and its use by decision makers. Overarching, all-hazards policy frameworks promote coordination of highly specific expertise, development of information-sharing arrangements, improvement of data integration capacity, investment in training civil servants and cooperation exercises across multiple agencies involved in country management" (OECD 2009b).

Supply chain security initiatives

We now turn to an examination of the various regulatory strategies that have been introduced since the 2001 attacks to address supply chain security risks. The United Kingdom's trade facilitation body, SITPRO,[5] has developed a useful categorization for the various types of recently introduced international trade security measures (SITPRO 2008):

- *Umbrella measures*—aimed at security risks in their broadest sense.

- *Goods specific measures*—aimed at risks specific to individual types of goods.
- *Control specific measures*—aimed at meeting narrowly specified control objectives.
- *Safety measures*—concerning the safety of staff and use of critical infrastructure.
- *Commercial measures*—business based initiatives to manage transport and supply chain risk.

The SITPRO categories are referred to in the following discussion of the various supply chain security initiatives that either have been implemented since September 11, 2001 or are now planned. It is important to note, however, that the categorization of a particular initiative neither confirms nor questions its validity. Other factors need to be taken into account before such judgments can be made, and these are examined later in the chapter; in this section the various strategies are identified and briefly described.

Many of the initial supply chain security measures may be described as umbrella measures, designed to deal with security risk in the supply chain at the broadest level. The first of these initiatives was the US Customs-Trade Partnership Against Terrorism (C-TPAT) program. In essence C-TPAT is a voluntary government-business program that encourages cooperation between United States Customs and Border Protection (CBP) and the international trading community in an effort to increase the level of international supply chain security. The intention is that businesses participating in the program, in exchange for meeting CBP-designed security standards and becoming C-TPAT certified, should receive certain benefits such as reduced inspections and priority processing. Manufacturers, importers, carriers, and service providers participate by submitting detailed self appraisals of their supply chain security practices, appraisals that are periodically verified by CBP.

Other initiatives are much narrower in focus. For example, the United States Bioterrorism Act[6] is a goods specific measure designed to help the United States Food and Drug Administration (FDA) determine the source and potential cause of any contamination of imported food and beverages. The act facilitates such identification by requiring registered food facilities[7] to provide the FDA with consignment information prior to importation into the United States. Depending on the mode of transportation, parties involved in importing these products are required to provide the information two to eight hours prior to arrival.

Another early initiative was the United States Container Security Initiative (CSI). Introduced in 2002, CSI involves bilateral arrangements between CBP and other customs authorities that are designed to identify high risk cargo containers before they are loaded on vessels destined for the United States. Economies agree to the posting of United States officials at ports that ship large volumes of goods to the United States, and for CBP to independently screen maritime containerized cargo (generally through X-ray and radiation scanning) before being loaded on board vessels destined for the United States.

The CSI is an example of a control specific initiative, its focus specific to goods that are exported to one particular economy. Those destined for other economies are not subjected to similar arrangements. At the time of writing 58 ports, accounting for 85 percent of container traffic bound for the United States, were participating in CSI.[8]

A number of shortcomings were identified in the CSI initiative due to its reliance on receiving "complete and accurate manifest data to analyze in deciding which containers to target for further inspection" (Sarathy 2005):

> In Rotterdam the CSI team found that manifest data was not complete. The data was limited to containers actually transferred from one vessel to another in Rotterdam. Manifest data did not extend to containers that remained on board a vessel bound for the [United States] which stopped in Rotterdam. Further, the CSI did not have manifest data on containers from Rotterdam which had arrived by truck, rail or barge from other countries (neighboring [European Union] countries as well as countries further afield in Eastern and Central Europe). Further, paper manifests were received at 40 different locations within the Rotterdam port. Dutch law sometimes prevented such paper manifests from being removed from their locations. These factors together made it difficult for CSI to receive accurate and complete and timely manifest data before the containers left Rotterdam.

According to Sarathy (2005), the information deficiencies that became apparent through the Rotterdam exercise led to the introduction of the United States Advance Manifest Rule (also referred to as the 24 hour rule). This requires all ocean carriers or nonvessel operating common carriers to electronically transmit cargo manifests and entry data to the CBP Automated Manifest System 24 hours before the United States bound cargo is loaded onto a vessel at the port of export. In essence, the 24 hour rule shifted responsibility for the provision of information from the foreign ports to carriers, forwarders, and brokers.

The 24 hour rule is a further example of a control specific initiative, one focusing predominantly on prescribed information and procedural compliance. Other United States control specific initiatives include the Secure Freight Initiative (SFI)[9] as well as the 10+2 rule and the practice of 100 percent maritime cargo container scanning under the United States Secure Freight International Container Security project (both mentioned earlier). Such initiatives are not solely being pursued by the United States— a fact evidenced by the widespread adoption of the 24 hour rule (and variations of it) by other customs administrations. Border related security initiatives are now ubiquitous. Even so, most responses to the threat of supply chain terrorism can be traced back to their United States origins. The C-TPAT initiative, for example, ultimately led to the development of the WCO SAFE Framework of Standards to Secure and Facilitate Global Trade—including the authorized economic operator concept, which has been or is being introduced around the world in one form or another. The C-TPAT focus on relatively broad supply chain security risks and the development of an overall framework for managing supply chain security have been further built on with the introduction of the International Maritime Organization International Ship and Port Security (ISPS) Code, the United States SAFE Port Act,[10] the International Organization for Standardization supply chain security standard (ISO 28000), and the United States Known Shipper program (mentioned earlier), which is being implemented by a range of transport security agencies around the world.

Governments outside the United States have adopted supply chain security regulations. The European Commission has its own advance cargo information regulation called Pre Arrival / Pre Departure (enacted in 2005 and to take effect in 2011), and it has the European Union authorized economic operator program (enacted in 2008). Japan's Advance Filing Rules on Cargo, Crew and Passenger Information, which took effect in 2007, covers cargo arriving by sea or air in Japan. China's 24-hour Advance Manifest Rule—which took effect in 2009—mandates that for all export, import, and transshipped cargo by any Chinese ports, ocean carriers must provide the manifest or the bill of lading to Chinese Customs 24 hours prior to loading. In addition, authorized economic operator programs have been launched by Japan (in 2006) and by China (in 2008; see Donner and Kruk 2009, pp. 11–13).

Two United States control specific initiatives that are currently being debated on their implementation, and which the international community is watching particularly closely, are the 10+2 rule and the 100 percent scanning initiative. Formally known as Importer Security Filing (ISF) and Additional Carrier Requirements, the 10+2 rule requires importers and ocean carriers to electronically submit data elements—in addition to the 24 or so data elements that they are currently required to provide— to the United States Department of Homeland Security Customs and Border Protection agency. The purpose of this initiative is to improve risk based targeting in relation to cargo destined for importation into the United States before the cargo is loaded on vessels at foreign ports.

The practice of 100 percent container scanning is requested by a 2007 United States law that involves the scanning of all United States bound container cargo at foreign ports by 2012 using nonintrusive inspection equipment, including radiation detection and imaging equipment.[11] A pilot program to test the feasibility of 100 percent scanning has been conducted at six selected CSI ports.

Appropriateness of the regulatory initiatives

A significant number of the security related regulatory initiatives that have been introduced since the 2001 attacks are representative of a risk management based regulatory approach and reflect many of the principles of compliance oriented regulation, of which risk management based regulation is a subset.

Partnership programs

The WCO SAFE Framework, the United States C-TPAT program, and the various national programs based on the SAFE Framework's authorized economic operator concept are all considered to fall within the management based regulation category. Importantly, all such programs are voluntary. Members of the international trading community are invited to join the various programs on the understanding that they will derive benefits not available to those who choose not to apply for membership. The various schemes do not impose any regulatory burden on industry participants that the participants are not willing to accept, and the decision to participate is based solely on considerations of commercial and social responsibility.

Each of the programs has a clear focus on supply chain visibility, but in a way that encourages industry participants to address the required security risk outcomes in a relatively flexible manner. This is achieved by leveraging business knowledge, operating practices, and information systems, with an opportunity for the regulators to verify industry's self assessed findings. Also, by leveraging existing commercial practices and procedures in this way, any disruption to business processes is reduced as much as possible.

The various programs also reflect sound principles of risk management by seeking to identify low risk members of the trading and transport community. The principal aim of C-TPAT, the European Union authorized economic operator program, and the Known Shipper program, for example, is to provide border agencies with a method of identifying secure elements of the international supply chain and so allow them to focus their resources on potentially high risk operators. Assessing the compliance levels of such companies, regardless of the result, provides the agencies with a clearer picture of compliance levels and the potential impact of noncompliance. This in turn greatly assists in determining where future compliance resources should be directed.

The notions of coordination, cooperation, and collaboration, which are at the heart of modern regulatory compliance, are well served by these compliance programs. Such programs help create a network of secure operations, they establish a base level of security standards, and they help raise the overall level of security for global operations. Also, participation in voluntary programs helps to further build the partnerships between the public sector and private industry necessary to create a secure environment (Purtell and Rice 2007).

There are, however, a number of concerns with these schemes, all related to the need to deliver the benefits claimed by authorities. Indeed, there is considerable doubt as to whether some of the identified benefits—particularly those associated with the mutual recognition of authorized economic operator status—will ever see the light of day. Given that all international trade has to take account of activities in at least two separate countries, there are obvious shortcomings for commercial operators in a situation where compliance and facilitation incentives apply only at export or import. Customs, looking for origin-destination supply chain security, and industry—particularly the exporters—are even more conscious of the benefits of intergovernmental cooperation to give authorized economic operator programs extended application and extra benefits to all concerned. Consequently, the mutual recognition of such programs and of authorized economic operator status becomes a quite important agenda for many customs administrations and economic operators (Irish 2009, p. 80; Buzdugan 2005, pp. 84, 99–100). According to the WCO (2007, p. 54):

> The Resolution on the SAFE Framework . . . calls upon Customs administrations to work with each other to develop mechanisms for mutual recognition of AEO validations and authorizations, and Customs control results and other mechanisms that may be needed to eliminate or reduce redundant or duplicated validation and authorization efforts.

> Mutual recognition is a broad concept whereby an action or decision taken or an authorization that has been properly granted by one Customs administration is recognized and accepted by another Customs administration. The standardized approach to

Authorized Economic Operator authorization provides a solid platform for long-term development of international systems of mutual recognition of AEO status at bilateral, sub-regional, regional and, in the future, global levels. In order for a system of mutual recognition to work it is essential that . . . there be an agreed set of common standards.

However, while some WCO members are interpreting the guidelines to require an authorized economic operator to demonstrate a high level of supply chain security (for example, Singapore), others are adopting a far broader interpretation that includes customs compliance generally. The European Union, for example, requires an authorized economic operator to demonstrate (European Commission 2007):

- An appropriate record of compliance with customs requirements.
- A satisfactory system of managing commercial and, where appropriate, transport records, which allows appropriate customs controls.
- Where appropriate, proven financial solvency.
- Where applicable, appropriate security and safety standards.

Clearly an unfortunate casualty of this failure to agree on basic authorized economic operator criteria is the concept of mutual recognition. If one administration requires an entity to demonstrate levels of both general compliance and security compliance before being granted authorized economic operator status, but another grants that status solely on the basis of security compliance, the achievement of mutual recognition is unlikely—unless the parties are prepared to adopt a lowest common denominator approach.

Another potential benefit that has attracted some attention is the potential for reduced insurance premiums, that is, the possibility that certification as an authorized economic operator or member of C-TPAT may result in a reduced risk profile and therefore lower premiums. However, measures to improve security do not necessarily lead to a reduction in insurance premiums, because insurance companies take a networked view of the supply chain (as they should) and are therefore concerned that a secure entity may be tainted by less secure entities that form part of their supply chain. This reflects the principle that any supply chain is only as good as its weakest link and risk attaches to the entirety of the supply chain, not just one entity within it (OECD 2009a). Indeed, it is not known if any participants in either C-TPAT or an authorized economic operator program have received cheaper insurance by virtue of that participation.

Partnership programs are strengthened in both their efficiency and effectiveness when they seek to incorporate a broader range of regulatory matters than those relating to a single authority. To achieve this a significant degree of interagency collaboration is required.

The OECD has recognized the dangers of a one dimensional, or silo, approach by government that fails to acknowledge the connections and interdependencies of modern society. As it states in its publication "Innovation in Country Risk Management" (OECD 2009b, pp. 4–5):

> Over time highly defined areas of competence tend to develop in which numerous ministries, departments and regulatory agencies at various levels of government carry out operations in parallel and separate silos. A modern networked society with increased connections and interdependencies may be exposed to unforeseen vulnerabilities when risks arise that do not fit neatly within the remit of one particular department. Indeed, government departments might focus on one phase of what is actually a multi-layered risk management cycle. . . . Policymakers, regulators and emergency services with narrow or short-sighted focus on achieving their individual mandates may also miss opportunities, fail to leverage the expertise of colleagues in different government departments, compare different types of risks and share lessons learned.

Supply chain security initiatives that fail to encourage interagency collaboration invite the same sort of costs and inefficiencies as initiatives that ignore the commercial aspects of the supply chain. The preferred governance model for risk management, as identified by the OECD from its various case studies, is therefore one characterized by an

The national security environment: strategic context

approach that addresses networked risk by (OECD 2009b, p. 11):

- Coordinating the many central, regional, and local government bodies in their various efforts to implement national policy goals related to public safety and security.
- Providing guidance to such bodies on how to conduct risk assessments.
- Streamlining and standardizing reporting requirements for risk assessment and emergency management plans through a common information sharing mechanism.

The WCO SAFE Framework—with its government-to-business and government-to-government pillars—is considered to be a good example of a governance approach that is relevant and effective in the international trade and transport security environment. Its effective realization is, however, likely to take some time.

Additional information requirements

The 10+2 rule (or ISF) is based on the same supply chain security philosophy as CSI—although in this case the initiative is related to the information associated with the cargo (in line with China's 24-hour Advance Manifest Rule). In essence the 10+2 rule extends the advance manifest requirement further into the supply chain, at least from a data perspective, and shifts the virtual border beyond the port of loading of the cargo back to the manufacturer. If the supply chain is examined from the perspective of the border management agency and it is assumed that the port of destination is the central node in the supply chain for a particular consignment, the data elements that comprise the 10+2 rule can be characterized as follows:[12]

- *Upstream in the supply chain* (importer or customs broker):
  - Manufacturer.
  - Seller.
  - Container stuffing location.
  - Consolidator.
  - Country of origin.
  - Harmonized System (HS) classification.
- *Upstream in the supply chain* (carrier):
  - Vessel stow plan.
  - Container status message.

- *Downstream in the supply chain* (importer or customs broker):
  - Buyer.
  - Importer of record.
  - Ship-to party.
  - Consignee.

The success or otherwise of the 10+2 rule as a risk management tool is totally dependent on its foundation, that is, the quality and timeliness of the data provided. If the data are false or inaccurate, intentionally or otherwise, the utility of ISF is compromised—as are the risk decisions that flow from that data. In this regard, the +2 component provided by the carrier does not really alter the risk equation, because while the container is moving there is less risk of illegal cargo being introduced into it than when it is stationary (see for example OECD 2005).

In this context it is important to note that any persons or groups intent on using the supply chain for criminal or terrorist activity are unlikely to advertise the fact through poor documentation of the trade and transport transaction. It is more probable that they will utilize legitimate sources and plausible data so as not to draw attention to the transaction. For example, they may set up a legitimate international trading company—or purchase one—and establish their legitimate trading credentials over a period of time. It is also likely that they may seek to use a well known and established carrier or logistics provider, perhaps even one that is C-TPAT certified or listed on the Known Shipper Database.

Anyone who may consider this scenario far-fetched need only refer to the example of the Khan network and the level of sophistication exhibited in that case (see for example Crawford and Stecklow 2004; Albright and Hinderstein 2005). The 10+2 rule is unlikely to detect anything unusual about a transaction in situations where the associated information has been constructed in such a way—and yet such a shipment logically falls at the very high or extreme end of the risk scale, at least as far as impact is concerned. If, on the other hand, the 10+2 rule data are unintentionally inaccurate (for example, through transcription errors or other carelessness), it is still unlikely to be detected by regulatory screeners but more likely to be detected than a carefully constructed scam. An economist once argued: "If customs insisted on more accurate manifest reporting, it would be far easier to identify shipments that posed a security risk."[13] However, the authors do not recall anyone actually describing their cargo as "weapons of mass destruction"!

Note also that investigations to uncover sophisticated illegal activities are extremely complex and take considerable time to complete, and consequently targeting under the 24 hour rule is completely reliant upon automated processing systems. For example, it took the authorities about ten years to uncover the activities of the Khan network, and there is little doubt that such activities would not have been identified within 24 hours even if additional data elements had been requested.

It has also been shown that even profiling is not a particularly successful technique for detecting sophisticated illegal activity of this type. For example, Press argues that "strong profiling (defined as screening at least in proportion to prior probability) is no more efficient than uniform random sampling of the entire population, because resources are wasted on the repeated screening of higher probability, but innocent, individuals" (2009, p. 1716).

Good intelligence and risk indicators based on that intelligence are now, and are likely to remain, the most effective and efficient means of detecting unlawful activity prior to arrival of a consignment. Requesting cargo related information as early as possible in an international trade transaction certainly provides extra time for border agencies to undertake a meaningful risk assessment of the cargo and decide whether or not to intervene, either by scanning, physical inspection, or import prevention—but to be effective, such assessments must be based on accurate information.

It is also pertinent to note that, from a compliance perspective, regulated entities can generally be divided into three categories:

- Those who will actively seek to comply.
- Those who will comply provided they are given appropriate incentives to do so (including appropriate incentives to avoid noncompliance).
- Those who will intentionally pursue a course of noncompliance.

Compliant members of the international trading community (including those who fall into the second category) will generally provide authorities with accurate information in relation to their consignments. The information provided facilitates the identification of the cargo, the means of transportation, and the various industry participants in the supply chain, and the fundamental data elements will provide a realistic, basic snapshot of the relevant consignment. While further data elements will assist in building a more comprehensive picture relatively quickly, there comes a saturation point at which additional information is unlikely to usefully contribute to the regulator's knowledge of the transaction.

Based on the assumption that deliberate noncompliers are unlikely to submit completely accurate information to government agencies, the authors believe that the saturation point for such noncompliers will be reached much earlier in the data submission process. In other words, given that certain data elements will be inaccurate, border agencies will at best have access to a handful of relevant information and will be unable to develop a true picture of the transaction beyond some very basic aspects such as the vessel, carrier, and the like. This is because noncompliers are unlikely to provide information that may attract attention from a risk targeting perspective.

This phenomenon is illustrated graphically in figure 18.2. The compliance assessment and regulation model addresses the utility of routine data collection relating to individual transactions from the perspective of identifying potential regulatory

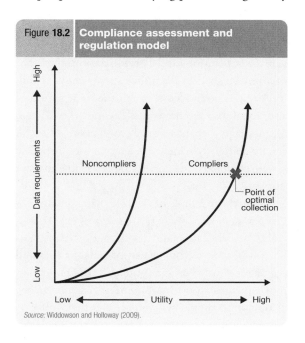

Figure 18.2 | Compliance assessment and regulation model

Source: Widdowson and Holloway (2009).

noncompliance. It postulates three basic principles that can be summarized as follows:

- As data requirements increase, the value added to the assessment process decreases exponentially.
- Beyond a particular point (point of optimal collection) the requirement for additional information adds a regulatory burden to noncompliers with minimal benefit to the regulator.
- The point of optimal collection is reached earlier for noncompliers than for compliers.

The model is qualitative and has not been tested by way of empirical research. The authors would encourage research designed to test the validity of the model.

It is therefore considered that as the provision of more information is mandated, such requirements are likely to add cost to an international trade transaction without a commensurate regulatory benefit. A more cost effective approach that is also more likely to identify supply chain security risk is through secure, real time access (that is, visibility on demand) to existing commercial data in the supply chain and through the leveraging of partnerships with the private sector to assist in identifying anomalies. In the absence of specific intelligence—such as evidence of an internal conspiracy—it should be recognized that industry participants are better placed than regulators to observe what is normal and abnormal as goods move along the supply chain.

Governments can add value by facilitating the process through appropriate regulation, international cooperation, and harmonization and standardization so as to maximize supply chain visibility. Value is not added through the prescription of additional data requirements.[14] As noted by Laden, "A good supply chain security program should retain the flexibility to achieve the goal of a more secure system of global trade . . . not simply become another 'paper tiger'" (2007, p. 80).

A further example of the role that governments can play is in the closely related area of export controls. The publication and dissemination to the public and private sectors of denied persons lists and red flag indicators provide guidance to supply chain participants concerning potential risks, and they also serve to supplement supply chain visibility. A particular advantage of this approach to regulators is that it treats the supply chain itself as an additional compliance management resource.

Examination levels

Many border agencies undertake 100 percent screening of consignments[15]—in the sense that the associated information is screened—and some have already introduced 100 percent physical screening initiatives through the use of radiation portals. Screening, which in many cases is now fully automated, forms an integral part of an appropriate risk management regime that assists in identifying those containers which may pose a security (or other) risk and are therefore candidates for scanning and inspection. The 24 hour rule and similar requirements for advance information contribute to the screening process and the early identification of high risk cargo.

No border agency, however, is physically examining 100 percent of its international trade, through the use of X-ray equipment or otherwise. Indeed, this would be impossible with currently available technology, physical infrastructure, and the volumes of container trade. Consequently, while in theory the physical inspection of the contents of every container may provide the best determination of a security risk, it is also one of the most costly and labor intensive measures to implement.

In this context it is the authors' contention that the concept of 100 percent examination (for example, scanning as opposed to screening), even in the environment after the 2001 attacks, represents the antithesis of risk management. Indeed, no 100 percent examination policy could be considered to represent a valid risk based regulatory control mechanism, as the absence of any form of selectivity excludes its qualification as a legitimate risk treatment. Furthermore, social expectations no longer accept the concept of intervention for intervention's sake. Rather, the current catchphrase is *intervention by exception,* intervention when there is a legitimate need for intervention—that is, intervention based on identified risk.

There has been strident criticism from both the public and private sectors with respect to the possible implementation of 100 percent scanning (see for example Ireland 2009; WCO 2008, 2009). Such criticism covers a broad range of issues including, but not limited to, potential costs and delays (Carafano 2008); staffing challenges (Straw 2008); the lack of physical choke points where large numbers of containers can easily be scanned on their way through ports (Straw 2008); the complexity of the task required of those viewing the scanned images (Straw 2008); and the shortcomings of available technology, regarding which Ritter comments (2009):

> . . . logic follows that there must be a direct relationship between quantity of scanning and risk mitigation. Unfortunately, a stronger relationship actually exists between risk mitigation and enhancing the quality of scanning. The global trade industry would be better served by focusing on mandating improvements in the type of cargo scanning rather than insisting that additional effort be focused on the quantity of scanning.

The portal monitors have proven to be an ideal technology for verifying that legitimate radioactive cargo is present in the supply chain—but little more. Trucks continue to trigger alarms by the thousand each day, and secondary inspections are being performed with increased frequency in United States ports and other select locations throughout the world. These secondary inspections ultimately serve to verify that commodities such as smoke detectors, fire brick, or cat litter are, in fact, emitting harmless amounts of radiation. But verifying *normal* is not the objective. And the actual utility of this approach, with regard to security threats, is still unclear.

It should be noted that the CSI program is not seen to fall into the same category as 100 percent scanning. It is selective in that it focuses on specific ports and adopts a risk based targeting strategy within those ports. As noted by Straw (2008):

> [The United States Department of Homeland Security] has long asserted that it screens 100% of US-bound cargo containers. That never meant a physical examination of each container, however. Rather, it referred to a risk-based screening, beginning with a review of all US-bound container manifests

at their ports of departure for information that indicated elevated risks. Only in cases where documentation gave reason to suspect elevated risk would a container be subjected to physical scanning or inspection.

Conclusion

Mandatory scanning requirements and increased information requirements are intended to form part of the broader suite of security programs which include such initiatives as C-TPAT and the European Union's authorized economic operator program. These initiatives are in turn designed to provide border agencies with a degree of confidence about the security of a participant's supply chain. This being the case, the question that must be asked is this: if a trader demonstrates a commitment to global supply chain security by achieving and maintaining authorized economic operator status, does there remain a genuinely risk based need for the trader to provide advance information to the authorities who granted that status, and for the trader's cargo to be scanned as a matter of routine?

As previously noted, any challenge to the validity of security initiatives can be quickly dismissed on the basis that it is seen not to be supportive of international antiterrorism efforts. However, it is the authors' belief that the time has come to critically evaluate the appropriateness of existing and proposed security initiatives, particularly in the context of contemporary risk management principles and commercial practicality. In this case, the evidence suggests, more is not necessarily better.

International attempts to retrofit security regulation into already overly complex cross border regulatory frameworks are resulting in particularly costly outcomes for industry, and this at a time when economic stimulation is supposedly high on the global political agenda. Regulatory initiatives must therefore be carefully scrutinized to ensure that they are achieving a cost effective outcome for both business and government that is consistent with:

- The desired policy outcome.
- The nature of the operational environment being regulated, including both its commercial practices and relative security risks.

- The extent to which the regulatory requirements are likely to affect the operational effectiveness of the activity being regulated, in this case international trade and transport.

In the authors' opinion the approach that is most likely to achieve these objectives is one of compliance oriented regulation—in which the elements of both enforcement and incentives to comply with regulatory requirements are present—as opposed to the more prescriptive approaches, which are less cost-effective and significantly more disruptive to commercial operations. Border managers are therefore encouraged to focus on the philosophy behind such initiatives when determining what may or may not represent an appropriate regulatory response to their identified security risks.

Notes

1. See "Security Filing '10+2'," United States Department of Homeland Security Customs and Border Protection, http://www.cbp.gov/xp/cgov/trade/cargo_security/carriers/security_filing/.
2. See "SFI: Secure Freight Initiative," United States Department of Homeland Security Customs and Border Protection, http://www.cbp.gov/xp/cgov/trade/cargo_security/secure_freight_initiative/.
3. See "Known Shipper Database," United States Department of Homeland Security Transportation Security Administration, http://www.tsa.gov/what_we_do/layers/aircargo/database.shtm.
4. Event and exception management provides authorized individuals with notification of events that have an impact on the decision-making process. In the business context this might be something like a shortage of inventory or shipment delay. In the government context this might be a change in transport route, origin, or company details. It can form an effective element of a profiling and targeting system.
5. On SITPRO see chapter 6, endnote 1.
6. *Public Health Security and Bioterrorism Preparedness and Response Act of 2002,* Public Law 107–188, 107th Cong. (June 12,

2002). Available at http://www.gpo.gov/fdsys/pkg/PLAW-107publ188/pdf/PLAW-107publ188.pdf.
7. The Act requires registration of all domestic and foreign food facilities that manufacture and process, pack, or hold food for human or animal consumption in the United States.
8. United States Department of Homeland Security, "Container Security Initiative Ports," www.dhs.gov/xprevprot/programs/gc_1165872287564.shtm, accessed 8 June 2009.
9. See "Security Filing with CSI, Megaports," United States Department of Homeland Security Customs and Border Protection, http://www.cbp.gov/linkhandler/cgov/newsroom/fact_sheets/trade_security/sfi/csi_megaports.ctt/csi_megaports.pdf.
10. See "Secure Freight Scanning at a Glance," United States Department of Homeland Security Customs and Border Protection, http://www.cbp.gov/linkhandler/cgov/newsroom/fact_sheets/trade_security/sfi/sfi_scanning.ctt/sfi_scanning.pdf.
11. *Implementing Recommendations of the 9/11 Commission Act of 2007,* Public Law 110–53, 110th Cong. (August 3, 2007). Available online at http://www.gpo.gov/fdsys/pkg/PLAW-110publ53/pdf/PLAW-110publ53.pdf. See section 1701.
12. "Security Filing '10+2'," United States Department of Homeland Security Customs and Border Protection, http://www.cbp.gov/xp/cgov/trade/cargo_security/carriers/security_filing/.
13. Quoted from discussions at the Round Table on Security, Risk Perception and Cost-Benefit Analysis, International Transport Forum and OECD Joint Transport Research Centre, Paris, December 11–12, 2008.
14. It should be noted that CBP has "softened" its stance on ISF recently—for example, by showing restraint in enforcing the rule until March 2010 and by relaxing some elements of interpretation and reporting timelines. However, the fundamental thrust of the initiative remains inappropriate in terms of risk management and commercial reality.

15. The terms *screening, scanning,* and *physical examination* need to be defined. For example, Martonosi, Ortiz, and Willis (2006) define them as follows: *screening* is "the initial assessment of the risk of [containerized cargo] based on the manifest, shipper, carrier, consignee and other information associated with the shipment," *scanning* is "the radiographical scanning of a container via an X-ray or a gamma-ray scanner to identify its contents," and *physical inspection* is "the hand inspection of the contents of a container by customs officers."

References

Aberdeen Group. 2006. "Industry Priorities for Visibility, B2B Collaboration, Trade Compliance, and Risk Management." Global Supply Chain Benchmark Report, Boston.

Albright, D., and C. Hinderstein. 2005. "Unraveling the A.Q. Khan and Future Proliferation Networks." *Washington Quarterly* (Spring): 111–28.

Bennear, L. 2007. "Are Management-Based Regulations Effective? Evidence from State Pollution Prevention Programs." *Journal of Policy Analysis and Management* 26 (2): 327–48.

Buzdugan, M. 2005. "Current and Emerging Air Cargo Security and Facilitation Issues." Institute of Air and Space Law, McGill University, Montreal.

Carafano, James. 2008. "Scanning for Common Sense: Congressional Container Security Mandate Questioned." WebMemo, The Heritage Foundation, Washington DC, June 13. Available at http://www.heritage.org/Research/Reports/2008/06/Scanning-for-Common-Sense-Congressional-Container-Security-Mandate-Questioned.

Closs, D., C. Speier, J. Whipple, and M. Voss. 2008. "A Framework for Protecting Your Supply Chain." *Supply Chain Management Review* 12 (2): 38–45.

Crawford, D., and S. Stecklow. 2004. "Supply Chain: How the Pakistani Nuclear Wing Managed to Skirt Export Laws." *Wall Street Journal Online,* March 23.

Dahlman, O., J. Mackby, B. Sitt, A. Poucet, A. Meerburg, B. Massinon, E. Ifft, M. Asada, and R. Alewine. 2005. "Container Security: A Proposal for a Comprehensive Code of Conduct." National Defense University, Center for Technology and National Security Policy, Washington, DC.

Donner, M., and C. Kruk. 2009. *Supply Chain Security Guide.* Washington, DC: The World Bank.

European Commission. 2007. "Authorized Economic Operators: Guidelines." Working Document TAXUD/2006/1450, European Union, Brussels.

INECE (International Network for Environmental Compliance and Enforcement). 2009. *Principles of Environmental Compliance and Enforcement Handbook.* 2nd ed. Washington, DC: INECE.

Ireland, R. 2009. "The WCO SAFE Framework of Standards: Avoiding Excess in Global Supply Chain Security Policy." *Global Trade and Customs Journal* 4 (11/12).

Irish, M. 2009. "Supply Chain Security Programs and Border Administration." *World Customs Journal* 3 (2): 79–85.

Kommerskollegium (Swedish National Board of Trade). 2008. "Supply Chain Security Initiatives: A Trade Facilitation Perspective." National Board of Trade, Stockholm.

Laden, M. 2007. "The Genesis of the US C-TPAT Program: Lessons Learned and Earned by the Government and Trade.'" *World Customs Journal* 1 (2): 75–80.

Long, S. 2009. "Port Community Systems." *World Customs Journal* 3 (1): 63–67.

Martonosi, S., D. Ortiz, and H. Willis. 2006. "Evaluating the Viability of 100 Per Cent Container Inspection at America's Ports." In *The Economic Impacts Of Terrorist Attacks,* ed. H. Richardson, P. Gordon, and J.E. Moore II. Northampton, MA: Edward Elgar Publishing. 218–41.

OECD (Organisation for Economic Co-operation and Development). 1997. "Report on Regulatory Reform: Synthesis." OECD, Paris.

———. 2005. "Container Transport Security Across Modes." European Conference of Ministers of Transport, OECD, Paris.

———. 2008. "Management-Based Regulation: Implications for Public Policy." Document GOV/PGC/REG5, OECD, Paris.

————. 2009a. "Security, Risk Perception and Cost-Benefit Analysis." Discussion Paper 2009-6, Joint Transport Research Center, International Transport Forum, Paris.

————. 2009b. "Innovation in Country Risk Management." OECD Studies in Risk Management, OECD, Paris.

Press, William H. 2009. "Strong Profiling Is Not Mathematically Optimal for Discovering Rare Malfeasors." *Proceedings of the National Academy of Sciences of the United States of America* 106 (6): 1716–19.

Purtell, D., and J.B. Rice, Jr. 2007. "Assessing Cargo Supply Risk." *Security Management Online,* June 15. Available at http://www.securitymanagement.com.

Ritter, Luke. 2009. "100% Cargo Scanning Mandate—Quantity, Quality and the Optimal Solution." Editorial, Homeland Security Innovation Association, n.p. Available at http://www.hlsia.org/editorial.htm.

Sarathy, R. 2005. "Terrorism, Security and the Global Supply Chain." Paper presented at the Conference on International Trade and Logistics, Corporate Strategies and the Global Economy, Le Havre, September.

SITPRO. 2008. "A UK Review of Security Initiatives in International Trade." SITPRO, London.

"The Stark Reality of iPod's Chinese Factories." *Mail Online*, 18 August 2006. Available at http://www.mailonsunday.co.uk/pages/live/articles/news/news.html?in_article_id=401234&in_page_id=1770, accessed 8 June 2010.

Straw, Joseph. 2008. "Outlook for Container Scanning." *Security Management,* October. Available at http://www.securitymanagement.com/article/outlook-container-scanning-004692.

UNCTAD (United Nations Conference on Trade and Development). 2006. "ICT Solutions to Facilitate Trade at Border Crossings and in Ports." Document TD/B/COM.3/EM.27/2, UNCTAD, Geneva.

WCO (World Customs Organization). 2007. *WCO SAFE Framework of Standards.* Brussels: WCO.

————. 2008. "Customs in the 21st Century: Enhancing Growth and Development Through Trade Facilitation and Border Security." WCO, Brussels, June.

————. 2009. "Joint Resolution of the Customs Co-operation Council's Policy Commission and the Private Sector Consultative Group Concerning the WCO SAFE Framework of Standards and the United States Legal Requirements for 100 Percent Container Scanning at Export" (Almaty Resolution). Document SP0292E1a, Policy Commission, WCO, Brussels, January.

Widdowson, D. 1998. "Managing Compliance: More Carrot, Less Stick." In *Tax Administration: Facing the Challenges of the Future*, ed. C. Evans and A. Greenbaum. Sydney: Prospect. 99–104.

————. 2005a. "Customs Partnerships: A Two-Way Street." Paper presented to the European Customs Conference organized by the European Forum for Foreign Trade, Customs and Excise, Bonn, June 10.

————. 2005b. "Managing Risk in the Customs Context." In *Customs Modernization Handbook,* ed. L. De Wulf and J. Sokol. Washington, DC: The World Bank. 91–99.

————. 2006. "Raising the Portcullis." Paper presented to the WCO Conference on Developing the Relationship between the WCO, Universities and Research Establishments, Brussels, March.

Widdowson, D., and S. Holloway. 2009. "Maritime Transport Security Regulation: Policies, Probabilities and Practicalities." *World Customs Journal* 3 (2): 17–42.

19 Border management considerations in fragile states

Luc De Wulf

In developing countries border management is a complex affair. Countries that recognize the need to improve their border management operations can draw on international experience and lessons from best practice—and on international support to initiate reforms. For customs, the World Customs Organization (WCO) has for years been a forum for detailing procedures and for helping members put these procedures in place. Other border agencies do not benefit from such international guidance, but their interventions are usually simpler and are focused on more specific objectives.

Until now international experience with projects to strengthen border management has often come from projects carried out in a normal operational environment for border agencies. Here the term *normal* implies that government provides basic security and that it provides a functioning legal and judicial environment. In such conditions traditional, time tested methods for supporting and assisting border agencies—when well designed and delivered—promise to yield results.

Different sets of problems arise for border management reform in fragile or weak states—the topic of this chapter. The chapter's first section describes the most frequently used criteria for identifying a fragile or weak state (henceforth a *fragile state*). The second section draws on the experience of the international community to help fragile states deliver services to their citizens, and it outlines key lessons learned from a variety of implemented projects—not only for border agencies. The third section details nontraditional customs management

reform programs carried out in recent years to help authorities in fragile states improve border management.

This chapter does not focus broadly on border management. Rather, it focuses more narrowly on the most important agency operating at the border—customs. On the one hand, revenue collection by customs is high on the agenda in fragile states (for which revenue is always a key priority)—as well as for the donor community that typically supports such countries. On the other hand, initiatives for customs in fragile states have already been implemented, and instructive lessons can be extracted from these experiences. Yet the same lessons may be applied equally to the improvement of other agencies operating at the border.

Definition of fragile states and lessons learned from past support

This section provides the widely accepted definition of fragile or weak states—and it argues that, for the application of nontraditional customs practices, a somewhat broader country grouping is desirable. Experience on the ground confirms that countries not covered by the traditional definition of *fragile state* have adopted many nontraditional customs practices and can provide guidance on how best to use these practices.

Definition of fragile states and countries targeted in this chapter

The term fragile state (or weak state) is used for countries facing particularly severe development challenges. The World Bank Independent Evaluation Group describes these countries as follows: "Most have poor governance and are embroiled in extended internal conflicts or are struggling through tenuous postconflict transitions. They face similar hurdles of widespread lack of security, fractured relations among societal groups, significant corruption, breakdown in the rule of law, absence of mechanisms for generating legitimate power and authority, a huge backlog of investment needs, and limited government resources for development" (IEG–World Bank 2006, p. xxiii). A working group advising the multilateral development banks recommended that they identify potentially fragile situations based on: "(a) an absolute cut-off point of an average CPIA [Country Policy and Institutional Assessment] country rating of 3.2 or less, or (b) the presence of UN [United Nations] and regional (e.g. African Union, European Union, Organization of American States) peace-keeping or peace-building missions during the past three years."[1] All observers agree that in the medium to long term countries move in and out of the fragile state category.

For analytical purposes—and to help the donor community tailor support most likely to provide results—development partners have converged around an approach developed by the Organisation for Economic Co-operation and Development (OECD), an approach that recognizes common characteristics (weak governance and vulnerability to conflict) along with differentiated constraints and opportunities in fragile situations. Inspired by this approach, this chapter distinguishes six sets of fragile states:

- Countries in prolonged crisis or impasse—military conflict is in full swing, and there may well be an absence of functioning government and of the rule of law.
- Postconflict or political transition countries, with phases related to the situation immediately after conflict and the transition situation that follows the immediate postconflict reconstruction phase (for example, Mozambique and Angola after the cessation of armed conflict).
- Countries that experience a gradual improvement.
- Countries where governance is deteriorating.
- Countries that experience episodes of temporary fragility in the stronger performers—at times, in only part of the country.
- Countries that admit to weakness of administration, with corrupt practices well grounded across the administration or in particular areas.

However, the above classification by itself does not allow the grouping of countries according to the cause of fragility. Such a grouping is important in helping to pinpoint the approaches with the best chance of success in remedying particular governance problems (in this case weak customs agencies). Accordingly, rather than simply using this or another classification of fragile states, this chapter proposes a detailed diagnostic for the problems of border agencies and customs operations in countries targeted for support—first to identify the dysfunctions of border management agencies, and then to seek out the most appropriate support, whether through traditional capacity building approaches or through nonconventional approaches.

Main lessons learned from earlier efforts by the development community to engage in development work in fragile states

The need to do good diagnostic work before engaging in support activities is also confirmed by the lessons learned in earlier efforts to assist fragile states. Past initiatives to assist border management agencies in fragile states often have not delivered the results expected. Sometimes this was because of unrealistic ambitions and the need to be seen as achieving results rapidly. At other times it was because insufficient resources were allocated. Periodic assessments of donor organizations' support to fragile states have somewhat improved the performance of

Border management considerations in fragile states

this intrinsically difficult set of support projects. A World Bank review of support to low income countries under stress in 2006 suggested that there had been a modest increase in the number of projects with outcomes rated satisfactory—from 50 percent in 2002 to 58 percent in 2003, 65 percent in 2004, and 82 percent in 2005 (IEG–World Bank 2006, p. xxv). Contributing to the increase were improved donor coordination, more realistic needs assessment, and better project monitoring. Below is a list of key lessons learned from the experience.[2]

- *Security.* Without basic security it will be impossible to deliver basic services, certainly in the areas of revenue mobilization and community protection. Local and foreign staff must be assured of the security of their life and property. No ironclad guarantees can be given in this area, but measures must be put in place to ensure that staff can execute their official functions without undue safety risks. The same is true for citizens that need to comply with basic legal provisions related to service delivery. Citizens should not have to fear retaliation, corrupt behavior, or the like. In some cases domestic security forces can be deployed. In other cases there will be a need to call on foreign peacekeepers.

- *Diagnosis of the key problems must precede policy formulation and implementation.* Projects benefit from a thorough diagnosis of situations—such as the political situation—that will limit what can be achieved and should inform the modalities of delivering support. Political sensitivities and the existence of clan loyalties—for instance—also need to be taken into account. Local expertise and experience need to be mobilized, and this can be done only after a detailed analysis of available human and financial resources and service delivery issues on the ground.[3] All too often this step has been skipped or shortchanged in favor of framing an urgent response.

- *Country ownership and absorptive capacity are at least as important as the technical quality of the knowledge products delivered.* Involve country counterparts to a degree. Even in deteriorating situations some state involvement should be sought. Where possible, international actors should avoid activities that undermine national institution building, such as the development of parallel systems without thought to transition mechanisms and long term capacity development. It is important to identify functioning systems within existing local institutions and work to strengthen these systems.

- *Work on a realistic vision of reform, and identify steps ahead to achieve the vision.* Reform design and sequencing need to be identified up front, not invented along the way. The lack of a vision has prevented many projects from achieving their ultimate goal of enabling local authorities to take over in due course. The vision should be realistic and shared as much as possible with the segments of the population most affected—where possible, with the population at large. Policy issues affecting the operations of border agencies should be addressed and announced transparently, not presented as donor driven priorities (an example from trade policy was the proposal to introduce a flat tariff rate when the Reconstruction Trade Policy Package was suggested for Iraq).

- *Donor coordination and predictable aid levels must be part of the support program.* The World Bank is working with the United Nations, the European Commission, and bilateral donors at the OECD Development Assistance Committee (DAC) to revise the guidance for integrated postconflict recovery planning, aiming at providing a shared platform to support greater coherence among political, security, development, and humanitarian actors in fragile transition situations.

- *Capacity building needs to start early.* It must not be launched as an afterthought.

- *Monitoring of progress is required, as there will be lot of learning by doing.* Without adequate monitoring it is not possible to identify what has been achieved, what the implementation problems have been, and how to adjust the project accordingly. The success of these projects depends largely on the capacity to adapt to changing circumstances and lessons learned in the field. Reviews of many projects have noted, though, that to remedy data shortcomings the projects need to include a data gathering component.

- *Sharing positive and negative experiences across similar projects improves project design.* This requires a dedicated effort, with contributions from people other than the task managers, who may not be in the best position to take the initiative in sharing. Sharing can lead to better guidelines for new operations. Narrative and problem solving notes, however, are likely to be more useful than formal guidelines.

- *Expectations for success should be realistic.* The World Bank's experience shows that the success rate of projects in fragile states—though it has been increasing over the years—is substantially smaller than in the rest of its portfolio. Projects implemented in countries with lower Country and Policy Institutional Assessment (CPIA) ratings have a lower probability of success. Staff working on these projects should recognize these constraints, and any later failures should not necessarily affect their career prospects.

If these lessons are kept in mind during project design and implementation, they are sure to improve the chances of success for projects aiming at border management improvement in fragile states.

Border management in fragile states: key elements of the institutional framework

Border management comprises the activities of all government agencies with responsibility for ensuring that imports satisfy environmental, security, industrial, and phytosanitary standards as well as customs requirements. The importance of these agencies shifts somewhat over time and with circumstances. Experience has shown that developing countries that rely heavily on customs revenues give customs great importance. Consequently, standards inspection often is given much less importance in such countries—as reflected in the scarcity of resources and staff for standards inspection, or even by the relevant agencies' total absence from border posts.

This emphasis on customs revenue generation is even more acute in fragile states than in developing countries in general. In fragile states the agencies responsible for generating domestic revenue often are incapable of functioning properly, leading local governments and donors to look at foreign trade as the sole tax base for necessary budget revenues. Donors—under pressure from their own constituencies to gradually reduce their financing in fragile states—operate under the strong belief that using foreign trade as the tax base is both expedient and, in the short term, the only alternative available. Hence they tend to concentrate on strengthening the role of customs in generating budget revenue, not on strengthening the roles of most other border agencies. Often the mission of customs to stem weapons smuggling is also very high on the priority list, as restoring national security is a precondition for normalizing economic activity and fostering development.

To many it seems that raising customs revenues is rather simple compared with levying income taxes—or most other taxes. Officers control the movement of imported and exported goods across the border, and they apply the statutory tax rates to the values of these goods; goods are released only when taxes and duties are paid. In reality, however, the procedures for raising customs duties and taxes are rather complex, and trader compliance often leaves much to be desired. Simplifying somewhat, one may say that customs clearance procedures comprise taking control of goods that traders intend to bring across the border, processing declarations, obtaining payment on duties and taxes, releasing the goods, and undertaking a postclearance audit. Processing customs declarations requires that customs determine the value of goods, the applicable tariff rate, and exemption status. If a preferential tariff applies importers must also present a valid certificate of origin. Some cargo enters the country duty free or for transit purposes, and special customs regimes deal with these trade flows—each with its own operational complexities.

These tasks require an adequate legal framework backed by a judicial system and an effective institutional infrastructure, as well as a functioning management structure and adequate resources. Much has been written on these processes and the enabling environment that permits customs to effectively and efficiently meet its responsibilities. But nearly all the available documentation pertains to countries in a position to implement the guidelines detailed in the World Customs Organization's Revised Kyoto Convention (see chapter 11)—or to countries where these guidelines are at least pertinent and their correct implementation has a realistic chance of success. Efforts by customs and by the donor community to support customs modernization in developing countries have broadly followed these guidelines.

In fragile states the situation is vastly different, and simplified procedures—at times deviating from documented best practices—may need to be considered. The rest of this section focuses on the extent to which customs' legal framework, control and clearance procedures, organizational setup, staffing, and management structure (given customs' key responsibility to mobilize resources) may need to be adjusted to take the circumstances of fragile states into account.

Legal framework

Where a customs administration is being established or reformed but no workable legislative framework is present, much can be gained by preparing a simple, transparent customs code. This can provide an adequate legal basis for customs functions.

Tariffs should be differentiated as little as possible. A single rate—already applied in Chile—may be feasible (such a flat tariff was recommended by the international community in Iraq immediately after the fall of the Saddam Hussein regime). If the change to a single rate is too drastic, one alternative is to set a tariff with very few bands. Another is to set indirect taxes applicable to imports and domestic production high enough to generate the required budget revenues, even if these taxes will initially be collected largely on imports.

The tariff rate differentiation should not be based on the degree of processing, as is often erroneously advocated by technical advisors. Such escalation results in higher effective protection for processed than for nonprocessed goods—a situation that later proves hard to reverse. Protection objectives should be clearly targeted, and they would be better accomplished by imposing a temporary higher tariff on a few well identified goods while their production is being stimulated. Fragile states sometimes rely on specific tariff rates or reference prices for the most common imports, given that customs valuation skills are scarce and compliance amongst the trading community is low (such prices are relied on, formally or informally, in Somalia). But such a practice is crude, unable to differentiate according to the value of goods. It also tends to be regressive. If applied in the short term and for pragmatic reasons, such an approach is understandable—but it should be replaced, as soon as this is

practical, by valuation practices in keeping with World Trade Organization rules.

Customs operations cannot wait until a new comprehensive customs code is prepared and enacted—a process that can be lengthy. In the initial stages of reform, the existing customs code probably can be used as the legal basis for customs actions, provided amendments are made quickly to eliminate excessively obsolete provisions and create a legal foundation for new procedures. But work on drafting a modern code should begin early on, guided by international conventions and agreements in the customs area (World Trade Organization and World Customs Organization) and by generally accepted modern customs procedures. Countries that belong to a customs union or other economic integration arrangement are bound to apply the common customs law of the regional arrangement. Others can be inspired by the legislation prevailing in other countries that have modernized their customs system.

Customs control and clearance procedures

Smooth border crossing procedures require that border agencies have effective control over goods that enter and leave the country—and that they operate with well trained personnel, properly operating information and communications technology (ICT) systems, and adequate infrastructure. These conditions often are not present in fragile states and will take time to put in place. Given the immediacy of the need for budget revenue, tradeoffs among some of the objectives of customs and of other border agencies will need to be accepted. Where other agencies are not present at the border, customs may sometimes act on their behalf with very little specific training—but trade facilitation and the protection of domestic economic activity may suffer. As more qualified personnel become available, as ICT systems become operational, as refined procedures are introduced, and as infrastructure improves, service to the trading community will gradually improve.

Most nontraditional interventions are activated to support customs control and clearance processes. In addition to those discussed in the next section, control and clearance procedures will most likely rely on physical inspection more than is warranted in countries with greater trade compliance and ability to undertake postclearance audits—and on a simplified duty drawback system, rather than on temporary admissions (which are difficult to control and restrict the use of duty exemptions). Security at the border often presents a major challenge for control, particularly in countries that suffer from internal conflict or are emerging from such conflicts. Where border officers are unable to take control of all goods arriving at a border or port because of pilfering or smuggling, it is very unlikely that many goods will be declared to customs and that duties and taxes will be fully paid. (Experience has shown that this often happens when the perimeters of ports and border posts are not well delineated, fenced, or guarded, and surveillance equipment is absent. This was the case in Monrovia when Liberia was liberated and the port was not yet under effective central government control. A similar situation now prevails at the eastern border of the Democratic Republic of Congo.) The geography and existing road infrastructure will dictate the precise nature—and effectiveness—of the intervention. Porous borders, with multiple entry points, will present greater challenges than borders with only one or a few crossing points to be secured.

Port security presents special challenges. The International Maritime Organization has established an International Ship and Port Facility Security (ISPS) Code that requires a security plan for ports, consisting of—among other items—perimeter security, personnel training, and drills. The ISPS Code can guide the implementation of key measures that should permit border agencies to function. The securing of ports in Haiti to enable border control agencies to operate, which has been supported by the international community, may offer a good example. Short term efforts to secure the customs premises—drawing on personnel outside customs, even United Nations peacekeepers—were combined with longer term initiatives to train personnel in security tasks, and finally with infrastructure investment for customs offices and installations (as well as for securing ports and border crossings). Customs should be trained and equipped to gradually assume effective control over import cargo from the military.

Any support activity to customs should take these requirements into account and budget for them.

Organizational structure of customs

Customs is best decentralized, with a central office assuming overall responsibility for customs administration, regional offices functioning as regional headquarters and assuming responsibility for administering customs in their geographical jurisdiction, and local offices for customs control and clearance activities. Decentralized organization requires proper delegation of authority, clear delineation of responsibilities, and effective lines of command and reporting. Broadly speaking, headquarters should concentrate on central management without getting involved in daily routine operations that properly belong to field offices. Experience shows that often this principle is not respected and that managers are often petitioned to make, or insist on making, detailed operational decisions. Thus, in crowded corridors in customs headquarters, importers, customs brokers, and others may wait at the doors of officials—including the customs director general—to obtain authorizations, request intervention in disputes with field managers, or ask for signatures for a variety of purposes. Such practices are greatly disruptive and prevent headquarters from concentrating on important central management functions. They also permit excessive face-to-face contact between traders and customs officials, contacts that all too often challenge integrity. Headquarters will be able to carry out its mandate effectively only if functions and activities are adequately decentralized and authority is adequately delegated to heads of regional and local offices, with appropriate controls in place to ensure compliance with rules and procedural requirements.

Fragile states will benefit from a simple administrative structure that allows them to carry out the most essential customs administration activities in an organized manner. They should avoid imitating the organizational setup of more developed countries, as trade flows initially will comprise only straightforward imports and exports. Below are some guidelines for the organizational structure of customs in fragile states, with the qualification that country variations—in terms of geography and in the role assigned to customs—will require flexibility.

At the headquarters level there should be four units providing local offices with resources and

Border management considerations in fragile states

technical support for revenue collection and control. These are:

- A human resource management unit, focusing on personnel recruitment and selection and the preparation and delivery of urgently needed trainings.
- A technical support unit responsible for the development of customs control and clearance procedures, valuation procedures, tariffs and nomenclature, the control of origin procedures, exemption control, and transit procedures.
- An ICT support unit.
- An internal control unit.

Depending on the available resources and the expected workload, these functions can be grouped initially in just one or two units—to be further split up later, when work volume and available resources permit.

At the regional office level. Depending on the size, geography, and trading activity of a country, a regional governance level may be needed. The initial structure of regional offices should be limited to the most essential support and monitoring functions, similar to what was noted in the previous paragraph for headquarters. The most essential operational support units will concentrate on valuation, classification, origin, internal control, training, and ICT.

At the local office level. This is where all control and declaration processing functions take place to ensure revenue collection and the processing of incoming and outgoing goods flows. Organizational arrangements are needed here for:

- Cargo manifest control and writeoff.
- Declaration reception and validation.
- Declaration checking, including the important duty assessment activities (particularly value, classification, and origin checking).
- The physical inspection of imports.
- The collection of duties and taxes.
- The prevention of smuggling and the securing of goods until they are released from customs control.

Staffing and training

Staffing border agencies in fragile states is a most challenging task—and one that will determine whether progress ultimately is made. A key step in providing for staffing and training is to make a systematic comparison between the staffing requirements (level and qualifications) for a simple customs operation—given the present circumstances of the country—and the staff engaged by customs before the country became a fragile state.

Some countries undertaking customs reform have chosen to pursue radical staff renewal, either by introducing an autonomous revenue agency (ARA; examples are Bolivia, Ghana, and Uganda) or by recruiting a management firm to temporarily assume many customs functions while preparing local staff to take over in due course (examples are Mozambique, Angola, and more recently the Democratic Republic of Congo). Such efforts are time consuming and extremely delicate—as well as costly—but they do have the advantage of being able to draw on the strong elements of the old staff and bring in new blood over time. In circumstances of high unemployment this permits customs to be very selective and recruit good staff. The process can, however, be very contentious—at times it will be impossible to remove the existing staff—and yet it must obtain both internal and external legitimacy. Such a radical program needs to be grounded in a thorough understanding of the forces at play in the country.

Whatever method is chosen to select the staff for border control activities, much will be gained from providing them with appropriate training. For immediate needs, urgent basic skills training should be organized for available personnel so that the new or reformed customs systems and procedures can be implemented without delay. These courses should instill the basic skills and attitudes of a civil servant, such as service orientation and integrity, and they should provide a basic understanding of the new customs system (concentrating on the most essential controls and procedures). More extensive training will need to be provided as soon as it can be organized. Therefore, the development of a comprehensive training system should begin early on. Obviously the duration and curriculum will depend on the severity of initial staffing constraints. Newcomers normally should undergo full time induction training. A part time arrangement, such as half a day of work and half a day of instruction, may work well, as it allows a larger number of staff to be trained early. Technical assistance from international or regional organizations, neighboring countries, or other providers can help deliver the training. In addition to classroom training, on-the-job training—side by side with foreign experts—should be arranged if possible.

Management structure

Key responsibilities of customs management include setting strategic and operational plans, establishing performance measurement and evaluation systems, developing personnel management and development systems, providing internal controls to ensure that procedures are followed correctly and ethical standards are adhered to, ensuring a good management information system, and ensuring that relations with the trading community are maintained. This is a tall order for customs in fragile states, for which the initial priority is to raise revenue.

Two issues stand out here. First, revenue targets should be realistic given the scale of trade, the compliance level of the trading community, and the risk that old habits (challenging to staff integrity) will linger. Overambitious targets will discourage management and staff even as they lead to overly optimistic expectations that, as history has shown, often result in the replacement of top customs management.

Second, customs staff members who are paid decently and on time will be a major strength to the organization—and will allow management to enforce discipline, as the risk of losing a decently paid job in a society with rampant unemployment is a strong incentive for avoiding disciplinary action. Fragile states often are plagued by the nonpayment or late payment of civil service salaries. This could be remedied by letting customs retain part of the revenues it raises to pay its staff—an earmarking practice that is contrary to budget orthodoxy, but that may well be accepted temporarily, as a pragmatic way to ensure that the key responsibility of customs is met (mobilizing the resources to finance government expenditures).

Border management in fragile states: nontraditional approaches

One of the major lessons learned from past support to fragile states is that their precarious circumstances require a pragmatic rethinking of traditional approaches to project definition, preparation, and implementation. What matters in these circumstances is not adhering to tested approaches, but searching for approaches that can promise results in the difficult circumstances of a fragile state.

Experience has shown that in these circumstances results can be delivered through a greater involvement of the local community and traditional power structures, through the use of private sector providers, and through a reliance on nongovernmental organizations for the delivery of key services. Testing the new approaches, monitoring them closely, and introducing modifications are all parts of this pragmatic approach, which has been tested selectively in countries facing serious constraints to the implementation of the traditional processes and techniques. This section first compares the traditional approaches used for strengthening customs with the techniques used in fragile states, where the traditional methods are unlikely to strengthen customs in its main revenue generating function. Second, the section presents the nontraditional techniques and illustrates their application with case studies and lessons from experience.

Support to customs in fragile states may rely on nontraditional approaches different from those used for other countries

Where traditional approaches are not expected to yield good results, several developing countries have relied on approaches that stood out for their pragmatism and promise rather than for their adherence to customs orthodoxy and consistency with international best practice. This section focuses on the approaches that differ most radically from a traditional customs model, including:

- Relying on management contracts with outside firms.
- Relying on a substantial presence of foreign technical experts.
- Creating an autonomous revenue agency (ARA).
- Hiring preshipment inspection and destination inspection companies.
- Relying heavily on reforms driven by ICT.
- In landlocked countries, requesting that customs clearance take place at the first port of entry.

- Obtaining advance notification from the departure port of arriving cargo.

The section describes each process in some detail, provides country specific examples (where adopted), and assesses the possible contributions of each approach—evaluating its conditions for success and its possible pitfalls, with a summary of the important lessons for fragile states.

Management contracts

A management contract is a time bound contract that country authorities make with a foreign company to manage its customs services—to raise substantially greater import duties than the country could raise itself, and to prepare the country to take over full customs responsibilities within a given timeframe. The contractor is paid on a fixed price basis or, more commonly, on a percentage of import values, possibly complemented by a performance related payment.

Three such contracts have been implemented: with Crown Agents in Mozambique (1997–2006) and Angola (began 2001 and still ongoing),[4] and with customs and Tax Consultancy LLC in the Democratic Republic of Congo (began in 2008).[5] Such contracts have also been considered by several other countries in recent years. Because the contract with Mozambique has been completed and its results can be evaluated with some benefit from historical perspective, it will be used to illustrate such contracts—and to draw lessons for other authorities considering such a contract.

Main features of a management contract: the example of Mozambique (1997–2006). In Mozambique the contract with Crown Agents was made after the country emerged from a long civil war that had seriously weakened its institutions.[6] The public sector operated at a serious deficit, and the donor community was urging the government to raise larger domestic fiscal resources to complement donor contributions. The International Monetary Fund (IMF) provided technical assistance and advice, but at that time no donors were ready to finance the long term technical assistance needs that would have been required to help Mozambique Customs upgrade its revenue mobilization capacities.

The Government of Mozambique, with the assistance of the United Kingdom Department for International Development (DFID), the IMF, and the World Bank, issued an international tender for management services that Crown Agents eventually won. The DFID covered 43 percent of the project cost, and the Mozambique government financed the rest of the total $37 million estimated project cost for the first three years using proceeds from a World Bank infrastructure project.

The objectives of the contract were:
- Sustainably improve customs receipts and introduce financial controls to prevent internal fraud and theft. Customs duties, representing about 60 percent of total budget revenues, would need to bear the brunt of revenue mobilization for some time to come; no quantitative targets were retained, in part because of the unavailability of a useful database and the great uncertainty about future economic development in the country.
- Develop an appropriate modern administration structure and organization and introduce effective, efficient customs control procedures.
- Assess staff qualifications and integrity, and take the needed steps to retrench redundant staff and recruit and train new staff.
- Review customs legislation and regulations, with a view to providing a basis for consistent, transparent customs operations.
- Introduce antismuggling techniques.
- Introduce a computer driven customs management system.

The contract specified that to undertake this assignment Crown Agents would take over the management of customs. Crown Agents recruited about 60 expatriate staff and gradually placed them in executive and operational positions. A senior Crown Agents consultant was appointed as delegated manager of customs and was responsible for carrying out the reform as specified in the contract. A Mozambique national was retained as deputy director of customs, to provide a legal basis for action in cases where the law did not confer necessary powers on a nonnational or on someone not belonging to the Mozambique civil service. A Technical Unit for Reconstructing Customs (UTRA, its initials in Portuguese) was created to monitor the implementation of the contract and take on the issues that required sovereign powers. The foreign experts were first assigned to the port of Maputo and later to other points of entry into the country.

The contractor claims the following outcomes:

- Despite a sharp reduction in tariff rates, customs duty receipts nearly doubled in dollar terms between 1997 and 2006. Duties as a share of imports rose slightly from 8.9 percent in 1995 to about 10 percent in 1999–2000, but they fell back to slightly over 4 percent of imports by 2006, largely as a result of the reduction in tariff rates. When the value added tax (VAT) was introduced in 2000, customs was well positioned to manage this tax; by 2001–02 the VAT on imports raised nearly a quarter of total tax revenue. Clearance times fell during the early years of the program—from more than a month when the program started, to 18 days in 2000, to about 8 days in mid-2002.
- Internal fraud, causing millions dollars of revenue loss, was documented and halted.
- Enforcement was strengthened and led to larger numbers of seizures—but staff corruption continued to plague the customs organization at the end of the contract.
- The program of staff renewal was undertaken through a retrenchment program and the systematic recruitment and training of new staff, with the result that by the end of the contract the skill mix of customs staff had substantially improved. Although the retrenchment program encountered serious delays and resistance, it was eventually completed in the last phase of the project.
- A basic computer based customs management system was gradually put in place.
- Customs clearance processes were reviewed and somewhat modernized, but manual procedures and paper based processes were still prevalent at the end of the contract—and basic elements of the customs control system, such as electronic manifest submission and Electronic Data Interchange (EDI), are still awaiting implementation.
- A new customs code and operational regulations were issued, in conformity with WCO best practices.
- Strengthening national customs management took more time than anticipated—the major

reason why the contract was extended beyond the timeframe originally envisioned.
- Customs authorities have positively assessed the management contract experience at international conferences.[7]
- Private sector operators have expressed satisfaction with the progress achieved, particularly with the reduction in clearance times and the reduction of blatant corruption.

Lessons from Mozambique and other management contracts. The Crown Agents project in Mozambique was the first of its kind and was initiated in very difficult circumstances. Donors, recipient countries, and contractors had no body of experience to draw on. Yet with the benefit of hindsight, the experience yields some lessons for similar projects:

- *Ensure political will and support* for the objectives of the program and its implementation modalities, including the extensive use of foreign experts in operational capacities. Such will and support are crucial for the acceptance of the program by all stakeholders, and thus for its success.
- *Get staff to buy in.* Special efforts should be made to ensure that the program is owned by the local customs management authorities and staff—not imposed from the outside, marginalizing the staff. The reforms should aim for a good understanding of the local cultural and juridical environment, not a replication of donor country practices. The implementation team should include change management experts.
- *Contractors should be accountable to local authorities*—not just to the donor community financing the contract. Care should be taken that this accountability has a structure ensuring clear lines of communication and authority.
- *Customs reform is best implemented as part of a more comprehensive trade policy and trade facilitation reform.* Customs operate within a given trade regime and given tariff regulations, both of which should be supportive of an effective customs operation (the case in Mozambique). Also needed to achieve the set objectives are supportive reforms in civil service employment, border control, judicial appeal, and the enforcement of sanctions and immigration.

Border management considerations in fragile states

19

- *The management contracts should attempt to ensure that contractors are paid based on performance and that the government interferes as little as possible in daily management.*
  - A performance based contract needs milestones that are clear, objective, measurable, and achievable. In the absence of an adequate information base this is easier said than done. Yet a special effort should be made to set performance criteria for revenues raised (taking tariff changes and trade flows into account), for training provided and skills transferred (particularly management skills), and for the time to release import and export cargo.
  - A balance must be established between government oversight of the program and interference in customs management. In Mozambique UTRA was set up for this purpose—but was not fully successful, as some responsibilities, reporting lines, and accountabilities were blurred.
- *Respect the dividing line between taking on operational responsibilities, and exercising sovereign power.* Contractors should restrict themselves to operational responsibilities.
- *The transfer of management skills needs to have very high priority.* This objective should be reflected in the composition of the team of foreign experts and in the team's working method. Hands-on operational customs experts will contribute to achieving the short term objective of raising revenue, while others will need to focus on the training and capacity building objectives of the project. The mandate of the second and third Crown Agents contracts in Mozambique addressed this issue head on by establishing a one-to-one mentoring program. Recruiting a balanced team of foreign experts with the required skills will remain a challenge, as it requires recruiting customs experts who are available on short notice and willing to work extensively in a difficult environment.
- *An explicit customs modernization strategy is needed.* Contractors should be guided by such strategy, informed by a detailed diagnostic.
- *Contractors should abide by established civil service regulations*—particularly when dealing with staff retrenchments and dismissal for corruption, for which labor legislation stipulates particular processes (due process, proof of evidence). Failing to abide by established regulations can lead to appeals that are acrimonious and expensive to settle.
- *A well thought through and implemented communications campaign* should inform all stakeholders—staff as well as the trading community—of the program objectives. The implementation details will benefit program outcomes.
- *The management contract should specify a clear exit strategy.* As the contract is a temporary solution for a crisis situation, the exit strategy should provide for the transfer of management skills, for country ownership and maintenance of the new electronic customs management system, for infrastructure acquisition, and for maintenance and future financing.
- *Various financing formulas can be drawn up for management contracts.* In the Crown Agents contract with Mozambique costs were shared between DFID and the government, with the contractor fees set up as a fixed management fee. An alternative would pay the contractor out of the additional revenue resulting from its intervention. Calculating such added revenue is not simple, as revenue developments are also affected by exchange rate fluctuations, tariff changes, and changes in trade policy and trade flows. A clear understanding on an accepted methodology would need to be reached in advance. Another alternative is for a private company to invest in the venture and be paid through levying a transaction fee (much as the Ghana Community Network is entrusted with managing the single window in Ghana; see De Wulf 2004).

Heavy reliance on foreign experts from donor countries

For some developing countries the development community decided that the best way to strengthen revenue performance was to send a heavy contingent of technical experts to build capacity in customs—or even, for the short term, to do hands-on work in customs operations. The approach and the difficulties encountered are illuminated here by three case studies:

- The experience of Australia in supporting reform and modernization in Papua New Guinea.
- The experience of Australia in supporting reform and modernization in Solomon Islands.
- The building up of customs services in Timor-Leste.

Papua New Guinea. Support to customs in Papua New Guinea was part of the border management and transport security sector of the broader Enhanced Cooperation Program (ECP), financed by the Australian Government. The ECP aims at improving national security through the strengthening of the country's capacity to collect revenue, facilitate the lawful movement of people and goods across the border, and regulate the safety and security of international transport links. Australian officials were placed in advisory positions in various departments and agencies of the Papua New Guinea government, working with its customs to a logical framework that was negotiated and agreed with its authorities. The framework, which was to last until 2009, set forth the program's goals, purpose, component objectives, outputs, assumptions and risks, key performance indicators, and monitoring indicators. Based on this framework, each technical assistant defined his or her area of responsibility and worked out a detailed work program against which he or she would be evaluated.

Under ECP, Australian Customs has four staff working within the Papua New Guinea Internal Revenue Commission. Although some ECP positions are in-line positions, at customs the technical assistants are in an advisory capacity—they are there to assist the reform process through a combination of technical assistance and capacity building within the organization. The customs ECP team leader acts as the deputy commissioner of customs and provides high level mentoring and advice to the executive staff. The other advisory positions under ECP focus on issues such as investigations, revenue, and border security. In-country advisors are complemented by work placements for Papua New Guinea officers in Australia and by training in both countries. The ECP strategy was expected to move away from hands-on, operational activities

and to gradually focus more on developing government capacity.

Solomon Islands. Since July 2003 Australia has been setting up the Regional Assistance Mission to Solomon Islands (RAMSI), responding to a request for assistance from Solomon Islands Government to restore security and law and order. Following four years of tensions in the country, the program aims at both providing stabilization assistance to Solomon Islands and developing longer term institution strengthening and peace building. Among its objectives are to transform Solomon Islands Customs into an administration capable of delivering revenue and community protection programs and reduce compliance costs through trade facilitation. The program log framework, jointly developed by Australian and Solomon Islands Customs, details activities until 2009, but assistance is likely to continue after this date. The framework gives priority to management development, policy, legislation (including a new tariff schedule, implementing the HS 2002,[8] and revising the exemption schedule), improving business processes (such as compliance and risk management), and ICT (including a cargo management system). In 2005 Australian Customs deployed two officers to Solomon Islands in advisory positions and made resources available for the purchase of equipment. The officers provide advice on operational issues, provide technical assistance, and build capacity. Australian Customs also provides short term work placements and training for Solomon Islands officers in Australia. Corporate governance remains a key issue to be addressed. Capacity and skills within the organization are still limited, and resistance to change makes reform difficult. That is why advisors took substantial operational work even though the emphasis of the program is on capacity building.

Timor-Leste. As in Solomon Islands, so in Timor-Leste a creation or relaunch of customs services benefited from secondments of international customs staff in a comprehensive donor community effort to assist the country. Timor-Leste gained its independence in 2002. Following the 1999 civil unrest in East Timor a United Nations multilateral peacekeeping mission had been established there with executive, judicial, legislative, and administrative

Border management considerations in fragile states

authority. In 2000 the United Nations Transitional Administration in East Timor (UNTAET) comprised approximately 9,000 personnel, including a small number of international customs officers whose charter was to reclaim and rebuild customs services for East Timor.

The Border Service of East Timor (BSET) was one of the first government agencies created, responsible for the critical border services of customs—immigration, quarantine, and assisting with revenue collection and security. In its early development the BSET focused on the basics of creating an administration, determining a mandate, developing legislation, establishing facilities at Dili Airport, Dili Port, and land border crossings, developing processes, and recruiting and training local staff.

Between 2000 and 2002 the customs administrations of Australia, Finland, New Zealand, Portugal, and the United States provided officers to support and guide the BSET's development of organizational and management capacity through tailored training programs, mentoring, and direct supervision. During this time robust procedures and systems that were practical, effective, and tailored to meet the needs of the new customs administration were fully implemented across core competencies. The BSET's capability covered airports, ports, border posts, marine activities, examinations, goods and passenger clearance, intelligence, auditing, and training. In essence, a basic but fully functioning customs service was established.

The program's reliance at its outset on non-Timorese staff in customs was due to a severe shortage of indigenous capacity. The shortage existed largely because customs services previously had been staffed by Indonesian nationals, who had left the country during the independence troubles. The non-Timorese staff were expected to focus on re-establishing key administrative functions and on performing line responsibilities.

In 2001 BSET became the Customs Service of East Timor (CSET), and immigration was established as a separate government service. Following independence in May 2002, under the United Nations Mission of Support in East Timor (UNMISET) peacekeeping and rebuilding mission, three customs officials from Portugal and Myanmar were engaged to lead and manage the emerging Timor-Leste Customs Service in the Director and Deputy Director positions. Successive Portuguese advisors remained in place until September 2007.

Unfortunately the officials from Portugal kept existing systems in place, developing no clear vision for a future organizational structure or for modern clearance procedures. The urgency of their intervention and their fast deployment largely account for this shortcoming. Because Portugal financed the intervention, the selection of staff was left wholly to its officials, not subjected to a competitive process. Only in 2004 was a customs code issued—one that is largely aligned to the procedures advocated by the World Customs Organization, yet still fails to address certain key modern customs procedures. The blame for this deficiency appears to fall on restricted consultation with operators and with experts in the field. A revision of the code was recommended soon after its adoption. Advisors often did not work in a team. Where capacity building was provided it was largely the result of the advisors' interpersonal skills and motivation. Inadequate attention appears to have been paid to training in some key customs skills, such as valuation and classification.

In April 2002 UNCTAD agreed to provide its customs clearance ICT system, ASYCUDA, to help Timor-Leste modernize and streamline its customs operations. The system became operational in late 2003, but the introduction of the modern procedures was plagued by funding shortages—as well as by resistance from the externally provided customs staff to implementing the automated clearance system. Also, staff trained in ASYCUDA procedures were deployed elsewhere, undermining the usefulness of their training. Until recently the desired results of the ASYCUDA system thus were not achieved, as several of its crucial modules remained inoperative—in particular the manifest, warehousing, and risk modules.

In 2006 a new action program was launched to roll out all the modules of ASYCUDA in Timor-Leste and to place much greater emphasis on capacity building. The World Bank has supported this second phase of the program.

Lessons learned from Solomon Islands, Timor-Leste, and similar experiences. Many other customs services have benefited from donor support that included

Border management considerations in fragile states

technical assistance and the provision of selectively experienced customs officers for extended in-country assignments. These other experiences have much in common with the case studies above. Some of the lessons learned are listed below.

- *Political support from the local authorities needs to be assured and nurtured.* This implies sharing a vision and strategy, as well as providing timely information on progress achieved.

- *A minimal enabling environment should be the first priority.* The customs organization should function with the minimum required effectiveness before more advanced customs features—such as risk management, internal audits, and postclearance audits—are introduced. Minimum effectiveness includes having electricity, staff who arrive on the job when required, decent buildings, reasonable security for the staff and for goods under customs control, reasonable salaries paid on time, and the like. At the same time, other government agencies with border control responsibilities—and the business community—must move forward with modernization.

- *Technical assistance staffing is key.* Staff profiles for advisors should match their assigned tasks. Clear job descriptions and systematic competitive recruitment—not only from the country that provides the funding—will pay off handsomely. Staff with project and change management skills should be included in the team to obtain buy-in from local authorities, the donor community, and the private sector, and to assume financial and accounting responsibilities. Also, staff will need the flexibility to accommodate their working methods to both progress and the lack of progress.

- *Local customs staff are key.* Identify, early on, the local counterparts who will take over in customs—and train them. Motivate them to stay with the customs service with realistic promises of training and career development. Keep them in positions where they can apply their training. Keep them fully informed about program objectives and modalities.

- *Apply the results of training.* Trainees should be supported to pass on their knowledge or to foster change within the organization. To overcome inertia and the rivalry of superiors and colleagues,

a full endorsement from management is required for the introduction of lessons learned in trainings abroad.

- *Donor coordination should ensure that the approach adopted is shared by all participants—and that it is implemented.* Clear, agreed performance criteria and donor leadership will pay off. Avoid fragmentary, donor driven subprojects that do not mesh with the program's overall vision.

- *Predictable funding levels should ensure that the strategy can be smoothly implemented and that technical assistance staff turnover is kept as low as possible.*

- *Be realistic.* Adjust customs control, clearance processes, and ICT use to local circumstances. Avoid a doctrinaire insistence on the most modern processes and procedures, even those that are internationally endorsed, as this might risk jeopardizing the introduction of approaches that are more pragmatic given local constraints. The organizational chart should be as simple as possible, not a copy of what exists in the home country of the technical assistance providers. Integrity can rarely be much better in customs than in the rest of the economy—though process simplification and transparency will help. Realize that even in the best circumstances, reform takes time.

Autonomous revenue agencies (ARAs)

Since the mid-1980s several countries' revenue agencies have been granted greater autonomy. Although this approach is not designed especially to assist with revenue mobilization in fragile states, it deserves attention, as it has sometimes been presented as an option.

Autonomous revenue agencies (ARAs) defined. An ARA is a governance regime for an organization engaged in revenue administration that provides for more autonomy than that afforded a normal department within a ministry. There are various degrees of operational autonomy in government services. At one extreme are agencies that operate with very little autonomy (such as an education ministry), and at the other are state enterprises with large autonomy. Because taxation is a very intrusive government function and is at the core of government sovereignty, revenue agencies have never been given more than partial autonomy. Nevertheless, most literature uses the term *autonomous revenue agency,* so the same term is used here.

Under the ARA model, the governments that make policies assign the responsibility for the policies' execution to agencies with greater day-to-day autonomy and accountability. An ARA responsible for revenue mobilization can act as a single purpose agency, separate from the finance ministry—and thus can remain focused on a single task, free from political interference in day-to-day activities and from more general civil service constraints.

With greater accountability and greater operational flexibility, ARAs were expected to operate more effectively and efficiently. A 2006 survey for the IMF that reviewed the experiences of ARAs in revenue agencies suggested that the ARAs' creation had responded to perceived shortcomings of established revenue agencies, in particular (Kidd and Crandall 2006, p. 27):[9]

- Low operational efficiency.
- The perceived need for a catalyst to launch broader reforms in the revenue agency.
- Impediments caused by the application of civil service rules to revenue agency staff.
- Poor communication and data exchange among the existing revenue departments. Perceptions of political and ministerial interference.
- High rates of corruption.

That the initiative to eliminate corruption was listed last is probably because the survey respondents were ARA staff. Case studies suggest that the desire to stem corruption was a major argument for finance ministries granting greater autonomy to revenue agencies. Experience has shown that corruption is a major problem in the revenue agencies of fragile states.

About 40 ARAs now operate, largely in Africa and Latin America (the first, created in the late 1980s in Peru, was followed by another in Ghana). The main characteristics of an ARA can be analyzed under three headings: management structure, financial autonomy, and human resource management.

Management structure. To ensure greater autonomy, in all cases ARAs combine the customs department, direct taxation department, and indirect revenue departments into one authority. In Latin America most ARAs are headed by a chief executive officer, while in Africa and Asia most ARAs are headed by a commissioner general backed by a board of directors. Invariably the finance minister appoints the head of the board, and board members represent the finance ministry and other public sector agencies. Some boards (for example, in Zambia and Uganda) include private sector representatives. The day to day management of ARAs with boards of directors rests with a chairman or commissioner. The ARA is entrusted with the administration of taxes (customs, direct, and indirect)—though at times it is also given responsibility for tax policy, possibly creating confusion and conflicting with the finance ministry. Foreign nationals often have been selected to head new ARAs, as to secure technical expertise and management skills not otherwise immediately available on the domestic market. Also, at times foreign managers have been thought better positioned to resist political and social pressures for special consideration.

Financial autonomy. Resources available to ARAs are set either as budget allocations negotiated annually, as a fixed percentage of total revenue, or as a variable percentage based on revenues collected.[10] In Peru a fixed share was set at 3 percent of customs revenue collections, but customs was also allowed to charge fees for services. Some ARAs have gained greater autonomy in procurement, thus avoiding detailed scrutiny by the finance ministry for each and every expenditure item—a stifling practice in many countries. At times, as a reward for exceeding revenue targets, customs obtains a premium to be shared between staff and ARAs. This provides an incentive only when targets are realistic (Fjeldstad, Kolstad, and Lange 2003; Therkildsen 2003). Conversely, ARAs underestimate likely revenue to capture such premiums.

Human resource management. The freedom from restrictive civil service rules for staff recruitment and compensation has been a major advantage of ARAs, permitting several to remove staff who were not sufficiently competent or honest. Bolivia took a very systematic approach to ensuring that its staff matched the desired profiles for professionalism and integrity.[11] Peru and Tanzania also undertook drastic staff renewals at the creation of the ARAs. Most countries that did likewise were able to upgrade the skill mix of their staff substantially. When other countries were less forceful in renewing staff, several observers noted this as a missed opportunity. Other countries failed to deliver adequate training programs, partly undermining the quality enhancement gained by revamping recruitment procedures. The salaries of ARA staff were raised substantially in all ARAs, to allow the ARAs to recruit and motivate qualified staff—in many cases the salaries were raised tenfold. The raises helped to attract specialized staff, especially those with alternative employment opportunities in the private sector (such as ICT staff, finance and budgeting staff, and investigation and accounting staff). Better salaries—and salaries paid on time—also helped reduce corruption. Not only are well paid staff less likely to engage in corrupt practices, but when one is fired for corruption it is worse to lose a well paid job than a poorly paid one. The new salary scale in an ARA can also allow greater differentiation between higher and lower level staff, akin to private sector practice.

Lessons for fragile states. Some fragile states have investigated the ARA model as a promising approach to improving customs revenue performance. The evidence from implementation so far does not justify unambiguous support for this option. Quite a few ARAs have led to higher revenues—certainly at first—but that result cannot solely be attributed to their newly acquired autonomy, and it may have resulted from operational changes introduced simultaneously with and independently of the granting of autonomous status.

As in development assistance for the most part—and for customs reform especially—it is difficult to generalize about the desirability of ARAs for fragile states. Each case responds to a very special situation and environment, so each requires its own solution—there is no one size that fits all.

The introduction of an ARA that merges all revenue agencies into one runs the risk of ignoring the substantial differences between the approaches of customs and of the department of direct taxes or domestic indirect taxes, and between the specific skills required for each—with the result that customs modernization is neglected. Customs operates on a transaction basis. In contrast, the other taxes are managed on a retrospective (ex post) assessment basis. Zimbabwe's ARA, the Zimbabwe Revenue Authority (ZIMRA), merged operations and staff to such an extent that specialization was diluted, undermining customs' operational effectiveness and efficiency—even though the avowed objective of the ZIMRA structure was to prevent the marginalization of customs operations. The ARA structure has since reinstated the position of a deputy commissioner of customs.

The ARA approach to reforming customs tackles only the management of customs, not the operational issues that affect revenue generation. Whether this approach is better than alternatives will depend on the causes of the present organization's performing below expectations and on whether those causes can be addressed by giving customs greater operational autonomy. If security issues are the main challenge to effective customs operations, it is unlikely that a traditional ARA will provide a solution. A good diagnostic of the local situation should tell decisionmakers whether an ARA can contribute to raising higher revenues in fragile states, if higher revenues are the prime reform objective. The following reflections in four categories—management autonomy, human resources, financial resources, and the drive for operational efficiency—are based on experiences with ARAs.

- *Management autonomy:*
  - What are the chances an ARA will be able to exercise its new managerial flexibility? Will the finance ministry and civil service continue to dominate the minutiae of running the ARA?
  - Is a nonnational manager acceptable if a national cannot be identified in the early years of the ARA? How receptive would a national institution be to hands-on managerial leadership by an outside director or commissioner?
- *Human resources:*
  - What are the chances a real staff renewal program and new recruitment program will be put in place—not just the recontracting or recruitment of old staff who have been proven incapable of achieving desired objectives, or who have a reputation for corruption? The

Border management considerations in fragile states

19

history of ARAs has shown that both outcomes are possible, with longlasting effects on the organization.

- Is there an external perception of legitimacy for the policies of paying revenue agency staff more than other civil servants and widening the pay differential between higher and lower level staff? Can the argument be used that revenue agency staff need higher pay because of their crucial role in financing government expenditures?[12] Can a compensation policy be agreed with the finance ministry to prevent the erosion of staff salaries, with periodic external audits?
- Managing incentive pay is very difficult in any circumstance largely for two reasons: because the output of a revenue agency and the contributions made to it by individuals and by teams are difficult to measure, and because the policy lacks external and internal perceptions of legitimacy. Would an ARA be better equipped than a less autonomous revenue agency to deal with these difficulties?
- What are the chances that the higher pay will be coupled with effective disciplinary action for poor performance and bribery? In the absence of such discipline an increase in salaries may merely replace poorly paid, corrupt staff with well paid, corrupt staff.
- *Financial resources:*
  - What is the likelihood of instituting a financing plan for the ARA that assures adequate resources?
  - Will the ARA be given greater procurement autonomy, to avoid the protracted procedures that often characterize traditional budget expenditure authorizations? Is there an antecedent capacity for adequate oversight and audit capacity, to ensure that expenditures are well guided?
- *The drive for operational efficiency:*
  - Would granting ARA status improve the chances that management adopts an appropriate vision of a modern customs service and implements it—as opposed to seeing the ARA as little more than a source of higher pay? Can the creation of the ARA be a catalyst, enhancing the chance of real operational

changes—a view that seems supported by the survey taken in 2006?[13] Results are best when customs uses its autonomy to pursue full modernization (as was the case in Peru), and where autonomy is respected over the years. Results are weakest—even wholly unsustainable—where customs delays such fill modernization.

In summary, granting a customs agency ARA status is no panacea for strengthening customs operations and raising larger revenues. At best it can provide an enabling environment for actions that can be difficult in a traditional organization, such as introducing effective human resource management, ensuring adequate financial resources, and even overhauling customs control procedures. Yet an ARA cannot guarantee any of these. Only a good diagnostic analysis, integrating the perspectives of political economy and of border security, will tell policymakers whether the ARA model improves the chance of raising much needed revenues in a fragile state.

Preshipment inspection and destination inspection

Correct valuations are crucial in customs clearance. While a core task of customs, valuation is also one of the most difficult, as customs often does not have the information or expertise necessary to ascertain the validity of import values noted on customs declarations or accompanying invoices. Under World Trade Organization valuation principles, countries are committed to applying the declared transaction value or invoice value unless there is reasonable doubt about its truth or accuracy—in which case the countries are authorized to use alternative valuation principles.[14] The difficulty of valuing imports and the belief that undervaluation leads to great revenue losses have led some developing countries to contract preshipment inspection companies for assistance. This section describes such services as they have evolved over the years, discusses their application, and provides advice on how best to use them.

Preshipment inspection and destination inspection defined. In preshipment inspection (PSI) specialized private companies are hired to check shipment details—essentially the price, quantity, and quality of goods ordered overseas. Developing countries use PSI to safeguard national financial interests, for instance, against capital flight and commercial fraud, as well as against customs duty evasion—and to compensate for inadequacies in administrative infrastructure. A PSI program has four steps:

- The importer requests that the PSI company provide an export certificate detailing the normal price of such a good exported from the given country of origin to the given destination country; the classification of that commodity; and, at times, the origin and duties and taxes due.
- The PSI company inspects the goods in the exporting country before they are shipped, and it issues a verification certificate.
- The importer includes the verification certificate in the customs declaration.
- Customs can use these data for valuation purposes—to challenge the valuation provided by the importer, or to accept the importer's valuation with greater confidence.

There is no standard PSI contract. Some PSI contracts allocate the trade from different parts of the world to different companies. Others allow the trader to choose among companies with whom the country has a contract. Most do not require PSI certificates for low value imports (creating a risk that the trader may split shipments into smaller consignments to avoid PSI intervention), for the government's own imports, for exempted goods, or for categories of goods in which customs believes it has the necessary capacity to verify prices. Fees for PSI services can be borne either by the government of the importing country or by the importer. They typically range from 0.6 to 1 percent of the value of the inspected shipments. The activities of PSI companies are subject to a World Trade Organization PSI agreement that recognizes General Agreement on Tariffs and Trade (GATT) principles and obligations as applying to the activities of PSI agencies mandated by governments. The obligations placed on governments using PSI include nondiscrimination, transparency, protection of confidential business information, avoidance of unreasonable delay, the use of specific guidelines for price verification, and the avoidance of conflicts of interest by the inspection agencies.[15]

Reliance on traditional PSI services has declined over the last few years and has been partly replaced by a new generation of PSI and PSI type contracts. One example specified a phased reduction of the PSI intervention. PSI variation, called destination inspection, draws on the information gathering capacity of inspection companies once goods have landed in the importing country. The destination inspection investigates the postentry declarations included in the contract. Destination inspection contracts can be as comprehensive as the traditional PSI contract, or they can be very selective and based on a risk analysis undertaken in the importing country (Mexico is an example). The findings from these interventions are expected to give customs greater confidence in making valuation decisions.

Evaluating preshipment inspection services on the ground. In early 2009, 12 countries had entered into PSI contracts with members of the International Federation of Inspection Agencies (IFIA) for explicit revenue protection objectives. An additional 14 countries held contracts with IFIA members for customs support services in the form of destination inspection services or more selective PSI and risk assessment services.[16]

There has been much debate among development professionals about PSI intervention for customs purposes. Proponents argue that the PSI intervention helps customs raise larger fiscal revenues and speeds up customs clearance, and that these benefits exceed the cost of the service. In contrast, critics contend that:

- Inspecting shipments at export is a burden on exporters and importers, creating delays and additional costs.
- There is no guarantee that goods imported are the same as goods inspected.
- The requirement for exporters to entrust sensitive information about their transactions to PSI companies is an intrusion into commercial confidentiality.
- The scarce foreign exchange spent on PSI could be better used to finance deep and sustainable customs reforms.
- Inspection results are erratic and untrustworthy.

Still other critics argue that PSI agents abroad are no more above integrity problems than local customs officers are, and that PSI companies often use undue influence and financial incentives to obtain contracts.[17] Finally, hiring PSI companies is often characterized as counterproductive to customs reform, particularly if PSI services are substituted for efforts to improve customs services.[18] The services of PSI companies often were regarded as a temporary solution to alleviate weaknesses in customs services. When weaknesses are alleviated, it was said, the contracts would not be renewed. However, PSI interventions have been a stable feature in customs operation for many years in some countries—and, often, little skill transfer is noted.

The outcomes of a particular PSI intervention can be judged against its impact on revenues, trade facilitation, and the customs administration.

Revenue impact. Authorities in fragile states, as well as donors, will attach the greatest importance to the intervention's revenue raising capacity. But the revenue impact of PSI interventions is not straightforward. It is difficult to separate the impact of introducing PSI from the impacts of trade liberalization, customs reforms, and shifts in trade patterns. A PSI company provides authorities with detailed statistics on its interventions, revenues, valuation uplifts (by category of product and by origin of the goods), and so on, and it reports revenue gains as a result of the intervention. Companies tend to claim credit for revenue improvements and for trader compliance increases (much as the presence of a police officer deters drivers from running a red light without requiring a higher number of traffic citations).[19] Opponents of PSI, including traders as well as some customs officers, tend to discount the claims of increased revenue. Experience, also, has shown that customs officers often ignore the data in PSI certificates or—worse still—use the data to extract bribes from traders (Anson, Cadot, and Olarreaga 2006). Few countries relying on PSI contracts systematically use the data provided by the PSI companies for monitoring, nor do many periodically evaluate or audit the PSI intervention and customs' use of the service. A detailed econometric study on the impact of PSI intervention on revenues in 19 countries does, however, suggest a positive impact on revenues—despite implementation shortcomings.[20]

Trade facilitation. The PSI intervention requires that traders undertake a few more steps before importing their cargo, and it may require that customs consult additional information before clearing goods. Critics claim that these extra steps complicate overall trade procedures and lead to errors that are difficult to challenge at the import stage. This is echoed in a recent trade logistics survey finding that, in Sub-Saharan Africa, 56 percent of respondents cite the intervention of PSI companies as causing major delays (Arvis and others 2007, p. 35). On the other hand, private sector representatives in some countries approved of the PSI requirements, claiming they have reduced customs bribery and harassment, shortened clearance times, and provided a degree of certainty.

Impact on customs administration. The use of PSI services can demoralize customs personnel and may affect their cooperation with PSI companies—perhaps because most PSI contracts are entered into by the finance ministry without the full support of customs. Also, PSI intervention may hamper customs modernization efforts, as it reduces the pressure on customs to build up experience in valuation. Although some contracts stipulate that PSI companies provide valuation training and transfer valuation databases to national customs, this rarely works out in practice. The PSI companies usually are not good at training local staff—and the companies' added value comes from their access to data in the goods' country of origin, access that is denied to national customs officers.

Lessons for fragile states. In fragile states for which revenue generation is a top priority, it may be worthwhile to establish PSI contracts for a specific period while expertise is developed. Data provided by PSI companies can give customs information it does not have and is unlikely to obtain on its own. The weaker the customs organization, the greater this contribution can be. But the outcome of such a contract will depend on a number of factors. To avoid a negative impact on trade facilitation it is necessary to build practical approaches and incentives into the customs clearance process.

Based on broad experience with PSI services, the following list captures some of the issues to be examined when considering PSI or when evaluating PSI programs already in place.

- *Contract only PSI companies that have a good reputation.* The IFIA provides a code of conduct for PSI companies.

- *Use transparent competitive bidding procedures* to select PSI service providers and to renew their contracts.[21]
- *Contract a single PSI company for only a few years* and, if needed, renew the contract under competitive conditions. Avoid split contracts—supervising multiple companies adds complexity and tends to increase contracting costs, while the country represents a smaller profit for each company so that headquarters supervises activities somewhat less carefully. Also, split contracts have led importers to adjust their import patterns to benefit from the inspection service providers they find to be most helpful.
- *Ensure that PSI contracts are fully endorsed by customs, not imposed on customs by the finance ministry or central bank.* Achieving this may require a change of management at customs.
- *Link the PSI contracts with a customs modernization project* that clearly delineates the responsibilities of customs and those of the PSI company.
- *Make the PSI contract explicit:*
  - Clarify the services to be rendered (price, classification, duties paid, special import regimes).
  - Provide for a time limit without automatic extensions.
  - List the goods to be inspected, with exceptions detailed.
  - Require assistance to customs in setting up valuation databases.
  - Set clear performance criteria that will allow the government to verify PSI performance, with penalties for failing to adhere to the retained criteria.
  - Commit the company to training customs staff and transfering technology.
  - Set reporting requirements including the numbers of inspections of irregularities addressed, of adjustments made to values, and of resulting additional assessments—as well as the number of complaints received.[22]
- *Record the PSI inspection findings in the customs declaration as well as in the automated customs management system.* Reconcile the data, explain any difference, and take appropriate action.[23]

- *Apply the penalties provided in the law for undervaluation offenses*—to enhance importers' compliance.
- *Set up an arbitration or appeals procedure*—to provide importers with an avenue to contest PSI assessments.
- *Create a steering committee*—located outside customs, but with customs participation—to oversee and audit PSI activities and to determine on an ongoing basis whether the contract provides value for money. Periodic reports should be made available to civil society. The WTO guidelines for a dedicated PSI audit service (WTO 1999) should be consulted.
- *Commit to an exit strategy ensuring a smooth transition when customs fully assumes valuation responsibilities.* A PSI company, following its exit, could be retained to assist in dealing with fraud sensitive goods or in other cases where valuation poses particular problems.
- *Manage a good publicity campaign*—to inform traders and the public about the PSI system.

Heavy reliance on ICT

Customs control and clearance all over the world have come to rely heavily on ICT for more efficient revenue mobilization, trade facilitation, and security.[24] Customs management systems assist traders and customs through the clearance process; the Internet and intranets are used to connect with traders and staff; and scanners provide information on the contents of a container, information that can be used for security and to confirm elements important for calculating duties and taxes.

Transit systems at times are supported by truck tracking systems for the central monitoring of transit truck locations, supplemented by mobile customs response teams ready to intervene when irregularities are detected. Trucks also may be fitted with electronic seals or with other electronic devices, such as special motion detectors and cameras that permit transit authorities to verify whether seals have been tampered with. And a single window—a new generation of ICT—permits declarants to electronically submit declarations containing all data required by the border agencies concerned, while providing a mechanism for these agencies to issue permits and clearances online (chapter 8).

Border management considerations in fragile states

Much as modern customs operations generally depend heavily on ICT, so the potential contribution of ICT to border management in fragile states is also very important—largely because it requires much streamlining in the cargo release process. Where clearance procedures are largely manual and accommodate much bureaucratic complexity (with local and historical idiosyncrasy) the adoption of clearance procedures driven by ICT will force the introduction of new working methods. When modern processes are forced on the customs administration and its staff without having to be included in a formal redesign of local procedures, the avoidance of such a redesign can undermine potential local opposition to procedural reform—a strategy sometimes compared to that of the Trojan horse. In addition to streamlining customs procedures, the adoption of ICT in fragile states can lead to greater transparency, faster customs clearance, and the production of better and timelier statistics.

All electronic cargo clearance systems available or designed for use in fragile states will provide the basic customs clearance modules. But they differ somewhat in the technology used, module strengths, and other operational details. Not all systems come with the same expertise and experience for implementation and maintenance—crucial considerations for fragile states.

Customs clearance systems can be either commercial off the shelf (COTS) or custom built, and although some countries have successfully designed their own customs clearance systems, this has taken a lot of work and plenty of resources—while other countries have initiated such an exercise only to abandon it and acquire a COTS system after delays and costly modifications. Thus the World Bank advised a small Eastern European country that had initiated the process of designing a dedicated customs clearance system to abandon its effort and instead look for a COTS system. The main points of this recommendation are informative. It concluded that the proposed custom built system had six disadvantages:

- It retained a functional architecture that did not provide for key operational processes and information processing for core customs functions.
- It failed to provide for thorough re-engineering of the customs control and clearance procedures to ensure compatibility with modern processes.

- It had deficient program management and process control.
- It failed to specify a methodology to assist with migrating from the present, antiquated system to the new system.
- It did not contain provisions for testing and quality assurance.
- It had no provision for partnering with external project resources, in contrast to most system development efforts in highly developed countries (which currently outsource 70 percent of major system development).

It is recommended that fragile states adopt a system that has been tested on the ground in a variety of countries, that is not overly complex and not too demanding on communication infrastructure, and that ensures implementation support will be provided as and when needed.[25]

ASYCUDA in Afghanistan and Timor-Leste. Initiatives to provide Afghanistan and Timor-Leste with ASYCUDA illustrate the donor community's conviction that a strong ICT component is essential to overall customs strengthening in fragile states. The PC Trade customs clearance system, promoted by New Zealand in the Pacific islands, is another good example of adequate clearance technology—it made a good stepping stone to the islands' later adoption of more sophisticated systems.

In Afghanistan the World Bank's Emergency Customs Project financed a component of the Afghan Customs Department's five year development plan—a plan that was prepared in cooperation with the donor community and thus was not a standalone project (as too many other ICT projects have been). The ASYCUDA rollout was gradual, aiming initially at covering the major transit routes and then at covering the declaration process in Kabul. Modules have been introduced slowly.[26] Implementation is strongly supported by top customs management, yet staff mobility and the reluctance of customs directors to abandon manual processing have slowed it down. The fragile security situation may also hamper full, timely implementation by restricting the capacity of central leadership to ensure staff adherence.

In Timor-Leste UNCTAD agreed early on—in April 2002—to provide the ASYCUDA customs clearance system, as it was considered most

Border management considerations in fragile states

appropriate for the local circumstances. Early tests, in September and October 2003, were successful. But funding problems slowed the rollout, as did the reluctance of the foreign advisors to adopt ICT based clearance. In the first phase it was noted that not all clearance posts were connected to the system—and, more important, that customs was not using many of the included modules (risk management, manifest recording and clearing, valuations support, electronic declaration lodging). A second phase was launched in 2006 with additional funding.

PC Trade in the Pacific countries. PC Trade was first conceived as a standalone, low cost tool specifically targeted for use by Pacific island countries to produce official trade statistics. A review of customs operations in the region suggested that the usefulness of PC Trade for automating customs operations, and for strengthening customs administration and customs duty collection, could be substantially enhanced with some modifications to add functionalities. Using funds provided by the Australian Agency for International Development (AUSAID) under the South Pacific Customs Development Program, Australian Customs and Statistics New Zealand expanded the existing system with operational functions that small countries needed to effectively and sustainably enhance customs operations without placing too heavy demands on skills and resources. The expanded PC Trade has been found well suited to its purposes and, in many cases, has provided an excellent bridge from totally manual approaches to a full suite of automated business processes. In several countries the system has now been replaced with ASYCUDA++.

Information and communications technology in fragile states: lessons learned. Based on the experience with customs ICT use in developing countries, the following conclusions are particularly relevant for fragile states.

- *Relying on ICT for customs clearance is essential for all customs administrations.* It increases transparency, fosters the adoption of simplified procedures, promotes their uniform application, and limits the face-to-face contacts that many customs officers use to solicit bribes. In seeking staff acceptance for the new system, much can be gained from a professionally designed and implemented communications strategy directed to staff and to the trader community. Customs may want to draw on outside resources to manage such a campaign.

- *The introduction of ICT should support a new, streamlined customs clearance process—not the computerization of existing clearance procedures.* Staff may be more tempted by modern, ICT driven procedures—and thus be more inclined to accept streamlined clearance procedures.

- *The introduction of ICT should be geared to the capacity of the country.* At times the design of the ICT system exceeds the country capacity. The proposal for a single window in one East Asian country is a case in point. While the window design called for the submission of a single declaration that would satisfy all regulatory requirements at all government agencies, several agencies were not ready to relinquish their prerogatives and operational modalities—nor did they have the required in-house ICT systems. So the project had to be redesigned and limited to introducing ASYCUDA, with an option to bring the other agencies in later. A more careful readiness assessment would have determined whether all the targeted agencies were prepared to submit to a more centralized clearance procedure, saving time and energy for everyone involved.

- *Adherence must be gained in customs.* The move to ICT involves changes. Adherence should be sought from those who are expected to gain. The opposition of others—those who benefit from existing inefficiencies and entrenched positions—should be contained.

- *Full political and management endorsement must be sustained over time and backed up with close supervision.* This may require personnel changes. The finance ministry, whose support is essential to ensure adequate lifetime project funding, should be convinced that more selective cargo inspections will not mean reduced revenue but will permit better utilization of scarce resources in the areas where revenues are most at risk.

- *Staff need to be brought on board.* Retraining should be offered—and complemented with early retirement and other compensation for staff who cannot be retrained. Efforts to instill collective pride will pay off.

- *Consult private sector stakeholders and assist them with ICT adoption.* They will be the prime beneficiaries of a more transparent, speedier release of goods. Experience has shown that their active support can greatly help the ICT rollout.

For landlocked countries, clearing import cargo at the first port of entry

Landlocked countries are faced with a special problem when importing goods. The goods arrive at a port in a neighboring country—or even two countries removed from their final destination—and need to transit towards the destination country, where full customs clearance must take place. A well functioning transit system could deal with this easily—yet transit systems do not function well, even in countries without the structural problems faced by fragile states.

These difficulties could be reduced if the landlocked country were to undertake some or all customs clearance procedures at the first port of call on the foreign territory. This is the practice in Djibouti, where since 1950 Ethiopian Customs has operated a preclearance facility for goods destined for Ethiopia (World Bank 2005).[27] Transit through the territory of Djibouti is unencumbered by the escort services and traffic sharing obligations that characterize transit trade in so many other countries. Final clearance then takes place on Ethiopian territory. A similar procedure has been proposed for Chad and, more recently, for the Central African Republic. In both cases customs clearance would take place in Douala, Cameroon, and cleared cargo would be forwarded to its final destination under a transit regime. With duties and taxes paid in Douala, and with broadly harmonized customs duties and indirect taxes among the countries, the risks of fraud during transit would be drastically reduced, eliminating the need for escorts. A similar proposal has been made periodically for Eastern African countries such as Uganda, Rwanda, and Burundi.

The recent decision to clear goods destined for the Central African Republic in Douala illustrates the issues with preclearance. Since January 1, 2006 all goods destined for the Central African Republic arriving at the port of Douala have been precleared

in Douala, and estimated import duties, value added taxes, and any other taxes on the goods are paid before they begin their journey on. When they arrive in Bangui, the process of customs clearance recommences and additional duties may be payable—but hardly any additional taxes are in fact collected at this stage. The process, it is claimed, has resulted in much better revenue performance for the Central African Republic and reduced leakage during transit in Cameroon. Traders, however, complain bitterly of the complexity of the operations and multiple controls. A more efficient process would be to strengthen the Central African Republic Antenna in Douala and proceed with full customs clearance and duty payments there, then send the goods on their way to their destination, where a simple verification would suffice once the goods had crossed the border. Once operational, the process could also be applied to cargo destined for Chad.

Advance notification, advance clearance

Some countries find it particularly difficult to take control of arriving cargo—largely because of their inability to control their borders and to judge the veracity of some declarations, together with the temptation for traders of landing cargo in uncontrolled areas and so taking advantage of a weak customs administration. Islands with weak border control are particularly vulnerable to such smuggling. Requiring that prearrival information be sent to customs in the destination country would help these countries to assert more control over their imports. The information could be provided by customs in the country of departure, which has the export declarations from which to extract and forward it. A mutual assistance agreement between the two countries' customs could stipulate which pieces of information in exporter declarations should be transferred—a practice akin to that mandated by the United States Container Security Initiative, which requires exporters of containers destined for United States ports to provide detailed cargo data in advance of the containers' departure from foreign ports.

In Albania the Pre-Arrival Information System (PAIS) was in effect from 1998 to 2002, following a 1998 crisis that drastically disrupted customs operations. A one way communications system designed to function during the crisis, PAIS was abolished once the crisis was over. The customs authorities of Italy, Macedonia, Greece, and Slovenia agreed to send prearrival information to Albanian customs for all consignments arriving at its borders by sea or by road, allowing the Albanian customs to better exercise cargo control. Albanian customs made good use of PAIS, which enabled it to better secure its customs revenues during a particularly difficult period.

A prearrival notification system has been investigated for Haiti—but implementation has had limited success because of a lack of cooperation from the United States, where most of Haiti's imports originate. To succeed better, the system would have required an agreement of mutual assistance between customs authorities in the United States and in Haiti, possibly drawn up broadly along these lines: United States port authorities or customs provide Haiti customs with basic information on cargo shipped from the United States and destined for Haiti (name of vessel, owner of cargo, nature of the goods, expected and timing of arrival in Haiti, even export value). Then the information would be transferred electronically to Haiti customs. This information would prepare Haiti customs if the vessel were not to land as expected or cargo not to be declared as in the departure notice. Export values could be compared with declared import values as an indicator for customs valuation.

A variant of such a prearrival information system—one that relies on the exporter, rather than customs or port authorities, providing the prearrival information to the destination country—has been initiated in the Republic of Côte d'Ivoire and Madagascar. In the Republic of Côte d'Ivoire the present scheme originated from the request of the Association of Maritime Transporters (OIC, for Office Ivoirien des Chargeurs) that all cargo destined for Abidjan be preceded by an advance copy of the export declaration in the country of departure. The declaration, called Bordereau de Suivi des Cargaisons (BSC), contained—among other data—information about the mode of transport, time of the ship's departure, and details of the ship, as well as a description of the goods and their declared export value. The document was sent by the exporter at the importer's request. In 2005 the OIC asked an expatriate logistics firm to help

put this information on the Internet. Customs expressed interest in the export data, considering that this information could help in its verification of declared import values. In 2006 customs began requesting that the BSC accompany all import declarations for sea shipments. The program having now run for several years, customs declares itself very satisfied with the progress achieved and the value of the information received. A similar program in Madagascar, launched in April 2007, is ongoing. In both countries the findings of these initiatives and the adjustments made to declared import values are reflected in the risk profile module used by customs.

Paying customs officers out of customs revenues

Customs salaries often are paid late in fragile states, a result of liquidity problems in the treasury. In the Central African Republic customs officers, along with other civil servants, have faced long payment delays for many years. Customs could be authorized to set aside, from its customs receipts, enough resources to pay its staff (as in an ARA). The practice would be an exceptional case in which earmarking—usually frowned upon by economists—is justified by the special circumstances of fragile states. An emergency procedure, it would need to be audited carefully and would be eliminated after the fiscal situation finds a firmer footing.

Conclusion

Mobilizing fiscal resources in fragile states is a high priority for both national authorities and the donor community. In most developing countries import taxation constitutes a major part of overall fiscal revenues. This is likely to be even more so in fragile states. But successfully levying import taxes is not simple—it requires among other things, the use of interlocking processes and a competent staff. Customs must be able, at least, to effectively require that traders declare their imports and exports. That assumes some security and a basically staffed, operational customs service. Traditional customs working methods, as spelled out in the Revised Kyoto Convention (chapter 11), often are impossible in fragile states.

The inherent difficulty of carrying out projects in fragile states—documented in periodic reviews—accounts for the substantially lower success rate for these projects compared with projects in less stressful settings. The periodic reviews have provided useful lessons that should guide the design of projects to improve their chances of success. Since not all fragile states share the same weaknesses, a project design should rest on a thorough diagnostic of the situation on the ground. Factors that must be analyzed include those specific to customs and those that may affect political support, acceptance by traders, and acceptance by customs staff. The coordination of donors, and their commitment to sustainable financing for the project's expected duration, will need to be reviewed. Where either is lacking, the project will be plagued by duplication and a lack of resources.

The nontraditional approaches to supporting customs operations discussed in this chapter range widely in scope. Some rely on information sharing between the customs of exporting and importing countries. Others simply suggest that customs staff be paid out of the import taxes raised. Still other approaches imply more substantial departures from traditional ways of operating: entering into a management contract with a foreign enterprise, for example, or contracting one or more enterprises to provide classification and valuation data on subsets of imports. The success of any of these approaches will be registered by the payment of taxes and duties on imports and by the degree to which smuggling is contained. Each country presents unique challenges, and no two projects will be identical.

Notes

1. From "Report of the MDB Working Group toward a More Harmonized Approach to MDB Engagement in Fragile Situations," 2007 Meeting of the Heads of Multilateral Development Banks and Multilateral Financial Institutions. The Country Policy and Institutional Assessment (CPIA) is the primary tool used by the World Bank to assess the quality of country policies and the main input to the World Bank's Performance-Based Allocation system.

2. These are very much in line with the OECD's "Principles for Good International Engagement in Fragile States & Situations" (OECD 2007).

3. For guidelines on diagnostic work in the area of customs see "Customs Modernization Project Preparation and Implementation Guidelines," The World Bank, http://siteresources.worldbank.org/ INTCUSTOMPOLICYANDADMIN/ Resources/Customs_Modernization_Project _Preparation_Guidelines_January_26_ 2006.pdf.

4. Crown Agents is an international development company providing direct assistance, consultancy, and training for public sector modernization, particularly in financial management, procurement, and logistics. It provides technical assistance in customs administration and other areas to developing countries and transition countries. See the Crown Agents Web site, www.crownagents. com.

5. Customs and Tax Consultancy LLC was created in 2008 especially in the context of managing the Democratic Republic of Congo customs management contract.

6. On the topic addressed in this and the following paragraphs, see also Mwangi (2004).

7. An example was Tivane (2008).

8. For the WCO's Harmonized System for classifying import and export goods, see "HS Nomenclature 2002 edition," WCO, http://www.wcoomd.org/home_wco_topics _hsoverviewboxes_tools_and_instruments _hsnomenclaturetable2002.htm.

9. The reasons listed by Kidd and Crandall include—in addition to these revenue agency shortcomings—a desire to create islands of excellence in the public sector.

10. The Kenya Revenue Authority receives 1.5 percent of collections, plus 3 percent of the difference between actual collections and the collection target for a three month period— subject to a total maximum of 2 percent of collections (Talierco 2004).

11. For a description of the Bolivian case see IDB (2001).

12. The case in Brazil; see Kidd and Crandall (2006).

13. See Mann (2004). Kidd and Crandall concluded: "Most countries clearly believe that they had a sound basis for establishing their ARA . . . an intuitive leap was made that the ARA was the best solution to solve those problems and address those deficiencies . . . in some countries, this leap may well have been in the right direction given the political context and the need for a dramatic catalyst for change, particularly where other reform initiatives had failed."

14. For a full treatment of this and other subjects discussed in this section see Goorman and De Wulf (2005).

15. See "Preshipment Inspection," WTO, http://www.wto.org/english/tratop_e/preship_e/preship_e.htm.

16. See the Internatinal Federation of Inspection Agencies Web site, www.ifia-federation.org.

17. A notorious case was the PSI contract granted by Pakistan in the early 1990s, which led to a management overhaul at the PSI company.

18. See Low (1995). The paper explains what PSI is, how it works, how it can benefit user countries, its drawbacks and pitfalls, and under what conditions it can benefit user countries. It contains various case studies and recommendations regarding the design, implementation, and monitoring of PSI programs.

19. For an example of a study that suggests that PSI intervention helped revenue mobilization in Argentina see Cristini and Moya (1999).

20. See Yang (2008). Presented in January 2005 at a workshop organized by the International Monetary Fund in Washington, DC, the paper is available online in a prepublication version at http://www-personal.umich.edu/~deanyang/papers/yang_psi.pdf. It concludes that PSI inspection programs lead to increases in import duties of 15–30 percentage points during the five year period after program implementation, an improvement that does not appear to be due to concurrent macroeconomic or policy changes or changes in national or bureaucratic leadership. The study suggests that reductions in underinvoicing and in misclassification are likely to be the cause of these increases. Results achieved in a particular country setting will differ depending on the trader compliance with valuation and classification rules before PSI began, and on how customs use the information provided through PSI.

21. Bidding documents should detail services to be procured, request price proposals, instruct bidders to spell out their prior qualifying experience for the task, and specify an exit strategy. The evaluation criteria and weights to be assigned should be made available to bidders in advance. An evaluation committee should be established with representatives from government agencies concerned and with private sector representatives involved in trade. Its composition should be made public before the bidding documents are issued. Companies should be prohibited from contacting individual committee members from the time of publication of the tender to announcement of the results. The committee should communicate to all bidders the results of the technical and financial evaluation, which should be published in the local press. If the tender document calls for the committee to submit a recommendation to a higher authority, the recommendation should be made public ahead of the final decision.

22. A WTO working party on preshipment inspection has proposed a model PSI contract that could be used as a guide in drafting these contracts (WTO 1999).

23. Noel Johnson (2004) argues that weak countries will have a difficult time undertaking this reconciliation and benefiting from its findings. This finding supports the hiring of an independent audit firm, as discussed below.

24. This section of the chapter draws on De Wulf and McLinden (2005) and Baioni and Bhatia (2005).

25. For details see "Guidelines for Evaluating Information Technology Solutions for Customs," Luc De Wulf, http://www.gfptt.org/uploadedEditorImages/00000343.pdf. Guidelines for procuring a customs clearance system are provided in De Wulf and Sokol (2005, pp. 304–309).

26. The creation of a central database, the preparation of a management information system, the preparation for declaration through the Internet, and the design of efficient trader and broker registration systems all enhance transparency in operations—permitting traders and their representatives to follow the process of their declarations without having to track paperwork and exchange customs information with neighboring countries.

27. In another example, imports into Finland and Sweden that landed in Norway were cleared at the Norwegian port and forwarded to Finland and Sweden using a simplified transit system—one without bonds and based on a high level of trust. The system was abolished with the advent of European Union procedures, as Norway is not a member of the European Union.

References

Anson, J., O. Cadot, and M. Olarreaga. 2006. "Tariff Evasion and Customs Corruption: Does Pre-Shipment Inspection Help?" *Contributions to Economic Analysis & Policy* 5 (1), Article 33. Online at: http://www.bepress.com/bejeap/contributions/vol5/iss1/art33.

Arvis, J., M. Mustra, J. Panzer, L. Ojala, and T. Naula. 2007. *Connecting to Compete: Trade Logistics in the Global Economy.* Washington, DC: The World Bank.

Baioni, P., and D. Bhatia. 2005. "Customs Information Systems Implementation." Staff Working Paper 5, Information Solutions Group, The World Bank, Washington, DC.

Cristini, M., and R. Moya. 1999. "El Control Aduanero en una Economía Abierta: El Caso del Programa de Inspección de Preembarque en la Argentina." Documento de Trabajo 62, Fundación de Investigaciones Económicas Latinoamericanas, Buenos Aires.

De Wulf, L. 2004. "Ghana." In *Customs Modernization Initiatives: Case Studies*, ed. L. De Wulf and J. Sokol. World Bank Trade and Development Series. Washington, DC: The World Bank. 19–32.

De Wulf, L., and G. McLinden. 2005. "The Role of Information Technology in Customs Modernization." In *Customs Modernization Handbook,* ed. L. De Wulf and J. Sokol. Washington, DC: The World Bank. 285–310.

De Wulf, L., and J. Sokol, eds. 2005. *Customs Modernization Handbook.* Washington, DC: The World Bank.

Fjeldstad, O.-H., I. Kolstad, and S. Lange. 2003. "Autonomy, Incentives and Patronage: A Study of Corruption in the Tanzania and Uganda Revenue Authorities." *CMI Report* R 9: 2003. Bergen: Chr. Michelsen Institute.

Goorman, A., and L. De Wulf. 2005. "Customs Valuation in Developing Countries and the World Trade Organization Valuation Rules." In *Customs Modernization Handbook,* ed. Luc De Wulf and Jose Sokol. Washington, DC: The World Bank. 155–81.

IDB (Inter-American Development Bank). 2001. "Bolivia: Institutionalizing Human Resources Management in Bolivia's Customs Administration." In *Customs Best Practices in East Asia and Latin America.* Washington, DC: IDB.

IEG–World Bank (World Bank Independent Evaluation Group). 2006. "Engaging with Fragile States: An IEG Review of World Bank Support to Low-Income Countries Under Stress." The World Bank, Washington, DC.

Johnson, N. 2004. "Committing to Civil Service Reform: The Performance of Pre-Shipment Inspection Under Different Institutional Regimes." Policy Research Working Paper 2594. The World Bank, Washington DC.

Kidd, M., and W. Crandall. 2006. "Revenue Authorities: Issues and Problems in Evaluating Their Success." Working Paper WP/06/240, International Monetary Fund, Washington, DC.

Low, P. 1995. "Pre-shipment Inspection Services." Discussion Paper 278, The World Bank, Washington, DC.

Mann, A. 2004. "Are Semi-Autonomous Revenue Authorities the Answer to Tax Administration Problems in Developing Countries? A Practical Guide." United States Agency for International Development, Washington, DC.

Mwangi, A. 2004. "Mozambique." In *Customs Modernization Initiatives,* ed. L. De Wulf and J. Sokol. Washington, DC: The World Bank. 49–64.

OECD (Organisation for Economic Co-operation and Development). 2007. "Principles for Good International Engagement in Fragile States & Situations." OECD, Paris, April. Available online at http://www.oecd.org/dataoecd/28/5/43463433.pdf.

Talierco, R. 2004. "Organizational Design Profiles of Semi-Autonomous Revenue Authorities in Developing Countries." Mimeo., The World Bank, Washington DC.

Therkildsen, Ole. 2003. "Revenue Authority Autonomy in Sub-Saharan Africa: The Case of Uganda." Paper presented at the Workshop on Taxation, Accountability and Poverty at the Annual Conference of the Norwegian Association for Development Research, "Politics and poverty," Oslo, October 23–24.

Tivane, Domingo (General Director, Mozambique Customs). 2008. "Customs Reform in Mozambique." Presentation at International Finance Corporation Conference on Trade Logistics, Washington, DC, May 5.

World Bank. 2005. "Republic of Djibouti—Transport Sector Review." Report 32575-DJI, The World Bank, Washington, DC.

WTO (World Trade Organization). 1999. "Draft Final Report of the Working Party on Preshipment Inspection." Document G/PSI/WP/W/24, WTO, Geneva.

Yang, D. 2008. "Integrity For Hire: An Analysis of a Widespread Customs Reform." *Journal of Law and Economics* 51 (1): 25–57.

20 Integrity risk modeling in the border management context

Amer Z. Durrani, Michaela A. Prokop,
and Michel R. Zarnowiecki

Governance, in this chapter, denotes the ability of the systems that enable a country to operate under the rule of its law (a more specific definition appears in box 20.1). Poor governance significantly impairs many countries' revenue generation, and it makes their trade facilitation less effective. Moreover, poor governance is recognized as a major barrier to success for many border management reform initiatives.

Earlier approaches to assessing and addressing poor governance as a barrier to border management reform had three main weaknesses. First, the earlier approaches were often more or less subjective in connecting corruption risk mapping to the overall governance environment (whether through a value chain analysis or through some other method). Second, the impact of the overall governance and social environment on reform efforts was often disregarded because that environment was discounted as an area where projects could have little influence. Third, a clear monitoring and evaluation tool was seldom provided.

These shortcomings of earlier approaches prompted a search for new methods to help identify all organizational vulnerabilities and comprehensively understand the governance dimensions of border management reform, both from a bottom up perspective and from a top down perspective. Such methods were needed to secure long term improvements. The result was a mechanistic tool, developed to adapt available risk assessment and management techniques (both generic and sector specific) for mapping corruption vulnerabilities—and then, using a simple governance analysis, to infer a governance accountability action plan (GAAP). The tool would help identify short, medium, and long term actions required, not only from project entities, but from other influential stakeholders as well. It would also be used to assess the extent of any reduction in corruption opportunities achieved through changes in governance.

The proposed tool would use generic business transformation audit and the governance controls assessment based on the Committee Of Sponsoring Organizations of the Treadway Commission (COSO) internal control integrated framework.[1] In addition, it would use the World Customs Organization (WCO) integrity framework

Box 20.1	What is governance?

Governance has been defined as ". . . the tradition and institutions by which authority in a country is exercised. This includes (1) the process by which governments are selected, monitored, and replaced, (2) the capacity of government to effectively formulate and implement sound policies, and (3) the respect of citizens and the state for the institutions that govern economic and social interactions among them" (Kaufmann, Kraay, and Zoido-Lobatón 1999, p. 1). The present chapter employs this definition.

(see WCO n.d.), a modified "Gartner Magic Quadrant,"[2] and World Bank guidelines for developing GAAPs. By using all these techniques it would enable graphic depictions of the governance topography and of the magic quadrant of action, clearly showing high priority areas for the present as well as for the evolving governance environment.

Because this approach appeared best for projects in the highly sensitive area of customs modernization, it was adopted to develop a vulnerability mapping and GAAP for a World Bank customs project in South Asia (box 20.2). Several years of experience in customs reform around the world had shown the limits of traditional modernization projects centered on customs. Many such projects were too focused on a specific function of customs activities. Some essentially yielded patching up procedures with a limited effect on overall institutional capacity. Others were all encompassing but rapidly found their limits, as customs systems (unlike other fiscal institutions) depend on many externalities that affect the agency's ability to reform—and over which it has limited control. Above all, the traditional projects did not extend beyond the limited domain of customs, even though most identified blockages were outside that domain.

Among the limitations of traditional modernization projects, three may be especially noted:

- *A specialized reform theme, such as valuation control,* implies technical competences and an organizational model (also based on computerization) that can be optimized only if strong control issues (such as postclearance reviews, audits, and severe penalties for forging invoices) are addressed in parallel. A self contained valuation project, therefore, will not wholly deliver. Instead the valuation project must fit into a much broader reform programme.

Box 20.2 Developing a governance accountability action plan (GAAP) for Afghan customs

Customs is widely seen to be among the most corrupt institutions in Afghanistan (World Bank 2009). Concerns include interference from provincial and local power holders, resulting in a considerable diversion of customs revenues and a lack of compliance with—and enforcement of—customs procedures and control systems. There are widespread allegations of political appointments, of pressure leading to the rehiring of dismissed staff, of preference given to individuals with links to the political elite (at the central or local level), and of the sale of lucrative posts. Rentseeking and demanding facilitation money is said to be widespread among customs officials and among other agencies at the border. (In 2009 Afghanistan ranked 179 out of 180 on Transparency International's global Corruption Perceptions Index.[a])

In postconflict Afghanistan—with its complicated donor relations and its many pre-existing donor initiatives—the challenge from the onset has been to design a cost effective customs project within a comprehensive strategy. The World Bank has been assisting the Afghan Customs Department since 2003 with the Emergency Customs Modernization and Trade Facilitation Project, which prepared the ground for establishing a more efficient customs and transit regime. However, governance concerns have continued to hamper further progress.

To better understand and address these concerns a governance accountability action plan (GAAP) was developed during preparations for the Second Customs Reform and Trade Facilitation Project. Several other assessments had been done—for example, a World Customs Organization Integrity Development Guide self-assessment and evaluation (WCO Secretariat and WCO Asia/Pacific Region n.d.), an information and communications technology (ICT) transformation audit, and a governance controls assessment using the Committee Of Sponsoring Organizations of the Treadway Commission (COSO) internal control integrated framework.[b] However, to identify priorities and entry points for intervention a more comprehensive understanding of vulnerabilities and responsible agencies was needed. The GAAP mapped vulnerabilities and identified priority reform areas, not only in customs but also in spheres of influence well beyond customs, by identifying other government and nongovernment actors at the border.

Notes

a. See "Corruption Perceptions Index 2009," Transparency International, http://www.transparency.org/policy_research/surveys_indices/cpi/2009.

b. See further the COSO Web site, http://www.coso.org/IC.htm.

- *Computerization* is the backbone of customs reform—yet it implies a whole range of reforms, such as declaration format and processing, legislation, organization, transit management, postclearance checks, risk management, business process transformation, and change management (to name a few). Thus, the information and communications technology (ICT) reform must also fit into a wider package of reforms.
- *Infrastructure development* can be effective only if it takes into account all the border agencies' operational mandates, fits into a comprehensive reform package, and is used to set reforms in concrete. It does not make much sense to consolidate existing procedures into a modernized layout—or to use modernized procedures with an existing layout, as the layout should reflect the ambitions of the reform program.

A holistic approach is thus needed, with final objectives corresponding to a real development strategy. Yet in the past such strategies have—more often than not—simply combined a shopping list with much wishful thinking. Comprehensive reform programs face two major difficulties. First, such programs typically are delivered through a multi-donor scheme, with donor coordination issues that are sometimes complicated. Second, the programs may prove overambitious given the timeframe and absorption capacity of the customs institution—or they may ignore, for pragmatic reasons, everything outside the immediate competence of customs (such as interaction with other agencies), yielding an incomplete or unsustainable reform.

Thematic approaches thus seem more promising. They may cover more than the customs area, or they may address issues from a more functional angle. That is how anticorruption projects were initiated—in a way that cut across the entire customs administration, and sometimes beyond customs. Yet those projects (for reasons of visibility) essentially addressed perceptions of corruption and of its roots, rather than focusing on overhauling the systems conducive to corrupt practices. Targeting corruption directly, as a theme, has seldom worked and is fairly inefficient. Either it buries corruption more deeply, making it more difficult to detect and unseat, or it leads to a direct confrontation with the corruption mafia, creating debilitating legal, political, and administrative obstacles—or it does both. The best way forward is, instead, to reduce corruption opportunities in the system. Accordingly, improving border management requires a review of the governance environment, and it must focus on systematic, outcome based approaches (box 20.3) rather than thematic or simply opportunistic ones.

The most effective thematic threads used in preparing the GAAP for border management reform were the World Customs Organization's (WCO) Revised Arusha Declaration and its associated Integrity Development Guide,[3] which set the standards for integrity in the customs environment and outlined a practical basis for developing and implementing integrity or anticorruption strategies. Based

| Box 20.3 | The first combined and outcome based border management reform approach: the World Bank's Trade and Transport Facilitation in Southeast Europe project |

The first combined and outcome based approach to designing a border management reform project was used for the World Bank's Trade and Transport Facilitation in Southeast Europe (TTFSE) project. It addressed customs and overall border management—not just customs corruption—as one element of the transport and trade chain, and it based its outcome on improved commercial and transport connectivity. Subprojects of the TTFSE project were thus enabled to focus on noncustoms agencies and on participants at the regional level (border police, food, health and standards, the business communities).

The TTFSE project was the first step toward what was called, at the time, integrated border management. Its approach was to set a highly visible set of outcomes (for example, border clearance delays slashed by half) and then—working backward from those outcomes—to identify the key elements that would enable the outcomes, the effect of those key elements on overall processes, the existing flaws in the key elements, and a few needed remedial measures that would be most effective. With this approach as its backbone, the TTFSE project was then split into country and thematic components.

Integrity risk modeling in the border management context

on a self assessment process focused on central issues affecting the development of an efficient integrity program, the Integrity Development Guide provides a framework to examine management, administrative, and integrity strategies already being employed and to identify further improvement opportunities.

The challenge for the border management reform GAAP was to adapt tools initially designed for general customs reform to a specific area of customs work—the border. Most previous projects had a top down approach and often ignored, or simply could not address, difficulties on the ground. In contrast, the Integrity Development Guide self assessment helped to bridge core customs functions—as usually perceived by international donors—with the application of those functions in field operations. The TTFSE project formed local project teams for the self assessment.[4] It was one of the first projects to successfully integrate all stakeholders (not only customs officials) in a comprehensive review of border processes from a functional perspective.

Governance and border management

With customs revenues constituting a substantial part of domestic revenues in many developing countries, efforts to address governance and accountability in customs are crucial to sustained economic growth—and are even more significant for postconflict and fragile states. But the central government's idea of revenue generation often differs greatly from the way revenue is collected at borders and other clearance locations. When the main responsibility of field officials is to meet revenue targets, opportunities for corruption increase.

Customs—over time and around the world—has been associated with corruption. Unlike most other civil servants, customs officers hold direct and discreet power over tangible and significant wealth. In addition, control and accountability systems at the border are often weak. These problems are often further compounded by weak judicial systems and low capacity in law enforcement.

However, the association of corruption with customs also reflects the special visibility of customs. Often it is the most visible agency at the border, so it is often associated with corruption involving other agencies. Finally, customs officials are often the best placed to collect and redistribute bribes on behalf of all the other border agencies.

Depending on the country, types of corruption prevalent in customs include one or more of the following.

Rentseeking is, literally, rent sought to recover the cost of acquiring or retaining a lucrative position. It includes petty or routine corruption (also called tea or facilitation money), whereby a trader pays a bribe at various stages to get goods cleared (box 20.4). Sometimes called survival corruption (as poorly paid government officials try to make ends meet), petty corruption is pervasive and often almost accepted as a necessary evil in some countries. The overall rent may be almost fixed, the size and frequency of bribes depending on the bargaining powers of payer and recipient. Though mainly associated with increased business costs, rentseeking can have a large and immediate fiscal impact when rents are considered too high and so encourage evasion. Petty corruption often can be reduced by using automation to limit interactions between customs officials and traders.

Two things are required to combat rentseeking in border management. One is an adequate working relationship among agencies. The other is a release by default approach—based on a risk management approach, which often can exist before full computer-

Box **20.4**	**Assessing the financial level of petty corruption: rentseeking at customs in a fragile state**

A major customs house in a fragile postconflict country was inspected by an audit department. Rapidly it became clear that practically every transaction was corrupt. A majority of customs staff faced arrest.

The local manager offered the auditors a $45,000 bribe to drop the investigation. As the auditors accepted it the staff scrambled to the importers, asking them to produce $45,000 in 20 minutes. The importers agreed—on the condition that the customs officers would cease collecting petty bribes for two weeks. These facts suggest that the rent paid to customs officers, in that customs house at that time, was about $90,000 a month.

ization is rolled out—to eliminate some rentseeking opportunities.

Patronage is the making of appointments as part of a reciprocal exchange of favors among political or other interest groups. Patronage networks impede the emergence of an efficient, modern bureaucracy. They facilitate evasion, so they have high fiscal as well as social impacts. And they often extend to law enforcement agencies, leading to pervasive impunity. While there are no technical methods for dealing with patronage, it is possible to introduce alert mechanisms into customs systems to point out patronage patterns.

Collusion occurs when a trader or agent evades all or part of a fiscal obligation and a customs officer receives a share in the unpaid amount. Leading to direct—often major—revenue leakage, collusion is largely a political and social problem. Yet it can be partly checked through simple but effective, real time alert mechanisms that bring suspicious transactions to the attention of a network of managers and auditors inside and outside the customs agency. Examples of such transactions include systematic valuation queries or waivers, the repeated processing of imports from the same importer by the same customs officer, and the like.

Collusion at borders can be addressed through:

- Checks and balances using external data (for example, data obtained automatically from across the border) to validate processing.
- As much as possible, automatic capture of basic data that cannot be interfered with later.
- Downstream control.

Grand (or criminal) corruption occurs when criminal interests pay or otherwise exert pressure to protect their illegal operations, such as drug trafficking. Often such corruption amounts to state capture by criminal networks. Assessing its impact is difficult, as family or tribal networks—sometimes intricate—collude in corrupt practices that allow large revenue leakage and the passage of illicit and hazardous goods (drugs in particular). The greatest costs of corruption to state and society are not the rents and bribes as such but the underlying distortions, revenue leakages and criminal activities that they

reveal and facilitate on a larger scale. Indeed, in fragile states grand corruption does not cause large fiscal leakages—rather, in more severe ways, it threatens the writ of the state.

Grand corruption can be partly addressed through an overhaul of procedures, legislation, and institutional mandate with auditing tools to help detect corruption levels. Such an overhaul can be only partly effective, because the deep social and political roots of criminal networks undermine any attempt at overhauling systems—especially in fragile states and countries in conflict, where the rule of law is generally extremely weak.

Designing a tool for mapping vulnerabilities to corruption and identifying mitigating actions: the governance accountability action plan for border management reform

Given the need for holistic, outcome based approaches to improving governance in customs and border management—and the landscape of corruption just described—how should interventions to improve governance in these areas be designed? This section outlines a possible approach. Like all attempts to find solutions, this one starts by identifying problems in relation to the desired outcome: better governance in border management.

Considering the complexity of donor initiatives, a cost effective border management intervention must do four things:

- Build on all existing activities.
- Prepare for longer term solutions, such as an overhaul of legislation or institutions.
- Optimize results for stakeholder ownership.
- Provide quantifiable results that validate the roadmap for further reform.

To design such an approach a methodology is required that assesses the overall governance situation and that identifies vulnerabilities as well as responsible actors. The setting of reform priorities then becomes possible through quantifying corresponding risk levels and determining governance dimensions.

The GAAP for border management reform was designed to be less subjective than earlier assessments and to allow the effects of poor governance on border management reform implementation to be monitored through a transparent, mechanistic approach. First piloted for the development of the Second Customs Reform and Trade Facilitation Project in Afghanistan (see box 20.2), the approach is described in greater detail below.

Mapping corruption vulnerabilities

The first part of the approach was to map corruption vulnerabilities for each customs process step and function. This entailed breaking the customs processing chain down into simple steps, which generally are consistent globally (though they may vary by country, or by point of entry and means of transport). As an example, the main steps identified in a landlocked, postconflict, fragile state appear in figure 20.1.

For each step and its substeps a corruption risk level was calculated—the product of a corruption impact rating and a corruption probability rating (box 20.5). For example, the levels calculated for arrival, landing, and cargo reporting at the border in a landlocked country identified the more substantial risks for that country and for each agency involved in this customs process step (table 20.1). Other corruption risk levels were calculated for the other steps: immediate customs control, compliance checks, violation detection and reporting, violation processing and adjudication, duty assessment, duty payment, exit, the transit regime, warehousing, re-exporting,

postclearance verifications, and customs investigations. (Aggregate risk levels for these steps appear in table 20.2.)

From mapping corruption risks to developing the governance accountability action plan

Mapping corruption risks, and calculating risk levels for each customs process step, helps identify the main bottlenecks and interdiction points. But underlying governance issues need to be addressed—and these issues must be understood before mitigating actions can be designed and priorities assigned to each action. (A further aim is to conveniently match various categories of mitigating actions against the various projects funded by donors.)

First, four broad organizational categories of mitigating action should be distinguished:

- *Enforcement* (defined as the ability to credibly impose obligations or detect violations).
- *Rules of business* (comprising all operating procedures).
- *Statutes and institutional mandates.*
- *The achievement of revenue objectives.*

Second, each vulnerability identified should be classified under one of four governance dimensions (according to the governance issue to which it is functionally related):

- *Policy* (unclear policies and objectives, inconsistent strategies).

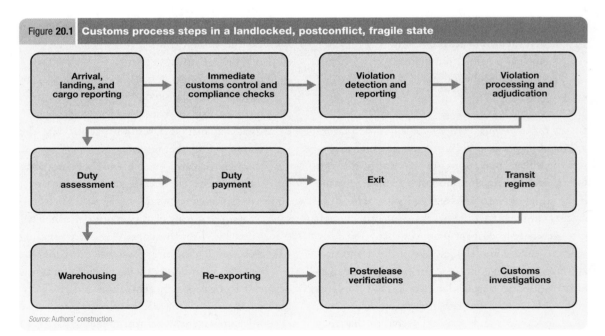

Figure 20.1 **Customs process steps in a landlocked, postconflict, fragile state**

| Arrival, landing, and cargo reporting | → | Immediate customs control and compliance checks | → | Violation detection and reporting | → | Violation processing and adjudication |

| Duty assessment | → | Duty payment | → | Exit | → | Transit regime |

| Warehousing | → | Re-exporting | → | Postrelease verifications | → | Customs investigations |

Source: Authors' construction.

Integrity risk modeling in the border management context

20

Box 20.5 Calculating corruption risk levels for each customs process step and substep

In mapping customs corruption vulnerabilities—part of the governance accountability action plan (GAAP) for border management reform—aggregate corruption risk levels were calculated for each customs process step. The aggregate risk level for a step was based on levels calculated for each of its substeps.

For the substeps, risk levels were calculated and high, medium, and low risk levels defined as follows:

- *High (red)* meant that corruption impact × corruption probability = from 7 to 9.
- *Medium (orange)* meant that corruption impact × corruption probability = from 4 to 6.
- *Low (green)* meant that corruption impact × corruption probability = from 1 to 3.

Corruption impact ratings reflect the impact of corruption in each substep on the three primary functions of customs—the collection of revenue, the facilitation of legitimate trade, and the protection of society (for example, the prevention of movements of hazardous goods). Corruption probability ratings reflect the likelihood of corruption in each substep (that is, of a given corruption vulnerability being exploited).

Customs corruption risk levels generally are determined drawing on existing quantitative and qualitative analyses and based on extensive experience and lessons from other countries. If such analyses are not available, an alternative approach is to conduct stakeholder surveys at border posts.

Once corruption risk levels are calculated for each substep within a customs process step, an aggregate corruption risk level for the customs process step is determined.

Table 20.1 Example of corruption risk mapping summary for each substep in a customs process step (arrival, landing, and reporting), with corruption risk levels

Substep of arrival, landing, and reporting	Nature of corruption risk or vulnerability	Agencies involved	Corruption impact	Corruption probability	Corruption risk level
Foreign release	Exiting cargo (unreported or misreported)	Foreign customs	3	2	Medium (orange): 6
Border infrastructure	Ineffective control	All agencies	3	3	High (red): 9
Immigration and other controls	Identity checking	Customs, border police, specialized police agencies (for example, counternarcotics, commerce, ministry of health, ministry of agriculture, ministry of transport, provincial agencies)	1	1	Low (green): 1
Driver and passenger checks	Inadequate risk management	Customs	3	3	High (red): 9
Border release	Delay during release	Police agencies, customs	3	3	High (red): 9
Isolated police checks	Delay by police checks	Police agencies	1	3	Low (green): 3
Cargo control by specific agencies other than customs	Unnecessary checks and delays		2	3	Medium (orange): 6
Reach the approved customs House	Deliberate avoidance of customs control (smuggling)	Army, border police, customs, customs police, commerce	3	3	High (red): 9
Reporting	Undeclared or misdeclared cargo	Customs	3	3	High (red): 9
Transshipment	Delay, diversion, revenue loss, concealed goods	Transport (policy), commerce, traders, transporters, police	3	2	Medium (orange): 6
Weighing	Redundant weighing	Road administration, provincial administration	1	2	Low (green): 2
Weight ticket	Unreliable weight ticket		2	2	Medium (orange): 4
Queue	Delay in queue		1	3	Low (green): 3
Rentseeking	Cost of rentseeking		2	3	Medium (orange): 6
Transit control	Diversion	Customs, police	3	3	High (red): 9
Total					High (red): 91

For the calculation of corruption risk levels for each substep in a customs process step—and for the subsequent calculation of an aggregate risk level for each step—see box 20.5.
Source: Authors' compilation.

20

Integrity risk modeling in the border management context

Table **20.2**

Example of corruption risk mapping summary for all customs process steps, with aggregate risk levels and linkages to the customs reform program

Customs process step	Aggregate corruption risk level	Linkage to the reform program
Arrival, landing, and reporting	High (red): 91	To ensure compliance throughout the customs territory, the customs agency would need powers of control, search, and arrest akin to police powers—including the use of weapons—and adequate computerized data exchange across borders. That would require a change in the interpretation of the constitution, some changes in penal legislation, and adjustments of the customs law. A parallel requirement would be a clarification, in the government's rules of business, of the various agencies' roles and responsibilities. For appropriate enforcement, customs would require an increased budget and resources for a 24-7 presence.
Immediate customs control	Medium (orange): 46	To achieve efficiency, customs checks must be supported by a credible customs agency—one with adequate powers to directly obtain information, share information with other agencies, and enforce penalties on defaulters.
Compliance checks	High (red): 72	Professional operating procedures need to be introduced to ensure adequate compliance checks. Such procedures can be effective only if clearance operations are well coordinated with other agencies, if customs is not subject to unnecessary interference by other departments, and if customs has the ability to prosecute and punish deliberate, repeated, and serious violations in the declaration, description, and evaluation of imported goods. This in turn would require: Adequate penal legislation. A clarification and amendment of customs' rules of business. The establishment and refinement of customs internal procedures—implemented by appropriately trained staff—to ensure adequate checks and balances. Proper reporting, measurement, and mechanisms for management feedback.
Violation detection and reporting	High (red): 30	There is currently no deterrent effect from the detection of violations, as penalties—when paid—are too low and are not properly accounted for by customs personnel.
Violation processing and adjudication	Medium (orange): 9	In the absence of a streamlined judicial process, cases are either delayed or not taken to court, further encouraging a sense of impunity among offenders.
Duty assessment	Low (green): 3	Revenue target objectives encourage arbitrary duty assessments, made with the aim of increasing collected revenues as much as possible (regardless of the amounts actually due).
Duty payment	Medium (orange): 24	Payment mechanisms are designed to capture traffic, with customs houses competing to offer the highest discounts in order to meet revenue targets—while there is little guarantee that duties will not be diverted.
Exit	High (red): 21	In the increasingly computerized environment, exit procedures provide a remaining opportunity for rentseeking—by delaying the exit of goods, and by creating an opportunity for face-to-face encounters between importers and customs officials.
Transit regime	High (red): 19	While great progress has been made in securing transit, customs still needs adequate powers of control and enforcement to ensure that the system is not abused.
Warehousing	High (red): 24	In the absence of clear provisions and adequate organization, warehousing schemes are not used to their full potential and can be seriously abused.
Re-export	Low (green): 1	Inadequate transit systems generate nontransparent substitution procedures.
Postclearance verifications	High (red): 28	It is important to establish strict and effective rules for the control of transactions after the release of goods—an essential feature of modern customs operations, but one that can operate only in a well defined organization.
Customs investigations	High (red): 27	Investigations should provide a safety net—a balance to upfront facilitation measures. This is possible only if customs has adequate powers. For abuse to be avoided, such powers of investigation need to be carefully managed and controlled.

The color coding of aggregate risk levels for customs process steps does not always match that of risk levels for customs process substeps, as color coding for the aggregate risk levels depends partly on the number of substeps in a step. A customs process step's linkage to the reform program indicates the relevance of particular sets of mitigating actions for that step within a comprehensive customs development strategy.

Source: Authors' compilation.

- *Institutions* (weak institutions with overlapping roles and responsibilities).
- *Procedures* (outdated regulatory framework, overly bureaucratic procedures).
- *Human resources and administrative capacity* (the lack of knowledge, skills, and human and administrative capacity to implement reforms).

Table 20.3	Levels of mitigating actions needed to address vulnerabilities, by organizational (action) category and functional (governance) dimension			

| Organizational (action) category | Functional (governance) dimension | | | |
	Policy	Institutions	Procedures	Human resources and administrative capacity
Enforcement	Political decision	Legislation	Border agencies	Interagency
Rules of business	Government guidelines	Interagency	Administration	Internal
Statute	Political decision	Government guidelines	Legislation	Interagency
Revenue	Government guidelines	Finance	Budget	Finance

Source: Authors' compilation.

For each combination of an organizational (action) category and a functional (governance) dimension, the level of the mitigating action needed is shown in a matrix (table 20.3). The matrix also brands project input categories in a way that allows crossreferencing among various donors. In designing this matrix it was recognized that most vulnerabilities to corruption are attributable, or related, to deficiencies in all four functional dimensions. To allow the setting of priorities, only the most important dimensions were identified for each substep. Human resources and administrative capacity affect all processes and were recognized as an important crosscutting issue, but they were included in the matrix only when they had an unusually large impact on the ability to implement reforms. It was also recognized that any mitigation action plan would require strong capacity and institution building measures.

For the example introduced earlier (see tables 20.1 and 20.2) a comprehensive table was constructed (table 20.4), correlating corruption risks and vulnerabilities to possible mitigating actions and the agencies involved (broken down by the various levels of mitigating action) and setting priorities for each mitigating action. The comprehensive table was then transformed into an overall governance surface diagram showing the vulnerability of customs processes to corrupt practices (figure 20.2).

Given the high interaction between processes, mitigating actions in one area usually have downstream effects on later processes. Such effects can be updated automatically by the model. Links were therefore established in the matrix between measures taken under one process step and any later steps that would be affected by the same measures.

The example in table 20.5 shows the impact on corruption risk of one customs process substep (border infrastructure) within the arrival, landing, and reporting step. This impact is assessed in terms of the issues and risks, the agencies concerned, the probability of corruption, and the mitigating action identified in the particular context. The mitigating actions are assigned to four major customs functions (preventive, investigative, postclearance, and online checks) and to other checks and audits. The impact of the mitigating actions is assessed in terms of functions affected and overall contribution to reducing the risk.

As each action may have an impact on other areas later in the process, dealing with one aspect of the reform may have a greater than proportional result in terms of downstream operations. For example, border station design must take into account interagency and cross border cooperation—identified under a previous step in the matrix—which will also contribute to solve some later compliance issues. Each time such an action is completed under the project, the table is automatically updated to change the value in the corresponding cell to 0, thus reducing the total impact of mitigating actions for this substep on corruption risk (shown in the right column of table 20.5, with a starting value of 25 in the example).

The impact on corruption risk levels of a given aspect of reform is accordingly reflected in a specific governance surface diagram for (figure 20.3, using the border infrastructure example). Each time an action is completed under the substep (or an earlier substep), one of the peaks on the diagram is flattened. Ideally, when all mitigating measures have been introduced, the entire surface bottoms out and becomes flat.

| | | Table **20.4** | Example of comprehensive risk mapping summary for all customs process steps, with mitigating actions, agencies involved, and priorities set for each step | | |

Process step	Nature of corruption risk or vulnerability	Average corruption risk level of process substeps[a]	Mitigating actions and agencies involved	Ease of implementing mitigating actions	Priority[b]
Arrival, landing, and reporting	• Entering cargo remains unreported or misreported. • Additional checks from other agencies cause delays and provide opportunities for rentseeking. • Unreliable weighing leads to delays and provides an opportunity for rentseeking.	Medium (orange): 91/15=6.0	Policy level: • Customs department and finance ministry—providing sufficient budget resources to ensure 24-7 presence for customs and border line control. Institutional and procedural level: • Customs department and neighboring countries' customs—ensuring adequate cross border computerized data exchange and cross border coordination.	24	MT
Immediate customs control	• Manifest is not available. • Declarations are prepared improperly or by customs. • Customs may accept improper declaration in return for bribe, or may refuse declaration.	Medium (orange): 46/9=5.1	Institutional and procedural level: • Customs department—introducing prenotification and automatic link to transit document. Human resources level: • Customs department and clearing agents—training of clearing agents.	7	H
Compliance checks	• During document controls, customs officers misuse their discretionary powers. • Goods are undervalued. • Incorrect tariff regime is applied. • Importers are subject to excessive rate of control. • During physical control goods may be subject to pilferage, inadequately or excessively examined, or control affected in return for a bribe.	Medium (orange): 72/11=6.6	Policy level: • Customs and other agencies present at border—agencies delegating power to customs to ensure compliance . • Customs, civil service commission, and judicial agencies—amending and clarifying rules of business and penal legislation for customs. Institutional and procedural level: • Customs—establishing and refining internal customs procedures; ensuring that clearance operations are well coordinated with other agencies; computerizing valuation process. Human resource level: • Customs—training customs officers in valuation.	8	H
Violation detection and reporting	• Penalties are too low to have deterrent effect. • Irregularities are not reported. • No distinction is made between minor and severe irregularities. • Customs abuses discretionary powers.	High (red): 30/4=7.5	Policy level: • Customs, civil service commission, and judicial agencies—enhancing legislation to increase penalties and strengthen enforcement capacity of customs. Institutional and procedural level: • Customs—introducing computerized reporting.	17	H
Violation processing and adjudication	Delays in judicial processes encourage impunity among offenders.	Medium (orange): 9/2=4.5	Policy level: • Judicial system—introducing expedited judicial treatment and administrative penalty schemes. Human resource level: • Judicial system—providing adequate training of judges.	21	LT
Duty assessment	Revenue target objectives encourage arbitrary duty assessments, made with the aim of increasing collected revenues as much as possible (regardless of the amounts actually due).	Low (green): 3/1=3.0	Policy level: • Customs and finance ministry—revising policy of revenue targets. Procedural level: • Customs—computerization.	10	MT

Integrity risk modeling in the border management context

Table **20.4**

Example of comprehensive risk mapping summary for all customs process steps, with mitigating actions, agencies involved, and priorities set for each step (continued)

Process step	Nature of corruption risk or vulnerability	Average corruption risk level of process substeps[a]	Mitigating actions and agencies involved	Ease of implementing mitigating actions	Priority[b]
Duty payment	Payment mechanisms are designed to capture traffic, with customs houses competing to offer the highest discounts in order to meet revenue targets (port shopping). Duty paid is not accounted for in treasury.	High (red): 24/3=8.0	Policy level: • Customs and finance ministry—Revising policy of revenue targets. Institutional or procedural level: • Customs, finance ministry, and central bank—introducing and encouraging electronic payment.	20	LT
Exit	Issuance of release note—and thus, exit of goods—is delayed in return for a bribe. Management reviews declaration; final signature can cost a substantial amount.	High (red): 21/3=7.0	Policy level: • Customs—introducing default green channel release. Procedural level: • Customs—introducing electronic signature and direct printing of release note on importer and clearing agent systems.	8	MT
Transit regime	Goods in transit are diverted and released for domestic consumption.	Medium (orange): 19/3=6.3	Policy level: • Customs—strengthening inland enforcement; customs, commerce ministry, transport ministry, interior ministry: Ensuring adequate border control. Institutional and procedural level: • Customs—computerization.	17	LT
Warehousing	Goods are pilfered. Control over goods entering warehouse is inadequate.	High (red): 24/3=8.0	Policy level: • Customs—introducing licensing. Procedural level: • Customs—strengthening inventory control; introducing document linkage and computerization.	23	LT
Re-export	Inadequate transit systems generate nontransparent substitution procedures.	Low (green): 1/1=1.0	Policy level: • Customs, finance ministry, commerce ministry, and transport ministry—amending legislation.	21	LT
Postclearance verifications	Payments are solicited or accepted to influence outcome of audit findings. Importers are harassed. Postclearance audit has limited access for on site visits.	High (red): 28/4=7.0	Institutional and procedural level: • Customs department—establishing strong coordination between customs and tax authorities; introducing and conducting management audits; introducing approved importer scheme.	20	LT
Customs investigations	Importers are harassed.	High (red): 27/3=9.0	Procedural level: • Customs department and tax authorities—introducing tight management control; improving intelligence and interagency coordination; computerization.	16	LT

Priority is as follows: H=high, MT=medium term, LT=long term.

a. The average corruption risk level for customs process substeps is a mean, calculated by dividing the aggregate corruption risk level for a customs process step (see table 20.2) by the number of process substeps.

b. Priority is determined through a calculation based on two variables: the aggregate corruption risk level for a customs process step (reflecting the importance of addressing the step; see table 20.2) and the ease of implementing mitigating actions. (See also figure 20.6, below, with discussion.)

Source: Authors' compilation.

Using the tool to monitor progress

Through assessing the ratings for each process step on a regular basis it is possible to evaluate any improvement in the governance situation. Using an interactive model showing the linkages among process steps, simulations can be done to evaluate the immediate and induced effect of any given remedial action—and the cost effectiveness of the action becomes more evident.

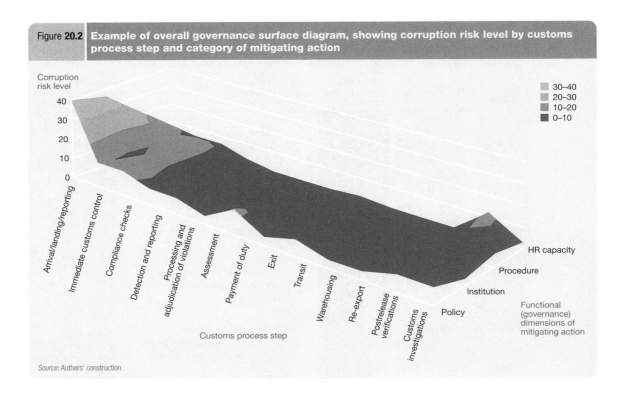

Figure 20.2 Example of overall governance surface diagram, showing corruption risk level by customs process step and category of mitigating action

Corruption risk level

40
30
20
10
0

30–40
20–30
10–20
0–10

Arrival/landing/reporting
Immediate customs control
Compliance checks
Detection and reporting
Processing and adjudication of violations
Assessment
Payment of duty
Exit
Transit
Warehousing
Re-export
Postrelease verifications
Customs investigations

Customs process step

HR capacity
Procedure
Institution
Policy

Functional (governance) dimensions of mitigating action

Source: Authors' construction.

The GAAP can therefore be used as a monitoring tool. In addition, when combined with performance indicators devised for the TTFSE (clearance performance at local level, overall departmental performance), it can provide quantitative data on any specific result that might be sought as part of the overall reform. For example, figures 20.4 and 20.5 show what the overall surface diagram would look like before and after mitigating actions for border infrastructure and related upstream mitigating actions are 40 percent implemented. (Shading denotes corruption risk level ranges.)

Setting priorities
The GAAP helped to identify and set priorities for needed mitigating actions from a systems perspective (table 20.6). For Afghanistan the tool showed that 10 high priority, indispensable categories of mitigating action could achieve 60 percent of desired results (table 20.7).

Ease of implementation, the expected level of difficulties anticipated to address a particular risk, is then calculated by multiplying a value assigned to each governance dimension[5] with the sum of whether it is within the prerogative of the customs department to change or whether it requires concerted action or action by other agencies.

Based on the ease of implementation and the aggregate risk level (reflecting the importance of addressing a given customs process step), priorities for implementation were determined. They are charted in figure 20.6 as a Gartner magic quadrant.[6] In the top right corner are high priority customs process steps, those that are highly vulnerable to corruption risk and are easiest to implement. In the bottom right corner are medium priority process steps that are less vulnerable to corruption risk but are expected to be among the easier steps to implement. In the top left corner are other medium priority process steps that are highly vulnerable to corruption risk, though they are expected to be more difficult to implement. In the bottom left corner are long term priorities, those that have lower vulnerability to corruption risk and are expected to be more difficult to implement (requiring substantial resources to overcome resistance and challenges). Decisionmakers can use such a diagram to identify high priority steps in a given political context.

Identifying reform ownership
In many countries several agencies, and representatives of provincial governors and local power holders, are present at the borders. Such presences can

Table 20.5	Example of impact mapping for recommended mitigating actions in a customs process substep (border infrastructure)

Nature of corruption risk or vulnerability	Agencies involved	Corruption impact	Corruption probability	Corruption risk level	Levels of mitigating action	Area for recommended mitigating actions[a]	Mitigating actions				Number of recommended mitigating actions in other checks and audit[a,b]	Total number of recommended mitigating actions (= their total impact on corruption risk)
							Number of recommended mitigating actions by major customs function[b]					
							Prevention[a,b]	Investigation[b]	Post-clearance[b]	Online checks[a,b]		
Ineffective control	All	3	3	9	Statutes, rules of business	Funding					1	25
						Design	1	1	1	1	1	
						Cross border coordination between neighboring countries' customs	1	1	1	1	1	
						Presence 24-7	1					
						Interagency coordination	1	1	1	1	1	
						Maintenance	1				1	
						Management control				1	1	
						Computer checks				1	1	
						E-link				1	1	
Number of recommendations							5	3	3	6	8	
Number of recommendations as percentage of total							20	12	12	24	32	100

For border infrastructure as a customs process substep within the arrival, landing, and reporting step, see table 20.1. For corruption impact, corruption probability, and the use of both to calculate corruption risk level, see box 20.5.

a. Recommendations in blue are specific to a particular substep (examples include interagency coordination, maintenance, management control, and computer checks). Those in black have already been identified under an earlier substep.

b. Numbers of recommended mitigating actions in boldface denote that a similar recommendation exists in an upstream process. Each time such an action is completed under the project, the table is automatically updated to change the value in the corresponding cell to 0—thus reducing the total impact of mitigating actions for this substep on corruption risk, as indicated in the total number of recommended mitigating actions (shown in this example with a starting value of 25).

Source: Authors' compilation.

Figure 20.3	Example of specific governance surface diagram for border infrastructure, showing corruption risk level by recommended mitigating action and category of mitigating action

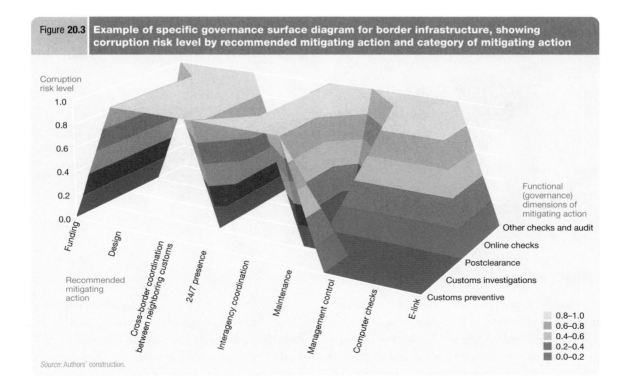

Source: Authors' construction.

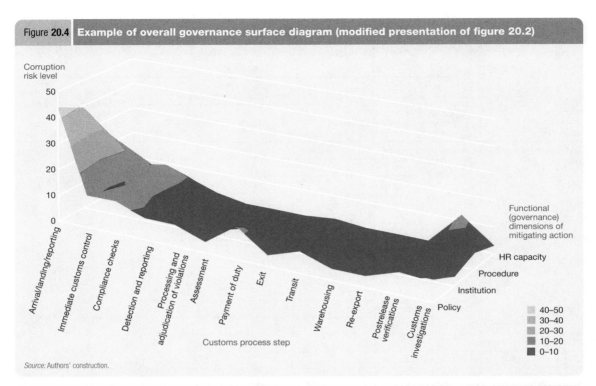

Figure 20.4 Example of overall governance surface diagram (modified presentation of figure 20.2)

Corruption risk level

Functional (governance) dimensions of mitigating action

HR capacity
Procedure
Institution
Policy

Customs process step

Arrival/landing/reporting
Immediate customs control
Compliance checks
Detection and reporting
Processing and adjudication of violations
Assessment
Payment of duty
Exit
Transit
Warehousing
Re-export
Postrelease verifications
Customs investigations

40–50
30–40
20–30
10–20
0–10

Source: Authors' construction.

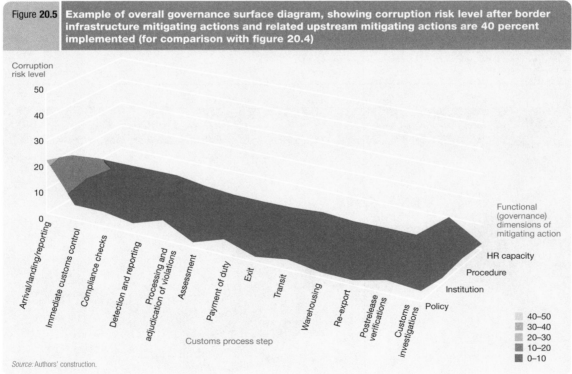

Figure 20.5 Example of overall governance surface diagram, showing corruption risk level after border infrastructure mitigating actions and related upstream mitigating actions are 40 percent implemented (for comparison with figure 20.4)

Corruption risk level

Functional (governance) dimensions of mitigating action

HR capacity
Procedure
Institution
Policy

Customs process step

Arrival/landing/reporting
Immediate customs control
Compliance checks
Detection and reporting
Processing and adjudication of violations
Assessment
Payment of duty
Exit
Transit
Warehousing
Re-export
Postrelease verifications
Customs investigations

40–50
30–40
20–30
10–20
0–10

Source: Authors' construction.

interfere with customs, and often they are heavily involved in corrupt activities. The absence of effective coordination and efficient border management procedures, combined with unclear and conflicting roles and responsibilities at various border agencies, increases the risk of corruption and smuggling. Under such circumstances introducing and implementing checks and balances becomes especially difficult. In certain cases, particularly in fragile states, a mapping of key actors may be required—identifying

Integrity risk modeling in the border management context

20

Table 20.6	Example of prioritized results from an analysis of influence, corruption opportunities and risks, and governance risks, by customs process step

	Influence				Governance risks attributed to:			
Customs process step	Customs	Other	Both	Corruption opportunities and risks	Policy	Institution	Procedure	Human resources and administration
Compliance check	9	3	2	67	5	4	7	5
Arrival, landing, and reporting	4	8	2	50	6	6	7	1
Customs control (immediate)	6	2	1	35	3	2	5	4
Payment	5	2	2	33	5	2	3	0
Enforcement	3	3	3	27	3	3	0	3
Transit	3	3	2	24	2	2	3	0
Warehousing	3	3	3	24	1	3	2	0
Release	3	1	1	21	1	1	3	1
Irregularities	5	2	2	19	4	3	2	2
Postclearance activity	2	1	1	8	0	1	2	1
Re-export	0	1	0	1	1	1	0	0

Source: Authors' compilation.

Table 20.7	Example of figures simulating the results achievable by 10 high priority, indispensable customs mitigating actions

	Occurrences	
Category of mitigating action	Number	Percentage of total
Computer checks	40	14
Management	25	9
Audits	22	8
E-link	14	5
Inland checks	13	5
Performance measurement	13	5
Cross border coordination between neighboring countries' customs	11	4
Interagency coordination	10	4
Legislation	10	4
Risk management	9	3
Total mitigating actions listed under the categories above	167	59
Other mitigating actions	114	41
Total mitigating actions	281	100

Number of occurrences is the number of times a category of remedial measures affects the different functions identified under the matrix. *Percentage of total* is the weight of a category in overall project completion.
Source: Authors' compilation.

potential winners and losers and the strategies that can be used to deal with such issues. In Afghanistan, for instance, a conflict and crime assessment was conducted to assist in managing risks related to the reform process for various actors.

The circles of influence that shape the governance environment of a project are social processes, government actions, and customs activities (figure 20.7). Distinguishing among them helps in determining which issues can be addressed by the project and by the customs agency—and which actions will require concerted efforts and support from other government agencies, as well as close dialogue with development partners and other stakeholders.

20

Integrity risk modeling in the border management context

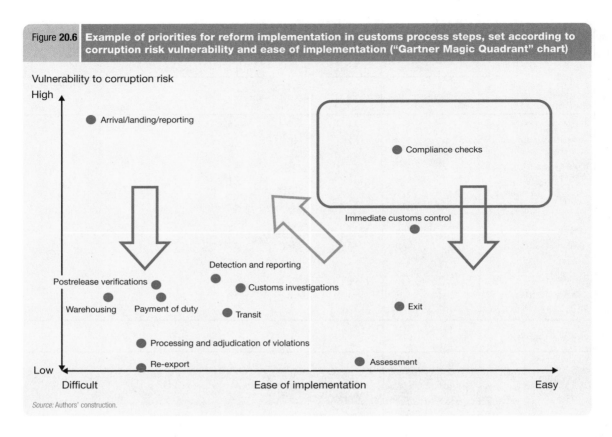

Figure 20.6 Example of priorities for reform implementation in customs process steps, set according to corruption risk vulnerability and ease of implementation ("Gartner Magic Quadrant" chart)

Vulnerability to corruption risk

High

- Arrival/landing/reporting
- Compliance checks
- Immediate customs control
- Detection and reporting
- Postrelease verifications
- Customs investigations
- Warehousing
- Payment of duty
- Exit
- Transit
- Processing and adjudication of violations
- Re-export
- Assessment

Low

Difficult   Ease of implementation   Easy

Source: Authors' construction.

Many actions necessary to improve the overall governance situation for border management are outside customs' direct control and can be successful only with strong political commitment at a senior government level. In Afghanistan, for instance, more than 70 percent of necessary actions are not under the direct control of customs (figure 20.8).

Conclusion: the governance accountability and action plan for border management reform

The risk mapping and implementation priority matrices illustrated in this chapter show which mitigation actions are required at each process step and identify the agencies responsible. The GAAP thus identifies key crosscutting governance challenges and presents a corresponding reform agenda in an integrated, strategic, and prioritized way, while it identifies which areas can be assisted by a particular project and which can be supported by leveraging the broader World Bank portfolio and through policy dialogue. Often many of the mitigation measures identified are already integrated into various government action plans.

However, such action plans often are not very focused and are not prioritized. The risk mapping approach therefore helps in identifying crucial reform measures, measures that may then trigger further progress.

The GAAP for border management reform outlined in this chapter was developed for, and applied to, the design of the World Bank's Second Customs Reform and Trade Facilitation Project in Afghanistan (see box 20.2). A comprehensive tool, the GAAP could take into account Afghanistan's multilayered donor approach, its severe interagency interference problem, and its existing weaknesses in legislation and organization while giving the government a reform dashboard and effectively enhancing its performance. Approved by the Afghanistan Minister of Finance in November 2009, and endorsed by other donors supporting border management, the GAAP will become a project monitoring tool for the government and for all donors as soon as the World Bank project becomes effective.

The GAAP is easily adapted to contexts other than Afghanistan. It can be used to identify organizational vulnerabilities and responsible actors and analyze governance dimensions and crosscutting governance challenges (table 20.8) in practically any

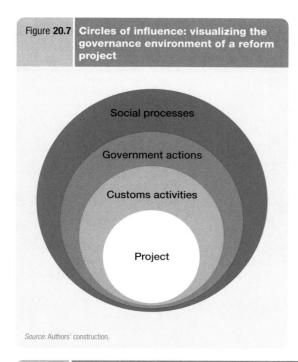

Figure **20.7** Circles of influence: visualizing the governance environment of a reform project

Source: Authors' construction.

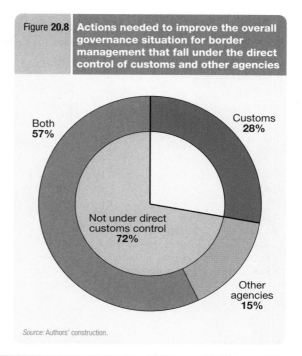

Figure **20.8** Actions needed to improve the overall governance situation for border management that fall under the direct control of customs and other agencies

Source: Authors' construction.

Table **20.8** Example of crosscutting issues summary from a GAAP for border management reform

Governance issues	Mitigating actions required	Agencies	Project level intervention	Other actions and actors	Timeframe
Cumbersome, opaque procedures leading to delays, smuggling, and rentseeking	• Computerization • Awareness campaign on fees, procedures • Revision of customs legislation to streamline procedures • Supporting infrastructure and equipment	Customs	• Automation of processes with supporting infrastructure improvements and equipment • Support to legislative and regulatory revisions and improvements in administrative and institutional framework • Process and skills survey and reform	• Support of legislative and judicial agencies • Close coordination with other development partners in revising and implementing laws	Immediate
Lack of adequate data exchange and coordination across borders	• Data exchange between neighboring countries • Supporting infrastructure and equipment	• Customs • Neighboring countries' customs	• Cross border links to capture reliable information on shipments • Establishment of transit tracking system with supporting infrastructure improvements and infrastructure provision • Facilitate dialogue and trade with neighbors	Support for regional cooperation mechanisms, bilateral discussions between the country and its neighbors on issues related to trade	Immediate
• High level of discretionary powers for customs officers • Frequent interaction between customs officers and clients	• Computerization and related change management process • Supporting infrastructure, equipment • Enhancement of disciplinary actions • Support to postclearance audit	• Customs • Finance ministry • Civil service commission	• Clearance operations computerized countrywide with support infrastructure improvements and equipment provision • Executive information systems allowing real time monitoring of operations and greater accountability • Support to postclearance audit function • Process and skills surveys and reforms	Within wider public administration reform, support for the development of disciplinary action and enforcement mechanisms	Immediate

(continued)

20

Integrity risk modeling in the border management context

Governance issues	Mitigating actions required	Agencies	Project level intervention	Other actions and actors	Timeframe
Limited ownership of reform process	Support for overall governance reform, public administration reform process	• Government • Development partners	• Strong donor coordination • Assist customs agency in designing and organizing awareness campaign on governance	Support of development partners and World Bank overall assistance portfolio and leverage	Immediate
Unclear customs agency mandate, focusing on revenue objectives	Review of revenue targets and of how they are internalized as operational targets	• Customs • Finance ministry • International Monetary Fund	Policy dialogue with development partners to review revenue targets and the way in which they have been internalized by the government	International Monetary Fund to assist finance ministry in review of revenue target policy	Immediate
Statute of customs, low salary levels, and lack of proper incentive schemes lead to rentseeking	Improved status for customs officers (through offering incentives or a clear career path, for example)	• Customs • Finance ministry • IARCSC[a] • Interior ministry	• Within wider public administration reform process, prepare ground for new statute of customs • Assist in revision of code of conduct and design and implementation of rewards and incentives schemes	• World Bank support for public administration reform • Leverage through joint policy dialogue between development partners and government	Medium term
Interference by other agencies at the border and by local power holders	• Improved interagency coordination • Delegation of other agencies' powers to customs, to ensure compliance	• Finance ministry • Interior ministry • Agriculture ministry	Prepare realistic strategy and action plan for effective compliance, prevention, and control function and capacities	Solicit the support of relevant government agencies and of development partners	Medium term
Human resource practices, including: • Nepotism • Selection and promotion based on relationships and favors	• Public administration reform • Transparent, merit based recruitment	• Customs • Civil service commission	• Prepare action plan for human resource policy, rewards and incentives schemes • Identify gaps in staff capacity, develop capacity building and on-the-job training curriculum	• Support to public administration reform • Policy based loans and grants • Support of International Monetary Fund	Long term

a. In this example IARCSC refers to Afghanistan's Independent Administrative Reform and Civil Service Commission.
Source: Authors' compilation.

country where a diagnostic survey of customs vulnerabilities has been conducted. Matrix parameters may change with local circumstances, so a careful analysis of steps, substeps, and interactions is required. Yet such an analysis can readily build on existing project reviews and feasibility studies. In sum, the GAAP offers a comprehensive monitoring and simulation tool that is also flexible enough to address any administration's needs. Moreover, it can be transposed from the national to the regional—or even the local—level.

Notes

1. See further the COSO Web site, http://www.coso.org/IC.htm.

2. See below, note 6, and "Methodologies: Magic Quadrants," Gartner, http://www.gartner.com/technology/research/methodologies/research_mq.jsp.

3. See "Programmes: Integrity," WCO, http://www.wcoomd.org/home_wco_topics_cboverviewboxes_programmes_cbintegrity overview.htm.

4. Local project teams under the TTFSE were panels consisting of midranking officials from all border agencies and private sector representatives at designated pilot locations. The teams were to monitor performance (clearance and processing delays), map all local operations and procedures, and make

recommendations to their various headquarters for improving processes.

5. For human capacity issues the value was 1 (least difficult to change). For procedural issues it was 2. For institutional issues it was 3. For policy issues—those that require, for instance, changes in legislation—the value was 4 (most difficult to change).

6. Developed by the Gartner Group, a research and advisory firm, the "Gartner Magic Quadrant" uses a chart with perpendicular x and y axes to analyze firms by plotting completeness of vision on one axis and ability to execute on the other. (The original version of this technique, introduced by the Boston Consulting Group management consultancy firm in 1968, used such a chart—with different variables plotted on each axis—when trying to decide whether or not a product should be continued, further developed, or discontinued; see "BCG History: 1968," The Boston Consulting Group, http://www. bcg.com/about_bcg/history/history_1968. aspx.) In the World Bank Second Customs Reform and Trade Facilitation Project for Afghanistan, the GAAP team used a modified Gartner chart to set priorities for customs mitigating actions. The team replaced the Gartner variables with, on the one hand, impact and effectiveness of measures, and, on the other, ease of implementation (while preserving the Boston Consulting Group's original four quadrant analysis technique).

References

Kaufmann, D., A. Kraay, and P. Zoido-Lobatón. 1999. "Governance Matters." Policy Research Working Paper 2196. The World Bank, Washington, DC. Available online at http://siteresources. worldbank.org/INTWBIGOVANTCOR/ Resources/govmatrs.pdf.

World Bank. 2009. "Fighting Corruption in Afghanistan: Summaries of Vulnerabilities to Corruption." Assessment, The World Bank, July 2009.

WCO (World Customs Organization) Secretariat and WCO Asia/Pacific Region. n.d. "Integrity Development Guide Self-Assessment and Evaluation." WCO, Geneva. Available online at http://wcoweb04.wcoomd.org/ie/en/Topics_ Issues/CustomsModernizationIntegrity/Integrity %20Development%20Guide%20E%20%20 Final.PDF.

Editors and contributing authors

Editors

Gerard McLinden is the convener of the World Bank's Customs and Border Management Practice group. He joined the International Trade Department of the World Bank as a Senior Trade Facilitation Specialist in January 2004. He is responsible for the design, development, implementation, and supervision of a range of customs, trade facilitation, and border management initiatives and projects. Prior to joining the Bank he worked in the World Customs Organization, where he was responsible for the World Customs Organization's (WCO) Customs Reform and Modernization program as well as a range of good governance, capacity building and training, and technical assistance initiatives. Prior to joining the WCO he served as the Senior Australian Customs Representative for the Asian region, based in the Australian Embassy in Japan. He has over 25 years' experience in Australian Customs, including senior appointments at the Director level in a variety of disciplines, and was the Project Director for a number of multimillion dollar customs reform and modernization projects in the East Asia and Pacific region. He holds a Bachelor's Degree in Economics and Political Science, an Advanced Diploma in Quality Management, and a Master's Degree in Management. Gerard has worked in over 80 countries and has undertaken border management reform assignments on behalf of a range of national and international organizations.

Enrique Fanta Ivanovic is a Senior Public Sector Specialist in the World Bank's Poverty Reduction and Economic Management Department for Latin America and the Caribbean. His expertise includes institutional capacity building, tax and customs administration, electronic government, and public expenditure management. Prior to joining the Bank he served as Deputy Director of Chilean Internal Revenue Service and then as head of the Chilean Customs Service. During his term as Director General of Chilean Customs he was also elected as Chairman of the World Customs Organization Council. He then served as the Deputy Director of the Chilean State Modernization Project, in charge of e-government. Enrique holds a Civil Industrial Engineering degree from the Universidad de Chile.

David Widdowson is the Chief Executive Officer of the Centre for Customs and Excise Studies, Canberra, Australia. He has more than 30 years' experience in his field of expertise and previously served with the Australian Customs Service for 21 years, including seven years in the Senior Executive Service. He is the President of the International Network of Customs Universities; Editor-in-Chief of the *World Customs Journal*; an Advisory Group member of the World Customs Organization's Partnership in Customs Academic Research and Development; and a founding director of the Trusted Trade Alliance. David holds a Ph.D. in

Customs Management. His research areas include trade facilitation, regulatory compliance management, risk management, and supply chain security.

Tom Doyle is a Senior Border Management Specialist in the International Trade Department of the World Bank. He has spent 32 years working within the domain of customs and border management and has held a number of positions within the Irish Revenue Commissioners, within the European Commission, within the Cyprus Government, and with the international consultancy company Accenture. During this time he has worked extensively in all areas of customs policy and strategy, but he is best known for his work within the information and communications technology (ICT) environment, where he has provided technical assistance and support to a number of countries in Asia, Africa, and Europe as an official and as a consultant. He has also authored a number of papers, including "Customs 2020," "Outsourcing as a Strategic Delivery Option for Customs," and "Collaborative Border Management."

Contributing authors

Jean-François Arvis is a Senior Transport Economist with the International Trade Department of the World Bank and has been leading the development of advisory work and knowledge products in the area of trade facilitation and logistics. Prior to joining the Bank he worked in senior positions with the French Ministry of Economy and Industry (regulation, trade, finance, and development aid). He is a graduate from the Ecole Normale Supérieure in Paris and Ecole Nationale Supérieure des Mines and holds doctorate degrees in physics.

Olivier Cadot is a Senior Economist at the World Bank's International Trade Division, Washington, DC, on leave from the University of Lausanne, where he is a Professor and Director of the Institute of Applied Economics. He was formerly Assistant and Associate Professor at INSEAD, Fontainebleau, and has also taught at institutions including the Paris School of Economics, Sciences Po, UCLA and the University of Geneva. He is a fellow of the London-based Center for Economic Policy Research (CEPR) and of the Paris-based CEPREMAP; a

research associate of CERDI; and a member of the editorial board of the Revue d'Economie du Developpement. He has published numerous academic papers on trade and development.

Luc De Wulf obtained his economics degree from the Katholieke Universiteit, Leuven in Belgium and a doctorate from Clark University, Massachusetts, US. After teaching at the American University of Beirut, Lebanon, he joined the Fiscal Department of the International Monetary Fund. He moved to the IMF Asian Department and worked for six years focusing on China before joining the World Bank, where he worked in both the Africa and Middle East and North Africa Regions. Since retirement he has co-edited the *Customs Modernization Handbook* and *Customs Modernization Initiatives* and has worked on several projects and studies related to trade facilitation, fiscal policy, and trade integration financed by the World Bank, the UK Department for International Development, and the European Commission.

Amer Z. Durrani is a Senior Trade Facilitation and Transport Specialist in the World Bank, currently working on regional trade and transport facilitation issues in the South Asia Region, in addition to working on the resident transport sector cluster for the World Bank in Pakistan. His work in this area also covers postconflict country environments. He has been leading the Bank Dialogue with Pakistan and Afghanistan Governments on Transport Services, Trade Facilitation, Customs, Ports and Shipping, Railways, Roads, and Aviation. In Afghanistan he has also led the work on Standards, Metrology, Testing, and Quality. He has previously covered these areas for the Bank in Bhutan, Lao People's Democratic Republic, the Philippines, Georgia, and Nepal. Before arriving at the Bank he worked on projects in the transport sector with construction companies, consultants, academia, and government in Pakistan, Italy, and the US. In recent years Amer is acknowledged for providing transport policy advice and opinion formulation assistance to a large range of clients in the public and private sectors in various countries and to organizations such as the United Nations Conference on Trade and Development (UNCTAD), the Chartered Institute of Logistics and Transport (CILT), the International Union for the Conservation of Nature (IUCN), various chambers of commerce and industry, the International Multimodal Transport Association (IMMTA), the WCO, GAC Shipping, the University of Birmingham, National Defense University (Pakistan), and Iranian Customs (IRICA).

Andrew Grainger is a recognized expert in the wider area of trade facilitation and trade logistics and is the founding Director of Trade Facilitation Consulting Ltd. In January 2009 he joined the University of Nottingham as Lecturer in Logistics and Supply Chain Management. His recent publications include work for the World Bank, the European Commission, and the European Parliament. Between 2002 and 2006 as Deputy Director at SITPRO, the UK trade facilitation agency, he held the post of Secretary at EUROPRO, the umbrella body for European trade facilitation committees. There he also participated as an expert within the European Commission's (DG TAXUD) Trade Contact Group. Other experiences include world trade and customs consultancy with PricewaterhouseCoopers and freight forwarding in Germany and Southeast Asia. Andrew holds a Ph.D. in Management from Birkbeck College, University of London, an M.A. (Distinction) in International Political Economy from the University of Warwick, and a BSc (Honours) in International Transport from Cardiff University. He is a Chartered Member of the Institute of Logistics and Transport.

Stephen Holloway is the Dean of Studies (Education/Research) and Principal Director of the Centre for Customs and Excise Studies and an Adjunct Professor in the Faculty of Law, University of Canberra. He has 25 years' experience in customs and international trade, including 20 years with the Australian Customs Service. He has worked closely with international organizations, customs and revenue administrations, and the private sector on international trade and border management, including customs reform and modernization, international logistics, the international regulation of intellectual property, legislative reform, and strategic export controls. Steve holds a Bachelor of Laws from the Australian National University and a Master's degree in International Customs Law and Administration from the University of Canberra, and he is admitted as a Barrister and Solicitor of the Australian Capital Territory Supreme Court and a Barrister of the Federal and High Courts of Australia.

Laura Ignacio worked on food safety and agricultural health issues as a consultant for the World Bank (2003–10) and the Standards and Trade Development Facility (2007–08). Major work included the preparation of action plans on sanitary and phytosanitary (SPS) measures for Lao People's Democratic Republic, Vietnam, and Ghana, and a review of SPS-related technical cooperation in Cambodia, Lao People's Democratic Republic, and Vietnam. She holds a Ph.D. in economics from the George Washington University in Washington, DC.

Robert Ireland currently works in the WCO's Research and Strategies Unit within the Office of the Secretary General, where he conducts research on customs and international trade subjects. From 2005 to 2009 he was a development advisor in the WCO's Capacity Building Directorate. Before his WCO employment, he worked as a policy analyst at US Customs and Border Protection, Office of International Affairs, where he worked on supply chain security and other enforcement matters. Prior to his US Customs employment he was an investigator for 11 years with the US Federal Trade Commission. Robert has a B.A. in Political Science with an emphasis in International Relations from Drew University in Madison, New Jersey and an M.A. in Public Administration with an emphasis in Policy Analysis from George Washington University in Washington, DC.

Frank Janssens is currently responsible for the Customs Trans-European Systems at the European Commission, where he is working as a Principal Administrator. He is also the team leader of a temporary structure to define the business process models for the new customs ICT systems to be established under the Modernized Customs Code. He is a trained economist specializing in international trade and a confirmed ICT project manager. He has spent over 20 years working within the domain of customs, international trade, and information technology projects, where he held different positions in the European Commission, the Belgian Ministry of Finance, and the private sector. During this time he has worked in several areas of customs policy, such as trade facilitation, international affairs, and assistance. In recent years he has focused on customs modernization projects which make extensive use of information and communication technology. He is the chairman of a number of electronic customs working groups composed of participants from the European Union Member States and Candidate Countries, with occasional attendance of economic operators associations.

Darryn Jenkins is recognized for expertise in restructuring and change management in the public sector environment, having spent much of his career designing and leading complex change processes. He was previously Commissioner–Customs and Excise in Zambia, Regional Comptroller in New Zealand Customs, and Customs Ombudsman in Australia, and he has held various positions at Director level in the Australian Public Service Board and the New Zealand State Services Commission. He works regularly as a member of the IMF Panel of Fiscal Experts, largely on reviewing revenue administration and making recommendations for changes in structure and management in customs administration. He has overseen customs and tax administration modernization projects in Vietnam, Indonesia, Uganda, Zambia, and Jamaica, and he has advised on a number of others as a project director. He has been engaged on assignments for the major donor organizations, including the World Bank, UK Department for International Development, and IMF, as well as for national governments. Jenkins holds an M.B.A. (International Business) from the University of New England, a P.G.D. (Policing and Public Order) from the University of Leicester, and an M.A. (International Studies) from the University of Sydney. He is a Member of the Australian Institute of Company Directors and a Member of the New Zealand Institute of Directors.

Erich Kieck is currently the Group Executive for Customs Strategy and Policy at the South African Revenue Service (SARS), responsible for advising the Commissioner on International Trade and Customs policy and legal issues. Previously he was head of International Relations. Erich joined SARS in 2001 as Advisor, International Economic Law in the Office of the Commissioner. Before joining SARS he worked at the Department of Trade and Industry in the capacity of Head, International Trade Law. He has participated in the negotiation and drafting of the Southern African Development Community Trade Protocol, the Southern African Customs Union Agreement, and various bilateral trade, customs, and investment treaties and has worked extensively on cross border trade, customs, and transport issues. He holds B.Iuris and L.L.B. degrees from the University of Pretoria and an L.L.M. (International Economic Law) degree from the University of South Africa. His professional and academic focus areas are international trade and customs law, regional economic integration, and developmental studies. He was elected to the position of Director, Capacity Building at the WCO in June 2010 and will join the WCO in January 2011.

Yue Li is a Young Professional of the World Bank Group, having formerly been a consultant there. She joined the World Bank in 2007, first in the International Trade Division within the Development Economic Research Group, and then in the East Asia and Pacific Region–Poverty Reduction and Economic Management Unit. Her work has been focusing on trade facilitation, services trade, foreign direct investment, and investment policy issues. She obtained a Ph.D. in economics from Rutgers University, a master's degree in economics and political science from Syracuse University, and a bachelor's degree from Peking University.

Maryla Maliszewska is currently a consultant with the International Trade Department of the World Bank. She has been working as a research fellow at the Center for Social and Economic Research (CASE, for Centrum Analiz Społeczno-Ekonomicznych) since 1996. Her research interests cover the modeling of international trade flows, the implications of regional integration using computable general equilibrium (CGE) models, the location of production, and agglomeration externalities. She has coordinated studies on the economic implications of a free trade agreement between the EU and Russia, EU and Georgia, and the EU and Armenia, and on economic integration in the Euro-Mediterranean Region and has contributed to several other research studies for the European Commission. She obtained a Ph.D. in economics from Sussex University and master's degrees in international economics from Sussex and Warsaw Universities.

Tadatsugu (Toni) Matsudaira joined the World Bank in 2009 as a Senior Trade Facilitation Specialist in the International Trade Department. He is an expert on customs and border management reform and modernization, as well as trade facilitation, and has contributed to several projects in these areas. Prior to joining the Bank he worked for the Japanese Government on international customs matters and trade facilitation policy formulation and was the Tokyo based head delegate on trade facilitation to the World Trade Organization from 2001 to 2003. He also served three years with the Organisation for Economic Co-operation and Development, specializing in border procedural barriers, and five years with the WCO focused on trade facilitation. Toni holds a bachelor's degree in Information Engineering from Keio University and a diploma in Quantitative Development Economics from the University of Warwick, UK.

Jean-Christophe Maur is a Senior Economist in the Growth and Competitiveness Program at the World Bank Institute. His current responsibilities there include leading the regional integration program and contributing to the Development Debates platform. Jean-Christophe joined the World Bank in 2008 from the UK Department of International Development, where he was in charge of UK trade negotiations in several areas and also of managing multilateral trade assistance. His research interests are regional trade integration and public goods, trade facilitation and nontariff barriers, intellectual property rights, and trade institutions. Jean-Christophe has a Doctorate from Institut d'Etudes Politiques de Paris and is a graduate of Essec business school. He was also a Visiting Fellow at Harvard University.

Monica Alina Mustra is a Trade Facilitation and Logistics Specialist with the International Trade Department of the World Bank. Since joining in 2004 she has worked on a number of the Bank's trade and transport related flagship projects, including the Logistics Performance Indicators (LPI), as well as on the organization of policy dialogues, workshops, seminars, and distance learning courses. She is currently Coordinator for the Global Facilitation Partnership for Transportation and Trade. Prior to joining the World Bank she worked for the Harvard Center for International Development, the European Commission, and the Romanian Ministry of Finance. She holds a Master's in Mathematics and Information Technology from University of Craiova, Romania, a Certificate in International Tax Policy and Administration from Harvard Law School, and a Master's Degree in Public Administration from the John F. Kennedy School of Government at Harvard University.

Michaela Prokop spent three years (2004–07) as Afghanistan country economist for the Asian Development Bank, where she was in charge of several governance reform programs and regional cooperation and trade facilitation projects. She subsequently joined the World Bank team working on the Emergency Customs Modernization and Trade Facilitation Project and contributed to the development of the Governance and Accountability Action Plan for Afghan Customs. She is currently working as a freelance consultant focusing on governance issues. She holds a Ph.D. in Political Economy from the University of Durham, UK.

Sebastián Sáez is a Senior Trade Economist working at the Trade Department, Poverty Reduction and Economic Management (PREM) Network at the World Bank. He studied economics at the University of Chile. He earned his Master in Public Sector Economics at the Catholic University of Rio de Janeiro, Brazil, and studied at the Programme de Specialisation en Diplomatie Multilateral at the Institute Universitaire de Hautes Etudes Internationales in Geneva. He has published several articles on international economic relations and the book *Estrategia y Negociación en el Sistema Multilateral de Comercio* (Dolmen Ediciones, 1999). He is co-editor with O. Cattaneo, M. Engman, and R. Stern of the book *International Trade in Services: New Trends and Opportunities for Developing Countries* (World Bank, 2010). He also edited *Trade in*

Services Negotiations: A Guide for Developing Countries (World Bank, 2010).

Ramesh Siva is a Lead e-Government Specialist in the e-Government Practice of the Global Information and Communications Technologies Group of the World Bank and has been involved in designing, developing, and operating ICT solutions for over 25 years. In the East Asia and Pacific Region his focus has been on public sector reform and modernization in World Bank projects with major e-Government and ICT components. His expertise includes integrated financial management systems, treasury systems, revenue administration systems, business systems, capacity planning, and design and development of e-government strategies. His current portfolio of projects includes national treasury and financial management projects in Indonesia, Vietnam, and Sierra Leone; customs and tax administration projects in Indonesia, Lao People's Democratic Republic, Cambodia, and the Philippines; judicial systems projects in the Philippines, Russia, Armenia, and Mongolia; and a technical assistance program for the implementation of Indonesia's National Single Window for trade.

Cornelis (Kees) L. J. Van der Meer has extensive expertise in the fields of standards and trade, private sector development in rural areas, and markets and agribusiness. From 1999 to 2006 he was a Senior Rural Development Specialist with the Rural Development Department of the World Bank. Prior to this he worked in the Netherlands Ministry of Agriculture, with responsibilities for policy and management of research and technology. He studied agricultural economics at Wageningen University and received a Ph.D. in economics at the National University at Groningen in 1981, teaching agricultural and development economics as an associate professor until 1988. He is a much published author and has significant experience working in developing countries. Kees is currently the leader of a consultant team for the Greater Mekong Subregion Sanitary and Phytosanitary (SPS) Action Plan at the Asian Development Bank.

John S. Wilson is a Lead Economist in the Development Economics Research Group of the World Bank. He joined the Bank in 1999 and directs empirical and policy research on trade facilitation, aid effectiveness, and regulatory reform issues, as they relate to economic development. He also provides expertise in Bank operations and spent two years in the Bank's Infrastructure Vice Presidency. He has participated in Bank projects (under preparation and completed) totaling over $1.3 billion, and he has provided leadership for the Bank in the establishment of the interagency Standards and Trade Development Facility. He also developed the initial concept for the Bank's Trade Facilitation Facility in 2009 and is a member of its Program Committee. Mr. Wilson is currently working with the Trade Department in the establishment of a new public-private partnership on "Aid for Trade Facilitation" for the Bank. Prior to joining the Bank he was Vice President for Technology Policy at the Information Technology Industry Council in Washington, DC from 1995–99. He has also been a Visiting Fellow at the Institute for International Economics, a Senior Staff Officer at the US National Academies of Sciences and Engineering and National Research Council, and Adjunct Professor of International Affairs at Georgetown University. He has degrees from Wooster College and Columbia University in New York.

Michel Zarnowiecki is a consultant and Customs Specialist. Previously he was a Senior Regional Coordinator for the Europe and Central Asia Region at the World Bank, in charge of programs focused on customs and other border agency reforms. He also participated in the Southern European Cooperation Initiative (SECI) working group on cross border issues, which later evolved into the Trade and Transport Facilitation in Southeast Europe program, and was subsequently involved in customs and border modernization programs in Russia, Turkey, the Caucasus, and Central Asia. Before joining the World Bank Michel worked in the International Monetary Fund's Fiscal Affairs Department and participated in customs reform programs in over thirty countries. Prior to his employment by the International Monetary Fund he was a regional commander in French Customs, and he holds the rank of Brigadier General in the French Customs Service.

Index

Index

Index

Index

Index

TradeNet, Singapore, 133, 144t

Trade Single Window Project, 133

TRAINS (Trade Analysis and Information System), 217

transit regimes

control mentality and convoys, 290

corridor management, 295

corridor performance monitoring, 295–96

described, 279

documentation flow, 282–83

guarantees, 283

guarantor, 283

implementation issues, 280, 289–91

information systems, 289

international law provision, 284–85

management requirements, 283–84

open markets and, 294–95

principal, 283

procedures, 281, 282f

regional carnet systems, 290–91

regionally integrated transit systems

carnet transit regimes, 285–86

European system, 288–89

TIR, 286–88

regulation of entry, 290

requirements for good function, 281

seals, transport, 282

time to initiate transit, 289–90

transit vs. trade facilitation, 291–94

types of transit, 280–81

Transit Routier Inter État (TRIE), 291

transport function at a border station, 40–41

Transports Internationaux Routiers (TIR), 29, 80, 188, 286

TRIE (Transit Routier Inter État), 291

TTFSE (Trade and Transport Facilitation in Southeast Europe), 347–48

U

UCR (Unique Consignment Reference), 192–93

UN/CEFACT, 133, 134, 160, 190, 192–93

Unique Consignment Reference (UCR), 192–93

United Kingdom, 133, 201–02, 203

United Kingdom Joint Customs Consultative Committee (JCCC), 163

United Nations

Centre for Trade Facilitation and Electronic Business (UNECE), 160–61, 270

Conference on Trade Development (UNCTAD), 31, 96, 217, 301, 329

Economic Commission for Europe (UNECE), 31, 80, 185, 286

Electronic Data Interchange for Administration, Commerce, and Transport (UN/EDIFACT), 134, 185–86

Layout Key, 185, 192

Mission of Support in East Timor (UNMISET), 329

Statistical Division (UNSD), 217

Trade Data Element Directory (UNTDED), 134, 184

Transitional Administration in East Timor (UNTAET), 329

United States, 134, 142t, 203

Customs-Trade Partnership Against Terrorism, 169

Government Accountability Office, 44

UTRA (Technical Unit for Reconstructing Customs, Mozambique), 325–26

V

value added tax (VAT), 239

violations section of a border station, 57

W

weighbridges at border stations, 60

World Bank, 24, 31

World Customs Organization (WCO), 4, 12, 31, 80, 96, 301, 347

Data Model, 186

Diagnostic Framework, 190–91

Recommendation on UCR and guidelines, 184–85

World Economic Forum, 24

World Health Organization (WHO), 264

World Organization of Animal Health, 263

World Trade Organization (WTO), 31, 80, 233–34, 264

WTO disciplines for nontariff measures

exceptions, 221–22

under GATT and TBT, 220

legal rules, 219

nondiscrimination and the GATT, 220–21

X

X-ray sheds at border stations, 59

green
press
INITIATIVE